Bert

English Folk Dance and Song Society

For over 100 years the English Folk Dance and Song Society (EFDSS), and its parent organisations, have been preserving, protecting, disseminating and promoting the English folk arts. EFDSS is the national folk arts development organisation for England, aiming to place the indigenous folk arts of England at the heart of our cultural life. Through programmes of performance, outreach and education at its headquarters, Cecil Sharp House in north London, and around the country, EFDSS seeks to support folk artists' and practitioners' development. EFDSS aims to promote the best of folk arts through a range of mediums including dance, music, song, film, exhibitions, and publications. Cecil Sharp House is also home to the Vaughan Williams Memorial Library – the national folk music library and archive – which contains a vast collection of books, manuscripts, films and audio-visual materials, serving as a touchstone for anybody working in the folk arts.

www.efdss.org

BERT

The Life and Times of A.L. Lloyd

Dave Arthur

Foreword by Richard Thompson OBE
Preface by the Rt. Hon. Sir Stephen Sedley

PlutoPress
www.plutobooks.com

in association with the English Folk Dance and Song Society

First published 2012 by Pluto Press
345 Archway Road, London N6 5AA

www.plutobooks.com

Distributed in the United States of America exclusively by
Palgrave Macmillan, a division of St. Martin's Press LLC,
175 Fifth Avenue, New York, NY 10010

British Library Cataloguing in Publication Data
A catalogue record for this book is available from the British Library

ISBN   978 0 7453 3252 9   Hardback
ISBN   978 1 84964 670 3   PDF
ISBN   978 1 84964 672 7   Kindle
ISBN   978 1 84964 671 0   ePub

Library of Congress Cataloging in Publication Data applied for

10   9   8   7   6   5   4   3   2   1

Designed and produced for Pluto Press by Chase Publishing Services Ltd
Typeset from disk by Stanford DTP Services, Northampton, England
Simultaneously printed digitally by CPI Antony Rowe, Chippenham, UK and
Edwards Bros in the United States of America

For Rowan, Caitlin and Holly,
Jay, Tim and Lou

Contents

List of Plates

Foreword

I first saw the name A.L. Lloyd on *The Penguin Book of English Folk Songs* in the school library, and thank heavens it was there. Not only did it give the school's budding folk singers better verses for 'John Barleycorn' or 'Banks of the Sweet Primroses', it was consulted by the music department, and spared us having to sing the more prim Victorian versions of our national folk songs in class. Over the next five years or so, I became aware that a sizeable chunk of the repertoire out there on the folk scene, being sung by Anne Briggs, Bert Jansch, Martin Carthy and just about everyone else, owed something to the collecting, interpreting, or just tweaking of Bert Lloyd. In my old band Fairport Convention, as our interest in the tradition grew, *Folk Song in England* was regularly consulted as the standard work, and when we started electrifying old ballads and giving them a backbeat, Bert was one of the few figures from the folk establishment who was open-minded and supportive. When we were putting together the *Liege and Lief* album, rehearsing deep in the Hampshire countryside, working on ballads such as 'Matty Groves' and 'Tam Lin', Bert was on the end of the phone to give us help and encouragement.

I only met him a few times, and I suppose my impression is of generosity – generous with his time, knowledge and voice – such a warm, giving instrument. If you could say a voice could smile, that's my impression of Bert's. Most of what I know about him I learned from Dave Swarbrick, who worked with him on many projects, and I realise what a mere drop in the ocean that knowledge is. I am thrilled to now have Dave Arthur's book to fill in the rest of the story of a quite extraordinary man.

Richard Thompson OBE

Preface

Few lives intersect with so many others, and even fewer with so many lives interesting in their own right, as did the life of A.L. Lloyd. In writing his biography Dave Arthur, whether he set out to do it or not, has found himself mining a rich seam in the history of twentieth-century Britain.

It is a seam which runs from the depression that drove youngsters like Bert Lloyd to the colonies, through the political turmoil of the 1930s which fuelled a migration of artists and intellectuals towards the Marxist left, on through a cold war against communism which followed the military defeat of fascism, to a realigned political culture in which idealism was required to adjust, sometimes reluctantly, to harsh realities.

Bert Lloyd was part of all of this, an autodidact, a polyglot and (in Cecil Day Lewis's view) a polymath who, having somehow traversed the space between the Australian outback and the Bloomsbury Set, moved on into print journalism and radio, pioneering a new form in sound broadcasting and playing a leading role in the recovery and dissemination of Britain's and Europe's traditions of oral song. Not bad for one lifetime, and remarkable for a lifetime mostly spent swimming against the tide.

But what most of us who knew him recall when someone mentions Bert is not this seam of history: it is the amiable, rotund, unfailingly generous dispenser of an apparently bottomless fund of information; the critic who was always kind and positive; and the singer, in a quirky, high-pitched voice, of a seemingly limitless repertoire of traditional songs. Of course there was more to him than this; of course he was a complex man; of course he had and has his critics; and of course not everything his critics say is unfounded. It's pretty clear, for instance, that he couldn't always bring himself to admit that he had rewritten some of the folksongs he sang.

Dave Arthur sets out to paint Bert warts and all. If what nevertheless emerges is at once a remarkable historical figure, a profound scholar and an approachable and decent man, it is because Bert Lloyd, whatever his faults, was all these things.

The Rt. Hon. Sir Stephen Sedley

Acknowledgements

I am well aware that I have probably done those things I ought not to have done, and left undone those things I ought to have done, and that my perspective on Bert's *life* and *times* will not necessarily be how someone else might have done it. This is not an in-depth critique and analysis of his work; I leave that for those more qualified than I to engage in. But I think the articles, both popular and academic, which have been written about Bert since his death have been full of factual errors and false assumptions.

Whether or not you agree with my view of his life, and particularly his part in the folk revival, I believe that the hard facts of dates, places and so on are accurate, and that a few longstanding and oft-repeated myths have been put to rest. I have been especially interested in detailing those areas of his life about which little is known – Australia, whaling, 1930s, the army, *Picture Post*, radio etc. This is as comprehensive a framework of a complex life as space and time allowed and a Lloydian resource for present and future Bertologists.

It has been an exciting and fascinating eye-opener. I hope you find the story as interesting to read as it was to write. I also hope that, wherever Bert is, he won't look down, or up, too harshly on my efforts to tell his story as honestly as I know how. I thank everyone for their patience, especially Malcolm Taylor at the Vaughan Williams' Memorial Library, who initiated this book and argued its case on my behalf. He has been a paragon of patience, help and understanding. Without him it wouldn't have happened.

Also, as Bert would say 'I offer a bow' to his daughter, Caroline Clayton, who generously gave me access to family letters. Without them it would have been a poorer book. A huge thank you, as well, to Malcolm Hay, who agreed to cast an initial judicious editorial eye over the majority of the book.

A further list of thanks covers twenty-seven years of interviews, phone calls, conversations, help and advice, journeys long and short, hospitality and generosity far beyond my hopes and expectations. Every morsel of information, as well as every scrap of opinion and advice has been gratefully received, even if there was insufficient space to use it all. Sadly, many of the following are no longer with us, but I am deeply grateful to everyone for their kindnesses:

Paul Adams, Hugh Anderson, Frankie Armstrong, Tim Arthur, Toni Arthur-Hay, Sir David Attenborough, Anne Beech, The BBC, Kenneth Bell, Steve Benbow, Georgina Boyes, Kevin Bradley, Sheila Burch, Alan Bush, James Cameron, Bernard Campbell, Jim Carroll, Martin Carthy, Norma Carthy (Waterson), Ted Clayton, Douglas and Nest Cleverdon, Shirley Collins, Gill Cooke, Pete Cooper, Bob Copper, John Copper, Peter Cox, Jennifer Cutting, Bob Davenport, Dan and Winnie Davin, Rosie Davis, Lucy Duran, Dusty, The EFDSS, Tony Engle, Faber and Faber, Christina Foyle, Hans Fried, Vic Gammon, Barrie Gavin, Goldsmiths' College, Reg Hall, Bert Hardy, Dave

Harker, John Hasted, Mary Helton, Sir Tom Hopkinson, Alun Howkins, Dr H.G. Alun Hughes, Stan Hugill, Sir Edward Hulton, Ken Hunt, Dave Hurst, Peter Kennedy, Louis Killen, Bill Leader, Humphrey Lyttelton, Pat Mackenzie, The Marx Memorial Library, Leslie and Bron Morton, Barry Murphy, Dr. P.J. Nixon, Paul Oliver, Tom Paley, Roy Palmer, Mike Parry, Bob Pegg, Carole Pegg, Ben Perrick, Michael Pickering, Elise Pin, Maddy Prior, Camilla Raab, Arnold Rattenbury, Chris Roche, Colin Ross, Steve Roud, George and Doreen Rudé, Willy Russell, Raphael Samuel, Derek Schofield, The School of Scottish Studies, Sir Stephen Sedley, Peggy Seeger, Julia Seiber-Boyd, Leslie Shepard, Brian and Sally Shuel, Hylda Sims, Vic Smith, Dan Stewart, Madeau Stewart, Dave Swarbrick, Sydney Public Library, Barry Taylor, David Toop, Richard Thompson, Jeff Towns, Vaughan-Williams' Memorial Library, Ursula Vaughan-Williams, Prof. Diane Waller, Steve Warnick, Edgar and Ann Waters, Mike Waterson, Peta Webb, Ben Weinreb, Colin and Shirley Wilkie, Edward Williams, Paul Wilson, Eric and Audrey Winter, Michael and Betty Wippell, Martyn Wyndham-Read, Mike Yates.

Thanks to Alex Bingham and the Ukelele Orchestra of Great Britain for financial support.

A special thanks to editor Rab MacWilliam and Pluto's Robert Webb whose skill helped me painlessly reduce the original manuscript by some thirty thousand words!

To those I've inadvertently missed, my sincere apologies and gratitude for your unacknowledged help.

Finally, a huge thank you and an abject apology to my family and friends who have suffered over several years of Lloydian obsession with good humour and support for a project they (and I) at times feared would never end.

Tunbridge Wells
2012

For further information on A.L. Lloyd please visit www.bertlloyd.org

Introduction

Put in everything you know, and then riddle out the fire and get rid of all the bits you don't need.

Rudyard Kipling on biography writing

These are my friends and my enemies. Start with the enemies, dear boy, and you'll get a better book.

Noel Coward to his biographer, Sheridan Morley

This book has been some twenty-five years in gestation. It has its origin some forty years ago, when I first discovered that A.L. (Bert) Lloyd lived a few minutes away from me across Blackheath, in south London. I wrote to him with all the enthusiasm and ignorance of youth, inviting him round to dinner to talk about my researches into the Anglo-American history of the 'Derby Ram'/'Didn't He Ramble' family of songs. Bert resisted the temptation to tell me he'd been there and done that two decades previously. He courteously accepted my invitation.

Sadly, a trip to Hungary got in the way so we never did discuss the 'Derby Ram'. He did, however, on his return, invite my wife and myself up to his book-lined first-floor study, overlooking Greenwich Park, to share the fruits of his recent expedition. Bert enthusiastically operated his reel-to-reel Revox tape machine, and kept up a running commentary on the trip, while we sat on the floor and listened to exotic epic ballad singers, while attempting to follow the song text (in Hungarian) that Bert thoughtfully provided for us.

From then on, for the rest of his life, our paths occasionally crossed, either at his Queen Anne house at 16 Croom's Hill, at clubs, festivals, concerts, Topic Records, or a couple of times a year in my car when I drove the pair of us up to London for editorial board meetings of the *Folk Music Journal* at Cecil Sharp House.

Bert Lloyd had a huge early influence on what I, and most of my generation of folk music enthusiasts, sang. This came partly from his albums, articles and radio programmes, and partly from his artistic influence at Topic Records, and sometimes from the beautifully written music and song lyrics that dropped through many of our letterboxes, because he felt they 'might suit us' or we had indicated an interest. He also encouraged our enthusiastic delving into the lesser known highways and byways of folk song, folklore, dance and storytelling and later 'electric folk'.

If this looks as if it's shaping up to be a hagiography, don't worry. I see no value in diaries and biographies that only tell half the tale, especially of people in the public eye – the movers and shakers of the world. If a person has affected our lives, then I believe we deserve to know who that person is, or was. A half-cut diamond is no diamond at all. I would rather know all the

1

facts, or facets, and make my own assessment of the life and achievements of someone who has in their own way changed my world. As Michelangelo knew, it was difficult, if not impossible, to carve a perfect statue before he had taken his block of marble up to the top of the quarry and watched the sun rise behind it to expose any flaws that lay within the stone. We are all blocks of marble, capable of transformation into lesser or greater works of art. Some are flawed beyond redemption. Some are flawless. Most of us are somewhere in between.

Despite Bert Lloyd's public life as a writer, performer and broadcaster, and despite his enormous influence on thousands of lives, most people know very little about the Bert Lloyd behind the round, genial, bushy-eye browed, sometimes quizzical public face. He was a private man, who succeeded in keeping his personal and public lives carefully separate. According to photographer Bert Hardy, Bert never mentioned politics or music in all the ten years they worked and travelled together as a photo-journalistic team. Hardy was very surprised when he eventually found out that Bert was a singer.[1] The folk world knew little or nothing about his earlier writings and political life in the 1930s and 1940s. In interviews he chose to ignore them. For some people, this imbued him with an air of mystery. Had he something to hide? Someone who knew him well once suggested that he might have been a spy – a not unreasonable supposition in view of his avowed communism, and since at least two of his several careers (*Picture Post* journalist and folk song scholar) had given him the opportunity to travel the world, including the Soviet bloc countries which were generally inaccessible to all but trusted Party members and fellow-travellers. The possibility also occurred to the security services who kept an eye on Bert, along with other communist folk music singers and collectors such as Ewan MacColl and the American Alan Lomax, who was working in Britain in the 1950s. One loses confidence in their credibility, however, when in a Secret Service memo dated 31 March 1955 we see: 'Extract from Special Branch Report: re *Daily Worker* Silver Jubilee Celebrations held at the Albert Hall on 27th February 1955. There followed a musical interlude with songs sung by the Choir of the Workers' Music Association, conducted by Bernard Stevens, with A.L. Lloyd accompanying them on the accordion.'

Bert on the accordion? As far as I know, and according to all he said, he played nothing beyond the little keyboard he had in his office for picking out the top lines of tunes, and a bit of closet guitar. The idea of a rather sedate Bert pumping away on a squeezebox is difficult to imagine. In fact he had no love of the accordion. Once, when reviewing a Bulgarian virtuoso accordionist for *Recorded Folk Music*, Bert declared the performance to be 'an education in what the usually beastly instrument can sound like'.

From the 1930s through to the 1950s MI5 must have had their time cut out keeping tabs on the Reds who lurked under so many artistic beds. The majority of creative thinkers in the 1930s and 1940s – poets, painters, cartoonists, musicians, writers, historians – seem to have been on the anti-fascist left.

In 1939 Special Branch noted that when the biologist and science populariser Professor Julian Huxley travelled away from home he 'invariably takes with him a complete set of the *Encyclopaedia Britannica*, a code book used by leading Soviet agents'! Some communists and fellow-travellers, such as Victor Gollancz, Derek Kartun (Foreign Editor of the *Daily Worker*), John Strachey, Christopher Hill and Stephen Spender, ultimately became disenchanted with the Communist Party, and many more followed after the brutal suppression of the Hungarian uprising by Moscow in 1956.

Gabriel (aka Jimmy Friell), the *Daily Worker* cartoonist for seventeen years, resigned from the paper when his cartoon comparing the Russian tanks in Budapest to the Anglo-French invasion of Egypt was rejected: 'I couldn't conceive of going on cartooning about the evils of capitalism and imperialism, and ignoring the acknowledged evils of Russian Communism.'[2]

Some, however, like Bert, were '100 per-centers'; faithful to the Party in political sickness and health, until death did them part. But this doesn't make him a spy. He was so busy for the whole of his life that I doubt he could have found time for regular meetings with Soviet spymasters in back-street cafés, or amongst the bushes of Hampstead Heath or Greenwich Park, dropping off the latest folk revival gossip in dead letter boxes.

Barrie Gavin, the TV film director who worked regularly with Bert for the last decade of his life, described him as 'sheltering behind a sheet of amiable plate glass'.[3] I think that sums him up very well. He was always amiable, always friendly and helpful, generous with his knowledge, but usually reticent and self-effacing where his own life and achievements were concerned. A casual remark about children whistling through blades of grass could set him off on a lecture about related musical forms, from Aboriginal gum-leaf bands that he'd seen as a youth in Australia to Romanian pear-leaf virtuosi. Ask about Bert Lloyd, however, and he'd say, 'Oh no, I don't think anybody would be interested in me'. On at least a couple of occasions Gavin broached with Bert the possibility of making a film of his life. Bert rejected the idea out of hand, insisting there were a lot more interesting and important subjects than him. He felt that the sort of work they'd been doing together, documenting traditional folk arts and working-class culture, was what mattered – its importance transcended the cult of personality.

It seems likely that modesty, rather than espionage, or more skeletons in his cupboard than is usual, prompted this personal reticence – which maybe also explains his extraordinary funeral, or non-funeral. He wanted no service, nor any ceremony so, according to Gavin, when he died, Greenwich council officials came round to the house, zipped him up in a body-bag, laid him in a zinc container, and took him away for 'disposal'. He slipped away from life in as unassuming a way as it must be possible to go.

So when Bert's modest opening words in *Folk Song in England* are 'This is a book for beginners not specialists', or, in *The Singing Englishman*, 'I know there are people better qualified than I am to write a book of this kind ... I know this is a sketchy book.' Or when he refers to the first edition of *Come All Ye Bold Miners* as 'skimpy in content, poorly edited as it was', perhaps he is being genuinely humble and not indulging in self-deprecation as the subtlest form of vanity.

He could surely have been in no real doubt about his own intellectual and artistic achievements. But possibly, as an autodidact, he suffered from what would be a lack of confidence in a world where an Oxbridge First is the accepted intellectual bench mark, and where self-deprecation spikes the guns of would-be critics. Anyway, despite his protests, he is arguably the most influential figure in the postwar folk music revival in England: the benign godfather of folk song.

Since his death in 1982 there have been major changes in politics and folk music. He missed seeing the break-up of the USSR. He missed the Blair years, so joyfully welcomed in by those on the left in 1997 and ending a decade later in disillusionment for many. He also missed the burgeoning in the new millennium of interest in folk music, especially instrumental music, amongst a considerable number of young people who, while looking back at their cultural roots, were reaching out to new audiences and taking the music on to new levels of musicianship undreamt of in the very early days of the revival when, after English-concertina player Alf Edwards, banjo- and guitar-picker Peggy Seeger, harmonica man Johnny Cole, guitarists Fitzroy Coleman, Brian Daly and Steve Benbow and, a bit later, fiddler Dave Swarbrick, it became somewhat of a barrel-scraping exercise to come up with many other competent accompanists.

Many of today's folk musicians weren't born when Bert died, so this book may, as Bert might have said, 'blow a few cobwebs away' and help put the current folk and world music scene into some sort of cultural and artistic context. As for the earlier generations of folk music performers, enthusiasts, academics (there are now more of *them* than you can shake a stick at), lefties old and young, and general readers who might have picked this up by chance, we can explore together a remarkable life, and pick our way through the myths and apocryphal Bert stories that have been circulating as fact for decades. Some, it must be said, perpetuated by Bert himself.

1
The Beginning

As a narrator my one task is to depict the given events in as accurate and lively a manner as possible.

Georgi Valentinovitch Plekhanov

Some of my friends think that when retelling an event or piece of news, I am inclined to alter or over elaborate. Myself, I just call it making something 'come alive'.

Truman Capote

What do we think we know about Bert's origins?

The BBC folk music catalogue credits Bert with an 'inherited folk song repertoire from his parents'. These included, according to the biographical notes on his 1950s American albums, 'sea songs' from his father. The BBC producer Douglas Cleverdon, who knew Bert well from the 1940s onwards and produced many of his classic radio programmes such as *Songs of the Durham Miners*, *Epic Survivals* and *Voice of the Gods,* reckoned that Bert was the illegitimate son of a Welsh cook and a Greek shipping tycoon! According to Cleverdon, this bizarre pairing provided Bert with a good Welsh tenor voice from his mother's side and the attributes of a Balkan folk singer (whatever they might be) from his Greek father.[1]

It's hardly the sort of lineage that you'd conjure out of thin air, so presumably someone (Bert?) had given him this information. Song collector and researcher Mike Yates had been told by Bert that his mother was a Suffolk girl with quite a repertoire of songs. His father was also said to have been a native of Barton-on-Humber, a fisherman who trekked around the country collecting folk songs. So we've got a Greek or Lincolnshire father, and a singing Suffolk lass or a Welsh cook, who was living proof that 'it's the rich what gets the pleasure, and the poor what gets the blame'.

The truth is somewhat more prosaic. Bert's parents were both Londoners. His grandfather, Albert Lloyd, an accountant, married Cornelia Anne McDowell in September 1870. Their first daughter Cornelia Anne was stillborn in 1871, other children came at regular intervals: Albert Frederick (1873), Annie Kathleen (1874), Beatrice Amy (1876), Walter James (1877), Florence Cornelia and Ernest Lancaster (1879), John McDowell (1881), Harry (1883).

Bert's father, Ernest Lancaster Lloyd, was born at 59 Huntingdon Street, Islington. Bert's mother, Mabel Emily Barrett, the daughter of Charles Barrett, a Battersea printer, first saw the light of day a couple of weeks before Christmas in 1881, at 33 Robertson Street West, East Battersea. They were married in St Faith's parish church in Wandsworth on 30 March 1902. At the time Ernest was a despatch manager. Interestingly, Bert's maternal grandmother,

Harriet Hannah Barrett (formerly Baber), was born in 1853 in Allandale, Northumberland, famous for its traditional New Year Tar Barrel burning (but I never heard him mention this folkloric connection). His maternal grandfather, Charles Barrett, born in 1855, was a compositor and came from Winslow in Buckinghamshire.[2]

Bert said that his father was quite a good singer of comic songs and the more popular folk-type material such as 'Barbara Allen' and 'The Bailiff's Daughter of Islington' (quite appropriate, as that's where he came from). His mother apparently burlesqued the singing of Sussex gypsies during the family's stay in the county when Bert was young. Of course, in those days most people knew a few songs, because they were accustomed to making their own entertainment. Working-class Londoners were famed for their knees-ups at any seasonal or family celebration when 'Come into the Garden, Maud' might rub shoulders with 'Jeanie With the Light Brown Hair', 'To Be a Farmer's Boy' or 'Polly Perkins', but it didn't make them folk singers in the narrow sense in which some of us use the term today – unless you go along with Louis Armstrong's all-encompassing definition: 'All music's folk music, leastwise, I ain't never heard a horse sing.'

Albert Lancaster Lloyd was born on 29 February, Leap Year Day, 1908, in a small late-Victorian terraced house at 93 Trevelyan Road, behind Tooting High Street, in south London. At the time of Bert's birth his father was a draper's packer, but according to Bert he'd also been a trawlerman, a dockworker, a failed poultry farmer and an Automobile Association patrolman. The trawlerman claim was probably a bit of romanticising. In 1911 the Lloyds were living on a Sussex poultry farm belonging to Ernest's brother, and an AA patrolman he definitely was: his army records have his job down as 'motor patrol' (cyclist), and on his death certificate he is noted as 'Ernest Lancaster Lloyd, AA scout and army pensioner'.

Both the Royal Automobile Club and the AA pioneered nationwide patrols, initially by bicycle and later by motorbike, to scout out the roads and to give their members advance warning, by saluting them, of any police speed traps. Eventually, when the AA came under fire from the police for aiding and abetting offenders they changed their methods and the scouts saluted everybody, unless they had seen a police ambush in which case they forgot to salute.

Bert had two older sisters – Beatrice Florence (Trixie), born 8 January 1903, and Kathleen Mabel (Kathie) who was born on 4 September 1904. His childhood as the baby boy in the family was seemingly a very happy one, because he always spoke very fondly of his parents and said what spirited creatures his sisters were and how surreal was their sense of fun.

He remembered being taken up to their bedroom as a small boy and stood at the foot of the bed while they faced him, holding on to the bed rail, and bounced up and down as if galloping on horseback. They would demand to know the time and Bert would solemnly announce 'Eight o'clock!', or whatever time he chose, to which his sisters would fling themselves back on the bed crying 'Too late! Too late!' Bert never understood the significance of the game but its surreal quality remained a vivid memory for the rest of his life. He also vividly recalled the time his father rigged up a series of hosepipes to the family gramophone, the ends of which the children held up to their ears in order to hear the music without disturbing the neighbours. Perhaps this was one of Bert's earliest experiences of his favourite word – 'ingenious'. Sadly, with the exception of these tantalising snapshots of his childhood, Bert's references to his early family life are scarce.

An early photograph shows Bert as a chubby, bright-eyed three- or four-year-old child with a mop of blond flyaway hair, dressed in a short-sleeved smock, standing seriously to attention, hands behind his back, with a large St Bernard dog at his feet. Another picture from the same period, taken in an orchard, has him sitting in a small two-wheeled pony cart, peering out from under a large upturned-brimmed, Christopher Robin-type sun hat. Next to him, holding the reins, sits his mother: a very smartly dressed, round-faced woman, wearing a dark Edwardian suit, a high lace-collared blouse, and an enormous flower-bedecked straw hat. She had, according to Bert, once worked in service for a Greek millionaire, where she developed a taste for the nicer things in life. At the pony's head stands Ernest Lloyd, small, thin-faced, dapper, with a moustache, in hacking-jacket, gaiters and flat cap. He could pass for a head gardener or gamekeeper on a large estate. At his feet lies the St Bernard. The photograph was taken on a sunny summer day a couple of years before the First World War cast its shadow over the Lloyd family.

One of the few early biographical snippets he mentions in album sleeve notes is that when he was about eight years old he was attending meetings of a juvenile temperance guild called The Rope-holders (similar to the Yorkshire Band of Hope which was formed in Leeds in 1847 to teach and impress on children the importance of sobriety). At these meetings he remembers lustily joining in the chorus of a popular temperance hymn:

> Sign the pledge, brother,
> Sign, sign, sign,
> Asking the aid of the helper divine.

Later he heard the tune attached to an American Civil War song, a revival hymn, and, in Australia, to the shearing song, 'Click Go the Shears'. But that was all a few years off.

In September 1914 Ernest Lloyd answered Lord Kitchener's call and joined the army. At Shepherd's Bush, West London, he signed a short-service contract (three years with the colours), swore 'by Almighty God to be faithful and to bear true allegiance to His Majesty King George the Fifth', allotted a portion of his army pay to support his wife and family, passed a medical – 'Physical Development: Fair. Many defective teeth upper jaw (consents to see dentist)' – and was appointed to the Essex Regiment 8th Cyclist Battalion, based in Colchester. He was soon transferred to the Royal Sussex Regiment, possibly with the 6th Cyclist Battalion, whose headquarters were in Brighton.

In July 1916 Ernest was sent to Belgium as part of the British Expeditionary Force (the Old Contemptibles) and was returned to Shoreham Depot two months later with a gunshot wound to his right arm, just one of the 290,461 wounded soldiers evacuated to the United Kingdom for 'further treatment' in that year alone. In June 1917 he was back on the Continent to participate in the bloody fiasco that was the Flanders, or Passchendaele, offensive. By August he was in hospital in Sheffield, being treated for nephritis (inflammation of the kidney). By the end of the year he was invalided home as 'unfit for future military service' due to 'debility'. He was discharged from the Royal Sussex Regiment in November 1917 with a disability pension of fifteen shillings and nine pence.[3]

In the last few weeks of his life Bert reflected on his father and the First World War. He told his family how Ernest had been sent back to fight in France when he was still weak from his earlier wounds and that, so Bert felt, was how TB had arrived in the Lloyd household. He was still angry sixty–five years later at the incompetence of the military authorities who treated their men as cannon fodder, and sad at the repercussions of their stupidity on his and other working-class families.

Ernest was a little man, just five feet five inches tall, with a thirty-one inch chest, and weighing only eight stone (112 pounds). Before joining the army he was, according to the army doctor, 'healthy in wind, eye and limb', if not teeth. By the time he'd finished with the army he was far less healthy, although he hadn't quite completed his service because in November 1920 he was found to be fit enough for the Territorial Force, and was attached to the 7th Auxiliary Middlesex Regiment for a year.

Private Lloyd, E.L. was finally discharged from the army at Hounslow in March 1922, and settled down with his wife, Mabel, and two surviving children, Beatrice and Bert, at 25 Mayfield Road, Hornsey, north London. He had just three years to live.

Here Bert was bright enough to get into the local grammar school, presumably the Stationers' Company School, which was just at the top of Mayfield Road. In those days the old grammar schools provided clever middle- and working-class children with all the benefits of a classical education. He would have had a good grounding in Latin, as well as in at least one modern language, which in his case was Spanish. Both of these would prove useful in later life.

The Lloyd family were destined to develop an unhappy familiarity with undertakers, a familiarity that carried through into Bert's adult life. His baby brother Eric, born in May 1916, died in July 1917; both of Bert's sisters died from tuberculosis, Kathie in the winter of 1917/8, Trixie in 1927. On 17 February 1924, two weeks before Bert's sixteenth birthday, his mother, Mabel, died of pulmonary tuberculosis in Clare Hall Hospital, South Mimms; she was forty-two years old. Ernest, whose occupation was entered on her death certificate as 'Book-keeper, Woolwich Arsenal Army pensioner', was with her when she died.

Bert's father died in 1925. It would be surprising if the loss of his whole family at such a young age didn't have serious repercussions on Bert's emotional development. Would losing one's loved ones with alarming regularity eventually inure you to the pain of loss?

DOWN UNDER

On the ninth day of October
From London we did steer,
And everything being safe on board
We sailed down the river clear;
And every ship that we passed by
We heard the sailors say,
'There goes a ship of clever lads,
And they're bound for Botany Bay'.
(Traditional)

With Ernest's poor health making it increasingly difficult for him to look after Bert, and the constant worry that Bert himself might contract the illness that was killing his family, it was decided, with the help of the Royal British Legion, to send him to live a healthier life in Australia.

Eight months after his mother's death, on Thursday, 9 October 1924, Bert left Mayfield Road with his suitcase and made his way to the King George V dock to join the other 914 passengers on the SS *Euripides*, under the command of Captain P.J. Collins, as one of the assisted migrants heading for New South Wales that year. In the ship's register he was entered as: 'Mr Albert Lloyd, male, age 16, scholar, contract ticket No. 491. Destination Sydney.' Some of the other passengers were getting off earlier, to start *their* new lives in Cape Town and Melbourne.[4] It was a good week to be leaving England and heading for the sun: wet in the south with widespread gales.

Four months before Bert left England, the folk song collector Cecil Sharp, who had also spent some time in Australia, died of cancer in Hampstead, North London. His pioneering *English Folk Song: Some Conclusions*, published in 1907, was to remain the standard analytical work on the subject until Bert's *Folk Song in England* was published some sixty years later.

In the nineteenth century, and the early years of the twentieth, several schemes were tried out to attract agricultural workers to Australia. In the mid-1800s the Family Colonization Loan Society assisted families to emigrate, and charitable institutions and poor-law authorities sent boys and girls from Ragged Schools, and girls and young women from the workhouses, to work as domestics and to help on farms.

In 1912 the 'Dreadnought' scheme was taking British boys between the ages of fourteen and eighteen and training them on Scheyville Farm in New South Wales, while the Child Emigration Society of Oxford sent *very* young children out to an establishment in Western Australia and maintained them until they were old enough to go to work. Henry Freeman took boys from the English Ragged School Union to a holding farm and from there they were distributed to other farms. Agents in Britain, usually working for the shipping companies, also acquired migrants, for which they received a bounty. Others, like Bert – an assisted migrant, had their passages arranged through philanthropic agencies such as the Royal British Legion.

In 1917 a Dominions royal commission had declared that the development of Imperial resources was being hampered by the unsatisfactory distribution of manpower, and that the success of Empire development was dependent upon the successful organisation of emigration to assist 'the progress of the immense territories of the Dominions and the increase of power of the Empire as a whole'.[5] Bert's ship, along with the other liners, *Sophocles*, *Diogenes* and *Themistocles*, regularly made the six-week trip down to Australia filled with assisted-passage migrants, many of them orphans.

He never saw his father again: the following September Ernest Lloyd died of pulmonary tuberculosis and haemoptysis. It was obvious to the doctors by the coughing up of blood that it was the most common form of active TB – and a post-mortem wasn't considered necessary. Ernest was forty-six and had been working as a motor scout until he became too sick to continue.

As sixteen-year-old Bert leant on the ship's rail, along with dozens of other excited and apprehensive emigrants, and watched London and his childhood disappear into the distance, he could have had no idea of the sort of life he'd be living on the sun-baked plains of New South Wales for the next few years, and he had yet to hear the oft-quoted description of the outback as 'a long agony of scrub and wire fence'. They steamed down the cold, grey, English Channel and headed into the rough waters of the Bay of Biscay, where the plunging of the ship in the choppy waters must have sent many of the town-bred emigrants crawling for their bunks, their stomachs in their mouths.

> All the while that it was calm
> I felt quite gay and frisky,
> But, oh! how pale and ill I looked
> When in the Bay of Biscay.
> ('The Voyage to Australia', traditional)

First stop was a couple of hours' lay-over in the Spanish port of Vera Cruz on the island of Tenerife, where the passengers could, for a ten shilling return fare, go ashore for a spot of sightseeing in one of the dozens of tiny bumboats, piled high with bananas, and manned by dark-skinned, shouting, gesticulating islanders that swarmed out to the ship. Soon, after a couple of warning blasts on the ship's siren, they were back at sea and ploughing down the West African coast for a thirty-six-hour coaling stop in Cape Town, and to drop off the first batch of passengers.

Here, sensible travellers took the advice offered them to stay ashore to escape the inevitable clouds of coal-dust that would envelop everything while the bunkers were being filled by the army of African labourers, who ran up and down the gangplanks hauling baskets of coal on their backs. Like the roustabouts who loaded cotton on the big paddle-steamers on the Mississippi levees, they somehow found enough wind and energy to sing to help them with their work. These must have been the first work songs that Bert heard, although at sixteen, and on his first trip to what was still referred to as the Dark Continent, the singing would have been just one of a myriad of extraordinary new experiences. It was certainly a far cry from a winter's day in Hornsey, and exciting enough to kick-start a lifelong fascination for exotic travel, and, perhaps, subliminally, folk songs.

Finally, on 21 November, after some forty-four days at sea, the *Euripides* rounded North Head, entered Port Jackson, sailed down the deep, 770-feet-wide water channel and tied up at one of the large wharves. Bert had arrived in Sydney. Ranked as the fifth port in the British Empire, it had a population of over one million, electric street lighting, an underground railway system being built and lots of huge impressive Victorian buildings. A new bridge over the harbour had recently been commissioned.

On the *Euripides* 'Incoming Passenger' list, prepared for the Australian immigration officials, Bert, along with a number of other teenage boys without a specific trade, was registered as 'farm labourer' – the 'scholar' on the passenger boarding-list cut no ice once he got 'down under'. After being herded ashore with their luggage, the 'New Chums' were taken to the Customs House (now a branch of Sydney Public Library) at Circular Quay, and given a cursory inspection by the Customs Inspectors, before being marched off to the Immigration Dispersal Centre.

Eventually, along with many of the other young assisted migrants who needed to be placed on farms, Bert found himself taken to George Street, Australia's oldest street, named after King George III in 1810: originally a mere track used by convicts fetching water, but by 1924 a busy road in the Rocks area, at the heart of Sydney, where, in the old Commissariat Stores (demolished in 1930), was situated the George Street North Labour Exchange. Here the new arrivals were registered and given the once-over by a bunch of small farmers or 'cockies' – so called, legend has it, because their farms were considered too poor to raise anything but cockatoos, as Bert explained to the audience at Dingles Folk Club in 1973:

> Cockies are small farmers, wheat farmers, nearly always very poor. Over much of Australia unless you owned a lot of territory you starve, and so it is with cockies in many parts. They're called cockies because all they can raise on their farms are cockatoos that, of course, eat all the wheat-seed as soon as you've planted it. Still, you can always eat cockatoo. There's a recipe for it, it says, you take your cockatoo and you pluck it and clean it and put it in the saucepan. You put a horseshoe in the saucepan, too, and fill it up with water. Put it on to boil, and when the horseshoe's soft you give it another ten minutes.

The cockies who gathered, vulture-like (as Bert described them), to grab some cheap Pommy labour were as like as not Pommies themselves, as the National Library of Australia's Kevin Bradley explained:

The small farms were, in fact, a nineteenth-century initiative which was intended to recreate English yeomanry in Australia, and in its first stages was designed to attract English settlers (who were to the early colonists, the epitome of the best stock). In later years it was recast as the soldier-settler scheme, but it is pretty likely nonetheless that the cocky farmer was a Pommy himself. The scheme was a disaster because most of the allotted farms were not big enough to support their owner, being based, as they were, on an appropriate English size.

Bert was finally allocated a job on one of these small farms in the Cowra district, a mixed farming area in the heart of central west New South Wales, on the edge of the western slopes, and about 140 miles southwest of Sydney. He was handed a railway travel voucher, and the £3 start-up money he'd deposited for safe keeping before embarking in London.

To his disappointment, after travelling half way round the world, when he got down to Cowra he spent a dismal time as farm dogsbody – milking, mucking out, digging, chopping and hauling.

> At daylight you must milk the cows,
> Make butter, cheese, an' feed the sows,
> Put on the kettle, the cook arouse,
> And clean the family shoes.
> The stable and sheep-yard clean out,
> And always answer when we shout,
> With 'Yes, Ma'am', and 'No, Sir', mind your mouth;
> And my youngsters don't abuse.
> 'The Squatter's Man' (Traditional)

The native Australians didn't want to know about this sort of general farm work with its low pay and long hours, but it was considered eminently good enough for the new chums straight off the ships from Britain. Australians preferred work in the big cities like Sydney, Melbourne or Brisbane, or fancied the hard-living, hard-drinking, romantic life of a shearer or stockman, where they could flash a blade in the shearing sheds, or crack a kangaroo-hide stock-whip on the huge cattle and sheep stations out west, where you had to be good with your fists if you refused to accept a drink, or called a bloke a liar, and where your wages were protected by the Pastoral Workers Union, which Bert would eventually join, marking his first involvement with politics. Thirty years later Bert used to talk about Old Dad Adams from Cowra, who sang the song 'Bluey Brink':

> Now it ain't in the history, you won't find it in print,
> But that shearer drunk acid with never a wink,
> Saying, that's the stuff Jimmy, why strike me stone dead,
> This'll make me the ringer of Stephenson's shed.

As Bert said: 'Rumour had it that the pubs didn't stock anything strong enough for Old Dad. It was said he would bore a hole in the bottom of a silo and suck out the fermented juice of the ensilage through a straw. To one expressing disbelief, the answer was, All right, look for yourself. All the silos around Cowra have got little holes bored in 'em.'

Cowra wasn't exactly the cultural centre of the universe. In the 1933 census, nine years after Bert's arrival, it boasted just 1,000 homes – and that was after a building boom. One thing it did have, however, was the small Cowra District Hospital on Liverpool Street, in the centre of the town (now a substantial private house), and it was there that Bert spent New Year's Day 1925, the high spot of which was an impromptu party held in the ward in the matron's absence. A vaudeville actor sang a song entitled 'One of the Has-Beens', to the tune of 'Pretty Polly Perkins', and Bert liked it sufficiently well to record it thirty years later on his 1957 Wattle album *Across the Western Plains*. However, according to Bert, it wasn't quite so popular with a pair of old bushwhackers at the other end of the ward who thought that the singer was having a personal dig at them:

> I'm one of the has-beens, a shearer I mean,
> I once was a ringer and used to shear clean
> I could make the wool roll off like the soil from the plough,
> But you may not believe me, for I can't do it now.

> I'm as awkward as a new chum, and I'm used to the frown,
> That the boss often shows me, saying, 'Keep them blades down'.
> ('One of the Has-Beens')

On leaving hospital, Bert was relieved to find out that he'd lost his job. He hotfooted it to the Labour Exchange and, in his newly acquired Aussie drawl, asked for work on a sheep station. He always claimed, half jokingly, that it was because he was mistaken for an Australian that he was offered work as a station hand at Frampton, near Bethungra, on a station called Ferndale. Bethungra's population today is fewer than 400, in Bert's day it was probably less. Its main claim to fame among pastoral-workers was the corrugated-roofed, veranda'd, sandstone-and-brick Shirley Hotel, with its promise of shade and cold beer. It was at Frampton, Bert's first big sheep station, that he would have joined the Pastoral Workers' Union: 'On the big stations you become a member of the Pastoral Workers' Union, and you are protected, as it were, and also the work is much more agreeable.'

In the sleeve notes of his Topic album *The Great Australian Legend* Bert said he learnt the songs 'The Lime Juice Tub' and 'Flash Jack from Gundagai' from a one-eyed shearer named Robert 'Bob' Turnbull in the shearing shed at Bethungra around 1930. This seems late if, as it appears, he went to Bethungra in early 1925, and went on to spend time on sheep stations at Bogandillon and White Cliffs, before leaving Australia in early 1930. In Bert's papers at London's Goldsmiths College, where his books and files were deposited after his death, there is a note referring to a song 'Take it Off', got from Robert Turnbull, Ferndale, Bethungra, 1927. This is the right sort of date for his time at Ferndale.

It has been popularly believed, mainly because Bert said so in interviews and in his song notes, that he left Australia around 1933 or 1934. However, according to acquaintances from the period, the general consensus is that he was back in London earlier than that. The historian Leslie Morton once said that when he and his wife first met Bert in the early 1930s they were living at the top of Hornsey Rise – just a few roads west of Ferme Park Road – and that Bert had lodgings nearby. Also, Bert's daughter Caroline remembered that Bert had told her he was twenty-one when he returned to England.

On passenger lists of travellers entering Britain during the 1920s and 1930s, there is a Lloyd who fits the bill. Albert Lloyd, aged twenty-one, left Australia aboard the White Star liner *Demosthenes* and landed in London in May 1930. In the register he is listed as 'farmhand' and his given address in England is 114 Fernpark Road, Hornsey (a misspelling of Ferme Park Road, just three streets from Mayfield Road, from where Bert set out in 1924). So we can safely say that Bert was back in England by the spring of 1930 after a six- to eight-week trip – Brisbane, Sydney, Melbourne, Adelaide, Albany, Fremantle, Durban, Cape Town, Tenerife or Las Palmas, Southampton and London.

Within a year of settling in at Ferndale it was, with the exception of the large stone and brick main house, completely destroyed in a bush fire, three or four weeks before Christmas in 1926. Bert escaped with a few minor burns. In a letter home to his sister Trixie, Bert said that the rebuilding and re-fencing of Ferndale would take several months, and then the place was to be sold, so there was no immediate rush for him to look for another job. So it's probable that he moved on to his next job sometime in 1927. Then he went further out west to a station called Bogandillon, on the plains of western New South Wales. His first impression was that it looked a bit bleak and barren compared to the towns he'd come from in the southeast.

According to Bert, his previous bosses had been 'tigers' and, when he was picked up in a Ford utility truck at the train station at Condobolin, he was keen to find out from the bloke who collected him what the new boss was like. For the twenty-mile journey out to the station he gave his driver a bit of a grilling and asked some 'pretty penetrating questions', which he later thought might have given the impression that he was a bit 'finicky' about bosses. His companion was fairly non-committal for most of the journey. It was only when they arrived at their destination that Bert discovered that his driver was in fact the boss, Mr A.H. Stevenson. Luckily he turned out to be someone with whom Bert got on rather well: better in fact than with Stevenson's father, Alexander George Stevenson, who actually co-owned the place – the Stevenson Pastoral Company – along with five others. Bert, who had several stories of his high-handedness with his son and the workers on the sheep station, nicknamed Stevenson senior the 'Napoleon of Pastoralism'. Luckily he lived at Hay, about 300 miles away, so he wasn't a frequent visitor.

Although there was work around the area for station hands it *was* the time of the Great Depression, which began in 1929, bringing class and political conflict to New South Wales, and financial ruin and mass unemployment for both city and farm workers with the collapse of commodity prices. According to Bert, there were 'an awful lot of swaggies passing through all the time. Some of them eccentric old boys with long beards, some of them eccentric young fellers at odds with society.'

On one occasion, when Bert was butchering a sheep, a couple of these 'young fellers' who had been working on the Darling Downs were walking back home to Port Adelaide following the Lachlan River. They called in at the station for rations and stood around watching Bert, hoping for a handout of a chop. It was the custom in the outback to offer transient workers some rations, even if you couldn't offer them any work. Since, according to Bert, he was interested in bush songs by this time, he decided they should sing for their supper, so he asked if they knew any songs, and was delighted to be treated to a pre-prandial, albeit rather garbled, rendition of 'Wallaby Stew', which he would add to his repertoire nearly thirty years later and 12,000 miles away, when Edgar Waters of Sydney, on a visit to England, showed him a coherent set of the words. Unfortunately, after they'd left the next morning, Bert discovered that the young swaggies had waltzed off with his best skinning knife. But he'd heard an interesting song, so, all things considered, he didn't think it was 'too bad a bargain'.

In a letter to the singer Martyn Wyndham-Read in 1977, Bert gave Martyn the lyrics and tune for the song 'The Midnight Ride', which he said he collected in Bogandillon in 1933. But as we now know, by 1933 he had been back in England for three years. Incidentally, this is one of the songs in the A.L. Lloyd Archive at Goldsmiths that shows evidence of several textual changes from an original typescript.

About once every six weeks, on a Saturday afternoon after work, Bert and his fellow station hands would ride the twenty miles into the nearest town, Condobolin. They'd arrive in the late afternoon and hitch their horses up at the back of the Commercial Hotel, which was the first pub they came to when they hit town. They'd wash the trail dust from their throats, get a haircut, do a bit of shopping, and then settle in the bar for a few beers until it was time to leave late on Sunday evening. Unlike the travelling shearing gangs, Bert and his mates were only moderate drinkers: 'The shearers used to put us to shame in that respect. They were much more diligent drinkers than we were.'

The landlady of the hotel had a soft spot for Bert – a fresh-faced, handsome, young lad thousands of miles away from home and, as far as she knew, family – and one evening when he was sitting in the bar, she invited him up to her first-floor front veranda that overlooked the wide tree-lined main street. It was a quiet, balmy night, and while Bert sat sipping his beer she tried to cheer him up by playing Frank Crumit's rendition of 'My Grandfather's Clock' on her wind-up gramophone. The event was one of Bert's abiding memories of his youth in Australia. As he said: 'It just shows what silly things hang in your memory, and all sorts of important things fall out.'

As the station hands rode out of town late on Sunday evening, the townsfolk were getting ready for bed. On hot nights, before the advent of air conditioning, many of them pulled their beds out onto the verandas and slept there. Bert and his mates would wave and wish a cheery goodnight to the nightgown-clad women and girls, before racing each other back to the station.

Londoner Bert obviously had a lot of catching up to do when it came to horse riding, especially compared with the Aussie stockmen, most of whom had been riding from childhood. But he was a quick learner, he was fit and athletic, and would have gone about the job of riding with his usual concentration and determination. An essential skill to master was how to survive a 'buster' – suitably descriptive Oz slang for a fall. The usual advice was to keep your hands above your head and 'fall like a bag of shit'. Not, perhaps, English pony club language, but no less effective for that.

Despite the butch, manly image of the typical bush-worker, there was also a sentimental side to him. As Kevin Bradley pointed out: 'Australian yarns are full of stories of riders who loved their horses, gave them the last of their water, lamented them when they died, praised them for saving their lives.' Bert was no exception and became very attached to his mounts. He apparently did several drawings and paintings whilst still in Australia, one of which, depicting two feral stallions (Brumbies), he sold to the historian A.L. Morton on his return to England. He also wrote a poem for a favourite mare:

> The Sun is Unmentioned
> I loved a mare – which was it? – she looked me straight
>   in the face from beneath her forelock.
> The living holes of her nostrils were two lovely things to
>   see, and the living hollows curving above each eye.
> After running, she sweated – she glistened! – and I pressed
>   moons against her flanks under my young knees … .
> I loved a mare – which was it? – and sometimes (for an animal
>   knows better of which forces we are proud)
> She lifted to her gods a brazen head; screaming,
>   honeycombed by a petiole of veins!

Rather than live in the men's bunkhouse on the Stevenson station 'amid the smell of greasy wool, fried lamb chops, shag tobacco and old newspapers', Bert chose to stay in a little weather-boarded shed in a yard next to the forge, behind the horse yard where the hands gathered to receive their early morning instructions for the day. Bert's hut, with its truck bed in one corner, and potato sacks nailed to the walls to keep the drafts out, was pretty primitive by any standards, but with the wind-up gramophone that he'd saved up for out of his wages, his box of 78rpm records, the books on loan from the Sydney library, and a few pictures nailed up, it was probably the most artistic and sophisticated roustabout's hut in New South Wales. When Bert went back and saw it again in 1970, he found it used as a dump for bits of machinery, and overrun with mice. Sticking his head in and looking around, he said: 'It seemed to me (at the time) very cosy. Looking at it now, it's bleak and bare, and you might say it was rough living, but it's always possible to make that kind of place snug.'

Leslie Morton said that knowledge just adhered to Bert and that he soaked up information like a sponge. This was certainly the case during his time in Australia. Taking advantage of the bush-workers' postal loan scheme run by the Sydney Library Service, in which rural workers could order up to a dozen books at a time, with the library paying the postage one way and the borrower paying the return, he went through the Chatto & Windus Phoenix Library catalogue like a locust, mopping up Proust, Tolstoy, James Joyce, Mark Twain (one of his favourite authors) and dozens of others. He had an amazing memory, which he didn't consider to be a sign of intelligence, just a fortunate skill with which he was born. In later life he could hear the first couple of notes of a piece of classical music and name the composition. He could also remember the book title and often the page number for most of the songs in his extensive library.

If there is any truth in the saying 'we are what we eat' then after several years working on sheep stations Bert should have been a Merino sheep. Perhaps 'we are what we read', which is why autodidacts like Bert are frequently such interesting people. Not bound by any 'official' canon or university reading list they are free to follow their noses and inclinations through half a millennium of printed books, and in the process explore bookish tributaries and bibliographic cul-de-sacs often missed by those more orthodox literary travellers who stick to the main routes.

Autodidacts have a passion for learning, an unquenchable desire to know, a need to understand, all the more impressive because it is self-motivated. It would have been so easy for Bert to get back to his shed after a hard day's work (fencing, boundary riding, tree cutting, clipping the ears and docking the tails of 6,000 lambs in four-and-a-half days, riding dozens of miles under the blistering sun moving mobs of cattle and sheep to different paddocks, and the dozen and one other back-breaking, hand-blistering, joint-wrenching jobs that he did on the western plains) and collapse on his bed till the next morning, when the cycle began again. But, no, after he'd looked after his horse, eaten, done whatever washing and mending needed doing, re-soled his boots, etc., he'd put a Mozart adagio on his wind-up gramophone, stretch out on his bed and in the lamplight write ten-page discursive letters to his family, or read a book. This was not the sort of pulp fiction found lying about in the men's barracks, but the latest novels, classics of travel and exploration, Russian literary histories, contemporary studies in literary criticism, poetry, philosophy, biographies, and all because he had to know. It was literature, music and art that sustained him when he was subject to the occasional concern about his future:

In a letter I received some time ago from a chap I knew at school, I read the fates of several of my erstwhile companions. One has a job in the Stock Exchange, another is in a bank, the writer has a meteorological job in the employ of the Government. Half a dozen others have snug permanences. From my lofty pedestal of disinterestedness I look down at them with a superior smile. At least, I'd like to, but you know, ideals and ideas aside, I'm an incorrigible suburban. Despite all sorts of theorisings, I'm forced to admit that I'd be much more content if I were in the stock exchange or civil service, or a bank, because all this swinging about on a loose end, with nothing firm or permanent in sight or ever likely to be – I see myself an old man with frayed clothes and unlaced boots, sitting on a seat in a park all day long – it's rather disquieting to my suburban self. I like to write of what a splendidly free and easy young person I am, but ... the hard slats of park seats are uncomforting to bones yet, in the meanwhile, there is Bach, Beethoven, Mozart, there is Picasso and Derain, Jacovleff, and even Eric Gill and Mestrovic, there is Milton and Flecker, even Baudelaire, Rimbaud and Mallarme, even Chekhov, Gogol, Pushkin, Lermontov, and Anna Akhmatova. And there is, too, that flesh which has to be sustained, who now remains your affectionate nephew – Bert.

This thought-provoking list was addressed to a couple of obviously sophisticated, literate aunties – unless he was simply writing above their heads, which seems doubtful. In October 1929 he wrote to his aunts, giving them his latest reading list, including *Life and Letters* which that month was devoted entirely to Richard Hughes' *A High Wind in Jamaica*:

It is the best child study I've ever read. I've been reading quite a lot lately – Hudson's *Green mansions*, Richard Jeffries' *Amaryllis at the Fair* and *The story of My Heart*, Martin Armstrong's *The Sleeping Fury*, H.M. Tomlinson's *Sea and the Jungle*, Wyndham Lewis's *Tarr* (which I liked very much), Liam O'Flaherty's *Spring Sowing*, James Joyce's *Dubliners*, Bekker's *Beethoven*, Baring's *Outline of Russian Literature*, Gosses' *Books on the Table*, Middleton Murry's *Discoveries*, and several others, all within the last few weeks.

The literary magazine *Life and Letters*, edited by the Bloomsburyite Desmond MacCarthy, was a monthly gift from his aunties which he enjoyed, feeling that he'd grown 'too stodgy and serious' for *John O'London*, *Everyman* and *Punch*. It always contained several pages of reviews and a listing of recent publications in the arts, sciences, politics, and travel and a section devoted to readers' reviews of books that weren't included in the main review section. This little magazine was a literary lifeline to Bert, keeping him up to date with what was happening in the outside world and giving him ideas on what to order from the Sydney library including art books. Unfortunately, many of the book illustrations were in monochrome. Undeterred, he familiarised himself not just with classical art but also with modern movements such as Fauvism, Expressionism, Dada, Cubism and Surrealism – the Surrealist Manifesto was published in 1924, the year he arrived in Australia. This was a movement he was to criticise a few years later in the pages of *Left Review*, as having no bearing on proletarian problems.

Nor was music neglected. An old school friend, with whom he'd stayed in touch and exchanged lengthy letters, sent him the *Musical Times* and *Musical Opinion*. Although he later claimed to have been happy enough sitting round the bunkhouse table joining in a singaround, in which two or three circuits of the table would produce some eighteen songs (popular songs of the day such as 'My Blue Heaven' as well as shearing, droving, drinking, and bush-ranging ballads), his real love was classical music. He scoured the HMV (for whom he would eventually record) and Columbia catalogues for 78rpm records to play on his gramophone.

What is recorded in his letters home to his aunties is the tremendous enthusiasm and passion he developed for classical music.

> My musical taste is fast improving. It's now about half past nine at night. Just a few minutes ago I was sitting on a flat rock about fifteen yards away from my hut. From the open doorway, my lamp poured out a long pale rectangle of light onto the dark ground, and I had set my gramophone going right in the doorway. You know, it sounds so much better that way, where the sound has room to spread, and when one is not too near. It doesn't sound mechanical or artificial in the least. Well, there I sat, with my elbows on my knees and my chin in my hands, while Mozart's adagio made glorious little arabesques of sound in the still hot air, like minuscular festoons of cool cascading pearls.

There's no mention in the half dozen or so letters we have from the late 1920s of a particular liking for the music played by the ordinary Australians he met through work or on his visits to towns or country fairs. In fact, the couple of times he mentions working-class music and taste his remarks are distinctly disparaging and superior, as in these descriptions of a country fair where he wandered through 'the smell and press of stupid animal people', in Condobolin in August 1929: 'When the showman [who had a menagerie] shouted out 'Reptiles! Reptiles! – to the crowds … They may have, some of these people, some of the loathsome aspects of reptiles, but they're far too stupid to be classed with those coil geniuses, the snakes. Lizards, perhaps, but not snakes.' And of the local Bush Band: 'at a given signal they commence to scrape squeaky violins, to elongate concertinas, to blow a flute, to thump a rattly piano.'

At this time, as a studious young man, he obviously hadn't developed any particular love of the working classes and their entertainment, but for Mozart and Bach he is full of praise. A Bach chorale could take him on flights of reverie away from the lamb chops, the newspaper-strewn floor of the men's barracks, the girlie magazine pin-ups pasted to the walls, their cheap dog-eared paperback novels, washing-lines of drying work-clothes, and a 'fool' playing a mouth-organ.

You sense in his long rambling letters home to his aunts and others, in which he talks about religion, philosophy, music and literature, as well as his everyday life, that he is as much speaking to himself as to his family. A young man with Bert's keen intellect would in normal circumstances have been attending college or university instead of herding a thousand head of sheep across the plains of New South Wales, and would have had similarly bright people with whom to discuss art, life and the universe. Starved of this dialogue, Bert tends to use his writing to explore his thoughts and opinions.

As far as classical music was concerned, he had no plan or knowledge of what to listen to initially, so he selected titles from the catalogue that looked 'interesting', or ones recommended in *The Musical Times*. He was disappointed with 'The Firebird', which he'd expected to be a lot more modern and avant-garde. He described some of his 'finds' to Mark Gregory in a 1969 interview that appeared in *Overland* No. 45, October 1970:

> I used to buy gramophone records ... mostly on spec, out of the catalogue. Some titles seemed very attractive – 'L'Apres-Midi d'un Faune', an absolutely irresistible title; I felt sure it must be smashing music even though I didn't know what was in store ... And I understood Mozart was a melodious composer, so I thought that he should be within my reach. HMV had just issued a cheap set on Plum Label, their cheap label – three records of the G Minor Symphony, the 40th. So I sent for that and found sure enough that I could grasp it; it was very charming music, too. And then there was big publicity for a Bach record conducted by Stokowski – the D Minor Cantata and Fugue, arranged for orchestra. Looking back, it seems very flashy, but it had big publicity, and I thought – well, I ought to try Bach, even though I'd heard he was rather difficult and severe. So I got this Bach thing. It wasn't difficult and severe at all; it was very exciting – flashy, but exciting. So there it was, I was educating myself.

This thirst for musical knowledge didn't come cheaply. The old HMV Red Label twelve-inch 78s were 10s 6d each, which was a lot of money in the 1920s. But, as Bert said, he had little else to spend his money on except a monthly haircut and a booze-up.

It would be interesting to know whether or not Bert's exploration of the HMV catalogue included listening to the English baritone John Goss and his Cathedral Quartet. Goss, a close friend of folk song collector, arranger, composer and noted drinker E.J. Moeran (1894–1950), and himself a folk song editor, recorded a number of 78s in the mid-1920s of folk song arrangements including various sea shanties ('Lowlands', 'Roll the Woodpile Down', 'Stormalong', 'Hog Eye Man', 'Haul Away, Joe', 'Drunken Sailor' etc.), taken from R.R. Terry's *The Shanty Book* (1921) and Joanna C. Colcord's collection *Roll and Go, Songs of American Sailormen* (1924). On a couple of the shanties Goss, for all his lieder background and concert hall enunciation, sounds eerily like Bert.

It's more than likely that Bert actually got to know Goss in London in the 1930s. Goss was involved with the left-wing Unity Male Voice Choir, which he conducted on 'Red Cavalry Song' at a Communist Mass Rally at the Empress Stadium in London in November 1938. The song, plus an extract of a speech by the Communist Party of Great Britain (CPGB) leader Harry Pollitt, was produced on record by the Russia Today Society.

Despite being a serendipitous, hit-and-miss affair, Bert's unorthodox self-education was obviously successful. By the time he returned to England in 1930 he was able to hold his own intellectually and artistically with some of the brightest, most enquiring minds of his generation.

Even if intellectually frustrated out in the bush, and having little empathy with the townsfolk of Condobolin, Bert took pride in his skills as a pastoral worker, and was very keen to point out the superiority of the stockman over the farm labourer in one of his letters home, with reference to someone who had obviously lumped farm labourers with stockmen, and although he finishes with a joke, the body of the letter shows how seriously he viewed his job, and his youthful snobbish attitude towards the 'smelly drudgery of a hob-nailed farm labourer'.

Bert conceded in later life that, as a young man, he got impatient with the station hands with whom he worked because he couldn't talk to them about the music, literature and art that excited him, and they found him unsociable for not joining in the card schools. But in retrospect he realised that, if he'd stuck it out a bit longer, he could have actually learned a lot more from them than he did. In consequence, years later, when he was earning his living from folklore, he had to acquire a lot of his 'bush' knowledge from books, as he once, perhaps unwisely, but honestly admitted in a letter to the Australian collector John Meredith:

> Your suspicion that most of my acquaintance with Australian folklore comes from printed sources is quite correct. In my years in the bush I wasn't looking for folklore. I doubt if I knew there was such an animal. Such songs as I picked up were not 'collected' but merely learned because I fancied singing them. Some I wrote down at the time (the texts, that is) others I memorised. Most of them ['most' had been changed from 'all' by Bert] have got so added to and altered about, consciously or involuntarily, in the course of time, that I imagine their scientific value to be small.

Meredith never failed to point this out whenever the opportunity arose.

One of the books that Bert later mined for yarns, traditions, legends and bush humour was Bill Wannan's first (1954) publication *The Australian*; 'the bush bible'. William Fielding Fern-Wannan (1915–2003) collected much of his Australiana from correspondents, through his 'Come In, Spinner!' column in the popular weekly magazine *Australasian Post*. Bert had dealings with the *Australasian* while working at Condobolin, as he told Brad Tate in 1972, in a letter about the provenance of the song the 'Maryborough Miner'/'Murrumbidgee Shearer' which he claimed to have learnt in 1934:

The singer (Bob Bell) took the song very seriously. He was an old man (in his 70s) employed as rabbiter on the station I was working on, and he was himself obsessed by the idea of making a gold strike. He had a rattly old Ford truck, and his dream was that he and I should pile some gear into his truck and set out for the 'Snowy Ranges of South Australia' where he knew there was gold waiting for us. He used to knock on the door of my hut after midnight sometimes, saying 'Boy! I'm just makin' me list. Do you like tinned beans?' He asked me to write to the *Australasian* (the fellers on *The Bulletin* are all ignorant bastards) asking for the precise location of the Snowy Ranges. They answered that no such mountain existed in South Australia. Bob said: 'By Christ, boy, we're on to a good thing here. Even the bloody newspapers don't know about it!'

> Oh the snowy, snowy mountain,
> This story has no end;
> For just like that old river
> I've gone half way round the bend.
> (Roy Lister, 'Snowy River')

Bert never did make the trip in search of the fabled Snowy Ranges in Bob's old Ford truck. Instead, he ended up working way out on the Western Plains near White Cliffs, a place that took its name from the outcrops of white shale in which opals were found, and where he said the trees were so scarce that the birds nested on fence posts, and the sheep spent much of the day fretting about how to stand in each other's shade. Not much different from the country around Condobolin according to Bert's jaundiced description of the area in 1929, after a prolonged period of drought: 'Miles and miles of parched plains without a blade of grass to be seen, of tottering sheep and cattle, of bleached skeletons, of innumerable carcasses and of the exhilarating scent of decaying flesh.'

A local saying had it that 'the rain hereabouts is dust'. A confirmation of Bert's description of the western line of New South Wales appeared in the Melbourne *Argus* in 1949, and was reprinted in *The Australian*:

On the Wallaby in Western N.S.W. a sundowner came upon the crumbling remains of a hut in a desolate location. Tacked to the door was a still legible notice: 'Twenty miles from a neighbour, 40 miles from a post-office, 50 miles from a railway, 50 miles from a pub, 10 miles from wood and water, 1,000 miles from a city. Whoever finds this homestead can have it. The missus wants to see life. She has left for the city. So have I.'

Out there, roustabouts (or, in Oz speak, 'rousies') like Bert could spend hours, days, months and years boundary riding with nothing but 100,000 sheep for company and the same few blokes in the barracks when, or if, they got home in the evening. There apparently came a time, and usually very quickly, when all conversation was chewed to shreds and every scrap of literature had been read, and suddenly the station-hand was 'alone in the vast empty valley of his own thoughts'. According to Bert, he'd seen men grab for a new sauce bottle and stare eagerly at the label, only to slam it down on the bare wooden table, crying in disappointment 'I've read that baaaaaaastard!'

The vast, open spaces with a scarcity of human companionship were ideal breeding grounds for many eccentrics who had 'gone bush', such as the 'bluey-pushers', who rolled in the dust and fought with their blue blanket bedrolls at the least provocation. There were the 'hatters', who strode alone across the country in their cork-ringed hats, and who could be found at night deep in conversation with the hat, which they had balanced on a stick on the other side of the campfire.

Years later, in a November 1950 *Lilliput* magazine, in an article entitled 'Wild and Woolly', Bert recounted an incident in which a mailman gave him a lift one night across the plains to Condobolin. The man's wife had just died and he seemed to have no heart for conversation. They drove for hours in silence then, just as dawn was rising, he said, 'Bunk a bunk a bunk! What's that, banjo or what?'

'Come again,' said Bert.

'Bunk a bunk a bunk. What's that, banjo or what?'

Bert hazarded a guess, 'Banjo?'

The mailman gazed absentmindedly across the plain which 'early in the morning looked like a ghostly ocean', and said at last, 'That's right. Banjo.' And spoke no more for the rest of the journey.

The boredom was occasionally broken by the arrival of the seasonal shearing gangs or by drovers, the 'overlanders', passing though on their way to the railheads with mobs of cattle or sheep. It was from these itinerant song carriers that Bert claimed to have heard a lot of the material he later recorded on such albums as the 1956 *Australian Bush Songs, The Banks of the Condamine and Other Bush Songs* (1957) and later *Across the Western Plains* (1958) and *The Great Australian Legend* (1971):

> Oh there's a trade you all know well, it's bringing cattle over,
> I'll tell you all about the time that I became a drover;
> I wanted stock for Queensland, to Kempsey I did wander,
> And bought a mob of duffers there and began as an overlander.
>
> So pass the bottle round, boys, and don't you leave it stand there,
> For tonight we'll drink the health of every overlander.
> ('The Overlander')

In the interview with Mark Gregory, Bert explained how and why he acquired his Australian repertoire:

> A great many of the songs caught my fancy, and I wanted to learn them. They amused me; some of them struck me by their poetry, some struck me by their tune, and I began to write them down. Not at all as a collecting

thing – at that time I'd never heard of the business of folk song collecting. So it was entirely to suit myself that I used to write the songs down in exercise books.

At that time I couldn't write music, so I used to memorise the melodies as best I could. I must have had many lapses of memory, and a complete absence of discipline, because I wasn't concerned as a folklorist, I was concerned mainly to take the songs into my own cultural baggage. What with the lapses of memory, the tendency to tinker with the stuff, and also the fact that when you've been singing a song for a long time, you find the song has undergone a lot of involuntary changes as well as the voluntary ones. I'm sure that the songs I learned in the bush now emerge melodically (much more than textually) fairly different from what I originally learned.

THE LLOYD CONTROVERSY

'Bert created the verses that the people should have sung but carelessly forgot to do so.'

Terry MacDonald

Bert's 'tendency to tinker with the stuff', allied to the 'involuntary changes', lies at the heart of what has become in Australia the 'Lloyd Controversy'. Where, when and from whom did Bert get his bush ballads? How much of his recorded repertoire is 'authentic' and how much was put together by him? Certain Australian collectors and researchers including Alan Scott and the acerbic John Meredith, who was capable of waxing apoplectic over Bert's Australian material, style of performance and folklore standing with some Australians, stoked up this controversy. This was brought to a head in 1983, a year after Bert's death, when the Australian Folk Trust announced: 'To assist in the collection of folklore, the AFT has established what will be an annual grant of $4,000 to fund worthwhile collection projects. We will be contacting the family of A.L. Lloyd and asking permission that this grant commemorate his collection work in Australia.'

Meredith responded to this news with a lengthy critical article on Bert in the magazine *Stringybark and Greenhide*, in which he said: 'In my opinion, the best memorial A.L. Lloyd could have would be a bonfire of all the phoney concoctions he has passed off as Australian folk songs over the last twenty-five years or so, the bulk of which has little in common with Australian traditional material collected in the field.'[6]

One can understand why someone like Meredith, who spent some fifty years collecting, performing and publishing Australian traditional songs and music, would be put out to read in the *American Folklore Society Journal* (No. 286) Professor Dr John Greenway naively describe Bert, a short-term pommy immigrant, as the Francis James Child of Australian folk song (Child being the editor of the definitive five-volume nineteenth-century collection *English and Scottish Popular Ballads*), and to find out that the AFT was setting up an A.L. Lloyd Memorial Fund for field collecting.

However, Meredith's vitriolic outburst in *Stringybark and Greenhide* was an unpleasant personal attack against a man who, however much Meredith and others might not care to admit it, had been a genuine bushworker for a number of years, and must have heard, and probably sung, authentic bush ballads twenty-five years before native Australian folk song enthusiasts and collectors such as, Meredith, Nancy Keesing, Russell Ward, Douglas Stewart, and Australian Folklore Society archivist, Harry Kay started collecting.

Bert's repertoire, according to Meredith and others, had little in common with the traditional Australian material that was being collected in the 1950s – many of those tunes, Bert felt, were not as interesting as the ones he recollected hearing in the 1920s. But it might have had things in common with the bush repertory and style of the 1920s as experienced by Bert.

I'm not so sure there is that much difference: a number of the songs collected since the 1950s share a similar working class language, content and defiant attitude to Bert's. Bert's vocal style and the personalising of his repertoire (however idiosyncratic, and however un-Australian to Meredith's and singer Duke Tritton's ears) was that of a genuine, though perhaps atypical, bush worker.

One of the things that vexed Meredith, a stickler for 'authenticity', was that the versions of Australian songs that Bert came up with were 'too good to be true' – they invariably had superior lyrics and tunes to the material that Meredith was finding. Worse still, Bert's recorded songs (his 1956 Riverside album *Australian Bush Songs* was the first LP of bush songs) were often the ones that caught the imaginations of a number of Australian folk singers in the 1960s and 1970s – singers such as Gary Shearston who recorded ten of Bert's songs on his 1963 album *The Springtime it Brings On the Shearing*, complete with Bert's vocal mannerisms and song accompaniment.

Another singer influenced by Bert was Chris Kempster, a Henry Lawson authority and founder member, with John Meredith in the early 1950s, of the bush-band the Bushwhackers. Kempster, less of a purist than Meredith, eventually formed the Rambleers with a couple of other ex-Bushwhacker members, and they took a lot of their inspiration from the American Weavers folk group and Bert Lloyd. In addition there was the Wild Colonial Boys who, according to ex-member Jim Fingleton, performed many of Bert's songs 'in a style unashamedly modelled on Bert'.

Fingleton explained:

From my early teens I had been mad on 'bush music' as we call it. When I came across Bert Lloyd's *Across the Western Plains* around 1964 it was an eye-opener for me. The songs available on record till that time were mainly performed by artists who had little or no knowledge of the bush, or how the songs were sung. My first exposure, for example, was Burl Ives singing 'Click Go the Shears' on an old wind-up gramophone in the 1950s. Then there was William Clauson, who sang in a very 'proper' manner, with perfect diction. Also Bush Music Clubs performed in Sydney and Melbourne, mainly made up of 'lefty' schoolteachers, but with a rather uninteresting plodding singing style. Then along came Bert, and what a breath of fresh-air he was! With his expressive singing style, new range of songs and clear feel for the lyrics, he brought an authenticity which had previously been lacking. I just doted on his stuff.[7]

Bert's records provided singers like Shearston, Kempster and Fingleton with the sort of material they were looking for, as Ron Edwards pointed out in 'The Cult of Lloyd' (*Northern Folk*, September 1966), his critique of Bert's recorded material: 'His collection is far more than unique, it is almost miraculous. Every song and every tune is exactly what we would wish for; soppy lines found in earlier versions have gone, and all is sun-tanned, sardonic and bushy, exactly as we like to imagine ourselves.'

In December 1968, in a poll conducted by the magazine *National Folk*, Bert was voted 'Best Performer of Traditional Australian Material', an award that must have stuck in John Meredith's craw. As, too, must the Settlers winning the Best Group award and the Seekers taking the honours for Best Track On Any Album with 'The Overlander'. Not much support from the folkies for bush bands and traditional singers!

Bert was obviously too successful for his own good. But he always insisted that his Australian songs were merely his own 'personal cultural baggage' and not intended to be an exercise in folklore scholarship. It seems unfair to castigate Bert because other people chose to sing his songs and placed him uncritically on an Oz folk-music pedestal that was not of his making. I'm sure he would have been as embarrassed by the A.L. Lloyd Memorial Collectors' Fund idea as Meredith was embittered. He would have been the first to acknowledge that any such fund should be named after Australian traditional singers, such as Sally Sloane and Duke Tritton, or indeed an Australian collector like John Meredith himself.

Brad Tate was right in his comments in a letter to *Stringybark and Greenhide* magazine in 1983:

Bert served to direct those so inclined to the authentic Australian folksingers. After the flash-in-the-pan of *Reedy River* [a 1953 bush music play], the revival here deteriorated into coffeehouse music until around 1965, when there was an influx of singers from the British Isles. To them Bert Lloyd was God. To some others he was, with his status as a folklorist, the inspiration to delve further into Australian tradition ... The bush items were only a small part of his total recorded output: and surely even they have done the folk revival here [Australia] much more good than harm.

It's not surprising that Bert's versions of Australian bush ballads took the fancy of young Australian singers. As became obvious during the heyday of the *British* folk revival, he had, with his writer's ear, a knack of 'tweaking' songs to give them more bite, as in his ballad 'Reynardine', one of his most successful folk song recreations. From a couple of fragmentary Irish verses, some adapted broadside stanzas, and the key line 'his teeth did brightly shine' (originally 'his eyes did brightly shine'), Bert turned a run-of-the-mill outlaw ballad into a much more exciting exercise in potential lycanthropy – a mysterious, ambiguous song that caught the imagination of singers and audiences, and spawned a plethora of performances, recordings, articles, poems and even paintings.

> Day and night she followed him,
> His teeth did brightly shine,
> She followed him o'er the mountain,
> That sly bold Reynardine.
> ('Reynardine')

Bert also recognised a good tune when he heard it. He was adept at 'fitting' tunes, often well-known melodies, to texts and creating a new exciting piece, where the total was usually greater than the sum of the parts. Who'd have thought the jokey melody that carried the self-parodying Scottish 'Donald Where's Your Troosers', when grafted on to Bert's modernisation and reworking of the ancient ballad 'Glasgerion' (or 'Glenkindie'), could produce the chilling 'Jack Orion'?

> Jack Orion he swore a bloody oath,
> By oak, by ash, by bitter thorn,
> Lady I never was in this room
> Since the day that I was born.
>
> Oh then it was your own boy Tom,
> That cruelly has beguil-ed me,
> And woe that the blood of that ruffian bold
> Should spring in my body.
>
> Jack Orion took off to his own house,
> Saying, 'Tom my boy, come here to me.'
> And he hanged that boy from his own gatepost,
> As high as the willow tree.
> ('Jack Orion')

In the notes to his 1966 *First Person* album, he had this to say about 'Jack Orion': 'The ballad of "Glasgerion" dropped out of tradition long ago but the story it tells is an engaging one and it seemed to me too good a song to be shut away in books, so I took it out and dusted it off a bit and set a tune to it and, I hope, started it on a new lease of life.'

Bert's problem lay not in the fact that he 'improved' songs but that in many cases he wasn't as transparent in acknowledging his creative input as he was with 'Jack Orion'. In Stephen Sedley's book *The Seeds of Love* (1967) 'Reynardine' is credited with having been collected by A.L. Lloyd from Tom Cook of Eastbridge, Suffolk. Yet, despite considerable research in Eastbridge, no one came up with a Tom Cook from the village. And yet on at least a couple of other occasions Bert refers to Tom Cook as being one of his informants. On a list of 'song sources' for amatory songs in the Goldsmiths archive Bert had typed: 'Gentle Johnny My Jingalo' words: T. Cook, Eastbridge, Suffolk, 1939, tune from Sharp, *English Folk Songs*, Vol. 1. He also credited T. Cook as the source of his 'Arthur McBride', which was, according to John Hasted, one of Bert's early songs.[8] If not true, why would he go to so much trouble to create a character and include him in notes to himself on sources?

A few years later Bert admitted in the sleeve notes to Anne Briggs's eponymous 1971 Topic album that he had adapted the 'Reynardine' words and tune from an Irish original. He had obviously originally given Sedley the Tom Cook provenance. Perhaps it's not that Tom Cook didn't exist, but that Bert, who had got material from him in the 1930s, used his name to validate his re-working of 'Reynardine'. In the *Anne Briggs* notes, Bert also discounted any vulpine connections, but by this time it was too late – the song was already up and running with its bushy tail waving behind it.

Sedley doesn't know why Bert felt the need to invent sources for songs he had rewritten himself:

I think that both Bert and Ewan were unnecessarily embarrassed about admitting that they were adding or improving when, of course, the whole folk process had always been a process of adding and improving. In 'Reynardine' I think the 'teeth so bright did shine' line is the best line in the song. Ewan did the same thing with 'Tramps and Hawkers' when he added the verse about working with the dockers on the Clyde, at least I've never seen that verse from oral tradition, and it's terrific. With Ewan the verse about the dockers was what Ewan felt ought to be in the song. Bert was frequently simply making a better job of a received text. We all have this problem of texts which have been received in damaged form, partial form or, even though good, could be made better. I don't know a single folksinger who hasn't either consciously or unconsciously modified received stuff. I collected 'Dido Bendigo' from a slate-quarry worker in Westmorland called Frank Burkett and took the tapes, on my way back to London, to the Watersons and they copied them. Then, I'm sure without thinking about it they modified both the words and the melody. In fact they ironed out one note in the melody which, in fact, made it less interesting. When the album came out Topic got Paul Carter to write the sleeve notes and he didn't enquire where the material came from and he gave a reference to a version collected by Baring Gould in Devon.[9]

Bert often used 'we' in his sleeve notes ('we find that …'), thus distancing himself from the act of creation, and subtly implicating us by implying that we, the listeners, have a hand in authenticating the union.

Sometimes he simply said 'sung here to the lively tune …', without mentioning that it was he who had put it to the 'lively tune', as in his marriage of a 'Turpin Hero' melody and the words of the nineteenth-century American minstrel piece 'Old Bob Ridley', which he came across in Alfred Williams's

Folk-Songs of the Upper Thames. There was no mention anywhere that he had fitted the tune to the words. Interestingly, there was actually a perfectly good tune available, probably very close to the Christy Minstrel original, sung by the old Norfolk fisherman Sam Larner, but Bert put his 'Bob Ridley' together before he'd heard Sam Larner, who wasn't 'discovered' by BBC producer Philip Donnellan until 1958.

Whatever Bert did to songs in the way of 'improvement', before sending them on their way to start a new life in the folk clubs, was done from the best possible motives – a love of traditional song, and a desire to see it flowering again; a 'people's-music' antidote to the worst aspects of pop music, and an example of home-grown culture that could prove a bastion against American cultural imperialism. And politically, a poke in the eye for capitalism and commercialisation.

Vic Gammon said that Bert's 'unashamed love of the material made him a reassembler and tinkerer'.[10] Bert's life in folklore seems to have been a permanent juggling act between scholarship, romanticism and performance. In his Eastern European work, his romanticism and desire to find thriving manifestations of an earlier authentic peasant culture led him to ignore the fact that much of what he saw and heard was to a certain extent 'stage-managed' by apparatchiks. He saw what he hoped to see; they let him see what he and they wanted him to see. The most intelligent and clear-sighted people can become blinded to the truth if the truth contradicts a preconceived belief or desire.

What did Bert really hear in the bunkhouses and round the campfires back in the 1920s? According to Mark Gregory the first song that Bert claimed to have learnt in Australia was 'Bold Jack Donahoe' which Chris Sullivan points out in his book *Castles In the Air* 'was available in W. Roy Mackenzie's *Ballads and Sea Songs from Nova Scotia*, a publication Lloyd referred to as early as 1946'. This doesn't prove that Bert learnt it from Mackenzie, but it's considered a bit of circumstantial musical evidence by Sullivan and others in the attempt to prove that most of Bert's Oz repertoire came later from published sources. In his 1969 interview with Mark Gregory Bert said that, when he bought a copy of Patterson's *Old Bush Songs* around 1930, he found therein versions of several songs that he'd known, which he'd acquired and put into his exercise books. Some of these texts were, apparently, very close to the Patterson versions and Bert thought they might well have been learnt from print. Some Australians might ask, 'but learnt from print by whom? Bert or his supposed informants?'

In various interviews Bert is quoted as saying that he acquired around 500 songs while in Australia. Yet, apart from the twenty-five or so recorded titles and a couple sent to Ron Edwards and published in *The Big Book of Australian Folk Song*, and one or two given to the English singer Martin Wyndham-Read (who also spent some years working and singing in Australia), few of these 500 have ever materialised. There's no bundle of Australian song manuscripts, or evidence of the school notebooks in which he said he noted the songs down, in the A.L. Lloyd collection at Goldsmiths.

Ron Edwards pointed out in *Northern Folk* (September, 1966) that of the twenty-five individual songs (some were recorded more than once) that appear on Bert's first three Australian albums, versions of twenty-one of them are to be found in Stewart and Keating's *Old Bush Songs,* and of the remaining four, one is by Henry Lawson, one by Banjo Paterson, 'The Derby Ram' may be found in *Singabout* (Spring 1956), and 'Bluey Brink' was on a 1940 Tex Morton record. He goes on to say: 'Nearly all Lloyd's songs differ from other known versions, and the differences are always improvements or, to put it more bluntly, his songs are all variations that we would like to collect ourselves but never do.'

Of course, this doesn't prove that these were the sources of Bert's songs. In fact, it would be a quite remarkable achievement had he rewritten and 'improved' all those songs on the albums. But without the notebooks it's difficult, if not impossible, to prove otherwise. Bert did indeed jot things down in exercise books throughout his life. His daughter Caroline still has a red school-type notebook filled with small fine handwriting. It contains notes on a range of topics, much of it in Spanish, but none of it dealing with Australia. It was not uncommon for Australian bush workers to use school exercise books in which to jot down information that took their fancy – songs, poems and toasts, along with recipes for use in animal husbandry, and other useful titbits. But these were not specifically 'collections' of songs. Anyway, no such Lloyd Australian commonplace book has so far materialised.

Professor David Gregory mentioned the phantom (and for him 'treasured') exercise books in his article 'A.L. Lloyd and the English Folk Song Revival, 1934–44' (*Canadian Folk Music Journal*, 1997), where he says: 'By the time Lloyd left Australia, these treasured exercise books apparently contained the words of several hundred songs (but no tunes). Still in his possession during the mid-1960s, when two student reporters from Oxford University interviewed him.' The reporters were Michael Rosen and Tony Coombs and their interview was published in the university magazine *Isis* in February 1966: '… he wrote out 500 songs from the sheep shearers and farmers, because he wanted to "take them into his head". He has still got the exercise books he wrote them down in.'

Mike Rosen later claimed he had in fact *not* seen the elusive books. He was merely, as usual, repeating what Bert told numerous interviewers to be the case.[11] There are two reasons for assuming that the books no longer exist, and haven't existed for a considerable time, possibly since Bert was in Australia. Firstly no one, as far as we know, has ever examined them. Secondly, if Bert still possessed them when he was performing and recording Australian songs in the 1950s and 1960s, he would have known exactly how much he'd altered the texts (a thing that he always claimed not to remember), and when, and from whom, he had learnt them. This was information that he either remembered incorrectly, or consciously changed, as is evident when we find him giving dates for songs when he could not possibly have still been in Australia, and informants' names and places crossed out and changed on typescripts of songs. Which are we to believe, when a manuscript note on the song 'One of the Has-Beens' states 'I heard this from a vaudeville actor, in hospital in Cowra, NSW, on New Year's Day' and yet, on publication, the 'vaudeville actor' has transmogrified into 'a teamster from Grenfell' who 'sang the song', thus providing a much more 'bushy' provenance?

It's possible, despite his good memory, that he became entangled in a web, not necessarily of intentional deception, but in a miasma of half-remembered lyrics and tunes, and fugitive dates, places and faces that recent, rigorous researchers, particularly in Australia, have found less than satisfactory. Bert was usually a meticulous cataloguer of his notes and references. If he had possessed the exercise books in later life, surely he would have known exactly where they were and what was in them. He would have been able, had he so wished, to tell the world exactly what he had heard in Australia in the 1920s.

Unless, of course, he didn't want to let the world know? Why didn't he, in later life, admit that he'd left Australia early in 1930? Perhaps it was simply that he would have had another three years to account for in London before he went whaling. And why did he claim to have collected songs as late as 1933 and 1934, when he could have given any date from 1924 to 1930 and nobody could have disproved it?

To many people, both in Australia and in Britain, the whole 'controversy' that has now lasted for some fifty years (since John Meredith's first letter to Bert querying the authenticity of much of the material on the Riverside album *Australian Bush Songs*) could seem to be a lot of fuss about very little. There are more pressing issues in the world than two- or three-dozen songs that Bert Lloyd might or might not have learned in the bush, and with which he tinkered to a greater or lesser degree. Perhaps much of the 'controversy' stemmed from Aussie sour grapes and an anti-Pom-imperialism stance. Although, we have Ron Edwards' explanation of his concern over Bert's material:

Younger folklorists, and a number of older performers, have asked what the fuss was all about, and some have defended Lloyd on the grounds that his versions are generally more singable than the originals. It must be remembered that there are very few folklore collectors in Australia and the numbers who have collected any quantity of material are fewer still. Some of us have not always seen eye to eye, but what Anderson, Meredith, O'Connor, the Scotts and others, including myself, were always very particular about was in transcribing the texts exactly as we collected them. We knew that the material was both rare and precious to our cultural history and therefore it was important to us that we preserved the material as accurately as possible. Lloyd's versions hit us like a bombshell, his vague attributions, some of which appeared to have been produced ad lib in order to please the publishers of the record notes, combined with his frank admissions of text alterations seemed to us at the time to be nothing less than sabotage to our whole aim of accurate collecting.[12]

No one could argue with that. Surely Bert himself would be sympathetic to Edwards' concerns. However, he had a valid point when he defended his position to Edwards in a letter in 1972:

> You ask which of the Australian songs I sing have been 'restored'. I suppose all of them ... At the time I took the songs into my head I was a bush worker pure and simple. A folklorist arriving at any station I was working on might have been interested to find an informant who wasn't a passive receiver but who had a recreative attitude to the songs – the process is common enough, otherwise variants wouldn't arise ... At best all I can claim for my bush-ballad stock is that they are 'Australian songs as sung by me'.

Bert would surely have given one of his wry smiles had he been alive to read Alan Scott's 'Bullshit!' letter, printed with John Meredith's 1983 'Depreciation of A.L. Lloyd' in *Stringybark and Greenhide*, and remembered what Scott had said about his own treatment of traditional songs in the introduction to his 1970 *A Collector's Songbook*: 'I was a singer before I was a collector. As received the songs were often fragmentary and incomplete ... to this end I have bent, cobbled, twisted and bashed, even written new lines. I believe however that the spirit of each one is still intact, that I have done no more than was necessary to turn them into singable songs.'

Although Meredith's *Depreciation* was arguably an ill-considered, bilious piece of writing, Kevin Bradley asserts that professional jealousy was not his prime or even major motivation in criticising Bert:

> Meredith was primarily a folklorist and a searcher for the 'real folk' of Australia. He was brought up in a small country town where he played accordion for dances and his father was an itinerant shearer. Born in 1920, he was only a decade or so younger than Lloyd, so it would be the same Australia they were talking about, and he didn't recognise veracity in Lloyd's description of Australia.[13]

True, but there's also a case to be made for the Meredith pot calling the Lloyd kettle black. Meredith himself was not above 'assembling' songs; one of his 'concoctions', as Edgar Waters termed it, was his 'The Old Bullock Dray', the lyrics and tune of which were put together from various sources. Also, the Australian bush-song tradition was, as in England, primarily an unaccompanied one, so Meredith's bush-band accompaniments represented no bench-mark of authenticity.

All of this will continue to be discussed for many years to come. The bones will be picked over and chewed on until the last vestiges of musical marrow have been extracted. The traditionalists/survivalists will continue to attempt to draw a time line where 'authentic' Australian traditional material became diluted by contact with the 'folk music revival'. Re-creationalists such as John Manifold, Bert Lloyd and academics like Edgar Waters believed that the folk process was 'creative and constructive'.

Surely any cut-off point for what constitutes 'traditional' material is actually quite arbitrary and artificial? Like it or not, what is considered by some collectors, writers and academics to be the authentic voice of the people is a voice that has been in a state of constant flux down the centuries. It has frequently taken inspiration from 'higher' art and literature, as with the hundreds of examples of 'traditional' British songs which, in fact, had their origins in the garlands, theatre productions and pleasure garden songbooks of the eighteenth and nineteenth centuries.

Think, also, of the popularity amongst working people of such Australian poets as Henry Lawson and 'Banjo' Paterson (who also 'patched together' texts for his *Old Bush Songs*), the American 'folk' bard Woody Guthrie, Virginia's A.P. Carter of Carter Family fame and the British Grub Street scribblers of broadside ballads. All of these produced, influenced, 'borrowed' and inspired myriad versions of songs and ballads which were being orally changed by the 'folk', for the better and for the worse, until pinned like butterflies between the pages of song collections, set in an amber-like prison of printer's ink for future generations to marvel at.

This being the case, some might feel that Bert Lloyd and other creative singers represented a healthy and thriving continuation of a process, rather than the death knell of some fading tradition that had run out of steam and was ready to become a museum artefact. Australian folk song collector and singer Warren Fahey believed this to be the case: 'In folk song we find a music that can be performed without imitation or bounded by conventions. It is a personal creation. Folk song is only folk song when it is part of a living tradition in a state of constant metamorphosis. From an "unconscious" collector A.L. Lloyd became a conscious interpreter and song craftsman. He wrote songs, he rewrote songs and he crafted unwieldy texts into singable songs.' Wendy Lowenstein, editor of *Australian Tradition*, the magazine of the Victoria Folk Music Club, considered Bert a 'fine singer and a brilliant folk song scholar, and a good, radical, honest bloke.'

Bert wasted few experiences. Most of what he saw, heard and did ended up repackaged in articles, radio and TV programmes, album sleeve notes, talks and anecdotal introductions to his songs in folk clubs, festivals and concerts. His experiences were regularly re-cycled for BBC schools broadcasting, for which he wrote dozens of entertaining, informative scripts in the 1950s and 1960s, on geography, travel, history, music and work. His professionalism and skill at presenting complex and unusual material in an accessible way was greatly appreciated by his producers, who regularly forwarded him excellent audience survey reports.

Of the Australian programmes for schools, which included *A Sheep Station* (1962), *A Small Town in New South Wales* (1963) and *Harvest in New South Wales* (1964), one of the liveliest was *A Bush Fire in Australia*, which was broadcast in June 1959. The programme starts with the narrator, Albert, played by actor Nigel Stock (who became a household name in the 1960s as Dr Watson in the popular BBC TV Sherlock Holmes dramas), saying: 'The best way to give an idea of what a bush fire is like is to tell you something that really happened to me. It was when I was working on a sheep-station about twenty miles from Condobolin on the western line of New South Wales. It was around Christmas time – that's when the real hot weather is.'

In the script Bert changed the scene of the fire from Ferndale, from where he wrote to his sister, to Bogandillon, and, for some reason, continued to place the fire there when he talked about it in May 1970 on his return visit to Bogandillon for the ABC programme *Ten Thousand Miles*: 'I was sent to muster a lot of sheep out of a paddock here on Bogandillon. When the fire came over the hilltop it was quite clear that I wasn't going to be able to get through the gate myself, let alone run the sheep out. I hopped off the pony and started running, and I became aware that there was a fox running beside me, almost tripping me up. Just running for company.'

In the TV documentary Bert gave more details of what happened to the animals than would have been appropriate for the schools programme, but neither were as graphic as the details in his letter to Trixie just after the fire. By 1970 his pony had miraculously resurrected itself from the 1926 pile of cinders and found its own way back safely to the sheep-station, even though: 'Most of the horses out there looked like rhinoceroses, they'd lost their ears, and their heads were so swollen up we had to shoot them.'

It's illuminating to have three versions of the same story told over the space of forty-five years, so we can see how memory and invention can change the elements of a narrative. The fox companion, one of the most charming details, didn't appear in his original letter so we must assume that it was added for the 1959 schools radio programme and, being such a nice touch, Bert couldn't resist adding it to the story for the 1970s retelling. And did he keep the Bogandillon setting simply because he was at Bogandillon with the film crew and it would have been less relevant if he'd said Ferndale? Bert was never one to let veracity stand in the way of a good story when some embroidery would suffice.

The 1970 TV documentary came about thanks to Ian Turner, an Australian historian, co-founder with Wendy Lowenstein of the Victoria Folklore Society, and an admirer of Bert. When he heard Bert was being brought over on a lecture tour by Peter Mann (who ran Melbourne's famous Discurio folk and transcendental record store), he thought it would be interesting to take him back to the sheep station near Condobolin, where he'd worked in the 1920s, and to film his memories and reactions to the inevitable changes over the intervening forty years. Turner, a long-time fan of Bert's singing and scholarship, and who considered Bert to be 'a good bloke', had visited him in London the previous year and looked forward to meeting up again.

Bert flew in looking fit, dapper, and cheerful. They set off with the film crew and folklorist Edgar Waters, on the 400 or so mile drive to the station, passing through a landscape that had changed considerably since Bert first arrived in Condobolin. Later Bert said that all the way up to the station he was:

a bit discouraged because in bush town after bush town we went through I couldn't identify anything at all. There was this place of motels, drive-in-cinemas and supermarkets, and this and that, just like American country towns. Different from what I remember of bush towns in the past. For one thing there were infinitely fewer cars [then], and horses hitched in the back of the stores, and weatherboarding, a lot of it unpainted, quite different from the snazzy, go-go, bush towns of today.

When they reached Condobolin, things didn't seem quite so strange. For one thing the Commercial Hotel, with its fancy iron-traceried first-floor balcony, sitting squarely at the end of the main street, appeared unchanged, although now it was an Aussie nightmare – a pub with no beer. It had been closed down for some time. And the motherly landlady who had played Bert 'My Grandfather's Clock' was long gone. But, when they made the twenty-mile drive out to Bogandillon, the old Stevenson station, it looked much as Bert remembered it from his youth. He got the chance to revisit his little hut, to reminisce in the old shearing shed, where he'd listened to the visiting shearers sing, and to stand in the yard and demonstrate his old skill of cracking a long stock-whip. A lot had happened to him, and to the world, since the last time he'd walked across that yard nearly forty years before.

The programme proved a bit disappointing. It was an interesting travelogue interspersed with Bert's reminiscences, but it didn't provide any folkloric nuggets, and it did little to throw new light on his Australian repertoire, or indeed on his day-to-day work as a pastoral-worker.

By 1929 he was fed up and frustrated with Australia. He tried to get out of the country by applying for a job in West Africa (which didn't materialise), and asking his aunts for the whereabouts of a family acquaintance who was a missionary in the Belgium Congo, on the off chance that she might be able to suggest some work for him. He didn't consider New Zealand because it was 'as bad as Australia'.

By 1930, Bert could no longer resist the urge to get out and return to Europe, which represented books, art and music, and a hoped-for career as a writer. According to his second wife, Charlotte, he worked his way back to England via South Africa on passenger liners, which he hated. Bert claimed to have stayed for a year in the Transvaal, putting his Aussie know-how to good use in the newly developing Merino sheep industry: '... around 1934 or '35 I left Australia and went to Africa. I'd had several years' experience with merino sheep, and they were just starting with merinos in the Transvaal, so I knew I could get a decent job there. But the country was so horrible I only stayed there just over a year. I preferred to face unemployment in Europe, rather than stay there any longer.'

Shantyman Stan Hugill once pointed out during a conversation that, if Bert worked on sheep stations in South Africa in the early 1930s, he certainly wouldn't have done any labouring work, since black Africans would have done it all.

Merino sheep had, in fact, first been introduced into South Africa in 1789 when William of Orange sent four ewes and two rams to his friend the Dutch naturalist and explorer Robert Gordon, who commanded the garrison in Cape

Town. In 1795 a ship heading for Australia bought twenty of the sheep: this was the start of the Australian merino sheep industry.

How Bert's South Africa sheep-station story can slot into the facts as we know them is a mystery. There's no indication in the *Demosthenes* passenger register that he did anything other than travel from Australia to England via South Africa. He was writing letters to his aunts from Australia in August 1929 with no indication that his departure was imminent and he was back in England by May 1930, so it doesn't give him much of a window of opportunity to have spent a year in South Africa! And if he'd worked his way back on the *Demosthenes* it's doubtful that he'd be included on the ship's 'passenger' list.

Bert settled back in north London with a thirst for knowledge, a head already full of information, a 'magnificent unbelief' in God, no ambition to follow his old school friends into banking or the Civil Service, and a developing left-wing political awareness, partly fuelled by his recent union experiences in Australia, where the pastoral social system had been described as 'a patriarchal despotism tempered by Bryant and May'. If the squatters on the sheep and cattle stations, with their thousands of acres of tinder-dry grass, failed to appreciate the mutual respect expected between themselves and their workers, a disgruntled labourer could always jog their memory with a box of matches. This was the subject of Bert's first piece of professional writing for *Left Review* in 1934. Bert's social conscience was also influenced by memories of his father's experiences in the First World War, a new circle of communist friends, and stoked up by what he read in the *Daily Worker*, which was founded the year he arrived back in the UK.[14]

Daily Worker, Wednesday, 8 February 1933
Unemployment has now reached the highest point in the history of the crisis. Ministry of Labour figures for January show that there were 2,903,065 unemployed on the Labour Exchange Register on January 23. At least 170,000 people have signed on at the Labour Exchange owing to being cut off by the Means Test.

2
A Telegram to Hitler

Every revolution evaporates and leaves behind only the slime of a new bureaucracy.

Franz Kafka

London in the 1930s was bubbling over with energy and excitement from the young idealistic left-wing intellectuals who thought that the great socialist revolution was just around the next corner, and a Communist Utopia was over the next hill. According to Professor John Hasted, physicist and folk singer: 'Everybody who was anybody was a Communist in those days.' That, of course, was an opinion and not necessarily a fact, but it sums up the view from the left, a view with which Bert would have concurred. When he got back into the country after six years in the wilderness, he had a lot of catching up to do. A lot of people to meet. A lot of ideas to discuss.

Leslie Morton remembered quite clearly that he first met Bert in 1932 when he wandered into Morton's little second-hand bookshop at Finsbury Park, north London: 'We met about 1932, when he was in his early twenties and I in my late twenties, both hard up and struggling to find a foothold in the difficult London world. But if he found things difficult he never showed it: always he was cheerful, alert, composed, interested in all that went on, on the lookout for new experiences.'[1]

He had already become a regular visitor and friend before Morton closed the shop in 1934 and took up the job of proprietor of the *Daily Worker,* which according to him meant: 'I was the chap that went to prison if anything went wrong. I was expendable. I remember Lord Haw-Haw, who was working for [Oswald] Mosley at the time: brought an action against us for incitement to violence regarding a big Hyde Park rally. But we won the case. I was lucky, but most of my predecessors ended up in prison.'

Morton and his first wife, Bron (Bronwen), were living at the top of Hornsey Rise, in north London, in the early 1930s. Bert had lodgings nearby and, being a young man, seemingly, alone in the metropolis, was taken under the Mortons' wing (although, in fact, his aunts were both very much alive and living in the area). He got into the habit of 'drifting' into the Mortons' house in the evenings, with armfuls of 78rpm records of American cowboy songs and blues, which he'd sit and play. He'd talk on every subject under the sun for hours. He told them that he'd recently got back from Australia, although Morton didn't remember him having any marked Australian accent. According to Morton, at that time: 'He was a very handsome young man, quite slim and well made. It was quite a bit later that he put on weight. He was a very neat dresser, very presentable, I never knew him to be a womaniser. He was very much the intellectual; he knew all about music, painting, and literature. There was nothing about which he didn't seem to know something. He was a remarkable man.' They found it hard to believe Bert's story that he'd been sent to Australia because he'd failed to pass his exams – 'A man who could collect languages like postage stamps!'

Bert always had a marvellous memory, but sometimes, in later life, he complained to Charlotte that his head was just 'too full of facts, too crowded'. If, as everybody agreed, he had such a good memory, this would imply that the numerous contradictory stories that he passed on throughout his life were intentional, and not simply examples of mild amnesia. It's probable that Bert was more fabulist than forgetful.

The Mortons and their good friends Allen and Norma Hutt, who lived round the corner in Hornsey Lane, were all active workers in the Holloway Group of the Islington Local of the Communist Party. Their headquarters were opposite Hornsey Baths, in a disused workshop in Andover Yard. Allen was a journalist on the *Daily Worker*, Norma (whom Bert would eventually marry) worked at the offices of ARCOS (All Russian Cooperative Society Ltd) as a secretary, and Leslie was on the CP Executive Committee. They couldn't have been closer to the heart of the Party, unless they'd been sharing a bed with the Secretary, Harry Pollitt. Pollitt, Rajani Palme Dutt, who was the CPGB's chief theoretician, and communist politician Willie Gallacher were regular visitors to the Hutts' home, where their young daughter, Jenny, found the tough Clydeside trade unionist, Gallacher, 'more fun' than the intransigent Stalinist Dutt.[2]

Morton thought that he was one of the first Party members Bert met on his return to England, and although, according to Morton, they didn't talk much politics (which is difficult to believe), they obviously had a big political influence on him and he became a Party member, remaining so for the rest of his life, although in later years he had little time, or inclination, to attend Party meetings. In the 1950s he'd send his daughter, Caroline, to the front door to pay his Party subs when the local rep came knocking, to avoid getting drawn into Party chat.

Morton's influence also extended to social history, which they occasionally discussed. Morton was preparing his classic, Marxist work *A People's History of England* (1938) at the time, and it had a seminal effect on Bert's evolving theories concerning folk music. Morton noted: 'In the little book *The Singing Englishman* (1944) he [Bert] does refer to a number of my ideas.'

In the *History Workshop Journal* for Autumn 1980 Morton spoke of the work the group did in the 1930s in the notorious Campbell Road area of north London:

Much of our work was concentrated in the area lying in the angle of Hornsey Road and the Seven Sisters Road. We canvassed most of the streets in the area, and at last were persuaded by two comrades living in the nearby Pooles Park to tackle Campbell Road. As they said, it was the poorest street in the district and the one where people lived in the worst conditions.

We were not, of course, unaware of Campbell Road's reputation and I think approached it with some trepidation. In fact we were pleasantly surprised at the friendly way we were received. Everyone we saw seemed ready to talk and we gathered a stack of information about bad housing, high rents, lack of amenities and so on. This we passed on to one of our number who undertook to prepare a piece for the *Daily Worker*, which he did in a style not lacking in colourful detail.

In 1933 Martin Lawrence published Hutt's *The Condition of the Working Class in Britain*. Frances Gillespie had this to say: 'Although this work is frankly designed as Communist propaganda it nevertheless deserves serious consideration as a carefully documented account of conditions prevailing among the working classes of Great Britain in the largest centres of industry ... .'[3]

The USSR believed these conditions were a potential prelude to a revolution they were happy to encourage and support. A huge amount of money (gold) was passed on to the CPGB from Moscow over the years for distribution to worthy causes such as striking unions. The surprising thing is that the revolution never materialised despite regular *Daily Worker* stories of angry protests at the poverty, sickness, exploitation and deprivation:

Daily Worker, Monday, 6 February 1933
250,000 DEMONSTRATED AGAINST HUNGER!
MASS DEMONSTRATIONS AGAINST UNEMPLOYMENT!
A feature of the demonstration was the enormous number of Trade Union banners that were displayed. Close on 1000 were on display. Slogans seen everywhere were RELEASE THE MEERUT PRISONERS! DOWN WITH THE MEANS TEST! RELEASE TOM MANN! A tremendous expression of working class determination to fight unemployment and all that it brings in its train of poverty and suffering.

Party members like Bert were expected to be 'active proselytisers', and to get out into the streets, factories, canteens and depots, selling the *Worker* and spreading the CP gospel. Anyone with any special skills was eagerly brought into the fold and put to work for the Party – writers, graphic designers, artists, cartoonists were all pressed into service at the King Street headquarters, producing pamphlets, posters, marching banners, articles, cartoons, illustrations and reviews for the *Worker*, *Left Review*, the Working Men's Association, and the popular working-class *Reynolds News*, for whom, in the 1930s, Bert wrote book reviews and even reviewed modern kitchen design ('Modern Design, Woman's Friend', 25 December 1938). *Reynolds News* is also where Britain's most well-known twentieth-century newspaper cartoonist, Giles (1916–95), began his career in 1937.

Bert also helped Morton out on the *Worker* with the occasional cartoon:

Bert did a few cartoons for us. We had a cartoonist called Desmond Roney, who drew under the name of Maro, he was killed in Spain. He was a nice man, a very dear man, but, like many cartoonists, very irresponsible. He drank a good deal, more than was good for him. We used to pay him for each cartoon, and then we made the mistake of putting him on a weekly wage. He'd draw his money and disappear for a few days, and the cartoons became very irregular. Occasionally when we were stuck and particularly needed a cartoon Bert would draw one for us. I think Bert had a great potential as an artist.

Nice though it must have been for the young Bert to have his drawings printed in the *Worker*, it probably didn't bring in much, if any, money. The following year, 1935, when Scottish political cartoonist Jimmy Friell (1912–97) sent the *Worker* some sample cartoons, assuming correctly that it was the only paper radical enough to print them, they liked them but couldn't afford to pay for them. Friell let them use the cartoons anyway. In March 1936 he was taken on as 'official' cartoonist, under the pseudonym Gabriel, and he developed into one of the most perceptive and hard-hitting cartoonists of his generation. He, of course, knew Bert, and later remembered him 'returning from an Antarctic whaling trip with a series of articles and a magnificent set of photographs'.

Morton's assertion that Bert was actually 'bumming around London' (as Morton phrased it) at least as early as 1932, and not 1934 or 1935, as Bert often claimed, was corroborated by the bookshop owner Christina Foyle (1911–99), who said that in her recollection Bert was safely ensconced as the manager of her foreign book department by 1933 (where Morton remembered dropping in to see him). 'He was here [Foyle's] in the very early '30s,' recalled Foyle. 'I was only about twenty-three when I got to know Lloyd well. I expect I employed him, because very early on, when I was about eighteen, I used to engage all the staff, my father couldn't be bothered.'[4]

Bert told Morton that it was he who had sent the famous telegram to Adolf Hitler from Christina Foyle: 'PLEASE BURN NO MORE BOOKS. STOP. WE WILL PAY HIGHEST CASH PRICES. STOP. WILL GIVE MONEY TO GERMAN RELIEF.' The notorious 'cleansing' book burnings took place at midnight on 10 May 1933, when a torchlight procession of thousands of students marched into the square in front of the university in Berlin (and in thirty-three other university towns). Watched by Goering and Goebbels, they made a bonfire of over 20,000 books whose authors, many of whom were Jewish, were considered to display an 'un-German' attitude. In her personal correspondence files Miss Foyle kept Hitler's response, courteously declining her offer, saying that he would no sooner corrupt the morals of the English than he would the Germans.

Another of Bert's favourite Foyle's anecdotes was the apocryphal story of Essex girl Christina asking her bookseller father, William, what the antiquarian value would be for a signed first edition of the Bible. William was a renowned collector of early bibles and had in his collection the bible presented by Samuel Pepys to Charles II on his restoration: but not a 'first edition'.

It's interesting that William Foyle, the bible connoisseur, who chose to live in the 800-year-old Beeleigh Abbey, once home of the White Canons, was a seventh child of a seventh child. He had a fascination for the occult and parapsychology – and was a friend of the notorious Aleistair Crowley. In the early 1930s Crowley was sliding into penury, and he was finally declared bankrupt in 1934, after unsuccessfully suing the writer Nina Hamnet for dubbing him a 'black magician'. He was a regular visitor to Foyle's when Bert was there and, according to Christina, Bert knew him well. Crowley who 'practically lived at the shop' was always borrowing money from William Foyle, and was invariably given a good price for the books he sold to raise a few pounds to help pay for his heroin addiction.

Despite Christina Foyle's reputation in the book trade as an unpredictable, snobbish autocrat – at least among her floating army of low-paid bookselling assistants – she could also be a charming if 'regal' woman, who sounded and looked disconcertingly like the Queen. In 1984, in her plush penthouse apartment on the top floor of the Foyle's building in Charing Cross Road, for 'afternoon tea and biscuits' served on a silver tray, she spoke very warmly of Bert, and remembered him then as 'fresh-faced and charming, and very good in the department' and capable of 'being able to talk the hind leg off a donkey on foreign authors'. Being roughly the same age, she also enjoyed his company socially:

I was very keen on Lloyd. He was with us for several years in the early thirties. He was a very curious person and I liked him very much. He was so gentle and had a most charming smile. ... I remember him for his funny clothes, not exactly shabby, but as if he lived in a fourth-floor back room south of the river at a rent of 3/6d a week and tried to look as if he was fairly respectable. He had a curious walk, he rather shambled along, and his overcoat collar was always rucked up around the back of his neck, and his hair used to stand up a bit, it was always untidy. He was thin faced, looking very ascetic. He was a very bohemian character, the bohemian of bohemians. He could mix quite freely with any of the bohemian groups. He could fit in with anybody, sailors, poets, anybody. He always wore a collar and tie but then so did everybody else, all the artistic types wore ordinary clothes. The girl poets and writers looked like office workers in grey or blue skirts. It was well before bohemians wore sweaters, jeans, and sandals and things like that.

In fact Christina was so keen on Bert that in the summer months she and her future husband, Ronald Batty, the manager of Foyle's rare-books department, would invite Bert to stay with them on their small yacht, to spend sunny weekends sailing up and down the east coast:

What was so marvellous about him was he seemed to know everything about any subject under the sun and we were very impressed – we were very young at the time.

In those days we had a small yacht on the River Crouch and he often came sailing with my brother [and] Ronald Batty, to whom I am now married, and myself, and another person who was with us at the same time, Ledig-Rowohlt, then in his early twenties, now [1984] the foremost publisher in Germany. We had some marvellous times in Essex in those far off days.

Heinrich Maria Ledig-Rowohlt was a good friend of Bert's during their time together at Foyle's and, if not a communist, was very left-wing. An illegitimate child, born the same year as Bert, he was eventually recognised by the famous German publisher, Ernst Rowohlt, as his son. On leaving Foyle's Heinrich went back to Berlin and worked in his father's company. During the Second World War the Nazis closed them down for publishing left-wing and other politically unacceptable literature and sent Heinrich to fight on the Russian Front. After the war Heinrich restarted the company and built it into one of Germany's largest publishers. He was also a respected translator of, among others, Harold Pinter, Henry Miller, James Baldwin and Nabokov.

How Bert reconciled his Jekyll-and-Hyde existence of alternating weekends on the water with Christina and communist street-rallies in the East End is uncertain. But one could see how he might wish to keep the two separate, just as he probably didn't announce from the stage of the Singers' Club a few years later that the second entry on the 'H' page of his telephone book was Harrods, or that he employed a cleaner whom he could blame for the mislaying of BBC books: 'The cleaner had tidily put it away among my books somewhere.'

At Christina Foyle's behest, Ben Perrick, Foyle's publicity manager, divulged his memories of Bert:

I joined Foyle's a few years after Bert and we were fellow-employees here until he left in (I think 1936 or 1937). After he managed the foreign books department he moved to the art books department. I was the publicity manager and we became very good friends. When the shop closed each day we used to walk to the tram terminus in Holborn as we both lived in north London. That walk each evening in his company was a great joy to me. His knowledge of so many subjects and his unquenchable desire to expound on them helped enormously to further my education. He was like a walking encyclopaedia. Whatever subject you mentioned he knew all about it, but I never heard a word about folk music.

He introduced me to the books of a wide range of authors – especially John dos Passos, John Steinbeck and William Faulkner. He passed on his views on art and poetry – and he would be wittily critical of people whose work or politics he opposed. Knowing him was akin to having a kind and knowledgeable tutor.

Apart from his erudition, my most vivid memory of him is of his rather high-pitched chuckle and of his very amusing mimicry. His mimicry of George Lansbury was really superb.

Sadly, I lost touch with him after he left Foyle's, although I did lunch with him a couple of times – I think it was while he was at *Picture Post*.

Bert and Ben Perrick also attended classical music concerts together at the Queen's Hall, London's favourite concert venue, a few yards south of Broadcasting House, next to John Nash's All Soul's Church. Sadly, the wonderful Queen's Hall was completely destroyed by an incendiary bomb on the night of 10 May 1941. Perrick remembered walking back through Soho after concerts there, with Bert keeping up a running commentary on the very latest, little known, avant-garde and foreign composers. One particular evening stuck in his mind. They were walking back through Bateman Street after having attended a Bach concert at the Queen's Hall, conducted by Thomas Beecham.

I started whistling a tune and Bert said, 'That's not Bach. I'm astonished at you. I could understand Debussy or even Cesar Franke, but Pierne, and from *Cydalise et le chevre-pied*! Where did you get it from?'
'I don't know. I just pick up these tunes without really knowing what I'm whistling. I think that was the "Entrance of the Little Fauns".'
'Yes, it was,' said Bert, 'It's from his ballet *Cydalise*. Pierne, of all people!'
Gabriel Pierne was hardly known in England at that time but Bert knew all about him – when he was born, all the ballets and song cycles he'd written, the fact that he'd studied under Debussy. Amazing.

Actually, Jack Payne and the BBC Dance Orchestra had recorded 'Entrance of the Little Fauns' (premiered in Paris in 1923) for Columbia in 1931, which is probably how Perrick heard it. So it wasn't quite as obscure as he thought, but to give Bert his due he recognised it and was able to give chapter and verse on the Frenchman. He had a photographic memory for tunes (and probably much else) and used to play a family version of 'Name That Tune', in which he would successfully name many classical pieces by the first two or three notes.
Another bookseller at Foyle's, with whom Bert became quite friendly, was Ben Weinreb (1912–99), who worked in the theology department. Weinreb always insisted that bookselling was the last refuge of the otherwise unemployable, although he eventually did very well out of it, becoming one of the world's leading dealers in architectural books and author, with Christopher Hibbert, of *The London Encyclopaedia* (1983). A few years younger than Bert, he was very much part of Bert's circle of friends and acquaintances, even though at the time he wasn't one of the group who looked like he was going anywhere.
After the shop closed in the evening, if Bert wasn't going straight back home to north London, the pair of them sometimes dropped into the Admiral Duncan in Old Compton Street – where another regular was the advertising copywriter, Jack Hargreaves – or the Fitzroy Tavern in Charlotte Street, a favourite with Dylan Thomas – but then where wasn't? Or they went for a bite to eat in one of the nearby cheap Soho cafés (bookselling then, as now,

being notoriously badly paid), such as the Chat Noir or Mrs Buhler's café in Rathbone Place, or maybe Meg's Arts Café over in Parton Street. If they fancied something a bit more exotic there was always the popular Nanking Chinese restaurant at 4 Denmark Street, which advertised itself in left-wing magazines as 'A place for the Internationalist'.[5]

According to Weinreb, 'everybody came into Parton Street in those inter-war days. It was a village with Meg's café in the centre'. A short, narrow street, now built over by the Cochrane Theatre, it ran from the northwest corner of Red Lion Square to the junction of Theobold's Road and Southampton Row, and through it the writers and journalists who lived in Bloomsbury walked every day on their way to and from Fleet Street.

At number 4 the old-Wellingtonian dropout, and supremely inept businessman, David Archer, ran the legendary Parton Bookshop, specialising in 'LEFT Novels, Poetry, Criticism, Marxist Literature, Education, etc.' as well as the *Daily Worker,* the monthly *Left Review*, and on Fridays the *New Statesman*, for whom Cyril Connolly, a shop regular, was the literary editor. The second floor of the narrow eighteenth-century building was rented to the Artists' International Association. In the basement the Stanley Brothers managed the distribution of the precocious Esmond Romilly's rebellious public school magazine *Out of Bounds: Against Reaction in Public Schools*. Bert was a regular visitor to the shop and knew Archer and the *enfant terrible* Romilly.

A nephew of Winston Churchill (known as 'Winston's Red Nephew'), Romilly was a determined pacifist and refused to join the Wellington College Officer Cadet Corps. At fifteen he ran away from the school and published *Out of Bounds* from the Parton Bookshop. The first issue appeared on 25 March 1934. Eventually his abhorrence of fascism overcame his pacifism and, at eighteen, he joined the Thaelmann Battalion of the International Brigade and fought in the defence of Madrid. In 1937, soon after being shipped home with dysentery, he met and married Jessica Mitford. In 1941, whilst they were living in America, he joined the Canadian Air force and was killed when his bomber was shot down over the North Sea.

The handsome, charismatic, rebellious young Romilly who died a hero's death at just twenty-two years old was the thinking girl's James Dean. One such girl was Bert's daughter, Caroline, who, although not born when Romilly gave his life in the cause of freedom, was fascinated by him and very much admired his romantic image. Bert's street cred went up several notches when one day, as Caroline was extolling Romilly's virtues, he casually let it drop that he had known the young 'rebel *with* a cause' in the heady Parton Street days.

However, the ex-Wellington master T.C. Worsley, in his autobiographical novel *Flannelled Fool*, saw Romilly somewhat differently as: '... a tough, ruthless, wholly unscrupulous, iron-hearted youth, practising already in relentless fashion the communist doctrine that the end justifies the means.'

Ben Weinreb went to work at Archer's shop in the spring of 1935 after having left Foyle's and unsuccessfully tried acting. He was offered a pound a week to keep an eye on the till and the shop, and given the attic room to sleep in, which he was to share with Dylan Thomas when Dylan was in town.

Having no lavatory up at the top of the house, they kept a tin bath in the centre of the room for night-time emergencies, and more than once Ben woke up to find an inebriated Dylan had been unable to find the bath in the dark and was peeing over his head. In December 1934, Archer, in conjunction with the *Sunday Referee*, published Dylan's first collection, *18 Poems*. Archer sold his shop to Winnie Barham in 1939 and moved to Glasgow to escape the Blitz. Here he opened another bookshop and the Scott Street Arts Centre. Finally, after returning to London and unsuccessfully reopening in Old Compton Street, he gassed himself.

A copy of Thomas's *18 Poems* turned up for sale a few years ago in Jeff Towns' Dylan's Bookstore in Swansea with a nice dedication from Bert: 'Herewith, the first book of a new very good young poet who sometimes works at the BBC, and he has signed it for you, too.' Infuriatingly, we don't know for whom it was intended – obviously not one of the literary Soho/Fitzrovia crowd who would have known Dylan. It sounds the sort of thing one might write to a female friend or maybe a family member.

Bert knew Dylan well. They wrote for the same magazines and frequented the same pubs, cafés, and parties. George Rudé remembered the two of them talking poetry at one of his soirees, with Dylan asking Bert's advice about a particular poem and both of them discussing their friend Roger Roughton's surrealist poetry, of which Dylan opined that it was 'a pity he doesn't get on with it. Trouble with him is he's got too much bloody money.'[6]

When word got back to England that Roughton, a pacifist who had moved to Ireland at the beginning of the war, had also committed suicide by gassing himself, Dylan contacted his friend, the writer John Davenport, in April 1941 to suggest a response to the news of Roughton's untimely death, and proposed that Bert should be approached to contribute: 'And get a few chaps – Bert Lloyd, maybe Enoch Soames & Henry Moore, you'll know who to get – to put their names.'

Bert and Roughton had been good friends and Weinreb remembered the day in 1935 that the pair of them went to see T.S. Eliot who was regarded with awe and respect by many of the younger writers: 'I can remember Roger Roughton and Bert Lloyd going off on a special occasion to see T.S. Eliot: Parton Street was buzzing with this famous interview. I think they just went to see him in the hope of getting something published.' Roughton obviously impressed Eliot because he published his story *The Journey* and several poems in the literary journal, *The Criterion*.

Next door to Archer's bookshop, on the corner of Drake Street, at 2 Parton Street, were the offices of the Communist Party publishers Lawrence and Wishart, and the Party's literary magazine *Left Review*. The company came about in 1936 when wealthy arts patron and publisher Ernest Wishart (who held the lease on number 2) joined forces with Martin Lawrence, a name invented by the Party to front their publishing operations – Martin Lawrence being a code for Marx and Lenin – M & L.

Across the road at number 1 was the Arts Café ('Open 9 a.m. to 10 p.m. – lunches, suppers, home-made cakes and morning coffee'), rendezvous of poets such as George Barker, Geoffrey Grigson and John Cornford, students from the nearby Central School and, of course, Bert. Above the café in a couple of rooms lived the well-heeled Roughton. From here he published slim volumes of surrealist literature and his self-funded magazine *Contemporary Poetry and Prose*, to which both Dylan and Bert were early contributors. Although Dylan may have thought Roughton was too affluent for his own good, he didn't let it deter him from accepting Roughton's largesse of half a guinea a page for his poems.

According to the poet and early British surrealist David Gascoyne (1916–2001), Roughton had 'an unusually open and receptive mind, together with a distinctive flair for quality'. He certainly published some original and fine writing by Dylan, including the remarkable short story *The Burning Baby,* as well as stories and poems by Gavin Ewart, William Empson, Isaac Babel, Antonia White and Bert, who Gascoyne believed was also the source of some 'novel material of anthropological interest'.[7]

ENGINEERS OF THE HUMAN SOUL

'All that dreary tribe of high-minded women and sandal-wearers and bearded fruit-juice drinkers who come flocking towards the smell of progress like bluebottles to a dead cat.'

George Orwell, on middle-class socialists

In 1933 a small group of leftish young commercial artists and illustrators had been in the habit of getting together a couple of nights a week at James Fitton's evening classes in lithography at the Central School of Arts and Crafts in Southampton Row. For the members of the group, which included the communists James Boswell (1906–71) and Pearl Binder (Lady Elwyn-Jones née Pearl 'Polly' Binder, 1904–90), as well as James Holland, Edward Ardizzone, and the older German sculptor William Ohly, the stimulating political discussions and the general camaraderie were as important a part of the proceedings as the classes. In fact Fitton later admitted that most of them knew as much about lithography as he did.

By 1933 many artists were feeling the effects of the economic depression. The 1931 census had revealed that only 700 of the 10,000 informants who declared themselves to be 'artists' were managing to support themselves by their art. Students who had spent several years studying at art college were being forced to accept such mundane jobs as painting lampshades, decorating plates and copying zoological specimens, for very little money. In his essay *The Artist Speaks,* published in R.S. Lambert's *Art in England* (1938), William Coldstream, co-founder of the left-leaning Euston Road School of painters, said: 'The 1930 slump affected us all very considerably. Everyone became very interested in economics and then in politics. Two very talented painters who had been at the Slade [School of Fine Art] with me gave up painting altogether, one to work for the ILP (Independent Labour Party), the other for the Communist party. It was no longer the thing to be an artist delighting in isolation.'

The rising tide of fascism across Europe was another cause for concern for many socialist-minded artists. One evening, an excited Pearl Binder turned up to the Central class and announced that they must all go up to Misha Black's studio at Seven Dials, to meet Cliff Rowe, who had recently returned from the USSR and who, fired with enthusiasm, wanted to start a group of left-wing painters.

Misha Black (1910–77), a then struggling twenty-three-year-old Azerbaijan-born artist, who would ultimately rise to giddy heights in design and architecture as Sir Misha Black, lived and worked at that time in a bohemian top floor studio in Little Earl Street (now Earlham Street), furnished with orange boxes salvaged from nearby Covent Garden market, and lit by candles, the electricity having being cut off. In the nineteenth century Seven Dials was a notorious rookery noted for its ballad printers, chaunters, patterers, criminals, whores, pugilists and gin-houses, and as the possible birth-place of so-called 'cockney' rhyming-slang. By the time Black and his wife moved into the studio the Cambridge Theatre had just been built across the road and things were beginning to look up, although it was still very much a working-class neighbourhood of cold-water flats, actors' digs, small traders and local businesses.

In the flickering candlelight the group sat around and listened to Rowe's enthusiastic report of life and art in the Soviet Union, where, in Moscow, he had exhibited a realist painting of hunger marchers entering Trafalgar Square at night. The Red Army, a noted patron of painters, had sponsored his work. He told them how all big organisations, such as trade unions, were expected to patronise some aspect of art, and he spoke fervently of the need for artists to organise in support of the working-class movement. He was preaching to the converted, at the end of the evening it was agreed to set up the International Organisation of Artists for Revolutionary Proletarian Art; not a name that tripped off the tongue, but one that summed up their radical left-wing enthusiasm.

Of the original group of a dozen or so only three or four were Party card-carriers; many of the others joined later. It was agreed to spread the word around to sympathetic friends and acquaintances and to hold another meeting in October. By October, after some advice from more experienced CPGB members, they were ready to get things rolling. The Blacks, who had by then moved into a couple of rooms on the second floor of a house in Charlotte Street, again acted as hosts. New Zealander James Boswell described the meeting:

> We went to the later Charlotte Street meeting with some more coherent notions and got the name whittled down to the Artists' International. 'Association' was added to the name a couple of years later when Moscow suggested the group should be more inclusive.

We had only the crudest ideas about art and Marxism and we nearly all felt the need to do something practical so we painted banners, posters and drew cartoons and gradually drew more support.

At this second meeting the Association could be said to have been founded. A.L. Lloyd was there and took part in the first exhibition at Charlotte Street in 1934 showing four small but very interesting drawings.[8]

The exhibition inspired the sculptor Eric Gill to write an article entitled 'Art and Propaganda' for the *Catholic Herald* which was reprinted the following year in *Left Review* (9 June 1935).

Bert had tried his hand at painting when he was still living in Australia, as A.L. Morton remembered:

He brought back from Australia a quantity of paintings and drawings which gave a remarkable sense of the strangeness of that strange land and of the new cultural developments there in the early years of the century. I bought one from him for a pound or two – a serious sum of money for us both in those days – of two wild horses in a stony desert. I wonder what happened to the rest of them?

The enthusiasm and commitment of the members of the new association outweighed any initial ideological naiveté, as they threw themselves into producing banners, posters, newsletters, pamphlets and books such as the 1934 collection *Hunger March Cartoons,* and arranging their first exhibition *The Social Scene*, in which Bert exhibited. A year later, they organised the exhibition *Artists Against Fascism and War.*

Although Communist Party members such as Bert, Boswell, Binder, James Lucas and Rowe were always in the minority, their influence and energy were a driving force, as Robert Radford pointed out in *Art for a Purpose*: 'The Communists did tend to be the most active in organising propaganda events and on committees and it was recognised that much of the overall dynamism of the AIA and many of its specific events were generated by its Communist members.'

Most of the artists involved in the early days of the AIA were graduates of British art colleges whose training and aesthetic values weren't designed to produce revolutionary artists. But they were all determinedly anti-fascist and pro-working class: 'Today when the Capitalist system and socialists are fighting for world survival we feel that the place of the artist is at the side of the working class.'[9]

They were keen to use their art and expertise to help fulfil the stated 1934 aims:

The International Unity of Artists Against Imperialist War on the Soviet Union, Fascism, and Colonial Oppression.

The uniting of all artists in Britain sympathetic to these aims into working units ready to execute posters, illustrations, cartoons, book jackets, banners, tableaux, stage decorations, etc.

The spreading of propaganda by means of exhibitions, the Press, lectures and meetings.

The maintaining of contact with similar groups already existing in 16 other countries.

In the *Dictionary of Labour Biography* Boswell is quoted as having described the AIA as 'a mixture of agit-prop body, Marxist discussion group, exhibition organiser and anti-war, anti-fascist art.'

Although the AIA never laid down any hard and fast rules as to what their frequently iconoclastic fluctuating membership and supporting artists could or could not exhibit, or what was deemed suitable 'revolutionary art', Soviet Socialist Realism (art that was realistic in form but socialist in content), as seen by Rowe and Binder during their sojourns in the USSR, had a definite influence on some members; as did the line drawings of the German political and social caricaturist, George Grosz (1893–1959), especially on the younger James Boswell.

If the AIA members weren't too clear on the interpretation of revolutionary art when they initially threw themselves into the struggle, neither were some Soviets. In 1934 when Stalin's son-in-law, Andrei Zhdanov, addressed the All Union Congress of Soviet Writers and decreed that artists would henceforth be required to provide 'historically concrete depictions of reality in its revolutionary development' combined with the task of 'educating the masses with the spirit of Communism', there was a certain amount of head scratching and beard tugging amongst many older painters, all of whom from then on were also required to join the State-run Union of Soviet Artists. But, unlike the AIA whose membership and supporters covered a wide spectrum of political belief and commitment including, as it did, anarchists, Catholics, communists and Marxists, and where for many the abhorrence of fascism was the only common denominator, Stalin's totalitarian Soviet Union appointed the Academy of Arts in St Petersburg the arbiter of taste, and empowered it to 'implement' the communist party-line on fine art, which included protecting the Soviet body from infection from the 'alien microbes' of the avant-garde. In his essay on Soviet art history in *The Art Bulletin* (December 1989) John Bowlt says: 'One of the most destructive critics of Modernism, Osip Beskin (1892–1969) even compared deviations from Realism to the 'decomposition and disintegration of a human body.'

The result was several decades of Socialist Realism (term coined by Stalin), in which the USSR was largely cut off from many of the modern trends in art, during which time artists produced countless portraits of Lenin and Stalin. Powerful propaganda paintings and absolute state censorship succeeded in keeping many people both inside and outside the USSR unaware of the scale of Stalin's atrocities for so long. Some people, of course, even if they did know, had no qualms about Stalin's ruthless tactics. The Comintern's man in the

CPGB, Palme Dutt, merely shrugged and said: 'That there should be spots on the sun would only startle an inveterate Mithras worshipper.'

It's not difficult to see how intelligent, sincere, socially conscious people like Bert, Binder and Rowe would want to be seduced by the Soviet promise of peace, prosperity, equality and culture for everyone. Some people, such as the writer e.e. cummings, saw through Stalin's regime from the start. The American cummings compared his 1931 trip through Russia to the descent into Hell in Dante's *Inferno,* and in *Eimi* (1933) attacks the Soviet regime for its dehumanising policies.[10] Malcolm Muggeridge pointed out in *The Thirties* that:

> The cost of a tour in the U.S.S.R., though moderate, was beyond the means of most manual workers, so that those who availed themselves of the exceedingly competent Intourist organisation were predominantly income-tax payers. Their delight in all they saw and were told, and the expression they gave to their delight, constitute unquestionably one of the wonders of the age. The almost unbelievable credulity of these mostly university educated tourists astonished even Soviet officials.

Stalin would have been right, and uncharacteristically honest, if he really made the 'reputed' remark, 'Lenin left us a great inheritance and we, his heirs, have fucked it all up!' The artists of the AIA, viewing life through, if not 'deepest red', then at least, rose-tinted spectacles, saw none of this.

The AIA, opting for the carrot rather than the stick (or perhaps the borscht rather than the belt), as befitted its disparate membership, hoped to come to a consensus over what constituted revolutionary art by discussions and lectures. In November 1935 Wishart published some of these lectures in the small AIA-sponsored collection *5 On Revolutionary Art.* The contributors were the anarchist Henry Read ('What is Revolutionary Art?'); Marxist art historian, F.D. Klingender ('Content and Form in Art'); Catholic sculptor, Eric Gill ('All Art is Propaganda'); A.L. Lloyd ('Modern Art and Modern Society'); and Marxist literary critic Alick West ('On Abstract Criticism').

In her foreword the AIA secretary Betty Rea said: 'Revolutionary art is at present an extremely controversial subject among those artists who are interested in the theory and history of their craft. In this book there are five considered opinions on the nature of revolutionary art, which will stimulate the reader either to draw his own conclusions, or at least to further a more vigorous discussion.'

One of Bert's problems, then, as a budding Marxist aesthetic theoretician, was the lack of any stone tablets etched with a cohesive set of Marxist artistic precepts. Marx and Engels did, however, leave a considerable body of writing on art and literature scattered through countless letters, manuscript notes, reviews, articles, and in passages in the major works. Unfortunately it wasn't until 1933 that Mikhail Lifschitz and E.P. Schiller assiduously gathered many of these fugitive pieces for publication. By 1967 the collection, now edited by Manfred Kliem, had reached 1,500 pages and was republished in Berlin as *Uber Kunst und Literatur*.

There's no indication in Bert's essay that he had seen the original Lifschitz 1933 collection by the time he worked on his 1935 AIA lecture. 'Modern Art and Modern Society' represents his first major piece of writing (his short story 'The Red Steer' plus a couple of reviews had been printed in *Left Review* the year before), and what first hits you is the confidence with which he launches into his subject. Bert's writing style appears to have sprung into life fully formed. It would be difficult to distinguish this piece from examples of his 1970s folklore writing. It's less adjectival, perhaps, although he does manage to slip in 'Yury Plekhanov, that intelligent, highly cultured and "peppery" old gentleman'. 'Peppery' is a Bert word. Then there is the transferred epithet of 'the long-nosed gallantry of feudal aristocracy', which is a typical Bert phrase. Also his simile of Seurat's bowler-hatted men as being 'formal as a limited company' is reminiscent of his oft-used 1970s line regarding the successful treatment of his arrhythmic heart, which he declared to be now 'as four-square as Bach'.

Did he perhaps have a chest full of early exercises in style and rhetorical device, similar to the Chinese brush artist who, when questioned about his ability to produce a masterpiece with just half a dozen quick brush strokes, opened a large cupboard out of which fell thousands of earlier practice pieces? The nearest equivalent would be his lengthy, consciously literary letters from Australia written in his teens and early twenties and obviously influenced by his reading at that time. Despite his frequently chatty, journalistic writing style, there was often an underlying late Victorian/Edwardian formality of phrase and language.

After commencing with a nod to Marx, and a bow to Georgi Valentinovitch Plekhanov (1856–1918), one of the founders of Russian Marxism, for providing a formula with which to understand the economic bases to the ideological superstructure of society, he leaps in feet first. There's more to it, insists Bert, than simply economics, and he slaps the wrists of 'some' Marxists for having the arrogance and the temerity to assume that merely being a Marxist confers on them some divine right to criticize 'any damn thing', whether it be 'psycho-analysis, physics, art, or what you will'. Without a considerable knowledge of the subject under criticism 'the advantage which their materialist standpoint gives them is immediately discounted'.

He goes on to show that he, at least, has done his homework; all those hours studying art books in the Australian outback weren't wasted. For the next fifteen or so pages, we are given a potted history of Western art from classical Greece, through the Middle Ages, the Italian Renaissance, French and German classicism, up to the movements of the twentieth century, and the forces that shaped each artistic epoch.

Along the way he shakes his head with disappointment at the failure of Epstein, who had initially shown a lot of promise, 'to find an effective mythological theme, and (being) unable to work without one'. He patronises Renoir's 'bright vulgarity' and his 'sweet-haunched little burgesses' – making them sound like bourgeois suckling pigs. Picasso, Braque and Gris come in for some stick for taking Cubism up a blind alley from where they could not recover 'concrete and material reality'. Needless to say the 'fascist Chirico' gets hammered for persisting in his 'feeble and frail' outdated neo-Hellenism. Being a fascist, Chirico was on a hiding to nothing to begin with. At least the others were basically good blokes, and talented artists, who had, hopefully, temporarily lost their way.

The problem with modern bourgeois art, Bert concluded, was the exclusion of materialism and dialectics. But: 'The existence of a proletariat conscious of its class and fighting for it – however little this may have entered the consciousness of the artist – is indicative of the rising of a new social order which will require a new order of art adapted to its needs.' Unfortunately, Bert doesn't tell us what form the new revolutionary art would take, but then neither did the other contributors to the book. However, as Betty Rea suggested in her introduction, the essays provoked plenty of soul-searching, navel-gazing, and discussion in many cafés, studios and pubs. And the racy, erudite essay, published in such respected company, could have done Bert's reputation no harm whatsoever.

A couple of months after the publication of *5 On Revolutionary Art*, the *Left Review* for January 1936 printed Bert's review of the book *A Calendar for 1936* with drawings by the three Jameses – Fitton, Boswell and Holland. In the same issue Douglas Garman, Wishart's brother-in-law, who in the 1920s had assisted Edgell Rickword edit the celebrated literary review *Calendar of Modern Letters*, reviewed *5 On Revolutionary Art* and complimented Bert and Alick West on contributing the two most balanced essays:

> Both write as Marxists whose intellectual convictions are sufficiently assured to allow them to approach the aesthetic problem freely. The former's [Bert's] stimulating survey of modern painting does much to support his contention that abstract art is largely the result of the artist's failure to solve the problem transmitted to us by Courbet, the materialist, and Cezanne, the dialectician ... .

In May 1935 Bert had been a signatory, along with many of the usual suspects, in the *Left Review*'s criticism of the Silver Jubilee celebrations for King George V:

PROTEST AGAINST THE JUBILEE

The celebration of the Jubilee is in effect a call to the nation to rejoice over the twenty-five years of our history from 1910–1935. It is the opinion of those who sign this paper that the events of this period have been of a character which forbids rejoicing. These events include a war in which out of the population of Great Britain and Ireland 812,317 men were killed and 1,849,494 were wounded. It has been a period of growing unemployment. In 1913 when three per cent of the total number of trade unionists was unemployed the problem was thought to be serious. In 1935 when 2,397,000 are unemployed we are bidden to official rejoicings. Those in Great Britain dependent on Poor Law Relief who already numbered 903,509 in 1915 were 1,498,247 twenty years later. We consider that rejoicing is out of place, and we protest against the arranged celebrations.

Signatories included: Pearl Binder, James Boswell, Hugh MacDiarmid, Eric Gill, Allen Hutt, A. Lancaster Lloyd, Edgell Rickword, Douglas Garman, Tom Wintringham (who, five years later, would be the mastermind behind training the Home Guard in street fighting and covert killing techniques!) and Ralph Fox, who just two years later would be killed in Spain fighting with the International Brigade.

Ben Weinreb decorated the Parton Street bookshop's window with an anti-royalty display in sympathy with the protestors: 'In July 1935 it was King George's Jubilee and I acquired some sweets called Golden Humbugs for the window, which we dressed with all the anti-royalist pamphlets we could find, in particular a virulent and witty one by T.A. Jackson [Tommy Jackson]. We were warned to expect a brick through the window but it never came.'[11]

A bit of good news that no doubt cheered Bert and the rest up was that the King, 'wishing to share in the sacrifices that the nation was called upon to suffer as a result of the financial crisis', agreed to a reduction of £50,000 from the Civil List. It must have been comforting to know that they were all in it together.

Retrospection can be a subtle re-arranger of truth. In most literary histories and biographies of the 1930s, the Parton Street bookshop is spoken of in reverential terms. The reality, when seen from the other side of the counter could at times, according to Ben Weinreb, be somewhat less romantic:

This romantic view of Archer's bookshop is just not so. The shop was just one small room, with shelves around the edges. It would have been the thickness of the house except for the corridor that went down the side of it. David had no head for business and after a year the unpaid bills began to mount, publishers stopped their credit, and bailiffs were an ever-present threat. If anyone wanted a new book we would ask for the money in advance and I would go off to the trade counter of the publisher concerned and purchase the book for cash, as all credit had been stopped by our suppliers. Two of his friends, David Abercrombie, at that time a lecturer at the London School of Economics, and Vicki Darragh, the wife of a journalist on the *Daily Express* [and *Daily Worker* reviewer], stepped in with a little money just enough to pay the bills and restock the shop. The conditions were that David shouldn't handle the money, and that my pound a week wage was the first thing to come out of the week's takings. My duties were minimal, for indeed the stock was minimal; we opened about 9.30, and there was the intermittent trickle of regulars, who bought the *Daily Worker*, which had been delivered the previous evening. These included Cyril Connolly, who never paid his bills, and other writers and journalists who lived in Bloomsbury.

The Parton Street poet George Barker could look down years later from the summit of Parnassus and say loftily: 'What a bore all those politically affiliated young men at your Parton Street Bookshop were, David, in those forgettable thirties.'[12] But he can't deny, and we shouldn't forget, despite Weinreb's dampener, the psychic creative energy that obviously emanated from the shop, and David Archer's commitment to encouraging young literary talent. It's difficult nowadays, standing outside the Cochrane Theatre and looking south across the bustling postwar, one-way traffic system to Red Lion Square, to picture beneath the buses, taxis and tarmac, the narrow alley, the small shop, the clatter of trams and the bright idealistic writers that gathered there almost eighty years ago, enthusiastically examining their latest slim volume published by the Parton Press. Politically affiliated certainly, bailiff-beleaguered possibly, but boring? Perhaps only to an older man who'd 'matured' beyond his idealism.

As well as publishing the Neo-Romantics, Dylan Thomas (*18 Poems*) and the ingrate Barker (*30 Preliminary Poems*), in the mid-1930s Archer also published David Gascoyne's surrealist collection *Man's Life is the Meat*, and a little known 1937 English edition of Franz Kafka's *The Metamorphosis* (*Der Verwandlung*) by one A.L. Lloyd[13] (a first edition of which was up for sale in America in 2008 for $5,000). Along with *The Hobbit* and Kafka's *The Trial*, *The Metamorphosis* appeared in the *New Statesman*'s list of the Best Books of 1937. Bert, Barker, Gascoyne and Thomas were an exclusive quartet who, in contrast to many other leading English writers of the 1930s – Day Lewis, Spender, Empson, MacNeice, Auden – were not university graduates.

Although Bert's was the first English translation to use the title *The Metamorphosis*, the story had, in fact, been published four years earlier by Secker and Warburg as *The Transformation* (1933) in a translation by Willa and Edwin Muir. In 1930, six years after Kafka's untimely tubercular death at forty, the Muirs had translated *The Castle* and over the next few years went on to translate the rest of Kafka's oeuvre. They were largely responsible for introducing and promoting his existential tales of political and social dislocation to English-speaking readers.

In July 1937 Evelyn Waugh, book reviewer for Graham Greene and John Marks's newly launched weekly magazine *Night and Day*, wrote a favourable, if brief, review of Bert's *The Metamorphosis*, which he described as 'a grim little story' but one which 'in its small horrifying way' was 'unmistakably stamped with the genius of *The Castle*'. Many years later, the BBC Third Programme wanted to broadcast the Kafka novella and, having decided on the Muirs' translation, had the temerity to ask Bert if they could use his title because the producer preferred *Metamorphosis* to the Muirs' more prosaic *Transformation*. Bert acquiesced.[14]

This was also the year which saw the publication of Bert's edition of Federico Garcia Lorca's *Death of a Bullfighter*.[15] It was quite an achievement for Bert to have had two important literary translations published in one year. We know Bert learned Spanish at school, but where and when he learnt German well enough to handle Kafka is not known. There is no mention of learning

German in the few surviving letters from Australia, but there would doubtless have been opportunity and motivation when he was managing Foyle's foreign book department.

If the Soho and Fitzrovian artistic left had taken the young working-class intellectual to their bosoms the incestuous upper-class Bloomsbury set were too preoccupied with each other and their own work to bother with him. Bert told film director Barrie Gavin about a Bloomsbury party he'd once attended soon after returning from Australia, clutching a written introduction to John Middleton Murry, the prolific writer, critic and founder of the literary magazine *The Adelphi*, and who in 1932 was to declare himself 'finally and forever a Communist'. Bert, at that time a nobody, was completely ignored by Murry, Virginia Woolf and the rest of the guests, and was made to feel most uncomfortable and unwelcome. He was obviously too 'working class' and insignificant to warrant attention, despite the fact that Virginia occasionally wrote for the *Daily Worker* and the Woolfs' library contained the works of Marx, Lenin, William Morris, various Communist Party pamphlets and booklets and, later, Morton's *A People's History of England* (1938).

Luckily, what Leonard and Virginia Woolf and the rest of their narcissistic Tavistock Square clique thought, or didn't think, about Bert was largely irrelevant to the less rarefied left-wing swell that was washing around the pubs and studios of Soho and Fitzrovia. In James Friell's Dickensian description:

> It was the best of times, it was the worst of times, a grim, poverty-stricken, callous time which many poor souls did not survive. In the face of the incredible complacence of the establishment it was also a time of great gusto, vehemence and vitality especially if you got into 'the struggle.' There the prevailing mood was one of irony. Not the classic detached irony so beloved of literary critics. It was bitter, caustic and deep rooted.[16]

Bert certainly threw himself into 'the struggle' and became a regular presence at CP meetings, rallies and social get-togethers. His face even appeared on political posters urging everyone to 'Unite For Democracy', and he became a recognised name in print.

THE POET IN THE CUPBOARD

If, as Friell said, 'it was the best of times, it was the worst of times', the 'best of times' were doubtless better if you had a flat in Berkeley Square, rather than the damp, overcrowded, back-street rooms of Salford, so vividly portrayed in Walter Greenwood's *Love On the Dole* (1933), and the 'worst of times' less easy to bear by an unemployed Durham miner and his hungry family than by a Parton Street poet. But all pleasure and suffering is relative, and when Bert spoke of experiencing periods of unemployment in the 1930s, and of 'shuffling between the dole office and the warmth of the British Museum Reading Room', he was, presumably, as disconsolate, in his own way, as the miner.

It's impossible to know just how 'unemployed' Bert was during the 1930s, and what he did for money. He seems to have spent several of those years comfortably working at Foyle's. He was certainly artistically busy and politically involved in the Communist Party between arriving back from Australia, working in Foyle's and going off to the South Atlantic for the 1937/8 whaling season, but how much money his artistic efforts generated is impossible to tell. He almost certainly wasn't rolling in cash, or, to paraphrase Dylan Thomas, 'Lack of money probably kept pouring in'.

Bert's friend David Gascoyne, the surrealist wunderkind, despite his numerous books and contributions to magazines, could not afford to rent a place of his own. So every night when the pubs, clubs and parties wound down, and all conversation was expended, the young literary rebel slunk back to his parents' rather pokey little flat above a suburban branch of the Midland Bank in East Twickenham.[17] High profile and critical acclaim did not necessarily equate with a large, or even, moderate income. So if Bert was relying solely on his pen to earn a living after leaving Foyle's, he might indeed have been on his uppers by 1937.

Busy though he was, establishing himself as a man of letters, Bert also led an interesting social life, forming friendships and future working relationships that would last for the rest of his life. It's fascinating, when following Bert's life, to see the same faces surfacing over and over again in a range of disparate situations and combinations through nearly fifty years – James Boswell, Misha Black, Alan Bush, Pearl Binder, Edgell Rickword, Tom Wintringham, Laurence Gilliam, Leslie Morton, and many more: a left-wing web of highly intelligent, creative, committed people whose politics and comradeship were forged in the working-class struggles of the inter-war years. Unlike Bert, the working-class autodidact, most of them were graduates, from middle- and upper-middle-class backgrounds, with little economic necessity to join the 'struggle', but who committed themselves to the 'cause' from a sense of intellectual conviction that it was simply the right thing to do, and in a belief that society could, and should, be changed for the better. Fascism – capitalism with the gloves off – shouldn't be allowed to win.

George Rudé (1910–93), a respected Marxist historian, joined the Communist Party in 1935 following a trip to Russia a couple of years earlier. In the 1940s he became a member of the CPGB Historians Group along with Christopher Hill, Eric Hobsbawm, Leslie Morton and E.P. Thompson, and several more. George studied history 'from the bottom up' and, as a good Marxist, took as his special area of interest the 'crowd' (to non-Marxist historians 'the mob'), social unrest and revolution. Revolutionary crowds are made up of individuals and his detailed archive research sought to put faces and names on these individuals. His first study, *The Crowd in the French Revolution* (1959), utilised Parisian police and court records to find out who the actual people were who took the Bastille, and what they thought they were doing. Nearer to home he wrote, with Eric Hobsbawm, the classic early work on nineteenth-century southern English rural unrest, *Captain Swing*.

As a communist in the 1950s Rudé was frozen out of the British university system, so in 1960 he and his wife Doreen went into academic exile in Australia and Canada where they stayed until their return to England in 1987. From the mid-1930s Rudé had shared a large top-floor flat at 14 Berkeley Square with Humphrey Haigh, a mathematician with whom he'd been at Cambridge, and whose parents owned the building, and Bertie Thomas, the son of an *Evening News* cartoonist. George remembered with amusement the effect that Bert Lloyd had on the younger Bertie:

> Bertie looked on Bert as Jesus. Bert was the great guru. One day when we were all sitting around, Thomas suddenly said, 'Bert, what d'you think of Michelangelo?' Bert replied, 'Oh, he's all right.' He was reading a paper at the time and didn't want to be bothered. Then Bertie said, 'What d'you think of Leonardo?' And Bert grunted. So he said, 'What about Raphael?' Bert said nothing. Bertie nodded and said, 'Oh, didn't make the grade, eh?'

Doreen described the flat as a regular and popular party venue for young leftish writers, artists, and interesting pretty girls, one of whom was the surrealist icon, Sheila Legge.[18] Legge didn't do a great deal but was years ahead of her time in managing to be famous for being famous. Or, as Doreen put it, 'she wasn't an artist as such, but she was a person who was multi-talented doing nothing. There were a lot of them about'.

Roger Roughton, Dylan Thomas and Bert were also often at the flat. Dylan was found there one morning after a late-night party. As George and Doreen were clearing up the dirty glasses and emptying the overflowing ashtrays they heard a porcine-like grunt from a broom-cupboard in the hall. On gingerly opening the cupboard door they found a crumpled snoring Dylan curled up amongst the shoes and boots, dead to the world.

When Doreen started going out with Rudé she had been warned by Sheila that she was wasting her time trying to develop any sort of permanent relationship because 'all George ever thought about was politics and work'. Bert, who was standing with them when Legge delivered her advice at one of the Berkeley Square parties, looked the gorgeous young Doreen up and down and said with a smile, 'Oh, I don't know, I think she might have a chance'. And so it proved. They eventually married in 1940 and remained happily together for over fifty years.

Sheila and Bert got on very well and she occasionally accompanied him to galleries, lectures, and more interestingly to the Frith Street nightclub where the teenage Doreen was employed for a while as a singer and exotic dancer. Soho's Frith Street has a long history of harbouring interesting people, including John Constable, Mozart, John Logie Baird, William Hazlitt and the Victorian novelist Mary Elizabeth Braddon. Just before Doreen became the toast of the street, the black American dancer Josephine Baker had debuted her famous 'banana dance' at the glamorous Art Deco Prince Edward Theatre, whose stage door opened a few doors along from Doreen's club. It was also at 29 Frith Street in 1952 (the year coffee came off ration) that the Scotsman Maurice Ross opened the Moka Bar, the first Soho espresso bar.

Doreen arrived in London from Ireland in 1938 and moved into a flat with three other girls in Marchmont Street, Bloomsbury. She was just seventeen years old, and very beautiful, as Eric Hobsbawm remembered when he wrote George Rudé's obituary for the *Guardian*:

> I first met George Rudé on the banks of the Cam in 1939. On that occasion I and other (male) student communists of the Party were more impressed by the extremely attractive and leggy girl he had brought with him, rumoured to be from the Unity Theatre, than even by his membership of the London District Committee of the CPGB. She was Doreen de la Hoyde of Dublin, whom he was soon to marry.

She had some idea of being an actress or a dancer, but until the big break came she had to earn money to pay her share of the rent on the Bloomsbury flat so she devised a bubble dance for the Frith Street club – one of the 'less sleazy ones', as she was always quick to point out in later life.

Her 'nom de bubble' was Sandra, a name selected for her by the club owner to give the act a bit of 'class'. Word soon got around Soho and Fitzrovia about the gorgeous young bubble dancer and needless to say in no time at all it was standing room only. One of the most enthusiastic punters was Bert who went along every night for a week, sometimes with Sheila Legge, George Rudé and Humphrey Haigh. They regularly commandeered the front row seats, from where they cheered, applauded and sang along lustily in the choruses: 'Sheila, George, Humphrey and Bert all came along. They thought it was hilarious, they loved every minute of it, it was so kitsch and unbelievable. Sheila wasn't a nightclub type, Bert certainly wasn't, but they came to see me and thought it was very funny. I suppose seeing as how I didn't have many clothes on was an added attraction.'

After the show Doreen would go round the front and join Bert or whoever was there. After one performance Bert told her that she had a nice voice and she should sing ballads, to which Doreen replied that there was more money in bubbles than ballads. A year or so before she died, Doreen still remembered the 'bubble' song that Bert and the others had sung with such enthusiasm some fifty years earlier; it was Sammy Fain and Lew Brown's jazz/blues number *That Old Feeling* (1937):

> I saw you last night and got that old feeling.
> When you came in sight I got that old feeling.
> The moment that you passed by I felt a thrill
> And when you caught my eye
> My heart stood still.

After a couple of months Doreen had got some 'legit' work, understudying Myrtle Stewart in *Dick Whittington*. The Frith Street nightclub wrote a string of letters begging her to come back because business had plummeted since she'd hung up her balloons, but she was by then too busy performing with Hattie Jacques and Ben Weinreb's sister at the left-wing Unity Theatre.

Bert, who was a few years older than many of the Berkeley Square group, had an aura of manly authenticity about him, from his years boundary riding and sheep herding in the Australian outback. This, coupled with his wide-ranging general knowledge – everybody who met him agreed there were few subjects upon which he couldn't hold a serious and knowledgeable discussion – imbued him with an air of authority, which, as we've seen, certainly impressed Bertie Thomas.

He was often to be found sitting quietly in a corner with his trade-mark quizzical smile watching the proceedings which George Rudé described as 'very exciting and involved a certain amount of womanising, drinking, talking politics, art. The whole thing sort of went together in the loose-living days of the thirties.' Doreen Rudé remembered Bert at that time as 'an ageless man':

He was never a bohemian, he was always casually smart. He'd wear a crew-neck jersey or a tie – the inevitable left-wing homespun tie. They were almost a uniform. When you walked into a place and looked around you saw the ties, usually orange like the Left Book Club book jackets, sometimes red. When he was at home he'd be respectably dressed; he wasn't a way-out dresser. If you went to the house he'd wear a suit jacket, not necessarily matching trousers, and some sort of jersey – he wore jerseys a lot. Fair Isle sweaters.

The flat became a centre for all sorts of people including Henry Moore, who knew Bert well, John Betjeman once lunched at the flat, as did T.S. Eliot. Roger Roughton tried unsuccessfully to entice Bernard Shaw along. One day a 'lionizing' party was thrown for the American author and humourist James Thurber (1894–1961), whom Roughton had brought back with him following a transcontinental road-trip in the United States.

According to Doreen, Bert had great success with the ladies, who found him very interesting and 'fell about the aisles with admiration'. He certainly found Doreen and Sheila Legge entertaining and enjoyed their company, although by 1938 he was seriously involved with Norma Hutt. 'He would come to the parties but never contributed much in the way of party spirit. He was rather a one-to-one person. He would remain with anyone he wanted to talk to. He talked a lot to George, and at one time tried to encourage him to take up writing for films and documentaries, which were a big part of the left-wing scene in those days.'

There was a general feeling that he didn't suffer fools gladly, but if you had something interesting to say you had his undivided attention. To give Doreen an air of mystery on her arrival in London, a girl friend had let it drop to Bert and the others that she was a fiery Irish revolutionary – a Celtic hybrid of Esperanza and Lenin. Years later Doreen admitted that Bert had seemed more amused than impressed with her revolutionary pretensions.

One gets the feeling that at this time Bert was feeling his way round, trying to find a niche for himself. Would it be creative writing? Journalism? Art or literary criticism? Painting? Drawing cartoons? Translating cutting-edge poetry and prose? All of these he successfully tried, and he was capable of practising them all to a significant level, but so were most of his friends and associates. There was no shortage of talented linguists, and certainly no dearth of accomplished painters and illustrators. The pubs and clubs of Fitzrovia were bursting at the seams with poets and writers who would read you their latest work at the drop of a hat or for the price of a beer. Bert needed something uniquely his own, that would slot into the left-wing ethos of the times – an area where he could reign supreme, the one-eyed man in the country of the blind.

Eventually he found it in folk song, the ultimate proletarian music. It was an area of working-class culture that his time in Australia, and his subsequent folk music researches in the British Museum, made him eminently qualified to adopt as his own. By the mid-1930s he was familiar with British traditional balladry as printed verse, and in February 1937 he wrote his first article on the subject for the *Daily Worker*, under the title 'The People's Own Poetry'. Alongside the article he gave a brief recommended reading list of some of the books that he had studied since returning from Australia: *The Oxford Book of Ballads* (edited by Quiller Couch), *Reliques of Ancient Poetry* (Percy), *The English Ballad* (Robert Graves), *Songs and Ballads of the Appalachian Mountains* (Cecil Sharp and Maude Karpeles) and *The English Ballad* (Francis J. Child).

Not having heard living English traditional singers at this point in his life, Bert writes of ballads in England in the past tense, although he was well aware that they were alive and well in the Appalachians:

Even today the English ballad still goes on developing, no longer, alas, in England, but in primitive communities of English origin and culture, such as in the Appalachian Mountains of the United States, or in Newfoundland.

My space is too limited to give more examples of this magnificent poetry. But surely the existence of such ballads and the splendid tunes to which they were sung emphatically disproves the theory that the masses are by nature unable to create artistically.

And, more than that, the superb quality of English folk-poetry is a foreshadowing of what the masses will be capable of when they are at last free of the stultifying miseries of capitalist industrialisation.

It is a romantic, political fantasy in which noble illiterate savages transcend their serfdom with moving poetry of 'terrific intensity':

Isolated by class barriers and often by geographical remoteness, as well as their inability to read, the peasants were unable to become acquainted with the culture elaborated in the cities for the more privileged classes.

They were obliged to make up their own songs, and being unable to write, they could only hand them down by word of mouth.

If the earlier 'peasants' had been capable of transcending cultural, geographic and educational isolation, one wonders why Bert didn't credit the contemporary proletariat with the artistic gumption to transcend the 'miseries of capitalist industrialisation' with equally moving poetry of terrific intensity. As he was to later discover, it was in the cradle and the very heartlands of the industrial revolution – the Midlands, the North West, and especially the northeast of England – that musical folklore continued to evolve after its decline in the more rural parts of the country.

The article is more interesting as a demonstration of Bert's class-conscious politics by that time than an academic analysis of folk balladry:

> Few ideas are more deceptive, more calculated to undermine the self-confidence of the working class than the present-day conception of culture.
>
> From our school days onward, we are taught to believe that humanity is a troop of beings incapable, in the main, of any real creative activity, especially artistic activity. In this troop, from time to time, there spring up as if by miracle, certain geniuses.
>
> These are the thinkers, the inventors, the poets and artists.
>
> Nearly always these geniuses come from the ranks of the middle-class intelligentsia. Occasionally they are from the aristocracy.
>
> And how about the masses? 'Bah!' Our teachers say, 'working-class poets and artists are so exceptional as to prove the rule that the masses are naturally inartistic, congenitally lacking in all those fine qualities of temperament and intelligence that make the artist and the poet'.

The 'present day perception of culture' to which Bert referred was a fighting retreat by the cultural elite in the face of an advancing and growing popular mass audience. The Elementary Education Act of 1870, aimed at bringing education 'within the reach of every English home', primarily to provide the working class with enough education – and no more – to be easily trained in the skills deemed necessary to maintain the nation's international position in trade and industry, also provided a popular mass market for literature and the other arts. For the middle and upper classes 'culture' was their prerogative, and they had no desire or intention to hand it over to the working classes. John Carey, in *The Intellectuals and the Masses: Pride and Prejudice Among the Literary Intelligentsia, 1880–1939*, describes the writings of such 'modernists' as T.S. Eliot and the critic F.R. Leavis in the face of the literate, if 'uneducated', masses, as 'shrill with panic'. So it's little wonder that, as a *Left Review* writer, Bert's visit to Eliot in 1935 in the hope of a commission had proved fruitless.

THE EDITOR IN THE BASEMENT

In 1959, when I was sixteen, I worked for a while in Collet's Political Bookshop at 64–66 Charing Cross Road, known in an earlier anarchic bookish incarnation as the revolutionary Hendersons' 'Bomb Shop'. Bought in 1934 by the rich communist Eva Collet Reckitt (1890–1976), it was never officially a CPGB bookshop, although the managers were invariably Party members.

Down the narrow spiral staircase in one corner of the shop was the out-of-print and rare-book department which had opened a few months earlier and was presided over by a large, rumpled-suited, elderly man, Edgell Rickword, who was blind in one eye. At lunchtime, I'd take my sandwiches downstairs into the musty second-hand-book-smelling cellar, sit next to him on a set of library steps and chat about books, mainly.

One day he surprised me by presenting me with an inscribed copy of *Rimbaud: The Boy Poet*, which he'd written in the 1930s. It was the first English biography of the French symbolist poet who had spent some of his wild youth in Soho. Edgell mentioned that also, in the 1930s, he'd edited a magazine called *Left Review,* a title that, at that time, meant nothing to me. That evening after work I crossed Charing Cross Road, and walked up into Soho to hear Bert Lloyd sing at the recently opened socialist (anti-espresso) coffeehouse The Partisan in Carlisle Street.

It was many years later that I discovered that these two men who had so impressed me as a teenager, and in many ways inspired a (questionable!) lifelong interest in books and folk music, were great friends and had worked together on the *Left Review* – Edgell Rickword as a renowned editor, and Bert Lloyd as contributor and group co-founder. When interviewed in the 1970s by Professor John Lucas for his book *The 1930s: A Challenge to Orthodoxy*, Rickword reminisced about the founding of *Left Review*: 'Well, the only thing I can remember is meeting in a room over a pub in Fitzrovia. There were about fifteen of us, Hugh MacDiarmid, I think, Bert Lloyd, Ralph Fox, Amabel Williams-Ellis, Tom Wintringham, and others. Someone had the idea of founding the Society for the Defence of Culture, as I now think it was rather childishly called. And we had the notion of setting up a group of Revolutionary Writers. Yes, it was as political as that.'[19]

Again, as in the founding of the AIA around the same time, it was the few Communist Party members of the group who provided the impetus. The principal instigator here was ex-Royal Flying Corps veteran Tom Wintringham (1898–1949), who had spent time in prison for sedition and inciting soldiers to mutiny. A military journalist, he was on the Central Committee, and was another of the Party members to have spent time in Russia. The group was unanimous in its disillusionment with contemporary literature quality and the commercialisation of the publishing industry. They could see the day arriving when books, as commodities, were no different than a pound of sausages, and about as intellectually stimulating.

A revolutionary literary society needed a publication. The magazine was started but, as Rickword said, 'the society rather faded out'. And that, as he said, was 'how *Left Review* was born'. What was probably Bert's first piece of professional writing appeared in the first issue of the magazine in October 1934 – the short story 'The Red Steer'. The story involved a couple of disgruntled Australian stock-hands who planned revenge on the boss by burning down the station – running the 'red steer' across his property.

This first issue of *Left Review* also included work by Hugh McDiarmid, Randall Swingler (the 'official' poetry voice of the CPGB and the 'money' behind *Left Review*), and the artist Pearl Binder (with whom Bert would collaborate twenty-five years later on the children's book *The Golden City*): not bad company for the first published writing of a young man who a few years before had been an Australian bush-worker. In October 1936 Cecil Day Lewis and Stephen Spender agreed to become regular contributors to the magazine. Day Lewis would write on a Topic of the Month, while Spender would write on poetry or literary criticism.

The magazine had various editors including Montagu Slater (1902–56),[20] and Rickword, and in 1938 Randall Swingler, who pulled the plugs on it, in the mistaken belief – or so Arnold Rattenbury (1921–2007), the poet and exhibition designer, thought – that it was going to be taken over and financed by John Lane at Penguin and become the *Penguin Left Review*:

> In the last issue there was an announcement that it was to be succeeded by *Left Review* in a 'new form', one of the most exciting developments in British publishing, and all subscriptions will be honoured. And nothing happened! Another contributor to the last issue was Penguin's John Lane who was keen on magazines. But the whole thing got caught up in the Spanish defeat and the imminence of war, and what could have been *Penguin Left Review* became *Penguin New Writing*. *Left Review* and *New Writing* were the obvious contenders, because Lawrence and Wishart had produced *New Writing* until that time, so it was another Communist stable thing. And *Left Review*, although, again, it was independent of the Party, was regarded as a Communist stable publication. And I think the two were in competition and Randall lost.
>
> When I met Randall the next year (1939) and lived with him and his wife whilst waiting to be called up for the army, he was trying to turn *Poetry and the People* into *Our Time*. Because he had this terrific guilt that he'd stopped *Left Review*, a viable left-wing publication, and he had to replace it.[21]

3
1936 and All That

We've lost when old ladies tip their chamber-pots on our heads.

Victor Hugo, *Les Miserables*

In 1936 Europe was balanced between peace and war, communism and fascism, dictatorship and democracy.

> Hitler and Mosley, what are they for?
> Thuggery, buggery, hunger and war!

This was chanted by hundreds of anti-fascist demonstrators as they marched down Tottenham Court Road in the mid-1930s. The *Daily Worker* cartoonist James Friell, along with James Boswell and any other Communist Party members who could be pressed into service, was on the march and he remembered 1936 as a political watershed: 'Thirty-six was the year Franco started the Spanish Civil War, Mussolini thought he had finished the Abyssinian War, and Hitler, by marching into the Rhineland, took his first step towards the Second World War. It was quite a year!'

It was also 'quite a year' on the domestic front, starting with the death of King George V and finishing with what Friell describes as 'the grotesque irrelevancy of the Abdication of King Edward VIII'. These royal exits neatly sandwiched a year of means tests, Mosley rallies, left-wing protests and skirmishes with the police, while an ineffectual Baldwin government stood by, watched the rise of fascism and tried to appease its way out of trouble.

One result, with a united left demonstrating against the British Union of Fascists, was the 'Battle' of Cable Street on Sunday 4 October. Many of the Fitzrovian radicals took part. They included George Rudé, David Gascoyne (who had joined the Party just two weeks earlier, thanks to Bert) and Bert himself who somehow, in the confusion of running street battles with an estimated 10,000 police, managed to get a bicycle 'wrapped round his neck'![1]

Much popular history of this period is from the left so we tend to get a one-sided view of public opinion. It should be remembered, therefore, that Bert and his Party comrades didn't speak for the whole of the working class. Many thousands of discontented workers, as well as a considerable number of the middle and upper classes, sympathised with Mosley's authoritarian fascist solutions to the country's undoubted ills. In fact, attendances at British Union of Fascists (BUF) rallies in the East End rose considerably in the immediate aftermath of Cable Street.

The day after the Battle of Cable Street, 207 Jarrow 'hunger marchers' set off from the Tyneside 'Town that was Murdered' to the accompaniment of harmonicas and kazoos, on their 300-mile protest march to London. They carried a petition for Government aid to alleviate the poverty brought about by the collapse of the steel, mining and shipbuilding industries of the northeast. They arrived on 31 October.

1936 was also important culturally for the left, with the founding of Party publishers Lawrence and Wishart, the foundation by the Marxist composer and pianist Alan Bush (1900–95) of the Workers' Music Association (WMA), the starting up of Victor Gollancz's Left Book Club, the appearance of Roger Roughton's *Contemporary Poetry and Prose*, and the first Surrealist exhibition in Britain – all these involved Bert in one way or another.

Lawrence and Wishart were later to publish Bert's two major folk song works – *Folk Song in England* (1967) and *Come All Ye Bold Miners* (1952, revised and enlarged 1978) – and his essay 'On an Unpublished Irish Ballad' in *Rebels and their Causes: Essays in Honour of A.L. Morton* (1978). The WMA, for whom, in 1944, Bert would write *The Singing Englishman*, his slim first attempt at synthesising folk song with his Marxist world view, came about when several choirs in the Co-Operative Musical Association and the London Choral Union got together to coordinate workers' musical activities under the direction of Alan Bush. As WMA member Aubrey Bowman explained in the *Morning Star*:

> Hitherto, music had been thought of as having to be brought 'to' the workers, to elevate them and immerse them in the 'beauties' of song and so alleviate the drudgeries and miseries of work and everyday living. It could, as one 19th century writer cogently put it, help stave off disaffectedness and revolution. But, in the WMA, there was a complete reversal. A revolution, in fact. Instead of music being brought to the workers, it is the music of the workers' struggle, of workers battles and of their triumphs that is brought to the musical arena.
>
> From its inception, the venture was a resounding success.

Over the years the WMA published a lot of material for workers' choirs, often using Eastern European traditional tunes, some collected by Bert, with either translated or new lyrics, and in 1937 the *Left Song Book* as part of Gollancz's Left Book Club. The WMA also started Topic Records, now Britain's oldest independent record label. Its worldwide reputation as Britain's premier folk music label is due in large part to Bert's artistic influence through the 1960s and 1970s. Alan Bush remained WMA President, and continued to arrange and compose, for the rest of his long life.

For Bert, the autodidact, the Left Book Club (LBC) was tailor-made. Here were the kinds of new titles that a Marxist such as he would have sought out even if they weren't being selected and offered as the 'Book of the Month' for a mere 2s 6d. His bookshelves, like those of so many other left-leaning readers of the time, were soon filling up with the orange softback club editions. A favourite, and one that he would discuss at length over many a dinner table when he returned from the Antarctic in 1938, was Edgar Snow's *Red Star Over China*, which came out in October 1937. It detailed the 6,000-mile 'long march' of Mao Tse-Tung's communist army to the north west of China to avoid extermination by Chiang Kai-shek's Chinese Republican Army. It was one of the club's most popular titles.

Another influential book in the Lloyd household, a copy of which much later turned up in a London second-hand bookshop with Bert's signature inside the front cover, was Leo Huberman's *Man's Worldly Goods: The Wealth of Nations* (1937). Still published today in India, and still read as a Marxist economic classic on the exploitation of humanity by capitalism, it's an 'attempt to explain history by economic theory, and economic theory by history'. Huberman took the LBC reader from feudalism to capitalism and on into a socialist future.

A couple of years earlier, the Fabian socialists and social reformers Sidney and Beatrice Webb published their huge (1,073 pages) apologia for Stalin, *Soviet Communism: A New Civilisation?*. After some forty years of dedicated work on social reform they grew disillusioned with the slow results of their gradualist political evolutionary policies and, following an extensive and blinkered trip across Russia, jumped into bed with Stalin, and decided that revolution not evolution was the way to get things done to create a socialist Utopia. People 'disappearing' and the shooting and starving to death of several million kulaks (the mainly Ukrainian farmers who resisted collectivism), could be excused as an anti-communist invention. A single-volume private subscription edition was brought out in 1935 by the Worker's Educational Association. Also in 1935 Gollancz published Emile Burns' *A Handbook of Marxism: Being a Collection of Extracts from the Writings of Marx, Engels, and the Greatest of their Followers*. This included Stalin. Both these titles took pride of place on left-wing bookshelves, including Bert's, alongside the LBC publications. In the 1950s Burns edited *The Marxist Quarterly*, for which Bert wrote 'Folk-Song for our Time' (July 1954).

All of the above titles and others were mulled over in the 1950s and later by Bert and Alun Hughes when they got together at executive meetings of the British Rumanian Friendship Society at 40 Great Russell Street, London, or met up at the Institute for Folklore in Bucharest where they were both working in the mid-1960s. Hughes recalled:

As a CPGB member myself, I found myself often in agreement with Lloyd's approach to matters being discussed. He and I had been influenced by many of the same books in the 1930s and later, and we had conversations on for example C. Day Lewis's Marxist symposium *The Mind in Chains*, on George Thompson's *Marxism and Poetry*, on the Critics Group pamphlets [Critics Group Press, New York, 1937/8. 12 Marxist pamphlets] and, often, on *Romancero de la Guerra Civil* [Madrid 1937]. Some of the romances taken from *El mono azul* he regarded as truly in the millennial tradition of such popular poetry in Spain. He admired much of Miguel Hernandez' poetry, some of which he translated, but was not greatly interested in my favourite, Antonio Machado.[2]

The Left Book Club was founded in May 1936 by the socialist educator and publisher Victor Gollancz, writer and Marxist theorist John Strachey, and Harold Laski, Professor of Political Science at the London School of Economics. The LBC was a publishing phenomenon. By the end of the first year the club had 20,000 members. This rose to 57,000 by 1939, along with 1,500 Left Discussion Groups. Robert Graves described the club titles on politics, history, science, poetry, and reporting as being 'like an armoury from which a weapon could be selected for argument on any conceivable subject'.

Its aim was the provision of information and theoretical analysis on the political problems of the day from both Marxist and democratic viewpoints and: 'help in the terribly urgent struggle for World Peace and against Fascism by giving all who are determined to play their part in this struggle such knowledge as will immensely increase their efficiency'. With its attendant discussion groups, summer schools and newsletter, *Left News*, the club struck a chord with thousands of concerned individuals who were looking for an alternative society. It was very influential in forming left-wing opinion in the late 1930s.[3]

A number of Bert's Party comrades wrote for the LBC. These included Leslie Morton (*A People's History of England*, 1938), Allen Hutt, Edgell Rickword, and the prolific Australian writer and critic Jack Lindsay (1900–90), with whom Bert remained good friends over a long time despite Lindsay's eventual communist apostasy. In February 1936 David Archer's Parton Press published David Gascoyne's surrealist poetry collection *Man's Life is this Meat*. The title is a meaningless phrase, an example of the surrealist fascination with the 'found object'. This verbal 'found object' was picked out of a typographic manual in which Gascoyne found the phrase 'Man's life is' and at the top of the next page the words 'this meat'. The surrealists, following on from the earlier Dadaists, and agreeing with Freud's theory that 'accidents are very largely predetermined by psychic necessity', saw the chance juxtaposition of words, ideas, dreams and images as a potentially revolutionary tool to break down bourgeois perceptions of the world.

Bert was less than convinced and said so in public discussions and print. He didn't, however, allow his scepticism to affect his friendship with many of the London surrealists, especially Roughton, Sheila Legge and Gascoyne, with whom he used to joke about his otherworldly surreal preoccupations. It was Bert and Roughton's friendly, if underlyingly serious, banter that persuaded Gascoyne to join the Communist Party, as Gascoyne later recalled in his *Journals*:

Looking back on this period, I was amused to recognise that I had probably been teased into joining the Party by Roger's and Bert's tendency to be satirical at my expense, regarding me as too interested in dreams and introspection to concern myself responsibly with the toiling masses or face the necessity for 'the expending of power on the flat ephemeral pamphlet and the boring meeting'.

Under Bert's influence Roughton was already a dedicated Party member and, as Michel Remy says in the *Dictionnaire General du Surrealisme et de ses environs*, was attempting to create 'a united front in which art and social progress, Surrealism and communism would cease to be mutually antagonistic'.

In 1936, before he officially reached his majority, Roughton finally got his hands on the substantial inheritance which had been left in trust since his father's early death. He used the money to finance *Contemporary Poetry and Prose* and other small press publications including, surprisingly, a collection of poems by the American e.e.cummings, who, a few years earlier, had denounced Stalin's machinations. In April Roughton also got an article on surrealism published in T.S. Eliot's literary journal, *The Criterion*.

In June 1935 Gascoyne had gone across to Paris to meet his surrealist heroes. His first stop was at the small apartment of the poet Paul Eluard, with whom he'd corresponded, and some of whose plays he had translated. He also spent time with the author of the Surrealist Manifesto, Andre Breton, who, favourably impressed with the teenage poet, invited him to sit in on the daily surrealist meetings at the Café de la Blanche. He even found a week's work translating an essay for Salvador Dali, to accompany an upcoming New York exhibition. He arrived back in England fired with enthusiasm and carrying a case full of brochures, pamphlets, poems, manuscripts and illustrations – gifts from the French surrealist group to help him with his book *A Short Survey of Surrealism*, which appeared in November.

While in Paris he'd met up with the English artist Roland Penrose and, along with their fellow French surrealists, they decided to put on an Anglo-French exhibition in London the following year. Excited by the prospect of a London exhibition by the leading French and British surrealists, Roughton printed the second number of *Contemporary Poetry and Prose*, which appeared in June 1936, as a 'Double Surrealist Number' to coincide with the opening of the International Surrealist Exhibition at the New Burlington Galleries in Bond Street.

Despite his reservations as to the validity of surrealist art in the 'struggle', Bert contributed four translations for his friend's special issue: 'Cradled Pamphlet' by Salvador Dali, 'Fable' by Alfred Jarry (the Breton absurdist writer and absinthe addict), Charles Cros's 'The Smoked Herring' and a 'Spanish Folk Song':

> Not last night but the night before
> Joroba gave birth
> To twenty-five rats and a pigeon.
> The pigeon had a little mill
> Where Joroba might grind her corn.
> Behind the mill was an old woman
> Wiping her arse on a tile.

> Behind the old woman was an old man
> Wiping his belly on a sheepskin.
> Behind a boy there was a girl ...

The fourth issue of *Contemporary Poetry and Prose* contained more work from Bert, along with Arthur Calder-Marshall, Dylan Thomas, Humphrey Jennings (the documentary film pioneer), Gavin Ewart, David Gascoyne and others.

In later life Bert sometimes pondered on how he'd got in with this bunch of intellectual and precocious high-flyers. In 1936 Dylan Thomas was still only twenty; George Barker, declared by W.B. Yeats to be the best poet of his generation, was twenty-four; the undergraduate Gavin Ewart was reading English at Cambridge and contributing to *New Verse* and *The Listener*; Roughton was just nineteen, and so too was the remarkable Gascoyne, considered by some to be 'England's only wholehearted surrealist', and already the author of two collections of poetry, a novel and the youthfully enthusiastic *A Short Survey of Surrealism* (1936), which is still in print.

What Bert's inherent modesty didn't let him realise was that many of these writers held him in great respect and, in Roughton's case, something approaching awe. Gascoyne who, for a few months in 1934, had shared a dingy top-floor flat with Roughton in Great Maze Pond in Southwark, noted in his journals that, once Roughton moved to Parton Street, he spent more and more time hanging out with Bert:

> It became obvious to me from the time when Roger moved to his Parton Street rooms that he found Bert Lloyd a more captivating and compatible companion than myself. Had he (Roughton) been homosexually attractive to me and I become emotionally involved with him, no doubt this situation would have led to bitterness and jealousy on my part; but nothing of the kind occurred ... . I too admired Bert Lloyd, and enjoyed his company; it would have been difficult to dislike him. But even before the outbreak of the Spanish Civil War it had become patent that he had developed a powerful political ascendancy over Roughton.

At this time Gascoyne was coming to terms with his ambiguous sexuality, and Bert was obviously a persuasive apologist for the Communist Party. The Surrealist Exhibition, which had eventually been organised by a committee which included Gascoyne, Penrose, Henry Moore and Herbert Read, opened on a sweltering Thursday afternoon and ran at the New Burlington Galleries from 11 June until 4 July. Over a thousand people squeezed into the gallery to hear the Father of Surrealism, Andre Breton, deliver his opening speech. The large crowd milling around the gallery brought the traffic to a halt the length of Bond Street.

Over the following three weeks some 25,000 visitors attended the event. Their reactions ranged from amused to bemused, enlightened to shocked and outraged, and as the *Bystander* said in its review on 17 June the exhibition 'set more tongues wagging in passionate disagreement than any exhibition since the Post-impressionists first bewildered London.' Critical reviews of the nearly 400 paintings, sculptures, objects and drawings by sixty-eight artists from a dozen countries were generally derisive. 'The dream value of a shrimp' jeered the *Daily Telegraph*. Herbert Read's claims of the 'dawn of a new age' began to look more like a sunset. A subsequent piece in the *International Surrealist Bulletin* admitted that Surrealism 'will only be successful in the degree to which it leads, not to social entertainment, but to revolutionary action'.

Although politically critical of surrealism, Bert was at the opening along with Roughton, the writer Arnold Rattenbury and many of the other left-wing London artists and writers. Love or loathe surrealism, it was a major event, not to be missed and a subject that would engage the art world in debate for decades to come. Dylan Thomas wandering around offering people cups of boiled string and enquiring whether they wanted them weak or strong enhanced the 'surreal' atmosphere. George Rudé's then girlfriend and Bert's sometime companion, Sheila Legge, drifted through the crowds dressed as the 'Surrealist Phantom', carrying a false leg and a pork chop, a publicity stunt dreamt up by David Gascoyne. A photograph of Legge standing in Trafalgar Square, her face covered with roses, pigeons balancing on her outstretched arms, heralding the surrealist assault on London, became one of the iconic photographs of the 1930s. It appeared in newspapers and magazines the length and breadth of the British Isles, and was subsequently reproduced in countless books. This, apart from her looks, was really Legge's only claim to fame. It made her a surrealist celebrity. In the exhibition catalogue she is photographed, minus the rose mask, with a group of the leading practitioners including Dali, Eluard, Penrose and Read. Running concurrently with the exhibition was a series of evening lectures. On 26 June Eluard gave a reading in French of surrealist poems by Alfred Jarry, Cros, and others. Gascoyne, Humphrey Jennings and George Reavey then read recent English translations, including Bert's translations from *Contemporary Poetry and Prose*.

During the 1930s, modern art fell between the twin stools of Soviet communism and Nazi fascism, both of whom suppressed it, insisting on propagandist realism. For the Nazis it was Bolshevistic, degenerate and un-German, and the Soviets declared it nihilistic and bourgeois, amongst other things. Through the 1920s and 1930s the Surrealists, particularly in France, attempted to resolve the dichotomy of wanting artistic freedom on one hand and the sublimation of art in the cause of revolution on the other. By the mid-1930s their absorption with psychology and parapsychology made it increasingly difficult to justify their relevance to revolutionary politics, as Bert argued in the Surrealist Debate that was put on at the Conway Hall during the run of the Exhibition.

Not being a working artist, Bert's main contribution to the work of the Artists' International Association was that of lecturer, speaker and art critic. At the Conway Hall he argued that surrealism wasn't revolutionary because its lyricism was socially irresponsible, a subtle form of fake revolution: 'These frivolous games of automatism and newspaper-clipping-creation, of goosy ghost-hunting and hazardous preoccupation with chance, though in many cases of undoubted scientific interest and value, can play no serious part in making the proletariat conscious of its social and revolutionary responsibilities.'

Not wishing to be too hard on the perpetrators of these 'frivolous games' (many of whom were fellow-travellers, anti-fascist sympathisers or friends like Gascoyne, Roughton and Legge), he acknowledged that: '… the Surrealists, particularly the English group, who have already issued an admirable proclamation calling for "Arms for the people of Spain" and have collected a considerable sum of money for the support of the Spanish Government, have no sort of Fascist motives behind their work. But for them to claim revolutionary activity beyond that is, I feel, a piece of self-deception.' He excuses them for being innocent and not realising the movement is a fake, but understands that their hearts are in the right place. The talk was later printed in the July 1936 *Left Review*, and again in January 1937.

Herbert Read and Hugh Sykes Davies submitted a 'Reply to A.L. Lloyd' to *Left Review*, in which they accused him of misinterpreting their motives and of using the language of literary criticism, when in fact the Surrealists had stepped outside the bounds of bourgeois criticism with their study of dream activity. Despite the unresolved differences between the surrealists and the AIA core-membership of politically-left artists, in August 1936, following the outbreak of the Spanish Civil War, the surrealists accepted an invitation to join forces with the AIA in the face of the perceived growing threat to world peace from fascism, and in the light of their joint desire to raise money for Republican Spain.

LONG LIVE THE REVOLUTION

> The bullfighters are monarchists,
> The monks are preachers of fascism,
> And the miners of the Asturias?
> Long live the revolution!
>
> My grandfather came from Mieres,
> His wife from Pola de Siero.
> The capital city of my blood
> Must surely be called Oviedo!
> (Gonzalez Tunon)

On October 4, 1934, following the collapse of the general strike called by the Alienza Obrera (Workers' Alliance) in protest at certain right-wing appointments to the government, the miners in Asturia, in the northwest of Spain, took matters into their own hands and rose up and took control of the province, armed only with hunting rifles, agricultural tools, and dynamite taken from the mines.

> The Moors are outside Oviedo,
> Oviedo they'll never take
> Though they kill all the Spaniards and threaten
> Their wives with murder and rape!
>
> The Regulars are bathing
> In the Covadonga flood.
> The lords swim at Majorca,
> While the miners swim in blood.

The Government sent an army of Moroccan mercenaries under General Francisco Franco to put down the uprising. After several days of bitter fighting Franco reached the miners' stronghold of Oviedo where, on 18 October, after bloody street fighting, the insurrection collapsed. Brutal reprisals were taken against the captured miners who were mutilated, tortured, and shot at the whim of their captors. Three thousand workers died, 7,000 were wounded, and 40,000 thrown in jail.

> In October there are no fiestas
> Except those of the season.
> But October only means to us
> 'LONG LIVE THE REVOLUTION!'

As news of the massacre of the miners spread slowly across Spain it divided the country and helped precipitate the Civil War, which began a couple of years later when Franco brought those same Moroccan mercenaries onto the Spanish mainland to overthrow the legitimate government.

'Long Live the Revolution', written by the Argentinean communist writer and poet, Gonzalez Tunon, was translated by Bert for Stephen Spender's collection *Romances of the Spanish War* (1936). In spring 1937 John Lehmann reprinted 'Long Live the Revolution' in Lawrence and Wishart's *New Writing 3*, and in the same issue included Bert's translation of 'Against the Cold in the Mountains' by José Herrera Petere, another poet who, as Lehmann says, had 'arisen among the anti-fascist forces in Spain, and whose 'Romances' have been on the lips of workers, soldiers, and peasants all over the country'.

Bert used his time as manager of Foyle's foreign book department to keep up to date with who was who on the Republican poetry front, such as Tunon and Petere. He gleaned the latest news on the Spanish literary scene from friends and acquaintances, such as John Gili (the Catalan bookseller and translator who, in the 1930s, ran the Dolphin bookshop at 5 Cecil Court, off Charing Cross Road specialising in Spanish and South American literature), and David Gascoyne and John Cornford, who travelled there in the mid-1930s. Another Republican poet whom Bert admired was the communist shepherd Miguel Hernandez, who died in prison in Madrid in 1942. After his death, scrawled on the wall above his prison bed, were found the poignant lines: 'Goodbye brothers, comrades, friends, Let me take my leave of the sun and the fields.' In 1939 Lehmann and Stephen Spender in *Poems for Spain* (Hogarth Press) included Bert's translation of his 'The Winds of the People'. Powerful and pertinent as these poems were, Bert's most significant work at this time was the introduction and promotion of Federico Garcia Lorca to English readers through the first British translations of his poetry and laudatory articles, such as 'Lorca: Poet of Spain' in *Left Review* 3, No. 2 (March 1937):

> Not since the time of Gongora had there been a poet of such stature in Spain. Never since the days when the common people had rushed to kiss the hem of Lope de Vega's cloak had a great Spanish poet been so loved. For Lorca, musician and folklorist as well as poet, had gone to the living tradition of popular Spanish poetry for the form and often the inspiration of his verse. The grace, the power and barbarous vitality of that kind of folk song called *cante hondo*, which is composed and sung in all the cities and villages of Andalusia, has had a tremendous influence on many of the greatest poets of modern Spain, but particularly on Lorca.

And earlier, in a full-page article in *The Listener* (27 January 1937) entitled 'The Tragedy of Lorca', Bert wrote:

> Nothing can stamp out the flame of poetry that is sweeping through Republican Spain at this moment. The last few months since Lorca's death have seen an astonishing revival of poetic interest. Literary differences have been dissolved, the poets of Spain are united to exalt and encourage the fight of the people. These poets have found in the mediaeval form of the *romance,* so brilliantly used by Lorca, the most suitable vehicle for their expression. How glad Lorca's heart would be had he lived to hear his friend, Rafael Alberti, at the microphone, reading these *romances* of the Civil War to enthusiastic crowds of 50,000 assembled in the football stadiums of Barcelona and Madrid. Lorca may be dead, but Spanish poetry lives as never before.

Shortly after the Asturian miners' insurrection had been so viciously put down, Lorca, when interviewed for the Madrid daily newspaper *El Sol*, unequivocally aligned himself with the workers: 'I will always be on the side of those who have nothing, of those to whom even the peace of nothingness is denied. We – and by we I mean those of us who are intellectuals, educated in well-off middle-class families – are being called to make sacrifices. Let's accept the challenge.'

Sadly, the sacrifice Lorca would be called on to make was the ultimate one. Although not a member of any political party, the article, plus the publicising of his democratic sympathies by the left-wing paper *El Defensor*, added to the fact that he'd signed two anti-fascist manifestos in 1933 and 1935, gained him many enemies on the right, marked him down in their eyes as a 'red intellectual', and sealed his fate.

A few days before the Civil War broke out in July 1936 between Franco's Fascist Nationalist army and the legitimate Republican Popular Front Government, Lorca had travelled south from Madrid to his parents' home in the historic Andalusian town of Granada. On 16 August, just four weeks after arriving in Granada, he was arrested and held in the gaol of the barracks of the First Granada Spanish Falange. Three days later he was taken before sunrise, along with two bullfighters and a schoolmaster, to an olive grove outside the town, where all four were shot and their bodies buried in unmarked graves. His books were banned and it was to be twenty years before his plays began to be performed again in Spain.

In 1937, when Bert wrote his *Left Review* article, there was very little, if anything, known outside Granada of the details surrounding Lorca's recent death, so Bert had to use his journalistic ingenuity and imagination to come up with a dramatic, satisfactory, story:

> Federico Garcia Lorca has told how once, when he was on tour with La Barraca, his theatrical company, in the bitter Estremadura countryside, he was unable to sleep and rose before dawn and walked out to the barn in which his actors were staying. Before long he found himself at the gateway of a ruined manor. Around him in the thin grass lay a number of broken statues; classical figures which in the eighteenth century had ornamented the park of some feudal grandee. The winter sun was rising, and out of the dissolving mist Lorca saw a lamb come towards him. The lamb began to graze among the statuary. But from behind a ruined marble torso, up started a family of black pigs, who rushed at the lamb; and speedily tearing it to pieces before Lorca's horrified eyes, they devoured it in this vague wilderness of fallen masonry.
>
> Surely Lorca must have remembered this scene on that blazing day in August 1936 when he, the finest and proudest poet in Spain, was dragged through the walled streets of Granada to face the Fascist firing squad.

Bert, along with the majority of British left-wing intellectuals, didn't feel it necessary to go to Spain to do his bit for the republican cause but, instead, went along with the old dictum about pens being mightier than swords. Despite this fact, the Civil War was often, romantically, dubbed the 'Poets' War' (perhaps that should be the stay-at-home poets' war?) and, although there has been an inordinate amount of publicity for the writers who *did* go, such as George Orwell, Laurie Lee and Stephen Spender, the fact remains that in the main the 30,000 or so foreign fighters from over fifty countries who made up the International Brigades were ordinary workers mainly from the trade unions and traditionally militant groups such as the Welsh and Scottish miners. The Republicans did, however, have overwhelming *moral* support from the European intellectual community, with so many prominent 1930s writers and painters having left-wing sympathies, and a shared fear of the rise of fascism in Germany, Italy and, to a lesser extent, in Britain and other European countries. Civil War 'tourism' was quite fashionable and thrill-seeking voyeurs returning from a few days in the bars and cafés of Barcelona or Madrid could become instant pundits in the media.

Bert's first literary volley for the Republicans was, arguably, Lorca's greatest poem 'Llanto por Ignacio Sanchez Mejias', published in Madrid in 1935. It's a lament for Lorca's friend, the matador Sanchez Mejias, who was gored in the Plaza of Manzanares, and died of gangrene poisoning two days later in Madrid, exactly two years before Lorca himself was to die.

Heinemann published Bert's bi-lingual edition *Lament for the Death of a Bullfighter and Other Poems* in 1937 to generally favourable reviews. The American critic Eda Lou Walton enjoyed the book, and her endorsement was typical of most reviews. V.S. Pritchett writing in the *New Statesman* called Lorca 'the most acclaimed poet of his generation' and that 'A.L. Lloyd has translated several of the later poems and has written an intelligent introduction.' *The Birmingham Post* thought that 'Mr Lloyd's renderings convey the feeling and the rich imagery and in some part succeed in suggesting the grace and sonority of the originals'. *The Listener*, which had printed some of the poems as early as late 1936, believed that 'Mr Lloyd has done us a great service, for there is no poetry like this in English … . Here we have all the exotic verse of the *cante hondo* combined with a perception as subtle as that of the French Symbolists.'

At this time in Wales a precocious sixteen-year-old schoolboy, Alun Hughes, was actively involved in the Aid for Spain movement, and *inter alia* translating poems from Spanish and Catalan for reading to meetings and for the *Daily Worker*. In his local library (courtesy of an enlightened librarian) Hughes kept up to date with the latest poetry through the pages of the prestigious magazine *Poetry London*, founded in the late 1930s by the charismatic, bohemian Tamil poet Tambimuttu, After reading Tambi's comments on *Death of a Bullfighter* which, according to Hughes, he 'praised to the skies', Hughes acquired a copy of the book. He wrote to Bert, care of Heinemann, enclosing a holographic copy of his own version of the poem. He remembers: 'His [Bert's] reply was friendly, congratulating me on "a good rendering", but disagreeing with my questioning of some of his versions as being too "free". I remember he said "What's important in a translation is that it is true to the spirit of the original, suggests the rhythms, and reads naturally in English".'[4]

A few others had their reservations, such as Alberto Palaus, head of the Latin American Service of the BBC in the 1980s:

> The translator [Bert] himself says that it is 'impossible to find any poet more difficult to translate adequately than Lorca' and that he is 'only too well aware' that his 'translations fall far short of the originals'. He is, of course right. He has tried mainly to convey the meaning and that is often intimately bound up with the sound of the words. The process of translation kills many of the images. He has been, I think, too literal, too respectful, but perhaps only another great poet would have the boldness to be otherwise. I think very little – if any – of the resonance comes over. Yet I admire anyone who attempts anything so difficult.

And musicologist and linguist Harold Dennis-Jones felt compelled to learn Spanish after reading Bert's translations and feeling something was missing: 'Looking at the translations in the 1940s I felt I ought to learn Spanish, which I did. Because I felt that though Lloyd talks about music and rhythm he puts none in!'[5]

They have a point, in as much as any English translation, especially of poetry such as Lorca's, which depends so much for its effect on the music – the rhythm, colour, pulse – of the language, and the Andalusian cultural images and references, will only ever be able to convey an 'impression' of the original. As Robert Frost said, 'Poetry is what gets lost in translation'. That being said, Bert's translation of 'The Dawn' – one of Lorca's New York surrealist poems – works very well, and captures the poet's bleak vision of 'Nueva York' perfectly; a society submerged by industry, pollution and divorced from nature. Lorca's few months in New York in 1929, ostensibly to learn English (although once there he didn't bother to try) brought home to him the debt he owed, and the love he had, for the simple life, the landscape and the language and traditions of his native Andalusia.

Influenced by his friendship with Salvador Dali and other Spanish surrealists, Lorca had been dabbling with surrealist art and poetry before he went to New York, but it wasn't until he experienced this city of 'extra-human architecture and of furious rhythm, geometry and anguish' that he found a subject ideally suited to this form of poetry. So far removed from his Andalusian experiences, New York required a new voice and surrealism was that voice.

Bert was right, if perhaps a tad hyperbolic, when he asserted in his 1937 *Listener* article, 'The Tragedy of Lorca', that 'Spanish poetry lives as never before.' It certainly flowered in Republican Spain and became hugely popular among both Spaniards and the foreign fighters and, according to Valentine Cunningham in *Spanish Front: Writers on the Civil War*: 'Ordinary people on the Republican side were apparently much gladdened by the support they were getting from foreign writers.'

So those stay-at-home writers were, indeed, helping the cause, even those such as C. Day Lewis who wrote stirringly (and guiltily) from the safety of their armchairs. As Cunningham points out there was 'intense pressure upon writers and writing to take sides, for or against the Republic', and with few exceptions they came down on the Republican anti-fascist side. So much so that Hitler admirer Wyndham Lewis, whose writing Bert had so much enjoyed in Australia, complained that it was seemingly compulsory for writers to be left-wing. Doreen Rudé once said 'they thought Russia, and all it represented, was the be-all and the end-all, but it just turned out to be the end-all'.

In June 1937, the enthusiastic and energetic socialite Nancy Cunard, a rich woman with a social conscience, threw her hat into the ring for the Republican cause. She decided to raise awareness of the Spanish War by producing a pamphlet in which writers would pin their flag to the mast and give their opinion on the conflict. Cunard, along with the rest of the British left, saw the war as an oppressed peasantry fighting capitalist landowners, the church and the army. A questionnaire was sent to every author in Cunard's large and impressive contact book, and then to everyone else who could be tracked down:

To the writers and Poets of England, Scotland, Ireland and Wales.
This is the question we are asking you:
Are you for, or against, the legal Government
And the People of Republican Spain?
Are you for, or against, Franco and Fascism?
For it is impossible any longer to take no side.

There were a dozen signatories to the 'Question' including W.H. Auden, Pablo Neruda and Stephen Spender. Hundreds of invitations were despatched, and followed up in the case of a non-response. One of those contacted was a spiky George Orwell, recently back from fighting in a POUM (the Trotskyite Workers' Party of Marxist Unification) unit, and smarting from a neck wound, and the hostile reaction of the CPGB to his exploits and his criticism of the communists' conduct in Spain. Never one for a platitude when an insult would suffice, his reply to Cunard was suitably boorish:

Will you please stop sending me this bloody rubbish. This is the second or third time I have had it. I am not one of your fashionable pansies like Auden and Spender, I was six months in Spain, most of the time fighting, I have a bullet-hole in me at present and am not going to write blah about defending democracy or gallant little anybody.

The results of the mail-out appeared in a *Left Review* pamphlet in the autumn of 1937 under the title *Authors Take Sides on the Spanish War*. It cost sixpence and contained 10,000 words from 148 contributors. A surprising omission among the names of the great and good who responded is that of A.L. Lloyd, who was usually well to the fore when it came to openly supporting this sort of thing. Those who did reply included many of his friends such as David Gascoyne, Jack Lindsay, Edgell Rickword, Harry Pollitt, John Lehmann, Alick West, C. Day Lewis and Douglas Garman. Cunard and Bert would almost certainly have known each other through *Left Review*, or at social get-togethers. This was especially so in the light of Bert's Spanish articles and translations, including his recent 'Lorca: Poet of Spain' in the issue of *Left Review* which also contained Jack Lindsay's 'On Guard for Spain' and John Somerfield's war report, 'Spanish Diary'. Even Bert's 'black magician' acquaintance Aleister Crowley contributed a response – written, by the look of it, under the influence of his favourite narcotic: 'Do what thou wilt shall be the whole of the law. Franco is a common murderer and pirate: should swing in chains at Execution Dock. Mussolini the secret assassin, possibly worse. Hitler may prove a "prophet"; time will tell.'

But, despite all the jingoism, fundraising exhibitions, marches, bravery, idealism and the deaths of thousands of republicans (including those of British intellectuals such as John Cornforth, Christopher Caudwell, Ralph Fox, Julian

Bell, Charles Donnelly and the first British volunteer to die, Bert's fellow AIA member, the young Slade-trained artist, Felicia Brown) it all came to nothing.

In his 1938 poem 'The Volunteer', C. Day Lewis paid tribute to those young, middle-class intellectuals who *had* felt compelled to stand up and be counted in the war against fascism, and who died for their convictions:

> It was not fraud or foolishness
> Glory, revenge or pay;
> We came because our open eyes
> Could see no other way.

Thanks to the British and French Non-Intervention Agreement, which denied supplies of arms and military support to the legitimate Republican Government, while allowing Hitler and Mussolini to provide Franco with troops, aircraft, tanks and guns, and to the political machinations of Stalin, who pursued his usual policy of intimidation and assassination to wrest control of the various Republican factions, after three years of bloody fighting Madrid fell to the fascists. On All Fools' Day, 1939, the victorious General Franco announced the end of the Civil War.[6]

The following Wednesday saw the first performance of Benjamin Britten's *Ballad of Heroes (Opus 14)* at a Festival of Music for the People organised by Alan Bush at the Queen's Hall, London. Originally to be called *Anthem for Englishmen*, it was composed to honour men of the British Battalion of the International Brigade who had died in Spain. Randall Swingler and W.H. Auden set the music to words.

At the end of 1938 the Republican Government decided to repatriate all the brigadistas, in the vain hope that world opinion could compel the withdrawal of German and Italian forces. Before their withdrawal from Spain some 13,000 members of the International Brigades were addressed in Barcelona's main street by the communist Civil War heroine 'La Pasionaria': 'You can go with pride. You are history. You are legend. You are the heroic example of the solidarity and the universality of democracy ... We will not forget you; and, when the olive tree of peace puts forth its leaves, entwined with the laurels of the Spanish Republic's victory, come back!'

4
Down to the Sea in Ships

In 1937, as well as his Lorca and Kafka translations and his *Left Review* article, 'Surrealism and Revolutions', Bert had a piece in the *Daily Worker* (10 February 1937), 'The People's Own Poetry', on traditional balladry and the influence of capitalism on folk art. 'In the *AIA News Sheet* he attacked Bernard Causton's article in *The Studio* 'Art in Germany Under the Nazis'. In the autumn he translated his first play, *The New Spectacle of Wonders: A Masquerade in One Act,* by the Galician writer Rafael Dieste. Although Dieste was one of the leading writers of the Galician language literary revival, this particular play was translated from the Spanish and published by Lawrence and Wishart in John Lehmann's *New Writing 4,* as was Bert's translation of Lorca's poem 'The Dawn'.

In an interview with journalist Michael Grosvenor-Myer for the magazine *Folk Review*, in September 1974, Bert came up with a greatly abbreviated version of how he had spent the 1930s: 'So back in England (from Australia) and all I had to market was a knowledge of sheep and that didn't get me very far. So I went to work at sea and in 1937–38 I was working in the whaling business.' He implied that he spent time at sea after coming back from Australia and before the whaling trip. No mention of working at Foyle's here. No reference to writing and drawing cartoons for the *Daily Worker.* Not a word about exhibiting paintings. No mention of his Spanish poetry translations. His version of Lorca's *Death of a Bullfighter* was published whilst he was in the Antarctic.

He does, however, appear to have returned to the sea, however briefly, in merchant ships *after* his whaling trip – even though his daughter Caroline, who admittedly wasn't born then, thinks not. In the Grosvenor-Myer interview, talking about his first radio script, *The Voice of the Seaman,* and his meeting with the producer Laurence Gilliam in 1938 to discuss the possibility of the BBC taking up his (post-whaling trip) unsolicited offer of the script he said: 'So we met for lunch; it happened that the ship I was working on was in port [London] at the time.'

Another reference to Bert's seafaring appeared in the Chicago-based folk music magazine *Come for to Sing* in 1983, in his obituary by the English singer Louis Killen: 'He then returned to England (from Australia) and joined the ranks of the unemployed. Except for occasional periods at sea on Antarctic [whalers?] and Black Sea oil tankers.' Black Sea oil tankers? Actually that one's a bit of a red herring. It was based on Killen's memory of a shaggy-dog story that he'd heard Bert tell which involved Black Sea oil tankers, and which had been told with such vivid detail that Killen had at the time assumed it to be based on personal experience. Now he's not so sure. But it shows how these biographical anecdotes get around and how, after a couple of printings or repeatings, they can become 'facts'.

Bert decided to sign on with the Southern Whaling and Sealing Company, a subsidiary of Unilever, for a six-month trip to the Antarctic whaling grounds for the 1937/38 season. This was a dramatic and macho decision, a job as devoid of cultural stimulus as his time in the Australian outback. It is apparent from letters that Bert wrote to Norma Hutt at the time that the main reason for his whaling trip was money. Whether he chose whaling as a source of money purely for financial reasons, for theatrical ones (being a whalerman has a picaresque air about it), or out of a genuine fascination with hard physical work, or a mixture of all three, we'll never know. Once committed, however, he certainly threw himself into the work and derived enormous satisfaction from a job well done, as can be seen in these lines to an aunt back in England: 'We've been whaling for some weeks and have been very busy – and I'm an excellent hook-man now. The hookers on the night team are the best the ship has had. We get through a lot of whales, usually ten or twelve a shift ... I like my job very much, and feel earnest about it as I have not felt for years. I never think about pictures or books or things now.'

In the *Australian Folklore Society Journal* for September 1996 a note appeared from Ron Edwards entitled *Lloyd on Whalers*:

A minor footnote on A.L. Lloyd but one that is of some interest shows how a publicist may state a fact but angle it in such a way that it suggests something different to what really happened. On the jacket notes to the Wattle record *Shanties and Fo'c'sle Songs* (1957), there is a note to the effect that 'A.L. Lloyd has worked on whaling ships', and on the sleeve note to *First Person* (Topic Records 1966) there is mention of 'a spell of labouring in the Antarctic whaling fleet'. Reading this it gives the picture of Lloyd standing there covered in blood and blubber and clutching a harpoon, or at least a flensing knife.

Lou Clay, art director at J. Walter Thompson, Melbourne, in the 1950s, told me in 1957 when I showed him one of Lloyd's records that he was a friend of Lloyd's and that they had both worked for the soap manufacturer Lever Brothers in the publicity department some years earlier in Britain. Lever Brothers maintained a whaling fleet which killed whales for use in the manufacture of soap and, according to Lou Clay, Lloyd's whaling experiences had been to go out on a whaler while writing publicity articles for the company.

This is not to belittle his knowledge of whaling lore but to put it in context.

It seems unlikely that Lou Clay would say this if it weren't true, and it seems hardly the sort of thing about which he could be mistaken. If he's correct, then his memories put a different complexion on why Bert went whaling. We know that Bert did work for a while as a copywriter. He always said how much he hated it. Later he would write corporate manuals and publicity material to finance his folklore research. In a letter to Edgar Waters he mentioned that he was 'grappling with a short book which I've been commissioned to write for Dunlop (about disc brakes, of which I know less than nothing). If ever it's finished, Dunlop will pay me enough money to enable me to spend a month or two getting some more interesting if less profitable work done.' He was obviously a pragmatic Marxist, and prepared to exploit the capitalist system for his own ends when necessary.

As for the whaling, whether Bert went in some sort of fact-gathering capacity or purely as a labourer is uncertain. But he definitely worked some of the time as a labourer, as his whaling diary and letters home indicate. Even if he wasn't a flenser or a harpoon-gunner (which were specialist jobs performed by Norwegians), he certainly got his hands dirty and was no stranger to 'blood and blubber'.

According to Bert he heard that the Southern Whaling and Sealing Company was hiring men – even though their recruiting seems to have been mainly on the northeast coast of England, around Newcastle and Hull, and on the Isle of Anglesey. Early in October 1937 he made his way to Liverpool to join the factory whaling ship *Southern Empress* at Bromborough Dock, the largest private dock in the world, built just six years earlier by Lever Brothers to facilitate the transference of oil from their tankers to their nearby factory at Port Sunlight. 'In the company of my shipmates I came up the gang-plank with heavy heart, light suitcase, and a donkey's breakfast.' The 'donkey's breakfast' was not an equine equivalent of a 'full English', but rather a straw-filled hessian bag which had, for hundreds of years, been the merchant seaman's palliasse, purchased before boarding ship from a dockside ship's chandler.

Bert and the others were piped, or rather squeezed, aboard to the Laurel and Hardy theme tune, performed by accordionist Albert Gommersal, whom Bert later described as 'a fat boy from Hull'. One grumpy, non-musical whaler apparently came aboard, heard the music, spat, and said: 'I see we've joined a floating orchestra.' In addition to Albert, there was a fiddler, an ocarina player, a mandolin player, two banjoists, spoons players, and a drummer whose drum was improvised from a barrel with canvas stretched tightly across the top.[1]

The *Empress* left Bromborough Dock at 11.30 a.m. on 6 October, and steamed down the Mersey, past New Brighton and out into Liverpool Bay and the Irish Sea, heading for the Caribbean island of Aruba, off the coast of Venezuela, in what was then the Dutch West Indies. As soon as the crew had their gear stowed away in their cabins, and had taken an exploratory wander around the ship, Nat Roberts, a well-known Holyhead ex-BBC entertainer, who specialised in bird impressions, took control of the ship's entertainment, and put an 'orchestra' together – what in the days of sail would have been known as a ship's 'fufu' band.

A couple of months later, a Christmas Day concert was organised and broadcast to all the other boats in the area over the ship's radio, as Bert remembered:

One night in the Antarctic when the whales were scarce, we gave a concert over the ship's wireless, for the benefit of any other factory-ships or catcher-boats in our neighbourhood. There was a lot of weather blowing, and it's doubtful if anyone was picking us up, but in that bloodstained ship we imagined ourselves to be radio stars throwing our voices on a spangled wind, and it was a memorable night for us.

The *Southern Empress*, like all factory ships, was as much a floating town as a ship. It was large, with its own engineering workshops, smithy, surgery, laboratories and hospital, as well as a pigsty with thirty pigs. Then there was the machinery – the winches, cranes, hooks, giant mincers, vast boilers, heated rollers and steam saws, all of which could convert a ninety-foot-long blue whale into barrels of oil, liver flakes and bone meal, in less than an hour. To give some indication of the size of the blue whale: an average specimen weighed as much as twenty-five fully-grown elephants.

In 1936 Norwegian whaler-men, having boycotted the Unilever ships that were being overhauled in Sondefjord, Norway, lost their crew monopoly when Unilever retaliated by having the annual overhaul of their fleet done in Newcastle upon Tyne, and started hiring British seamen for their ships. An agreement was reached between the British and the Norwegian governments that one third of the factory ships' crews should henceforth be British. This is how Bert ended up shipping out with a mixed crew of Norwegians, Welsh and English. He spent most of the trip living in the Norwegian quarters, partly, so he said, to learn the language and partly because the English quarters were so dirty. Perhaps Bert was being a bit finicky, because other seamen on the trip thought the conditions excellent, or maybe they just had lower standards, and rats in their boots were, for them, par for the course, as described by Hull whaler-man, Bernard Campbell:

In the morning you got up at five o'clock, if you were on at six. You'd get a swill – wash your hands and your face, and then get your overalls and big boots on. One morning I put my foot in one of the boots and I thought what the hell's happened here? I thought my foot hadn't swollen all that much, and I put my hand in and there was a bloody great rat in there. I never put my boots on the floor any more, I hung them up. In fact you had to swill your boots out at night 'cos there was all congealed blood inside. It was a very dirty job, blood, oil and guts all over the place. Terrible. But you got used to it.

Apparently, they even got used to the constant awful smell of the blubber being rendered down, which impregnated every fibre of the whalers' clothes and frequently caused raised eyebrows, and guaranteed plenty of space on trains and buses on the way home from the ship at the end of a trip.

Except for the specialists, all other seamen like Bert signed a contract of employment as 'labourers' for an agreed wage of £9 10s a month, plus a whale oil and liver-flake bonus of '0.235 old pennies' per 170kg barrel, plus a shilling an hour overtime. As Campbell said: 'Everyone served as a labourer. It didn't matter what you were – carpenter, joiner, quartermaster, pig man (we had a pig-man on board), everyone signed on as labourer. They could call you up to any job they wanted: knife-sharpener, he was a labourer, boiler man, he was a labourer, the lot.'

In those days the labourers wore no special protective clothing, just lots of it, which gave rise to one of Bert's most enduring memories of the trip – the hassle he had when it came to taking a pee and, in his words 'trying to find two inches of frozen gristle through four inches of clothing'. Overalls, jackets and boots were purchased from the ship's 'slop-chest'. The boots with their three-inch spikes, which gave some purchase on the slippery deck, were the only concession to safety. A pre-war whaler was a health and safety nightmare, a tragedy waiting to happen, and happen it did, although not as frequently as one might expect. One man on Bert's trip had his head 'snapped off' when a grab slipped off a whale's tail. Another had a leg ripped off at the hip by a hawser, and a third was crushed between a whale and the side of a boat. It's surprising that serious accidents were so few in the chaos of the butchering deck, half obscured by dense white clouds from the fifty boilers and frequent snow flurries, unguarded machinery, and decks slippery under foot with blood and oil.

But before they began the butchery, they had to get to the whaling grounds. This was done by what at first seems a surprisingly circuitous route via South America and South Africa. The reason for the zigzag journey was that the best deal in fuel oil was to be had at the Caribbean island of Aruba, where the Royal Dutch Shell Oil Company had a base, with refineries and oil installations on nearby islands. Here they sold cheap heavy fuel oil under long-term contracts. It was a deep-water port, where the factory ships could take on 10,000 tons of fuel oil in twelve hours, and was a regular fuelling point for the Antarctic whaling companies. It was cheaper for the *Empress* to make the detour to the Caribbean to fill up with cheap Dutch oil, despite adding a couple of weeks and several thousand miles onto the voyage, than to buy the oil in Britain.

Aruba, like all ports around the world, also catered for the alcoholic and sexual needs of visiting sailors. However, it was not on the scale of the famous nineteenth-century sailor-town in Honolulu, which at the end of the season could accommodate the most demanding needs of up to 3,000 whaler-men (!), most of them suffering from 'Arctic virginity', after two years at sea. The area round the oil jetties on the south coast of Aruba, with its corrugated zinc-roofed wooden drinking huts, music bars and pick-up joints, did its best to give Jack a good time, as he wandered or staggered through the crowded, noisy, sandy streets of the shanty town that had mushroomed a mere 100 yards or so from the dock gates.

The *Southern Empress* tied up amongst the oil storage tanks on 22 October. As this was to be a twenty-four-hour turnaround, the captain decided against granting shore leave. Frustration built up amongst the crew until a Scouse entrepreneur forged a batch of shore passes and sold them off for sixpence a time, allowing a 100 or so whalers 'unofficial' shore leave. Waving their 'passes' they streamed past the Dutch police guards on the gates in the chain-link and barbed-wire-topped security fence, and hurried to join the American, Norwegian and Heil-Hitlering German whalers, whose ships were also in port that evening.

Later, as the inebriated, carousing crew of the *Empress* staggered back to their ship, they were surprised by mounted and motor-cycle and sidecar police who appeared at the dock gates, ostensibly to 'quieten them down'. A riot broke out, with the police firing guns in the air and laying about them with sticks and sabres. The whaler-men fought back with their fists, aided by piles of ship's crockery thrown at the police by those men who had stayed on board ship. They also lowered nets over the side to pull up the injured. Several men were slashed with swords and canes, and one man lost an ear. Some were arrested and were bailed out by the captain the next morning, before the ship sailed for Durban to meet up with her catcher boats, and head down to the ice. What part Bert played in the 'riot' is uncertain but he was definitely amongst the crew that went ashore because he took some photographs of the desolate area of ramshackle huts and scrubby wind-sculpted trees around the docks.

On 19 November the *Empress* arrived in the port of Durban, where her eight catcher boats were waiting for her. This marked a brief return to South Africa for Bert. That evening the whaler-men were allowed official shore leave and many of them wandered along the Bluff, the quay area from where, up to the First World War, some six whaling companies had operated. By the time Bert arrived in 1937 there was just the South African Whaling Company running two shore-based stations where the Durban whale-boats brought their catch to be processed. After taking on provisions and fresh water, and bunkering her catcher boats with some of the Aruba oil, the fleet of ships steamed out of Durban on 20 November heading for the Antarctic.

Bert saw his first whale a couple of weeks later, on 5 December, when they hauled a sperm whale up the slipway and onto the false pine 'whale-deck' that had been laid on top of the real deck to protect it from damage during the next few months' operations. The sperm whale was the only type of whale the catchers were allowed to shoot out of season. On 18 December they reached the whaling grounds. Antarctica consisted of five-million square miles of ice, a fifth of which had still not been seen by man and twelve-and-a-half-million square miles of sea with sub-zero temperatures. It was subject to sudden squalls and fogs that could last for several days, and persistent numbing west winds with no land to break their force.

The whaling season had begun officially on 8 December and from then until the end of the ninety-eight-day season on 15 March, it was non-stop work around the clock, twelve hours on and twelve hours off of bloody, stinking, back-breaking, noisy work. In his tiny black 1938 diary Bert wrote:

2 January. Sunday 6 a.m. Very bad weather, fog, snow. Worked very hard. Filled all the boilers.

3 January. Monday. Transport arrived and hove to some way off. A catcher
brought the mail about 2 a.m. this morning. Elation on deck.
6 January. Mail at coffee time.
8 January. 4 wires broke – not fatal!

While his frozen fingers and aching body were going through the motions,
beneath his cap Bert's creative brain was observing, analysing, and filing away
these images, sounds and smells, for possible future use. In a letter home
he said: 'It's exciting to see a whaler in action. It's a very cinematographic,
even exotic, business. In the working of it there's such a mixture of efficiency
and conspiracy. The deck at times resembles a slaughter yard manned by
calculating lunatics.'

The most skilled of these 'calculating lunatics' were the spike-booted
Norwegian flensers, who, wielding their razor-sharp, long-handled flensing-
knives like bloody hockey sticks, crawled and clambered over the huge pale
carcasses like so many black crows, and sliced down through the inches of
blubber, which was then peeled off in long strips, before being cut up by
the 'blubber gang' and dropped into large grinding machines prior to going
into the boilers. The decks were permanently covered with enormous bloody
chunks of meat, piles of steaming, stinking, intestines, and heaps of bloody
bones. Above the winches' rumble and the howling of the wind there was the
incessant chatter of the bone saws.

10 January. Few whales. Washed clothes. Read some of Our Village by
Miss Mitford.
11 January. Helped cast off transport. Not too many whales till after 12
then they came in.
12 January. Wednesday. Day watch (as usual) had few whales. We worked
about 9.

The butchering and processing production line on which Bert worked was
a far cry from the early days of pelagic whaling, when the little sailing ships
set out from London, Hull, Whitby, New Bedford and Nantucket 'for to hunt
the Greenland whale', or to spend two or three years on the sperm whale
grounds off the coast of South America, hunting down their prey close up in
rowing boats with hand-held harpoons.

On the catcher boats that serviced the *Southern Empress*, the closest the
gunner needed to get to a whale was fifty yards, from which distance a
156-pound exploding harpoon, invented by Norwegian Sven Foyn in 1864,
if skilfully placed just behind the last rib, exploded amongst the vital organs,
killing the whale instantly. However, this precision required ideal calm weather
conditions and most whales required a couple of harpoons to finish them
off. The gunners, who were usually also captains of their catcher boats, were
considered the aristocracy of the whaling trade, an honour befitting the men
on whose skill depended the success or failure of the whole mission.

13 January. Cold, snow again. Day gang had 2 whales. We worked steadily till 5, then I knocked off. Nearly broke Fred's leg with winch.

15 January. No whales. Worked in tank till 12. Did nothing in tank but talk politics – Spain, China, USSR with Oswald and shop steward.

16 January. No whales still. Everyone talking dirty, making score cards of number of girls and whores etc.

That season the *Empress* killed over a thousand whales to provide 103 barrels of whale oil for soap and margarine, and 1,700 barrels of liver flakes. The undoubted cruelty and wholesale slaughter of whales caused few pricked consciences in those pre-conservation days. It was simply a job for which they were all well paid and looked after. Bert was never an apologist for the whaler-men, believing that you can't judge past events and practices in the light of modern perceptions and sensibilities. He was known to get uncharacteristically cross when people asked him if he was ashamed of having gone whaling, pointing out it was 'just a job of work', done in the days before conservation was fashionable. Although he *was* well aware of the short-sightedness of the practice of intensive modern commercial whaling, as he pointed out in an article in the *Leader* in January 1946, entitled 'Whale-food for Starving Europe?: How the World has Idiotically Squandered the Treasure of the Antarctic Oil Supply':

If the whaling industry were to take a pre-war amount of oil out of the Antarctic over the next few years, it would cut its own throat … This season there are only seven factories working in the Antarctic (in 1938/9 there had been thirty four) … The seven factories will be fortunate if they bring back as much as 150,000 tons of oil. That 150,000 tons of oil is about as much as the whale companies will dare to take for several seasons to come, if they want to stay in business … During the pre-war years in the crazy scramble for profits, an idiotic and wasteful slaughter went on almost uncontrolled (there were restrictions, but they meant little). Now the situation has to be faced: for the big eyes and the hollow cheeks, the whaling industry can do precious little.

Even here, Bert is more concerned with the squandering of a resource than with any sentimental idea of whale preservation for its own sake. It's a simple mathematical fact 'too many ships kill too many whales'. In January Bert was suffering from a 'very bad back' and was feeling very miserable. But a whaler's no place for self-pity, and a few days later he noted in his diary: '26 January. Worked 15 whales with ease. Despite back.' A week later he narrowly escaped death when he fell into one of the boilers full of whale tongues.

4 February. Fell into boiler – just did not break my neck.

5 February. Very bad weather, snow and sleet. Big whales worked 10.

9 February. Wednesday Worked 14 whales some big. Very busy. Pat came to see me.

On the whaling grounds the floating factories were serviced by transport ships which collected the oil and took it back for processing. They also brought provisions and, more importantly, letters and news of the outside world from the wives, children and girlfriends at home. This was how Bert received news that Heinemann had published his slim translation of Federico Garcia Lorca's *Lament for the Death of a Bullfighter and Other Poems*.

In February 1938, Bert, in his black spiked boots and cap was on the butchering deck slicing blubber or cutting up the prehistoric-sized skeletons with powerful steam-saws. Several thousand miles north, in her Greenwich Village apartment Eda Lou Walton, poet, critic and Professor of English at New York University, sat at her typewriter and wrote a glowing review of *Lament for the Death of a Bullfighter and Other Poems* for the *New York Times*:

... These translations keep the meaning intact and do not force the English into a version which might be perfect in meter and assonance and yet but a garbled version of Lorca's original. Spanish poetry with its continuous rhyme or assonance is very difficult to translate. Only in the romances does Mr. Lloyd try to give the feeling of the form used. One has here the original poems which are easy to follow and the very excellent English versions.

Bert couldn't have hoped for a more sympathetic reviewer. Walton was a left-wing intellectual, and lover of the Jewish-American communist writer Henry Roth, who a year earlier had written an article for the communist journal *The New Masses* entitled *Where My Sympathy Lies,* in which he defended the Stalinist 'trials': 'There are several things about this trial about which I am confused. Nevertheless, enough and more than enough has been revealed to convince me of the guilt of the accused; and by guilt, I mean that all their efforts were calculated to nullify or destroy the very growth of the safeguards that would ensure the freedom and fraternity of millions of men.'

This was a sincere, if misguided, opinion on Roth's part and one with which Bert would have concurred. Roth went on to attack Trotsky and the Trotskyites, who were no more loved by the CPBG and Bert, and who had also been 'purged' by the Communist Party in Spain, as reported by Orwell when he returned to London from the Spanish Civil War. So it's no surprise that Lorca, with his folkloric peasant influences and interests and his martyrdom at the hands of the fascists, was one of Walton's, Roth's and Bert's literary heroes.

While the outside world was admiring Bert's published work, on board the *Southern Empress* he was finding it increasingly difficult to focus his mind on writing in the face of relentless back-breaking physical work, twelve hours on and twelve hours off, seven days a week. On 21 January he had attempted to write a letter to his old friend Roger Roughton but the next day he tore it up in frustration:

21 January. Worked 15 whales. Began letter to Roger.
22 January. Destroyed letter to Roger. Worked 10 whales but all small.
23 January. I am inarticulate as I never have been before in letters.

If Bert was finding it difficult to balance the intellectual life with the labouring one he was supported by Norma Hutt who, having come to terms with Bert's prolonged absence, sustained his spirits with letters, telegrams and the latest books.

7 February. Monday. Norma telegram 8 days coming!
19 February. Saturday. Worked very hard. 15 whales. Port side team prepared for transport.
20 February. Sunday. Transport came around 3 (I think) Got letters and books from my sweetheart xx

On March 15 they caught their last whale. The season was declared over, and at 11 p.m. Bert was on his way home: '15 March. Last whale! A sperm. Got some teeth (rather Fred did). Very bad weather, fierce wind, seas over deck.' The last job to be done at the end of the season was the dismantling of the wooden flensing deck that had been laid over the real deck. After several months' use it was saturated with oil, blood, fat, flesh and dirt, and was broken up and thrown overboard before the *Empress* reached warmer latitudes on her homeward journey and the filthy decking started to smell.

16 March. Changing watch. Did washing.
17 March. Fred and I shifted timber from boat deck – very cold! Stacked coke in pigsties.
18 March. Friday. Scraping on boat deck. Lovely morning, but bitter wind in afternoon.
21 March. Cleaning between boilers. Cleaning rooms.
26 March. Saturday Durban.

After the cleaning, scrubbing and scraping, the crew could take some time out for sunbathing, swimming in improvised canvas pools, and boxing, which was a popular pastime on board ship. The *Southern Empress* tied up at Liverpool's Bromborough Docks at Port Sunlight on 22 April 1938, after six months and twenty days at sea, with her tanks filled with 17,547 tons of whale oil. The 1937/8 season was described by economist Harold Salvesen as 'phenomenally lucky with weather, and supply and condition of whales'. It ended with the second largest volume of oil ever recorded with British ships taking a total of 19,542 fin, blue, sei, sperm and humpback whales.

Bert's share of the spoils on discharge, if he was indeed being paid as a labourer, would have been around £170, less deductions for National Insurance, boots, overalls, jackets etc., purchased from the ship's 'slop-chest', as well as any advance he might have spent ashore on Aruba or Durban, and postage for letters home. It doesn't sound a lot for six months' work in one of the most inhospitable and dangerous environments on Earth, but it was two or three times the money that a labourer would have earned on shore. To some of the impoverished Anglesey whalers, who had been on the dole before the trip, a take-home pay of around £100 was a small fortune.

Despite the relentless, hard, bloody work, and the fact that, once he was home, he vowed he'd never go whaling again, Bert actually loved the Antarctic. Like so many before him, he had been captivated by the light and the chance to see such unique sights as a group of penguins standing on a blue whale's back. Unfortunately, the trip didn't actually provide Bert with many sea songs – 'Bonny Ship the Diamond' ('Tich Cowdray's speciality'), 'Greenland Bound' ('a favourite of Fred Clausen, from Stoneferry, Hull, a meat-cutter on the *Southern Empress*'), 'The Balaena' ('well-known amongst the *Empress* crew'), and 'Off to Sea Once More'/'Old Jackie Brown' (Bert credited Fred Clausen for most of the words, which were published in *Sing* (January/February 1955) with the note that 'gaps in Fred's memory were filled chiefly by Ted Howard of Barry'). Another song he submitted to *Sing* (August/September 1957) was a version of 'Lord Franklin' collected, so he said, from Edward Harper, a whale-factory blacksmith from Port Stanley in the Falklands.

The crew, many of whom were Welsh, tended to sing hymns and popular songs of the day, and were habitual harmonisers, as Bert described in the notes to his album *Leviathan!* (1967):

We had a vocal harmony group; well several of them. We'd a lot of Welshmen aboard, from Holyhead and Amlwch, mostly small fellows destined for the liver-gang. They sang all the time: hymns, Nelson Eddy numbers, 'Just before the battle, mother.' If two met, they sang in harmony. If one was on his own, like as not he'd sing just a harmony part – the bass of the piece, or an alto line. On the way down to the ice, some of the Englishmen went nearly scatty, chipping rust or, worse, cleaning oil-tanks (they boom like a cathedral) all day alongside a Welshman who never let up on 'The Indian Love Call', but sang *round* the tune all the time and never came out with the melody. In self-defence, some of us English also took to singing in parts, often without blend, but we found it thrilling. At Fo'c'sle sing-songs we mostly sang film-hits, Victorian and Edwardian tear-jerkers, and only a few whaling songs.

Although Bert did not pick up many folk songs, the whaling experience did provide him with a rare insight into aspects of the working lives of the earlier whalers, which informed his performance of whaling songs on record and in the folk clubs of the 1960s and 1970s, an experience he didn't want to repeat:

I swore I'd not go back again
Once we were homeward bound;
For the pleasures they are few me boys
On the bitter whaling grounds.

It also provided him with source material for future writing, recording, and radio scripts. However, his first attempt at putting his experiences into a radio programme would prove unsuccessful. Bert arrived back in London in April

1938, just in time to participate in the large May Day procession which was awash with banners from all the left groups and which AIA member, William Townsend, described in his journal:

> Red flags and Communist Party banners, memorial banners for comrades lost in Spain, Trade Union, Labour, Christian Socialists, Co-op Guilds, Left Book Club and Marx House banners. About 200 artists followed the AIA 'Unity' banner, including a group of surrealists wearing top-hats and Neville Chamberlain masks, who gave Nazi salutes to the lines of spectators. A loudspeaker van played the 'Internationale' and Spanish republican songs.

5
Working for Auntie

On his return to England Bert lost no time in trying to get back into writing. He immediately dropped a line to a useful acquaintance, the journalist and innovative BBC producer John Pudney (another Parton Street poet, who gave Ewan MacColl his first radio writing job, and later became famous for his Second World War Air Force poem, 'Do not despair ... For Johnny-head-in-air'). In 1934 he had been one of the first BBC producers to use recorded 'actuality' speech in his documentary programme 'Opping 'Oliday.

'Dear John, I have been working on a whaling ship and have just come back from 7 months in the Antarctic. Do you think there's a radio talk in whaling?' Bert asked Pudney, in the event he couldn't help himself, to kindly pass the enquiry on to someone who might be interested. This he did on 4 May, in an internal BBC memo with this note: 'Albert Lancaster Lloyd, the writer of this letter, is a most intelligent man, though he possesses rather a squeaky voice.' Unfortunately for Bert, the BBC had just approached members of the crew of the RSS *William Scoresby*, which had been in the Southern Ocean between 1935 and 1936 on a scientific whale-marking expedition, to provide a talk on whaling.

The BBC's disappointing answer was forwarded to Bert at the Pension Louise, Le Lavandou, Provence, in the south of France, where he was staying for a week or two, until mid-June. Today, Le Lavandou has a sizeable marina, and is a rich person's sport-fishing centre, but in the 1930s it was a small fishing port, famous, if known at all, for its fifteen kilometres of sun-soaked coastline, lavender, and cicadas. Perhaps Bert had taken Norma off to the sun on the proceeds of the whaling trip, as compensation for his seven-month absence.

A few months later, on 16 August, he heard a BBC radio programme about unemployment in the United States, entitled *The Job to be Done*. It was written by Para Lorenz, produced by Laurence Gilliam, and based on the original American production by William Robson. Robson was a major writer-producer in the 'Golden Age' of American radio, and a prominent member of the 1930s American Popular Front Movement, the left-wing cultural renaissance in art, theatre, music, literature and radio. With Irving Reis, Robson wrote and produced radio programmes for the CBS Columbia Workshop, including *The Job to be Done*. In 1942 he was one of the writers for the thirteen-part joint CBS/BBC series *This Is War*, intended to give Americans a better understanding of their British ally. In the 1950s, along with Aaron Copland, Leonard Bernstein, Pete Seeger and countless other 'red' artists, he was up before the Committee on Un-American Activities.

The Columbia Workshop radio show ran from 1937 to 1957. It declared itself 'Radio's foremost laboratory of new writing and production techniques' and pioneered the use of sound effects and music in drama productions. Bert was very impressed with the artistic way *The Job to be Done* was put together without losing its social message. He wrote to Laurence Gilliam suggesting a similar kind of programme showing the conditions and life of the ordinary British seaman – not the officers or the capitalist ship-owners, but just ordinary seamen, a subject on which Bert had first-hand knowledge. Bert told Michael Grosvenor-Myer:

I had a letter back from Laurence Gilliam, who had produced *The Job to be Done*, saying that he had had an idea for a long time of doing a documentary about seafaring which would cover the sort of ground that I had mentioned. But he hadn't been able to find anybody who could write it from first-hand knowledge. He would like to meet me. So we met for lunch; it happened that the ship I was working on was in port at the time and he asked me to have a stab at writing such a piece. I'd never thought of myself as a writer, certainly not as a writer of dramatic documentaries, but however I did. I wrote an hour-long dramatised documentary about seafaring.

On 4 November 1938, Gilliam sent an internal memo to the copyright department saying he had now read and accepted a script that had been submitted by A.L. Lloyd, entitled *Voice of the Seamen*. The programme, which was Bert's first radio writing, was broadcast from 6.45 to 7.30 p.m. on Saturday, 17 December 1938, for which, despite haggling for more (he'd asked for £50), he received a fee of twenty-five guineas, and was credited as 'author and actor'.

It must have been quite a revolutionary piece of radio for the conservative BBC, whose presenters still donned evening dress to read the news. Here was a programme presented by working-class voices (although they were actually actors and not real seamen), using working-class language. Perhaps even more remarkably, they were complaining publicly against injustice, dangerous working conditions, and mismanagement by the large shipping corporations.

There was an outcry from the ship-owners, and questions were raised in the House of Commons. But *The Times*, soon after, ran a series confirming Bert's bleak depiction of the merchant sailors' lot. The BBC, or perhaps certain members of the corporation, was impressed with Bert's script writing, so different from most BBC writing at that time. It must have been a breath of fresh air in the staid corridors of Broadcasting House for those with the nose to smell it. 'They asked me to write more. It was difficult to write at sea because there was no privacy. I was reluctant to give up seafaring for the speculative business of writing. So they offered me a contract. So I entered the ranks of the intelligentsia at a relatively advanced age.'[1]

On 17 January 1939, the BBC Programme Contracts Executive, P.E. Cruttwell, wrote to Bert offering him a six-month contract as a scriptwriter in the features and drama department, 'subject to everyone being able to reach a satisfactory agreement'. This presumably refers to money because, as we've seen, Bert had already tried to haggle over the twenty-five guineas fee for his seamen script. It was to be the first of numerous skirmishes with the BBC accounts department over the coming years. The mutually acceptable agreement they reached was that Bert should be paid £6 a week. He moved into an office in Broadcasting House, and two weeks later was writing a feature programme about the discovery of gold, entitled *Who Wants Gold?*, for which the programme planners had allocated £185 to make the programme. Later in the year he wrote English dramatisations of the Dutch legend of *The Little Woman of Stavoren,* and the Swiss writer Blaise Cendrars' novel *L'Or,* a fictionalised story of John Sutter, a Swiss pioneer who started the Gold Rush in northern California.

Over the next few months the Accounts Department tried to work out how much, and when, to pay Bert for specialist translation work on scripts. Did it come under his normal job expectations? Or did he deserve a translator's fee on top of his salary? And what happened when he worked with other people on a piece? It was finally resolved and Bert was paid an extra fee on top of his salary for translation, and certain other 'specialist' work beyond the normal call of duty.[2]

An important and influential BBC radio series which Bert heard and enjoyed in 1938 was the twelve-part *I Hear America Singing*, written and presented by the English journalist and broadcaster Alistair Cooke, and produced for the BBC by Charles Chilton. Cooke, who had emigrated to the USA in 1937, was back in England for six months during 1938. In those days, according to Charles Chilton, you had to leave the States for six months while applying for naturalisation. Cooke, who had a real love and knowledge of folk song and folklore (his son eventually became a member of the bluegrass band the Charles River Valley Boys), had made several visits to the Archive of Folk Song at the Library of Congress from as early as 1932, and in 1936 had produced a half-hour programme for the BBC on American hobo songs entitled *New York to the Golden Gate.*

During 1937 Cooke began to think about putting together a radio series on the history of American folk song. Finding that there was a dearth of commercial recordings of authentic performances, he approached Alan Lomax, at that time Assistant-in-Charge of the Archive of Folk Song, and with his help persuaded Herbert Putnam at the Library of Congress to lend him material from the Archive. Cooke was obviously very persuasive because, until then, no other radio producer had managed to acquire this material for broadcasting. He was allowed to borrow recordings and bring them over to England on the understanding that the programmes would be one-offs and that the discs would be returned immediately to the Library of Congress, along with any copies made by the BBC. The series which was broadcast just once live, and was never heard again, was the first time that many people in Britain had heard authentic American folk music.

The producer Charles Chilton, known to 1950s and 1960s radio audiences for two hugely popular series, *Riders of the Range* and *Journey Into Space*, both of which he wrote and produced, joined the BBC in 1932 as a fifteen-year-old messenger boy. He soon transferred to the gramophone library where he remained until he went into the Forces in 1941. At that time there were a lot of jazz recordings in the BBC archives that no one knew much about. Chilton, who was a jazz fan and read the music papers, started putting together jazz programmes which were accepted for broadcasting. He thus became, uniquely, a gramophone librarian *and* producer. On his return to the BBC after the war he became a full-time Light Entertainment producer.

He first met Bert through their mutual interest in, and support of, the Unity Theatre. They became good friends and Chilton regularly searched out records for Bert in the BBC sound library. He worked on several programmes with Bert but when asked in 2009, when he was in his nineties, he couldn't remember which ones they were. The pair often dined in the BBC canteen or one of the many cafés around Oxford Street and Mortimer Street, and also visited the library at Cecil Sharp House together to research material for programmes. Chilton wrote a number of programmes on popular culture and music including: *A Ballad History of Samuel Pepys, London's Pleasure Gardens, Cries of London* and *The Long Long Trail* which, after collaboration with Joan Littlewood and Theatre Workshop, became the hit stage show *Oh! What a Lovely War*. In the 1950s Chilton also got to know Peter Kennedy and Alan Lomax through their work for the BBC.

In September 1939 the BBC moved much of its wartime production and production staff, including Bert, out of London to the safety of the quiet Worcestershire town of Evesham, where in April 1939 they had bought Wood Norton Hall, once home of the exiled Duc d'Orleans. Throughout the summer the BBC building department put up huts in the grounds of the large stone and timbered country manor to house stores and workshops, and converted the main building into offices and emergency studios. The whole scheme was conducted in the utmost secrecy. However, in spring 1939 a BBC engineer who was in Berlin for a radio exhibition was shown photographs of Wood Norton by a German friend who knew all about the place!

The house, which dated back in parts to the Middle Ages, was known by the code name 'Hogsnorton', the imaginary town created by the comedian Gillie Potter (Hugh William Peel), a 'wireless' favourite from the early 1930s, who began his reports from mythical Hogsnorton with the words, 'This is Gillie Potter speaking to you in English'.[3] In a letter written to Igor Vinogradoff in October 1939 Bert refers to the place as 'Hoggers', a most uncharacteristic-sounding diminutive – it sounds more like some ex-public school 'chinless wonder' than ex-whaler-man, ex-roustabout Bert Lloyd.

From September, Schools, Music, and Features and Drama, all departments that had moved out of London following the declaration of war on 3 September, used the recently finished studios. As there were no facilities for accommodation at Hogsnorton, Bert and the rest of the staff (by 1940 about a thousand people) were billeted around Evesham, for which their sometimes unwelcoming hosts were paid a guinea a week. Bert must have been at Hogsnorton before war was officially declared because by the time the Prime Minister, Neville Chamberlain, made his radio speech Bert had already managed to find lodgings with Mrs Hall at 8 Cambria Road, just a few minutes' walk from Evesham railway station at the top end of the High Street, and a couple of miles from Hogsnorton. On hearing the news, Bert wrote a concerned letter to Norma (by now his wife) in London to let her know that he had arranged for her to stay with him.

My Dearest Wife,

Are you frightened? Old Chamberlain has just made his speech. I have just arranged with Mrs Hall – that's my landlady's name – that you shall come down here as soon as you can and share my room. It isn't like a war at all, is it? Last night I went to the pictures, the GB Newsreel was very wild. Flags fluttered, Londonderry [Honorary Air Commodore, Lord Londonderry] spoke. The King and Queen stood smiling in their garden while the little princesses tugged their hands. And not a soul in the audience cheered, clapped or even stood, and this on the eve of war! It's a great sign. Another sign is that you don't hear a breath of criticism of the German people, nor any aspersions on them. Though, no doubt, people will feel different when the bombs start falling. Wear your gasmask, darling. Find out where your shelter is.

Evesham is very crowded of course. Because there are evacuated kids and the High Street is choked with cars. So I am lucky to find a place so soon. The river – the Avon – is very pretty here. There is a Norman arch, an old monastery where Mrs Hall has a flower and vegetable garden.

Reynolds [*Reynolds News*] was good this morning. I do hope Allen is kept on, because *Reynolds* is, in a sense, the most important paper in the country just now [Allen Hutt was night editor for a time during the war].

The fact that the BBC staff could not divulge what they were doing up at the hall, behind the huge golden gates, didn't help to cement relations between the incomers and the locals, many of whom regarded them with suspicion, especially when it became obvious that, contrary to earlier rumours, the house was not going to be a home for the Duke and Duchess of Windsor. It seems to have been Bert's lot to be regarded with suspicion at various times in his life. Later on in the war he was questioned on suspicion of being a German spy, after he had been seen by a fellow traveller writing German words on the steamed-up window of a train.[4]

If BBC staff wanted to visit the Regal or Clifton cinemas which, along with a weekly dance, were virtually the extent of entertainment in Evesham, and were coming from, or had to return to, Hogsnorton they had to cycle in, and leave the bike in the courtyard of the Northwick Arms, for any other BBC staff member to pick up if they needed to get back, or catch one of the two green double-decker London General Omnibuses that had been bought by the BBC and driven down to ferry the staff the three miles or so along the A44.

It's interesting how primitive life at the BBC was in the 1930s – solid-tyred buses, a pendulum master clock on the control room wall that was adjusted by having bits of silver paper stuck on the pendulum, and up the hill from the main house in the huts used by the Monitoring Service (before it moved to Caversham) they were still recording intercepted foreign broadcasts on wax cylinders, which were shaved and re-used.

In contrast, German engineers as early as 1934 had perfected magnetic recording tape, on a cellulose acetate base. This, in conjunction with an earlier American device, Ultra-Sonic Bias, made it possible to increase the frequency range, reduce distortion, and eliminate background noise. The BBC first became aware of the German advances in recording when the Caversham monitoring service picked up simultaneous speeches by Hitler from two different places. Obviously, at least one had to be a recording, but the sound quality of both transmissions was identical. Despite being very busy scriptwriting, recording interviews, and helping produce programmes, Bert was missing Norma, and on the morning of Sunday, 24 September, he dropped her a quick line before dashing off to work on *The Home Front (1) Children in Billets* with Stephen Potter.

My darling love,
It is very lonely without you so don't be long. I can only write a short note as I am just going to Stephen's to work on next Saturday's programme. We played the records back and some of them are very charming. Out of about 24 minutes of recording, we can use 17 minutes, which must be a record. Shapley[5] usually takes three hours recording for the same result. Shows what the war can do.

The *Daily* [*Daily Worker?*] comes now. They sent a subscription card.

All the Regional boys, Gough, Bridson, Dillon and co., came up yesterday to discuss their future. Walter is still in bed (9.15 am) singing 'A tisket a tasket' very loud. Margaret woke up about 7 and sang 'Hold Tight' [Andrews Sisters' April 1939 hit] at the top of her voice.

We got some very interesting records, one of the Anchor in Fladbury, including a long political dialogue between two near drunk fruit pickers and a soldier. One of them kept butting in to say 'Do yeou know what Oi'd do with that ole 'Itler? Oi'd roll un up in woire and scrape 'un down!' Others proposed running him through the chaffcutter. Among other remarks: – 'It was real fine about them Czechs, but it's goin' to take more than boards and nails.' Altogether it is an interesting record. A similar record made in Napoleonic times would have sounded rather like it, I think.

Now love I must go, because I have a lot to do. I hope you won't have difficulty in getting the Spanish dictionary. Of course you'll be writing before Friday. Let me know if you want any more money. Goodbye darling. Don't hang about in town once the house is dismantled.

The Anchor Inn, to which Bert went with one of the new Direct Disc Cutting vans to record the locals, is on the village green in Fledbury, less than a mile away from Hogsnorton along the Evesham Road. The Anchor and the other village pub, the Chequers, were popular with airmen from the nearby airbase at Tilesford/Throckmorton. The villagers knew when the aircrews were off on a raid over Germany by the empty bars.

THE SHADOW OF THE SWASTIKA

'This is the BBC Home Service. Tonight we present *The Shadow of the Swastika*, the story of the Nazi Party.'

By October 1939 Bert was back at Broadcasting House, which by then resembled the *Marie Celeste* with so many staff having been evacuated for safety. He was preparing to start work on the marathon drama documentary series *The Shadow of the Swastika*. The BBC wanted the first episode written and researched in just ten days. Bert wrote an urgent letter to his BBC research partner, the Russian historian Igor Vinogradoff:

Dear Igor,
I have come down from Hoggers to work on the Nazi History. Laurence [Gilliam] thinks of calling the series *The Shadow of the Swastika*.
    It has been decided that the first of the series shall be a panorama of the entire history of the Nazi Party (1920 to now).
    I gathered from Laurence that he wanted the first one in ten days or so. I am in B.H. room 524. I have arranged for us to have a secretary from Thursday on.

He asked Vinogradoff if he was free to start work on the programmes the following day, once they'd decided on how to 'manage the collaboration'. He added that Gilliam wanted the first two scripts to be written 'during this visit of mine', so he obviously intended returning to 'Hoggers'. At first sight, Bert and Vinogradoff might appear an oddly matched couple – Bert a committed working-class communist and Vinogradoff with his aristocratic connections through his wife, Julia (the daughter of the famous arts patron Lady Ottoline Morrell), and his father the world's leading Russian medievalist, Sir Paul Vinogradoff. But, despite their widely differing backgrounds, Bert and Vinogradoff pooled their writing and research skills and produced a drama-documentary masterpiece.

The first programme in the series was broadcast from Wood Norton on the evening of Friday, 10 November, featuring Marius Goring as Adolf Hitler. Dozens of wannabe Fuhrers (including a woman) had unsuccessfully auditioned for the part. Producer Laurence Gilliam described the programme's opening: 'In the studio a red light flickers violently and then glows steadily: the announcer turns from the microphone, and with one vigorous stroke of the conductor's baton the orchestra crashes into the opening bars of the 'Horst Wessel Song'. In millions of homes in Great Britain and overseas sets are tuned to another episode of the B.B.C. series which are re-enacting in dramatic form the fantastic history of the Nazi Party and its Leader.'[6]

It was a resounding success, and Bert's most prestigious piece of writing so far. It made compelling, if disturbing, listening, for as Gilliam said: 'It is telling them the facts about the man and the forces that have cast the monstrous shadow of war over all their lives.' According to the Listener Research Department, the show attracted one third of the adult population, and scared many old ladies half to death. Twelve million people tuned in; no other feature programme, with the exception of *The Maginot Line*, had been listened to by anything like so many people. According to Gilliam: 'In a certain army barracks all except two of the soldiers quartered there gave up their one night out to listen. The two "joy-birds" came back noisily before the programme had finished; they were quickly and unceremoniously silenced.'

The researching and writing of such a vast and complex story in such a short time – the programmes were booked for broadcasting at fortnightly intervals – was a remarkable achievement. Not only was it written so quickly, it was also well written. Bert and Vinogradoff set the scene in the foreword to the book of the scripts that was published by John Lane of the Bodley Head Press in 1940:

In October 1939 we were asked to prepare, on a basis of austere facts, a series of radio-dramas which would describe the origins of the Nazi Party, its rise to power, and the developments which eventually led to the Allies' declaration of war. Time was short.

The Features and Drama Department had already been evacuated to the provinces. We, like a lonely outpost installed in a temporary office in Broadcasting House, began to sift material from a hundred books, as well as from newspaper cuttings, confidential reports and magazine articles, in English, German and French, in order to work out an authoritative dramatic treatment at once historical and topical, of the history of the Nazi Party. We made no statement and dramatized no incident without good authority.

Another source of material for Bert and Vinogradoff was the *Daily Worker*, which had been documenting Hitler's rise to power from the early 1930s. In addition, in November 1939 Sidney Solomon, Secretary of the Board of Deputies of British Jews, wrote to Vinogradoff offering 'facilities to consult the most complete set of files, letters, magazines and books dealing with the Nazi regime'.

It's impossible to please everyone. The *Daily Sketch* for 1 January 1940 complained 'Horrible Music Spoils the Swastika Series'. The writer went on to explain that 'the horrible noises – supposed to be music' – and which he didn't recognise – were in fact new arrangements of the 'Horst Wessel' song, Wagner's Wotan theme and the German folk song 'Die Lorelei'. 'Being told I ought to have known brings from me the reply that the rescoring not only spoils whatever melody there might have been, but the discordant results are unworthy of so interesting a series.'

A Mr Harry Carr wrote to *Truth* asking, in light of the BBC claim that 'every incident recorded is based on ascertained facts', who ascertained the 'facts' of conversations between Hitler, Goebbels and Goering that went on behind closed doors. He said it seemed unlikely that Goebbels and Goering supplied the information!

As an ardent anti-fascist of long standing, Bert would normally have been delighted to have been handed such a prestigious and important piece of proselytising work – a chance to spread the word, and the sort of opportunity that he and the CPGB could only have dreamed of a few months earlier (before, that is, the August 1939 signing of a non-aggression pact between Stalin and Hitler). Communist parties around the world, who received their orders (and money) down the line from Moscow, were obliged to go along with this unexpected about-face, and support Soviet 'neutrality'. The CPGB initially supported the war on an anti-fascist stance but, when the Communist International declared it now to be an 'imperial conflict' which should not be supported by the working classes, decided to oppose the war. This was a period in which, according to Leslie Morton, 'the Party was in a bit of a confusion'.

This must have left Bert between a rock and a hard place, but, behaving as the professional that he had become, he got on with the job. Harry Pollitt, the Party Secretary, refused to make the U-turn and stepped down from office. It was this sort of CPGB yo-yoing on the end of the Soviet string that might have offered George Lansbury, the Labour leader, the opportunity to make the alleged remark: 'That lot run a revolution? They couldn't run a whelk stall!'

It wasn't just Bert who was between a rock and a hard place. Stalin was there, too. However disconcerting and puzzling, not to mention embarrassing, the 1939 Nazi–Soviet Pact might have been for many CPGB members it was understandable. In signing the Munich Agreement with Hitler and Mussolini and handing the Sudetenland over to Germany in the naive belief that it would put an end to German expansionism, Neville Chamberlain and the French Prime Minister, Edouard Daladier, betrayed Czechoslovakia in the hope of appeasement. Seeing this, Stalin must have thought that if, or when, Hitler decided to invade Russia (a stated intention in *Mein Kampf*), he could expect no help from the West, so a Soviet–Nazi pact would at least give him some breathing space.

The script consultant for the BBC series was E.L. Woodward, Fellow of All Soul's College Oxford, and lecturer in modern history at New College. He was paid a miserly £20 to check all nine complex scripts before broadcasting. Drafts of the scripts were also sent to the Foreign Office for vetting. On 16 January 1940, after script number seven had been read, it was 'suggested' that critical references to the Munich Agreement should be cut out 'simply on the ground that it seems undesirable now to revive the controversy about the Czech question'. The FO suggested that the Russians signed the pact with Germany not because of the Munich Agreement but because: 'The German offer to hand over the Baltic States to Stalin was more than the British were prepared to do, and it kept Russia out of the war. Whereas a pact with us not only might have involved Russia in war, but would have subjected Russia to the peril of being attacked on a large scale by Germany.'

It was probably a bit of both. Either way, Stalin was covering his back and buying time, and had no reason to want to jump into bed with Chamberlain, particularly as (he must have realised) the British Government hated and feared communism more than they did fascism, and were hoping that Hitler would invade the Soviet Union and wipe out communism. In fact, research by Richard Bassett for his book *Hitler's Chief Spy: The Wilhelm Canaris Mystery* (2005) suggests that Chamberlain got wind of a Nazi Party plot to depose Hitler to avert a war with Britain and France over his claims to the Czech Sudetenland and that he rushed across and signed the Munich Agreement to spike the plotters' guns and to give Hitler the chance to destroy the Soviet Union. Also, of course, his 'peace in our time' agreement with Hitler bought Britain an extra year in which to build fighter planes to defend Britain against what Chamberlain had been warned by his experts would be a catastrophic bombing campaign by the Luftwaffe if, or when, we went to war with Germany. So perhaps Chamberlain was not so much an appeaser as a political wheeler-dealer, as was his successor, Winston Churchill.

The new political situation put Bert, and other known communists like Ewan MacColl and Joan Littlewood, who were also working for the BBC, under even closer surveillance. A note on MacColl's Special Branch file for 12 October 1939, read: 'I do not understand why the BBC continues to use them. Could they be warned to drop them if other people are available?'[7] They certainly could. Within a few months all three found themselves out in the cold. However, Bert was allowed to get on with *The Shadow of the Swastika*. The nine programmes were considered to be such a powerful propaganda tool that the Ministry of Information made an arrangement with the BBC to have copies made 'with a view to the recordings being used for M.I. purposes'.

Plaudits for the series came in from all sides. Publishers wrote to Bert and the BBC wanting to issue the book of the scripts. Pyramid Pictures saw great potential in it as a film. A letter from a W.A. Mullen in Northern Ireland offered a possible American radio airing: 'To be quite frank, I think this programme is one of the finest I've ever heard, and I should like very much to have the opportunity of submitting it to a friend of mine who is Radio Director of a large advertising company in New York.'

In his reply Bert thanked Mullen for the interest, and pointed out that two or three American radio stations (including NBC and Columbia) which had wanted to air the series 'have been obliged to abandon the idea because America is a neutral country and its Government, not unnaturally, is not anxious to tread on anyone's toes'. The weekly newspaper *Reynolds News* ran Bert's *The Shadow of the Swastika*, 'an exclusive serial presentation by the part-author of the most-talked-of radio feature since the war', for six weeks from January to March 1940. At this time, Bert must have been one of the best known and most talked about writers in Britain, certainly amongst the literary, political and artistic communities, which helps explain why a little later *Picture Post* and the Ministry of Information were so keen to use his writing skills.

In the 1940 *BBC Radio Handbook* Val Gielgud, Director of Features and Drama, referred to D.G. Bridson's *Harry Hopeful* series and then continued:

> Nor must another type of documentary be neglected; the documentary that is literally based on documents. Here too there is great advance. Mr Laurence Gilliam's Shadow of the Swastika series has brought to full stature a type of programme hitherto represented only fitfully in such productions as Twenty Years Ago and The Russian Revolution. Such programmes have been condemned as propagandist but whatever their intention, one thing about them has been axiomatic from their inception; accuracy of fact has been their sine qua non.

Despite this enthusiastic endorsement from Gielgud, Bert's enthusiasm and skill in denouncing Hitler and the Nazi party didn't outweigh his communist affiliation, and his days at the BBC were numbered, at least for the next few years. According to *Picture Post* editor, Tom Hopkinson, at that time in the BBC you had to be reasonably anti-fascist, balanced with a reasonable degree of anti-communism.[8] Bert, who had never made any secret of his communism, failed to have his six-monthly contract renewed in 1940.

There were obviously certain influential people within, and without, the BBC who were not altogether unsympathetic to the fascist viewpoint. The communist journalist Claud Cockburn, in his mimeographed magazine *The Week,* had reported the high-level meetings of Nazi ambassador Ribbentrop with leading Tories. He also kept an eye on the 'Cliveden Set', as he dubbed the group of Nazi sympathisers who congregated at Lady Astor's house, Cliveden. Just four years earlier the BBC, under pressure from the Foreign Office, had been forced to cancel a series of educational programmes entitled *The Citizen and his Government* because Sir Oswald Mosley, founder and leader of the British Union of Fascists, had been invited as one of the listed speakers. The Government, if not the BBC, perceived Mosley as a constitutional threat, through the pamphlets and nationwide discussion groups that were planned to coincide with the series.

Bert was certainly thrown in at the deep end when it came to radio scriptwriting. Between June 1939 and February 1940 he wrote eight scripts: *National Service Roll Call 1* and *2, The Eel's Foot* (with Maurice Brown), *Aeatoroa, Eleven Thousand Whalermen, The Home Front (1) Children in Billets* (with Stephen Potter), *The Empire's Answer* (with Laurence Gilliam), and *Cockneys in the Crisis* (with Gilliam and Olive Shapley). He translated two plays: *La Cite des Voix* and *Les Aveugle;* assisted with the translation of the Czech play *Cavalry Patrol* and he knocked off nine instalments of the *Shadow of the Swastika.* He was certainly earning his £6 a week.

Laurence Gilliam's judgement in employing Bert in the first place was amply justified. In January 1940, just before Bert's six-monthly contract came up for renewal for the third time, Gilliam wrote a glowing commendation to the

Director of the Finance Department, recommending that Bert's contract should be renewed and at a substantially increased figure, and, if possible, for a longer period than six months. He praised the quantity and quality of Bert's work:

> With the outbreak of war his usefulness, already great, was considerably intensified and the series *The Shadow of the Swastika* which has been officially endorsed as an outstanding programme of the war period, owes a very large degree of its success to his ability. ...This rate of work at such a high standard, coupled with the very high degree of political tact displayed, makes this in my view a very remarkable achievement and one that fully deserves generous recognition from the Corporation.

However, Bert's contract wasn't renewed, despite the fact that plans were already underway for him to write a new series using a similar format to *The Shadow of the Swastika* and provisionally titled *Hitler's Victims*. There is no doubt that his overt communism was the reason for his dismissal. A memo was circulated saying that he was not to be employed without prior permission from the powers that be. Whether or not he was being spied on by his secretary and reported to MI5, and his file marked 'premature anti-fascist' (as a former policeman once claimed) we don't know.

'Premature anti-fascist' is a term surrounded by hearsay. It was popularly believed to be an FBI euphemism for 'communist subversive', used to describe left-wing American Spanish Civil War veterans on their return to the US – International Brigaders who had the temerity to oppose fascism before the Second World War, when it finally became respectable to be anti-fascist. Many Spanish Civil War combatants claimed to have experienced prejudice when they later attempted to sign up for the US Armed Forces to fight the Nazis, because of the words 'premature anti-fascist' stamped on their files.

Bert did manage to get the odd bit of freelance radio writing, but it wasn't until 1949 that a note went round the BBC letting producers know that it was once again acceptable to book him, and he immediately started getting offers of scriptwriting and translation work from his old leftist friends in Features and Drama (although, according to the BBC television producer Barrie Gavin, Bert later confessed to feeling let down by many of his BBC friends). This continued into the 1970s when he was 'discovered' by Gavin with whom he worked on a number of TV documentary films for the last twelve years of his life. He was lucky to have cut his radio teeth in the 1930s and 1940s, which was a Golden Age for BBC radio. Tom Cheesman describes Bush House at that time as: 'A nest of poets: internationalists, cosmopolites, translators from classical and modern languages, bohemians. Many a man of the pen (and they were nearly all men) kept the wolf from the door with the Reithian shilling: W.H. Auden, Dylan Thomas, C. Day Lewis, Stephen Spender, F.R. Higgins, and others.'[9]

The other Reithian beneficiaries included Louis MacNeice, W.R. 'Bertie' Rogers, Olive Shapely, Felix Felton, Stephen Potter, Francis Dillon – and Bert Lloyd. Laurence Gilliam credited the 'diverse and stimulating essays' of the last five writers as being fundamental to the development and success of the Features Department, and helping to shape innovative experimental radio forms. Features also had a list of some seventy composers that they could draw on for programmes.

Producers had much more flexibility in programme making in those days. They could commission freelance writers to go off half way round the world if necessary to research a programme idea. The Features Department consisted of around twenty-five staff producers who were all contracted as writers also, several of whom were communists, including the well-known producer Reggie Smith (eventually transferred from Features to Drama to keep him as far away as possible from potential political programmes), the radical journalist Claud Cockburn (editor of *The Week*) and Bert.

Many of them were serious social drinkers. From the 1930s to the 1950s a lot of the Features planning and programme shaping went on in informal conversations in the Stag public house, or the baroque bar of the George, the 'Gluepot', at 55 Great Portland Street, just round the corner from Broadcasting House. The pub's nickname was coined by Sir Thomas Beecham, whose orchestral musicians got 'stuck' there during breaks in rehearsals at the nearby Queen's Hall. It was where actors, writers, composers, poets, musicians and producers all congregated, and where beer flowed, ideas flowered, deals were struck, and producers put people together. The George was a cultural and intellectual melting pot and the BBC was a real patron of the arts.

AS I ROVED OUT

There is in Suffolk, within the sound of a Trinity House foghorn, a remote hamlet reached by narrow, high-hedged lanes. Among its few cottages and farms is a single inn, the Eel's Foot. To the passer-by this beer-house, for that's all it is, is like many another country pub; it's small and undistinguished apart from its curious name. But on Saturday evenings the Eel's Foot is the scene of a dramatic rite which after years of acquaintance is still exciting.

BBC *East Anglia Sings*, 19 November 1947

A little while after he started working for the BBC in 1938 Bert had what was probably his first encounter with live rural English traditional singers. How it came about was that by the end of 1937 Leslie Morton, having finished *A People's History of England,* had moved back to his native Suffolk and, with Vivien Jackson, had rented a cottage on Leiston Common where Bert and Norma (Hutt) would visit them.

A couple of miles down the road at Eastbridge was the Eel's Foot Inn where every Saturday night the local fishermen and farm workers would get together in the small bar for an evening of song, music and step-dancing. Morton, who had been brought up in Suffolk and knew a number of popular local songs such as 'The Foggy Dew', 'Rap A Tap Tap' and 'Five Night's Drunk', used to regularly wander down to the pub for the sessions. One weekend when Bert and Norma were staying, they accompanied him to the singaround.

Bert was blown away. Here were working-class people doing their own thing, singing songs that had been handed down to them possibly for generations – a thriving folk culture on his own doorstep. Now it was no longer sufficient to simply take the songs into his own 'cultural baggage', as he said he had done in Australia as a young man. This was what he'd been reading about in the British Museum and the *Folk Song Journal*. Here were living, breathing examples of the working-class culture he'd been discussing with Morton during the preparation of *A People's History of England*. Something had to be done with it. As soon as he got back to London and the BBC, Bert put in a programme proposal to go down to Suffolk and record a Saturday night session at the Eel's Foot.

The possibility of making an outside broadcast recording was a new idea. It was first made possible with the development of the direct disc-cutting machine. The BBC had been slow to pick up on advances in sound recording, preferring to broadcast 'live'. This was partly because it was felt that, if artists and presenters knew they were being recorded for later transmission and could, if necessary, do retakes of the scripted speech, it would make them less focused and sharp with their presentation and lose the immediacy of a 'live' performance. Also, early recording equipment was expensive, cumbersome and not terribly efficient. The system used by the BBC in the early 1930s was the Blattnerphone, which used steel tape 6mm wide and 0.08mm thick, a mile long spool of which weighed in at 21 pounds, while tape edits had to be welded or soldered.

Commercial recordings had, of course, been made on records for many years, but the process was complex and expensive – about £50 a finished disc for the BBC. The first part of the process, the recording onto wax discs, was of little use for broadcasting or archiving because the wax discs could only be played once before they deteriorated. This all changed when musician Cecil Watts developed an aluminium-based and lacquer-coated disc and recording machine in his first-floor flat in London's Shaftesbury Avenue. His original intention had been to come up with a system that could directly play back durable recordings for use in band rehearsals. His system became known as Direct Disc Recording, and it was soon taken up by publicity companies and advertising agencies for use on commercial radio stations. The BBC finally got round to borrowing one of Watts' machines for trials in 1934, and was impressed enough to buy six machines for their Maida Vale studios a year later.

In 1935 Laurence Gilliam used a Direct Disc Recorder set up in a 30-hundredweight Morris van, powered by 24-volt accumulators and charged by a generator driven by the engine, to record part of his Features programme *Gale Warning*. This amounted to the BBC's first outside broadcast unit. The idea caught on with the BBC mandarins and in 1937 they announced: 'A small fleet of recording vans has been designed and constructed for collecting programme material from all parts of the country for subsequent inclusion in the programmes.'

It was one of these Direct Disc Cutting travelling studios that Bert and a BBC engineer took up to the Eel's Foot on 13 May 1939. Bert, Norma, Leslie Morton and Vivien Jackson, and a producer descended on the Eel's Foot with a pocketful of BBC petty cash to ensure that enough drink flowed to banish any inhibitions. They needn't have worried, because so much free beer flowed that by the end of the evening a state of near anarchy was reigning in Mrs Morling's little pub. At times the Chairman of the evening, Phil Lumpkin (known locally for his rendition of 'My Father Kept Two Rabbits'), with his cribbage-board gavel, had difficulty keeping order. Despite the chaos, Bert came away with his first folk song programme. On 29 July 1939, the BBC broadcast *Saturday Night at the Eel's Foot*, its first full-length programme of genuine traditional singing.

As Mike Yates said in his 2002 review of *Good Order*, the Veteran CD of the BBC recordings from the Eel's Foot: '... these BBC recordings are important, because they were made at a time when the singers and listeners were all part of a *living* singing tradition. It was, in a real sense, *community* singing, where the singers, songs and audience were all part and parcel of the same thing. True, the tradition was on its last legs – which is another reason why these recordings are so important.' 'It was an important historic moment musically speaking,' said Leslie Morton. 'Before that most people had thought that natural singers and folk songs were dead, but here were a whole lot of people doing it every Saturday night for the hell of it.'

They were, of course, in pubs all over the country at that time. But, as Yates said, the writing was on the wall for the old country singers and musicians who would eventually succumb to changing musical tastes, jukeboxes, television and radio itself. The old Norfolk singer Harry Cox succinctly summed it up: 'The young blokes come in here; they shove the wireless on singing this 'ere squit!' Singers like Cox were finding less and less of an audience for their music, until he and the relatively few other English tradition-bearers still singing were 'discovered' (many by Peter Kennedy and Bob Copper, two of the 'collectors' employed by the BBC for their 1950s folk music collecting scheme), and taken up by the folk revival of the 1960s and 1970s, when they and their music found a new audience and took on a new, if different, lease of life.

All of the singers that were there that evening in 1939 have long since passed on to that singaround in the sky but, thanks to Leslie Morton, who fired Bert's enthusiasm for the Eel's Foot, we can still hear the voices of 'Velvet' Brightwell declaiming 'The Bold Princess Royal', 'The Indian Lass' and 'Pleasant and Delightful', Albert 'Diddy' Cook's 'Blackbird', 'Poor Man's Heaven' (Tom Goddard) – which Bert correctly identified as an American workers' song – 'The Foggy Dew' (Douglas Morling), 'The Farmer from Cheshire' (Alec Bloomfield), 'The Old Sow' (Fred Ginger), and the step-dance tune 'Jack's the Boy' played on the melodeon by Jack 'Dot' Button. Other singers on that heady alcoholic May evening included Harry 'Crutter' Cook, the landlady's daughter, Eileen, who gave a moving performance of 'Among My Souvenirs' (Eileen ran the pub with her husband Stan from 1945 to 1958) and Leslie Morton, who remembered singing 'McCassery' ('McCafferty').

6
Bertie Badfruit

Imagine how splendid and much more humanly truthful the early collections of sea chanteys might have been had the collectors been able to print what was really sung.

George G. Carey, Folklore Forum, 1971

The next time you hear somebody singing without embarrassment about the 'Seeds of Love' or 'The Bonny Black Hare', maybe it was A.L. Lloyd who persuaded him to drop his inhibitions.

Jean Aitchinson

When Philip Larkin wrote 'They fuck you up, your mum and dad', he wasn't propounding a universal law, but for some people it's true. It may be unintentional, which in some ways is worse, in that it demonstrates a lack of empathy that can condemn a child to an emotional limbo, a lifetime searching for reasons, explanations and absolution.

Jenny Stein (née Hutt), Bert's stepdaughter, experienced some of this when she was nineteen and her mother, Norma, committed suicide. Sadly, neither her father, Allen Hutt, nor Bert seem to have been very emotional men, given to overt demonstrations of affection. Tom Hopkinson once described Bert as a 'bit of a cold fish', although some people disagree with this (Caroline, Bert's daughter from his second marriage, remembers him as loving, warm, tolerant, supportive and respectful). Perhaps, mistakenly, the two men felt that at nineteen Jenny was mature enough to cope without a comforting arm. Not so. At the age of eighty, she still spoke of not being cuddled back in 1945:

I don't know why, but nobody cuddled me. I think I really needed a cuddle. I couldn't do anything. I couldn't even cuddle Joe [her half-brother]. I was just there smoking, and feeling abandoned and lonely. Thinking about it now, I don't think it was the worst thing my mother could have done. I think she thought it was for the best. She was a brave little person. Although it was rough on Joe and me of course at the time. Joe was five and old enough to know what happened. We were all in the house when she did it. It was horrible. Bert woke me up and told me and I could smell the gas straight away.[1]

Norma's own childhood had not been an easy one: 'She was illegitimate, you know, which in those days was considered a terrible thing,' said Jenny. 'Grandpa Garwood was a bit of a bugger and he finally abandoned Granny Garwood and Norma when Norma was about six. So she was kind of fucked up by that. She was a brave little girl, you could tell that from the photographs. I think deep down I knew she was going to kill herself. Initially there'd been scenes, then they stopped. That was when she'd accepted that their relationship was over.'

Bert met the Hutts soon after he arrived back in England from Australia, through his early friendship with the Mortons. Allen Hutt, tall, gangly, bespectacled, a few years older than Norma, and not the archetypal family man was, according to Jenny, 'a bit weak as a father, and we didn't have a great family life'. Most of his time and energy was put into his politics, and his work as a writer, journalist, and chief sub-editor of the *Daily Worker*. He was highly intelligent, a dedicated communist, an apologist for Stalin (whom he described as Lenin's best disciple), a brilliant award-winning typographer, sometimes rude and brusque, and, like Bert, a good linguist, speaking Russian and French and reputedly able to swear in five more languages. Eric Scott, Allen's assistant from 1946, remembered him as a 'newspaper man of the front rank'. Hutt did, however, have an erratic side:

He always seemed two people, on the one hand a dedicated professional of acute sensibility and deep emotional understanding and on the other a clown who could not resist exhibitionism. He was sometimes rude without purpose and affected a World War One type hatred of Germans. A remark of his that would now be considered racist was that the best cure for a cold was a 'bottle of Burgundy and a black girl'. It was an irresistible desire to shock.[2]

Bert also displayed at times this desire to shock. We have to assume it was intentional, because both men were intelligent enough to realise the effect that their words might have. Kaye Webb, who worked on *Picture Post* with Bert and eventually became assistant editor of *Lilliput* magazine from 1941, was no great fan of Bert from the time he told a questionable sexual story in mixed company at a *Lilliput* editorial meeting. Tom Hopkinson recalled a similar incident in the pub in Watford where journalists and editorial staff regularly congregated for lunch on printing day:

We'd all got our lunch at the Rose and Crown, the town's best pub – lots of farmers and business people and so on. Bert in this mixed company would tell very loudly of the whaler-men in some South African port and some Salvation Army lass who came aboard and was cornered by two or three roughies and was raped and pushed ashore weeping. This is a story which anyone with experience of the war and life under rough conditions might well tell to a pal, but not in a crowded bar room, and not seemingly as though it were funny. This was rather distressing. An odd quirk.

Perhaps Bert and Allen Hutt said things that were inappropriate to the setting to shock middle-class listeners out of their perceived complacency and not, as Hopkins thought, simply Bert's interest in his own stories and an unawareness of how people were reacting to them.

Norma was a small, dark woman, elegant and dainty. She was very reserved, shy and a bit prim, and dubbed 'The Parson's Daughter' by Vivien Morton's father, Tommy Jackson, the communist theoretician. Leslie Morton recalled an evening with Bert and Norma in the Eel's Foot pub when he (Morton) sang a faintly suggestive Suffolk version of 'Five Nights Drunk'. Norma begged Vivien three times to stop him singing. It was done in a light-hearted way but with an undercurrent of seriousness. Jenny remembered how she and her mother would curl up in embarrassment when Bert sang bawdy songs for their dinner guests:

'When he sang that famous song about Sam Hall, who only had one ball, we would die of embarrassment. He'd sing it for whoever was there.'

Norma, a communist, probably through Allen, was, like Bert, a voracious reader and an excellent shorthand typist. She worked with Leslie Morton's first wife, Bronwen, for ARCOS (All-Russian Cooperative Society Ltd), a British-registered trading company that in the 1920s was based in Moorgate, and later moved to Kingsway, near Bush House. The prime object of ARCOS was to be a channel for trade between the USSR and Britain. All orders and contracts between the two countries were handled by ARCOS. The company shared offices with, and was inextricably linked to, the Russian Trade Delegation, the Chief of which enjoyed diplomatic privileges.

In May 1927, three years before Bert returned to London, ARCOS, which was used as a front for Soviet Intelligence in the inter-war years, was the centre of an international incident which led to the severing of diplomatic relations with the USSR, and the claim by Rykov, Chairman of the Council of Peoples Commissars, that the British Conservative government was trying to provoke a war with Russia. It was serious stuff, financially as well as politically, because the USSR, just about to embark on its first Five Year Plan, had intended spending millions of pounds on British industrial equipment.

Over seventy policemen, acting on a tip-off, and ignoring diplomatic protocol, had raided the ARCOS offices looking for a stolen British Army Signals Training pamphlet, which was reported to be 'in the hands of the Russians'. Nothing especially incriminating was found, despite the fact that a number of safes were cut open, and hundreds of files confiscated. Eventually, as invariably happens, in the cynical world of politics and diplomacy, expediency won the day, things settled down and ARCOS and the Trade Delegation got back to trading under the watchful eye of MI5.[3]

Jenny, who lived with her mother and Bert in her teens – rather than with her father and his new wife, Sheena, whom she didn't particularly get on with – remembered Russians from the Delegation visiting and sometimes staying at Bert and Norma's Highgate home several years later. She had been sent off, aged five, to be a boarder at A.S. Neil's progressive school, Summerhill, at Leiston in Suffolk. Leslie Morton ended up teaching at the school after he left London, and became Jenny's history master. In the absence of her parents, the school, its pupils and teachers became her family. It was from her group of ex-school friends and Norma's best friend, Jessie Simpson, that Jenny received the most support over her mother's subsequent suicide.

Jenny left school in 1942 aged sixteen with an ambition to get into filmmaking. Luckily, through the freemasonry web of communism Allen Hutt knew the right people to contact. In July he wrote to his old friend Humphrey Jennings (1907–50),[4] the AIA painter turned documentary filmmaker who was running the Ministry of Information's Crown Film Unit based at Pinewood Studios at Iver in Buckinghamshire: 'I am trying to get Jenny a cutting room job on which I thought perhaps you might be able to give me some further dope and possibly suggest ways in which she might start in the cutting room of some documentary outfit like your own. I haven't seen you around town lately and hope we shall run into each other soon.' Needless to say Jenny was soon working for Jennings, who wrote a glowing letter to Hutt saying he hoped she liked working for the Crown Film Unit as much as they liked having her on board. She worked on several prestigious wartime documentaries (including the noted 1944 documentary *A Diary for Timothy*, for which she was the film-cutter).

On the night she died, Norma had spent the evening in a local pub talking to Jessie, while Jenny was at the cinema watching the Bob Hope, Bing Crosby and Dorothy Lamour comedy *The Road to Utopia*. Bert passed the evening reading in a rocking chair in front of the fire, babysitting their son Joe and Joe's friend Sam Hutt, Allen and Sheena's young son, who was having a sleepover. Joe Lloyd and Sam Hutt (better known these days as the singer Hank Wangford) were to remain friends for the rest of Joe's short life.

The Hutts would appear to have been a separation waiting to happen when Bert came on the scene. He was handsome, fit and a charismatic young man with a prodigious intelligence, a sense of humour and a colourful and romantic background – there probably weren't many handsome ex-Australian stockmen in north London at that time, especially ones who could discuss art, literature and music with such passion and enthusiasm. It's no great surprise that Norma, approaching forty, and in a marriage that didn't seem to be going anywhere, should be attracted to Bert, some eight years her junior. The attraction was mutual. One day, so Norma later told Jenny, Bert had turned up at the front door and they simply fell into each other's arms and rushed upstairs to bed, where they remained for twenty-four hours, with snack breaks for baked beans, toast and tea. They had no idea of the chain of events they were setting in motion, or of the lives that would be affected down the generations as a result of those twenty-four hours.

Bert and Norma's relationship had begun some time before his 1937/8 whaling expedition. Bert once told Barrie Gavin that Norma had begged him not to go, but he insisted he had to for the money. Norma apparently intimated that there was someone else who was interested in her and she might not be around in six months' time if he went. Whether this was true or not we don't know, although there is a family rumour that at one time Norma did go away to Prague for a fling with Roger Roughton. Perhaps this happened during Bert's trip. Anyway, she *was* still waiting when Bert returned in April 1938, clutching his six months' pay.

For many intellectuals, artists, and political radicals, the 1930s was a time of sexual and social latitude – the sort of freedom and rebellion one usually associates with the 'swinging Sixties'. There was the same disregard for the mores of bourgeois society or, as Jenny more succinctly put it: 'They were young, it was the thirties, and people fucked like stoats.' This laissez-faire attitude was exemplified by the ménage-a-quatre that Allen, his new girlfriend (and wife to be) Sheena, Bert and Norma set up in the Hutts' old house. Bert and Sheena simply moved in and the two couples occupied half the house each until Bert and Norma finally got their own place. As a young teenager, Jenny found this an uncomfortable and unsettling arrangement. When she came home from Summerhill for the holidays, she was never sure with which part of the house and which couple to identify.

Despite the somewhat bohemian set-up, there came a point when the women at least wanted to be made 'honest'. Norma, who was devoted to Bert, had, as Jenny described it, put all her eggs in one basket where he was concerned and wanted to get married. Everyone who knew them agreed that she adored Bert:

I think my father had a girlfriend or two. I think Mum had had rather a hard life, and perhaps felt that Bert was the way out of it. And then he wouldn't marry her. They eventually married but Norma had to push him into it. He was happy to live together but not the commitment of marriage. Then when Norma found out that she was two months pregnant that tipped the scales.

On 14 February 1940, Bert married Kathleen Norma Hutt (formerly Garwood) at St Pancras Register Office, London. Norma was thirty-eight and Bert, who was registered as 'Employee, British Broadcasting Corporation', was thirty-one. They lived at Flat 4, 1 Holly Terrace, West Hill, N6. Norma was two months pregnant at the time and Joseph was born on 5 September, at Middlesex Hospital. On Joe's birth certificate Bert's job was entered as journalist. By then they were living at 11 Highgate West Hill, N6, between the Highgate Ponds on Hampstead Heath and Highgate Cemetery (where Karl Marx and Bert's old bookshop boss, William Foyle, are buried). George and Doreen Rudé sometimes dined with the couple in the early 1940s and Doreen was surprised at how earnest Norma was: 'I thought that Bert's humour was never what I would have described as earnest at any time, even if he occasionally had an earnest intensity. When I met Norma I felt she had a school-mistressy aura of earnestness, and I thought how extraordinary.'

Jenny, who chose to live with Bert and Norma, had no problems with Bert as a stepfather and they all got on well. Bert bought her presents, took them on trips to the cinema and played them his music, talked about books (of which there was no shortage in either household, with a special place, as in all left-wing households, for the orange- or yellow-wrapped Left Book Club publications), and took more of an active interest in her life than Allen had found time to do.

Norma and Jenny's affectionate family name for Bert was Bertie Badfruit, although now Jenny can't remember the significance of the amusing title. When they had people round for dinner Jenny tended to do the cooking as Norma 'hated it'. As if to demonstrate how civilised they all were, Allen and Sheena were regular dinner guests. But the civility was on the part of the men. Norma didn't like it: Sheena didn't like it. They didn't like each other. But Bert and Allen were good friends and they either didn't appreciate the undercurrent of latent hostility, or didn't care, or, more likely, weren't even aware of it. Neither of them, at that time, seems to have been blessed with an advanced emotional radar system.

The fact that Bert was a good stepfather made it all the harder for Jenny, and presumably for him, when the marriage started falling apart, culminating in Norma's suicide. The beginning of the end was when Bert began an affair with Charlotte 'Lottie' Ohly, a very beautiful young German refugee who was one of their social group. The film director Uri Weiss had introduced her into the Lloyd household. In the mid-1930s London was a popular haven for political exiles escaping Nazism, many of whom were artists who made a considerable cultural impact on Britain. They faced common problems of social integration, assimilation and language, which fostered strong emigré solidarity.

Various British artistic groups, including the AIA, offered practical help with accommodation and work. Some, who had managed to get themselves established, set up their own support groups. A number of artists, including Lucie Rie and Hans Coper who were destined to become internationally acclaimed potters, congregated around William Ohly, a (Yorkshire-born) German sculptor and the wealthy owner of the exclusive Berkeley Galleries at 20 Davis Street, London, where he exhibited their work. This is the same William Ohly who had attended James Fitton's lithography classes at the Central School in 1933 and was in with Bert on the founding of the AIA.

Charlotte Maria Adam, who was staunchly anti-Nazi, had met Ohly, some thirty years her senior, while she was a sculpture student in Germany. They had intended to marry in Germany, but after 1935 it was not possible for Ohly to stay in the country. Charlotte agreed to emigrate to England and marry him in London. Before leaving for London the twenty-two-year-old Charlotte had second thoughts about the marriage, but she decided to go anyway and tell him face to face that the marriage was off. Arriving in London in 1935, she found that Ohly was ill and had lost his memory. In a scene straight out of a romantic novel Charlotte made a vow that, if he could be restored to health, she would marry him. He did recover and Charlotte, on 23 October 1935, true to her promise, became Mrs Ohly and set up home in Ohly's house in Chelsea, leaving behind her friends, family and the possibility of fighting the rise of Nazism in her own country.

Despite the age difference and the difference in their ways – Ohly's gregariousness versus Charlotte's natural reserve – there was genuine affection between the two of them. Some acquaintances said that Charlotte's relationship with the cultured, charming and urbane Ohly appeared more like that between a daughter and a father than a wife and husband, but this might just have been an outsider's perception due to their age difference. Although, as it turned out, the marriage was short-lived, they remained good friends for the rest of Ohly's life.

Ohly, who had a philanthropic nature, had organised social events with musical recitals, tea and buns at his gallery, as a distraction from the bleakness and blackouts of wartime London. After the war he opened the residential Abbey Arts Centre and a Museum of primitive art in New Barnet, where visiting foreign artists could live and work. Bert and Charlotte's daughter, Caroline, remembers Ohly with affection from the times she and Joe were taken as children to events at the museum, where she was allowed to dress up in grass skirts and other exciting costumes. They also occasionally stayed at the Centre for short holidays, and Ohly was a welcome guest at Greenwich. It sounds a very civilised and agreeable set-up. Ohly died in Islington in the summer of 1955, aged seventy-one.

It was considered prudent by the Jewish Board of Deputies that German Jewish refugees should keep a low profile to avoid inflaming anti-Semitism. Non-Jews, like Charlotte, who were seen as 'enemy aliens' were also advised to keep their heads down, particularly after the fall of France when anti-German feeling grew. Although, when Bert conducted a survey for the army newspaper *The Turret* at Catterick Garrison in 1942, nearly 80 per cent of the troops said that the German people should not be punished for the war. How much that sentiment was reflected in the population at large is hard to tell.

Charlotte was soon plugged into the emigré support network and, although Ohly was a wealthy man and she had no real need to work, she was determined to be financially independent and looked around for a job. Her first unsuccessful attempt to get work in the UK was at a munitions factory. Needless to say, an attractive young woman with a strong German accent in a bright red coat stood out like a sore thumb, and she was lucky not to have been arrested. As well as her art training, she was a fine seamstress and a skilled dressmaker, and she eventually got a job working for another German exile, Sigmund Freud's daughter Mathilde, who in 1939 opened the up-market dress shop Robell in Baker Street.

The shop interior, designed by Mathidle's brother, the well-known Hampstead architect Ernst Ludwig Freud (father of the painter Lucian, and broadcaster and politician Clement), had a chic minimalist look. It was not quite *haute couture* because everything was off-the-peg, but, once an item had been selected, with solicitous help from the staff, it was Charlotte's job to make any alterations required to make it feel like a handmade garment. Her knowledge and appreciation of the human body through her training as a sculptress proved invaluable when it came to draping, folding, cutting, sewing and fitting. She had impeccable taste and refused to let women buy dresses that she felt were wrong for them.

Later, when she was married to Bert and living in Croom's Hill, Greenwich, Charlotte made all her own clothes and most of the clothes for the rest of the family. Jill Day Lewis (Jill Balcon), wife of C. Day Lewis, who lived a couple of houses down from the Lloyds, often saw Charlotte walking down Croom's Hill on her way to the shops and said that she always looked impeccable, elegant and had great style.[5] Erika Bach, one of Robell's customers who became friendly with Charlotte, confirmed Charlotte's elegance and taste: 'She had great beauty and dignity and a superb skill as a dressmaker. She first worked in a dress shop in London and later worked at home for a few friends, myself amongst them. I have many memories of visits to Charlotte's house, meeting their children and hearing her husband's hoarse voice as he sang some of his foreign folk songs to us.'[6]

By the end of the war, when Bert left his job at the Ministry of Information and went on the army reserve, his relationship with Charlotte was well established. Jenny remembers the winter of 1945 as one of rows, tears and recriminations at St Alban's Villas. Norma, and presumably Charlotte, demanded that Bert make a decision between the two of them. He had broken the news to Jenny that the marriage was on the rocks, not that she needed to be told. It wasn't exactly a closely guarded secret. Towards Christmas, Norma seemed resigned to the break-up and became calm and much quieter. In retrospect, Jenny realised that she was closing herself off and mentally putting her house in order in preparation for suicide but between her busy job at the Crown Film Unit and boyfriends, the teenage Jenny was too busy with her own life to recognise the calm before the storm. Norma had, as Jenny said, 'put all her eggs in one basket'. Life without Bert was unthinkable.

Marital breakdowns and separations of any kind invariably pose problems for friends and relations. It's difficult not to take sides, and people often fall into two camps depending where their sympathies and perceptions of the rights and wrongs of the case happen to lie. In the case of a suicide, the ultimate demonstration of pain and despair, this must be even truer. This certainly seems to have been the case over Norma's suicide. Jenny, despite having had a good relationship with Bert up to that point, found herself unable to forgive him. She felt that in some ways Norma's death was a relief to Bert. After the inevitable arguments and tears, with Norma asking Bert to make up his mind and to decide between herself and Charlotte and his prevarication, Norma had taken the decision for him and, as Jenny saw it, let him off the hook.

A little later Jenny asked Bert for her mother's diaries and Bert told her he'd burnt them. The diaries were a daily record of the family's life in wartime London, conscientiously maintained, in meticulous handwriting, written in part for Bert, who had often been away on *Picture Post* assignments, army training or conducting research for the Ministry of Information's magazine *Britanski Soyuznik*. One can understand how the last few months of the diaries could have made uncomfortable reading. We don't know what Norma might have written as she saw her marriage dissolving. It's difficult to be balanced and objective in this situation if you see yourself as the injured party. Things are often said or written in the heat of the moment, or from the depths of despair, that can be painful, sad or accusatory. Few situations, especially emotional ones, are as clear-cut as we would like to believe. Even so, Jenny felt that burning the diaries was a final betrayal and cut Bert out of her life from then on, moving out and only seeing him when she wanted to meet up with Joe.

Norma committed suicide on the night of 28 December 1945; she was forty-three. The next morning, a Saturday, was to be Leslie and Vivien Morton's wedding day. When Vivien rang to tell Bert and Norma not to forget the wedding, Bert answered the phone and said that Norma had 'put her head in the gas oven'.

Charlotte moved into the house soon after to help Bert look after Joe, now that Jenny had gone. Bert and Charlotte were married a few months later, at St Pancras Register Office. Charlotte was thirty-three; Bert was thirty-eight and registered as a journalist. Outside the family, friends and political associates also had opinions on Norma's suicide. Some, like the Mortons, were surprised at what they perceived as Bert's lack of concern and they tended to drift apart. Leslie Morton remembered an occasion several years later when he again met up with Bert:

> There was a long gap when we didn't see him after Norma's suicide. When I met him years later I put out a hand to greet him. I didn't think of kissing him, and he said, 'Oh, are we so distant now?' It horrified me, I didn't mean anything. He was obviously very self-conscious, after Jenny had cut him off, and he probably thought I was in Jenny's faction. I always remember that, it made me very sad.

UNDERNEATH HER APRON

Because of her devotion to Bert, Norma was prepared to share his enthusiasm for folk song but embracing erotic and bawdy songs was a step too far for the rather prim Norma. Bert, on the other hand, had a distinct interest in erotic songs, and for many years ploughed a lone furrow through the British folk revival, lecturing on and performing the type of traditional song that had caused the Rev. Baring Gould to rewrite lyrics and which the Victorian and Edwardian folk song collectors found themselves unwilling (for personal reasons), or unable (for social reasons) to publish unexpurgated – songs such as 'The Husband With no Courage in Him':

> It's seven long years I've made his bed,
> And six of them I've laid agin him,
> And this morn I rose with my maidenhead,
> Now that shows he's got no courage in him.

Or the 'Wanton Seed':

> I said to her, 'My pretty maid,
> Come tell me what you stand in need.'
> 'Oh yes, kind sir, you're the man to do the deed,
> For to sow my meadow with the wanton seed.'
>
> Then I sowed high and I sowed low,
> And under the bush the seed did grow;
> It sprang up so accidentally without any weed,
> And she always remembered the wanton seed.

It wasn't just Victorian and Edwardian audiences and editors who wished to cover up the piano legs. In the US as late as 1971 an outraged reader of *Folklore Forum* complained of erotic and scatological articles in folklore journals, describing the research as 'the scholarshit of fucklore'. And in Britain there were those on the contemporary folk scene who didn't share Bert's liking for erotic song. A reviewer in *Spin* magazine in 1966 reproached Bert for a 'boring over-emphasis on the sexual joke'. In his reply a couple of issues later Bert gave a persuasive defence of his reasons for singing such songs:

It's true I do sing rather a lot of songs of erotic content. I like them. Behind the light surface there are often considerable deep, ponderable sobrieties. The roots of many such songs are found in the religious intuitions of early agricultural civilizations and these intuitions – such as the identifying of ploughing and poking – have often doggedly survived more or less unaltered over the last – what? – three thousand years or more, up to our own time; so it's clear they have a tenacious grip on the imagination of man, and are not to be lightly shrugged off as insignificant. It's in the favour of the folk songs that few of them adopt the idea of sex as sin. The message tends to be about increase, rather than naughtiness, with laughter rather than guilt and despair. (I'm speaking now of the solidly traditional erotic songs, not the sad pornographic Eskimo Nellery). I suppose the reason why I incline to sing rather a lot of amatory–encounter songs is to reassure young listeners that relations between the sexes don't have to be – as the pops pretend – a matter of despair, loss and frenzy. Perhaps attempts to redress a balance tend to seem like a 'boring over-emphasis'?

This might, indeed, have been Bert's motivation for singing his erotic songs, but his obvious enjoyment (and that of most audiences) of the songs led some people to believe that there was no smoke without fire and that he had an eye for the girls.

His sense of humour might, in the wrong hands, have been misinterpreted. Signing himself, on occasion, A.L. Lewd[7] was a joke that would have done nothing in some quarters to dispel rumours of lechery. Martin Carthy has an anecdote concerning Bert's humour and the ballad 'Jack Orion'. When Bert sent Dave Swarbrick a typed set of words for the ballad he changed 'velvet glove' to 'velvet sock' which would have implied that the following rhyme was not 'love' but 'cock'.

Ewan MacColl was in agreement with Bert's attitude to erotic song. He accused some folk club singers of substituting 'risqué' songs for honest bawdy. They were right, of course. In general, traditional song does treat the subject with 'honest bawdy', a natural earthiness frequently absent in the loveless, often misogynistic, creations of students and those described by Bert as 'uprooted men-without-women', or in the 'art' songs popular with certain young men about town that appeared in collections like Thomas d'Urfey's *Pills to Purge Melancholy* (1698–1720), such as 'As Oyster Nan Stood by her Tub', which lives up to the collection's subtitle of *Lewd Songs and Low Ballads*:

As Oyster Nan stood by her tub,
To show her vicious inclination;
She gave her noblest parts a scrub,
And sighed for want of copulation:
A vintner of no little fame,
Who excellent red and white can sell ye,
Beheld the little dirty dame,
As she stood scratching of her belly.

It might be said that, like some other aspects of Bert's folklore vision, when it came to erotic songs his eyes were perhaps twinkling through rose-tinted spectacles. Many of the erotic folk songs were not necessarily simply celebrating a tumble in the hay or the spirit of fertility. They could also be taken as warnings to young women (generally the partner 'left holding the baby') and, less frequently, young men (who might find themselves in need of 'pills of white mercury') about the dangers of promiscuous sex. Sexual relationships might not, as Bert said, be matters for despair, loss, or frenzy, but they should, perhaps, be about responsibility as well as laughter, and many amorous folk songs were potentially as admonitory as amusing.

Bert was astonished when in a 1966 review of *The Bird in the Bush* in *English Dance and Song* he was accused of 'trying very hard to shock'. 'Nothing was further from my mind', he told his audience at the 1966 London Folk Music Festival at Cecil Sharp House. He suggested that this non-acceptance of sex in love songs was a middle-class prejudice, since folk songs were originally created by a different social class. In the sleeve notes to *The Bird in the Bush* he also suggested that:

With misplaced sympathy, modern city writers have remarked on the 'disconcerting ease' with which young women in the folk songs become pregnant, forgetting that for societies in healthy condition the arrival of children is vital and joyous because, among other things, it means more hands to help with the work. So it's not surprising that the idea of trying out a girl to be sure of her fertility lies within many an amatory folk song, where pregnancy is only unwelcome if the girl is deserted, and not always then.

I'm not sure that the unmarried mothers in folk songs who succumbed to the wiles of Bold Dragoons, Gentlemen Soldiers and philandering Jolly Jack Tars, and the thousands of servant girls used and abandoned by their 'masters' with their bastards would have seen it quite like that.

7
Picture Post and Army Life

Along with the Left Book Club, Mass Observation, the documentary film movement, Unity Theatre and the AIA, *Picture Post* was part of a cultural movement for social change, brought about by the mass unemployment and the international and national political turmoil of the 1930s. This was a movement in which the major players drank in the same pubs, ate in the same cafés, read the same literature, were invariably left-wing if not always communist, and a group of which Bert was very much a part.

The Hulton Press had started *Picture Post* in 1938, when Edward Hulton commissioned Stefan Lorant, a Hungarian-born Jewish refugee from the Nazis, to create a new magazine for him. An ex-photographer and film director, Lorant had a remarkable eye for, and understanding of, photographs. Earlier in the 1930s, before being imprisoned by the Nazis, he had edited a German picture magazine, *Munchner Illustrierte Press*. On his release in 1933 Lorant fled to London where he started up *Weekly Illustrated*, the first popular British picture magazine.

A little later, in August 1937, he borrowed £1,200 from his girlfriend and brought out the 100-page pocket magazine *Lilliput*. Its lively mix of jokes, cartoons, photographs, the occasional tasteful pin-up, articles and stories, made it an immediate hit. In June 1938 Lorant sold *Lilliput* to the Hulton Press and agreed to create for them a new large-format picture magazine, which as Robert Kee explained in *The Picture Post Story* would involve: '... the use of the camera to unfold a journalistic story through its own eye rather than (as had been the general magazine practice until then, and still was in Britain) the publication of pictures from press and other independent sources labelled with informative captions.' The original staff consisted of Lorant, assistant editor Hopkinson (poached from Odhams press), a secretary and two German refugee photographers Kurt Hutton (Kurt Hubschmann) and Felix Man (Hans Baumann).

The large format of the magazine was decided upon by Lorant who explained to Hopkinson that it was based on the natural enlargement of a 35mm negative with suitable margins. The 35mm lightweight, flexible, camera was the *Picture Post* camera of choice: 'It wasn't necessarily the cheapest way because there was always going to be some wastage on each reel of paper, but it meant that we could use a variety of layout patterns, with combinations of landscape and portrait shots for either single pages or across double-page spreads.'

The magazine title came from two lists of relevant words made by Lorant. The team picked one word from each list, the two favourites being Picture and Post. And so *Picture Post* – a populist, anti-fascist, liberal magazine – was born. The first issue appeared on 1 October 1938. It soon acquired a pool of some of the best journalists and photographers in the country: a list that years later would read like a who's who of the journalistic great and good: James Cameron, Macdonald Hastings, Anne Scott-James, Robert Kee, A.L. Lloyd, Fyfe Robertson, Kenneth Allsop, Trevor Philpot, Woodrow Wyatt, and photographers of international repute such as Bert Hardy, Thurston Hopkins, Grace Robertson, Kurt Hutton, Hayward Magee, Bill Brandt (a close friend of Bert) and many more.

It was always a photo-led paper; it didn't matter how good the journalist was, if a team came back to the Shoe Lane office without pictures, it was a disaster. As Bert Hardy explained:

On *Picture Post* the photographer took pride of place. It didn't matter how good the written story was if you didn't have good pictures. The journalists had to make sure the photographer got good pictures by talking to the subjects so that they weren't conscious of the camera. This was very important and it was very much what a journalist had to do. Bert Lloyd was very good at that, and at the same time he was making written and mental notes for the article. He had a wonderful memory. Also he was used by me to carry my bag around.

When Tom Hopkinson, who knew Bert from *Left Review* as well as from his radio programmes, heard in 1940 that he had become persona non grata at the BBC he had no qualms about getting Bert signed up as the *Picture Post* 'social expert'. This meant he was employed to produce articles showing how the ordinary men and women in the street were coping with the war, although his first article, appearing on 10 February 1940, 'The Story of New Zealand (1840–1940)', was in fact a lengthy piece celebrating the centenary of the founding of the Dominion of New Zealand, when the Maori chiefs 'ceded their country to the British' in return for 'protection'.

The mainly historical article was obviously based on library research, and perhaps a chat with Kiwi friends such as James Boswell, because the photos and illustrations are standard picture-library material, and the few contemporary descriptive pieces could easily have been picked up from a couple of guide books, although Bert does manage to make it sound like first-hand knowledge:

Deep south is Dunedin where every second street and every other shop bears a Scottish name. Solid, conservative, wealthy Dunedin is built not so much out of Scottish thrift as out of ruffianly gold-rush gold … . The other big city of the South island is Christchurch, with its lovely parks, its traffic belts, Gothic architecture all over the place and 16,000 bicycles all ringing in the streets at once … . There's not much of the sunny south about Wellington on her off-days, with her battlements of chimneys bristling in the wind and rain and the jagged hills behind her. North of them all is Auckland, elegant and snowy, with Byzantine towers, Moorish cinemas, Greek museums and flowering roof gardens on the tall hotels.

Other articles in this issue included one on the history of the rifle from Bert's *Left Review* and CP friend, the ex-soldier and military journalist Tom Wintringham; a photograph of mine-laying off the East Coast of Britain; a bizarre quote from right-winger Sir Nevile Henderson, Britain's former Berlin ambassador ('Goering may be a blackguard, but not a dirty blackguard'); and a piece on how France is guarding her coastline from German invasion, which ended: 'The French Navy guards the coasts of France, and guards them well.'

The following month, the 2 March cover photograph was of actor Marius Goring in the BBC studio recording one of his ranting Hitler speeches for Bert's *The Shadow of the Swastika*. The producer Laurence Gilliam wrote a behind-the-scenes look at the production of the series, with excellent studio shots of the cast and the BBC Northern Orchestra in the Manchester studios where the programmes were recorded. There was no photo of Bert although (of course) he and Vinogradoff did get credited as the writers. There exists a nice photo (see plate 15) of the pair of them hard at work in their office at Broadcasting House, sitting across from each other at their shared desk, reading, pencils poised, concentration etched on Bert's face.

On 28 September 1940 *Picture Post* printed the classic 'The East End at War': ten pages of evocative black-and-white photographs by Bert Hardy of rubble-strewn streets, flattened houses and people surviving and getting on with life; a sewing-machinist busy in a shop whose windows have been blown out; a man, sleeves rolled up, sitting amongst the ruins of his home sorting out an income tax demand; and a wonderful kitchen interior with four people sitting around a table drinking tea, a half-empty milk bottle, some side plates and a banana creating a still-life centre piece shot in the natural light from the lace-curtained, criss-cross-taped windows, as fine in its own way as any seventeenth-century Dutch interior by Vermeer.

Add to this a sensitive, perceptive and balanced complementary essay by Bert Lloyd, in which he simply tells it how it is – no mythologising, no attempt to paint everyone as chirpy heroic cockneys (although some of them were) – and you can see why the two Berts made such a hugely successful and formidable photo-journalistic double act. Here they showed ordinary people trying to come to terms with 'the aerial hell' into which they had been pitched – people suffering stress, fear, confusion, lack of sleep and trapped in some ongoing bad dream. Every homeless Blitz victim who was being pushed from pillar to post by impotent bureaucrats, and who frequently had to rely on the charity and good will of family, friends, strangers or the local vicar, knew how ill-prepared was the Government.

The Government was running its own propaganda war through its control over the BBC and by getting positive articles published in popular magazines, such as a feature in *Illustrated* on the role of the RAF in the Battle of Britain. They also planned to pay for extra pages in *Picture Post* for a propaganda article entitled 'The Might of Britain' but in the end decided to use the money elsewhere. The Ministry of Information film division commissioned lots of five-minute shorts as well as longer documentaries, such as Humphrey Jennings' Blitz documentary *London Can Take It*. The MOI kept a small army of scriptwriters, journalists, radio and film producers and directors in work and out of the services throughout the war.

'The East End at War' was the first story on which the two Berts worked together and was the start of a partnership that lasted for ten years, with four years off from 1942 to 1946 while Bert did his army training and his stint at the MOI. It's perhaps surprising how well the two Berts got on: in many ways they were as different as chalk and cheese. Bert Hardy was a very simple, no-nonsense, hard-nosed press photographer. Bert Lloyd, on the other hand, was highly intellectual, a gifted linguist, a connoisseur of food and good wine, deeply political, conscious of his image and inclined to keep many aspects of his life in strictly separate compartments. But the partnership worked, and Hardy soon realised the value of Bert Lloyd's presence when it came to setting up a rapport with the working-class subjects of many of their articles: 'From the point of view of *Picture Post*, his greatest asset was his ability to win people's confidence instantly, and to talk to anyone. This made him the best man to send along to places like the East End of London.'

In the early days of *Picture Post*, writers and photographers weren't always credited, so it's sometimes difficult to know just which articles the two Berts produced. Occasionally one can make an educated guess, as in the case of the 14 December 1940, article 'Christmas is Coming at the Eel's Foot'. This is a double-page spread of atmospheric photographs taken at one of the Saturday night sessions at the Eel's Foot in Eastbridge, the scene of Bert's first encounter with English traditional music a year or so earlier. These priceless photos show the chairman of the evening, Philip Lumpkin, brandishing his cribbage-board gavel, 'Good order, ladies and gentlemen please!', the melodeon player Mr Button (known as 'the fiddler') playing 'Jack's the Boy' for step-dancers Percy Denny and one-eyed Syd Cook to dance a hornpipe in the narrow bar-room, Mr A. Cook singing 'The Blackbird', and a young woman, Eileen Morling, the landlady's daughter, singing what, we don't know – possibly her favourite, 'Among my Souvenirs'. The final picture is of the company standing with linked hands around a table strewn with empty glasses, faces underlit by a glass-funnelled oil-lamp, finishing the evening with 'Auld Lang Syne'.

The two Berts had opened a window onto the rural musical past for the mainly urban readers of *Picture Post*. One wonders what the readers of the day made of it? This was Bert's first published first-hand article on English folk song:

> Folk Song is quaint now. Folk Song is arty. But once this was not so. Once, the farm labourers and the weavers, the road-menders and tinsmiths who made up these songs two hundred, three hundred years ago, were the fellows who sang them. And to this day there are still places to be found where the songs and style of the old traditional singers are still kept alive by the people themselves.

The Eel's Foot is such a place. The Eel's Foot is in Eastbridge. Eastbridge is in Suffolk. Where the weather is bleak, but the beer is good. On Saturday nights in the Eel's Foot, the little barroom is too crowded to play darts. The locals sit formally round two tables and sing. They sing in turn as they are called upon by the chairman.

They sing the songs of a forgotten time – songs about highwaymen and sailing ships, about deserting soldiers and servant girls betrayed. They celebrate the victories of Nelson, and lament the defeats in the American wars. 'The Foggy Dew,' 'The Indian Lass,' 'The Blackbird,' 'Pleasant and Delightful' – these are favourites.

As each song ends the glasses are filled up again, there is a burst of chatter until the next singer is on his feet. Then the customers are called to order by the chairman, and a new song begins. Not all are folk songs. Some prefer the jaunty irrelevances of the music-hall number of fifty years ago. Some young people choose to sing the modern romantic ballads and dance tunes they hear on the radio. But the folk songs are favourites. Their passing is regretted. Seventy-six-year-old Mr 'Velvet' Brightwell, shaking his ear-rings, declared, 'I used to be reckoned a good singer before them *tunes* come in!' So song after song passes away the evening, till 'Time!' is called and 'Auld Lang Syne' breaks the party up and they file into the cold night, after an evening of traditional singing as our forefathers knew it.

Other articles that Bert wrote before joining the army were 'The Life of an East End Parson' (another Blitz story), 23 November 1940; 'Committee in Revolt' (the work of a food Price Regulation Committee), 19 July 1941; 'Parish War Cabinet' (the work of village 'invasion committees'), 16 August 1941; and 'The Most Important Lunch Party of the War' (a lunch party arranged by the Russian Ambassador, Ivan Maisky, for an array of foreign ministers, including Winston Churchill and Anthony Eden), 13 September 1941. According to Bert Hardy they were the only 'British Press boys' to be allowed in, thanks to Bert's communist contacts at the Embassy.

Earlier that year, on 22 January, the British Home Secretary, Herbert Morrison, had invoked his wartime powers of censorship, and had banned publication of the communist *Daily Worker* and Claud Cockburn's popular, if incendiary, *The Week*, which the New Zealand writer and Rhodes Scholar Dan Davin (1913–90) remembered as being a favourite read of the more left-leaning Oxford undergraduates in the Balliol Common Room in the 1930s.[1]

The *Guardian* summed up the general feelings of the rest of Fleet Street in its leader column: 'No one likes the idea of the suppression of a newspaper even during a war, and least of all the suppression of a newspaper that is the sole organ of a legal political party.' That said, the *Worker* had pushed its luck, as the *Guardian* went on to say:

Yet no one who has read the *Daily Worker* and *The Week* during the war can doubt the extreme provocation they have given ... The *Daily Worker* began the war as a supporter of resistance to Hitler; it changed its tune when it found that Stalin wanted to be friends with Hitler.

Day after day it has vilified the British Government and its leaders to the exclusion of any condemnation of Hitler. Nothing that has happened in this country has been decent and right. But the *Daily Worker* did not believe either in the war or in democracy; its only aim was to confuse and weaken. We can well spare it.

One might argue that justifiable vilification of the British Government was easy to achieve as its conduct and record throughout the 1930s was certainly not above criticism, unless one was a *Daily Mail*-reading Conservative who chose to view the poor organisation for civilian welfare in the early days of the Blitz through rose-tinted spectacles. It's surprising that Bert's few-holds-barred critical *Picture Post* coverage of the war escaped censure from a jittery government. In fact, at the outbreak of the war he had apparently been reported to the authorities for being a communist and having 'a defeatist attitude'; he was investigated by MI5 and declared 'harmless', although, as we know, this didn't save his BBC job.

The Government and the MOI had been worried from the outset of the war that there might be a popular rising by a disgruntled and disaffected working class led by the communists, and reports that the *Daily Worker* was achieving high sales figures in the shelters did nothing to assuage their fears. In 1937 the *Daily Worker* had been directed by Moscow to broaden its appeal and try and attract the 'entire working class', not just the communist faithful, and by the late 1930s it was selling 100,000 copies a day, and 150,000 on Saturdays.

The Government was also well aware, through Security Services telegram decryption, and phone and letter interception, that Britain and Empire countries had long been targets for subversion, the 'forcible destruction of the bourgeois state machine'. This priority of the Comintern, and therefore the CPGB, which took its line directly from Moscow, was only put on hold in the mid-1930s by the threat to Russia of the rise of fascism in Germany and elsewhere.

In 1940 *Picture Post* sent the two Berts up to Liverpool to do a piece on the Birkenhead-Liverpool ferry and Bert Hardy related how the pair of them were mistaken for spies: 'On the way back we were sitting next to the door of a compartment on a crowded corridor train. I asked Bert about the funny type they used in Germany, and he wrote my name and some phrase in German on the dirty steamed-up train window.' When they went into the magazine on the following Monday morning two MI5 officers were waiting for them in the editor's office. They wanted to know why they had been writing in German on the train window. Another passenger had reported the incident and they'd been tracked down through their special railway Press passes. After an awkward half hour they convinced the security officers that they were merely harmless, if bilingual, journalists.

In June 1941, when Hitler invaded the Soviet Union and the Communist International took a pro-war stance, Harry Pollitt was reinstated as General

Secretary of the CPGB. The Party began vigorously campaigning for a second front to be opened up against Hitler. In August the Ministry of Information, attempting to 'steal the thunder' of the CPGB and sabotage their efforts, opened up an Anglo-Soviet liaison section. This became a period of Russian Fever. The Russians could do no wrong. The Red Cross 'Aid to Russia' Fund was hugely supported by the British public, and Mrs Churchill, as Chairman of the Red Cross, received suitably grateful letters from their Soviet counterparts: 'We appreciate your help for our people in their fight against fascist bandits.'[2]

On Sunday 26 October 1941, Bert and Bert went up to Edinburgh for *Picture Post* to cover a council meeting, but the re-routeing of passenger trains, also frequently being shunted into sidings to let more important munitions trains get through, meant wartime rail journeys were a nightmare and consequently they arrived too late to report the meeting. So they went the couple of miles across town to the docks at Leith on the east coast for their second assignment, which was to interview the crew of the first Russian ship to dock in Britain since Russia had entered the war. The ship was expected on the Tuesday. The two Berts met up with the female interpreter they'd been given, who was supposed to understand the various dialects spoken by the seamen. But, as Bert Hardy tells it, she got 'hopelessly confused with all the dialects and in the end Bertie Lloyd was interpreting for her'.

This is one of several examples of Bert's facility with languages. Charlotte Lloyd recalled the time several years later when she accompanied Bert on a collecting trip to Romania, where the folklorist from the Bucharest Institute who was to be their guide spoke only Romanian and Italian. In a couple of days with the help of a dictionary and his schoolboy Latin Bert was conversing happily with him in Italian.

The last feature the two Berts did together before Bert Lloyd went into the army was the genuinely hazardous 'At Sea With Our War-time Trawler Men', which appeared on 21 March 1942, and for which the two journalists braved U-boats, mines and enemy aircraft for a ten-day trip to the North Atlantic fishing grounds. Bert Lloyd set the scene:

The hands that hold the wheel are square, gnarled, grimy. The palms are scarred. The nails are broken. Above each wrist, almost obliterating the tattooed protestations of True Love to this girl and that, is a ring of saltwater boils. Young deckies ashore from their first trip wear these boils proudly, as a badge, a medal, a favour. The boils show they are fishermen, and being fishermen means they don't give a damn for anybody or anything.

The man at the wheel glances at the compass above him. Then he stares straight ahead. The winter sea is a thin green. The sky is the colour of paraffin. From the wheelhouse windows he can see the for'ard well-deck, glistening wet, where they sort and gut the fish; and for'ard, on the port and starboard side, just abaft the break of the Fo'c'sle, the great hoop-shaped steel trawling gallows rear up, which take the main weight of the net as it tows.

They sailed out of the Lancashire fishing port of Fleetwood in a boat that didn't inspire confidence, as Bert Hardy recalled in his autobiography:

Before we went on board, we took the precaution of buying a lot of second-hand clothes, so our own wouldn't permanently stink of fish. The trawler itself was a tiny, dirty, stinking little tub; all the best boats had been taken over by the Navy, to be used as minesweepers. When the crew turned up they were completely pickled. Some could barely manage to stagger up the gang-plank, but soon we got out to sea.

Bert H. remembers that the sea was particularly rough that week and was amused that Bert L., who had been to sea and had been giving Bert H. advice on sea-sickness, was 'sick as a dog' while Hardy remained unaffected by the pitching and tossing of the small boat.

The same year that Bert left *Picture Post* for the army, the MOI, in a fit of political pique, withdrew their overseas subsidy of the magazine which had enabled wholesale exporters to send 10,000 copies a week to the allied forces in the Middle East. This was in response to *Picture Post* articles critical of the Government's handling of the war in North Africa. Tom Wintringham had had the temerity to ask where were the Chiefs of Staff worthy of our troops and who could outwit Rommel, the German master of desert warfare? Edward Hulton had pointed out the firepower deficiencies in the armaments of the allies. The MOI accused *Picture Post* of demoralising the troops in the Middle East, to which Hopkinson replied that they were simply stating facts that the troops themselves already knew. In response to the effective banning of *Picture Post* to the troops, the magazine urged all its readers to privately send copies to any friends and family members fighting in the desert.

With its finger on the pulse of what the ordinary man and woman in the street and barrack-room was thinking and feeling, and the courage to campaign on their behalf, combined with world-class photography, excellent writing, and thoughtful, amusing, quirky, and always interesting articles on every aspect of life in Britain and abroad, *Picture Post* became as much an institution as a magazine. It was an essential part of the British way of life during the war years and into the 1950s. It helped get people through the Blitz and the dark days of the war and looked forward to the founding of a welfare state fit for those in the services and at home who had pulled together against the odds and defeated Fascism.

THE LONG AND THE SHORT AND THE TALL

> Little Imber on the Downe,
> Seven miles from any Towne
> Sheep bleats the unly sound,
> Life twer sweet with ne'er a vrown
> Oh let us bide on Imber Downe.
> (A early paean to the bucolic life on Salisbury Plain – anonymous)

Although not great poetry, the above lines pretty accurately summed up life in the village of Imber for a few hundred years up to the twentieth century. It had all changed by the 1940s when there were army garrisons all over the area, and thousands of troops regularly used the Plain for exercises, manoeuvres and tank and gunnery practice in preparation for the liberation of Europe.

On Monday 13 April 1942, on the Imber Ranges, a demonstration was organised by V Corps to show the effect of a low-level aircraft attack on motorised columns of troop carriers and other vehicles. Unfortunately, it all went horribly wrong and did, indeed, show the carnage that such an attack could wreak. According to a report in a diary in the Bovington Tank Museum: 'One of the pilots mistook his target and fired into the assembled spectators causing a large number of casualties (some 25 killed and 50/60 wounded). The resources of the Garrison and the civil authorities of Warminster in the way of ambulances, stretchers etc., were rushed to the scene without delay.'

Bert, whose barracks were opposite the Southern Command Military Hospital, saw the results of the 'friendly fire' accident being brought in and reported a more serious version of the incident in a letter to Norma the following day:

Tuesday 14 April,
Darling lovely wife, I see the High Command have issued a kind of communiqué about what I was going to tell you yesterday and didn't. So I can tell you now what happened. Some outfit was on manoeuvres near here – tanks, troop-carriers, etc. – a plane swooped down on a convoy of troop carriers and opened fire on them with all its eight guns. By some mistake it was firing live ammunition. The Southern Command Hospital is just over the road from our barrack-room. They had ambulances and lorries arriving all day yesterday with the wounded. They brought the dead, too, for laying out. There were 64 killed altogether, 28 of them being spectators, officers mostly (including a Brigadier). The spectators were the men whose names were in the paper.
Somebody will get into trouble, because so many officers were knocked off. I suppose it will be the RAF armourer who is supposed to examine all the ammunition before it is loaded.

Bert then goes on to thank Norma for the delicious cakes that she and Jenny had baked and sent him. He promised to return the cake-tin at the first opportunity.

With potential death around the next corner wartime soldiers have to live in the moment, otherwise they wouldn't be able to cope. Barrack-room black humour is one way to cope with the stress. As we see in the unintentional humour of Bert's story of a squadron suicide:

I think I told you most of my 'news' on the phone. The cross-country run. The Empire Rifle-test. Oh yes. Something I forgot. One of our fellows shot himself last night. Unless somebody shot him – it isn't clear. He isn't dead yet, but is not expected to live. Did I tell you about him? He comes from Cardiff; is about 23; used to work at sea as a cook; told me he was fed up and intended to desert; worked in the storeroom where (among other things) the revolvers are kept. About 7.30 last night he was found shot through the heart with a pistol by him. There are innumerable theories as to who shot him. I should think he shot himself. His name is Nakimura. People here are rather fed up about it because it leaves the squadron without a goal-keeper!

Bert enlisted on 19 March 1942,[3] the same week that the North Sea trawler article appeared in *Picture Post*. He went into the 60th Training Regiment, Royal Armoured Corps (RAC), which was based at Tidworth camp in Hampshire, on the eastern edge of Salisbury Plain. On arrival he was kitted out, inoculated, his already receding hair cut, and he was asked for his religion. The limited army options were Church of England or Catholic. I'm not sure what an army clerk would have made of atheist. 'Atheist? C of E atheist or Catholic atheist?'

His initial six-week basic training was the same as for all recruits in the British Army regardless of the fighting unit in which they ended up. It was designed to produce 'fit and hard' troops who knew how to obey an order (ideally blindly) and involved log-lifting, vaulting, rope-climbing, wall-climbing and ten-mile cross country runs before breakfast, plus hours of marching and parade-ground drill. This gruelling physical regime would have been less hard on Bert, with his years in the Australian outback and the Antarctic, than on the many recruits from more sedentary backgrounds. He looks tough and well in his army photographs and played football for his squadron: 'I am playing football for the squad tonight. Football here is very good. Two English and one Scottish international are in the regimental team.'

Despite throwing himself into the life of the regiment, and assiduously attending lectures and practical sessions in his determination to 'be a good soldier', he was not impressed with all the army 'nonsense' as he told Norma a couple of months after joining up:

I find there is just as much nonsense about the R.A.C. as there is about other regiments, e.g. you are issued with boots which have a terrific grain in them. But they insist that you polish your toecaps with a toothbrush handle till the grain is rubbed out and the toecaps are smooth. Of course it takes hours and hours. Luckily we have a defrocked priest among us – at least, a bloke who went through the OCTU [Officer Cadet Training Unit] early in the war and then got kicked out. He showed us how to smooth our boots out with a hot spoon handle. The results are terrific. We are the smartest squad among the newcomers.

We get up at 6, parade at 6.15. Knock off about 4.30. But after we knock off there is an enormous amount of equipment to clean and blanco. We also have to fold our blankets in a very fancy way, and lay out our beds most elaborately. It's all a relic of the old cavalry days. A lot of the NCOs still carry riding whips. The Regimental Sergeant Major gave us a talk, 'What you're here to learn is to kill and not be killed'.

After basic training, and having received the coveted RAC black beret with its mailed-fist cap-badge, he began a three-week advanced course involving driving various vehicles ('I can already drive Bedford lorries – 3 lessons – and have to go out on the road in convoy next week'), wireless operation and his first introduction to a tank. The Royal Armoured Corps was formed in April 1939 by amalgamating the Royal Tank Regiment with various cavalry regiments. Apart from adding some 'dash and verve' to the Tank Regiment, cavalry terminology was also carried over; Bert was a trooper instead of a private, and he and his crew didn't just 'get into their tanks' they 'mounted' them. And, as Bert said in his letter, some of the NCOs still carried riding crops! The three primary tasks of a tank crew were to drive the engine, operate the wireless and fire the gun, and each trooper was trained in at least two of these skills. Gunners were either gunner-mechanics or, like Bert, gunner-wireless operators, the wireless part of which he found 'deeply, deeply boring' and not as enjoyable as his gunnery training.

Frank Owen, a fellow trooper and friend of Bert's, and a brilliant newspaper-man, who before joining up had been the acclaimed editor of Lord Beaverbrook's *Evening Standard*, detailed the work of a 'tankie' in *The Royal Armoured Corps,* published in 1945:

> For the tank driver to drive his 30-ton monster up and down hillsides, through woods and streams, across sand, bogs and beaches, calls for strength and stamina as well as skill. It calls for something, too, from the gunner to squat for hours on end with his forehead glued to a rubber brow-pad and his eye glued to the rubber eyepiece of his telescope, with one hand working the power traverse which rotates the turret, with the other keeping a 6-pounder or 75-mm gun laid on a target from a swaying, jolting gun platform. As for the loader, who is usually the wireless operator, he requires all the concentration he can muster to stand up in a space just big enough for a man to squeeze into, and to fling shells into the breech with the mechanical precision and repetition of a piston. No, the tank is not a Rest Home.

In the event of the crew of a disabled tank having to fight its way on foot across a battlefield, they were also trained in field-craft, unarmed combat and infantry assault drill. This necessitated Bert becoming an expert in the use of all the weaponry carried in a tank, which included the Ack-Ack, Bren and Vickers K guns, Tommy gun, .22 rifle and his official personal weapon, the service revolver. In the light of this it's not as surprising as editor Tom Hopkinson thought when, at a *Picture Post* editorial meeting in September 1949, Bert evinced an interest in and knowledge of the Colt 45, the Westerner's favourite revolver. He subsequently wrote a colourful potted history of the

Wild West to go with the set of cowboy photographs that Hopkinson had brought to the table.

Bert had to learn to dismantle and re-assemble his guns blindfolded. He explained the reason for this to Norma:

> The idea of stripping the gun blindfolded isn't really as silly as it seems. With the turret closed the inside of a tank is pretty dark and you may have to take your gun to bits in the middle of a battle in a hurry. Both Bainwell and Brooke (the Sadler's Wells chorus singer you saw on the escalator) are both in my class. Poor Brookes can't make head or tail of it. The mechanism part of it, that is. Whenever the sergeant asks him a question Brooke shakes his head in despair and says 'I don't know, kid.' Which rather rattles the sergeant who isn't used to being called kid by anyone.

Tank gunnery practice was initially conducted indoors, where Bert 'fired' a laser-like beam of light from a mock-up gun turret onto a painted landscape cyclorama. He next advanced to shooting pellets from an air-rifle fixed above the barrel of a gun at a three- dimensional landscape on which target model tanks were moved by electrically operated wires. Finally, he was let loose with live shells. For live firing, the trainee gunners were often taken to the coast to fire safely out to sea at floating targets.

As well as Tidworth, where Bert spent his first three months in the army, and from where tank crews got the opportunity to career all over Salisbury Plain on day and night manoeuvres, he also went to South Wales where firing platforms were set up on the cliffs. He travelled down through Gloucester and Cardiff to Newton Camp on the Castlemartin Peninsular in Pembrokeshire. Newton Camp was just a collection of Nissen huts on the cliffs near the famous lily pools and the small chapel of St Gowens. It was a beautiful spot where Bert could pick cliff-top flowers and send them back to Norma carefully folded into his letters. It was also popular with the men because of the abundance of rabbits, which they caught to supplement their army rations.

Less idyllic was the huge Catterick Camp a few miles out of Richmond in North Yorkshire, the grimness of which was relieved by the occasional trip out to the coast at Hornsea where he attempted to hit moving targets towed behind boats. He also passed a few hours in the smoky, irreverent, atmosphere of the cinema: 'I have just come from the cinema – it wasn't much, Deanna Durbin in *Nice Girl?* Deanna has a young schoolgirl sister who was always on heat. Whenever she came prancing in, the licentious soldiery would shout 'Here comes electric arse!' It ended with Miss Durbin surrounded by sixpenny Union Jacks, singing "There'll Always be an England." The face was on the screen but you couldn't hear the song for raspberries.'

Catterick was reckoned by many soldiers to be the 'most miserable place on earth':

> We arrived at Catterick looking like colliers (the coaches were filthy and there was no water … Had to get up at 5.30, train from Tidworth about

8 arrived Catterick 10.30 at night then march 3 miles to camp. Spent till about 1.30 finding blankets, a bed, clearing our kitbags. Then we had to be up again at 6. It doesn't look as if we'll be able to get papers (newspapers) here. But I'll respond on that a little later when I'm more sure.

During his time at Tidworth Bert collected at least four songs, all amatory, typescripts of which are in the A.L. Lloyd Archive at Goldsmiths College, 'The Chiefest Grain' and the text of 'Lovely Joan' (from S. Harrison, Tidworth, 1943), 'Thame Fair' (from Harry Barclay, Tidworth, 1943), and 'Nottingham Fair' (from Trooper Wood, RAC Tidworth, April 1942):

> As I was a-walking to Nottingham Fair,
> I saw a fair damsel all on a grey mare,
> With her arse painted blue and a bull on her back
> And a bundle of fodder was stuck in her crack.
>
> The mare threw this damsel right off in the ditch,
> And I out with my prick and I mounted the bitch,
> But she drew back her foot and kicked me in the shin
> And before I got in her I was off her again.
>
> Well, there was the king and the company more,
> All riding on horseback and walking before.
> A stark-naked drummer beating the drum
> With his heels in his arsehole before them did run.
>
> Along came a giant as tall as a steeple,
> Pulled out his John Thomas and pissed on the people,
> With a mouthful of mustard to keep his balls warm,
> Ten thousand got drowned before they were born.

'Nottingham Town' is a version of the well-known 'Nottamun Town' recorded by, amongst others, Fairport Convention and Shirley Collins, who learnt it from the Kentucky singer Jean Ritchie. The Ritchies have preserved much of the repertoire taken by their family from the British Isles in the eighteenth century and in September 1917 the Misses Una and Sabrina Ritchie sang the song to Cecil Sharp:

> (Verse 2)
> I rode a big horse, that was called a grey mare,
> Grey mane and grey tail, and grey stripes down his back,
> There weren't a hair on him but what was called black
>
> (Verse 4)
> I met the king and the queen and a company of men,
> A-walking behind and riding before,
> A stark naked drummer came marching along
> With his hands in his bosom always beating his drum.

Not all versions of this strange song that found their way across the Atlantic and into the mountains were sanitised. The inveterate ferreter-out of bawdry, Vance Randolph, collected in the Arkansas Ozarks several 'Nottingham Fair' texts similar to Bert's. Traditional performers seem to have been less bothered by the surreal texts attached to 'Nottamun Town', and less inclined to try to analyse them, than academics and revivalist folk singers. In fact, according to Karl Dallas, Jean Ritchie was once told by an old Kentuckian: 'If twas understood, then the good luck and the magic be lost.' Who are we to disagree?

Between tank gunnery courses and 'pumping' (as he described it) his fellow troopers for songs, Bert somehow managed to find time to get some writing done. Apart from the seemingly endless round of boot-polishing (or dubbining), blancoing, lectures, morse-code practice and trying to learn 'in three days what would take a regular three years', there was no privacy or space to write, as he regularly told Norma in his letters home, written while lying on his bunk.

In May 1942 his 'The Cowboy and his Music' appeared in *University Forward*. This was a well-known student magazine, which was mostly circulated amongst left-wing students by the University Labour Federation. Its aim was to coordinate the students' wartime activities – pushing for a Second Front etc. The article was written in Bert's barrack room in March and he says in the last paragraph, '… forced to put down pen due to loud singing of companions!' It was reprinted in *Our Time* with more musical examples in April 1943. Also in 1943 the WMA's (Workers' Music Association) *William Morris Musical Society Bulletin* printed 'The Revolutionary Origins of English Folk Song', which by 1944 was expanded into the book *The Singing Englishman*.

Through his letters one begins to understand the difficulties Bert faced when trying to write, and realise what was actually involved when he tells us that *The Singing Englishman* 'was put together mainly in barrack-rooms, away from reference-works, in between tank-gunnery courses.'

> Our barrack-room is so crowded we haven't room for a table and a couple of forms. So, once again, we have nowhere to sit, and nowhere to put things down. It makes life very complicated. …
>
> … Two maniacs are blowing 'I Don't Want to Set the World on Fire' through combs covered with toilet paper, and it's hard to think. They have just changed to Beethoven's 5th *Symphony*. It's a nightmare.

He sent regular colourful letters and postcards home to Norma, Jenny, and baby Joe, full of news and information. One might not have expected some of these to get past the censor. This is partly explained by the fact that Bert mentions going down to the Post Office to send letters and returned cake tins to Norma. If he was posting stuff through the normal civilian channels, then it could easily get by unchecked, unlike letters from soldiers serving abroad who had no option but to send their mail through the army postal service and the military censors.

As we've seen, some of Bert's friends were surprised at his relationship with Norma, whom they described variously as 'prim' and 'school-marmy'. She was not the sort of person, they felt, ideally suited to the earthy, gregarious, highly intellectual, adventurous, man-of-the-world Bert. Leslie Morton said: 'We were all very surprised when he and Norma went off. I wouldn't have expected it of Norma who was a rather down-to-earth young woman. I would have said the last person to have a romantic affair with a young man like that.'

But despite other people's reservations, and although their marriage did ultimately end disastrously, for the first few years they were obviously very much in love and shared many interests, not least literature and politics. From his whaling diary entries of 1937, where he refers to her as his sweetheart and 'my love' and puts a kiss next to the entry, through to his army letters, his writing is full of affection:

Life is very flat, stale and profitless, darling. I try hard to concentrate on learning all I can and being as good a soldier as possible. But in my heart I only want one thing, sweetheart, and that is to be home and with you and that nonsensical baby. I get very miserable without you.' ...

... Went into Darlington, it's full of civilians, and particularly of girls (quite nice girls, too). I was never so much ogled. But I stayed faithful, darling. Faithful to you and to my determination not to miss the last bus to Richmond. ...

... My sweetheart, do you ever really think about us with the war really over? I hardly ever do. But I did last night in my hard, narrow, lonely bed. Only for a short while. I soon went to sleep. But while it lasted I could hardly bear it. We'll have such a lovely time.

When, in June 1942, he was posted to Catterick Camp he also provided editorial copy for a radical services newspaper, *The Turret*. The idea for *The Turret* must have been hatched up by Bert and Frank Owen soon after Bert arrived in Catterick, because by 19 July he was complaining to Norma about still being unable to bring out *another* issue due to lack of production space. This followed two earlier letters mentioning *The Turret*. The first explained its origins:

Owen and I are running a regimental wall newspaper. It hasn't appeared yet. It is planned for the week after next and weekly from then on. About six foolscap sheets on a board. We have quite a good commercial artist to draw the headings etc. I think it would be handy if you could send me two or three *Soviet War News* a week, as there may be usable stuff in there, don't you think? I've had evening classes every evening this week. Tonight I had a class then an editorial meeting of *The Turret* which is the name of the wall newspaper.

They obviously managed to bring the first issue out before hitting the space snag: 'We are having difficulty with the Turret because we can't get a room.

Things are so much in process of construction in here that even some of the classrooms are not rooms but tents. I am impatient to bring out the next issue, but without somewhere to put it together it isn't possible.'

When they did finally get it up and running, Bert waxed enthusiastically about a poll they conducted through the paper which confirmed the poet H.B. Mallalieu's contention that they had been 'called upon to fight against something we regarded as wrong without, at the same time, having a conviction that we were defending a way of life that was right'.

> This week's number is by far the best. The poll was: Do you want a new social system after the war, or is the present one good enough? 93% of the regiment said they wanted a new system. 7% said they didn't know. Nobody said the present system would do. A copy of *The Turret* is going to the Imperial War Museum each week. It ought to shake someone there.

If Bert did indeed send copies to the War Museum they seem to have been lost. The museum was closed down for the duration of hostilities, so it's possible that the papers never got through. Whatever the reason, the Museum, despite extensive searches, has no record of *The Turret*. Neither do the Tank or Army Museums. So the nearest we can get to it are the photos that one of Bert's pals took of him working on the paper and pinning a copy up on the camp notice board (see plate 21).

Service newspapers, of which there were dozens, ranged from the well-produced, illustrated, *Picture Post*-like *Parade* to broadsides run off on duplicating machines. Whatever the size or quality, they were all avidly read by hundreds of thousands of troops with a thirst for information and entertainment and with time on their hands in transit or barrack-room, and often little or no access to ordinary newspapers. The well-known service papers such as *Union Jack*, *Crusader*, *SEAC* and *Eighth Army News*, although officially sponsored publications set up to help maintain morale in the troops, had a decidedly left-wing approach to their reportage and editorials. They adopted a populist approach in keeping with the troops' favourite national newspaper the *Daily Mirror*. Editors such as Hugh Cudlipp, Warwick Charlton and Frank Owen were determined to give their readers what they wanted, and if this meant publishing articles and letters critical of the Government and the War Office, then so be it. It was this fact that made the papers so popular with the men, who felt that the papers truly represented what they thought and were not just Government mouthpieces.[4]

British Army commanders, realising that the papers acted as a safety valve for actual or perceived grievances, defended editorial freedom. The Government didn't see it that way. Winston Churchill referred to some of the ex-*Daily Mirror* journalists who worked on the service papers as 'malignant scum' and in a letter to Brendan Bracken, the Minister for Information, suggested that he was 'underrating the troops by supposing they only like the garbage on which they are being fed'. He felt the left-wing bias of the papers undermined morale, and that they should be batting for England by promoting the Government line and waving the flag of patriotism.

Bracken felt that the dangers were being exaggerated and declared 'Few people take their opinion straight from newspapers, and I imagine that hard-bitten troops are no less self-reliant'. The argument rumbled on unresolved throughout the war. In fact Churchill was right to have been wary of the service newspapers, because the fact that they facilitated widespread discussion of current affairs and encouraged soldiers to have an opinion on the postwar shape of the world was one of the main reasons that in the 1945 election the majority of soldiers voted Labour.

The soldiers certainly had plenty to gripe about, and communists such as Bert were not slow to pick up on this and to indulge in a bit of left-wing proselytising. Of course, some political prophets were less subtle than others, as Bert found out to his dismay when he attended a communist meeting soon after arriving at Catterick:

> I am very fed-up too because on Sunday I went to a Party meeting thrown by some fellows in another RAC regiment in this camp. (Miles and miles I had to walk). It was heartbreaking. The whole meeting was dominated by a Colour Sergeant who was obviously some kind of Party religious maniac, and who spoke so energetically and so recklessly I was horrified. Most of his audience were non-Party people. Most them didn't really know what was going on. This maniac assured them all it was their solemn duty to come again next Thursday and each to bring with them 10 recruits to the Party, and so on. He also spoke most indiscreetly (he didn't know half the people at the meeting) about how he had written to Gallacher (Communist M.P.) asking for help and money! It was more than I could bear. I need hardly say he tried to browbeat all these strangers into coming to his barrack-room for another meeting that same evening. He promised them a lively time and said that often the discussions went on long after midnight. After he had gone we managed to get the proceedings on to a more earthly plane and I suggested we should have an inter-regimental debate, in a large hall, on the Second Front. We might even be able to get the officers to collaborate. It will be difficult to get speakers against. But I can do that myself if necessary. I'm certain we could fill a big hall – we should be able to get 1000 people, I think. That sounds a lot, but this is an enormous garrison and most of the men drift around with nowhere to go. They would welcome an inter-regimental dogfight of this kind.

It's obvious from his letters that Bert certainly wasn't the only communist in the RAC although, being Bert, he was more subtle and circumspect in his proselytising than some of the others. It was also a general policy for Party members not to take their CP membership cards into the army with them. But in 1942 the Russians were still our chums and comrades could whistle the 'Internationale' with impunity, as Bert heard early one foggy morning at Catterick. He joined in but the fog was so thick that they failed to find each other, and in the end the CP whistlers went their separate ways in search of breakfast.

The 'Internationale' had been adopted as its national anthem by the newly formed Union of Soviet Socialist Republics in 1922, so when the USSR was forced into the war on the allies' side, many people on the left waited with interest to see if the BBC would include the anthem of international revolutionary socialism in its popular Sunday evening wartime radio programme *The National Anthems of the Allies*. They waited in vain. This was obviously a step too far: shortly afterwards the programme was taken off the air.

According to sources in the National Army Museum Archives: 'Early on in the war the War Office made arrangements for recording the qualifications on any person called up for military service so they could be posted wherever they could be most usefully employed.' Bert's qualifications would have been noted as writing, journalism and languages, and exactly a year after joining the RAC, he was plucked out of the regiment, put on reserve, and seconded to the Ministry of Information to work as a journalist on the Russian language magazine *The British Ally*.

He had spent a year preparing to go into battle in what most tank crews thought of as claustrophobic coffins. Stuck inside a metal box, with the turret closed, surrounded by ammunition, the chance of getting out alive if hit by an armour-piercing shell was very low. There were few sights guaranteed to chill a trooper's heart more than burnt-out battlefield tanks. Bert was lucky to have been seconded to the MOI before having to fire his 6-pounder gun in anger in the deserts of North Africa or some French village. Although, had he done so, he would have performed his job conscientiously along with the millions of other ordinary men and women, on all sides, who put their lives on hold for the duration of the war and performed unimaginable feats of bravery and endurance.

8
The Singing Englishman

Folklore forms don't depend on their original environment for their continued existence; sailing ships are gone but the sea shanty is still sung: the function is altered but the song remains. The stuff is transcultural.

Bert Lloyd

The Singing Englishman, published in 1944, was a commendable achievement. Since there was no folk revival scene as such in 1944 it planted musical seeds that would flower in the 1950s. The WMA commissioned it as No. 4 in their Keynote Series of Music Books, and followed *Twenty Soviet Composers* (Rena Molsenco), *Background of the Blues* (Iain Lang) and *Music and Society* (Elie Siegmeister). In the preface to his later *Folk Song in England* (1967) Bert explained how he had first come to dip his toe into the piranha-infested waters of folk song scholarship back in 1944:

> In America, late in the Depression and early in the War years, traditional song and its topical imitations were coming into vogue, particularly among young radicals, as a consequence of the stresses of the time, and the rumble of newly-found or newly-made 'people's songs' was rolling towards us across the Atlantic. The Workers' Music Association sensed that similar enthusiasm might spread in England, and they were eager to help in the re-discovery of our own lower-class tradition.

So they commissioned Bert to write a 'social-historical' introduction to folk song. The modest, pocket-sized, seventy-two-page, green paperback, priced at a shilling, had an impact beyond anything that Bert or the WMA would have imagined, but, as Bert pointed out, there was nothing else like it: 'It wasn't a good book, but people were kind to it perhaps because it was the only one of its sort: like the okapi, not much to look at but cherished as unique.'

Bert's book was a far racier, if politically subjective, introduction to folk music than Cecil Sharp's *English Folk Song: Some Conclusions* (1907), or Frank Kidson and Mary Neal's *English Folk-Song and Dance* (1915). Despite its faults, it's a good read; a very personal, enthusiastic work. Following in the tradition of A.L. Morton's *A People's History of England* and preceding by a year George Thomson's *Marxism and Poetry* (Thomson had read Bert's book), it was an attempt to redress the balance after decades of what Bert saw as middle-class folk song appropriation.

In his foreword Bert admits that it's 'sketchy', but believed it would 'help fill a gap until the real thing comes along'. It did just that, and for many postwar folk-revival singers and enthusiasts who hadn't actually seen a copy it acquired a reputation of mythic proportions. It is unavoidably polemical. Bert was a hard-line communist and the book was commissioned and published by the music wing of the CPGB, so it was hardly going to be a panegyric for capitalism. Bert once explained in an interview (*Folk Review* September 1974) why he thought Marxism relevant to folk music:

> Marx and many of his followers were very perceptive analysers of the movement of history and of society within history, and since folk songs are very closely bound up with the history of the underdogs, then Marxist applications are particularly valuable in arriving at how and why lower class society has changed in history and why the song styles have changed with these social changes.

The Marxist historian and sometime mentor to Bert, Leslie Morton, thought *The Singing Englishman* had: '... a sparkle and spontaneity and a boldness of attack which make it a model for the application of Marxist ways of thinking to cultural questions. It looks squarely at folk song as music and poetry, the peak of the cultural achievement of the English lower classes.'

It has become fashionable in academic folk music circles to subject Bert's folk song writing to critical reading, and there's no doubt that a certain amount of *The Singing Englishman,* doesn't stand up to scrutiny in the light of current knowledge. But it would be remarkable if it did. One would hope that over fifty years we have advanced in our researches and understanding of folk song. Virtually single-handed (well, with a little help from his friends) he, and they, wrested English folk song from the control of, as he would see it, the bourgeoisie – the conventional, conservative, middle-class that had appropriated it, emasculated it, and laid down their own rules for its definition, performance and dissemination through the auspices of the English Folk Dance and Song Society.

With notable exceptions, such as the 'Hammer-man' poet and song collector Alfred Williams, who generally collected what the people sang rather than what he wished them to sing, and Percy Grainger, whose early attempt at putting folk song study on a more scientific footing was seen by the Folk Song Society as more contentious than constructive, the cosy folk song world was due for a shake-up. So if Bert, in his enthusiasm to reclaim folk song for the working classes, made some unwarranted assumptions, and sometimes followed his heart rather than his head, perhaps we should cut him a bit of slack.

Ultimately, of course, in rescuing folk song from the bourgeoisie, Bert, MacColl, and others tried to impose their own ideas on the music and developed their own rules of performance, definition and historical relevance, and were not averse to bending the evidence to fit their vision of what a proletarian music should be. And if the proletariat didn't know what was good for them, it was okay because Bert and the rest could tell them, or in Bert's case 'show' them by example and the feeding of material. In MacColl's case it was more blatant; you did what he said or you were beyond the pale. The two men who were so influential in the development of the folk revival couldn't have been more different in their methods of attaining the same goal. The singer Louis Killen neatly summed up their differences when he said that whereas MacColl would bludgeon you to death, Bert was more of a stiletto man.

By the time he came to write *Folk Song in England* twenty years later, although no less political in its overall vision, Bert had dropped some of the specific statements and ideas that modern critics dispute in the *The Singing Englishman*. For instance, Bert's original unsupported claim that the 'Cutty Wren' was a fourteenth-century revolutionary song with its origins in the Peasants' Revolt (the 'Tyrant Wren' being symbolic of baronial property which, come the revolution, would be distributed to the poor), isn't mentioned. Also, his earlier enthusiastic references to a supposed politically subversive pan-European witch cult, organised into cells or covens, which were 'of course, wildly persecuted and had to work as strictly undercover groups', have gone.

Although generally discredited nowadays, that was the thinking in the 1930s and 1940s when everyone, including Bert, was seduced by Margaret Murray and her persuasive witchcraft studies *The Witch Cult in Western Europe* (1921) and *The God of the Witches* (1931), in which she posited a Neolithic nature religion that survived as an underground cult until at least the eighteenth century. Both books were bestsellers in the 1940s at the time that Bert was writing his own book. He had obviously read them and became quite excited with the idea of the witchcraft groups. Like Bert, Murray was out to find evidence that supported her theories. Many present-day followers of the Wiccan religion and other Neo-pagans are loath to drop Murray's exotic ideas, and her books are still considered essential reading for many in the modern pagan revival.

The assiduous folk music scholar Georgina Boyes, in her article *The Singing Englishman: An Introduction and Commentary*, asks, quite legitimately, why *The Singing Englishman* was ever regarded as influential and important: 'Even with generous allowance for over half a century of developing practice and research, its combination of doctrinaire political commentary and unsubstantiated historical generalisations make the book a problematic read. We tend to prefer our politics more subtly argued and sources transparently presented now.'

A problematic read? Well, yes, it is unless you simply accept that much of the earlier part of the book from the Dark Ages through to the end of feudalism is often romantic wishful thinking, and assumptions based on scant historical evidence. 'It [folk song] grew up with a class just establishing itself in society with sticks, if necessary, and rusty swords and bows discoloured with smoke and age.' The Saxon minstrels may well have been generally unemployed and forced to ramble around the countryside after the 'Norman's piled out of their assault craft on to the Sussex beaches'. And many of them were, no doubt, 'fine honest and talented men and in a bad business'. Bert acknowledges that 'by and large we know really very little about the folk music of this time' (i.e. the Middle Ages), but that didn't stop him from imagining.

He's on somewhat safer ground historically when he reaches the better-documented eighteenth and nineteenth centuries (poaching songs, sea songs, etc.). Although, influenced by Leslie Morton, he invariably puts a Marxist spin on the relationship between folk song and society – a small cry for the common 'man': invariably 'man'. And that's another thing he's been accused of – sexism. Yet Bert was merely typical of many, if not most, men in the 1940s, especially working-class men. It was to be another few years before Simone de Beauvoir stood up and declared: 'This has always been a man's world, and none of the reasons that have been offered in explanation have seemed adequate.'

The main areas of unease are not the romantic historical fantasies, but Bert's consistent affirmation of certain folk song 'facts' which simply don't stand up to even perfunctory examination such as: 'But the singer's feeling that this glamorised version of life is not real is nearly always underlined by the astonishing melancholy of the tunes. Even songs with the happiest words commonly have tunes full of sadness and pathetic longing.'

'... [A]nd incest, a common subject [in folk song].'

'When you hear folk songs of any period, behind all the recitals of love and anger ... the beauty of a country spring and the bitterness of country labour, if you listen there is something more, a deep longing for a better life, a longing that shows itself by plaintive turns of speech and by the melancholy of even the most idyllic tunes.'

Really? From the enormous corpus of songs and tunes available you could pick out countless pieces that suggest the complete opposite. If you pick the 'right' songs and tunes you can construct a folk song picture that proves almost any point of view. However, we mustn't forget that despite Bert's enthusiasm for the subject he was still learning, listening and reading. This is really a work in progress. Over the next few years he would have the chance to study many thousands more songs.

There's little point in trying to interpret the book in the light of current knowledge, attitudes and sensitivities. In the 1930s and 1940s, politics (and the sexes) were more polarised. Bert and those many intellectuals and artists on the left were engaged in a life or death battle with the 'dark forces' of fascism. The fact that they didn't apprehend the equally dark forces of Stalinism might make them gullible but doesn't diminish their essentially good intentions. Bert, as a Marxist and a communist, along with members of the Historians Group of the CPGB – Leslie Morton, Christopher Hill, Eric Hobsbawm – was attempting to bring about a revolution in historical interpretation. After millennia of history from above, they were looking at history from below, offering ordinary people a voice, and giving their opinions, their courage and their musical achievements, the credit so long denied them. Yes, Bert's standards of academic rigour in *The Singing Englishman* leave a lot to be desired but he wasn't an academic: he was a good journalist who could put across a story, and he put this story together under difficult conditions, in the middle of a war, off the top of his head.

As he also admitted in the foreword 'I know there are people better qualified than I am to write a book of this kind. But they do not do so.' Bert did, and it's not too strong to say that it's largely because Bert wrote *The Singing Englishman* at that critical time and nudged open the folkloric floodgates that the folk revival developed in the way it did. It gave today's academics – such as Boyes, with all the modern research tools at their fingertips – the opportunity to study the music in depth and to re-assess and build on the work of the pioneers such as Bert.

This work was regarded as influential and important because, for all its faults, it was a breath of fresh air. It was exciting and it was written in a popular style. Even if they didn't all go along with the polemic, the readers felt that these 'folk' songs were songs with roots, sung for sustenance and pleasure over the generations. It was romantic. It was a revelation, and for some, but by no any means all, political. But the main thing about these 'folk' songs – original traditional songs and ballads, adaptations and rewrites by Bert, and new and old songs by MacColl and others – was that they expressed many common experiences, thoughts and fears, they were peopled by interesting characters, they were great to sing and they brought people together.

However bizarre might be the idea of fifty people in an upstairs room in Nuneaton bellowing out sea shanties, they were, undoubtedly, fun, and every man and woman in the audience could be a romantic Jack Tar or a quick-witted sailor-town doxie without having to brave Cape Horn, eat weevily biscuits or catch the clap. There were as many motivations for singing folk songs as there were people singing them. Despite Bert and MacColl's attempts at stage-managing the revival, folk music soon meant whatever you wanted it to mean. It was endlessly adaptable and virtually indestructible.

Audiences eventually developed for every aspect of folk music. There were people singing in 'mummerset' accents with hands clasped to their ears. There were cowboys from Glasgow and Essex. There were music-hall exponents from Birmingham. There were professional Geordies, one of whom, famously, came down to London and sat under a grand piano to sing his songs because 'it felt like he was back doon the pit'. There were comedians – many of whom left to make careers in television. There were cockney singers, blues singers. There were shanty men who'd never left dry land. There were left-wing social commentators (right-wing ones were noticeably conspicuous by their absence). There were navel-gazing singer-songwriters crouched over guitars being paid for conducting their own psychotherapy in public. There were fashion victims in the best or worst that Carnaby Street could offer. There were 'farm labourers' from grammar schools all over the country, in Union shirts and neckerchiefs. There were pre-Raphaelite girls with long braided-hair in flowing, flowery frocks, others in hot-pants and tight t-shirts ('tit-hawkers' as MacColl called them). There were faded-denim-clad guitar and banjo-toting 'Dharma bums' hitching between Soho, Paris, and the south of France. There were Stetson-wearing bluegrassers from Sevenoaks. There were skifflers playing beyond their time in a Brave New World that had discovered a fourth chord, and there were many, many more, and what they all had in common, in fact often the only thing they had in common, was that they were enjoying themselves making music, and bringing pleasure to thousands of people every night of the week all over the British Isles, and throughout the summer at festivals. Remarkably they are still doing it.

So Bert and MacColl might not have achieved the political revolution they set out to achieve (the folk revival got away from them), and *The Singing Englishman* may be open to justifiable criticism, but they were, along with others, responsible for opening people's eyes and ears and the bringing of pleasure to countless people over the years. Leave all the analysing to modern academics who frequently write about folk culture in a language that makes anything pertinent that they might have to say completely beyond the reach of the 'folk', about whom they are so interested. That's a mistake that Bert never made; he always wrote in plain English, sometimes, admittedly, a little colourfully, for everyone to understand. He wanted to communicate. He had a story to tell which he thought was important.

That's why the *Singing Englishman* (like its later incarnation *Folk Song in England*) was a groundbreaking, if flawed, work, and the folk revival would be a lesser place without it.

THE BLOOMSBURY LIGHTHOUSE

On 16 March 1943, exactly a year after he enlisted, Bert was seconded to the Ministry of Information working for Peter Smollett in the Russian Liaison Department in Senate House, the University of London tower block in Malet Street, on the Russian language magazine *Britanski Soyuznik* (*The British Ally*). He stayed there until the end of the war.

Bert worked alongside writer and editor John Lehmann who had published some of Bert's Spanish poems in *New Writing* in 1937 and in *Poems for Spain* (1939). Lehmann mentioned the magazine in his autobiography, *I Am My Brother*:

> The Ministry of Information arranged for me to do much the same kind of work (he had been submitting monthly 5000 word articles to the Russian literary magazine *Internationalnaya Literatura* on the British literary scene) for *Britanski Soyuznik*, the British propaganda newspaper which the Russians allowed us to publish over there, and which had a phenomenal success: its circulation was severely restricted by a meagre paper ration, but copies changed hands on the black market at high prices.

Graham Greene, who also worked in the building ('in a silly useless job'), described in his *Ways of Escape* the imposing white tower of Senate House as a beacon that guided German bombers to King's Cross and St Pancras railway stations. He nicknamed it the 'Bloomsbury Lighthouse' due to the regular breaking of the blackout regulations. Also working in the 'Lighthouse' was an acquaintance of Bert's from the *Left Review* days, the poet C. Day Lewis. He had joined the Publications Division as an editor in 1941, along with the writer Laurie Lee. Later in the war when the MOI moved to the less conspicuous Russell Square House, Lee had the occasional unenviable job of 'spotter' for incoming German V1 and V2 rockets. This entailed crawling out of his office window and perching precariously on the ledge with a pair of binoculars and a police whistle which he blew vigorously if a rocket headed in their direction, warning the staff to take cover on the other side of the building. They lost plenty of windows from nearby blasts but escaped a direct hit. George Orwell, for whom Bert had no love, based the Ministry of Truth in his *1984* nightmare vision of a totalitarian Britain on Senate House.

The MOI had been formed on 4 September 1939, the day after war was declared, and was responsible for news and press censorship, home publicity and overseas publicity in Allied and neutral countries. Initially, at least, the Ministry of Information became, according to Norman Longmate in *How We Lived Then*, 'the first great national joke of the war'. Much to the embarrassment of the sixteen professional journalists employed by the Ministry, the other 983 Ministry staff with their mishandling of information, obfuscation and petty bureaucracy soon earned the Ministry such derisive titles as the Mystery of Information and the Ministry of Malformation. It also provided wartime comedians with gags like the one about the woman who, misunderstanding the Ministry title, rang up asking for directions to Clapham Common, only to be told that they didn't know the way, and even if they did they couldn't possibly tell her.

The MOI thinking on the complex situation of being allied to the Russians and a political system of which they were frightened but could not afford at this point in the war to criticise, was to simply point up all the advantages, such as they were, of the British democratic way of life.

In September 1941 the Director General of the MOI, Walter Monckton, wrote to Brendan Bracken, who had been appointed as Minister in charge of pro-Soviet propaganda:

> I do not think that we ought to hesitate to emphasise in our propaganda the divergence between our own political conception and communism any more than we ought to let the Communist Party in this country take credit for the help which the Russian defence is giving us. The CPGB did not support our war; they only support our war effort now because we are fighting the same enemy as the Soviets in whose war they do believe. But I think it would be a mistake to make our main-effort criticism destructive of the Soviet ideology. It would be better to throw up in positive contrast the enduring value of our own democratic way of political life.

This was the work on which Bert was engaged on *Britanski Soyuznik*. Although there can be certain advantages in a poacher turning gamekeeper, I'm not sure if that was how the MOI saw Bert's role. It's probably not how Bert would have described it, but promoting British democracy in the communist USSR does seem to present a conflict of interests for a hard-line communist such as Bert.

By the time he joined the ranks of the MOI writers (dubbed by Andrew Sinclair in *War Like a Wasp* the 'shysters and half-poets in London grovelling around the Ministry of Information') the department had got its act together, and *Britanski Soyuznik* became a great success. It was more of a success than the British Government ever realised, and more of a success than the Russians had ever visualised, and it presented them with serious propaganda problems.[1]

Following the signing of the British–Soviet Treaty in 1942, it had been decided that the MOI should produce something to encourage mutual understanding between the new allies and they came up with *Britanski Soyuznik* a well-written, well-illustrated magazine that promoted British culture and achievements. It was put together in London and published by the British Embassy in Moscow. Bert was in a position to commission work from his Party friends, as Leslie Morton related:

> I didn't see him but he got in touch and I wrote some articles for him for the *British Ally*. It was published in Russian for the Soviet Union. I'm sure Bert spoke Russian then. It was a kind of magazine journal with considerable cultural character. And there was a digest called the *British Chronicle*. I did a couple of articles on Jonathan Swift, and one on E.M. Forster's *A Passage to India*.[2]

With its first rate informative articles on science and technology, art and literature, military matters and industry, and the war effort, it soon became essential reading for not just the Russian elite (for whom it was originally intended), but Russians from all walks of life hungry for information of the outside world. The subscriptions came pouring in from all over the Soviet Union. At one time its circulation was around 50,000, with 7,000 of those going to the Red Army. Of course the magazine was passed from hand to hand so the readership was far greater than the number of magazines sold, and its influence was considerable. This subtle propaganda worried the Russian security services because they felt it gave an impression that Britain was better off, and was putting more into the war effort than Russia. However, the people's commissariat of foreign affairs thought that any attempt to stifle the magazine would be politically unacceptable at that stage in the war when Britain, the USSR and the USA needed each other and were all outwardly getting on so well.

There was talk at one time of the Russians producing their own version of a *British Ally*-type magazine in which they could put their own spin on life outside the USSR, but nothing came of it. By the end of the war, the magazine was an unwelcome propaganda guest in the country and it was widely believed by the Russians to be a cover for espionage activities. This was compounded by the fact that once the war was over the magazine put more emphasis on articles extolling the virtues and democratic advantages of everyday life in postwar Britain, not what the Russian state wanted its people to read. The propaganda department of the Central Committee cut down the allowed numbers of subscriptions, particularly to the Red Army where only high-up officials (who could presumably be trusted to remain uncontaminated) were allowed to read it. Word was put out in official articles and in behind-the-scenes chats to warn people off reading material deemed politically harmful.

As the Cold War grew ever frostier the *British Ally* finally disappeared from sight. But by then Bert was long gone, was widowed, remarried, and was travelling the world with a fist full of airline tickets and an expense account as a *Picture Post* roving journalist.

RETURN TO *PICTURE POST*

When the sun is in, the West of Donegal is a grey, uneven land of rains and mist. When the sun is out the rocks turn purple and the delicate oat-fields come to life, and the country shines like the rainbow-world of an Irish tale. Then the sun hides again, the fields turn dark, and what you see is the wet stones and the black bog and the cottages huddled behind hillocks, their roofs lashed down by ropes against the screaming wind.

Life hereabouts is like that, too – a day of hard work and grinding poverty: a brief escape of an evening into the coloured land of fairy-tales: and then, the grey old round again … .

Walk through Teelin of a winter night, and you will pass one dark cottage after another, because everyone is gathered into two or three kitchens where some fun is afoot. Favourite at such gatherings is the shanachie, the teller of traditional fireside tales, the recounter of dreams and visions and glittering escapades.

So begins Bert's wonderfully atmospheric and folklorically important article 'The Irish Storyteller', which appeared in the March 1947 *Picture Post*. Bert and photographer Hayward Magee were documenting the end of an era of Irish oral culture, soon to be changed forever as the twentieth century increasingly impinged on the way of life and the traditions of the Gaeltacht.

Most, but not all, of the Irish traditional storytellers are old men. There are still plenty of them scattered down the west coast from Donegal to Kerry and round the bend to Cork; but nowadays, in most parts, the shanachie lacks an audience: and if he wants to keep his hand in, he must tell his tales to a stone wall as he herds his cattle, or to the tail of his cart on the road from market. Where the tradition flourishes, is in villages like Teelin, which has half a dozen skilled shanachies, all fishermen or fishermen's wives. There, on any night from September to mid-March, you are likely to find at least two kitchens where storytelling goes on for hours to an audience of perhaps a dozen, perhaps a score, of villagers … .

Nowadays, when you hear a good modern shanachie like 70-year-old Michael Heaney, of Teelin, you get an idea of what the great court storytellers of the Middle Ages must have been like … .

Heaney is probably the best storyteller in a village of storytellers. He knows many Fenian tales, and he prefers to tell them in the homes of others. But 76-year-old Mary Donnegan, always tells her tales around her own hearth. As is usual with women, she tells no hero tales ('a woman teller of Fenian tales and a crowing hen!' is proverb hereabouts). Most of her stories are rather shorter affairs, of rich and poor people, of sober fathers and wild sons, of murderers and hangmen sometimes, or of women with soft words for seals, or of fishermen and fishermen's wives and what the sea has done to them … .

Her hands flicker in the lamplight. Her pale face shines out of the obscurity of her black shawl. Her firm old voice goes on unstumbling, though her tale may have all the coloured twists and curlicues you find in Gaelic art. The audience while the tale is on, make no sound except to draw their breath at some hellish happening, or suddenly laugh at a vivid and hilarious turn off plot.

It is strange to hear these tellers, reckoned ignorant, recounting tales full of the old culture of half the races of Europe – tales with something of Boccaccio in them, or of French fable, or of the wonder-stories of Byzantium and beyond; tales with all the heights and depths to be found in Shakespeare.

If you've anything of the Irishman's quick eye for a symbol, you may see something striking in the picture of that once-glittering tapestry of Gaelic culture, long since worn threadbare and trodden underfoot, whose remnants are still displayed in the firelight by a ghostly old woman in a black shawl and muddy shoes.

He'd been back with the magazine for a year since leaving the MOI and had written around fifteen articles. Most of them had been bread-and-butter stuff, such as 'The Disney Team at Work' (23 March 1946), 'The Most Popular Girl in Britain' (22 June 1946), 'A New Opera for Glyndebourne' (13 July1946), and 'Portraits from the King's Collection' (14 December 1946). But, whether the subject matter was serious or lightweight, Bert could be relied upon to turn in a well-researched, well-written, entertaining and informative piece, as attested by Tom Hopkinson: 'Bert was in many ways a fantastic journalist, his work was, of course, coloured by his political views, and therefore there were some areas which, if one wanted to keep reasonably near the middle of the road, one would avoid having him write about. But on anything he was interested in he had a marvellous touch, and he was a marvellous researcher, too.'[3]

His earlier interest in music and art came in very useful for pieces such as the Glyndebourne spread on Benjamin Britten's *Rape of Lucretia,* in which, although praising Glyndebourne for taking the opera on the road at prices affordable to 'that section of the populace who wouldn't know a hock from a hand-saw', he couldn't resist a little dig at the moneyed classes. He described the privileged audience that attended Glyndebourne Opera House as 'ladies in evening dress and gentlemen in tails picking their way gingerly through the common crowd' at the railway station, and returning to London, their breath 'fragrant with Forster Riesling Auslese, 1934'.

As a red-blooded male who, according to Hopkinson, Doreen Rudé and Stan Kelly, was 'a ladies' man', or at least attracted the ladies, Bert no doubt enjoyed the visit to artist Norman Pett's Cotswolds studio to watch him drawing his scantily clad *Daily Mirror* cartoon heroine, Jane ('The Most Popular Girl in Britain'), from two live models – one for the legs, stockings and knickers, and another for the mop of blonde hair and the bra.

In that first year back at *Picture Post* he also spent time in Argentina for the election of Domingo Peron, husband of the people's sweetheart, Evita, with whom Bert spent a day. Charming and fascinating though Bert found her, he still labelled her husband a dictator when he got back and wrote up the article 'Argentina Votes itself a Dictator' (April 1946). Any unashamed admirer of Mussolini, even if the unions liked him and he had a charismatic wife, was not going to impress Bert. (Years later he tried, unsuccessfully as far as we know, to sell his Evita experiences to BBC radio's *Woman's Hour*.)

He also visited Czechoslovakia: 'This is an unexpected story. It is the story of the expulsion of the Sudeten Germans by the Czechs. But, in contrast to last winter's expulsions, this one is quietly and peacefully carried out. This article is the first on present-day Czechoslovakia following a visit by A.L. Lloyd, journalist, and Raymond Kleboe, cameraman.' The Germans, who had settled in the Sudetenland around the fourteenth century, had never been part of the German Reich but had lived and worked untroubled for 600 years as a Czech minority, retaining their language and customs. In the 1930s the Czech Konrad Henlein, encouraged by Hitler, formed the Sudeten Deutsche Partie with the aim of acquiring independence from Czechoslovakia and of smashing Czechoslovakia's liberal democracy. Ninety per cent of Sudeten Germans went along with Henlein and aligned themselves with the Nazis. Following Hitler's defeat the Czechs felt that they could no longer trust the Sudeten Germans and sent two and a quarter million of them to Germany.

Bert and Kleboe were given complete freedom by the Czechs to enter the deportee transit camps and interview the Germans and photograph whatever they wanted. Bert saw nothing but 'consideration being shown and a decent respect for human dignity' on the part of the Czech authorities, unlike, as he pointed out, the treatment meted out by the Sudeten Germans after Hitler's annexation of the Sudetenland:

As their train bumps on towards the Reich, the Sudetens will perhaps recall the happy days when the Jewish shop-windows went flying into smithereens and the fires in the trade-union buildings were starting up, and the folk were running about looking for someone to take a smack at, and shouting: 'We want to be home in the Reich!' Soon they will get their wish. Soon they'll be home in the Reich. Czechs see it, not as an act of revenge, but as a necessary safeguard against a repetition of betrayal.

A month later, on 7 September 1946, *Picture Post* published another Czech article 'Czechoslovakia: A Peasant's Life' in which Bert looked at the life of the rural community living in and around the little Moravian town of Straznice, 'deep down south on the Slovak border', and how they were responding to the postwar reconstruction that was taking place across Europe. 'With their old-fashioned, uneconomical strip system and their low level of agricultural mechanisation (two factors which add up to a prize waste of much-needed man-power), the Moravian-Slovak peasantry are marching out of step with the general quick industrial progress of the Republic ... if Czech agriculture is to keep up with the progress of Czech industry changes there will have to be, sure enough.'

The dichotomy here was that the old rural ways, which he saw as moribund and a barrier to economic and social progress were the basis of the way of life, unchanged over hundreds of years, which supported, and found meaning in, the traditional songs, dances, costumes, and time-hallowed traditions that he was thrilled to witness at a festival in Straznice one weekend: 'Marie Kaluzovd has visitors. Singers and dancers from nearby villages, they've come in for the local festival. They pray at the local shrine before the fun starts. Rich young brides-to-be ... come in from Knezdub, a few miles away. They're young girls hoping to marry. They bring embroidered pillows with them as an indication of their wealth.'

An old man dressed in a traditional embroidered shirt had carried his double bass miles from Cicmdny in Slovakia, to play in the dance band and perhaps win a prize for his music. 'Work is forgotten. Politics too. All they think of for the next few hours is fun and dancing and an occasional swig of wine.' In the grey reporter's notebook that he used on the trip, he jotted down some tunes which for some reason didn't end up in 'A Folk Festival in Czecho-Slovakia' his first contribution to *English Dance and Song* (1946), the magazine of the English Folk Dance and Song Society. It was exactly this sort of East European music and celebration that as a professional folklorist he would be only too happy to record and film a few years down the line as precious, unique, examples of a living traditional culture, what he called 'deep folklore', that we in the industrial west had buried beneath our factories and 'dark satanic mills'.

Tom Hopkinson, a great admirer of Bert's journalistic skills, felt that Bert Lloyd worked best with the down-to-earth cockney photographer Bert Hardy. Although Bert produced a lot of good articles with many other photographers, some of the classic *Picture Post* stories were indeed done by the two Berts, as we've already seen. On 8 January 1949 the magazine ran their feature 'Life in the Elephant'. The two Berts' first exploratory trip to the Elephant and Castle in south London was on a foggy Thursday morning, 18 November 1948. As with many of their stories, the pair had no set plan beyond doing a feature on the Elephant. They would often wander around chatting to people, getting a feel for an area, until an image or a story presented itself and sparked them off. Bert Hardy recalled how they got into the Elephant story:

We'd been up there two or three times and couldn't get going. We used to catch a tram across Blackfriars Bridge and then wander around. All we were seeing was smog and trams. One day we were walking down a dismal street of drab terraced houses and there was a young couple sitting on a doorstep, arms round each other. I said, 'D'you mind if I take a picture?' and they said, 'No.' Then a young woman from across the street called out 'How about taking a picture of me, love?' I said, 'Oh, sure, what's your name?' 'Maisie!' And I made out I'd taken one. Then I said, 'What's it like at the back of these places?' She said, 'Bleedin' awful! Come and have a look,' and led us round to a dreary old yard with washing hanging up. And then through the window I saw a young couple sitting on a settee. I said, 'What's it like inside?' Bert's keeping her talking all this time. She took us in and there was this young couple and they couldn't care less and I took a lovely picture of them. It turned out she was a young prostitute and he was a Canadian just come out of jail, and they'd been at it all night.

Maisie was also a prostitute, who met her clients in and around the Lyon's Corner House restaurant in Piccadilly. Her husband was in prison and she shared the basement flat with the other girl. It's a mark of the trust that the two Berts inspired in their contacts that they easily gained access to personal and private worlds that would have been inaccessible to most journalists. Whether it was a decrepit single-end flat in the Gorbals, in which a gas-jet had to be left on all night to deter the rats, an Arab seamen's lodging house in the toughest part of Cardiff's Tiger Bay, or a south London prostitute's sad and dingy basement, they were made unconditionally welcome and they in turn treated their informants with respect and a natural empathy.

These articles set in the poorest and most deprived areas of Britain could so easily have descended into media voyeurism but instead the two Berts found dignity, humour, generosity and humanity in the lives of these working-class people surviving at the bottom of the social heap. Maisie became their contact and guide to the Elephant. She knew the street-corner bookies, the black-marketeers, the locals in the pubs, the shopkeepers, market-traders, street urchins, housewives and hard men. They took to dropping in at her flat before the day's work and would chat while Maisie sat up in bed, holding court, a Woodbine in one hand and a cup of tea in the other.

When 'Life in the Elephant' appeared, they had produced, with Maisie's help, one of *Picture Post*'s all-time classic features: a masterly social document in word and image. The atmospheric photographs of coal heavers, costermongers, blacksmiths, Salvation Army evangelists, Jewish tailors, horse dealers, hookers, housewives, eel stalls, pubs, paupers hostels, doctors' patients, mums with kids, and a host of other resilient, humorous, friendly people getting through life as best they could, won Bert Hardy his second Encyclopaedia Britannica Photographic Award.

Also, in 1948, the two Berts were in Eire for the elections, which they assumed would be a foregone conclusion, with Eamon de Valera the only real candidate after sixteen years of ruling, hence the title of Bert's article, 'Eire Takes Hobson's Choice'. De Valera lost. Before that they'd gone to Glasgow's Gorbals district for another expose of the plight of the inner-city working classes, 'The Forgotten Gorbals' (31 January 1948): 'Book and ballet brand it as an evil quarter of Glasgow. It is indeed. Not because of the people in it. But because of the way they must live. It's high time changes were made.'

Towards the end of that year they enjoyed the fresh air and freedom of the open road through Central France to the Loire Valley for the autumn wine harvest, a trip resulting in 'A Village in France' (18 December 1948). Piling their bags into Bert Hardy's old Ford Prefect, they motored down to Paris where they stopped overnight, dining at their favourite restaurant, l'Escargot, before heading south:

> All the way down from Paris to Orleans, the country is wheat country, as flat as your hand, but not half as interesting. Beyond Orleans, you are in the heart of France. The landscape comes to life, the vegetation changes colour, the valleys are wide and easy, the earth rolls as far as the eye can see, with vineyards, vegetable plots, hunting woods, the whole Trafalgar, as the local peasants say.
>
> When we came into Mont-pres-Cambord (pop. 1,100) it was evening, and the mist was coming up. The whole village seemed to be shaking with winepresses.

Bert Lloyd had a contact in the village, and when they found him he was with a few friends in the cellar where he kept a huge barrel of his own wine. He insisted the English visitors have the first swig of the new vintage from an old battered aluminium cup, which was then passed around for everyone to drink from. The farmer and his son gave up their only bed for the two Berts, which turned out to be 'all lumpy and bumpy, and most uncomfortable'. But this was a small price to pay for the fascinating portrait of vanishing rural village life with which they came away – and, of course, the excellent local wine much of which vanished while they were there.

In the late 1940s there were still restrictions on how much money one could take abroad. It was normally £5 a day for holidaymakers but being 'press' the two Berts were allowed twice that, and as Bert Hardy recalled:

> On £10 a day we lived like millionaires. And when we got to where we were going we could telegram back for more to be sent out. We had the time of our lives. We didn't stint on the food and wine, but we did do tremendous stories. When I was with Bert we used to go out doing the stories during the day and in the evening enjoy ourselves. He was a treat to be with. We were always talking. He'd always reminisce to me. He liked good food, and he knew his wines. It was a joy to be with him.
>
> I remember when we were down in the Camargue in 1947 doing a story on the cowboys, and the Gypsy festival at Saintes-Maries-de-la-Mer, we stayed in a lovely hotel in Arles, the Julius Caesar, and used to motor across to the Camargue each day. We were having such a good time we were in no hurry to get back until Bert got a telegram from Charlotte, who was pregnant with Caroline, telling him off like mad. Telling him it was time he came home because 'your baby's about to be born'.

In fact, the message that Bert received was a bit stronger than that. Charlotte, who was a bit of a hypochondriac, telegrammed to say that she was 'dying in childbirth' and he'd better get back if he wanted to catch her still alive. The Gypsy festival, in which the figure of Black Sara was taken from the church and carried into the sea, took place on 24 May. As soon as they'd got all they needed, they threw their bags into Hardy's Prefect and 'burnt rubber' back up through France, across to Kent and up to north London. Here they found a perfectly healthy Charlotte just about to give birth in a Golders Green nursing home. Caroline was born on Tuesday, 26 May 1947: Charlotte lived to tell the tale. Bert, not wishing to let Charlotte know how worried he'd actually been, was quite casual about the whole affair, and didn't admit to the mad dash across France. It was only after Bert's death, when Bert Hardy was at Croom's Hill for the making of a Lloyd TV tribute, that Charlotte heard the true story of the Camargue trip.

The Camargue series of articles was Bert's idea. The horsemen, 'les guardians', of the Camargue, and the gauchos of Argentina held a special interest for Bert, and with whom he felt an affinity, having been a 'cowboy' himself for several years in Australia. Although the wetlands, salt-marshes and lagoons of the Camargue, with its wild white horses, fighting black bulls, mosquitoes and flamingos was far removed from the sun-baked plains of New South Wales, Bert understood the horsemen and the skills required to work cattle. That probably also partly accounted for his interest in American cowboy song and lore. That, and the fact that the cowboys produced and performed politically satisfying, working-class musical folklore.

A couple of months after returning from the Camargue, with his daughter Caroline safely born, Bert was up in Manchester documenting the 'Life of a Prison Officer' (November 1948) at Strangeways prison: 'The notion of educating men in gaol and giving them a sense of purpose is winning small success because prisons are overcrowded (so that rooms for leisure are turned into cells), and there just aren't enough prison officers to tend men outside their cells after teatime.'

The *Picture Post* team were a very close-knit group, who cared and looked out for each other. The journalists all worked together in a large open office with half a dozen desks, and everyone attended the weekly editorial meetings, from the editor down to the tea boy. It was a leftish paper, so much so that after the war Tom Hopkinson remembered saying at one editorial meeting, 'We simply must get a hundred per cent Conservative writer on the staff. We're all too left wing. We're all in agreement. We must have somebody to give the opposite point of view.'

The gregarious Bert Hardy got on well with all the journalists and enjoyed going into the office about ten o'clock (when most of them drifted in) and chatting about 'every subject under the sun.' When they weren't away on an assignment Bert Lloyd, Bert Hardy, and anyone else who was around used to lunch together. They'd catch the bus from Shoe Lane in Holborn along to Oxford Street where they'd stop off at a little sherry bar before walking up Rathbone Place, past the Wheatsheaf pub, to their regular restaurant, the Little Acropolis in Charlotte Street. Over the years, according to Hardy, the Acropolis was the scene of some 'wonderful social lunches' – with the two Berts, Lionel Birch, Edgar Ainsworth (known as 'Grumpy'; a little man who looked like one of the Seven Dwarves), Ted Castle (Assistant Editor and husband of the Labour MP Barbara Castle), Charles Fenby, Sidney 'Jayco' Jacobson (later Lord Jacobson), Anne Scott-James (who married Macdonald Hastings), June Head, Fyfe Robertson, Robert Kee, John Ormond Thomas and many more.

Generally the magazine went to press on a Monday. Three or four of the journalists and photographers (those who had a major spread in the issue), plus the editor, would spend the whole day at Sun Engraving, the printer in Watford, putting the magazine to bed, up to whatever time it took at night.

> Next morning at half-past ten the dummy would have come up to the office all pasted up, and I'd put it on the table in the conference room and the whole staff would be there, photographers, journalists even the office boy. They were all expected to bring some ideas and we'd go round in turn and say what we thought about the week's paper and talk over ideas for future editions.[4]

Another important part of the magazine was the inevitable Readers' Letters column, by which the Editor could test the pulse of the readers' opinions. Sometimes, however, if there was a shortfall of correspondence the journalists would write a few letters of their own to stimulate a response. Stan Kelly remembers Bert telling him how he would make up pseudonyms such as 'Angry Major from Bishops Stortford' on topics guaranteed to elicit a response. One of Bert's favourites, which always worked, was 'Should pets be allowed into church during service?'

By 1948 the *Picture Post* owner, Edward Hulton, had reversed his wartime flirtation with the Labour Party and the left, and wrote an article in the summer of 1948 entitled 'Why I Am Not Supporting Labour'. Now that the fascist threat was eliminated and the Cold War was under way, he turned his attention to the traditional enemy of the moneyed classes and capitalist big business, and took a strong anti-communist stance, which he felt the paper should follow. Bert became his nearest 'Red under the bed'. Hulton asked Tom Hopkinson to sack him but Hopkinson wrote back in March taking full responsibility for Bert's actions:

> I want to confirm in writing the assurance I gave you today. I fully realise that a member of our editorial staff, Lloyd, is a Communist: he has never made any secret of it. This makes it unsuitable for him to be employed on any job of a political or especially confidential character.
>
> As editor I undertake the full personal responsibility for seeing that his views do not colour work of his that we publish. Nor influence the paper's attitude in general.

It wasn't just rich capitalists who had it in for the communists: also in 1948 the Labour Prime Minister, Clement Attlee, brought the Cold War into the open when he declared the Communist Party a menace. Timothy Neat makes the point in *Hamish Henderson: A Biography* that the fact that 'a major intellectual socialist like George Orwell was involved in McCarthyite plotting in 1947/8, shows how quickly anti-communist attitudes had penetrated British, as well as American, society within three years of the end of the Second World War'. Bert had no time for Orwell, and would have had even less had he known of the list of fellow writers that Orwell prepared for Special Branch.

After having lived around north London since returning from Australia, Bert, with every expectation of remaining at *Picture Post* with a regular income, moved south of the river and bought 16 Croom's Hill, overlooking Greenwich Park. He was unaware of the Fates conspiring against him at *Picture Post* and at the BBC. However, he must have got an inkling in 1950 when Hulton ominously wrote in the magazine: 'Nearly everybody is now persuaded that the Soviet Government constitutes a grave menace, not only to peace, but to our very lives ... Although it may very well be true that the Kremlin does not desire war at this particular moment, this is merely because it is waiting, crouching, for a better opportunity to spring upon us.'

Tom Hopkinson was sacked later that year, and Bert, realising that the writing was on the wall once Hopkinson's protection was removed, resigned in sympathy with his editor and also, presumably, to pre-empt his own inevitable exit. Bert Hardy recollected the day they heard about Hopkinson's dismissal:

> Bert Lloyd and I were up in Birmingham on the 30 of October to do a story on an ordinary shop-girl. We were still looking for the ideal girl when Bert rang the office and heard the news that Tom had been sacked. 'Right, we're going back,' said Bert. We went straight back to London. He refused to work for Hulton for sacking Tom and for trying to keep a true and honest story out of the media.

The reason for Hopkinson's dismissal was that he'd attempted to publish a story on the Korean War by James Cameron and Bert Hardy which showed the Americans, our South Korean allies, and the United Nations forces in a less than flattering light. Hardy and Cameron, who had been in Korea covering the war for *Picture Post*, had sent back a picture story showing the ill treatment of political prisoners by the South Koreans, with the connivance of the Americans and the other allies:

> Jimmy Cameron and I came out of Pusan Station one day and saw a load of political prisoners crouching in the road, heads bowed, all tied together and we guessed they were being taken off probably to be executed. We ran up the road to the United Nations office to try to get them to stop it. They said it was nothing to do with them, and to go and try the Red Cross. We hurried across town to the Red Cross headquarters and they said it was a United Nations' affair. We went back and got pictures of them being loaded

onto lorries by South Korean troops to be taken off to be shot. Young boys of about fourteen and old men in their seventies. It reminded me of what I'd seen in Belsen.[5]

The powerful pictures of shaven-headed prisoners, squatting, heads bowed, awaiting their fate like so many cattle at an abattoir, were sent back to *Picture Post*, where Hopkinson hung on to them till Hardy and Cameron returned. Realising how sensitive the story would be, Hopkinson got Cameron to excise any emotive content that might leave the magazine open to the accusation of political bias or sensationalism. He even found a photograph of an American being paraded through the streets of the North Korean capital, Pyongyang, which he put in to help balance the article. The final laid-out copy was shown to Hulton who made no objections at the time. Later, however, when the magazine was actually being printed, he decided he didn't want to antagonise the Government and the Americans, so he stopped the presses and told Hopkinson to remove the Korean pages and re-make the magazine. Hopkinson took them out and held them over for a week while they had discussions.

The two Berts were wandering around London looking for a photogenic Guy Fawkes for a Bonfire Night story when they heard that Hulton had stopped the presses for the first time. Many of the staff were disturbed by the news and there were murmurings of resignation if the interference continued. Bert Lloyd was especially concerned about the political suppression. The following week, when the two Berts were scouring Birmingham for the 'typical shop-girl', they heard that Hopkinson again attempted to print the article, and again Hulton stopped him, and finally sacked him. Despite all the earlier talk of mass walkouts, only two others beside Bert actually left, fashion writer, Marjorie Becket and Derek Wragge-Morley. According to Hopkinson: 'Sounds of incessant argument raged over all the floors of our Shoe Lane offices and the sight of distracted journalists rushing across the road to the Two Brewers and tottering more slowly back attracted much interest in Fleet Street.'

In the 1977 television documentary *The Life and Death of Picture Post*, the offices were likened to an ant-heap after been kicked. Things slowly settled down with associate editor Ted Castle taking over from Hopkinson, but it was the beginning of the end for the magazine which 'just lost its sense of direction and wandered off into the fog' and finally folded in May 1957.

9
Croom's Hill

The day Bert returned from Birmingham, from where he'd phoned in his resignation to *Picture Post*, he and Charlotte sat in the stone-flagged basement kitchen at 16 Croom's Hill discussing their future late into the night. The children were ten and three and they had a large house to upkeep. It wasn't going to be easy. With so many media doors closed to known communists, or even suspected communists, during the Cold War, they decided that Bert should devote his life to folklore and make a living writing, if or when possible, for the BBC, and 'articles for this and that'.[1]

Bert's Party contacts and his facility for languages would stand him in good stead. In the early 1950s there were a number of cultural exchanges with Eastern European countries, and through his involvement with the Workers' Music Association and the International Youth Festival Movement, Bert got the chance to visit Russia, East Germany, Albania, Romania, Bulgaria and Hungary, where he researched in the folklore institutes and developed cordial working relationships with Eastern European musicologists such as the eminent Bulgarian musicologist Raina Katsarova, with whom he went on at least one collecting trip, and the Romanian Constantin Brailoiu, whom he never met, but whose work he translated. According to Charlotte these were the two musicologists who had the most influence on Bert.

Charlotte would make their clothes, and do some freelance dressmaking, and would work with Bert on translating whatever prose, poetry and plays they could get. They managed, but, according to Bert, his family 'nearly starved in the process, as I began to devote myself more to studying folk music scientifically'. Being short of money was one of the main reasons for choosing Eastern Europe as his main area of research:

Collecting folklore from strictly folklore sources is a slow business in England, and that means it's a relatively expensive business. Whereas in Eastern Europe, where the traditions are in full flower, it's very easy to descend on a group of villages and in a very short time to have recorded several hours of artistically valuable, sociologically valuable music. And so it happened for economic reasons more than anything else that much of my study of folklore has been in southeast Europe. One can work scientifically on a firmer foundation because the folklore material is less altered, less affected by town musics, and so one can get a clearer notion of the character of folklore.

The Lloyds bought their impressive four-storey Queen Anne house long before Greenwich became a fashionable place to live. Thanks to Charlotte's impeccable taste, it always looked elegant, and it only cost a few thousand pounds in the late 1940s. The old house needed a lot of renovation, which was done cheaply by a recent graduate from architectural college. Many of the big houses on Croom's Hill were requisitioned during the war and used to house refugees from north London. By the end of the war some houses were in a parlous state of disrepair and were sold quite cheaply. Even as late as 1957 when C. Day Lewis bought 6 Croom's Hill, five doors down from the Lloyds, it cost just £5,000.[2]

On seeing their home, some people assumed the Lloyds were wealthier than was the case, and were somewhat puzzled that Bert didn't lavish wine on dinner guests, not realising that the family budget rarely ran to wine. If the visitors had examined the artworks that decorated the walls they would have seen amongst the oriental paintings, from the gallery of Charlotte's ex-husband and family friend, William Ohly, others that had been cut out of magazines and carefully framed by Bert. A couple of them were genuine Henry Moores (he knew Moore well and had written on him for *Picture Post*); one of which was sold to pay for a kitchen to be put in on the ground floor when Bert became unable to go downstairs into the large basement kitchen. As Caroline remembered: 'He only made it to the new kitchen twice before he was too infirm and had to stay on one level [first floor] with the bedroom, study and bathroom. Charlotte carried the meals up to him.'

In the 1970s his office was a spacious first-floor corner room, with large un-curtained windows allowing in the maximum of light and unhindered views in all seasons across Greenwich Park, a few yards away on the other side of narrow Croom's Hill. A long shelf down one wall carried his Revox reel-to-reel tape machine, a record deck, an amplifier, neat stacks of tape boxes and a little keyboard for picking out tunes. Above it, a couple of overhead shelves were stuffed with books and more tapes. On his desk between the windows was his portable typewriter, lit at night by an anglepoise lamp. Potted plants lined the window sills and across the room next to the floor-to-ceiling run of bookshelves sat a conveniently positioned comfortable, well-worn, armchair.

The six-shelf bookcase which ran the length of the wall from the window to the door, bulged fit to bursting, with files, folders and well-thumbed books. Many of them were gifts from friends and colleagues around the world in various languages: *Zeitschrift fur Anglistik und Americanistik* by Rolf Bernst, inscribed 'To Mr A.L. Lloyd with my best compliments of the author. Berlin 22 December 1955'; *Cantos Navidenos en el folkore Venezolano* by Isabel Aretz, signed 'Para A.L. Lloyd con el recherdo afecturso de Isabel Aretz, Caracas, 1963'; *Musical Instruments of India* by S. Krishnaswamy, inscribed 'A.L. Lloyd, Delhi 20.6.70'; *Oxford Dictionary of Nursery Rhymes* – 'Happy leap Year birthday to Bert from Charlotte, Joe, and Caroline, Feb 29 1952'.

For years, the family wore clothes made by Charlotte, an exception being a cashmere cardigan that she once bought Bert as a special luxury. They also took in lodgers to help make ends meet, including American Ralph Rinzler. Peggy Seeger, who also lodged with them, claimed that the Lloyds never charged *her* for staying. It should be said that the Lloyd's 'home-made' clothes were a cut above normal 'home-made' clothes as actress Jill Balcon (Day Lewis) recalled:

> They never had a car. I think they were living on very little. They didn't do extravagant things or have holidays. But it's nothing to do with wealth, how you live, if you've got style. Charlotte had great style. The house was very elegant, and Charlotte always looked wonderful. She could see something in a magazine and cut a dress from the photograph or drawing. She'd buy very good material and make these wonderful copies of Dior and designers like that. Unfortunately she felt that when she got to a certain age she shouldn't wear bright colours, which was a shame because she could have worn anything and looked fabulous. Everything about Charlotte was restrained. Their daughter, Caroline, was a very affectionate girl, ebullient, very close to her mother.

In 1957 when Jill Day Lewis told Ralph Vaughan Williams that the family were moving to Croom's Hill, Vaughan Williams said enthusiastically, 'That will be nice, you'll have Bert Lloyd for a neighbour. He's the greatest expert, alive, on folk music'. Cecil Day Lewis revelled in the working-class atmosphere of the area and took inspiration from it for the detective novel *The Worm of Death,* written under his pseudonym of Nicholas Blake. In the postscript to his autobiography, *The Buried Day,* he describes Greenwich at that time:

> J. [Jill] gave me a telescope. Now, sitting by the Thames, I can bring closer to me the great cargo liners rounding the Isle of Dogs, the tugs and their strings of lighters, the wharves, warehouses, power stations, the skyline restless with cranes, the blue-diamond lights of welding and the indigo smoke from tall chimneys – all the river life which, here at Greenwich, overlooked by the palace and the park, enlivens their elegance with a workaday reality. I am happy, living in this place where old and new can be focused together into a historic present.

The fascinating melange of bustling riverside community (with its local shops, businesses, factories, and Victorian terraced houses), Goddard's Victorian Pie and Mash shop, Bet's corner paper-shop, palaces, the busy central covered-market, elegant architecture, and centuries of historical associations, nestling between the Thames, Greenwich Park and Blackheath, appealed to Bert's proletarian sympathies, his appreciation of fine things and his romanticism. He enjoyed the area very much, and when Caroline was young and he was home, he always walked her to school up the steep hill alongside the oldest enclosed Royal Park in London (dating from 1433), and up onto the Heath (one-time haunt of highwaymen), from where he could look back at the panoramic view over London.

In May 1949 Bert enthused to Douglas Kennedy, Director of the English Folk Dance and Song Society, about the move to Greenwich:

You see by the address, we have moved. I blanched at the notion of moving south of the river, but now I find that is mere northern superstition. We are delighted with our house, situation, neighbourhood, and neighbours. You and your wife must come and see us, by river-bus if you want to save petrol. I'm going to Transjordania for a brief trip but I should be back early in June. Perhaps we can fix something then if you're not away.

Bert and Charlotte were early 'pioneers' in Croom's Hill. Over the next ten years other artistic couples discovered the pleasures of living here. The Day Lewises and their two children at number 6; actor Michael Aldridge and his wife, and their girls, across the road next to the pub at number 11; the Assistant Head of BBC documentary films, Norman Swallow and his wife Madie, up at number 30; next to them the painter Bernard Adeney (who might have predated the Lloyds), founder member of the London Group; and close by, the journalists Nicolas and Claire Tomalin and the painter John Bratby. At that time Bert Hardy lived just up the hill in Blackheath, and he used to pick Bert Lloyd up in the morning and drive the pair of them up to the *Picture Post* offices.

Although on good terms with the neighbours the Lloyd's tended to keep themselves to themselves. Norman Swallow never remembered seeing Bert in the pub across the road from their house, although Bert did run 'singaround' evenings in the Richard I pub just down the road in Royal Hill. The Lloyds don't seem to have been very active in the Greenwich Society, of which Day Lewis was the Chairman, and Charlotte was not a regular attendee of 'girls' coffee and chat mornings. A couple of possible reasons for her general reticence in socialising, which went back to her days with William Ohly, was that she had a severe hearing impairment and was naturally shy. Her German friend Erica Bach and Norman Swallow both said that Charlotte was very conscious of, and disliked, her German accent, which she did her utmost to lose. She was so anti-German that, when Caroline was at the Mary Datchelor School for Girls, she could not even be persuaded to help Caroline with her German homework (although she enjoyed working with Bert on translations of German books and plays).

Jill Day Lewis surprised herself one day by knocking on the door of number 16 to offer her sympathy when some drug-related 'scandal' appeared in the local paper concerning the Lloyds' son Joe, who ended up in Wormwood Scrubs. She didn't really feel close enough to them to do this but felt that they must be feeling lonely and very conscious of the 'scandal' and they were probably in need of a bit of support. She was pleased to have done it because Bert and Charlotte appeared appreciative of her concern.

One of the reasons that the Day Lewises and the Lloyds weren't actually 'chummy' was that Cecil never felt wholly comfortable in Bert's company, and he didn't enjoy, as he saw it, being lectured to. Whether this unease had some subconscious basis in politics – Bert being a staunch unrelenting communist and Day Lewis an apostate – isn't known. In 1934 Day Lewis had written 'Yes, why do we all, seeing a communist, feel small?' Day Lewis wasn't alone in feeling uncomfortable with Bert. The Australian folk music scholar John Manifold told Doreen Rudé that when he was living in England he always felt rather intimidated by Bert. I've heard the same thing from other people. Rudé said she didn't think that Bert was the kind of person who wanted to make you feel less than whatever you were, it was just the man himself; a man of so many parts and extraordinary knowledge in so many areas. How we respond to other people has as much to do with how we see ourselves, as with them.

As a young man, the playwright Willy Russell, despite youthful insecurities, found Bert anything but intimidating:

> Having come from a firmly working-class background, and desperately struggling to try and become something of a writer, I was gauche, unsure, insecure, easily intimidated, and highly confused when, through my involvement with the folk scene in Liverpool I began to listen to and even meet major figures such as Bert, MacColl, Charles Parker and others. I mostly found them intimidating and even terrifying and probably withered, hopelessly, beneath their gaze. No doubt this was due in part to the stature and esteem in which they were held but, as I latter came to realise, such figures tended to have the kind of egos, which when combined with their absolutism did make them rather unapproachable except to those who would willingly become unquestioning disciples. The exception was Bert who, regardless of his own position, never ever intimidated or demanded unquestioning loyalty to his beliefs. Bert was the most human of those major figures. To me he seemed always to be primarily interested in people rather than in 'the people' and in him I certainly saw that scholarship and wisdom were not the enemies of mirth, mischief and joy.[3]

After leaving *Picture Post*, Bert had suggested to Bert Hardy that, having been such a successful team on the magazine, they might start up their own photojournalist agency and work together as freelancers:

> Bert wanted him and me to work together as a team, but I couldn't see it so I didn't do it. He was fantastic at the working class stuff but to run a business you've got to be much more versatile. If I'd joined him as a team doing photographic journalism he probably would never have gone into music. We still stayed good friends and as I lived just up the road in Blackheath I used to go and see him a tremendous amount.[4]

Tom Hopkinson was of the same opinion:

> He was an oddball. He was very much a unique character. He was excellent as a journalist in his own field, with a fine command of English. He knew how to get at the facts and how to put them together in a very readable way. He was a really gifted journalist as a member of a team. I wouldn't have expected him to be a great success working on his own because his field was rather limited.

As a character I would say he was subtle and complex. Because of his upbringing and the loss of his parents in a society that didn't seem to give a damn it gave him a very leftward inclination. He would have been shaken by the Russian treatment of Czechoslovakia and Hungary but, knowing his attitude, I don't think his convictions would be basically altered.

He was a good and loyal comrade to the people he worked with, and he was a likeable fellow, but I'd say very few people would really have understood him, and I wouldn't claim to be one of them.[5]

SNOW ON THE WRONG FOOT

On 30 October 1945, the radio producer Captain Royston Morley wrote a 'private and confidential' internal memo to his superiors saying that Head of History Broadcasting, Harry Ross, had expressed a wish to use A.L. Lloyd as a scriptwriter on his forthcoming (schools history) programmes. Morley went on to say that if his memory wasn't playing him false he had a feeling that there had been 'policy objections against the use of Lloyd, although, as you know he is a first-class features writer'. The next day a reply came back saying that the producer had 'better look for another scriptwriter for these programmes'. This didn't necessarily mean that Bert couldn't do *any* work for the BBC, but it certainly meant that producers would have to jump through hoops to justify using Bert over other more politically 'acceptable' writers. This went on for about ten years without him realising why his programme ideas and initial offers of work fell through more often than not.

In February 1948 he was invited by A. Nicolaeff in the European Production Department to work on a programme on *The Near Eastern Music of the U.S.S.R.* When Contracts Department were contacted, Nicolaeff received a pencilled reply on his letter that said: 'Not to be used. Commission to be cancelled. Fee may be payable if work already done.'

Later, in the early 1970s, Michael Rosen, who in the 1960s had interviewed Bert for Oxford University's student magazine *Isis*, was one of many whose broadcasting careers foundered due to secret 'colleging' – BBC jargon for MI5 political vetting – when it was decided that 'he dug with the wrong foot!' or 'Didn't have snow on the right foot!'[6] In his book *Class Act* Ben Harker mentions that in 1953 Bert appeared alongside producer R.D. 'Reggie' Smith, Isla Cameron (the early revival singer, originally with Theatre Workshop, 1927–80) and Ewan MacColl, on an MI5 list of 'Communists prominently associated with the BBC'. During the Second World War, all BBC staff broadcasting to occupied Europe were automatically vetted by MI5 and, according to the journalists David Leigh and Paul Lashmar (who exposed BBC blacklisting in the *Observer* in August 1985), it was presumably at this time that MI5 first got its toe in the door of Broadcasting House. In 1985 Brigadier Ronnie Stonham was still conducting secret MI5 vetting out of the Orwellian Room 105 on the first floor of Broadcasting House. Following Leigh and Lashmar's disclosures (denied by the BBC for the previous fifty years) the BBC agreed in April 1986 that staff should have access to their personnel files.

On 19 December 1945, seeking to get his writing (other than journalism) back on track, Bert wrote to BBC Drama producer Lance Sieveking enclosing his translation of Lorca's *Blood Wedding*: 'It is a play of considerable beauty (I have not done justice to it of course in my translation); but it does present a lot of difficulties for English actors. It might be better on the radio than on the stage. Anyway, see what you think. I hope you like it.' Why he suggested that he might not have done the piece justice, or that it was 'difficult for English actors', is unclear. But it certainly wouldn't have inspired confidence in a potential producer. He asked for the eventual return of the manuscript, as it was his only copy and he wanted to submit it to a publisher.

Early in January the script was sent across to the drama producer and writer Peggy Wells for her opinion. She was less enthusiastic about the play than Bert:

This is a poetic drama telling the story of a family feud and how the son of one family runs away with the bride of the son of the other family. A chase follows the abduction and the young men kill one another.

It takes a tremendous time to tell this simple story and personally I don't think it's worth adapting. I don't think the writing is distinguished enough to make such a piece worth while.

At the end of January, Sieveking told Bert that he felt *Blood Wedding* took a tremendously long time to get anywhere, but that perhaps in the original the story was carried by the poetry. He didn't feel the English version sufficiently interesting to produce. He did, however, ask Bert if he had 'the time and inclination' to dramatise some short stories. Bert replied meekly on 1 February not attempting to defend the play, which would have been difficult in the light of his earlier negative comment. It's just another example of the puzzling self-deprecating attitude that Bert evinced throughout his life over his writing.

I'm sorry you didn't like the *Blood Wedding*. But no doubt you are right. Even in Lorca-Spanish it starts slow and takes a long time to get going. It's a bit hard to play too. As far as I know the only people who perform it often are the Gypsy Theatre Company in Moscow (though it's not about Gypsies of course). I haven't time to do any adaptations just now; I'm busier than I like to be. I don't really enjoy adapting either, unless there is scope to be very free indeed. But thank you for the suggestion all the same.

It's interesting that Bert didn't feel happy with the restriction of mere adaptation; he needed to be able to be much more creative with a piece, an attitude which was also reflected in his folk song work: 'I sing very few songs as I receive them. I like to alter them round a bit according to my fancy. Old Vaughan Williams once said to me, "The practise of altering folk song is an obnoxious one, and I trust nobody to do it but myself." I don't feel like that but I do like to alter, to remake songs.' Joan Littlewood had more confidence in his translation, than did Bert: having seen his script, she wanted to produce *Blood Wedding* with Theatre Workshop but was unable to acquire the performance rights.

Bert's regular employment at *Picture Post* gave him the rare opportunity, at least for a few years, of being choosy about his other writing. In July the BBC contracts department suggested a fee of five guineas for a thirty-minute script for *Radio Rhythm Club*. They agreed to increase it to eight guineas after Bert's initial protest, but Bert felt that this was still not enough for the work involved and he was in the enviable position of being able to decline the commission.

The following year, 1947, his old boss, and friend, Laurence Gilliam, Head of Features, arranged for Bert to translate Ernst Schnabel's play *The 29th January* from German into English for the Third Programme. For the ninety-minute play Gilliam was offering Bert a more reasonable sixty-five guineas for translation and adaptation. Charlotte who, although not down officially as joint translator as in later BBC work, witnessed the contract, and would almost certainly have worked with Bert on the play. Schnabel, an ex-German naval officer, became well known a few years later for his book, *Anne Frank: A Portrait in Courage*. In the late 1940s he was one of a small group of innovative German radio writers, experimenting with socially committed radio drama incorporating documentary and feature techniques. He was Head of Drama for North West German Radio (NWDR) from 1946–49. Schnabel pioneered interactive drama, inviting his audiences to work with him.

Bridson's production of *The 29th January* (broadcast originally by NWDR from Hamburg early in 1947) sounds somewhat ordinary today, technically. A Richard Burton-type deep brown voice leads the listener through the twenty-four hours of the day, during which time we hear how ordinary people are coping, or not coping, with the grim realities of a ruined postwar Germany, made all the worse by the freezing weather, with still over fifty days to go until spring. Voices weave in and out of the incidental music and sound effects, giving brief vignettes of what's happening at this moment in time – prisoners of war returning to bombed houses and dead families, prostitutes surviving courtesy of the occupying forces, TB patients dying in cold sanatoria, people selling their clothes for a slice of bread, or trying to sell useless household items, made from recycled gasmasks and other war surplus, that nobody wants, soldiers' graves with snow-covered tin helmets balanced on the wooden crosses, still too recent to have started rusting. It's a grim, although not self-pitying, picture of the devastation of war, and would have had a much more powerful impact when first broadcast, just over a year after the end of hostilities. Bert's translation works very well but is let down to a certain extent by the BBC 'actorish' voices that attempt a range of regional and working-class speech.

A significant piece of work that also came through in 1947 was the invitation by the writer and radio producer Geoffrey Bridson to research the songs for a proposed ballad opera, *Johnny Miner*. Bridson, a middle-class Mancunian, a couple of years older than Bert, had grown up and been educated at, the 'quietly pleasant oasis on the Lancashire coast', Lytham St Annes. At seventeen he returned to a Manchester 'wallowing in the backwash of the Cotton Slump'. Although the artistic group he fell in with, which included the painter L.S. Lowry, and *Love on the Dole* author Walter Greenwood, were not themselves impoverished, they couldn't fail to be aware of the grinding regional poverty, particularly in the smaller Pennine mill towns such as Bolton, Ashton, Burnley and Rochdale. The general hardships of working-class people plus the militant, red-bannered May Day parades, limping hunger-marchers, and fascist confrontations on the streets of Manchester stirred Bridson's social conscience.

In 1933, in the course of seeking outlets for his writing, Bridson had met Claud Cockburn, the *Daily Worker* journalist, and editor of the inflammatory political paper *The Week*. Cockburn suggested writing for radio and told him to get in touch with his communist friend Archie Harding, recently made BBC Programme Director, Northern Region, by Sir John Reith, who told him: 'You're a very dangerous man, Harding, I think you'd be better up in the North where you can't do so much damage.' A year later, encouraged and inspired by Harding's political vision for radio, Bridson wrote *May Day in England*, a programme which gave a local street busker, and political activist, Jimmy Miller (aka Ewan MacColl), his first radio job as a 'working-class voice'. In 1947, after having written and produced the nostalgic and celebratory *Mirror of our Times* to mark the 25th Anniversary of the BBC, Bridson felt the need to 'write something a bit more polemical'.

In 1943 Bridson had been working for the BBC in America and, with the Harlem poet Langston Hughes and some musical help from Alan Lomax, he had produced the first radio ballad-opera, *The Man Who Went to War*; a revolutionary piece of radio following the fortunes of an African-American family in a war-torn city such as London. Paul Robeson took time out from his Broadway portrayal of Othello to play the part of God, for a mere $100, as a goodwill gesture to the people of Britain. Sonny Terry, Brownie McGhee, and Josh White performed folk songs. We know Bert heard the programme because a couple of years later he included the song 'We're Gonna Move into Germany' in his book *Corn on the Cob*, giving *The Man Who Went to War* as the source.

Now, four years later, Bridson fancied trying his hand at the ballad-opera format again: '... building upon the theme of life in the coal towns that I knew, I sat down to write "Johnny Miner." The hero of the work, Johnny himself, was an archetypal figure – the essence of pitmen everywhere – and his story followed the fortunes of the miner from the bad old days of the early nineteenth century up to the recent nationalisation of the mines.'[7]

Set in the Durham coalfields, the songs were researched by Bert, who, as Bridson told the BBC copyright department in December, was 'a recognised authority in the British work-song field'. They were arranged for solo voices and choir by the Hungarian-refugee composer, and Workers' Music Association stalwart, Mátyás Seiber (1905–60), with whom, two years earlier, Bert had written the English texts and the notes for Seiber's arrangements of *Twelve*

Russian Folk Songs For Children (WMA 1945). The fifteen songs Bert selected for the programme were – 'The Collier's Rant', 'Down in the Coalmine', 'Bonny at Morn', 'Must I go Bound', 'Stand Out Ye Miners', 'Sair Fyel'd Hinnie', 'I Love My Miner Lad', 'Blaydon Races', 'Jesu, Lover of My Soul', 'The Miners' Dirge', 'Ma Bonny Lad', 'The Durham Reel', 'Johnny Miner', 'Geordie is Gone for a Soldier' and that old Durham pit-village favourite 'We Shall Not be Moved'.

About half of them he rewrote to make more specifically appropriate for the story. It was a mix of Northumbrian songs (not all mining songs) from standard northern song collections, songs given a Geordie twist ('Geordie is Gone for a Soldier'), a popular Wesleyan hymn, and some adapted from American sources. George Korson's song collection *Coaldust on the Fiddle* had appeared in the States in 1943 and we know that Bert was familiar with the book, and its predecessor *Minstrels of the Mine Patch* (1938), because in his 1952 *Come All Ye Bold Miners* he prints 'Stand Out Ye Miners' with the ballad opera and *Coal Dust On the Fiddle* as the source. He also references *Minstrels of the Mine Patch*.

The classical singer Owen Brannigan and the actress/singer Marjorie Westbury performed the songs. Brannigan from Northumberland had made a speciality of performing northeast folk songs alongside his operatic repertoire. The Opera Group of the Workers' Music Association (WMA) conducted by Alan Bush provided the choruses. This was not quite the singing you might have heard in a Geordie miners' social club, but in 1947 probably as close as you were going to get at the BBC, and according to Bridson, it was a 'lively, rumbustious show and despite its Geordie gutturals was well received by the listeners' (except by some former coal-owners, still smarting over nationalisation, who complained to the BBC).

Later Bert said: 'Brannigan, himself a Geordie, revives an ancient mystery: what prevents a good concert singer from singing folk songs satisfactorily? The singing is hearty, the dialect broad and accurate, and still it does not work.' The WMA later staged a performance of the show at the Steiner Hall in London. The selection of songs doesn't show Bert, at that time, to be exactly an 'authority' on Northumbrian mining songs, but it gave him food for thought and the chance to do a bit of research into an area of song generally unexplored by the bucolically-focused, middle-class folk song collectors and scholars, and to see the possibilities of industrial song in his quest for a people's music relevant to a postwar urban audience. The first result of this interest was his *Come All Ye Bold Miners: Ballads and Songs of the Coalfield*, published by Lawrence and Wishart in 1952.

It was an area of research that had been in his mind for at least a year before Bridson approached him, since he had reviewed B.A. Botkin's folklore anthology *The American People* for *Our Time* (September 1946). Benjamin Albert Botkin, folklore editor of the Federal Writers' Project (1939–41) and head of the Archive of American Folk Song (1942–44), was Bert's sort of man, an anti-fascist, and editorial board member of the radical *People's*

Songs (a forerunner of *Sing Out!*) and a prolific writer and editor of folklore anthologies. An academic renegade and populariser who believed that folklore belonged to the people and not to proprietorial scholars, Botkin was influential on Bert's evolving folk song theories, and Botkin's collections – *The American Play-Party Song* (1937), *A Treasury of American Folklore* (1944) and many more – were a welcome resource for song, anecdote, history and tale and stimulated Bert's interest in industrial and contemporary folklore. Of which Bert had this to say in his review of *The American People*:

> The [current academic] theory is that folklore is a thing of the past, the sturdy clodhopping peasant past. We have no folklore now because we have no folk, that seems to be the line; you can't have folk in an industrial society. Or rather 'in a Capitalist society'... the antiquarian boys, who don't know great A from a bull's foot about the folk culture of their own day and age, have evolved a myopic and snobbish theory that all the ancient orders of folklore (the Child ballads, for instance) are a kind of aristocracy, and all the newer order are something less than the dust.
>
> A case cited by Mr. Botkin is that of Cecil Sharp, who was delighted with the old style narrative ballads of the hill-billies, but who was unable to see anything in cowboy songs except evidence that 'the cowboy has been despoiled of his inheritance of traditional song' and has 'nothing behind him.'
>
> The viewpoint is a nonsensical one ... Years ago Carl Sandburg wrote 'If anyone wants a vivid presentation of the factors which constitute the folk element as connected with the making of folk art, let him read through a list of human occupations as given in the handbook of insurance men'... the proper study of folklore is the study of working people, now, as much as at any time; for industrialisation doesn't destroy either a folk or their lore though it may make pretty big changes in both.

And he finished up with this suggestion that the mines and mills would be a rich and, so far, largely untapped source of contemporary English folklore:

> *The American People* is a book of astonishing richness. Its counterpart, *The English People*, would be more difficult to compile, not because the stuff is lacking (I'm sure it's not), but because folklore has been studied here in such a cockeyed way that the ground for such a collection is ill-prepared. Nobody, to my knowledge, has been around the mines and the mills and among the fettlers ... collecting the stories and the sayings which must surely abound in such jobs.

He might also have had at the back of his mind Alan Bush's remarks in his *Left Review* article 'Music and the Working-Class Struggle' (September 1936), '... a return to folk song, with its romantic associations of an idyllic pre-capitalist era should be avoided'.

A CULTURAL UPSURGE

It was Communist Party policy in the 1930s to utilise members' skills for the benefit of the party. This resulted in various professional and cultural groups forming under the CPGB umbrella, centred in London. If you were, say, a member of the Victoria branch you might also be a member of the theatre, historians', journalists' or writers' group, or whatever, and you were expected to faithfully attend both your branch and your group meetings.

Bert would have had an interest in three or four groups (journalism, history, music, writing), although not necessarily as a full-time member. Vic Gammon remembers in the early 1960s seeing Bert sharing the platform with Leslie Morton at a meeting of the Historians Group, a group that had, according to Eric Hobsbawm, been 'decimated' in 1956, the CPGB's *annus terribilis*, but Bert and Morton were still hanging in there, old-style hardliners in a rapidly changing political climate. Arnold Rattenbury, a convener of the Writers Group, which Bert often attended, recalled that Bert 'wasn't as far as I can remember on my core list of members. But he definitely came along if he was in the office [MOI and, later, *Picture Post*]. The meetings were held once a month upstairs in a nice old pub, the Salisbury, in the alley between the New Theatre and the Wyndham's in St Martin's Lane. It was easily available for anybody who happened to be in town.'[8]

And, of course, they all published articles by Bert, he being one of the original Left group that had gathered round the AIA and Parton Street. It was politically and culturally incestuous. Everybody knew everybody else, and they all worked together in various combinations on a range of projects. Edgell Rickword said that they didn't want to fill the pages with their own stuff, and he hoped that through the WMA, WEA, the Unity Theatre and other groups, working people would hear about *Left Review* and send in contributions. Typical of the sort of material they were hoping to attract was the series of workers' articles describing 'A Shift at Work' which appeared in December 1934: 'Monday Morning in the Machine Shop', 'Threshing Day and it Rained', 'Lunch in a Restaurant' (waitress), 'Soap and Clothes' (washer-woman), 'By the Dancing Needles' (tailor's machinist), 'The Late Duty Porter' (hotel porter).

One of the original organisers of the CPGB Writers Group was the wealthy Oxbridge communist Randall Swingler who, along with Rickword, Rattenbury, Jack Lindsay, Bert and others involved in the various left-wing magazines were attempting to coordinate a literary policy, to do something about the quality and status of communist writers, and to think about the profession and make aesthetic judgements. Lindsay, whose wife Ann raised capital and managed the affairs of Fore Publications, explained in his autobiography *Life Rarely Tells*:

> Our activities were now for some years centred on the hopes of developing further what we called, with jesting seriousness, the Cultural Upsurge, the release of cultural energies and interests by the war, which we felt could be encouraged, expanded, powerfully linked together as a necessary part of a

large-scale social advance signalled by the 1945 [Labour-won] elections. I
was now chief director of Fore Publications with its monthly *Our Time*, in
which we sought to record and stimulate the cultural upsurge.

Swingler's leading role in furthering the 'cultural upsurge' can be seen in
the number of publications in which he was the prime mover and financer,
including *Left Review*, *Our Time*, *Arena* and *Seven*, and in 1938 he established
Fore Publications.

Although it's not suggested that Bert was 'allotted' folk music as his field
of 'upsurge' work by the CPGB, his interest in folk music and, after the war,
his growing interest in the development of a 'people's music' (inspired by the
work in America of Woody Guthrie, Pete Seeger, the Almanac Singers and
the folklorist Benjamin Botkin) fitted in well with the cultural upsurge idea
and his articles such as 'The Cowboy and his Music' (*Our Time*, April 1943,
reprinted with new musical examples from *University Forward*, 1942), 'The
Guerrilla Songs of Greece' (*Our Time*, December 1944), 'Sing Out America'
(*Keynote: The Progressive Music Quarterly*, 1945), 'Black Spirituals and
White' (*Modern Quarterly*, 1945), 'The Ballads of the Bad Men' (*Seven* Vol.
7:1, 1946), 'The Origin of Spirituals' (*Keynote*, 1946), and 'This "folk"
business', a review/article on Botkin's folklore anthology *The American People*
(*Our Time*, September 1946), were welcome contributions to the magazines.
Bert also wrote his history of the cowboy for *Picture Post* in the issue of 8
October 1949 (with photos by Leonard McCombe), in which he managed
to have a little dig at exploitative bosses:

In 1882, the price of steers on the range had jumped from 12 dollars to
35 dollars. That same year, the skilled cowhand's wages were 25 dollars
(about £5) a month and keep. Out of that he bought his own working gear
– boots, saddle, slicker, gun, etc. - from the company store. Sometimes he
ended up a season's work in debt to the rancher. He had a song about it:

> I went to the boss to draw my role,
> He figured me out nine dollars in the hole.
> So I took him aside and we had a little chat,
> And I hit him in the face with my five-gallon hat.

In February 1945 the celebrated jazz historian and music journalist Max
Jones edited a collection of essays on the theme of 'people's song' under the
title *FOLK – review of people's music. Part 1*. Jazz Music Books had intended
to publish a larger volume but 'production difficulties proving insurmountable,
it was decided that issue of a portion of the material in this form now was to
be preferred to a complete shelving of the project'. Some of the essays were
culled from other publications – William White's 'The Calypso Singers' had
appeared in *Esquire* and Preston and McCarthy's 'Poetry of Afro-American
Folk-Song' was from *Now*. Bert's contribution was 'The Revolutionary
Origins of English Folk-Song'. It was a reprint of the earlier WMA *William*

Morris Musical Society Bulletin article, which had already appeared in 1944 in its expanded form as *The Singing Englishman*. So this was nothing new from Bert, but a welcome bit of publicity for *The Singing Englishman*, which didn't sell in large numbers. There were still copies knocking around the WMA office seven years later during the Festival of Britain.[9]

That there was a buzz concerning vernacular music in England after the Second World War is apparent by the other essays included in *FOLK*, or held over for a second volume, which included 'Negro Music in Puerto Rico' (Maude Cuney Hare), 'English Songs of Revolt –The Luddites' (Reg Groves), 'U.S. Work Songs' (Preston & MacCarthy), 'Tribal Music of Africa' (Claude Lipscombe), 'John Henry – Folk Hero' (Rex Norton), 'Songs and Street Games of London Children' (Charles Chilton) and others.

Also between 1945 and 1948 Burl Ives, the American folk balladeer and actor (and subsequent betrayer of his communist folk singing friends to the Un-American Activities Committee), had hit records with such titles as the hobo fantasy 'Big Rock Candy Mountain', the 'Foggy Dew' (also one of Bert's favourite early songs), 'Lavender Blue, Dilly, Dilly' and the old antebellum minstrel song 'The Blue Tail Fly'. So Bert was not alone in his interest in Afro-American music and American folk songs generally, alongside his ongoing study of English folk music and its role as the possible corner stone of a radical revival of 'people's music'. But a people's music that reflected Bert, MacColl and Lomax's vision.

Incidentally, 'The Blue Tail Fly' and other popular American minstrel songs had been collected from agricultural workers in the villages of the upper Thames earlier in the century by Alfred Williams, showing that traditional 'folk' singers were more eclectic in their tastes than the majority of collectors would lead us to believe. Bert, who mined Williams's *Folk-Songs of the Upper Thames* for material for his 1950s recordings, was well aware of the people's catholic tastes, as he pointed out in a letter to Stephen Sedley in November 1961:

> I think we incline to over-estimate the rurality of 'classical' folk song, or rather to under-estimate the role played by the large towns and cities in the creation and diffusion of the stuff. At the beginning of the nineteenth century, the musical repertory of town and city working people (not necessarily displaced persons from rural areas) probably consisted to a considerable extent of folk stuff, along with a few more or less topical street songs, some hymns, some scraps of opera, and some sentimental or comic stage songs [including American minstrel songs]; after all, Sam Cowell, probably the most successful London comedian in the middle of the nineteenth century, had a repertory that consisted in the main of folk song and folk song parody, and his two biggest successes after 'Villikins', were 'Lord Lovel' and 'Lord Bateman'.

Cowell was an American actor and art singer who utilised his natural comic ability and vocal skills to develop a cockney stage persona, specialising in the cockney dialect being popularised in the mid-1850s by Charles Dickens. Another of Cowell's famous numbers on the London and regional theatre stage was 'The Ratcatcher's Daughter'.

A lot of the interest in Afro-American music, such as the blues and spirituals, came from jazz enthusiasts exploring the roots of the music and discovering folk-blues, gospel songs and spirituals, plantation hollers and work songs. In the same way a little later, many English skifflers looked at the roots of skiffle and American folk song and discovered British antecedents. Bert would have seen certain parallels between the blues and English folk music; each was essentially a rural music that drifted into the towns and cities with the influx of rural workers looking for jobs in factories, mills and other industries. Both underwent changes in their new environment, and in both America and England the early rural forms fell out of favour with the urban proletariat on the lookout for novelty, which was increasingly supplied by professional entertainment producers and promoted through the printed media and latterly radio and records. This is presumably what Bert meant when, in 1954, in *The Marxist Quarterly*, he said, 'Capitalism has made a sad mess of our folk song tradition'.

It didn't actually *kill* folk music, of course, which is always in a state of flux, but changes in society – social and geographical mobility, fluctuating affluence, changing work patterns, and the mass media – all conspired to make the old non-professional, community-based material and styles of performance appear dated. Traditional singers could then do one of three things: gracefully, or grudgingly, admit defeat and hang up their clogs; tenaciously hang on, despite the lack of an audience, as in the case of Norfolk's Walter Pardon who hung on to his repertoire in private until his music was taken up by a new audience in the 1970s folk clubs; or go with the times and adapt their music for the new audiences where, it mustn't be forgotten, there was possibly money to be made.

In Appalachia in the 1920s and 1930s a host of small string bands sprang up playing exciting hell-for-leather versions of traditional tunes and songs, or new material with its roots in the old music, in the hope of making a few dollars from the record companies such as Okeh that sent their scouts into the southern mountains to find and record these local bands and sell the records back to the rural populace. The same was happening on the other side of the tracks, where black rural performers were playing guitar and creating the blues out of their lyrical and musical roots, and were being recorded by the big record companies and issued on their 'race' labels for sale to the black community. A number that caught the popular imagination, like 'Trouble in Mind', could sell up to 700,000 copies.

However, race records and local white old-time records took a hammering during the depression of the 1930s and, by the Second World War, audiences, black and white, who had left their rural roots behind in the search for work in the cities, had generally abandoned the country blues, the rural string bands, and archaic-sounding ballad singing for smoother, more sophisticated types of popular commercial music. Max Jones detailed the process in his comprehensive history of the blues, written as part of the *PL Yearbook of Jazz 1946* (edited by A. McCarthy). Bert, who knew Jones, and had an interest in the blues (he wrote blues and jazz articles for *The Transatlantic* magazine in the 1940s) would certainly have read the essay. And he would have noted the similarities between the place of the blues and what he would have termed 'classic' English folk song in contemporary society, and would have taken on board Jones' comments on a musical revival:

> Blues singing is not a forgotten art by any means. It is alive today and can be made to flourish, and the radio networks are beginning to play their part. Whether it can survive away from its roots is yet a matter for conjecture, but it seems at least possible that a music so vigorous will withstand transplantation and continue to thrive if given a fair hearing. There is no reason why blues shouldn't tell the story of a large section of American people in present times, for the singer automatically brings his topics up to date, employing an idiom familiar to his audience.

If you just substitute 'English folk song' for 'blues', a lot of the above was relevant to England where a similar picture pertained. In the face of music-hall, variety shows, dance bands and crooners, cinema, radio and records, the older folk song material and style of performance had become less and less relevant. As we know, it hung on tenaciously in isolated rural pockets, such as some East Anglian pubs, Cumbrian hunt suppers, and in the repertoire of the atypical Copper Family of Rottingdean, Sussex (a county, incidentally, in which Mervyn Plunkett, Ken Stubbs and others managed to collect a considerable amount of material in the 1950s).

But by then the songs were a cultural anomaly surviving in the heads and voices of an increasingly aging and ever dwindling group of men and women and no longer (or very rarely) being created. But they were not, quite, beyond reviving, especially in the northern mining and textile communities – industries picked out by Bert in his Botkin review – where songs were still being created in a traditional idiom, or had been until much more recently, and would bloom again for a while in the folk clubs, largely through Bert's influence, and during the Miners' strike of 1984–85, too late, unfortunately, for Bert to hear.

So Bert saw what he felt was needed to bring about a contemporary flowering of working-class musical culture as an antidote to the 'dope of popular, and especially popular transatlantic, music'. What it required was authentic examples of the 'classic' English folk singing tradition on record and on the radio, and 'new measures' such as clubs, concerts, workshops and festivals to bring a revived, unadulterated, folk tradition to national prominence. Bert already had access to the WMA's Topic Records, and he had left-wing friends at the BBC and in magazine and newspaper publishing. He just needed the venues in which to build up an audience for 'a folk music for our time', based on what he saw as the best of the past, but with an eye and ear on the present and the future. It was something he'd touched on in 1944 in *The Singing Englishman*:

Some say things have changed and we will not have folk songs any more. They are the pessimists. And some try to revive traditional music that has nothing to do with social life any longer; and all that happens is they give you a recital of the popular songs of the past; and they try to make a living thing of it. They are the optimists. But that is not the whole story. Things do change, and they change again; and just because at this moment we have no great body of fine folk song that is bound close to our social life and the times we live in and the way we go about our work, that is not to say there will never be any more.

It should be remembered that the idea of folk song clubs (but not in pubs) did already exist, although from the various histories of the folk revival you'd be excused for thinking that they were an invention of Bert, MacColl, Lomax et al. There's a note in the July 1949 issue of the magazine of the English Folk Dance and Song Society, *English Dance and Song*: 'FOLK SONG CLUB. Please note there will be no meetings of this club during the Summer Session.' The sort of folk song performances that took place at the EFDSS headquarters at Cecil Sharp House in the late 1940s would probably have been rather twee affairs, run by such well-meaning (and musically literate) people as Patrick Shuldham-Shaw,[10] who was at the parlour and concert-stage end of the folk music spectrum, and represented the 'acceptable' voice of folk song.

It was middle-class renditions of traditional songs, along with American-influenced pop music, that the initially communist-led second folk revival set out to replace. However, it must be said, the WMA's idea of folk song presentation at the time was little better than that of the EFDSS-type concert singer. Choirs performing arrangements for various combinations of voices by Alan Bush, Matyas Seiber, Will Sahnow and others were the order of the day. Even as late as October 1952 the WMA put out a choral edition of Bert's *Coaldust Ballads* with the note:

Some of the songs chosen are for performance by men, others by women, and, in most cases, optional parts are added to enable singing by choirs as well as – or in place of – solo voices. This should make them of wide service to our singing people everywhere. A very interesting feature programme could be devised, making use of the twenty songs in a blend of solo and choral items. If any choirs are desirous of performing them in this way we will certainly consider the possibility of producing a suitable spoken commentary.

What Bert hadn't envisioned was the upsurge of interest in traditional music by the BBC in the 1950s and the large number of programmes that would introduce radio listeners to authentic folk singers, from the Western Isles to Cornwall, and East Anglia to Donegal. In fact, far from being a new innovation by the BBC in the 1950s, the corporation had already initiated a folk-music collecting programme in the 1940s, as the BBC's Marie Slocombe pointed out in a letter to *English Dance and Song* magazine in February 1964:

Lomax is undeniably a skilled and tireless collector and a fine broadcaster, but he did *not* persuade the BBC to start its scheme. Brian George, Head of Central Programme Operations, was planning the scheme as early as 1947 and himself carried out experimental field recordings in Ireland in the summer of 1947 and 1949. As a result of these pilot expeditions the BBC management endorsed his recommendations that the BBC should, with the help of the EFDSS and other recognised bodies, take the initiative in organising a systematic survey of the British Isles with a view to placing on record the best of what still remained. When Alan Lomax came on the scene (Autumn 1951) the scheme was already under way and the BBC was, in fact, able to give him information to help him make his own recordings for the British volumes in the Columbia World Library. He included some BBC recordings in this publication and, in turn, allowed the BBC to archive some of his. He was not at any time or in any way responsible for the BBC activities in the folk field.

When the folk club scene spread in the 1960s and 1970s to cover the entire British Isles, Bert, MacColl and the rest, became as prescriptive and proscriptive over what did and what didn't constitute folk music as all the early collectors, whom they had accused of cultural imperialism and of having a lack of understanding of the 'folk'. Both revivals – pre-war and postwar – were very selective in their cherry picking from popular culture, and both were intent on using it for their own ends. They were all on a political mission and felt that they knew what was best for the folk, and appear to have little sympathy for what real working-class people actually liked if it didn't fit their preconceptions. Cecil Sharp denigrated music-hall; and MacColl had the temerity to tell traditional performers what was musically acceptable at the Singers' Club, as shown in a letter to Bob Davenport from the singing miner Jack Elliott of Birtley: 'As for Ewan and Peg if they want to be on the outside looking in that's okay. I'll still keep singing for one reason, I like it. I was singing and playing a mouth-organ before I met them, so nuts.'

Also Bert's comment to Mike Yates when they heard Walter Pardon sing 'The Balaclava Charge' – 'Why is it that singers like Walter love to sing such appalling songs?' Although, in fairness, Bert would never have let Walter know what he thought of the song. Norma Waterson recalled the time that the Watersons were in Washington with Bert and Walter for the Bicentennial Folklore Festival and Pardon sang 'Balaclava': Bert rushed up to him and congratulated him. It was exactly what Pardon needed.[11]

The folk revival movers and shakers were disillusioned if they believed that the music they were promoting as a cornerstone of the second folk revival would have any real and long-lasting effect on the general public, the folk. Admittedly, by the mid-1960s there were folk clubs in most towns and many villages, but they often catered only for a few dozen people. Audiences of a couple of hundred or more were generally found only in the largest of the urban clubs. Although thousands of working-class boys, rarely girls, were caught up in the excitement and pounding rhythms of skiffle in the 1950s, most of them went on to play or jive to rock and roll.

MacColl, ever ready to attack the capitalist system and the big money boys, was out of touch with the real world beyond his quite limited sphere of influence, as was shown by his less than successful attempt to get down with the kids in the uncomfortable teenage radio ballad *On the Edge* and his attack in *Sing Out!* on Bob Dylan, whom he patronisingly referred to as Bobby Dylan, in which he declared that: 'Only a non-critical audience, nourished on the watery pap of pop music could have fallen for such tenth-rate drivel.' It was arrogant, and laughable, in the extreme for MacColl to set himself up as judge and jury on someone who was changing the face of popular music. Bert at least had the good grace, or the good sense, to say:

What Tin Pan Alley calls folk song, introspective, personalised, semi-cabaret song from the Dylan to Ralph McTell-type repertory is a perfectly respectable repertory but it hasn't got much to do with folk song in the folklorist's sense, but it has a great deal to do with folk song in the Tin Pan Alley sense. Tin Pan Alley has rather annexed the term so perhaps folklorists in retreat ought to find a new term for what they occupy themselves with, because so much bashing goes on about what is folk music and what isn't. The term was never a satisfactory one because 'folk' seems to imply a whole nation, or at least a large chunk of a nation. I don't know what the word means. The individual items of the folk song repertory often had a tiny circulation and were in the heads of very few people. You've got your 'Barbara Allens' that crop up in hundreds of variants, but on the other hand you've got your 'Brigg Fairs' that were only in the head of one singer, and *he* couldn't remember all the song.

Ultimately they lost control and the second revival became just another cul-de-sac off the main highway of popular commercial music, with its own 'star' system, its mindless hype, its sycophancy, its fanzines, and its subjection to market forces. Some people might not find the commercialisation of folk music particularly objectionable: that's what you get for living in a capitalist society where accountants are the new high priests, and idealism is a luxury few can afford. But it is what Bert and those other early communist folk singers had tried, unsuccessfully, to subvert with a more meaningful music for societal change: 'Ewan and I felt it was rather a shame that this simple exotic American material [skiffle] was hogging the scene and it would nice if we could introduce onto the musical scene more and more traditional stuff from our own islands.'

In 1958 in *Recorded Folk Music* Bert had referred to: '... a considerable resurgence of music-making, and not only on the primitive level of skiffle. That is to the good. And if the signs are read aright, it may be leading to the active exploration of our own native traditions. That would be better still. And if *that* gets under way on a truly broad scale, severe shocks and delightful surprises may be in store.' It was an optimistic dream that wasn't fulfilled in the way that Bert hoped. Some people did actively explore their own native British traditions, but there were more musical tremors than seismic shocks. Bert and MacColl failed to bring about a change in the musical consciousness of society at large, and failed to keep 'folk song' out of the hands of the large media corporations.

REMEMBERING OZ

It's significant that, despite Bert's later claims to have returned from Australia with notebooks full of work-songs and bush ballads, which would have been a unique resource for articles and talks for his 1940s preoccupation with 'peoples' music', they don't figure in any of his musical folklore (a favourite Bert term) writings in the 1930s and 1940s. Why not? The Australian songs he subsequently recorded are just as good, if not better, than the songs and lore of the Wild West that he was peddling at the time. There's really no sign of a body of Australian material until the mid-1950s.

In the early 1950s a couple of events seem to have sparked off Bert's interest in his song experiences in the Australian outback twenty-five years earlier. In 1953 Melbourne's New Theatre (Australia's equivalent of Unity Theatre) had commissioned a play from the playwright Dick Diamond. The resulting production, *Reedy River*, told the story of the Shearers' Union, and life in an outback community following the disastrous shearers' strike of 1891, which ended with thirteen of the union leaders being charged with sedition and sentenced to three years imprisonment on the island of St Helena. John Meredith's Bushwhackers Band (decked out in 'stage' bush-worker costumes) sang and performed the music for the play that kick-started an interest in bush music, ballads and bad outfits. Being a suitably radical play with the added advantage of folk songs and dance tunes, it was ideally suited for the London left-wing Unity Theatre, and Ivor Pinkus's production opened on 17 December 1954 at the theatre in Goldington Road, Camden. Bert provided some songs and music for the production, which was musically directed by John Hasted. Bert also turned up for some of the rehearsals and gave the cast a lot of first-hand information about life in the outback.

The young Australian communist librarian (and later folklorist) Edgar Waters and his wife Ann had arrived in London earlier in the year, and he wrote a background article on the Australian cultural scene (what little of it there was) and the influence of the Sydney and Melbourne New Theatres' productions of *Reedy River* for Eric Winter's *Sing* magazine.[12] Waters and his wife found a flat in Camden Town and Ann got a teaching job in a school in south London. Edgar embarked on his ambition to study folk music while in London. He acquired a reader's ticket for the British Museum and divided his time between the museum's Reading Room (where he went to study broadsides) and the basement of Cecil Sharp House, where he would don headphones and work his way through the EFDSS copies of the BBC's 1950s folk music collecting scheme.

At that time, Helen and Douglas Kennedy hosted a Saturday afternoon musical get-together at Cecil Sharp House with tea and cakes and usually a talk on some relevant topic. Peter Kennedy spoke of his collecting work for the BBC, and one Saturday Edgar chipped in with a chat about Australian song. Bert also gave one of these talks. Over forty years later, when recorded by Kevin Bradley for the National Library of Australia, Waters couldn't remember the subject of Bert's talk. He did, though, remember the congenial 'charming Helen Kennedy' as a lively hostess who surprisingly regaled them one Saturday with the mildly bawdy 'Nutting Girl', performed to her own concertina accompaniment.

It was at one of these Saturday afternoon soirees that the Waters first met Alan Lomax, who offered Edgar a position as his assistant, transcribing tapes from his recent field recordings. It lasted for three or four months and although it didn't bring in much money, it helped bring Edgar up to speed on live British folk song. One of his major undertakings was transcribing the two or three days' worth of songs and interviews that Lomax had recorded with Norfolk's Harry Cox – Cox having gone down to London and stayed at Lomax's Belsize Park flat for the sessions. According to Waters, Lomax, after seeing a number of Rising Sun pubs in Norfolk, was convinced that there must be a Norfolk link to the American bluesy brothel song 'House of the Rising Sun'. He quizzed Cox on the sex lives of English farm labourers, and Cox's sex life in particular, to try and establish a connection. But to no avail: Cox kept his sex life well buttoned up, although (probably out of pity for Lomax) he did come up with (or make up?) an East Anglian 'blues' verse which had a surprising similarity to the American song:

> If you go to Lowestoft
> And ask for the Rising Sun,
> You'll find two old whores there
> And my old woman's one.[13]

One evening Edgar and Ann Waters were invited to a party at the flat that Lomax and his girlfriend, Susan, shared with Ewan MacColl. As opposed to the rather genteel, respectable Cecil Sharp House gatherings this was a much more raffish 'bohemian' affair. Edgar and Ann Waters sat on the floor next to Seamus Ennis and enjoyed the music and easy camaraderie. Among the people who sang that evening were Ennis, Isla Cameron and MacColl. Then, Waters recalled:

Someone asked 'Bert' to sing and a man who had been sitting quietly in the corner got up and sang 'Bold Jack Donahue'. This was Bert Lloyd. Later he came across and talked to me about Australian folk songs. He knew a great deal more about Jack Donahue than I did, and was obviously well acquainted with Paterson's Old Bush Songs but also with more recent publications such as Old Australian Bush Ballads.[14]

Bert had bought a copy of *Old Bush Songs* in Australia back in the 1920s, as had many bush workers. Vance Palmer's and Margaret Sutherland's *Old Australian Bush Ballads* was a small collection of thirteen songs and tunes 'restored' to make them easily accessible for campfire or family sing-songs around the piano. Palmer restored the lyrics, some of which came from Banjo Patterson's *Old Bush Songs*, and Sutherland restored the music and arranged it for piano, 'calling on her own instincts for appropriate melody when there was no one who remembered the original tunes'. The collection received short shrift from the purists. Perhaps it should be said Bert didn't have to know a great deal about 'Jack Donahue' or Australian songs in general to know more than the younger Edgar Waters at that time. The Australian folk revival was very much in its infancy, and the handful of folk music enthusiasts (who were probably more familiar with the American songs of Pete Seeger and the Almanacs than they were with indigenous Australian material) were only just beginning to research their own musical folklore.

Edgar and Ann Waters struck up a warm friendship with Bert and Charlotte and were welcome visitors to Greenwich. During this time Edgar, who had had a role in instigating the setting up of the Australian Folklore Society, which actually happened after he had left for England (it was officially constituted on 16 January 1954), was sent the recently transcribed Society archives. Archives was a rather grandiose name for what was in fact the (at that point) modest results of the latest song collecting of tyro collectors such as John Meredith (whom Waters first met when he returned to Australia), Nancy Keesing and Russell Ward, plus a disparate collection of songs and ballads, many without original tunes, culled from old and contemporary newspapers, magazines and books. A lot of them had their origins in the music-hall and popular songsters, or were the work of known poets, and were not the songs from the oral tradition that Waters was interested in.

Years later Waters was surprisingly disingenuous in print about whether or not he'd shown Bert this song archive material that had been sent over to him during his eighteen months in London: 'It is quite possible that I showed material that was sent to me – some of it or all of it to A.L. Lloyd – from the Australian Folklore Society – and stated in its *Journal* to be "freely available to all who wished to study it."'[15] In fact, he did show it to Bert. In one of the Kevin Bradley interviews he mentions Bert coming round to his flat to look at the material, and comments specifically on Bert's interest in a version of 'The Banks of the Condamine'.[16] Bert later recorded a version of the same song to a different tune.

Waters showing and obviously discussing with Bert even a modest-sized, contemporary collection of Australian folk songs would surely have been quite a significant aspect of his relationship with Bert. One that, at the very least, would have stimulated Bert's interest in Australian folk song even if it didn't, as some Australians contend, necessarily supply him with the raw material from which to create or recreate some, or even most, of his own songs. Edgar and Ann Waters returned to Australia in October 1955, to escape the London smog and to enable Edgar to accept the invitation of his old friend Peter

Hamilton to join him in Sydney in setting up Wattle Records, an Australian version of Topic Records. He was instrumental in introducing Bert to the nascent Australian folk scene in 1957, issuing the ten-inch LPs *The Banks of the Condamine and Other Bush Songs*; *Singing Sailors* and *Shanties and Fo'c'sle Songs*, and the seven-inch EP *Convicts and Currency Lads*.

By the end of 1957, *Banks of the Condamine* had sold sufficiently well (about 350 copies) to nearly cover its costs, and was doing well enough for Wattle to contemplate a second Bert album of Australian material, *Across the Western Plains* (September 1958). Waters was keen to record the rest of Bert's Australian songs, which he thought was about another fourteen numbers. During his time in London they had obviously discussed Bert's repertoire, which Waters believed to be about two albums-worth in total, far short of the 500 songs that Bert has frequently been credited with collecting in Australia. Years later Waters admitted that, apart from a couple of songs, he never actually heard Bert's Australian repertoire during his stay in London. This could mean that Bert just never got round to singing for Waters after their initial meeting at Lomax's flat, or that any repertoire he might have had wasn't in a polished and singable state as early as 1954 and 1955.

Wattle were holding four tracks over from the first album and Waters wanted Bert to re-record a couple of them because he felt the quality wasn't good enough and that 'the "Lachlan Tigers" drags, and you and Peggy [Seeger] don't fit together too happily at some points'. On another, 'The Flash Stockman', he asked Bert to drop the word 'bloody' because radio stations wouldn't play songs containing any stronger language than 'blast' or 'flaming'. One or two record shops had already refused to stock *The Banks of the Condamine* because of the text of the 'Derby Ram'. Waters apologised for the bowdlerisation but felt that it would be of great benefit to the Australian folk scene to get Bert's recording as widely heard as possible. As an afterthought he suggested Bert drop the phrase 'by the living Jesus' from 'Click Go the Shears' and replace the Chinamen in 'Travelling Down the Castlereagh' with scabs or non-union men. Waters also promised to send Bert regular Australian Folklore Society archive texts and tunes which he was having transcribed by a volunteer. He had obviously already sent Bert some dubbed copies of the field recordings because he apologised for not having 'sent any further tapes', due to the fact that he never seemed able to get two tape-machines together in the same place to do the copying.

Waters was not impressed with some of the work of local Australian revival musicians such as John Meredith and Alan Scott from the Bushwhackers ('pretty dreary') or their offshoot, the Rambleers ('poor, but should sell well'), even though Wattle was recording them. By the end of 1957 the only Wattle record that he was happy with was Bert's *The Banks of the Condamine*.[17]

In the 2006 Bradley interviews, Waters confessed to being less than blown away when he first saw the Bushwhackers in *Reedy River*. He thought their idea of a 'bush band' was one of the worst things that had happened to Australian folk music. He described it as Thump, Rattle and Roll music, due to the remorseless jingling-thump of the lagerphone, which was a percussion 'instrument' introduced into the Australian folk music scene by John Meredith, whose brother had once seen something similar used in a pub music competition, but which had no precedent in bush dance bands. Having little good to say about the music was perhaps why Waters didn't go up and introduce himself to Meredith that night.

Although Bert has been hauled over the coals by certain Australian folklorists for what they see as his cavalier folk song editing and attributions, in one instance it was his friend Waters, wearing his Wattle Records hat, who suggested in a letter of August 1958, concerning Bert's sleeve notes for the forthcoming Wattle album *Across the Western Plains*, that Bert might be less than transparent about a song source:

> You are right in assuming the text of 'Wallaby Stew' that you had from me was collected by Percy Jones. Just the same, I would be happier if you could bring yourself to delete the reference to him from your note (hence my name also). Jones' publishers are nasty people, and I am not at all sure that Jones himself might not welcome the chance of making a nuisance of himself to us, over copyright. He is closely associated with the Industrial Groups and the Democratic Labour Party, both of which are Catholic Action-inspired. We'll take the risk, if your conscience pricks; it isn't such a big risk, probably. But we'd rather not take it.[18]

Percy Jones, a Catholic priest, was closely associated with Daniel Mannix, the fiery Catholic Archbishop of Melbourne who believed that Australia was in the 'gravest danger from Communism'. The pair of them would have had no time or sympathy for the communist Waters and Wattle Records. Bert, whose conscience was obviously 'pricked', compromised by saying in the sleeve notes that Waters had shown him 'a coherent set of the words, *probably* from the collection of Dr. Percy Jones'.

A 1946 article by Dr Jones was also apparently the main source of Bert's 'Click Go the Shears'. Douglas Stewart and Nancy Keesing printed Bert's recorded version in their *Old Bush Songs* with a note saying: 'From Dr Percy Jones' collection with one additional stanza'.[19] The folklorist Keith McKenry conducted a fascinating piece of detective work on the song and his persuasive conclusion was that 'Click Go the Shears' was probably written in the 1940s by the bush poet Jack Moses.[20] Moses gave it to Jones, Jones published it in 1946 and later gave it to Burl Ives (who recorded it in 1952), Bert's (recorded in 1955) is the Jones/Ives version with some tweaking of the odd line or two, and a doctored verse and chorus that John Meredith had collected in 1953. Meredith, who was furious when he heard Bert's recording, himself later published it and pinched Bert's rewrites of the Jones verses! In fact no-one comes out of the convoluted story terribly well except poor old Jack Moses, who was never credited or received any royalties.

It would seem to have been a combination of the Unity *Reedy River* production and the arrival of Waters with news of a burgeoning Australian bush-music scene and some copies of a few recently uncovered bush ballads that inspired Bert to dust off and tidy up some of the material that he had heard, or read, in his teens and early twenties in New South Wales. Just how much dusting and tidying up he had to do we don't know. But probably more than he admitted, and possibly less than Meredith and subsequent Australian folk music researchers would like to believe.

Before visiting Australia and New Zealand in 1952, Burl Ives had toured the British Isles playing, among other places, London (Royal Festival Hall), Newcastle and Liverpool. He was back again in 1953, by which time his concert repertoire would have included some of Jones's Australian material. Did Bert go and hear him? Or meet up with him? While in the UK in 1952, Ives possibly acquired a copy of Bert's *The Singing Englishman*, because when he was in Sydney he was reading it. Ives and his wife were staying at Sydney's upmarket Hotel Australia where the young folk music enthusiast Edgar Waters and a friend went to see them.

When they entered Ives's room they saw a copy of the conspicuous bright green paperback booklet on a chair.[21] It seems certain that Ives had only recently acquired it, it not being the sort of book that he'd have carried with him around the world from America, especially as it was a publication of the music wing of the CPGB, and back in the USA the Committee for Un-American Activities was hounding artists with communist connections. It was that very year, 1952, that Ives was summoned to give evidence to the Committee. He denounced Pete Seeger and other old friends as communists to save his own musical career.

10
The English Folk Dance and Song Society

When everyone else was listening to Cream, I was listening to A.L. Lloyd and Ewan MacColl. These were two old guys who used to record together, trying to replicate the original instrumentation of sea shanties ... Some of the words were absolutely unbelievable ... I loaned the LP to [Captain] Beefheart and he probably still has it.

Frank Zappa, liner notes to *The Lost Episodes*
(on which he sings Bert's 'The Handsome Cabin Boy')

Early in 1948 Bert wrote to the Scottish poet, songwriter and song collector Hamish Henderson (with whom he'd have many more dealings once the folk revival got under way in the 1950s and 1960s) complimenting him on his recent collection *Ballads of World War II*. The collection contained two songs which were destined to become folk club favourites a few years later – 'Ballad of the D-Day Dodgers' and Henderson's own composition 'The Highland Division's Farewell to Sicily'. In typical Bert fashion he enclosed a number of songs that he felt might interest Henderson should he publish a second collection: '... the German ones I got from a girl who played drums in a three-piece band at the British Officers Club in Aachen. She was an entertainer on the Eastern Front, and was caught at Stalingrad ... . There are, of course, a number of American songs; most of them have an author-made appearance ... .'[1]

Although appreciated by Bert, Henderson's collection of unexpurgated soldiers' songs had to be printed privately under the fictitious imprint of The Lili Marlene Club of Glasgow to avoid trouble from the censor. However, this didn't save Henderson from being banned for several years from appearing on the BBC by an outraged Lord Reith. Around the same time, Bert finally decided if you can't beat them, join them and in February he applied for membership of the English Folk Dance and Song Society (EFDSS): 'I would like to become a full member of the EFDS [*sic*]. Can you please tell me what the subscription is? I would like also to enter for the Folk Music Festival Competition on March 10 in class 1 (solo singers).'

He'd obviously decided that he was ready to start performing in public, and had been giving a lot of thought to English performance style, his own in particular. He'd read Percy Grainger's analysis of traditional singing in the *Folk Song Society Journal* and Cecil Sharp's *English Folk Song: Some Conclusions*, and over the years he had heard a fair bit of folk music. In his *A.L. Lloyd: A Personal Memoir* (1984) Leslie Morton remembered Bert in the 1930s as: '... developing his own distinctive singing style in these years, taut and unfussy. On the whole he preferred the traditional English style of unaccompanied song, but he was never pedantic about that or anything else and was prepared to accept an instrumental accompaniment if it seemed to add anything of value.'

Commercial recordings of traditional English singers were scarce – Bert could only give Gower singer Phil Tanner's two Columbia 78rpm recordings as being generally available in his 1944 'discography' in *The Singing Englishman*. However, by 1948 and the singing competition, he'd had ten years of listening to East Anglian singers (the 1934 HMV 78rpm disc of Harry Cox singing 'The Bold Fisherman' and 'The Pretty Ploughboy'; his own BBC Eel's Foot 1939 recordings and the East Anglian pub 'frolics', recorded in 1945 by E.J. Moeran for the BBC). Also, over the years he'd had the opportunity to go through the BBC archives, where he would probably have found the Columbia 78rpm discs of the wonderful Lincolnshire singer Joseph Taylor, if he didn't already own them, and recordings made by the producer Douglas Cleverdon in 1940 and 1941 of Cecil Sharp's informant Louie Hooper in her cottage in Langport, together with other West Country musicians, singers, and wassailers. This, plus the very few singers he'd met and collected from while whaling, and later in the army, and what he undoubtedly heard in Australia, provided him with enough pointers to develop his own unaccompanied style of singing.

Bert was a conscious 'revivalist' singer despite the seemingly indissoluble myth begun in the 1950s[2] and perpetuated by David Gregory in his *Folk Music Journal* article 'Lomax in London' (2002), where Bert is described as a legitimate inheritor of his own folk song tradition. Is Gregory inferring Bert was a 'traditional singer'? He was English, so that would make him a 'legitimate inheritor of his own (English) folk song tradition', but no more than any other English revivalist singer whose family knew a couple of popular folk songs. Everyone knew 'To Be A Farmer's Boy'. Bert wasn't a traditional singer, merely a singer of traditional songs.

The EFDSS Folk Music Competition took place on Wednesday 10 March 1948, at Cecil Sharp House. As a Class I competitor Bert had to sing two folk songs of his own choice, one of them English, with or without accompaniment. The Society was honoured that its President, Ralph Vaughan Williams, had agreed to adjudicate. Bert was the winner in his class, and, aged forty, was set to embark on yet another career – that of a professional folk singer. Annoyingly, the brief report in the May 1948 issue of *English Dance and Song* doesn't say what Bert or anyone else sang. This is perhaps an indication of the lack of general interest in singing by the EFDSS; if this had been a dance competition there would, no doubt, have been a full report.

Until well into the 1960s, song was the Cinderella of the English Folk Dance and Song Society. The regular Albert Hall festivals were 95 per cent dance, with a couple of token singers thrown in while dancers got their breath back. The Society's main London contribution to the 1951 Festival of Britain were three performances of the 'Folk Dances of the British Isles' on 21–23 June at the Royal Albert Hall and one performance at Parliament Hill. The main folk song contribution came from the Workers' Music Association with material chosen by Bert.

In an interview which Bert gave some twenty-five years later, he explained the EFDSS concentration on dance by the 1950s:

Over the years the EFDSS had come to concentrate more on social dance, and earlier schools, partly because the classic repertory of folksingers was dwindling. The collectors were finding it more and more difficult to come across material that was in any sense new or even valuable variants of what had been collected before. So as a study of surviving country folklore in the mouths of country singers that was becoming a very restricted activity. The EFDSS were perfectly willing to leave the performance of the songs that had been collected and piano arranged to concert artists who wanted to perform the songs. They felt that their value as an organisation lay in an extensive programme of social dance. So the branches of the EFDSS all over the country came to concentrate on dance and, once established, it went on and on, mostly with the same dancers who were getting more and more middle-aged and indeed the organisation was to some extent beginning to suffer from hardening arteries.

Having *The Singing Englishman* under his belt (notwithstanding its cool reception by the middle-class collectors and scholars of the EFDSS – he had called Cecil Sharp 'dumb'), having won the Society's singing competition, and creating a favourable impression on Vaughan Williams, Bert's next move was to establish a friendly relationship with the Society director, Douglas Kennedy, who was more forward-thinking and keener to build bridges with the outside world than many of the more reactionary older Society members. He established communication with Douglas's son Peter, who also worked for the EFDSS and who, over the next few years, would become arguably Britain's most important, and controversial, folk music collector.

In May 1949 Bert wrote to Douglas Kennedy and included a cheque for a 'five bob sub' towards the cost of the proposed publication of Margaret Dean Smith's *Folk Song Index*, and eight pence for a copy of the leaflet *May Day and the English Tradition*. He went on to offer his services as a possible contributor to the proposed 6 July discussion *How Should Folk Songs Be Sung* because 'It's something I have views about'. These views had been touched on in *The Singing Englishman*, where he'd said that, should his readers have the good fortune to hear a genuine traditional singer, they would 'get an idea how terribly far off the mark is the folk song as written in the arrangements and as sung on the concert platform'.

Kennedy replied a few days later. 'I very much hope that you will be able to take part in the discussion on July 6th. The Society is gradually becoming conditioned to accept some authentic guidance on this point.' This is a truly bizarre comment from the director of the English Folk Dance and Song Society. One would have hoped that over the fifty or so years of the Folk Song Society's existence it would be *they* who were in a position to give 'authentic guidance' on folk song style and performance. In the late 1940s the only employee who seems to have had experience and a real understanding of

1. Ernest Lancaster Lloyd (Bert's father).

2. Mabel Emily Lloyd (née Barrett; Bert's mother).

3. Kathleen (Kathie) Lloyd (Bert's sister).

4. Beatrice Florence (Trixie) Lloyd (Bert's sister).

5. Bert aged three, 1911.

6. Bert in a pony cart, with his parents, Sussex, 1911.

7. School photograph, circa 1920; Bert second row back, second from left.

8. Bert as a teenage schoolboy.

9. Bert photographed in Sydney, Australia, late 1920s.

10. Ferndale sheep-station, Frampton, New South Wales, after the bush fire of Christmas 1926.

11. Bogandillon, New South Wales, with his favourite pony, 1929.

12–13.   *On the Southern Empress*, 1937.

14.   Playing harmonica on the *Southern Empress*, 1937.

15. At the BBC, working on *The Shadow of the Swastika* with Igor Vinogradoff.

16. Bert on a political poster, 1938.

17. Norma picnicking on Hampstead Heath, 1930s.

18. On a North Sea trawler, 1942 (photo: Bert Hardy).

19. Norma with Joe, circa 1940.

20. With Joe, circa 1941.

21. Catterick Army Camp. Nailing up a copy of *The Turret*, 1942.

22. Trooper Lloyd at Catterick, working on *The Turret*, 1942.

23. In the Camargue, France, January 1947, interviewing a *gardian* (Camargue cowboy) (photo: Bert Hardy/Picture Post/Getty Images).

24. In the Camargue, France, January 1947 (photo: Bert Hardy/Picture Post/Getty Images).

25. Playing the guitar at home – a private passion.

26. Charlotte Lloyd (née Ohly) (photo courtesy of Caroline Clayton).

27. Caroline and Joe Lloyd, Greenwich Park, circa 1950 (photo courtesy of Caroline Clayton).

28. Bert, Charlotte and Joe, circa 1947 (photo: Bert Hardy).

29. With Ewan MacColl, 1962. Peggy Seeger's instruments in the foreground (photo: Brian Shuel).

30. With Ray Fisher and Anne Briggs, 1962 (photo: Brian Shuel).

31. Bob Dylan at the Singers' Club, December 1962. Bert sits behind Dylan (photo: Brian Shuel).

32.   With Ewan MacColl at the Singers' Club.

33.   Bert and Alf Edwards rehearse for Centre 42, Wellingborough, September 1962
      (photo: Brian Shuel).

34–36.   Bert with his books, 1970s (photos: Hedy West).

37. At home in 1966 (photo: Brian Shuel).

38. On the Isle of Lewis, 1978, notebook at the ready.

39. Bert in the 1970s.

traditional music on any practical level was Peter Kennedy, and that initially was village barn-dance music; he did, of course, later become one of our most important song collectors. In 1959 Bert commissioned him to write an article entitled 'British Folk Music on Record' for *Recorded Folk Music*. It is a very informative article which includes a fascinating and important analysis of traditional singing style as he had collected it:

> At first hearing, the singers appear to be intentionally producing what many educated musicians would consider an unmusical sound. There is certainly no sustaining of pure unaltered notes as taught at the music academies. This applies to singers both young and old; indeed, I have played recordings of twenty-year-olds who have been taken for eighty-year-olds by nearly every listener. Some singers seem rather to be speaking than singing, and if notes are held for any length, they are warbled. Most singers seem to prefer to put a harsh cutting-edge on their voice and they like to pitch the song as high as possible. Street-singers, gypsies and tinkers incline to sustain their notes more than ordinary country singers. If they do so, it is not with the level tone of the concert singers, but with slides, glottal stops and other vocal effects.
>
> In some parts of England, and still more often in Ireland, one occasionally comes across signs of a highly elaborate form of musical decoration. In a previous number of this review [magazine], A.L. Lloyd has referred to 'an ancient general European decorated style', and my own belief is that what now persists in England only in isolated examples is a survival of this once-widespread singing style.
>
> Another thing that may seem strange is that nearly all our singers use no form of instrumental accompaniment ... [Folk singers] were never concerned with harmonic implications but with the melodic variation of one note in relation to the next.[3]

This is the sort of information that the EFDSS should have been able to pass on to the nascent folk song revival, but seemingly couldn't. With its emphasis on dance (Douglas Kennedy had been a fine Cecil Sharp-taught morris dancer in his day), and its primarily dance membership, it's no wonder that the Society was seen as irrelevant (apart from the resources of the library) by the majority of folk song enthusiasts for the first couple of decades of the second folk revival. But from Bert's point of view, it was quite fortuitous. It meant that yet again he was in the right place at the right time and, like some communist Trojan horse, was welcomed into Cecil Sharp House as a folk song expert. The sad thing is that, once safely inside the gates, instead of razing the temple to the ground, he took his seat at the editorial board's library table, munched biscuits, drank tea, kept a low political profile and didn't do too much boat rocking.

In 1951 – the year that the rebuilt Cecil Sharp House was opened by HRH Princess Margaret – Frederick Keel, an original member of the old Folk Song Society (the Folk Song Society and the English Folk Dance Society amalgamated in 1932), retired from the editorial board of the EFDSS *Journal*. Bert was co-opted onto the board in 1952 to replace him, joining the chairman, Frank Howes (*The Times* music critic), Peter Kennedy, Douglas Kennedy, Maude Karpeles, Pat Shuldham-Shaw, Margaret Dean Smith, Vaughan Williams and several other pre-war folk music luminaries. Over the years, through their work on the editorial board and at other meetings and events, Ralph Vaughan Williams came to know Bert well and considered him a leading authority on English folk song. He had no problems with Bert's politics, or indeed the left in general.

Two years later Bert and Peter Kennedy managed to get Seamus Ennis elected to the editorial board. In 1958/9 Bert put himself up for election to the Society's Executive Committee but failed to get the requisite number of votes. Despite Bert's work at that time with the Society president, Vaughan Williams, on the *Penguin Book of English Folk Songs*, he was beaten to the first four places by Ron Smedley, Kenworthy Schofield, the Rev. Kenneth Loveless and the blind song-collector Fred Hamer.[4]

Although during his twenty-eight years on the editorial board Bert contributed only three articles of any length, he was a valued, and valuable, board member with his language skills and broad knowledge of world folk music, which he put to good use in book and record reviews and boardroom discussions. His earliest contributions to the *Journal* were some song notes in the 1953 issue. His first major essay, 'The Singing Style of the Copper Family', appeared in the 1954 issue and was full of good sense mixed with water-muddying as far as a definition of folk music is concerned. As one might expect from Bert, readers were treated to a succinct international tour of folk polyphony.

As Dave Harker has noted, he used the article to discreetly challenge some of the more old-fashioned notions of folk song. Bert concluded that English rural harmony, as performed by the Coppers, is not an aberration, but was probably quite widespread and almost surely 'evolved by singers with at least a nodding acquaintance with musical theory that was once common in our villages' (and towns). He admits that since the sixteenth century 'folk singers' have been learning their songs from print as well as by oral transmission, that musicians have availed themselves of printed tune-books, and many of them were perfectly capable of transcribing their tunes into their own manuscript books. However, he can't resist hanging onto Sharp's coat-tails and describing their skills as 'rudimentary', implying that they weren't sufficiently developed to interfere with their 'folk' status and were far enough away from 'art' practitioners as to be distinguishable as 'folk'. This can be seen as an example of the folk music scholar's attempt to make awkward facts fit popular assumptions.

In 1958 Bert contributed 'Notes to 5 Songs Collected by Peter Kennedy from Harry Cox'. In the privacy of his own mind it was probably a piece he wished he hadn't written, as it brought the public derision of the Australian collector John Meredith down on his head. In his note on Cox's 'The Maid of Australia' Bert had said: 'It [the song] does not seem to have persisted in Australia, and one Antipodean folklorist has suggested that this may be because, in at least one of its versions, the song appears to refer to an Aboriginal girl. Miscegenation [inter-racial sex] is a theme that Australian folklore inclines to avoid.'

Meredith, already dubious of Bert's Australian credentials and miffed at the high regard in which he was held by some Australians (e.g. Edgar Waters), jumped on Bert's *faux pas* and in the 1959 issue of the journal wrote a long letter enumerating many examples of miscegenation in Australian folklore, beginning:

> I must disagree with A.L. Lloyd's statement that 'miscegenation is a theme that Australian folklore inclines to avoid'. If this is his belief, then his knowledge of Australian folklore must be even sketchier than I had previously imagined it to be. If, as I suspect, A.L.L. has gleaned most of his Australian folklore from printed sources, then this is most likely the reason that prompted his statement, for most of the ballads dealing with miscegenation as their central theme are unsuitable for publication.

In reply, Bert explained himself by saying that the only two pieces mentioned by Meredith he had come across had been in student song books, or sung by students, and he had believed them to be 'marginal to folklore proper'. Now, having read Meredith's letter and realising that this was not the case, he courteously thanked Meredith for drawing his attention to 'so many pieces that I did not know.' As we saw earlier in the 'Lloyd Controversy' this was just the sort of ammunition that Meredith welcomed for his lifelong disparagement of Bert, and just the disarming sort of response that Bert invariably gave his denigrators.

The other two lengthy essays were both on Eastern European themes, an in-depth survey of 'Albanian Folk Song' (1968) and 'The Ritual of the Calus: Any Light on the Morris?' (1978). The article on the Romanian Calusari discussed a 1958 film made in the villages of Barca and Giurgita by Mihai Pop from the Romanian Folklore Institute, a copy of which had been loaned to the EFDSS and shown by Bert in 1976 to illustrate a talk. Bert's article gives a history of the Calus Whitsuntide dance ritual from the notes supplied with the film by Pop, and from a detailed, if rather dated article, 'The Roumanian Hobby-Horse, The Calusari' by Professor Romus Vuia, which had appeared in the special 1935 International Festival number of the EFDSS *Journal*. The Calusari group that performed in the 1935 festival was organised by one of Bert's later major influences, the Romanian born, naturalised French ethnomusicologist, Constantin Brailoiu (1893–1958).

Rather surprisingly, in his article Bert made no reference to the important, earlier forty-five-minute film of Calus dancers from Falfani in the Romanian province of Arge, filmed in 1938 by the remarkable artist, Egyptologist and musician Amice Calverley (1896–1959).[5] She gave a copy of this to Kennedy for the Society, which Bert would surely have seen. In the Calverley film the true magical, shamanistic heart of the Calus ritual is shown when sick babies are laid on the ground to be danced over in expectation of a cure. Twenty-three years later Pop's team, apparently, found no sick villager so the healing ceremony was staged, reconstructed for the film. This may not throw any light on the morris, beyond the season and the odd ribbon and bell, however there was enough ancient ritual, fairylore and solar mythology to keep the morris dancing 'ancient fertility' brigade happy.

From eighteenth- and nineteenth-century descriptions of the Calus ritual it's obvious that it has changed considerably over the years, and especially so under communism. Bert's explanation for a watering down of the magical element of the ritual was that 'the magic had leaked out,' contending that it's the nature of folklore 'that rituals become mere customs and customs end up as spectacles'. That may be so, but according to Dr Paul Nixon the process was accelerated with the help of Party officials who rounded up and imprisoned the faith-healers attached to the ritual, producing what he terms a neutered theatricalisation of Calus: 'The Party could not tolerate rival structures and personalities, local medicine men and extensive social alternatives – Calus were exactly that, *real* folk bound up in real power balances. They must be tamed by force and replaced, but Bert does not speak of these details.'[6]

No, he doesn't. But perhaps he wasn't as much 'in the know' as Nixon claims. We can't be certain how aware Bert was of the political machinations of the Culture Bosses. How much he actually saw from the cocooned environment of his 'privileged guest' status, with its free transport, comfortable hotels, compliant translators, folklorists, archivists and choreographed and handpicked performers. Or, maybe, he was merely being pragmatic and gratefully accepted what was offered to him.

In the autumn of 1951 Bert was invited to be a guest lecturer for the EFDSS 'Evenings in the Library' series of talks, along with MacColl (ballad recital), Peter Opie (children's songs), Peter Kennedy (village barn dance experiences) and others. His subject was 'The Raw Material of Folk Song'. Bert was now in the unique position of having one foot firmly in the WMA camp and the other in the EFDSS but, as we've seen, he failed to exploit this unusual position. Perhaps once he was accepted into this august, albeit mainly conservative, editorial club he didn't want to make waves, or maybe he was simply outnumbered.

Mike Yates (*Journal* editor, 1972–80) recalled the day that he asked for Bert's help with a song in an Eastern European collection:

I showed him a page in the book and he said, 'Well, I don't actually speak this language but it must be similar to …' and he mentioned some other language. He looked at it and said, 'This must mean this, and that would be …' and he translated the whole page for me. He did it with such modesty, with no idea of superiority or anything. It was just a fact of life. You felt he thought that it wasn't that difficult and that anyone could do it, really.[7]

It's not strictly true that Bert didn't attempt to rock the boat, but, having failed to breach the inner sanctum of the Executive Committee, where Society decisions were made, and with the editorial board being an inappropriate arena in which to conduct political battles, Bert was reduced to trying to effect change through the ballot-box as an ordinary Society member. But as any radical elements within the EFDSS were vastly outnumbered by the reactionary majority, he got little joy from his efforts. An example of this was the extraordinary general meeting called by Roger Marriott, Bert, MacColl and thirty-five other members in July 1960. Kennedy had announced that it was his intention to retire as director in 1961 and the National Executive Committee were looking around for a possible replacement. There had also been a Commission Report on the future artistic policy of the Society with various recommendations. The National Executive (which, incidentally included Charles Parker) seemed to feel that none of this was the affair of the membership. By 1960, two years after a statement of policy had been asked for by the more radical section of the membership, all that had appeared was a 'Stop Press' note in the Society magazine which gave a brief summary of the chairman's opinion. Hence the extraordinary general meeting in which the committee were asked what exactly was their policy, if indeed they had one, at this critical moment in the Society's history. They were also asked for clarity on the future duties of a director in a time of change.

In the Annual General Report for 1960–1 it was reported that, at the meeting, A.L. Lloyd (London):

> ... called the attention to the present very wide interest in folk song, especially among the Younger Generation. Those with whom he came in contact, were apt to regard the Society as a kind of amiable social club for middle-aged dancers. The members should realize that this was an important time for the Society, which in relation to this present widespread interest was in grave danger of missing the bus. It was trying to be popular and learned at the same time, but in fact one had to admit that it was 'neither truly popular nor truly learned'. The NEC were lacking in energy for encouraging folk song and scholarship and he held that this may be due to indecision and vagueness of policy. The Committee had a responsibility to channel the new enthusiasm of the Younger Generation and to give it a lead. There was a path that lay somewhere between fossilization on the one hand and Denmark Street on the other. Now that there was clearly a new revival, surely there was a need for a new policy. In his opinion the vagueness of our aims seemed a poor tribute to Cecil Sharp.

MacColl said much the same thing, asking whether the Society was going to provide a lead for the thousands of young people interested in folk music or was it going to go on being a gentlemanly club where members died peacefully and imperceptibly? The majority of members, led by Maude Karpeles, who asked 'all those with the welfare of the Society at heart' to vote against any motion of censure and to support the status quo, won the day, and Bert and MacColl left with their opinion of the EFDSS confirmed.

If Bert had little in common with much of the Society's membership and was unimpressed by its organisation, there were certain advantages in the early days of his folk music career in being welcomed into the bosom of the Society by Kennedy. As a professional singer and folklorist it gave him official credibility in the academic world – he was soon attending international folklore conferences and mixing with eminent western musicologists such as Charles Seeger. He already had Eastern European contacts through the Communist Party and the WMA. Apart from his academic work, his EFDSS connections occasionally came in useful for bread and butter performance work. For example, there was a time, in 1952, when he needed a reference for an Aylesbury choral society, and could offer Douglas Kennedy as his referee: 'Mr A.L. Lloyd, whom we are thinking of as a folk song singer at one of our next season's concerts, suggest I write to you for an opinion on his singing as it is somewhat of a departure from our usual type of concert, I should like to have the authority of your opinion to present to my committee.' They had no idea that Kennedy considered Bert's authority on the matter of folk singing to be far greater than his own, and were happy to receive Kennedy's unqualified (in both senses) recommendation:

> I can unhesitatingly recommend him as a folk song singer. He is one of the few singers I know who are [*sic*] capable of interpreting the folk song in its original form, or as near to it as an educated person can get. Whether that kind of singing will be applicable to normal conditions is another matter. A few years ago I should have recommended definite caution. Now, however, there is quite a body of informed taste ready to accept unaccompanied singing and the traditional style. You can at least assure your committee as to the acceptance of Mr Lloyd's style, for Dr. Vaughan Williams awarded him the first prize at the last Folk Song Competition we held at Cecil Sharp House, a year or so ago. I daresay your audience would be much more unprejudiced than a sophisticated town gathering where there might be an element ready to snigger at the unexpected.[8]

Kennedy obviously believed that uneducated people performed folk song in its 'original form', and also that unaccompanied folk song was potentially a sniggering affair. Perhaps Bert credited Kennedy and the EFDSS with more clout than was warranted, because in 1953 he was writing to Kennedy asking advice on how to go about getting funding for a project he had in mind concerning sea shanties:

> For some time past I have been turning a project over in my mind, and I would value your advice. I have been struck by the fact that we're all very proud and sometimes sentimental about our sea-shanties, but we really know very little about them. In fact, considering that there are many people still alive who were working at sea while shanty-singing was a living tradition, it is astonishing how poorly documented the study of the shanty is.[9]

He thought it would be well worthwhile conducting a proper investigation among old-time sailing ship sailors while there was still time, looking into singing styles, individual repertoires, the extent of improvisation, means of dissemination, the popularity or rarity of particular shanties, how they were used, the type of ship and route that provided the richest and most varied songs and issues concerning authorship:

> All of this would be most valuable data for the vexed and little touched-upon question of folk creation. Indeed, I believe the shanties are the only body of English folk song that allow such study.
>
> I should dearly love to undertake such an investigation, but of course I can't afford to. One would think it would be worth some Foundation's while to put up a bit of cash for it. Do you know of anywhere one might apply? I'm sure something valuable and lively would come of it. But it would need doing soon.

Kennedy, after showing Bert's detailed proposal to his son Peter agreed that it was a good idea. In reality, however, he had no more idea than Bert on where to get funding. He suggested that it might be done under the umbrella of the BBC folk music collecting scheme in which Peter was employed. He offered to drop a line to Marie Slocombe at the BBC suggesting that Bert be given the job of conducting the research. As far as we know, nothing came of the idea. However, in 1962 in the EFDSS magazine *Folk* there appeared a seven-page article entitled 'Lime Juice Songs and Shanties' by Peter Kennedy, based on his interview (as part of the 1950s BBC collecting scheme) with ex-sailor Commander Halliday on the history and art of shanty singing.

In 1953 Bert seems to have been unaware of the existence of the shantyman and maritime historian Stan Hugill (1906–92), who proved to be a walking encyclopaedia of shanties, shanty singing, and shipboard practice, and who in 1962 published the definitive *Shanties of the Seven Seas*. Hugill had actually been down to Cecil Sharp House in March 1955 when he gave a Library Lecture on 'Shanties and Shantying', but it was a few years later that he came to national prominence. A couple of years older than Bert, Hugill was adventuring and shanty-singing in the South Pacific and around the nitrate ports of South America on the *Garthpool*, the last British commercial sailing ship, when Bert was roustabouting in New South Wales.

After the Second World War, during which he was a prisoner of the Germans, Hugill settled down to life ashore as instructor at the Outward Bound Sea School in Aberdovey, Wales. By the time his book came out and he was appearing at the Spinners folk club in Liverpool and other places as the last of the deepwater shanty men, Bert and MacColl had already sewn up the shanty/sea-song market with *The Singing Sailor* (1956), *The Blackball Line* (1957), *Thar She Blows* (1957), *Blow Boys Blow* (1960), *A Sailors Garland* (1962) and *Whaler Out of New Bedford and Other Songs of the Whaling Era* (1962). Many of these were re-issued in a bewildering number of permutations, formats, titles and cover designs over the years in Britain, America and Australia.

As the genuine article, Hugill was not terribly impressed with what he considered, despite Bert's shanty-singing in the film *Moby Dick*, to be library shanty men and armchair experts, although he conceded that Bert always acknowledged his (Hugill's) expertise.[10] If Hugill was a little underwhelmed by the dry-land sailors, other less informed people took the shanties and sea-songs to their hearts and were inspired by Bert and Ewan's albums.

Stan Kelly, who recorded a shanty album for HMV with Stan Hugill, felt that Hugill's response was:

> The reaction of the real shantyman who objected to non-seafarers 'putting on the agony'. Hugill's voice, of course, had lost its edge when he started recording so I always assumed some sour grapes in view of Bert and Ewan's stronger and more vibrant vocal chords! In the other direction, Bert often scoffed at the lack of 'scholarship' in Stan's magnum opus, *Shanties of the Seven Seas*. Not in a nasty way but, again, you can see how clashes occur.[11]

By 1979, when Dave Harker was looking for financial assistance to publish the manuscript collection of John Bell, the nineteenth-century Newcastle bibliophile and song collector, Bert had given up on the EFDSS as a source of funding. As he told Harker:

> I'm not much good when it comes to suggesting sources that might put up money. I've never been lucky with any feeble overtures of my own, though once the Arts Council sent me a cheque out of the blue, without being asked. I've no idea if your venture would interest them, but I don't imagine it's up their street. I should think it's pretty hopeless looking toward the perennially impoverished EFDSS but the Vaughan Williams Trust has money for suchlike ventures, and it might well be worth approaching them.[12]

The unsolicited 'maintenance grant' fell through Bert's letterbox while he was working on *Folk Song in England*. C. Day Lewis was on the Arts Council Literary Panel in the mid-1960s and may have had a hand in securing the award for Bert. Harker, with his joint editor Frank Rutherford, finally got his book published in January 1984 by the Surtees Society.

THE WRITING CONTINUES

In spring 1939, Fore Publications had published their first half-dozen Key Books. These were pocket-sized pamphlets that promised 'fiction, biography, history, science and topical information by the best modern writers'. This was not dissimilar in intent from the Left Book Club but more closely associated with CPGB aims and ideas, with titles like Richard Goodman's *England's Best Ally* (an appeal for an alliance with the Soviet Union), Palme Dutt's *When England Arose* and Jack Lindsay's *England, My England* (on the English radical tradition). Then in 1945 they published a piece of Lloydian Americana – *Corn on the Cob: Popular and Traditional Poetry of the U.S.A.*

Corn on the Cob was a small, sixty-six-page paperback that, as Bert said in his introduction, had a lot to do in attempting to introduce British readers to the whole spectrum of American traditional verse. And it *is* verse, folk poetry without tunes that, as Bert acknowledged, is never wholly satisfactory. It's like 'listening' to ballet, or watching opera with the sound turned off. Folk song lyrics are intimately bound up with their tunes, even if many disparate tunes may exist for a particular song, and they only come alive in performance. There's nothing less inspiring than people 'reading' ballads. The 'enchanter of souls', the poet George Barker's party piece was a declamation of the ballad 'Tamlin', which went down very well with the arty-crafty 1930s London crowd, but then they'd never heard the Traveller Betsy Johnston or Bert singing it. As Bert says: 'It is hoped that the poems in this book are capable of surviving the cruel divorce from their tunes. Probably most of them can so survive; they are tough. But readers are reminded that however these poems read, they sing a thousand times better.'

So why publish them without the tunes? The fact that a convention had grown up over a couple of hundred years of publishing ballad texts without the tunes is no reason to perpetuate it. Economics no doubt came into it: as Marx and Lenin knew, it invariably does. However, the forty-three pieces that Bert selected for this intimidating task go some way to achieving their goal. Following a standard form of subject division we have 'The Old Songs from the Mountains', The Songs of the Shifting Frontier', 'Negro Spirituals and Negro Protests', 'Prison Songs Black and White', 'Songs of the Bad men and the Wicked Cities', 'Songs of the Great American Bum' and finally 'Songs of Modern Times'.

The sets of lyrics are well selected. Admittedly some of the songs are composite texts taken from more than one version of a song. And, as one of Bert's sources was John and Alan Lomax's *American Ballads and Folk Songs* (1934), which itself contained numerous composite texts, some of the songs must be quite a way from any original collected traditional set of lyrics. However a 'collected' set of lyrics has no intrinsic Grail quality; they just happen to be a bunch of lines sung and noted down, or recorded, on a particular day.

In his essay 'Starting Over: A.L. Lloyd and the Search for a New Folk Music, 1945–49' in the *Canadian Journal for Traditional Music* (1999/2000), David Gregory had this to say about *Corn on the Cob*:

It was, in fact, intended to stimulate in England the kind of political folk revival that the Almanacs (Almanac Singers) were leading in the U.S.A. The collection was the first cheap and convenient source book available to British Revival Singers, and it would not be superseded until Alan Lomax's *Folk Songs of North America* was published by Cassell in 1960.

Gregory, I believe, overestimates the importance of, or perhaps the impact of, the book on the British folk revival. Unlike America there *was* no folk revival in England in 1945. There were EFDSS-type recitals, also many community choirs, often left-wing, but they tended to sing choral arrangements of international, especially Russian, songs, light classical pieces, etc. At that point they rarely performed traditional folk songs, English or American. During the war the WMA choir sang a lot of international songs on the radio, Russian songs in translation, songs of struggle and Alan Bush's songs. There was a lot of interest in the choir because nobody else was doing this material.

The left-wing literati who would have read the 'folk poems' as credible, creative examples of working-class culture, would have favourably received *Corn on the Cob* and been unperturbed by the divorce of lyric from music. The collection would also possibly have been of interest to early blues and jazz aficionados, who were more often collectors and researchers than performers.

It was several years after the publication of *Corn on the Cob* before a few people started looking for folk material to sing, and the majority of the American songs (not including those by Woody Guthrie) that were sung in the early days of the folk revival, both in Britain and in America, are to be found in two Lomax collections: *American Ballads and Folk Songs* (1934) and *Our Singing Country* (1949). They were usually learnt in the UK from recordings of singers such as Pete Seeger and Burl Ives (and his paperback *Song Book*) and groups like the Almanac Singers, the Weavers and in the mid-1950s from Lomax himself and his skiffle/folk group the Ramblers. Other sources were 78s of American Old Time music picked up in junk shops, Ramblin' Jack Elliott, Lonnie Donegan, Russell Quaye's City Ramblers with their unique mix of blues, gospel, cockney, skiffle and jazz songs, Ewan MacColl (whose first recording for Topic Records was 'The Asphalter's Song'/'I'm Champion at Keeping 'em Rolling'/'Fourpence a Day'/'Barnyards of Delgatie', 1950), Bert himself in live performance and (from 1953 on record), John Hasted's skiffle and folk group, and eventually live and recorded British traditional singers like Harry Cox, Bob Roberts, 'Pop' Maynard, the Copper Family, Sam Larner and Phil Tanner.

All of these, with the exception of Tanner, came and performed in London. So too did Irish and Scottish singers living in London or passing through (Seamus Ennis, Dominic Behan, Maggie Barry, Jimmie Macgregor, Robin Hall and many more). The library at Cecil Sharp House was popular with Bert, but not the first port of call for the vast majority of the coffee-bar cowboys who emerged during and following the skiffle craze. But when asked today, no singers from the 1950s can remember using *Corn on the Cob* as a source of material, or even hearing of it. It was certainly no way as influential as Bert and Vaughan Williams's similarly modestly sized *The Penguin Book of English Folk Songs* (1959), or as widely known in the 1950s as *The Singing Englishman*.

Of course, throughout the 1950s there were numerous inspirational, if ephemeral (since most listeners were unable to record them) radio programmes on British, Irish, American and European folk music, frequently written and presented by Alan Lomax and also Peter Kennedy. This must have been very frustrating for Bert: the last thing he needed was a genuine American expert (Lomax arrived here under MI5 surveillance in 1951), who had actually collected and published song collections of the cowboys, gospel singers and bluesmen which Bert had made his own in his writings during the 1940s. Bert and Lomax were never as close as MacColl and Lomax seem to have been. MacColl and Seeger claimed Lomax as their 'best friend'.

1946 saw the American re-publication of Bert's translation of Kafka's *Metamorphosis* by the Vanguard Press. In 1999 the New York Public Library held an exhibition entitled *Nabokov Under Glass: Centennial Exhibition*. An item in the exhibition was Vladimir Nabokov's copy of Bert's translation of *Metamorphosis*, which Nabokov had annotated and re-translated in places. He considered the book second only to *Ulysses* in his critique of twentieth-century prose. Faber and Faber reprinted Bert's *Metamorphosis*, along with *Death of a Bullfighter and other Poems*, and *Folk Song in England* in 2008, as part of their Faber Finds print-on-demand series of important out-of-print books, to celebrate the hundredth anniversary of his birth.

In December 1946 *Picture Post* printed a feature entitled 'Some Carols You May Not Know'. Although no writing credit was given, it looks very much like a Bert article, including as it does one of his favourite carols, 'The Bitter Withy,' which he recorded for HMV in 1953. When he recorded it again in 1956 for the American Riverside album *Great British Ballads Not Included in the Child Collection*, presumably to give the recording more credibility, the sleeve notes by Kenneth Goldstein state: 'The version sung by Lloyd is primarily a family version "which has been amplified from printed versions over the years".'

However in the Christmas 1956 issue of *Sing* magazine, to which he contributed 'The Bitter Withy', Bert says: 'I've looked at all the printed versions of this song that I possess – about a dozen or so – but none is anything like as good as this one, either for text or tune. I don't know where I learned this one; certainly from print; but I've been walking about with it for more than twenty years so it may have got a little altered in that time.' Which must mean we can also discount 'family tradition' for 'The Bramble Brier' ('Bruton Town') on the same album: 'Most texts are of an extremely poor literary quality; the version sung by Lloyd, part of his family tradition, appears to be one of the finest versions around.' Similarly with 'The Shooting of His Dear': 'The version sung by Lloyd is largely from his own family tradition, but has been expanded from various printed sources.'

It's also interesting to read in the fanciful biographical notes that Bert's father was '… a trawler fisherman and dockworker of East Anglian origin with a fine store of East Coast folk songs particularly of songs relating to seafaring. His mother, who had a more formal musical education, accompanied her folk singing with a rather elaborate piano style.' In addition, Jimmy Miller's (Ewan MacColl) birthplace had shifted several miles north from Lower Broughton, Salford to Auchterarder, Perthshire!

Both MacColl and Bert obviously felt the need to re-invent themselves to give their pronouncements more authority, Bert seemingly even more than MacColl (who, as well as changing name and birthplace, reduced his age). Bert's differing accounts of his parentage are numerous, and his remarkably selective 'memory' of his early life in later autobiographical writing and interviews is puzzling. He once told Tom Hopkinson that, following his whaling trip, he decided it was time to educate himself, so he set off for Egypt with a box of books and, for six months, sat in the shadow of the Sphinx and read.[13] Let's hope the BBC didn't find out: they were paying his wages at the time. Of course, Bert and MacColl certainly aren't alone in creating their own life histories, and as Bert's old acquaintance Aleister Crowley would have said: 'And it hurt none, do what thou wilt, shall be the whole of the law.'

Bert created some wonderful songs, probably more than we realise. One he contributed to MacColl and Seeger's *The Singing Island* (1960) was the unique 'Farewell to Tarwathie', subsequently much sung as traditional Scottish and more recently recorded by the American singer Judy Collins for a television documentary about Moby-Dick. Bert claimed to have learnt it in 1938 from a John Sinclair in Durban, South Africa and recorded it on the Riverside album *Thar She Blows*. This was originally an 1850s poem by a Scottish miller, George Scroggie. A set of words based on the poem was collected by Gavin Greig and the Rev. James Bruce Duncan in Aberdeenshire and appear in the first of the eight-volume *Greig-Duncan Collection*, but with no tune. In 1938 these lyrics were only available in the Greig-Duncan manuscript collection which Mr Sinclair would have been unlikely to have seen. It's much more probable that Bert found the words some time before 1956, and tinkered with them a bit to make them fit a tune that he knew – 'Green Bushes', or a slowed down version of 'Rye Whisky'. He *was* in Durban in 1938 on his way back from his whaling trip, and this was probably used to provide a convincing provenance to 'Farewell to Tarwathie'.

'Lord Franklin' is another song, supposedly from that same trip which became hugely popular after Bert 'collected' it from Edward Harper, a whale-factory blacksmith of Port Stanley in the Falkland Islands, in November 1937. Bob Dylan liked the tune well enough to use it for his 'Bob Dylan's Dream', after hearing Martin Carthy sing it. If Bert did indeed collect them he was remarkably fortuitous. If not, he was remarkably talented. Either way they are fine songs and deserve their popularity. Had he really collected them in the late 1930s you would have expected him to at least mention them in *The Singing Englishman* where instead he said: 'Nowadays aboard the floating whale factories in the Antarctic the same songs are sung as you hear in any factory ashore, the same songs and *no* [my italics] others … . I have heard whalermen singing at work on deck and after work down in the fo'c'sle, but on top or down below I never heard them sing much but "Boohoo, you've got me crying for you".' As it is they don't get a mention until the 1950s, which is significant.

One Bert creation, before we leave this fascinating aspect of his work, is the wonderfully atmospheric 'The Weary Whaling Grounds'. Appearing on

Leviathan! (1967), it is another whaling song that Bert rewrote, fitted with a tune, and successfully floated on the revival sea without a ripple. It appeared originally in Gale Huntington's 1964 collection, *Songs the Whalemen Sang*, as 'The Wings of a Goney', from the 1859 log of the *Ocean Rover*, and was the only known text before Bert's British version surfaced with its more euphonic and folksy 'I'd rather be snug in a Deptford pub, a drinking of good beer' replacing 'I would sooner be at home in some Dutch grocery shop, eating crackers and cheese or drinking beer'.[14]

ROCK ISLAND LINE

> Jesus came to save our sins,
> Glory be, we're gonna need him again.
> Oh the Rock Island Line is a mighty good line
> The Rock Island Line is the road to ride.

When Norma committed suicide in 1945 their young son Joe was five years and three months old and bright enough to realise what was going on. Initially, he transferred his maternal needs to Jenny, Bert's stepdaughter. But then she, too, disappeared from his life, leaving Charlotte to help bring up Norma's son – a permanent reminder of the sad consequence of her relationship with Bert. Joe Lloyd was a bright boy who five years later sailed through his common entrance examination and, around 1951, after a satisfactory interview, became a pupil at St Olave's Grammar School. He had curly dark hair, and was described by an old school acquaintance as 'quite a "pretty" boy, liked by the girls for his looks'.

A year ahead of Joe at St Olave's was Neville Derbyshire, a young man with dandyish pretensions and also a proselytising jazz aficionado, offering an alternative to the music of such singers as Frankie Lane and Johnny Ray, both of whom were very popular in the school. So successful was he that one day a young acolyte, Mike Parry, commandeered the school record player, wheeled it into his form room and presented a programme of jazz recordings for his intrigued classmates. In 1956 Mike, who had recently left the school, was invited to join ex-classmate George Kennard and start a skiffle group along with Joe Lloyd and John Howlett. George and Joe played guitar, while eighteen-year-old Mike provided 'percussion' on the washboard – inspired by the Washboard Queen Beryl Bryden, who had played on Lonnie Donegan's recent 1956 chart hit 'Rock Island Line' – and John plucked away on the ubiquitous tea-chest skiffle bass.[15]

Skiffle was the first popular, grassroots, pluck it, strum it, blow it, bang it, do-it-yourself teenage music craze. It coincided with the growth of coffee bars and as ex-skiffler John Pilgrim said:

For a brief while in 1956 almost every Soho coffee bar and delicatessen seemed to sprout some kind of band or group. Music seemed to be emerging out of every window – the excitement was palpable. Then the Russians moved into Hungary, and in pale emulation the authorities in Britain decided that too many people were enjoying themselves for nothing. So they clamped down on the most innocent part of Soho. Soho's brief period as a wide-open music area ended.[16]

Teenagers were a new concept – the term first appeared in the *Readers Digest* in 1941. Neither children nor yet adults, they emerged from the grey, austere, post-war years in search of an identity, fun and a voice of their own. Skiffle, fashion, coffee bars, and then rock-and-roll gave it to them.

The advantage of having Joe in the group was they had access to a mouth-watering wealth of material from Joe's dad; they didn't just have to rely on the recordings of such popular professional skifflers as Lonnie Donegan, Bob Cort, the Vipers, and Chas McDevitt for their repertoire. As always, Bert was generous with his encouragement, time and the provision of suitable material. He opened their ears to a wide range of music through his American Library of Congress albums, including bluegrass, blues and cowboy songs, which the band listened to in the basement of the Lloyds' Greenwich house.

In the summer they were allowed to go up and practise on the roof. This had two advantages for Bert. Firstly it made him into a 'cool' father – not many parents would encourage their sons to go and play on the roof. Secondly, it kept the sound of rehearsals as far away from the rest of the house as possible! Martin Carthy, a year below Joe at St Olave's, was impressed with the group's material and asked Joe where they got it. 'From my dad.' What does your dad do?' asked Carthy. 'He's a singer.' It's interesting that in the 1950s Joe thought of Bert not as a writer or journalist but as a singer.

As well as exploring Bert's record collection, the band had the opportunity of meeting and listening to the numerous folk artists who passed through the Lloyd household – Peggy Seeger, a sometime lodger, accompanied Bert and Ewan MacColl on records, radio programmes and in clubs, and also taught budding folk musicians guitar and banjo for the Workers' Music Association in London. The fine bass player, Jim Bray, also an early visitor to Greenwich, was always happy to play along with them. Legendary bluesman Big Bill Broonzy, who in March 1957 appeared on the BBC television show *Six-Five Special,* turned up at Bert's one day and astonished the teenagers by managing to play some wonderful blues on one of their cheap skiffle guitars. Brooklyn 'cowboy' Ramblin' Jack Elliott arrived with his big Gretch guitar, cowboy boots and Stetson hat. Bert's daughter Caroline remembers the day that Rambling Jack and Bert turned up at her Greenwich primary school to perform for her classmates. She was relieved to find her fears and acute embarrassment unjustified, as Bert and Jack soon had the kids eating out of their hands with sing-along Woody Guthrie numbers and entertaining English songs like the 'Derby Ram'.

For the average skiffler, and early folk fan, the quality of affordable guitars generally available was abysmal. They tended to fall into two categories: cheap, lightweight plywood and nasty; and cheap, heavy plywood and nasty. The lighter ones tended to buckle and bow at the first sign of string tension or exposure to heat or cold, and the heavier ones could have doubled up as wardrobes and required a body-building course to hold and play for any extended period. Some enterprising youngsters decided to build their own guitars by trial and error. A few, like another Croom's Hill visitor, Barry 'Spud' Murphy (1938–2011) went on to become fine luthiers. The names Gibson and Martin, if known, were uttered in hushed, reverential tones, and the chances of getting one at that time were about as likely as a walk on the moon. The first two halfway decent steel-strung, flat-top guitars that tyro folk singers got their hands on were the Harmony Sovereign and the Swedish Levin Goliath, generally bought by young Londoners on Hire Purchase from Ivor Mairants' guitar shop in Rathbone Place, or (the long defunct) Scarth's music emporium in Charing Cross Road.

The Delta Skiffle Group, as they eventually called themselves, busked in Villier's Street beneath the arches of Charing Cross station, and also played in the window of Old Compton Street's Orlando's coffee bar run by 'Johnny the Pole' (who occasionally climbed onto the counter and recited Chekhov). This was next to the famous 2I's coffee bar at number 59 (now boasting a Green Plaque to celebrate its role in the birth of British rock and roll). Some evenings they'd go and hear Bert and Ewan MacColl at the Ballads and Blues club at the Princess Louise pub in High Holborn, one of the first London folk music clubs (originally opened as a skiffle club in April 1956 by Russell Quaye and the City Ramblers spasm band). Bert suggested that one or more of the skiffle group might accompany him on the opening night of the club but, although flattered, the lads declined, in the face of serious musical competition from Alf Edwards, Fitzroy Coleman, Peggy Seeger and others. Other Delta heroes included the twelve-string guitarist and blues singer Long John Baldry (1941–2005), once spotted by them playing on the steps of St Martin's-in-the-Field, and the pioneer bluesman Alexis Korner (1928–84), of whom Bert remarked to them, 'fine guitar player, but awful voice'.

Some weekends they would go to an office block in the City of London, where the parents of another St Olave's pupil, Dick Gough, were caretakers. They'd practise in the boardroom whilst, unknown to Dick's parents, helping themselves to drinks from the directors' fridge. At one point the Delta Skiffle Group was encouraged by Bert to enter the *Daily Worker* Skiffle Competition held in the Federation Hall in Abbey Wood. Bert, who was on the panel of judges, agreed, due to his vested interest in the group, to take no part in judging the Delta's performance. Their entry, a version of 'The Derby Ram', learned from Bert, won the prize for the most original song.

When Joe arrived at St Olave's he was expected to do well and was put in a class a year above his age. Unfortunately he failed to live up to his academic potential and left school at sixteen. When Peggy Seeger first came to England in 1956 and stayed for a couple of months with the Lloyds she remembered the young Joe as very friendly and likeable: 'The most fun of all four of the family. I liked him. He took me all around naughty London. We went to the dives and we drank, and did all kinds of things He was always very outgoing and very fast. I had the feeling that he may have been on drugs.'[17]

This proved to be the case. Indeed, Charlotte couldn't cope with her stepson's lifestyle and drug habit, and had little sympathy for the crises that Joe inflicted on the family. In the 1960s the composer Edward Williams and his wife Judy, who were old friends of Bert, had a smallholding at White Lackington in Dorset, and Bert asked them if they could possibly help him out by letting Joe stay with them in the country, away from the narcotic temptations of the London clubs. The Williamses agreed and took Joe in, looked after him and encouraged him to help out on the smallholding.[18] They were very fond of him, although the respite was short-lived and when Joe got back to the city he rapidly returned to his old habits with an ultimate tragic result.

Caroline seems to have been the only member of the family with whom Joe could discuss his addiction. He told her that he got into drugs through hanging out with jazz musicians. After leaving school Joe worked for a while for Joan Littlewood at the Theatre Workshop, then later as a BBC film editor. He eventually married and moved to Italy. In 1978, during a trip to the UK, Joe died of a heroin overdose in Better Books in Charing Cross Road – one of the most hip bookshops in the 1960s and 1970s, where one could pick up the latest James Baldwin or William Burroughs. It was a suitably rebellious shop, which suited Joe's lifestyle and personality. In future years Charlotte could never pass the shop without saying, 'That's the shop where Joe died.' Barrie Gavin felt that Bert never fully recovered from Joe's untimely death. Caroline said that despite Joe's drug problems Bert's love for him was constant and immense, and she agrees with Gavin that Bert's heart broke when Joe died. The hole left by Joe's death was enormous and the thing the family missed the most was his huge capacity for laughter – helpless giggles (like his father).

Joe and the other Delta Skiffle Group members began to find they had less and less in common, and eventually Joe drifted away from the band, which continued for a while with the addition of a pianist. But the skiffle craze evaporated as quickly as it had sprung up. By the end of the 1950s it had all but vanished, but not before it gave birth to a Golden Age of English rock and rhythm and blues bands. And, of course, there was a rapidly expanding folk revival movement (those musicians who eschewed electric guitars and clung to their acoustic instruments had to go somewhere) in which Bert and Ewan MacColl, aided and abetted by Alan Lomax, were determined to play a leading role. In later life Bert was surprisingly and, perhaps, unjustly dismissive of skiffle and claimed not to see much validity in it. It became quickly commercialised once the record companies and promoters, who had been caught on the hop, suddenly realised there was a large potential audience for it. A few people such as Lonnie Donegan, Chas McDevitt and Nancy Whiskey achieved a pop-like celebrity with the concomitant record sales, and people like Bert and MacColl got radio and concert work off the back of it, but the vast majority of the thousands of, mostly working-class, skifflers, were ordinary kids who suddenly discovered the pleasure of making their own music.

Here was a real nationwide cultural upsurge. A new world opened up for them. Most were never going to be virtuoso musicians, or any sort of musician, but it didn't matter. It was a grass-roots democratic movement which blossomed for a couple of years and without which the subsequent folk revival, of which Bert was one of the beneficiaries, would have been a very different affair, if it would have taken off at all. The ex-skiffler (the City Ramblers and the Vipers) John Pilgrim, has a more positive take on the skiffle boom:

> I sat in a London pub recently and heard Geordie folksinger Bob Davenport singing 'Bill Bailey'. He was accompanied by jazz pianist Johnny Parker, one of those who started it all. The pair went on to do 'Blaydon Races' and 'Cushy Butterfield'. Those two are senior figures in their respective fields. Yet it is impossible to imagine them performing together without the eclectic influence of the skiffle movement they helped create.
>
> Skiffle then had a number of virtues. But above all it enabled people to realise that music was for playing and singing, not just listening. People who play music tend to take a more active interest in music other people play and record. Some at least of the immense variety of music available today has a market because skiffle created an informed musical population who developed their own ideas of the sort of things they wanted to hear.[19]

11
Ramblers and Bold Miners

In 1950 when his position at *Picture Post* became untenable Bert decided to jump before being pushed. Suddenly he was free to put much of his time and energy into what had become an increasingly important part of his life: folk music. Although, as he has said, his family nearly starved in the process. But the time was right, even though neither he nor the protagonists in his immediate future were aware of their imminent conjunction.

Around 1949 Bert and John Hasted, who knew each other through the WMA and the Unity Theatre, discovered a mutual interest in People's Music as performed by the American communist propagandist Almanac Singers. Hasted had been given a copy of their Keynote album *Talking Union* (which included 'Which Side Are You On?', 'Talking Union', 'Union Maid' and 'Roll the Union On') by a merchant seaman friend who had stopped over in New York and met the group; this was Alun Hughes. Bert and Hasted got into the habit of meeting up for lunch once a week at a little Greek restaurant by Cambridge Circus, just off Charing Cross Road, to discuss putting the world to rights.

By a strange coincidence Bert and Hasted had originally both been introduced to the Almanacs in the early 1940s by the same person, many miles apart and several years before they actually met. From 1940 Hughes was serving as a merchant seaman on the Norwegian tanker M/T *Hoegh Scout*, occasionally sending Bert texts of songs he picked up from shipmates. In August 1942 his convoy docked in New York where he met the Almanacs and bought three Keynote albums; the Almanacs' *Talking Union* (released in June 1941), *Dear Mr President,* the Almanacs' 1942 topical album in support of the war effort, and the 1940 *Six Songs for Democracy*, songs of the Spanish Civil War and the International Brigade (originally recorded in Spain in 1938). Hughes wrote to Bert about the albums and Bert borrowed the two by the Almanacs, returning them by post to Hughes' brother's house in Cheltenham about five weeks later (Hughes being by then back at sea). In a letter to Hughes Bert said, 'I find them of tremendous interest, and they give me an idea of a new dimension in folk song'. Bert later published 'Round and Round Hitler's Grave' from *Dear Mr President* in his 1945 collection *Corn on the Cob*.

In the mid-1940s, Hughes introduced the three albums to fellow Oxford University student Hasted. Hasted told Hughes of his excitement at the discovery of a type of music wholly new to him, a music he would eventually sing with Bert and introduce into the repertoire of the London Youth Choir.

The Marxist composer Alan Bush was very much an enemy of all pop music at that time – it was 'all moon and June!' On hearing the popular song 'I Don't Want to Set the World on Fire', he thumped the table and said, 'Comrades! That's exactly what we *do* want to do!' Bert and Hasted felt the same. As Hasted said:

> We were all very conscious that 100 per cent of pop music is politics, so if you destroy pop music, it's a political act. Bert understood this earlier than I did. Which is why he was singing English songs while we were still singing skiffle. This was the point of agreement we had with Alan Bush, we were trying to start a movement, it wasn't just two guys in a café in Cambridge Circus.

Bert was still at *Picture Post* and had recently moved house to Greenwich. Hasted, a hard-working member of the Notting Hill Branch of the CPGB, was juggling his time between politics, being a research physicist at University College and singing in Bush's excellent choir, the Workers' Music Association Singers. He was also trying to come to terms with a dissolving marriage due to his political and musical commitments; he was out most evenings rehearsing or performing at meetings and political rallies. He was also taking lessons in conducting from Bush with the intention of eventually starting his own choir (he eventually ran the London Youth Choir), although, even then, he was beginning to have doubts as to whether large choirs were best suited for putting across political messages. He was coming to the conclusion that for any People's Song movement the whole audience must be able to hear every word and be able to participate, for which a small group might be more appropriate.

At that time in England small acoustic folk-type groups, if any existed, were generally unknown, unlike in America where there was a strong musical-folklore tradition of guitar and banjo-led trios and quartets which the original Almanacs – Pete Seeger, Lee Hays, Millard Lampell, Peter Hawes – adopted early in 1941 and used as the vehicle for their political song writing and radical proselytising. Woody Guthrie joined them a few months later in June. Despite the popular image of the Almanacs as initiators of a nationwide explosion of radical workers' singing and song-making, their union, peace and (after Germany invaded Russia) anti-fascist songs, styled generally on traditional folk song tunes and poetry, had little real influence on the mass of the 'people', who preferred the latest commercial popular music, and whose values were frequently not those of the Almanacs, who tended to follow the Communist Party line sent down from Moscow. According to Serge Denisoff the Almanacs' songs were 'better known in bohemian and communist circles than in the ranks of labour'.[1] Pete Seeger has noted that: 'Except for a few unions there never was as much singing as some people now suppose. From listening to the *Talking Union* record and reading a couple of novels about the labour struggles of the '30s one might jump to the conclusion that the United States was full of class-conscious harmonizing in those days. 'Taint true.'

And unions are generally too busy with their day-to-day work to bother about singing, songbooks and producing workers' records, as Bert and MacColl found when they attempted to get the TUC and the Labour Party aboard the folk-train. In 1961 Bert wrote a proposal asking for financial support to produce an anthology of working-class cultural traditions. For £7,500 Lloyd and MacColl (presumably the 'two good researchers' he had in mind in his proposal) would initially spend a year researching and setting up the project which would stimulate working-class culture. The proposal was submitted to Merlyn Reed, organiser of the Labour Party's 1962 Cultural Festival, in the hope that 'the organized Labour movement' could assist by first putting up the money. Secondly, making available its organisational resources (e.g. the investigators would have to rely heavily on the aid of interested people in trade union branches in various industries and localities; also they would need to be able to appeal for help through the columns of the working class press, especially trade union journals). And lastly, assisting or even undertaking the publication of a selection of the findings (though it might be hoped that a publisher such as Penguin might well be interested).

Bert continued: 'The investigation of our industrial folklore can only be carried out with the interest and benevolence of the working-class movement. The capitalist class has no part to play in this matter. Indeed if they had, it would be a disgrace for Labour to stand aside while capitalist foundations direct an affair that is so much Labour's intimate concern.[2] The TUC and the Labour party, however, could not be shamed into stumping up the cash. In November 1964, when Bert wrote to Hamish Henderson thanking him for an off-print of tales from 'the Coddy' (a mutual Scottish storytelling acquaintance), he was still trying unsuccessfully for funding: 'I'm trying to raise money from H.M. Government for a systematic industrial folklore project. No signs of success yet.'

Back in 1949 Bert and John Hasted couldn't foresee any of this; they had simply heard the Almanac's 'Talking Union Blues' and were hooked:

> Now if you want higher wages let me tell you what to do
> You've got to talk to the workers in the shop with you,
> You've got to build you a union got to make it strong,
> But if you all stick together, boys, it won't take long.
> You'll get shorter hours,
> Better working conditions,
> Vacations with pay,
> Take your kids to the seashore.

Hasted was still an Almanac enthusiast forty years later when he explained his work with Bert:

> I was very sold on 'Talking Union' and their other stuff and realised it was very different from what Alan Bush was doing. I played some of it one day

to Alan and it didn't seem to register at all, although he was very passionate about political singing in his own way.

When I first met Bert we got on very well because there weren't many people around that were interested in folk music. We were both interested in traditional music, I knew about Cecil Sharp and the EFDSS and had done a bit of folk song collecting when I was up in Oxford. But we were both very excited about the Almanacs. I didn't like folk songs to be sung in choirs and nor did Bert, so we were like long lost comrades when we met up. I can never forget the time I plucked up my courage and over lunch suggested that there should be an Almanac group in England, a labour-movement, trade-union group. I asked him if he wanted to form a group like that in England his eyes lit up, and he leant across the table and said, 'Passionately!'

It was only a matter of weeks before they were singing together for some of Bert's Hampstead CPGB contacts. But first they needed a group. In the summer of 1949 two young American students, Jean and Jay Butler, had arrived in London. Jay was enrolled at the London University Institute of Archaeology and Jean was taking up a place at the School of Oriental and African Studies. They planned to survive frugally on Jay's postwar G.I. Bill money, which was intended for one person. They found a flat to rent at 3 Gower Street, just a few minutes' walk from their respective colleges.[3]

As well as being interested in African music, Jean Butler (whose family came originally from Franklin County, Vermont) was also a banjo player and guitarist with a huge repertoire of American folk and union songs. She was, according to John Hasted, a tough, fiery character with a hard, raw voice to match. This isn't apparent on the Folktracks cassette *King Kong Kitchie,* a collection of children's songs from her family repertoire, recorded by Peter Kennedy in 1957 under her later, and more familiar, name of Jean Jenkins. Here she sounds rather like a cross between Shirley Collins and Jean Ritchie, but was, of course, singing this material with a Pete Seeger-ish up-picked banjo style before Shirley Collins had discovered the Southern Mountain songs and ballads and learnt banjo from Jenkins' fellow Rambler John Hasted, and before fellow Americans Peggy Seeger and Jean Ritchie appeared in Britain.

The Butlers started hosting informal 'hootenannies' where university friends and acquaintances interested in folk music would get together to sing or listen. These were hugely popular and well attended. Alan Hughes who occasionally dropped in remembered Jean as 'a magnificent guitarist, with a clear, true voice. Her audience in Gower Street were entranced by her music and were always loath to leave.' The couple were always short of cash, and would pass a hat round at the end of the evening for people to contribute a few shillings. This was similar to the hootenannies held by the Almanacs in their New York base, Almanac House, where visitors contributed thirty-five cents towards the rent on the premises.

Jean, from Arkansas, claimed to have performed with the Almanacs and Woody Guthrie, which was quite possible as she had been a CIO (Congress of Industrial Organisations) union organiser in Little Rock, from 1942 to 1945.

The Almanacs travelled thousands of miles performing at union meetings to facilitate labour militancy and class-consciousness. However, Pete Seeger did once say that if all the people who claimed to have sung with the Almanacs were laid end to end, they would circle the globe. She was particularly involved in campaigning for black rights in trade unions, work which brought her to the attention of the anti-communist brigade but, like Alan Lomax, she left for England and escaped their clutches.

Hasted had heard about the sessions on the university grapevine, and Bert and he became regular visitors to the Butlers' basement flat. It wasn't long (1950) before Bert, Hasted, and Jean, along with classical guitar player and research chemist Ernest 'Nesty' Revald, formed arguably England's first folk group. They took their group name, the Ramblers, from the Guthrie song 'Rambling Round Your City', which Jean sang for them. Their aims and repertoire were strongly influenced by the Almanacs and they were soon singing at union meetings, CPGB fundraisings and WMA events all over London, and occasionally in the provinces. None of them had a car, so they travelled to gigs by public transport unless something came up a long way out of London, in which case they'd try and get someone to drive them there. Hasted cut back his choir work to organise the Ramblers. One memorable performance was for a meeting of the CAWU (Clerical and Administrative Workers Union), where they shared the platform with the Prime Minister, Clement Attlee, and the young actress Miriam Karlin. Hasted remembers that Attlee 'got the bird' from the assembled members and that the Ramblers 'blew him off the stage'. As it was a Clerical Union meeting, Bert had started to write a song which went:

> Take a letter, Miss Smith,
> Take a letter, Miss Smith,
> We want a rise in wages.

The others dissuaded him from singing it. According to Hasted they had to regularly restrain each other because they had no experience whatsoever and had to learn how to run a folk group as they went along:

We wanted to emphasise our difference from the usual choirs. We were very relaxed in turtle-neck sweaters, casual clothes. We never used microphones unless we were at a very large meeting of maybe a thousand people then we might stand around the speaker's mic. Bert had quite a respectable strong voice. We sang in harmony. I'd write the arrangements. I was bass-baritone, Bert had a high tenor and Jean was authentic Almanac, she reminded me of some of those coal-camp women from Kentucky, like Aunt Molly Jackson. Guitar, banjo, and three voices. We sang Almanac material, Jean would sing Guthrie songs and some mountain ballads, and she had some really interesting original songs that never appeared in *Sing Out!* magazine or in the *People's Songbook*. Bert would sing some of his English songs, sometime solo, or if they had choruses we'd all sing along in harmony. One of Bert's favourites was 'Arthur McBride', and he'd do things like 'Seventeen Come Sunday' and the odd shanty.

As there was no one else around in England doing the same sort of thing, they had to work out even the most basic things from scratch. For instance, Jean liked to sit down when she sang, but in big halls where they needed to be seen, the others liked to stand. Hasted started writing to Pete Seeger for advice on running the group and also advice on guitar and banjo playing. Pete responded with help, encouragement and guitar and banjo tips and tablature. Although he finally tracked down a folk guitar (and later a banjo) and started to learn it, Hasted was never sufficiently good while with the Ramblers to be allowed to play with them on stage. He eventually ended up accompanying a young Shirley Collins on banjo. As well as the above-mentioned repertoire, the Ramblers also sang gospel songs taken from the *Fisk University Songbook* and the *Sacred Harp* and pioneered Shape Note singing in England. A favourite of the group was 'Amazing Grace' (long before it became a folk revival favourite), and they wrote or rewrote a number of songs including 'Keep-a-going and a-growing' and 'The City of Babylon' – Babylon as 'the centre of evil, the capital city of capitalism and nuclear imperialism':

> Bye bye, city of Babylon
> Bye bye, city of Babylon
> Bye bye, city of Babylon
> Your kingdom must come down.
>
> Calling all them idle sinners
> Down from the hills the fire shall roll
> When we march in the name of freedom
> What'll become of your poor soul?
>
> Over the plain came a million riders
> Stretching from here to kingdom come
> Calling to all the mischief makers
> You'll never get to heaven with the ATOM BOMB.

Thanks to Hasted's work with some of the world's leading atomic scientists – with their slogan, 'Einstein says he's scared … and when Einstein's scared … I'm scared' – the Ramblers were several years ahead of the CND movement.

The group used to rehearse in the evenings and at weekends in the Butlers' Gower Street flat; Bert always preferred the weekends so that they could get a good long rehearsal in. As Hasted related:

We, all of us, except Nesty, had material we got hold of from somewhere. Usually Bert's advice was followed. Once we'd decided on a song we'd sing it through a few times and then decide whether it needed harmonies and what sort of accompaniment. Bert was very knowledgeable but, of course, in those days nobody outside of Cecil Sharp House knew about folk music. There was no folk music scene as such.

The group lasted for two or three years until Hasted decided to leave and spend more time with his London Youth Choir and prepare it for the 1953 World Youth Festival in Bucharest. The LYC recorded 'Ballad for America' by John Latouche and Earl Robinson for Topic Records in 1952. To coincide with the Bucharest festival, at which Bert and MacColl sang together, the WMA produced a song collection entitled: *Youth Sings for Peace: Songs from the repertoire of the London Youth Choir. Songs sung by the Ramblers.* It was a collection of eleven union and anti-war songs, with crude hand-drawn music and guitar chords, stapled together on five foolscap song sheets. The titles were: 'The Duples Strike' (written by John Hasted), 'The Banks Of Marble', 'Union Maid' (Guthrie), 'Go Home Yankees, 'Hoist The Windows' (adapted by Bert from a Negro Spiritual), 'Poor Working Man', 'I Dreamed I Saw Paul Robeson', 'Johnny has Gone for a Soldier', 'Johnny I Hardly Knew You', 'Hold the Fort' and 'Are you Going off to War, Billy Boy?' (Adapted by Bert and Hasted):

> Did they tell you war's a game, Billy Boy, Billy Boy,
> Did they tell you war's a game, charming Billy?
> Yes, they tell me war's a game, but it's murder just the same
> I'm a young thing and ought not leave my mammy.

The WMA also published a more professional, sixteen-page songbook for the British delegation to take to the Festival. The front cover declared *Sing for Friendship, Freedom, Justice, Unity and Peace at Bucharest.* Inside was the usual strange, disparate mix of songs that the WMA thought appropriate for international occasions – a couple of British radical songs such as Johnny Ambrose and John Hasted's 'A Mighty Song of Peace' and Randall Swingler's 'Song of the Waking World', an obligatory Negro Spiritual ('Ain' Goin' Study War No More') and a Guthrie song ('Put My Name Down'), and then a mix of English ('Jerusalem', 'Blaydon Races' 'Don't Dilly Dally'), Welsh ('Land of My Fathers'), Irish ('Johnny I hardly knew yer') and Scots ('A Man's a Man for a' that') national songs and popular folk songs, all printed in broad dialect and in the case of 'Land of My Fathers', a Welsh language option. According to the foreword: 'By singing these songs you are expressing your desire for peace and a fuller life.' And the choice of song was made from songs 'that young people cannot be stopped from singing'.

In later life Hasted metaphorically beat himself up for being, as he said, 'a traitor'. Once he'd established and successfully run his youth choir and taken them to the Eastern-bloc youth festivals, he encouraged various members to split up into small skiffle groups: 'So I was really a double traitor – a traitor for leaving the Ramblers to work with the choir, and the Ramblers collapsed, and a traitor to the choir for breaking them all up into skiffle groups, and then a traitor to skiffle because I wanted it to be folk song, then a traitor to folk song by getting re-married and leaving it altogether.'

Around 1953 Jay Butler received a grant to study for a year in Scandinavia, and he and Jean were preparing to go when she was offered the job of Keeper of Musical Instruments at the Horniman Museum, at Forest Hill, south London. Jay spent the next year in Copenhagen and in 1954 Jean took up her post at the Horniman. When Jay returned, he found Jean involved with Clive Jenkins, the white-collar union official, later to be dubbed the 'champagne socialist'. By then the Ramblers had finished and Jean, whose eventual volatile marriage to Jenkins finished in 1961, was settled into her work. She became an eminent musicologist and later wrote and presented some marvellous radio programmes using her own African, and in particular Islamic, field recordings, many of which were issued on six LPs by Tangent in 1976 (some are now available on Topic Records).[4]

Jay stayed in England to finish his PhD and around 1957 he found a job in prehistoric archaeology in Groningen. Jean Jenkins and Bert obviously stayed on amicable terms after the demise of the group because Bert gave her book *Musical Instruments* (Horniman Museum, 1958) a glowing review in *Recorded Folk Music* and, according to Alun Hughes, Bert regularly consulted her on musicological matters.

It's a mystery how, in all the academic articles and biographies that have appeared over the last few years purporting to chart the second folk revival, the Ramblers are a virtually invisible group; the best kept secret of the revival. The only writer who seems to have given them a proper mention is Pete Frame, in his meticulous rock history *The Restless Generation*. Some authors have mistaken them for part of the later Alan Lomax group of the same name. They were around before tape recorders were generally accessible, and before there was a folk scene as such, but Jean Butler was playing banjo around London several years before banjo-toting Peggy Seeger arrived on the scene, and the Ramblers were a genuine folk group well before the skiffle craze and the subsequent folk revival took off, performing a repertoire that contained a lot of the material that would eventually become the staple of revival folk singers of all persuasions.

Much of it was passed on to the folk scene via Hasted's London Youth Choir and its various offshoots, and his Skiffle and Folk Song Group which was resident at his Tuesday night 44 Club in Soho's Gerrard Street, opened around 1954. Members of the group included at various times Hasted , Eric Winter, Judith Silver (Goldbloom), Hylda Sims, Shirley Collins, Marion Grey, Red Sullivan, John Cole and Martin Winsor, all of whom went on to play leading roles in the emerging folk scene. And, of course, Bert.

It is quite remarkable that such a recent and supposedly well documented phenomenon as the folk music revival is such a tangled web of misinformation, disinformation, supposition, contemporary myth, vested interest, hyperbole, ignorance and romanticism. Admittedly, some of Bert's Walter Mitty-ish tales don't help to clarify things. For instance there is the question of whether or not he met Woody Guthrie. In his 1948 letter to Hamish Henderson (already mentioned) Bert comments on Guthrie: '... Woody Guthrie, who worked in the U.S. merchant navy during the war. I met him once. He had a guitar hanging over his bunk with a notice on it saying: handle with care: this machine killed ten fascists.' If Bert was implying that he'd *seen* Guthrie's guitar hanging over his bunk, where and when could he have been on Guthrie's ship, or even met him? It was common knowledge by 1948 that Guthrie had anti-fascist slogans stuck on his guitar and they vary in different photographs. So Bert could have known that without having seen the actual guitar.

Guthrie had signed up for the Merchant Marine and made two initial trips to North Africa and the Mediterranean. By June 1944 he was washing dishes and (unofficially) musically boosting the morale of the young soldiers on board the Liberty ship *Sea Porpoise* heading for the Normandy beachhead. Towards the end of the month they were anchored off the Irish coast awaiting further orders. Early in July the order came to head for Normandy where they successfully landed three thousand troops. A little later the *Sea Porpoise* hit a mine but, although badly damaged, managed to limp back to Southampton. On arrival, Guthrie was routed by train through London to Glasgow and then back to the States.

When he changed trains in London, Guthrie took time out to drop into Broadcasting House where he announced that he had been in the recent BBC/NBC production of *The Martins and the Coys* (broadcast by the BBC on 26 June 1944), an Appalachian ballad opera devised by the BBC radio producer D.G. Bridson when he was working in the New York office in 1943/4 and produced by Alan Lomax following Bridson's return to the UK. Guthrie was invited to sing on Children's Hour, and on Friday, 7 July, after an autobiographical statement, he sang a couple of railroad songs, 'Wabash Cannonball' and '900 Miles'. He also recorded 'Stagalee' and 'Pretty Boy Floyd'. On a song manuscript dated 'July 13, 1944' he wrote, 'this train is carrying me outside from London now; on up towards Belfast and Glasgow'. So he was obviously around London for about a week.

By 1944 Bert was working in London for the MOI and it's not credible that he'd have been on the *Sea Porpoise* in the Irish Sea, or in Southampton, let alone by Guthrie's instrument-strewn bunk. He might, on the other hand, have met Guthrie at the BBC or somewhere else in London during his brief visit. But apart from the mention in the letter to Henderson, nobody seems to remember Bert talking about having met Guthrie. It's another one of those tantalising and probably now-unsolvable Bert mysteries.

WHEN ALBERT MET JAMES

'Lloyd was a genial old guy with a twinkle in his eye. MacColl could be a right bastard if you got on the wrong side of him.'

Karl Dallas

After the relatively stable *Picture Post* years after the war, the new freelance 1950s were as precarious for Bert as they were exciting. It was a time of establishing and nurturing contacts both in Britain and in Eastern Europe which would help to keep him gainfully employed and artistically fulfilled for the next three decades. The gravy-train days of the *Picture Post* plane tickets and a daily overseas subsistence budget that had taken him across Europe and to Jamaica, Brazil, Argentina, the Middle East and the Western Isles of Scotland (many of them more than once) were over.

In 1951, so it seems, while still working with the Ramblers, Bert first met Theatre Workshop's Ewan MacColl (or Jimmy Miller as he was then still widely known) and Alan Lomax, both of whom were to become seminal figures in his musical career, and he in theirs. As both MacColl and Bert suffered from selective memory syndrome, their later pronouncements on the early days of the folk revival are not always very helpful. In Barrie Gavin's television documentary *Bert: A Personal Memoir*,[5] MacColl remembered his first meeting with Bert: 'Who should come up to me after the show but this jolly, round little man who was Bert Lloyd. We had to clear out of the theatre … we didn't have it for long, before the caretaker got shirty. So we went out into the street. I remember it was a cold winter's night and we stood there for about an hour talking about music.'

In his autobiography, *Journeyman*, MacColl again recalled that first meeting with complete clarity: 'We met in Stratford East outside the Theatre Royal where I had been taking part in a Theatre Workshop production. It was a balmy summer evening and we stood there for an hour or more talking and singing snatches of songs at each other until we were moved on by a policeman.' At least he agrees with himself on the time involved, if not the season. As they apparently discussed mining songs we must assume that MacColl's memory was correct when he says that Bert was 'heavily involved in the compilation of his book of coal-miners' songs *Come All Ye Bold Miners*, which appeared in 1952. This would mean that they would have met in the 'balmy summer' or 'cold winter' of 1951. Bert 'remembers' that his first meeting with MacColl was in 1950 after a show at Stratford East. Theatre Workshop didn't move to Stratford East until 1953, but they did play the Theatre Royal over the Christmas period of 1949/50 with their less-than-acclaimed production of *Alice in Wonderland*. By 1950 MacColl had already recorded the two 78rpm records for the WMA's Topic label ('Asphalter's Song'/'Champion at Keeping 'em Rolling' and 'Four Loom Weaver'/'McKaffery').

As early as 1948 Bert's name appears in Theatre Workshop records as a signatory to the company's application to take over the David Lewis Centre in Liverpool to run it as a theatre school and arts training centre: 'Lectures on Social History, Art, Architecture, Linguistics, Appreciation of Music, and Stage Technique … Joan [Littlewood] would head the project, assisted by Laban, Jimmie [MacColl], Jean and Nelson Illingworth, Bert Lloyd and Hugh MacDiarmid.'

So, taking everything into account, it's inconceivable that Bert and MacColl were unaware of each other's work prior to 1951, and hardly credible that they hadn't actually met. On the other hand Alan Lomax didn't arrive in England until 1951, according to his Special Branch records. If, as according to MacColl, he was instrumental in getting them together, 1951 seems the most likely date for their meeting.

They obviously had much in common through their BBC scriptwriting, politics, theatre, music and desire to promote a working-class British alternative to American-dominated popular music, as MacColl pointed out in the Bert tribute documentary: 'Bert and I were both Marxists, Bert was a very, very, strong Marxist, a very good theoretical Marxist as well. I remember Bert saying "If we're going to make any kind of an impact with this music we have to start very close in time to the people of today. There's no use beginning with all those old country songs that I sing. We've got to start with something which is much closer to them in time, with the industrial songs, and there are plenty of them".'

This assumption had more to do with Bert and MacColl's personal political beliefs and aspirations than with the temperament and attitudes of many of the young people drawn to folk music. They were on a hiding to nothing in attempting to bring about any universal artistic change in the general consciousness. Any musical movement was only ever going to appeal to a minority of the population. Cinemas and dance halls were the new temples where the masses went to worship at the shrine of the Hollywood film and American music and dance, and a bit later television and pop records became the opiates of choice. But for those younger, romantic sections of the population who did follow Bert and MacColl into the folk-music cul-de-sac, it was in many cases exactly those 'old country songs' with *stories* that attracted them to the music, partly because, initially at least, Bert, MacColl, Lomax, Hasted and those singers within their sphere of influence (Steve Benbow, Jimmie Macgregor, Hylda Sims, Shirley Collins etc.) were presenting the traditional songs and ballads in a more accessible way than had hitherto been the case around the school piano.

Soon, too, these young folk fans got the chance to hear the real thing and were hooked by the simplicity, honesty and pride of the old country singers. It was the Copper Family, Harry Cox, Phil Tanner, Pop Maynard and so on, with their bucolic tales of 'jolly fellows that follow the plough', compliant milkmaids, fine hunting mornings, banks of sweet primroses, highwaymen and roisterers, that satisfied so many romantic yearnings for an earlier pre-industrial Eden before the Fall, before the threat of the Bomb, coinciding conveniently in the 1960s with the kaftan-wearing, flower-bedecked hippies, many of whom found relevance and meaning in rural song and traditions and such social gatherings as fairs and the nascent folk festivals.

It must have irked Bert and MacColl to find such conservatism and acceptance of the status quo in much folk song and certainly in many traditional singers, of whom the Copper Family are a prize example. It wasn't so much that the countryside had less potential for attracting people to folk music, as the fact that it had less potential for the more radical, confrontational, class-war material that expressed the proletarian ideology that the Marxist Bert was looking for and, in the mid-1940s, detected in the industrial north of England. Here in some of the songs of the miners, weavers, spinners and others, were the 'songs with teeth' that fitted into his revolutionary world view, songs which he frequently 'tweaked' and set off on a new life in the folk clubs, such as the bitter 'Blackleg Miner' with its militant, threatening last verse:

> So join the union while you may,
> Don't wait till your dying day
> For that may not be far away,
> You dirty blackleg miner.

According to MacColl he sang to Bert at their first meeting 'The Gresford Disaster' (which Bert once suggested MacColl probably wrote) and 'The Collier Laddie' – a song he said he'd learnt from his mother or, as he claimed on his Topic album *Steam Whistle Ballads*, from his grandmother:

> I've travelled East, and I've travelled West
> And I've travelled oe'r Kirkaldy,
> But the bonniest lass that e'er I spied
> She was following her collier laddie.

When MacColl finished 'The Collier Laddie' Bert enthusiastically said, 'You've *got* to send me that song'. It duly appeared in Bert's book, along with the other MacColl contributions – 'The Gresford Disaster', 'The Plodder Seam' and 'Fourpence a Day'.

Come All Ye Bold Miners came about thanks to the National Coal Board (NCB) and Leslie Shepard, who directed, scripted and helped edit a phenomenally successful monthly cinema newsreel of colliery affairs entitled *Mining Review,* which ran for twenty-five years. The newsreel had started in 1948, a couple of years after Attlee's Labour Government nationalised the coal industry, and it was shown in 700 cinemas in the coal-mining areas of the British Isles. At its height it had a regular audience of several million. Each month, four or five subjects were covered, ranging from the latest safety devices, increased coal production and health issues to social items such as female billiards players and pigeon-fancying. In the course of working on the series, Shepard, who was a folk song enthusiast and familiar with Bert's *The Singing Englishman* and *Corn on the Cob,* came across material that made him think of Bert: 'I had come across evidence of industrial folklore, and I had the idea of doing a story in which Bert Lloyd would talk about the subject and ask miners to contribute folk songs.'[6]

Shepard had met Bert and Charlotte earlier at a social evening at Jack and Gerda Chambers' house. Jack Chambers worked with Shepard at the cooperative Data Film Productions (which produced *Mining Review* for the NCB). Chambers had been a documentary film director through the war, and in 1952 would direct the first three-dimensional film about coal mining using the latest model BFI 3D camera. The Coal Board films officer was Kurt 'Lew' Lewenhak, an alternative-theatre enthusiast and an acquaintance of Ewan MacColl and other singers. He was later prominent in the CND and Peace Movement. So when, at the weekly editorial meeting, Shepard suggested using Bert in the *Review* to harvest some industrial songs before they died out, Chambers and Lewenhak were enthusiastic, although they did suggest a sound test before going ahead with the idea.

Chambers arranged another get-together during which Bert could record for them. Shepard borrowed an early 'portable' tape recorder (which weighed in at 50 pounds) and captured Bert singing the American miners' union song 'Which Side are You on' (with guitar accompaniment, although it's unclear if it's Bert playing) and an East Anglian 'Foggy Dew' (with a Harry Cox sounding 'doo' for 'dew'). Both were songs that Bert was performing at that time with the Ramblers. Everyone was happy with the sound test and an item, 'The Miner Sings', was scheduled for inclusion in the May 1951 edition of *Mining Review*. The Coal Board announced: 'To mark the start of the Festival of Britain in May 1951 *Mining Review*, in conjunction with *Coal* magazine, is sponsoring a prize contest to find some of the lesser known miners' songs.'

The film was screened at the A.L. Lloyd Memorial Conference at Cecil Sharp House, London in February 1984, when Leslie Shepard recalled making it: 'I directed Bert's *Mining Review* appearance in 1951 in a tiny set at Carlton Hill Studios, Maida Vale. It was my first sound dialogue item. We linked the item to a competition in the Coal Board's magazine *Coal*. It was on the basis of response to this short film item that Bert later developed his book *Come All Ye Bold Miners*.' The black-and-white film opened with concert singer Roland Robson singing 'The Collier's Rant' from a script, in a strong Geordie accent. Then Bert, in his usual collar and tie, swivelled round in his chair and, looking serious and slightly self-conscious, spoke to camera:

> Most miners, Geordies particularly, will know that song that Roland Robson is singing, its name is *The Collier's Rant*, and it's what we call a folk song. At one time there used to be a lot of these songs in the coalfields but few of them ever got written down, and now many of them are dying out. But I believe there are many miners who still know them and are perhaps making them up for themselves. The kind of songs I have in mind are about miners' work or his home life, his pastimes, about mine disasters or strikes or trade union struggles.
>
> We want to collect them before they disappear, so we're having a competition with prizes. If you know any of these songs of the coalfields please send them to me. My name is A.L. Lloyd and you'll find full details in the May issue of *Coal* magazine.

Prizes of ten guineas and six of £5 were offered for the best. In his preface to *Come All Ye Bold Miners* Bert tells us that over a hundred pieces were sent in, not all of them folk songs: 'Some were parodies, literary recitations, parlour ballads of the type of "Don't Go Down the Mine Daddy". Many were stage songs of the past, particularly from the Tyneside music-halls of a century ago. But a number of fine songs, not hitherto seen in print came to light.'

If, as we've seen, potentially several million people in mining areas all over the British Isles saw the film and read the magazine, then the resultant harvest of a hundred or so songs, many of which weren't the 'folk songs' that Bert was looking for, is actually a very insignificant response. Either many of the viewers couldn't be bothered to send Bert their songs, or the singing of what Bert would recognise as folk and folk-type songs in the coalfields had indeed virtually died out. It's perhaps significant that when the folk revival got under way there were hardly any traditional industrial folk song role models of the likes of the rural Coppers and Harry Cox.

With the exception of Jack Elliott of Birtley who, along with his family, was recorded by MacColl and Peggy Seeger and appeared on the Folkways album *The Elliotts of Birtley: A Musical Portrait of a Durham Mining Family* (1962) and the first Leader album, *Jack Elliott of Birtley* (1969), the vast majority of recorded industrial song in the 1960s and 1970s was performed by revival singers such as Louis Killen, Johnny Handle, Bob Davenport, Ray Fisher, Bert, MacColl, Harry Boardman and the Oldham Tinkers, many of whom got material from MacColl's 1954 WMA song book *Shuttle and Cage: Industrial Folk Ballads*, and Bert's *Come All Ye Bold Miners,* or from Bert himself. They nearly all recorded for Topic Records, considered by many the best-respected folk music record company in Britain (and certainly the longest running), where Bert, as Artistic Director, was in a position to influence, if not actually dictate, who recorded and what they recorded.

In a letter to Dave Harker in February 1973, answering Harker's suggestion for an album of songs of the northern music-hall performer and songwriter Ned Corvan, Bert said that he had, in the past, suggested such an album to the Topic directors but the idea hadn't been taken up. So, he obviously couldn't actually dictate all of Topic's recording policy. However, Bert's influence on artists, audiences, repertoire, the direction the revival took and the media was not inconsiderable, and no less pervasive for being conducted with a smile and a friendly self-effacing 'suggestion'. Behind the avuncular public face was a steely determined Marxist with a vision that he did his best to bring to fruition. Norma Waterson, grande dame of the influential Yorkshire singing dynasty, insisted that Bert did not dictate what the group could or should record for Topic, but she admitted that when Bert suggested their classic album *Frost and Fire* he sent them sheaves of songs and tunes from which to select material.

Bert was subtler than MacColl and in many ways more influential in the direction that the second folk revival took, but more on the repertoire than for any widespread take-up of Marxist politics, despite MacColl's opinion:

Bert was a great folklorist because he was also a good Marxist, there was no contradiction in the two positions. He had this extraordinary capacity of convincing his collaborators or his friends, and even his enemies, without appearing to do so. This is a tremendous virtue, with a thousand Marxists like him I'm sure we'd have had the revolution in Britain already.[7]

In some ways the folk song revival, as visualised by Bert and MacColl, was a victim of its own success. In *Education* (May 1959) Bert stated: 'Most of those taking part in the new folk song revival are secondary modern [implying working class], rather than grammar school products'. This might possibly have been true of the 1950s, but by the 1960s and 1970s, when there were hundreds of folk clubs around the country, instead of the 'workers' taking the folk baton and running with it the folk club movement would appear to have been hijacked to a certain degree by white, frequently middle-class school teachers, university and college students and graduates, and ex-grammar school pupils. One certainly came across more of them running folk clubs and performing in them (Tony Rose, Peta Webb, Martin Carthy, Shirley Collins, Pete and Chris Coe, Peter Bellamy, Bob and Carol Pegg, June Tabor, Robin Dransfield, Roger Watson etc.) than farm labourers, coal-face workers, paint-shop sprayers, car mechanics and Woolworths sales girls, and their interest was generally biased in those early days more towards the music than overt political proselytising.

Apart from performers such as Johnny Silvo, Cliff Hall from the Spinners and Fitzroy Coleman, black faces were not to be seen in folk clubs. There were, of course, pockets of left-wing, folk-enthusiast social workers, office workers and a few manual workers, at places like the Singers' Club (and some of the northern clubs) where MacColl and Peggy Seeger, and to a lesser extent Bert, ruled supreme, but in general the folk movement as a whole soon became less obviously party political, if spiritually on the left.

Many of the original communist firebrands of the early revival, such as Eric Winter and Karl Dallas, mellowed, or at least became less conspicuous (although in later life Dallas became very active again, and was in the national news during the Iraq war singing anti-war songs and acting as a 'human shield'). Some by the mid-1950s were disillusioned by Russian communism and the invasion of Hungary in 1956, and felt that thirty million lives was too high a price to pay for Stalin's transformation of Russia from agricultural nation to super-power. Some communists, like John Hasted, left the folk scene altogether. MacColl, on the other hand, went the other way. Feeling that the Party was going soft he became a hard-line Maoist. Bert simply remained an obdurate old-style communist, eventually out of step with many of the political changes in Eastern Europe and elsewhere. Marxist folk song editor Stephen Sedley became the Rt. Hon. Lord Justice Sedley. Some singers, such as Pete Coe and Roy Bailey, became more politically motivated over the years and, along with unashamed left-wing performers like Dick Gaughan and Leon Rosselson, continued to use their music to try to change society and the world, but they are exceptions to the general rule. For most people, folk music was simply fun and, particularly amongst the latest generation of virtuosic folk music instrumentalists, exciting.

When he returned to Australia in the 1970s Bert gave a lengthy lecture on *Songs of the Mine and Mill*, in which his memories of the events of 1951 which led to the publication of *Come All Ye Bold Miners* seem to be at variance with Leslie Shepard's:

I began my collecting business into industrial folklore around 1950, 1951, and I was convinced that our coalfields ought to be rich in songs even though nobody seemed to have explored them very well and there was precious little evidence that songs were still on the go. We knew that they used to be during the nineteenth century but didn't know what still remained or what was being made fresh. So I went to the Coal Board and the Mine Workers' Union to see if I could interest them in the notion and they were very lofty about it, 'We can tell you, son,' they said, 'that you're wasting your time. The, then, President of the Mine Workers Union said, 'I was born and brought up in the coalfields and I know the stuff isn't there.' I was a bit discouraged about that, not because I thought they were right but because they weren't giving me any money for it. So I started collecting colliery songs in just about the daftest way and most unscientific way possible, by correspondence. I persuaded the Coal Board (reluctantly they did this) to allow me to write an article for them about the coalfield balladry of the past and quoting some examples of what used to be on the go and encouraging any colliers who read this magazine and who happened to have songs in their head that they hadn't learnt from print or off records to send me at least the words, and if they could persuade some kind friend, music teacher or somebody like that, to dot the tune out for them to send the tune as well, and I, out of my own pocket, generously would award ten pounds for the song I reckoned was the best find. Well, we sat back and waited to see what would happen, and the Coal Board people were grinning very smugly to themselves sure that nothing much would happen. Within about two weeks we had received about a hundred songs and many of them completely unknown and many of them really interesting, and that gave me a considerable number of addresses of colliers who I could then visit and record.'[8]

'Many' should perhaps read 'some'. It seems very unlikely that the Coal Board would have run a newsreel item and a magazine article and expect Bert to pay the prize money out of his own pocket, especially as the collection was going to be part of their contribution to the Festival of Britain. Even if they weren't prepared to finance field-collecting trips to the northeast of England they were certainly supportive and enthusiastic over the idea of the film and magazine project initiated by Leslie Shepard.

Through the project Bert did acquire a number of mining contacts, which helped to get his industrial folk song research going and resulted in the publication in 1952 of Come All Ye Bold Miners and a BBC pilot programme on Miners' Songs. At the end of the year BBC North Region commissioned a thirty-minute feature entitled The Life of Thomas Armstrong. Tommy Armstrong (1848–1919) from Tanfield Lea, County Durham, the 'Pitman Poet', was one of the finest of the northeast dialect poets and songwriters and Bert printed eight of his songs in Come All Ye Bold Miners. The BBC agreed to finance a week's programme research on Tyneside, for which I'm sure Bert was very grateful, and he no doubt managed to fit in a lot of other research at the same time. Later, in 1965, Bert was instrumental in getting Topic to release Tommy Armstrong of Tyneside, a collection of fourteen of

Armstrong's most popular songs performed by some of the leading revival singers of the northeast. Yet again, Bert felt the need to tinker and change things, as Harker points out in *One for the Money* with reference to the song Bert called 'The Durham Lock-Out':

> In the third edition of his [Armstrong's] *25 Popular Songs*, published in 1930 and edited by his son, the song in question is called 'The Durham Strike'. In *Come All Ye Bold Miners*, in 1952, and even in 1978 [the enlarged revised edition], Lloyd titles the song 'The Durham Lock-Out. He also changes Armstrong's favourite tune, 'Castles in the Air', a variant of 'The Ball o'Kirriemuir', and replaces it with the maudlin 'Come All Ye Tramps and Hawkers', thus converting what had been a song with a smart cutting edge into one with a self-pitying tone.

Also in 1951, while he was sorting out the responses to the *Mining Review* project and starting work on *Come All Ye Bold Miners,* Bert put together a song collection, *Singing Englishmen,* for the Workers' Music Association (of which he was by then one of the Vice Presidents, along with such respected musical names as Paul Robeson, Benjamin Britten, Aaron Copeland and Hanns Eisler). The WMA *Collection of folk songs specially prepared for a Festival of Britain Concert given in association with the Arts Council of Great Britain*, consisted of twenty-three songs, including a couple where Bert's definition of 'folk song' is as flexible as a rubber band. He would, hopefully, have blushed in later life at the inclusion of Charles Kingsley's 'Face Your Game' (smuggled into the index as 'Labour Song'), despite its good intentions and such on-message sentiments as:

> Weep, weep, weep and weep,
> For pauper, dolt and slave,
> Hark! From wasted moor and fen,
> Fev'ross alley, workhouse, den,
> Swells the wail of working men.

The majority of the other 'folk' songs ('The Collier's Rant', 'Spermwhale Fishery', 'Cutty Wren', 'Dives and Lazarus' etc.) were carefully selected to 'mirror the life, work, and aspirations of the British working-population' and point out the futility and sorrow of war, the hardships of working life, and the eventual post-mortem consequences of being a rich uncaring capitalist like Dives:

> And it fell out upon one day, Rich Div'rus sickened and died,
> There came two serpents out of Hell, his soul therein to guide,
> 'Rise up, rise up, brother Diverus and come along with me;
> There is a place in Hell for you, for to sit on a serpent's knee.'

The Singing Englishman was also still available in 1951, claiming to be 'A Festival Re-issue of An Introduction to Folk Song'. In fact, it was a way to shift some of the back stock that the WMA still had in its cupboards. Camilla Raab, a friend of Bert's who worked in the WMA office at the time, recalled sitting at a table and pulling off all the original green paper covers and stapling on the new 're-issue' cover with its Festival of Britain logo.

Come All Ye Bold Miners was a welcome addition (despite, yet again, the paucity of tunes) to the available folk song resources, especially to singers and musicians from the northeast, that unique cultural enclave trapped between England and Scotland, fiercely proud of its musical traditions and culture. Interestingly, southerners who were quite happy to sing American, Scots and Irish songs in fond approximations of the original accents, rarely attempted the Geordie repertoire, beyond 'Blackleg Miner' and 'Wor Geordie's Lost His Penker' (marble), which was done as a tongue-in-cheek piece of nonsense.

Despite Bert's earlier distrust of literary 'folk song' composition, which went against all that he'd originally accepted concerning the general anonymity and dissemination of folk song, while working on *Come All Ye Bold Miners* he became increasingly aware of the huge influence local dialect songwriters and poets and broadside ballads had on the popular Northumbrian song repertory from the eighteenth century until the early twentieth century. He happily plundered the early collections to supplement the few anonymous folk songs sent in by miners, and ones that he'd acquired from MacColl, Lomax and Hamish Henderson.

As we've come to expect with some of Bert's published collections and recordings, after the initial acclaim there slowly developed a body of criticism about his editorial methods and attributions, as well as about some of his pronouncements and assumptions on working-class culture as a whole. More and more people, in particular Dave Harker (*One for the Money: Politics and Popular Song* and *Fakesong: The Manufacture of British 'Folk Song' 1700 to the Present Day*), originally inspired by Bert's industrial trail-blazing, began to conduct their own in-depth research into industrial folk song and to subject his work to academic analysis.

In his paper 'A.L. Lloyd and Industrial Song' (A.L. Lloyd Memorial Conference, London, 1984, printed in 1986 in *Singer, Song and Scholar*) Roy Palmer examined in detail Bert's editorialising and said: 'It is clear that Lloyd's editorial approach was not merely to reproduce the material sent to him. Sometimes the changes made were small, as with "Trimdon Grange", but others were far-reaching.' He goes on to deconstruct, amongst other songs in *Come All Ye Bold Miners*, the 'Recruited Collier', which Bert had rewritten from Robert Anderson's *Ballads in the Cumberland Dialect* (1808). It was, in fact, originally about a 'recruited ploughman' whose closest connection to mining would have been putting coal on the fire. The following verses, first sung with such feeling by Anne Briggs on the album *The Iron Muse* (1963), and subsequently by many other female folk singers, are seemingly pure Bert inventions:

> As I walked o'er the stubble field,
> Below it runs the seam,
> I thought o' Jimmy hewin' there,
> But it was all a dream.
>
> He hewed the very coals we burn,
> An' when the fire I's leetin',
> To think the lumps was in his hands,
> It sets my heart to beatin'.

In a letter to Roy Palmer in August 1975, Bert admitted fitting the tune to the song but could no longer remember whether he'd made up the melody or taken it from tradition. He added: 'I think the latter; but if so, what was it the tune of?' Following Professor Richard Dorson's 1969 definition of 'material created by authors and passed off as the folk tradition' as 'fakelore', it can't be denied that *Come All Ye Bold Miners* contains a fair bit of 'fakelore'. One's reaction to that fact depends on whether you take the word fakelore to be merely descriptive or pejorative.

In later life, Bert must have felt himself in an increasingly tight corner, with regular requests for more and more specific details about the songs he had published and recorded, and articles challenging his often unsubstantiated historical and sociological pronouncements. From the examples I've seen, he always answered good-naturedly and with disarming honesty concerning any earlier editorial shortcomings, as in this letter to Dave Harker (July 1972), referring to song transcripts that were sent to him by J.S. Bell, a coal-face driller from Prescot, Lancashire, for *Come All Ye Bold Miners*:

> I made quite a number of changes – dropping lines or stanzas where I thought the texts were too prolix, occasionally altering the dialect spelling, or making contractions (I'll, we'd, etc.) in the interest of metre. In particular I altered 'The Coalowner and the Pitman's Wife', to accommodate bits of the incomplete text I got from Jim Denison. I should have made it clear.
>
> Altogether, you see, not a reliable piece of editing. I would be more particular nowadays. If a new edition of CAYBM gets done, I'll review the pieces in the light of their originals.

By the time Lawrence and Wishart got round to publishing a 'new, revised and enlarged edition' in 1978, Bert had moved on and was involved in filmmaking with Barrie Gavin. He had been unwell for a number of years, but he did go back over his texts and notes of a quarter of a century earlier and 'correct' some of his earlier editorialising. However, he couldn't bring himself to admit in his notes for 'The Durham Lock-Out' (his title) that although directed by the author, Tommy Armstrong, to be sung to the tune 'Castles in the Air', the tune that Bert says is 'nowadays current' was put to it by Bert himself.

By the time of his death in 1982 Bert, tired and weak, was no longer the one-eyed man in the folk-music country of the blind. For his last few years he had fought a rearguard action against the bright young newcomers, intent on making their mark in the world of folk music scholarship. Many, if not most, of them initially stood on Bert's shoulders to see where they were going.

Regardless of subsequent academic opinion and discoveries in the field of British industrial folklore, no one can deny that Bert and MacColl single-handedly, or double-handedly, kick-started what has now become a recognised and reputable area of musicological and sociological research. They also stimulated interest in shanties and sea songs, erotic songs, ballads and Eastern European music. No one can take away the fact that *Come All Ye Bold Miners* was a pioneering work – the first collection of British mining songs which, as Bert said in 1972, stimulated interest in industrial song, in new songwriting, and the creation of a workers' music for the twentieth century:

> To my surprise this modest and rather slackly-assembled little book seemed to have good effect in stimulating the resurrection of colliers' songs, and in the creation of new ones of similar type, especially in the North-east. I remember Johnny Handle used to refer to it as 'the Bible' which always seemed to me to be pitching it a bit high, to say the least. It did inspire the Elliotts to some extent, I believe, and no doubt that started a kind of chain reaction. It's hard to say whether the present interest in industrial song would have come about simply through the impetus of the folk song revival without the publication of the book. Probably it would, but I feel the book played a part out of proportion to its intrinsic value. A matter of timing, perhaps. When I noticed its effect, I wished I had done it better.[9]

Remarkably knowledgeable though he was where folk song was concerned, he did have blind spots and, as he himself would have agreed, was not infallible. For example, when collecting material for *Come All Ye Bold Miners,* he took Welsh union officials at their word when they informed him there were no Welsh mining songs, when in fact there was a very sizeable body of mainly Welsh *language* mining material in books and on broadsides. Welsh was the main language of the nineteenth and twentieth centuries in the coalfields, and many examples were in the National Library of Wales collections and some county record offices. This serves to remind us that Bert, who arguably had more comparative knowledge of musical folklore than anyone else in Britain, was not omniscient and often not completely transparent.

In the same year that *Come All Ye Bold Miners* appeared, Bert and Charlotte worked together on a translation of the disturbed German writer Hans Fallada's (1893–1947) dark, fictionalised study of a man's descent into alcoholism, which ends with his incarceration in a criminal asylum for the murder of his wife. The story is less fictional than might be supposed. Fallada, the pseudonym of Rudolph Ditzen, was at various times in his life an alcoholic and a morphine addict, and spent time in prison for stealing to support his habit. In his youth he shot and killed a friend in a suicide pact which went wrong, managing to escape trial on the grounds of insanity. During the 1930s he wrote some highly acclaimed books while working for the publisher Ernest Rowohlt, whose son, Heinrich, Bert worked with at Foyles. He stayed in Germany when Hitler came to power and, although bitterly opposed to Nazism, he could not manage to leave the country and survived, when many of his artistic friends were arrested, by writing non-politically confrontational children's books. Later, in 1944, when he shot and wounded his first wife, the Nazi authorities committed him to a criminal asylum, from where he wrote *The Drinker*. It appeared posthumously in 1950.

While working on the book Bert had no idea that a few years down the line his son Joe would have much in common with Fallada.

12
Back to the Beeb

On 20 December 1949, W.L. Streeton, Head of Programme Contracts at the BBC, sent an internal memo to the booking managers of the various departments announcing that 'the bar on the engagement of A.L. Lloyd is removed'. But, notwithstanding this, reference had to be made to Streeton before 'effecting any engagement'. Bert was lucky throughout his forty-year career as a writer and presenter for the BBC in having the support and respect of several left-leaning and well-thought-of producers, starting in the late 1930s with Laurence Gilliam, and followed by Reggie Smith, D.G. Bridson, Douglas Cleverdon and finally, for his television work, a ten-year relationship with the director Barrie Gavin. He worked for many other producers (he wrote over 120 schools programmes and dozens of other programmes) but this group comprised his core supporters at the BBC. It was for them he did his most significant work. Although his television writing didn't kick off until the 1970s, he had been contemplating potential television work twenty years earlier.

In 1950, after leaving *Picture Post*, he had asked Gilliam for help in acquiring some technical knowledge in television production. He said he had a number of ideas for television plays (which didn't come to fruition) but could not get ahead with the scripting until he 'got the hang of the production set up'. Gilliam put him in touch with Wolf Rilla, BBC TV's first drama script editor. Rilla, a German-Jewish refugee from the Nazis, knew Bert from their time together in Features and Drama in 1939 where Rilla was a writer/producer. In 1942 he joined the BBC German Service. On the resumption of television production in June 1946, after its six-and-a-half year wartime closure, Rilla moved over to television. He went into films in 1952, directing the classic *Village of the Damned,* based on John Wyndham's sci-fi novel *The Midwich Cuckoos.*

Despite having one eye on television, Bert certainly wasn't going to abandon radio now that he was, if not *persona grata*, at least back on the air. In October 1950 he wrote a long letter to Alec Robertson in Talks department reminding him that it was a year since he'd given his last radio talk (*White Spirituals*) and offering him a 'reasonably scientific' piece for the Third Programme on the folk music of Argentina. After two closely typed pages of information on Argentinean music Bert finished with:

I have plenty of records to illustrate a half-hour talk dealing with all these different styles. The records I should use, while authentic, are commercial records, and not 'ethnographical' recordings. The ethnographical level of music exists in Argentina only among the savages of the Chaco, and among the folk of low cultural level in Patagonia and thereabouts. Elsewhere, folk music is very highly developed and even professionalised.

I spent some time with gauchos on the pampa (the country of the criollo dances) as well as with the Indians in the North (the country of the old colonial-style songs), so I'm able to give the background colour, as well as the social setting, of the music.

Do let me know what you think.

Unfortunately not everyone at the BBC, especially in the rarefied air of the Third Programme, appreciated Bert's colourful journalistic writing style. The Third Programme's Christopher Holme replied to Robertson's programme offer by saying that potentially the idea appealed to them and was something they'd been meaning to produce for some time. However, Holme had reservations about Bert's work. He'd had another look at *White Spirituals*, which 'was better than something else of his which I saw' but still seemed to be too much of a 'told to the children' attitude for the Third. He felt, unfairly, that Bert's journalistic style suggested a superficial and slapdash approach to the subject. However, if Bert had some 'good stuff' that the BBC could not get in any other way, then Holme would accept a programme consisting almost entirely of music 'with the barest linking script'.

When Robertson told Bert this, he assumed that Bert would turn it down. Although disappointed, Bert accepted the restrictions:

It's a bit disappointing. The music is moderately interesting in itself, but especially interesting by virtue of its background colour, and its musicological curiosity. That is, it's really worth treating seriously, and not just as if it were another of those programmes of Latin American café music a la Edmundo Ros. I'm keen to do the programme, anyway. So shall we try it?

Bert and other writers rarely, if ever, knew exactly what the various departments said about their scripts and ideas, and why they were sometimes turned down. It saved their egos taking a bashing, but gave them little chance to argue their case, or to change their style or treatment. Most internal comments were delivered via a mediator who invariably toned down or excluded much critical comment. The snobbishness of some Third Programme producers was summed up by the self-confessed 'intellectual' and 'man of letters' Henry Reed, when he wrote in the *B.B.C. Quarterly* that the launching of the Third Programme was to be lauded because it acknowledged 'that some listeners are fools and some are not, and that we cannot wait for the fools to catch up with their betters'.

Despite Holme's reservations about his writing style, Bert was considered by the BBC to be an authority on American folk music, and six months earlier Holmes himself had allocated a research fee for Bert to assess the programme possibilities of seventy 78rpm records that the BBC acquired from the Library of Congress. Surely Bert couldn't believe his luck – 140 recordings of traditional American music delivered to his door for him to play at his leisure, and to get paid for it! BBC jobs such as this must have made Alan Lomax's appearance on the scene the following year all the more frustrating. Not only did Lomax monopolise the BBC's American music output over the next few years, he also became an influential figure in the British folk music field.

In November 1950 Bert sent a rough draft of the first part of a script on the death of Abraham Lincoln to Geoffrey Bridson. It was an interesting script which, Bert explained, started out: 'Deliberately written flat and factual, and slightly stylised, because I wanted it to have some of the stiff black-and-white quality of an old-time newsreel. That way it will contrast better with the colour and fantasy of the real body of the programme, which begins the moment Lincoln opens his mouth.' The main part of the programme was to be a projection of sound images – sometimes coherent, sometimes delirious – of Lincoln's past life running through the dying President's mind. Bridson, who was Assistant Head of Features, liked the idea very much and tried to place it with the Home Service with a note saying that he thought they could get a good script out of it and that 'Lloyd is a writer that I feel we ought to encourage'. Unfortunately, the Home Service had in the recent past produced several Lincoln-related items and decided against any more for the time being.

In January 1951 Archie Harding commissioned Bert to make a translation and radio version of Lorca's *The House of Bernada Alba*. Harding also booked him to revise Ashley Dukes' translation of the 1900 play *Midsummer Fire* (*Johannisfeuer*) by the German nationalist playwright Hermann Sudermann, a prolific *fin de siècle* writer, surprisingly unknown to Bert. And in February Reggie Smith produced a programme of Lorca poems read by John Lehmann's actress sister Beatrix, from Bert's English translations in *Lament for the Death of a Bullfighter*. Bert, who didn't have a copy of his book, asked Smith if he had a copy that he could borrow so that he could re-read it and make a couple of corrections before the broadcast. In his letter of 24 January Bert was very enthusiastic about work: 'I am full of ideas today. I'll type them out separately and send them with this letter, for your comments.'

One of Bert's ideas concerned the Hungarian play *Murder in the Village* by Julian Hay. 'A vivid and exciting play,' so Bert thought, 'based on real events of 1935–6, when it transpired, during a murder trial, that the women of a village on the Tisza ... had been poisoning their husbands and re-marrying over and over again, to get hold of enough land to live on.'

He sent Smith his translation of the play. Around the same time he sent D.G. Bridson a selection of translations of Andalusian-Arabic poems for a possible programme, and also suggested something on the poetry of Neruda. To Douglas Cleverdon he sent a lengthy proposal for a radio series entitled *The Foundations of Folk-Music* (1. *The Sound of Folk-song*, 2. *Virtuosity and Folk-music*, 3. *The Shape of Folk-song*, 4. *The Themes of Folk-song*), and a list of single programmes on various aspects of American music using the Library of Congress and other records in the BBC Sound Archive that he had listened to for the BBC (*British Ballad Survivals in the USA*, *Songs From*

Prison, The Mountain Fiddler, Folk-Songs of the Industrial Age, Folk Music of Latin America, Negro Music of Brazil).

The music and poetry ideas were shot down in flames by Christopher Holme, the mouthpiece of the Controller Third Programme. Of the folk music series, they didn't feel that Bert was well enough qualified to speak on non-European music on the Third Programme. A miscellaneous scheme such as Bert suggested could prove 'confusing to the listener'. Nor was the conservative Third Programme interested in the Andalusian and the Neruda poems because they weren't 'mainstream enough' and represented the 'tributaries and the outlying marshes' of poetry. On the other hand, 'If some outstandingly interesting poet such as Auden were to translate something obscure then we could include the material under Auden and not under Andalusia'. At the bottom of the internally circulated letter Reggie Smith had added 'Coo!' and in his note to Bert he said: 'I am sorry about Neruda. It is sufficient comment on the people making the decision that they can refer to him as a backwater or marsh.' The play was eventually returned as unsuitable.

In January 1952, while casting around for suitable radio projects, Bert and Charlotte came up with the idea of a documentary dealing with an ear operation ('fenestration') that Charlotte had undergone in the late 1940s, which Bert thought might lend itself to the use of interesting sound effects as well as performing a service to listeners who might benefit from the information. Charlotte had impaired hearing from childhood, as Bert explained to Miss Pain at the BBC:

For her all noises, conversation, music, were just a blur. Early on, she had a noise in her head like a huge factory in which people were endlessly clashing together coils of wire. Later this became a blur too. The fact that it was difficult to talk to trades people, to hear traffic noises, to join in general social life, created a special set of embarrassments and suspicions, which were added to by the fact that one was never sure whether the threatening or enticing sounds heard in one's head were real or not. On the other hand it was possible to use deafness as a psychological defence: there was always a good excuse for isolating oneself from bores at a party, for instance; one could if necessary exploit the enigmatic aspect which deafness gives to one's character.

Following the birth of Caroline in 1947, Charlotte, who was afraid that she wouldn't hear the baby crying, and kept imagining that she could hear her when she wasn't crying, decided to opt for fenestration to correct her hearing and to save herself countless fruitless journeys dashing up and down stairs. For ten days, following the several-hours-long, extremely delicate and potentially dangerous operation, in which a tiny window was cut into the bones of her inner ear, Charlotte felt sea-sick, due to her centre of balance having been profoundly disturbed. During the slow process of the return to normality, Charlotte, her eyes and ears bandaged, experienced strange phenomena, such as not being able to stand and not being able to associate one thing with another – she couldn't imagine what her hand was grasping.

When the bandages were finally removed and Bert took her home, Charlotte had to adjust to all the familiar house and street noises that for so many years had eluded her. Everything was new – her children's voices, the noise of bath-taps, the rustle of clothing – and Charlotte found the whole experience initially a bit of a let-down to find out how unaesthetic most domestic noises were. She told Bert: 'Things look so nice and sound so horrid'. Eventually, of course, she grew accustomed to the banality of everyday sounds and was able to appreciate music for the first time. This must have been immensely pleasing to Bert, for whom music was such an integral part of life, and which hitherto they'd been unable to share. However, it was an interesting programme idea that the BBC didn't take up.

Other proposals turned down that year by the BBC included a piece on Eva Peron:

I wonder whether you would care for a short *Woman's Hour* talk on Eva Peron? To say <u>I Knew Her</u> would be stretching it too far, but I met her when I was in Argentina two years ago, and she gave me the opportunity, which I believe no other journalist, foreign or Argentinian, has had, of spending an entire afternoon in her private office in the Department of Labour, watching her methods of work and her manner of dealing with her various callers – heads of unions threatening strikes, place-seekers, personal friends, up-country women with domestic worries.

Of course, opinions differ about her, some saying she is the greatest saint of our time, while others believe she was the greatest racketeer; and in consequence I well realise that any broadcast about her is a delicate matter. At the same time I believe a personal description of this fabulous creature from the viewpoint of an average sensual man might well be instructive and entertaining, without offending either her admirers or detractors. Face to face, she made a curious, almost pathetic impression, quite unlike the conventional view of her (pro or con), and I believe this impression is possible to convey in a radio talk, better than in print.

Also rejected were two European play translations and adaptations. The first was the unfinished mini-masterpiece *Woyzeck* by the young nineteenth-century doctor/dramatist Georg Buchner. It is a study of paranoia and hallucinatory experiences, and one of the earliest examples of 'working-class tragedy' in which the anti-hero – the penniless, proletarian Woyzeck – treads an inevitable tragic path to his destruction. It's also an examination of the abuse and misuse of military and scientific power (a prescient picture of Nazi Germany) represented by the Captain, who pontificates about morality and philosophical ideals which are completely irrelevant to his poverty-stricken servant, and by the Doctor who conducts medical experiments on Woyzeck. It was way ahead of its time, both in its subject matter and fragmented structure.

The play had been adapted many times over the years before Bert got his hands on it, notably Alban Berg's 1925 opera *Wozzeck* (and, later, Werner Herzog's film adaptation). Bert felt that *Woyzeck* was 'virtually unplayable on the stage' but was perfect material for radio. He also felt that Berg's admirable music got in the way of a strong, simple story. Bert sent his adaptation to Archie Harding in June 1952. Surprisingly, script reader Helena Wood gave it the thumbs up; she thought it a 'good translation and an interesting radio adaptation'. The Assistant Head of Drama, Donald McWhinnie, said it was 'quite the best version of this piece we have had'. He felt that the play became a practical proposition for the first time, and was so enthused that he suggested getting Alec Guinness to play the eponymous anti-hero. However, after failing to persuade the Third Programme to squeeze it into an already full schedule for the rest of the year, McWhinnie sent a rueful letter to Bert, congratulating him on the piece, but explaining that the Third were unwilling to commit themselves to a future broadcast.

Bert had equally bad luck with his offer to Douglas Cleverdon of the fifteenth-century Spanish novel in dialogue *La Celestina* by Fernando Rojas. He did a great sales pitch describing it as 'a brilliant, romantic and mysterious work, partly grave, partly picaresque, full of passion and wit. Some scholars believe it had a great influence on Shakespeare'. He was hoping to work on the script with his friend, the Spanish poet Rafael Dieste (at that time a Cambridge lecturer). Cleverdon passed it all on to Christopher Holme and nothing came of it.

Few people perhaps realise the number of unprofitable hours that writers such as Bert spent on speculative scripts. Like another folk song enthusiast, the Rev. Sabine Baring-Gould (who at one time held the record for having authored the most books in the English language), Bert was a remarkably prolific writer, a lot of it unpaid. As well as time-consuming unprofitable speculative writing, he was an assiduously generous correspondent and produced copious numbers of free informative articles and notes for cash-strapped folk magazines around the world. By 1952 Bert had also lost the support of music talks producer Alec Robertson, who from 1949 till he left the BBC in 1952 produced the Third Programme's classical music programme *Record Review.* One of his last acts before retiring was to turn down one of Bert's programme suggestions: 'I don't want to use Lloyd again – he seems to me a very indifferent broadcaster. Try my successor!' A slight consolation is that in 1948 Robertson's reading of the programme notes for the BBC's projected monumental series *The History in Sound of European Music* had been described by Harman Grisewood, Acting Controller Third Programme, as 'wooden as an academic text book.'

In January 1953 Bert got a letter from the BBC Copyright Department confirming a commission to write a half-hour programme on the life of the nineteenth-century pitman poet, Thomas Armstrong. Earlier that month he had written to the BBC Contracts Department complaining about the five-guinea fee offered him for what had been his first TV appearance, in Alan Lomax's *Songhunter* series where he sang two mining songs and did a little more: '[I] took part in a two-sided discussion of some length on the subject of industrial folk song generally. Now, I don't know what television rates are, as this is my first appearance, but in view of the fact that the work involved was rather more than the contract indicates, I feel justified in referring the matter back to you.'

In February/March he was in Manchester recording songs for Ewan MacColl's six-part radio series, *Ballads and Blues,* which went out weekly on the Home Service from 10 March. Each programme dealt with a different theme – love, war and peace, the sea, railways, work, the city – and was sung by Americans (Big Bill Broonzy, Ma Rainey, Alan Lomax, Kentuckian Jean Ritchie) as well as Bert, MacColl and Isla Cameron. The Humphrey Lyttelton Jazzband was also in the programmes to 'provide instrumental colour'. As MacColl explained in *Journeyman*: 'The main objective of the series was to demonstrate that Britain possessed a body of songs that were just as vigorous, as tough and as down-to-earth as anything that could be found in the United States.'

What the British singers lacked in the railway department they more than made up for with the shanties in the sea programme. Although recorded in a rush, Bert enjoyed working on the series, as he told Ken Bell:

The radio series which I did with Ewan MacColl and others is unequal, as such things are bound to be, but it contains some very nice things. The programmes were recorded in a rush, under pretty chaotic conditions, without scripts being written etc., so it's hard to tell what they'll sound like. But we all enjoyed working on them, so perhaps they'll sound reasonably lively.[1]

The programmes were not as well received as MacColl later claimed, and the BBC, who couldn't justify the expensive shows, decided against a follow-up series. However, MacColl liked the idea of the format with its mix of folk, blues and jazz, and he and Bert with some of the others put on three Ballads and Blues Sunday afternoon benefit concerts for Theatre Workshop at their new premises, the Theatre Royal, Stratford East, which were well attended. Out of these came an offer from an agency for Bert and MacColl to tour Scotland with a Ballads and Blues group. They pulled in old stalwarts Alf Edwards, Fitzroy Coleman and Isla Cameron, and set off for Glasgow, Dundee and Edinburgh's Usher Hall.

Jean Ritchie has fond memories of Bert and her time in Britain. Ritchie had quite an influence on the early folk revival, not least due to her introduction of the Appalachian dulcimer to British audiences. She performed several times with Bert, on radio, in concert at Cecil Sharp House along with Doc Watson, and elsewhere: 'Bert was a good friend, both on our first stay in England in early fifties, and his visits to USA. He, Ewan McCall and Isla Cameron were many times at our flat, and we at theirs, all of us making music and enjoying each other's company.'[2]

In October 1953 Bert wrote to Josephine Plummer, Assistant Head of Children's Hour, whom he obviously knew:

Dear Jo, I'd very much like to sing on *Children's Hour.* The idea occurred to me the other day when I was making some records for HMV's Educational List (the first four sides are coming out next month, I think). HMV's Miss Davis was lamenting that there are so few singers with a decent repertoire of songs suitable for children. If that's your colleagues' experience, you might care to try out what I can do. I know a lot of traditional songs about animals, for instance, which might make a short programme. English-language songs, British, American, Australian, mostly very short. I like to sing them to a 5-string banjo, which seems to accentuate their curiosity and minimize their quaintness. Let me know what you think, won't you.

Plummer wrote back inviting Bert to come in and let them hear a few sample songs. He went along with banjo player Al Jeffrey and sang half a dozen numbers ('My Little Hen', 'Sally Buck', The Deer Chase', 'The Derby Ram', 'Whoa Pony' and 'Jack Can I Ride?') which went down very well. Plummer thought they were 'lovely, and good fun', and she described Bert in an internal memo as a 'sort of English Burl Ives, with a touch of John Jacob Niles. Grand for Children's Hour with a carefully selected programme.' She also found the banjo 'very attractive'. If Bert had played his cards right perhaps he could have *become* the English Burl Ives.

He also wrote several schools programmes for a new series entitled *Know Your Neighbourhood* with titles such as 'About Maps', 'Names and People', 'Making the Fields' and 'Caesar's Camp', plus a sprinkling of general schools scripts. At the end of 1953, in the damp, freezing, smog-swirling season of runny noses, colds and flu, Bert received a compliment from the Medical Research Council regarding his schools programme *The Common Cold.* They wrote to the BBC congratulating him for what he had made of the material, and concluded: 'We find it extremely rare for a layman to write a script without dropping any serious bricks.'

In January 1955 Bert's old communist friend, the BBC producer, Reggie Smith, introduced him to Talks Organiser Elizabeth Rowley and suggested that she might be interested in broadcasting Bert's experiences whilst acting as the shantyman in John Huston's film *Moby Dick,* which would finish filming in February. Rowley was obviously taken with Bert's anecdotes because the same day she wrote an internal memo to Talks Producer R.E. Keen proposing a fifteen-minute talk programme for the Light Programme.

Bert's hyperbolic storytelling skills had translated his two months' experience during August and September 1954, trapped on a small and uncomfortable boat with some eighty other people, into a Boccaccio-like tale of near disaster and high humour on sea and ashore. He had likened the conditions of this isolated community to that of a prison or prison camp, and his stories of how they passed the time when filming was impossible due to bad weather tickled

Rowley's fancy. She added a postscript to her memo: 'Mr Lloyd can sing the most beautiful shanty which you might like to include in the recording.'

Ben Weinreb claimed that Bert got the film job through the recommendation of their mutual friend Bernard Miles, who was also in the film. Bert's only appearance in the final cut is near the beginning of the story, as the whaler *Pequod* sails out of New Bedford (in reality the Irish seaside town of Youghal) at the start of the great and disastrous adventure. There's a close-up of Bert's bearded, eye-patched face looking through the rigging as he hauls on a rope and hollers out 'Blood Red Roses':

> Our boots and clothes are all in pawn
> Go down you blood red roses, go down!
> And it's mighty draughty round the Cape of Storm
> Go down you blood red roses, go down
> Oh you pinks and posies.

He then goes into an almost falsetto rendition of 'Heave Away my Johnny' off camera; a version of the song that Bert devised for the film.

It was during the filming of *Moby Dick* that Bert collected a couple of his more interesting shanties. The halyard shanty 'Roll Her Down the Bay to Juliana' (or 'Emma, Emma') was learnt from Eddie 'Ted' Howard who was on board the *Pequod* to lend his voice to the shanties, along with other members of the Welsh group the Barry Riggers, a club of old-time sailing-ship men. Ted, from whom Bert also collected a version of 'Off to Sea Once More', died later in 1954. Another club member, Dougie, whose fondness for the state of inebriation precluded him from actually sailing on the *Pequod*, spent much of his time in the dockside pub at Youghal where he sang Bert the shanty 'Bring 'em Down'. Bert was on board the *Pequod* while they were filming off Ireland but he can't be spotted in any crowd shots on board ship, unlike Bernard Miles who has several nice cameo scenes. Alf Edwards apparently performed the concertina music in the pub where the whalermen sang and danced before the trip, although it is unlikely to be Edwards on the screen, unless he was made up beyond recognition.

The screenplay by Ray Bradbury and Huston was finished in March 1954 and filming began in April. The Art Director, Ralph Brinton, had bought a 100-year-old three-masted wooden schooner in Scarborough, Yorkshire, and with a new stern and a false bow had turned it into Herman Melville's 1840s New England whaler, the *Pequod*. The beginning of the film was shot in Youghal, which had to be stripped of all modern power-lines and signs. The harbour-side houses were given false fronts to look like New Bedford.

Huston first took the *Pequod* down to the Azores where Portuguese whalermen still hunted whales with hand-harpoons from longboats. They allowed Huston to join them on a hunt during which they killed twenty whales. The sea off the Azores was rougher than Huston expected, and one of the three steel-framed, latex-covered, ninety-two-foot articulated whales broke its towline and disappeared into the sea mist. Due to the damage that the *Pequod* suffered in the rough seas, they headed back up to the St George's Channel between Wales and Ireland.

As Huston said in his autobiography *An Open Book*: 'That's when the real troubles began.' The winter weather off the Welsh coast was some of the worst on record. Another huge white whale broke loose and floated away, with the star, Gregory Peck, complete with ivory peg-leg, hanging on for dear life. Later, when rescued, he said that he had anticipated an ignominious death – drowned at sea with a rubber whale. According to legend one of the lost whales was reported as a hazard to shipping drifting somewhere in the English Channel before ending up in Holland.

Huston explained that they usually had men out in longboats when they were filming the whale: 'This was risky in bad weather, and when the seas got dangerously high we'd bring the longboats back to the ship. But it was in precisely this kind of weather that the cables would snap and the whale would begin to drift away.' He was faced with a difficult decision: whether to save the men or the whale. Apart from the $30,000 cost of each whale there was the added cost of not having a whale available for filming as soon as the weather permitted:

> Grave news, grave news, John Huston cried,
> To lose three of my crew,
> But the loss of a thirty-thousand dollar white whale
> Would break my heart in two, brave boys,
> T'would break my heart in two.

Hell-bent on authenticity, Huston shot the typhoon scenes in a real storm under full sail. Cameras were suspended on elastic ropes from the masts so that the crew could be seen battling the mountainous waves. The ship was de-masted three times, and a dozen of the crew were injured during filming. The final close-up shots of the whale were filmed in an 80,000-gallon water tank at Elstree Studios. One of Bert's *Moby Dick* stories involved the time that the *Pequod* was on the high seas when a modern passenger ship hove into view, Huston told the crew, in their period costumes, to lie about the decks as if dead. The passengers and crew of the passing ship were treated to the unnerving spectacle of an apparent nineteenth-century ghost ship drifting in the Irish Sea.

Moby Dick, which took two years to complete at a cost of $4.5 million, was Huston's favourite movie but was not a box-office success and failed to thrill the critics. Bert's BBC talk *A Film Extra at Sea* was recorded on 21 February and broadcast on 10 May 1955. In January Bert was booked to write *Whaling in the Antarctic* for the Schools Department *Travel Talks* series. He also wrote an introduction to modern whaling for the teachers' notes. The research, even for a programme about which Bert was quite knowledgeable, was considerable. It involved visiting company and other archives, tracking down reference books and reading them, as well as making personal contacts and interviewing them in person, by phone or by letter. Bert wrote on a small portable typewriter. As he didn't drive (although he'd driven trucks in the army), all research journeys had to be done by public transport. For one twenty-minute schools feature, *Air Sea Rescue,* he had to make two winter trips down to Gosport in Hampshire (24 January and 3 February 1955) to witness air-sea rescue demonstrations and conduct interviews.

At the end of February Bert received a letter from Ivan Gilman offering him dramatised history scripts for twelve-year-olds for broadcast in early 1956 – *Draining the Fens, The Hudson Bay Company* and *Oglethorpe and Georgia* (on America from the sixteenth to eighteenth centuries). The Hudson Bay Company were not best pleased with the BBC over their programme and wrote a tetchy letter to the Head of Schools Broadcasting when a changeover of programme assistants meant the archivist had not been sent the script for approval prior to recording, as agreed.

Although perhaps not a musician of the calibre of some of his professional musical associates over the years, such as Alf Edwards, Brian Daly, Fitzroy Coleman and Peggy Seeger, Bert could read and write music perfectly well, and could write simple arrangements of folk tunes if necessary. Surprisingly, Peggy Seeger, who worked with Bert on numerous musical projects, claims to have had no idea that Bert could read music, or that he had any interest in, or knowledge of, classical music. Caroline Lloyd is certain that when she was younger she saw Peggy and Bert sitting in his office poring over musical scores.

On 17 March 1955 Reggie Smith booked Bert to provide musical settings for 'The Devil's on the Prowl' and a couple of other songs, plus a few minutes of incidental music for violin, whistle, concertina and drums, and some verse narration for Smith's Home Service production of *Schinderhannes,* Carl Zuckmeyer's 1927 play about the famous eighteenth-century German Jesse James/Robin Hood, who was guillotined before an audience of 40,000 in 1803. Bert sent a sample top line for the singer, Marjorie Westbury, asking what key would suit her best so that Seamus Ennis could bring the right whistle along to the recording session! When the programme was finished to everybody's satisfaction, the powers that be decided to postpone broadcasting it because it wasn't deemed suitable to be aired before a general election. Later, in August 1958, Smith booked Bert to select some Greek folk tunes, and in some cases arrange the tunes for voice and violin, for his production of *The Bridge of Arta,* a programme about the famous stone bridge that crosses the Arachthos River near the Greek city of Arta. According to folk legend and ballad, the bridge's 1,300 builders, forty-five master-masons and sixty apprentices could not stop the bridge's foundations collapsing every morning until a human sacrifice was made – the wife of one of the builders.

Through the 1950s and 1960s, travel, music and history programmes for schools were a regular, if not huge, source of income. Bert wrote on a bewildering range of subjects and always succeeded, with his deft journalist's touch, in making them informative and accessible – the schools' listener reports were invariably enthusiastic and complimentary. Communicating with ordinary people was what he did best. In April 1955 he wrote a fully dramatised script for the Schools Department entitled *A Village in the Andes,* for which he also wrote the teachers' notes and researched suitable photographs that were not available to the BBC through their usual sources. On the 22nd and 24th he was commissioned to write a twenty-minute feature for schools on *The Cotton Crisis* and an eighteen-minute fully dramatised script, plus teachers' notes and photographs, on *Cattle Farming on the Pampas*. As a freelance writer he was constantly reprocessing and utilising earlier experiences, articles, and programmes. With *Cattle Farming on the Pampas* he had *Picture Post* to thank for paying for his trip to Argentina a few years earlier, when he travelled around the country soaking up information on regional occupations, folklore, costume, song and dance.

Bert was very proactive when it came to his BBC writing. As we've seen he regularly sent in programme ideas, not all of which bore fruit. His politics were never far from the BBC's consciousness, though, and references to Bert continued to crop up in memos into the late 1950s. On 30 November 1956, the producer Douglas Cleverdon felt obliged to write to the Head of the BBC's East European Service to let him know that Bert's programme *Folk Music of Rumania* would be edited on 11 December and, as had been suggested by the European Liaison Officer, the Romanian section might like to send along a representative to vet the material in case the songs contained some sort of propaganda. He also sent them a copy of the script with a transcription of the songs. A couple of days later he received a letter thanking him for the script of Bert's 'excellent programme', which the department had 'read with enthusiasm'. They were pleased to see that the songs were 'all authentic old Romanian Folk Songs, and there has been no smuggling in of politics'.

On 8 September 1955, Bert had written to Cleverdon suggesting a programme based on the material he had brought back from Bulgaria in the winter of 1954 whilst collecting music for Alan Lomax's *Columbia World Library of World Folk and Primitive Music*. The BBC had already bought sixty minutes of the material for their music archives but Bert said that he had several more hours of Bulgarian folk music of all kinds that would make an interesting programme. The Third Programme agreed to take a forty-five-minute programme selected from the Bulgarian trip. Cleverdon and Bert got together for lunch at Cleverdon's house, just up the road from Broadcasting House, to thrash out the format. When he wrote back to accept the lunch date Bert added a note: 'I didn't like to say it before, in case it sounded like sales talk, merely, but I believe you'll find the general level of items unusually brilliant.' The programme was eventually broadcast on 30 January 1956.

Bert was fortunate in having Cleverdon's enthusiastic support for his various folk music programme ideas. Cleverdon, who was responsible for making many of Bert's more important radio documentaries, was part of the leftish, iconoclastic group of features producers, writers and presenters which included the godfather, Laurence Gilliam, communists Reggie Smith (introduced into the Party by Anthony Blunt), Archie Harding and Olive Shapley, D.G. Bridson, Dylan Thomas (Cleverdon had originally commissioned *Under Milk Wood*), Bert and others. Cleverdon had been interested in folk music since the 1930s when, as a young West Region producer in Bristol, he had made folk music programmes featuring one of Cecil Sharp's old singers and concertina players, Louie Hooper, and the Marshfield Paper Boys group of mummers, or the Marshfield Gang, as he affectionately described them. In February and April 1944 he had even written a couple of articles for *English Dance and Song* entitled 'Adventures in Recording'.

Bert had initiated one of his major pieces of BBC writing earlier in 1955 when, on 10 January, after reading Kenneth Tynan's enthusiastic review of the Theatre Nationale Populaire's Paris production of *Mother Courage*, he wrote to Donald McWhinnie, the recently appointed Assistant Head of Drama:

> Tynan's column in last Sunday's *Observer* has reminded me about Brecht's *Mutter Courage*. A long time ago, Archie Harding mentioned this play to me. He told me the BBC had seen one or two unsatisfactory English versions of it, and suggested I might have a stab at it myself, to see if I could produce something better. For this purpose he lent me a copy of the book, which I confess I still have. After Archie's death, the idea went out of my head; but now it's back in again. Reggie Smith tells me this is not a very propitious time for trying to sell a translation of this particular play, but if it is decided to do *Mutter Courage* later on, I would be glad if you would bear me in mind as a possible translator.

Smith's claim that it was an inauspicious time to be trying to sell *Mother Courage* presumably stemmed from the fact that, when McWhinnie was appointed in 1953, he had made no secret of his concern about the lack of new British drama writing being produced by the BBC, and also his disquiet at the extensive number of European plays and adaptations of novels. Unlike the conservative Val Gielgud, Head of Drama, who confessed to having little sympathy with contemporary and avant-garde playwrights, McWhinnie was an enthusiastic supporter of the British New Wave writers who emerged in the 1950s and 1960s.

By 1953 televison was rapidly gaining in popularity and both Radio Features and Radio Drama were doing a lot of soul searching into how best to handle the competition. In 1953 Louis McNeice wrote an impassioned article entitled 'Plea for Sound' in the *BBC Quarterly* in which he claimed: 'sound can do so many fine things which will never be possible on television.' This would include poetry and forms of drama in which there could be a creative use of sound. The radio listener's imagination, if suitably stimulated, could often far surpass a TV director's and designer's interpretation of scenes and action.

McWhinnie's impact helped radio drama to flourish during the 1950s, and he encouraged dramatists such as Samuel Beckett to write for radio, and contemporary novelists such as William Golding to offer up their works for radio adaptation. He also approved several of Bert's German translations including *Mother Courage*. He wrote to Bert on 13 January saying that the German actress Maria Fein might be interested in playing the part of Mother Courage, and he'd very much like Bert to 'have a stab at translating the play'.

In May Bert was commissioned to submit specimen scenes for a possible radio production.

During this period he was also regularly supported by the Drama Script Editor, Barbara Bray, who was generally able to see the potential in Bert's various translations and adaptations, even when the initial drafts or outlines needed quite a bit of work to bring them up to scratch. She frequently ignored the often-negative reports from the play reader Helena Wood who, in the case of *Mother Courage*, declared that the translation was 'not really good enough', that it was often stilted and usually characterless. She felt the humour to be 'more often presented in phrases of donnish waggery, with nothing of the original punch and vigour'.

Bray, whilst agreeing that the script was stiff at times, was more hopeful and recommended that the BBC went ahead with it with Reggie Smith as producer. On 14 June Bert was officially booked to complete the translation and to adapt it for broadcasting as a ninety-minute radio drama. Charlotte witnessed the contract under the name of M. Ohly (Charlotte Maria Ohly was her previous married name), presumably to make the witness appear to be an independent person.

In July the Third Programme had the idea of sending Bert across to East Berlin for three days, if they could arrange a visa, to liaise with Brecht, since he was famously protective and controlling over his work. After the BBC managed to pin the playwright down and set up the meeting, it was for some reason cancelled, but Brecht was content for the project to continue. He sent Bert and the producer a few notes about the character of Mother Courage which he felt had been misinterpreted in some earlier productions, described by him as 'sob-stories'. Mother Courage, he wrote, as well as being a mother who loses her children to war, is also 'a business woman, shrewd hard-boiled she cannot think of a life without her business, that is without war'. Even though at times she curses the war, and thinks that she should be against it, she mechanically carries on with her trade: 'She does not learn her lesson – but the audience should learn theirs.'

In typical Lloydian fashion there is a bit of a mystery here. Bert had initiated the translation in January 1955 and it looks as if the BBC thought he was still working on it when they tried to set up the July meeting with Brecht. In that same month Joan Littlewood's production of *Mother Courage* went on in Barnstable as part of the 1955 Devon Festival of the Arts, where it was advertised as: Theatre Workshop in the English Premiere of *Mother Courage and her Children* by Bertolt Brecht in a translation with lyrics by A.L. Lloyd.

What *is* clear is that the translation turned out to be more work than Bert had anticipated. For a start, the twelve songs in the play contained 290 verse lines that had to be translated to fit the original musical score by Paul Dessau. Brecht sent a card to Bert in September congratulating him on the translation and pointing out that the music was quite complicated and that words would need 'some adjustment according to the bars'. Bert began to feel that the fee of £150 was inadequate. The producer Reggie Smith agreed and suggested that Bert be paid an extra £5 for having to modify the tunes and lyrics to enable actress Maria Fein to sing them. Five pounds doesn't perhaps seem a lot, but it represents over £100 today, and Bert's fee of £150 is equivalent to £2,800 today. A few years later, in 1960, Charlotte and Bert returned to Brecht and translated *St Joan of the Stockyards* for the BBC and the following year Brecht's *Refugee Conversations*.

On 2 September 1955 Bert was booked to write an eighteen-minute, fully dramatised script for School History, *Oglethorpe and Georgia*, and on 3 October another eighteen-minute script for a Country Schools series on *The Whirly Birds* (helicopters). Bert got plenty of mileage out of his translation of Lorca's *Lament for Ignacio Sanchez Mejias* (reprinted in 1953), despite subsequent translations by other well-known writers. It was still going strong in 1955 when the BBC wrote to him in October asking for permission for Reggie Smith to re-record Beatrix Lehmann reading Bert's 1937 translation for the Third Programme. The BBC were broadcasting two performances of Maurice Ohana's 1950 orchestral setting of the Lorca poem and wanted to precede the performances with a reading of the poem in English by Lehmann. Casablanca-born Ohana was a French composer who, in the 1950s, was destined to become one of the leading composers of his generation. He was particularly influenced by the melancholic Andalusian *cante jondo* with its sombre themes of death and disappointed love.

On Friday October 28 Bert flew to Belfast to take part in a BBC Northern Ireland Home Service Talks programme *Folk Song Forum*, for which he wrote and presented *The Origins of the Carol*.

In July 1956 Charles Armour from BBC Schools wrote to Bert congratulating him on a recent schools programme and asking him what areas of Europe he'd be interested in writing about in future programmes. Bert sent back an impressive list:

> Thank you for your compliments about the Cornwall programme. I'm glad it turned out all right. I'd like to see the school reports some time when I'm in the building. That may not be for a month as I'm going to South Germany for a folk music conference on July 24th, and if it's nice there I may stay on for two or three weeks.
>
> You ask what areas of Europe I'm interested in. Since the war I've visited the following places, mostly in order to write about daily life there (some of these places I have returned to more than once at intervals of two or three years):
>
> Norway: Particularly Lofoten at cod-fishing time, and the west coast; also the whaling towns on the Oslo fjord (where the Antarctic ships get most of their crews).
> Spain: Mainly Galicia and the villages of Estremadure and Andalusia (I don't know the towns so well; in Spain, I generally stay in villages).
> France: The wine country of Touraine and Burgundy; and particularly Provence – Aix, Nimes, Arles and the Camargue.
> Germany: Aachen and district, Rhineland, both Berlins.

Czechoslovakia: Northern Bohemia, Prague, Southern Moravia, Eastern
  Slovakia.
Hungary: Matra Mountains, Budapest, the Great Plain.
Rumania: Bucarest, Muntenia, Southern Transylvania.
Bulgaria: All over.

In these last four countries, my principal concern was with folk-music, so
I know more about village life there than industrial life.

The following January (1956) Bert was in the studio with Douglas Cleverdon
to record the programme on Bulgarian folk song, using the recordings he'd
brought back from Bulgaria and sold to the BBC. Then in February he
selected material and wrote a linking commentary for a schools programme
on American ballads. He wasn't presenting the programme but offered to sing
any of the ballads (except 'John Henry', which he said 'really needs a Negro
singer to do it justice'). As a guitarist for the programme, he recommended
his friend and accompanist, session musician Brian Daly, who 'knows the
idiom of these songs very well'. Bert occasionally tried out his school scripts
on his daughter, Caroline, although, as he admitted to his *Adventures in Music*
producer in 1956, it wasn't a fool-proof system of quality control.

In February Bert had been hustling for more drama work: 'The long article
about Zuckmayer in last week's *Times Lit. Supp.* has reminded me about his
circus play *Katherine Knie*. My wife and I feel it would make a first-class
Saturday evening play, for it is simple and rather sentimental, but full of
colour and charm and with sharper wit than usual.'

The corporation was interested in the idea and commissioned a detailed
report on the play from Bert. Reggie Smith was up for directing it and in
April they agreed to do it, subject to copyright clearance. Then, in May, Bert
received a letter telling him that Zuckmayer had made arrangements for a
new musical version of the play, and was therefore unable to dispose of any
broadcasting rights. For nearly four months the Lloyds had been waiting to
hear if they were back in the translation game, only to be frustrated at the
last hurdle.

Luckily, other radio work came in. In April he was contracted to write
two programmes for the Adventures in Music series on morris dancing and
square dancing, and another entitled *Czechoslovakia and Dvorak*. In October
he delivered a schools script on the life of the revered Northumbrian saint
Cuthbert, the one-time Bishop of Lindisfarne. Cuthbert had started life as a
shepherd boy in the borders. As shepherds across Europe have been known for
their pipe playing, Bert introduced a bit of atmospheric Romanian shepherd
music. He explained to the producer that:

The Romanian piece has close affinities with certain venerable Irish Gaelic
pieces, not because of direct culture-contact, but because once–universal
primitive models are nowadays found best preserved on the far fringes of
the culture area [which stretched from Ireland and Spanish Galicia to the

Crimea]. We don't know for sure what melodies Northumbrian shepherds played in the 7th century. But the chances are they were something like the piece I suggest. Anyway it's a nice noise. Sounds a bit like musique concrete.

It would have taken a brave and knowledgeable Schools producer to challenge Bert's argument. It was exactly this breadth of musicological and general knowledge that made him such a valuable scriptwriter, especially for schools. He could be counted on to know just the right bit of music and just the right bit of fascinating information to catch the children's imagination.

During January and February 1958 Bert was booked by the BBC producer Charles Parker (1919–80) for the six 'Hootenanny' programmes he recorded for the Midland Home Service. Three months later, Roger Fiske commissioned Bert to write and present the last of six programmes on British Folk Song. This was to be an overview, a summing up of the series, in which Bert was asked to talk about 'folk music as sung by the "bright young things" today – very up-to-date post-skiffle stuff, as done at the Princess Louise pub'. Fiske was two or three decades too late for London's 'bright young things' but Bert did his best and roped in a gaggle of folkie 'bright young things' in the forms of MacColl, Seeger, Alf Edwards, Ralph Rinzler, Bobby Clark on fiddle and Bert himself.

Fiske quaintly pointed out to the BBC Booking Manager Norman Carroll that 'they would all be 'vamping', without music in front of them, and I suppose, so far as there is a leader at all, it's A.L. Lloyd.' 'Vamping'! How anarchic and *ad hoc* it must all have sounded to the staid BBC who normally worked with 'real' musicians. To make matters worse Rinzler and Clark had 'never broadcast before'. The topping on the cake was Alf Edwards, a concertina-playing variety booking, 'who always asks for ten guineas for what Miss Heritage calls "pick-up groups" and I gather Miss H resists this'.

The idea of 'vamping' without music, or busking, would have been anathema to Edwards who also played the bagpipes, saxophone, drums, piano, trombone and ocarina. His mother who, while pregnant, had played the fiddle while standing on her head on a tightrope, paid him sixpence for every new instrument he learned. He could play any music put in front of him as long as he had the dots. Peggy Seeger remembered his later consternation while working on the Radio Ballads when she gave him forty-two bars of just chords and said, 'Improvise'.

Later, when he finally understood that these chord letters represented the background of a possible tune or countermelody he was jubilant. The penny had dropped and Alf went wild, musically filling those bars with material dredged up from his whole musical experience. He would abandon the tune totally and let his fingers fly and silence or a minim rest would be a rare commodity.[3]

Don MacLean, the BBC Music Organiser, Light Entertainment (Sound) was no lover of skiffle, hootenanys or folkbeat, and early in 1958, on hearing a

Charles Parker pilot programme of 'ballads, blues, skiffle and calypso, linked in a semi-professional but intensely exciting, free-for-all jam session', recorded live at the Princess Louise and featuring the usual gang of MacColl, Seeger, Bert etc., he wrote:

> The artists on that particular session at the Princess Louise have been on the go for many years and have made little impact on the public. I've always regarded Ewan MacColl and his comrades as the Ken Colyers of folk music in Britain: they intentionally sing 14-bar choruses because some infirm old negro used to do so unintentionally. In jazz broadcasting we give Colyer his share, but we've done a great deal more to foster the creative boys as opposed to the re-creative. So with 'folkbeat': the appropriate share for the copyists should be small – and there should certainly not be a weekly transmission of such contrived entertainment as this tape contains.[4]

Parker had more success later in the year with his radio ballad *John Axon,* in which Bert sang. Other BBC folk music work that year included singing on Dennis Mitchell's *Ballads and Blues,* and two programmes that Bert had suggested to Douglas Cleverdon, a programme on folk carols (*All Bells in Paradise*) and a forty-minute look at the music and ceremonials of prehistoric Europe (*Musical Pre-History*). Cleverdon had to battle with Peter Crossley-Holland (not a great fan of Bert) for the *Musical Pre-History* programme which Crossley-Holland believed was 'really a field for the scholar', and pointed out that 'Mr Constantin Brailoiu has for instance an expert knowledge of S.E. Europe and a large archive at Geneva and Marius Schneider is a specialist in prehistoric musical traditions'. Crossley-Holland saw Bert as a popularising, academic lightweight who was more suited to Schools and other less cerebral departments than the Third Programme. And he had a point when he said that it couldn't be assumed that the music now found in connection with traditional ceremonies in Romania and other South Eastern European countries, which were to be Bert's main areas of investigation, represents the music as it was in prehistory. He felt that a 'feature-like' treatment of this subject was unlikely to solve any problems and could possibly jeopardise the field of the genuine scholar.

Despite Crossley-Holland's poor view of Bert's scholarship, it was Bert who introduced the English-speaking world to thirteen of 'Mr Constantin Brailoiu's' major essays in *Problems of Ethnomusicology* (1984), which he translated from the French and edited for the Cambridge University Press. It was Bert's last work, and he didn't live to see in print what for him would have been one of his most important contributions to musical folklore.

In January 1959, out of the blue, Hilary Pym from the Gramophone Department offered Bert a great gig as a sort of folk music DJ presenting a series of programmes for the General Overseas Service. Pym had been reading the magazine *Recorded Folk Music* that Bert was editing for Collet's, and felt that as Bert had 'made a special study lately of the [folk music] records that are available', he might feel there was enough interesting material for a series of six programmes. Six programmes! Bert would happily have presented a couple of dozen. It was a good start to the year.

In April Bert wrote to the BBC Drama Script Editor Barbara Bray to draw her attention to Gerd Gaiser, who was establishing himself as one of the most important modern German writers, and whose book *Schlussball* Bert and Charlotte had just read. They felt it to be one of the best and most perceptive novels of the 'postwar plight'. He went on to talk about Gaiser's radio plays and said that if any of the radio pieces are found suitable for doing in Britain they'd like 'to have a shot at translating them'.

Two months later, Bert's *A Bushfire in Australia* was broadcast as a schools Travel Talk. The same month Charles Parker, Senior Features Producer, Birmingham, wrote to the BBC Copyright Department in London to tell them that the dramatico-musical radio ballad *The Floating Republic* (the story of the 1797 Nore Mutiny based on traditional music and ballads of the time) that he'd booked Bert to write back in 1958 was to be put on hold so that Bert could: 'devote himself exclusively to *Bold Nelson's Praise*, as this has been accepted by Home Service for Trafalgar Day, 21st October 1959.' Bert conducted the research for *Bold Nelson's Praise* in the library of the National Maritime Museum a few minutes' walk across Greenwich Park from his house.

Following the musical drama's airing on 12 October 1959, Peter Grant in *Ethnic* (Autumn 1959) gave the programme a very positive review:

This wireless programme, to celebrate Trafalgar Day, was in the form of a 'garland of songs and stories' that might have been heard in a fo'c'sle sing-song of the time ... the sound of those evocative, romantic names, Santa Cruz, Cadiz, the Nile, Copenhagen and Trafalgar, lead to the songs – to 'Bold Nelson's Praise', 'The Banks of the Nile', 'The Agamemnon Song', 'Says the Afterguard, Amen', a dozen or so in all – and to hear them like this, with some of the scraps of dialogue culled from contemporary letters and ringing out like newly-minted coins, is a splendid reassurance that they are part of the flesh and blood of living history. One shudders to think, though, what such a programme would have been like twenty years ago.

Bold Nelson's Praise is a good example of the argument for complete honesty and integrity when using folk song and contemporary material to illuminate historical events. If the letters and song texts are not taken from primary sources, the programme's value is considerably reduced. Of these lines, referring to women at the battle of the Nile ('One died of wounds, and on her birthday too. Death keeps no calendar. We buried her in the sand. She was from Leith', and 'One woman bore a son in the heat of the action. From Edinburgh she came') Peter Grant said: 'In the face of these epic simplicities, which surely come from original sources, one remains dumb.'

So far as we know these did indeed come from the original eighteenth-century naval letters and documents that Bert studied in the museum library when working on the script. When the programme was broadcast in 1959, the young singer Louis Killen recorded it on his new tape recorder with a microphone stuck in front of his wireless. Nearly fifty years later, in November 2008, when he sang at the Centenary Tribute to Bert at Cecil Sharp House, Killen related how the programme 'had a very strong effect on me and my repertory for the rest of my singing career ... and there were several songs from that which have stuck with me all the time'. One of them, 'The Death of Nelson', he sang at the concert. Killen is just one of hundreds, possibly thousands, of people whose lives were changed by hearing Bert or one of his radio programmes, and the ripples continue to spread as a new generation of folk music singers and enthusiasts discovers his work.

13
Writing and Recording in the Fifties

There is no point in putting music out if it isn't going to change the world. 78 revolutions per minute was something we aspired to – well, 78 revolutions a year would have been all right for us – as long as we had the revolutions we would be happy.

Bill Leader

In 1954 Bert was finally taken off the military reserve and discharged from the army.

In January of that year the first issue of Lawrence and Wishart's new *Marxist Quarterly* printed a ten-page article by Bert entitled 'Folk Song for Our Time?'. He starts off by suggesting that society was witnessing a revival of interest in folk music, more powerful and more significant than that experienced earlier in the century. It is more powerful, he says, because unlike the first revival which emerged 'mainly among middle-class folk, scholars, educators, parsons, givers of garden parties', this second revival has '... arisen more or less spontaneously among young people in youth clubs, rhythm clubs, trade union branches, night-school classes, in fact precisely among those people who are the true heirs to that lower-class musical heritage we call – for want of a better name – folk music.' 'Spontaneously', that is, with a prod from Bert and MacColl, and many years of planning and preparing the ground.

The aim of the article was 'to try to suggest what folk music may have to offer' the thousands of ordinary people, youngsters particularly, who have 'been turning to folk song in search of the satisfaction of some apparently deep artistic want'. And also, to see what they, in turn, may have to offer folk music. He then lets the reader know exactly what he is talking about; folk music, being such a fluid concept, means virtually whatever you want it to mean, and today it's no better – the term has become virtually meaningless as a musical definition.

Bert does no better than anyone else in defining what he's talking about. He theorises that folk music had two fundamental characteristics that for him distinguish it from other musics – *performance* (oral transmission, perpetual variation of the material, vocal and instrumental techniques) and *function* (what the singer hopes to achieve – propitiation of evil powers, solace for a baby's death or strengthening men's determination during a strike). He goes on to elucidate the multiple theories and academic spats about who or what actually are the 'folk' and comes to no conclusion himself. Then follows a few pages where he's dipping and diving into Marxist folk music research in the USSR, Congo pygmy yodelling, Negro chain-gang chants, and a whole lot of other stuff on functional work songs, plough cries, shepherds' calls and street cries.

Next he trashes John Meier's *Rezeptionstheorie* – art starting at the top and filtering down to the peasants, who gather up the crumbs and reshape it (badly) until it becomes folk song/music. He quotes Bartók's discovery of 'a wealth of music quite different from that created for the privileged classes, music with a direct social function – to still terrors, soothe longings, fill needs.' (Bert said elsewhere that he believed children's playground songs and rhymes were some of the few examples left in Britain of what could be classed real folk music.) The reader would have found the information interesting, but they might be excused for wondering what most of it had to do with England and an English folk revival. Eventually, he gets to the core issues and reiterates much of what he'd been thinking and saying since the late 1940s when he and John Hasted first got together to change the world. He said that 'if our folk song has any future, that future lies with the town worker'. Zoltan Kodaly felt much the same and said he thought folk music would be carried on by the educated urban youth. In addition, Bert thought the following could not be overlooked:

At least part of the newly revived interest in folk music has a strong political bias. There are many who believe that music may be a force to assist the progress of the human race; and since folk music is created directly out of the common experience and aspirations of working people, it follows that folk song is likely to be a powerful aid not only in mirroring man's condition, but also encouraging him on his forward march. Also, folk song is the most truly and deeply national aspect of our musical culture, and at a time when that culture is in grave danger of losing its independence it is well that we avail ourselves of what we can in the way of fortification.

Capitalism, he believed, has made a sad mess of our folk song tradition (something he'd been saying since the 1930s) but that:

The outlook for a revival not merely of interest in folk music, but of the actual creation of new forms of it does not seem so dark as it did in, for instance, Cecil Sharp's time. Our native musical idioms are among the most powerful as well as most beautiful in Europe, and there seems to be a wide audience, young [urban], hungry for culture, anxious to listen to folk song, and what is more important, to take it into their own repertoire, to make it part of their own cultural baggage.

Can these circumstances lead to a revival of folk music creation? It remains to be seen.

Both Bert and MacColl were interested as much in the creation of folk music as in its preservation. They were looking to create a primarily urban movement which, along with traditional songs and ballads, would include the creation of new songs, rooted in musical folklore and relevant to present day (political) needs. Both had done their fair share of song creating for radio, theatre and publication for a number of years before the folk revival took off. MacColl had been writing songs based on folk originals or new lyrics to folky tunes from his time in radio and agit-prop theatre companies in the 1930s and 1940s and eventually for Theatre Workshop. His songwriting for the Radio Ballads was simply a continuation of this. Bert had 'created' new 'folk songs', based on traditional tunes and lyrics, for Bridson's radio ballad opera *Johnny Miner* and regularly put new words to Eastern European tunes for WMA choirs and *Sing* magazine. With Hasted he wrote political songs for the Ramblers, based on traditional models, and for the rest of his life he wrote, rewrote, improved, tweaked or added a pinch of rhythm to the countless songs that he introduced into the folk revival.

Young people in the early folk clubs and coffee bars and on CND marches were happy enough to sing the left-leaning songs that were being written for them by MacColl, Hasted, Dallas, Winter, Stan Kelly and Peggy Seeger. But most felt less inclined, or perhaps less able, to write them themselves. Eventually, however, with Bert's encouragement (*Come All Ye Bold Miners* and Topic Records) and MacColl's songwriting example, there was, from the early 1960s a small flurry of new songs with an industrial theme, from northern English songwriters such as Keith Roberts, Johnny Handle and Ed Pickford, written in a style whose face was firmly turned towards traditional song, as were many of the songs of Matt McGinn, Jock Purdon, Graeme Miles, John Connolly, Bob and Carole Pegg and Jez Lowe. Some of these songs are still being recorded by folk acts, or reappearing on reissued albums; some, like Connolly's 'Fiddler's Green' and McGinn's kids' songs, achieved a degree of fame but, unlike MacColl's golden goose, 'The First Time Ever I Saw Your Face', most of the songs that surfaced from the more traditional end of the revival pond – songs Bert would have seen as lineal descendants of the old rural folk songs – remained firmly within the boundaries of the folk world and failed to breach the barrier surrounding 'popular' music and affecting the public at large. This was despite MacColl's attempts:

> There are no nightingales in these songs, no flowers – and the sun is rarely mentioned; their themes are work, poverty, hunger and exploitation. They should be sung to the accompaniment of pneumatic drills and swinging hammers, they should be bawled above the hum of turbines and the clatter of looms for they are songs of toil, anthems of the industrial age.

That polemical introduction to *The Shuttle and Cage* would have been more appropriate shouted through a (red) megaphone to a crowd of out-of-work 1930s miners or dockers than written for an urban youth that by the mid-1950s had found its voice and identity. And with an end to the immediate postwar austerity, had the money to buy such novelties as suede brothel-creepers, drape jackets, cut-away collar shirts, boot-lace ties, make-up and girls' teen fashions and cigarettes. Also radiograms and Dansette Junior record players on which to play 78s and 45s of 'The Father of Rock and Roll', Bill Haley, whose 'Shake, Rattle and Roll' was the first rock and roll song to enter the British singles charts in December 1954, and Elvis Presley, 'The Hillbilly Cat', whose Sun release 'That's All Right' appeared in July 1954. Hunger, poverty and Stygian darkness were not good selling points for the majority of teenagers who just wanted to have fun.

Another attempt to breach the popular music barricades was the electric-folk and folk-rock mini-movement of the late 1960s and 1970s, which had a degree of success and a couple of novelty 'hits' with Steeleye Span's 'Gaudette' and 'All Around My Hat', but was never really much more than a fad for that majority of young people outside the folk world, who jumped just as quickly onto the glam rock, punk or ska roundabout and hopped off after a few spins. The songs that were written within the British folk revival were written for, and sung to, the converted. Their impact rarely extended beyond the folk scene or very local audiences, such as members of the mining community who frequented County Durham's Birtley folk club. But, in general, most people would not have heard, or heard of, any of them.

Things were no better by the 1970s when Bert was invited to judge an *English Dance and Song* magazine National Song-Writing Contest. In the Spring 1972 magazine he gave his verdict: 'By and large the standards of melody and poetry were not of a sort to pull down the stars. However, a handful of entries were above the ruck.' He managed to find just three songs that justified publication and the £10 winner's prize.

Despite the disparaging opinion that Bert, MacColl, Bush, Hasted and the rest had of popular music, it did, and still does, in many ways fulfil the same needs that they were claiming as folk music's unique selling point. 'Teenager in Love', 'Dream Lover' and the Everly Brothers' 'Problems' for example, verbalised many of the dreams, desires, and fears of young people at the end of the 1950s and the beginning of the 1960s.[1] Even if Bert was right about 'a wide audience, young, hungry for culture', the vast majority of young people were perfectly happy with the youth 'culture' they already had. It might not have been Bert's, or the Young Communist League's, idea of 'culture' but culture it was. Despite MacColl's claims of an 11,000 Singers' Club membership, and many satellite folk clubs following the Singers' Club musical policy, the vast majority of ordinary working-class young people remained blissfully unaware of MacColl, Bert, Seeger, Lomax and the 'folk scene'. They were even less well known to the adult population.

Bert went on to say that oral/aural transmission was alive and well, thanks to the radio and records, and that the need was for musical material worth the listeners 'exercising their fantasy on.' This is the material that Bert and MacColl were intent on supplying. By 1954 MacColl had already recorded thirteen records for Topic – a mix of traditional songs and ballads and his own songs written in the simple, easily accessible, folk style such as 'Champion at Keeping 'em Rolling' and the infamous 'Song for Stalin', in which the man responsible for the deaths of millions of Russians is turned into some sort of benevolent superhero, a jolly red giant levelling mountains and diverting rivers for the benefit of mankind.

Despite the fact that one of the main reasons for Bert's musical crusade was the swamping of our indigenous musical culture by American music, he's happy enough to hold up the example of the American radical folk song movement as a source of inspiration:

> Those who feel that the springs of folk creation have dried up, as far as the industrial worker is concerned, may take heart from what happened in America in the 1930s. There, the great stimulus towards the creation of new folk song began when militant trade unionism swept through the textile mills and coalfields of the South, among industrial workers still living within a traditional folk culture. Folk bards arose such as the North Carolina cotton spinner Ella May Wiggins, Aunt Molly Jackson the Kentucky miner's wife, and most remarkable of all, the Oklahoma migratory worker Woody Guthrie, whom one folklorist has described as 'the best folk-ballad composer whose identity has ever been known'.

Later, Bert would demote Guthrie from traditional worker bard to a mere New York folk-scene singer. Britta Sweers, in her book *Electric Folk*, points out that in Alun Howkins 1981 TV documentary *The Other Muse*, Bert admitted that the British revival was 'set in motion by a contrary situation: it was, on one hand, a defensive reaction against the domination of American culture, yet, on the other hand, it was also inspired by American models'.

It always sounds xenophobic or nationalistic to talk of Bert's ideas on *English* folk music and his work in the *English* revival. Bert was certainly no xenophobe. His sphere of interest and influence extended across the British Isles, and beyond, but his particular area of work was England. Scotland had Hamish Henderson, Ireland had Seamus Ennis. Ewan MacColl floated between England and Scotland depending on which side of the cultural bed he got out of on any particular day. Alan Lomax worked with all of them, as did Peter Kennedy, although his main area of collecting was England.

There were, obviously, many other people involved in folk song collecting and reviving (Bob Copper and Sean O'Boyle to mention but two) but these six seem to have been the movers and shakers in the early 1950s. There was an unsubstantiated rumour circulating back in the 1960s that in the 1950s a folk music cabal of Henderson, Kennedy and Ennis had a meeting and agreed to carve up the British Isles, each taking his own fiefdom, and all that went with it, including copyright of material. Peter Kennedy was certainly very on the ball when it came to copyright. Few folk musicians brought out an album in the 1960s and 1970s without a claim dropping through the letterbox for half of the traditional material recorded. The claim invariably went in the bin.

The acquisition of copyright and royalties was certainly not the reason for Bert's writing and rewriting of traditional material. He clearly got more satisfaction from seeing his creations slip back into the corpus of frequently anonymous material which we call folk song. In a 1977 postcard to writer Roy Palmer he said: 'Yes, of course you can use "Trimdon Grange" and anything else of "mine". I consider anything I collect is Public Domain unless its authorship is traceable and copyright worthy.'

As early as 1962, in *Sing Out!*, Bert had written an article entitled 'Who Owns What in Folk Song?'[2] which begins: 'Almost unnoticed, the jungle is closing in. The amusement industry, which formerly ignored traditional music, begins to feel that there is money to be made from the folk song revival.' He went on to highlight the iniquitous behaviour of certain collectors as far as copyright was concerned. In particular he targeted Alan Lomax's tenuous claims in *Folk Songs of North America*:

> There is general agreement on one point – that a musician may claim copyright on a written arrangement of a folk song. In legal terms, 'arrangement' means that at least a bass-line is added to the melody. The simple alteration of text and melody-line, without harmonization (as for instance in many items 'arranged by Alan Lomax' in the recently published *Folk Songs of North America*) does not in itself provide a ground for claiming copyright.

He continued his dig at the Lomax collecting dynasty with a reference to the song 'Good-night, Irene', which everyone knew had been collected by John and Alan Lomax from Huddie Ledbetter, 'Leadbelly':

> When an obscure convict sang 'Goodnight, Irene' to a folk song collector the collector felt himself free to copyright the song. The song became a hit, but not before the convict had become a well-known public performer, wishing to exploit his own song. (The confusion was resolved out of court, to the collector's advantage.)

Bert couldn't have known the extent of the Lomaxes' appropriation of collected folk song. But American journalist Bart Bull has this to say: 'Currently, the BMI [Broadcast Music, Inc.] catalog contains 890 compositions with Alan Lomax listed as songwriter or composer; John A. Lomax is listed as the author of 694 titles; in both cases, based on legal issues or royalty revenue stream preferences, other songs are listed with ASCAP, PRS, or other international collection societies.'[3]

In spring 1967, Bert had been concerned enough about EFDSS copyright claims on Jack Elliott of Birtley's 'I am an old miner' ('The Banks of the Dee'), which had been printed in *English Dance and Song* (Winter 1966), to write a letter to *ED&S* pointing out that Elliott had learnt the song from Bert's *Come All Ye Bold Miners*:

> If the song is anyone's 'copyright,' it's Mr White's [from whom Bert collected it]. I have no claim on it. What claim has EFDSS?
>
> Does EFDSS mean to claim copyright on all the print-learned barely altered versions of songs it comes across? It will be busy. Every club singer's

head is full of such songs. I foresee jostling in the jungle, and splitting headaches for the Performing Right Society, M.C.P.S. and such bodies!

Around 1971, with so many people beginning to claim copyright on traditional material, and Gerry Sharp at Topic wanting clarification on the matter, a small group including Bert, lawyer Stephen Sedley and oral historian Bob Thompson got together to look into the matter. They hoped to establish a workable code of practice. As Bert explained: 'We felt that it would be a good idea if musical folklore words and music could be subject to copyright control, but that the fees accruing from that control, or the majority of it, should go into a common or national fund for research and such.'

Bert and Sedley formally put their proposal to an AGM of the English Folk Dance and Song Society, only to be met with stiff resistance from, amongst others, Maude Karpeles. As Cecil Sharp's executrix, Karpeles thought it would be too dangerous for control of the material to go out of the hands of the executors. She felt that the law as it stood provided protection to those who devoted their time and money to folk music collecting. The proposal ended in a stalemate. The idea, however, continued to nag at certain members of the EFDSS Executive.

In 1973 a government committee was set up under the chairmanship of the Hon. Mr Justice Whitford to consider what changes needed to be made to the law on copyright and designs. The committee's remit was to review the copyright laws and ensure that they remained in the public interest while, at the same time, being fair to both creators and users. Fearing that the presiding judge would have little, if any, knowledge of English folk music, those EFDSS Executive members who were concerned that there should be proper public domain established in which people couldn't appropriate the music, put their own committee together at Cecil Sharp House to examine the problem. Stephen Sedley being the only lawyer on the committee, put up some ideas and explanations of how copyright law worked, and what might be done to secure a public domain. Sedley later recalled that Bert, who was also on the committee, was quicker on the uptake than anybody else; he was more astute with his points and questions than the other committee members, and Sedley said that 'he saw a razor-sharp mind at work'.[4]

In February 1974 Bert wrote to Sedley:

After cogitation, I have produced this 'definition' of folk song in the hope that it will help to guide lawyers even if it wouldn't satisfy folklorists.

FOLK SONG

(a) consists of anonymous versified words and tunes, emanating mainly from the so-called common people, usually presenting some technical differences from the conventional creations of learned poets and composers;

(b) it is not restricted to its original form but is usually spread by oral means, and thus in its circulation undergoes sundry transformation in its travels (the appearance of certain song-texts in print, on popular leaflets, broadsides etc., may sometimes work towards 'fixing' a song-text, but the general truth of the above statement remains; a folk song is likely to exist in many variants, of which no one form is more 'authentic' than another);

(c) being subject to constant modification by successive performers, folk song may be described as 'collective' in authorship, in that it serves (or has served) as spiritual nourishment for more or less sizeable communities where individual creative traits merge and disappear if only on account of the uniformity of common taste and preference.

As you'll see, this 'definition' concentrates mainly on aspects of authorship, which I imagine to be the nub of the problem where law is concerned.

He had, in fact, long since rejected the idea of the composer/writer anonymity being the *sine qua non* of folk song, especially with regard to industrial or workers' song, but his 'definition' here was designed to help sort out a hypothetical situation where there was no obvious author and no natural entitlement to copyright claim. It was not an attempt at a comprehensive definition. Folk song and workers' song definitions have always been ultimately unsatisfactory, and back in 1961 Bert was toying with the idea that we were perhaps looking through the wrong end of the telescope:

The point of workers' song lies not in its forms but in its functions. Perhaps as Marxists we should divide our song heritage according to the social classes that create or receive it: that is instead of asking: Is this art song, stage song, folk song? We ask: Who is the bearer of this song and for what purpose does he use it?[5]

Six years later, in *Folk Song in England*, he contended that 'after three-quarters of a century of tune collecting and nearly two hundred years of text-study, we are still without a definition of folk song that really fits our local condition'. But, at the same time, he publicly threw his hat into the ring with the International Folk Music Council and their 1954 definition based on Cecil Sharp's theory of Continuity, Variation and Selection:

As we shall see, there are points to quibble about, but the formulation is valuable for its clear suggestion of the vital dialectic of folk song creation, that is, the perpetual struggle for synthesis between the collective and the individual, between tradition and innovation, between what is received from the community and what is supplied out of personal fantasy, in short, the blending of continuity and variation.[6]

The EFDSS deliberations on copyright were forwarded to the Whitford Committee, which finally presented *The Report of the Committee to Consider the Law on Copyright and Designs* to Parliament in March 1977. The EFDSS wanted the law clarified or amended to ensure that 'it is not possible for any private individual or company to, in effect, appropriate for himself or itself what is in its nature collective and communal property'. The Committee agreed that the mere transcribing of a work [song] should have no protection under copyright law unless the transcriber's [collector's] version involves sufficient skill and/or labour to qualify as an original work. Despite such rulings, copyright can still be a legal minefield.

1954 had started well. On New Year's Day a letter from BBC Music Bookings invited Bert to write and present a Children's Hour programme of 'Songs to the Banjo', to be broadcast on 1 February. Unfortunately, or, perhaps fortunately (depending on one's opinion of banjos), he had to turn the offer down because from mid-January to mid-February he was in Hungary, as he told Ken Bell in a letter of 18 March:

I have just been in Hungary, having a look at the work of the folklorists there. Things have altered a great deal since the information on which you based your remarks was prepared, but that should not worry your examiners! Impressive as their collecting and indexing departments are, the most striking and powerful folk-music organisation there now is the Folk Art Institute whose concern is not with taking folk song from the people, but in stimulating them to make more of it. In this respect they are doing colossal work.

It would be interesting to know what, if any, ideas Bert brought back from Hungary, which he felt he could incorporate into his own attempts to stimulate the English people to pick up what he saw as the remaining sparks of folk song and fan them back into flame. Although Reg Hall and Mervyn Plunket could point out in *Ethnic* that there were still hundreds of singers of traditional songs knocking around in the 1950s, the fact is that, even if it wasn't as dead in the water as Bert seemed to think, it *was* on its way out as a cultural phenomenon. When that last generation of country performers died – Pop Maynard, Harry Cox, Charlie Wills, Phil Tanner, Charlie Bates, George Townshend, Sam Larner, Scan Tester, Jinky Wells, Stephen Baldwin – the musical baton was rarely, if ever, taken up by their descendants and neighbours but instead by romantically (and/or politically) motivated revivalist performers, usually with little, if any, social, cultural, geographical or familial connection to the old source singers. A similar situation pertained in America in the 1950s and 1960s when many young Jewish romantics in New York and other northern cities discovered and immersed themselves in the Old Time music of the southern mountains. The result is not so much a revival of the old music in its original social setting but a bifurcation (or perhaps bifolkation), a splitting of the tradition into old and new, each with a different job to do.

Bert's letter to Ken Bell was in response to a copy of Bell's thesis *Folk Music Research*, which he was submitting for a B.Arch., degree from King's College School of Architecture, Newcastle upon Tyne. Bert had agreed to write a foreword. As Bert was a Member of the International Folk Music

Council, and an editorial board member of the *Journal of the English Folk Dance and Song Society*, his name on the foreword would give Bell's thesis a bit more authority.[7]

In 1952, after buying a copy of *Come All Ye Bold Miners*, Bell had written to Bert telling him about the thesis he intended to write on folk music research as part of his final architectural year design project for a Folk Music Institute:

> That September I pestered foreign embassies in London for information on their folk musics, researched in Cecil Sharp House, and visited Bert. Several letters of advice followed from him, Alan Lomax, who was in London, and Maude Karpeles. In September 1953 as a penniless student saving up to get married, I hitched a lift on a collier ship from my home in Hartlepool to London, docking at Greenwich Gas Works, so that I could visit Bert with the draft of my thesis. He agreed to write the Introduction to it. I qualified as an architect the following July. He was a lovely fellow, Bert, always ready to help.

In April 1954 Bert sent Bell the introduction, which began:

> For the musicologist, struggling with his present inadequate facilities, while the riches of the world's folk music accumulate around him in the form of cartons of magnetic tape which threaten to wall him up alive, it is indeed a relief and encouragement to find young architects are turning their minds to the needs of this peculiar and expanding science.

Bell got the opportunity to repay Bert in a small way for his support when he and his wife moved to Hertfordshire in 1957 and was involved in helping to organise the 1958 Hemel Hempstead Arts Festival. On 29 September he booked Bert and the American musician Ralph Rinzler, then lodging with Bert, to do morning and afternoon performances for schoolchildren in the village hall. Bell recorded the performances on a very primitive tape recorder with one static microphone taped to a broom-handle. The sound quality leaves much to be desired. However, through the rumbles, hisses, off-mic remarks and persistent rain on the hall roof, we get a rare fifty-year-old window into the past through which we can eavesdrop on Bert introducing kids to folk music. The response was enthusiastic enough and Bert and Rinzler were amiable, although Bert's vocabulary and introductions did seem to be a bit above their heads.

He was surprisingly formal, almost Edwardian in his approach, and you can't help wondering just how much of an understanding of folk music the children actually went away with. He seemed less comfortable working with groups of live children than when writing informative and entertaining radio scripts for them. Our attitude to presenting this sort of musical educational programme has loosened up considerably over the intervening years. Bert apologised to Bell for not being able to stay for the evening concert but he had to be back in London for the dress rehearsal of the play *Live Like Pigs* at the Royal Court, in which he was performing.

On 13 January 1954, BBC Schools Broadcasting aired Bert's semi-dramatised programme *The Whaling Industry* in their Current Affairs series. Although it had been some sixteen years since he'd been whaling, he had kept up to date with what was happening in the industry through the Norwegian Embassy. He received a complimentary note at the beginning of February from the Schools Department telling him that the programme had been 'very much a hit' with the schools and that they'd like to thank him 'for another first class script'. A couple of weeks later, he wrote to the Contracts Department saying that he wished there was no distinction between dramatic and semi-dramatic scripts, because he was paid as if for semi-dramatic work but invariably ended up doing an almost fully dramatised script.

Other school scripts that year included *The New Town*, *The Exhibition*, *On a Coffee Plantation in Brazil* and, for the History Department, two fully dramatised scripts; *Aethelric the Outlaw* and *The Peasants' Revolt*. He and Charlotte also translated Carl Zuckmayer's play *Schinderhannes*, which the Assistant Drama Script Editor (Sound) found 'vigorous, dramatic, and effective'. In November, when the script was finished and accepted by the script editor, Reggie Smith was asked: 'Would this appeal to you as a commitment?' He wrote back immediately: 'Very much thank you!'

One evening in the spring of 1954, in Eric and Audrey Winter's West Hampstead flat, John Hasted, Eric (a librarian at St Pancras public library), and the journalist and puppeteer extraordinaire Johnny Ambrose decided that the London Youth Choir needed a magazine. A lot of songs were being written but, before the days of easily available portable tape recorders, they were not being preserved in any organised way. The magazine would be a repository for these and other songs for future singers. It was to be magazine policy that the printed versions should not necessarily be definitive, or pin the songs down like dead butterflies – anyone could add to them, change them, try another tune, or whatever. They would be subject to the 'folk process'. They defined their areas of interest as traditional material from the British Isles and contemporary songs with a political slant, traditional and topical foreign material in translation, music-hall and choral: 'A song is a song. If it's worth singing we'll print it.'

Sing, as it was to be called, was to be an unashamedly political magazine, providing songs of international peace and friendship. It was influenced by the American magazines *Sing Out!*, which had started exactly four years before, and the earlier *People's Song Bulletin*. The *People's Song Bulletin* ('Organized to create, promote and distribute songs of labor and the American People') had come out of a meeting of some twenty-five singers and songwriters in December 1945 in New York's Greenwich Village when, as later described by Woody Guthrie, they all decided to pitch in their efforts 'to make out of all their little works one big union called People's Songs'. Guthrie said that 'unless we do hear the work songs, war songs, and love songs, dance songs, of all the people everywhere we are most apt to lose the peace and this world along with it'.

This was a statement with which the *Sing* editorial team heartily concurred. Guthrie's belief in the power of song was exemplified in the 'This Machine Kills Fascists' message stuck on the front of his guitar. As the only professional journalist, Ambrose was elected editor and the first issue was planned for May. Before then, however, he was offered a lucrative job in America working as a puppeteer on a film of Pinocchio, and had to pull out. Winter, who had done some writing, decided to take over as general editor with John Hasted as music editor. The first issue appeared in May 1954; Winter remained editor for the next thirty years.

Bert, whom Winter had first bumped into in 1953 at the Romanian Youth Festival in Bucharest, was a great supporter of the magazine and occasionally sent in an unsolicited article, which arrived with the usual beautifully transcribed musical examples. He was also always ready to write a few song notes or a bit of musical history. For the second issue (July/August 1954) Bert contributed 'A Folk Song of the Industrial Revolution' – notes and tune for 'The Poor Cotton Weaver'. He continued to help the magazine throughout the 1950s with songs and articles, including 'Old Jackie Brown' or 'Go to Sea No More' (January/February 1955); 'Paddy West' (April/May 1955); 'Some Notes On the "Which Side" Tune' (June/July 1955); 'Background to St James' Infirmary' (June/July 1956); 'The Bitter Withy' (December 1956); 'Johnny Todd' (February/March 1957) and 'Lord Franklin' (August/September 1957). *Sing* also published the occasional small song booklet, the first of which was an eight-page booklet entitled *Four Folk Songs from Rumania*. It included 'Mother Sent me to the Vineyard' (collected by A.L. Lloyd in 1950) and a choral dance from Transylvania with English verses by Bert.

Winter recalled an evening in 1957 when he went down to the Tuesday night sessions at Russell Quaye and Hylda Sims' Skiffle Cellar at 49 Greek Street to hear Bert sing. During the evening Winter was invited up to sing by Bert who explained to the audience that he was the editor of the commendable folk music magazine *Sing*, which they should all read. Winter, in turn, waxed lyrical about Bert's new album. At the end of the evening, Winter thanked Bert for the plug for the magazine, and Bert thanked *him* for the kind words about the new album. Bert then put a hand on Winter's shoulder and said: 'Eric, if we don't scratch each other's backs, who will scratch them for us?'[8]

The decade following the Second World War was for many young people, and some not so young, a time for consolidating the peace. The notion of peace generated the same enthusiasm and proselytising spirit that anti-fascism had brought about in the 1930s. As Doris Willens said in her biography of Lee Hays, *Lonesome Traveller*:

The time, in the victorious aftermath of a war fought for the right reasons, seemed gloriously auspicious. Fascism had been defeated by 'the common man'. Now the 'common man' wanted more than the economic hard times of pre-war years. Among workers in both countries (Britain and the USA) the war had left a residue of admiration and good will for the Soviets, the word socialism had a less threatening ring. Why shouldn't alliances continue?

But she goes on to say:

The period of good will would soon dissipate in an already building counter trend that would culminate in the dismal McCarthy years, when fear and loathing would equate such phrases as 'one world' and 'brotherhood' with Stalinism, and when every kind of liberalism would be thrown into long and dark disarray.

Despite the political rhetoric, the suspicion, the surveillance, the oppressive Eastern European puppet governments, and the 'democratic' oppression of the left in Britain and America, for some it was a time of innocence and naivety when anything seemed possible if we'd just all get together and sing songs. There's something in that. It's difficult to fall out with people with whom you're singing and sharing good times.

Just such an idea had kicked off as early as 1947 with the first World Festival of Youth and Students in Prague. Two years later Budapest was the host. By the 1950s the festivals, organised by the World Federation of Democratic Youth, whose headquarters were in Budapest and whose motto was For Peace and Friendship – Against Nuclear Weapons, were in full flower and attracting vast numbers of young people from all around the world – to Berlin (1951), Bucharest (1953), Warsaw (1955) and Moscow (1957). In Warsaw in 1955 Bert hung out for some of the time with the County Clare uilleann piper Willie Clancy and fiddler Martin Byrnes. According to Bert: 'Between them they electrified the town. Polish cheers and drinks followed every jig and reel, and I recall the two of them making their triumphal parade from one bar to another playing like angels, with vodka running out of their ears.'[9]

The World Peace Council, the International Union of Students, the British Peace Committee and others supported the Youth Festival Movement, an anathema to Western governments who saw it merely as a communist propaganda scam. It brought youngsters together in friendship and solidarity against the Cold War. The West was right, in as much as the festivals were stage-managed, flag-waving events promoting socialism, but they did attract thousands of sincere young people across the political spectrum from both sides of the Iron Curtain who were genuinely committed to brotherly love and international accord. The events were also great fun and a huge adventure for postwar youth unaccustomed to foreign travel.

However, getting to the festivals could be anything but fun, as 1,600 young singing British peaceniks, or Peace Doves as the communists called the festival delegates, found when they headed for the 1951 Berlin festival. In an article See You in Berlin! Flowers or Bayonets,[10] Bernard Parry detailed the history of the trip and told how the British Foreign Office, in collusion with the French, Belgians and Americans, did everything in their power to prevent people attending. Fifty years later, when official documents were made public, it was discovered that the British government had plans to send 'shock squads' of young people to infiltrate and disrupt the festival. A civil servant wrote: 'We should not try to compete with the communists in these monster youth jamborees. Youth *per se* is a concept which, to my mind, is repugnant to the Western way of life.'

Bert was a regular attendee of these festivals, and used the opportunities to consolidate his Eastern European contacts with musicians, academics and folklore institutes. By 1952 he was a Vice-President of the WMA (along with Benjamin Britten, Paul Robeson, Inglis Gundry and others), which was represented at many of the festivals by John Hasted's London Youth Choir. The choir was originally formed to participate in the 1951 Berlin Youth Festival where it was very successful. The LYC rehearsed on Monday evenings in the Warsaw Club at 81 Portland Place, just up the road from Broadcasting House. The choir members, who paid their own travelling expenses, raised the money for the train fare by busking around London and performing for peace committees, the London Fire Brigade, MP Sidney Silverman's 60th birthday party (thrown by the local Labour Party), and anything else that would put money into the choir coffers. It soon had more offers of bookings than it could fulfil and so a South London Youth Choir was established in Lewisham.[11]

In the early 1950s many Eastern European choirs visited Great Britain, and it became an accepted courtesy for these choirs to sing a British song for their hosts. Through his WMA connections Bert acted as advisor to the various embassies on suitable songs for the choirs to learn and perform. This provided him with more official contacts, which would prove useful when organising collecting trips to Eastern Europe and in providing him with a welcome source of income in the difficult days of the Cold War.

There were various ways in which the CPGB looked after their own when many communist intellectuals were blacklisted from certain jobs, and freelance writers fell on hard times with the postwar collapse of many of the popular wartime magazines. One way was to appoint needy members with positions in the various 'friendship' societies which were all CP front organisations. Arnold Rattenbury worked for the Romanian Society and Charlie Ringrose was Hungarian Society Secretary from 1952 till the society dissolved in 1986. As Rattenbury explained, a lot of this work was funded directly from Moscow in the shape of carrier bags stuffed full of used £5 notes, which were clandestinely handed over at London tube stations. Not exactly glamorous James Bond tactics, but practical. 'I couldn't get a job anywhere because I was a Commie. And that's why I washed up with the Romanians, that's the job the Party found me – Press Office for the Friendship Society. Pretty crummy job. They weren't really anything. They were giveaway jobs for old Party hacks.'[12]

Another scheme, from which Bert would have benefited, was the wealth of material in English, with excellent photographs, provided by Agerpres, the Romanian News Agency, which was made available to freelance communist journalists by Vianu, the press attaché at the Romanian Embassy in London.

Alun Hughes who, as a Cold War journalist, also benefited from the system explained how it worked:

> This was often high quality academic material written by Romanian scholars. Folk culture was a major theme in this 'handout' material. British journalists were paid, at piecework rates, per column inch for any Romanian topic rewritten by them and published in British and other periodicals. I used to visit Vianu once a month in Kensington, with my file of the month's work.
>
> From Agerpres, too, came translations (often clumsy) of Romanian writers, classical and modern. These would be reworked and then published as 'translations' by noted writers such as Jack Lindsay. Lloyd's 'translation' of Ion Creanga's *Recollections from Childhood* may have been the product of this virtually universal procedure of, especially, the 1950s and the Cold War years. Many East European works were subsidised by the respective government, and 'ghosted' in this way. Otherwise, little if any at all would have been published.[13]

All the journalist had to do was to rewrite the material up in his or her own style. What made the material valuable to the recipient was that it provided the latest information on agriculture, industry, sciences, literature, folk music or whatever – information unavailable to most Western journalists. The published articles were good propaganda for the Soviet Bloc countries. Typical of the sort of material that would be passed on was the series of articles 'Folk Instruments of Rumania' which Bert published in the *British Rumanian Bulletin* (1958) – the bucium, the bagpipe, the pan-pipes, the cobza, etc. – or, 'The Lantari, New Light on the Gypsy Musician' in *Recorded Folk Music* (November/December 1959). A couple of years later he placed another article on the Romanian cobza in the *Lute Society Journal*.

In Warsaw in 1955 Bert had been elevated to the Youth Festival music-judging panel, as Hasted reported in his Warsaw Notebook column in *Sing* magazine (October/November 1955):

> The International Folk Singing Competition, probably the first of its kind ever held, was an event of historical importance. More than a hundred outstanding singers from countries of widely differing musical traditions, competed before an international panel of judges, among them A.L. Lloyd from this country. The diversity of material was astonishing, and cannot be described in mere words – but every effort is being made to issue a representative collection of items in the form of a long-playing record, perhaps on Topic label. Liz Letsky of the London Youth Choir was the only singer from Western Europe to win a diploma in this contest.

Topic did issue an LP, *The Warsaw Festival 1955*, with Eileen Sweatenham introducing a selection of the choirs that performed over the two weeks. On hearing the bravura performances of the Balkan, Russian and Chinese folk singers, it's not surprising that Bert and his fellow judges only allotted one prize to singers from the West.

The 1957 Moscow Youth Festival took place just a year after the Hungarian uprising led by Prime Minister Imre Nagy, who had promised the Hungarian people independence and political freedom, and ended up dead. What the Russians described as 'the forces of reactionary conspiracy against the Hungarian people' were brutally put down by the invading Russian Army. The Russian behaviour was a step too far for many British communists and they left the Party in droves. Typical of the feelings of many Party members was the letter of 6 November 1956, sent to the *News Chronicle* and the *Cambridge Daily News*, by Peter Cadogan and Ivor Jordan, secretary and chairman of the Cambridge City Communist Party, condemning Russia's actions in Hungary, and saying that the CPGB should think for itself and not blindly follow the Moscow line. They also said: 'We believe that despite gross mistakes made in the Stalin era, communism has expressed, and in some ways still does and will again express, all that is best in human values.' They were thrown out of the Party as traitors.

Despite Khrushchev's remarkable 1954 speech condemning Stalinism, and his own crushing of Hungary, with the subsequent torture and execution of Hungarian activists, and of Nagy (as a lesson to all other leaders in socialist countries), hard-liners like Bert and Alan Bush, remained unmoved, at least in public. As Martin Anderson said of Bush: 'When it came to the Soviet Union he was no fool, but the sincerity of his beliefs was immune to reason.' This could apply equally to Bert. The ends justified the means. Of course, some intellectuals were simply naive. As Malcolm Muggeridge pointed out in *The Thirties*, Julian Huxley actually believed that Stalin used to go down to the rail-yards in Moscow and personally help the workers unload the trains![14]

Following the Khrushchev speech, and then the occupation of Budapest by Russian troops, there was a demand in the CPGB for rank-and-file voices to be heard questioning Soviet orthodoxy. This in the Communist Party in those days meant a demand for a recall Congress. There was a weekly Party paper called *World News and Views,* the organ to which one addressed such branch resolutions, which were then supposed to be listed. However, the editor, George Matthews, a member of the Party Executive, ensured that critical articles and letters in favour of a recall weren't published. In view of this the communist academic historians Edward (E.P.) Thompson and John Saville let it be known that if people sent them material that had been rejected by *World News* they would print it in their fledgling magazine *The Reasoner*, an oppositional publication which was growing in influence within the Party. Following the third issue which demanded that the Executive Committee of the CPGB should 'dissasociate itself publicly from the action of the Soviet Union in Hungary', Thompson and Saville were called in by the Political Committee and suspended for three months for 'disobeying their specific instruction to cease publication'. In the light of this, according to Rattenbury, he and Montagu Slater pulled together a number of the old Writers Group including Jack Lindsay, Doris Lessing, Herbert Nicholson, John Sommerfield,

Hamish Henderson (who was in London at the time) and Bert, and encouraged Thompson and Saville to continue publishing, but suggested instead of putting their own names at the top to use Lessing, Rattenbury, Lloyd, Lindsay etc., and to continue changing the name until the executive decision was seen to be ludicrous, and rescinded.

However, Thompson and Saville after long discussions joined the 7,000 (one in five) other CPGB members who resigned from the Party following the Soviet crushing of the Hungarian 'uprising'. They got hold of some capital and decided to take *The New Reasoner* into print as a formal journal. It ran for three or four years before amalgamating with *University and Left Review* at the end of 1959 to become *New Left Review* – a bridge between the old sloganeering 1930s and 1950s/1960s welfare Britain. A forum of the New Left 'where different fruitful traditions of social discussion are free to meet in open controversy'.[15] Two of the main discussion points of the early 1960s were undoubtedly 'the Bomb' (the Cuban missile crisis was in 1962) and Labour's third successive election defeat.

As far as is known, Bert never wrote for any of the above journals (although he did perform a 'Ballads and Blues' evening for the ULR Club's skiffle social in July 1957), and even if in principle he might have agreed with the idea of the rank-and-file of the CPGB being allowed to voice critical opinions, the fact that he remained a Party faithful when many of the above were jumping ship makes it surely unlikely, despite Rattenbury's assertion, that he would have thrown his hat in the ring with Thompson and Saville.

Surprisingly, the 1957 Moscow Festival went ahead as if nothing had happened in Hungary the year before. The festival fell right in the middle of the British skiffle craze, and Russell Quaye's City Ramblers, England's most original skiffle group, and residents at the famous Soho Skiffle Cellar (later Les Cousins), which had opened in April 1957, were invited guests, along with John Hasted's Skiffle and Folk Song Group, and Ewan MacColl's Ballads and Blues folk ensemble featuring Peggy Seeger and guitarist/singer Steve Benbow. Shirley Collins was also there, but singing in a play with Theatre Workshop. Collins insists that, despite published statements to the contrary, she was not there as part of MacColl's group, but was working for Joan Littlewood, replacing a sick Isla Cameron.[16] The play that Littlewood took to Moscow that year was her modern-dress, updated *Macbeth*. It was set between the First and Second World Wars with Macbeth as a general who becomes a dictator and ends up being shot by a firing squad. It didn't go down well.

With all the above musicians away, plus Bert who, according to John Hasted, was also there, Soho must have been left bereft of singers for three weeks. It's perhaps worth pointing out that despite what George Melly described as the 'choreographed bacchanalia' of the 1986 film of Colin MacInnes's novel *Absolute Beginners*, 1950s Soho was not yet overrun with sex-shops and strip shows. As Melly continued in his *Literary Review* (April 1986) article: 'The tarts stood on the streets at prescribed intervals [the younger ones under the lights, the older ones in shadowy doorways] and despite the presence of the criminal world, the general feel was both cosy and a bit staid. The real point about the teenage revolt was that it stuck out *because* of the postwar gloom it emerged from.'

The City Ramblers busked in Red Square, entertaining the crowds who were basking in a June heat wave, while Hasted's group performed for an admiring Khrushchev inside the Kremlin, as did Shirley Collins. Afterwards the event generated an inevitable 'Moscow Talking Blues' in *Sing* – that seemingly easy to write, play and sing musical genre that reached its apogee in the 1940s with Woody Guthrie and went rapidly downhill from then on to its nadir as:

> Well Britain sent, God bless my soul,
> Skiffle, jazz and rock and roll,
> Says Comrade Shepilov, 'Man alive!
> I don't dig this bourgeois jive'
> But N.K. Khrushchev, he's the man
> Wants more skiffle in the five-year plan.

Various 'talking blues' were popular in England in the 1950s thanks to the live performances and Topic recordings of Ramblin' Jack Elliott, who learnt them from Guthrie. Dating back to the 1920s, the talking blues originated with Chris Bouchillion, whose record company decided that he was better at talking than singing. The style was taken up by Robert Lunn, from whom Guthrie learnt it. Guthrie used it very effectively for his social commentary. The 'Moscow Talking Blues' was not an outstanding example of the genre but, amazingly, was one of the least toe-curling songs that appeared in *Sing* at that time. It was a veritable Shakespearean sonnet compared to Martin Winsor's take on 'The Gypsy Laddie', 'The Wraggle Taggle Cool Kats':

> There were three cool cats came to the door,
> And asked for this young chick, you know,
> And one played alto, one played bass,
> The other sang 'Yippee-i go-man-go!'

Later, in October and November 1954, Bert went on a collecting trip in Bulgaria with the folklorist Raina Katsarova (1901–84). Katsarova as Head of the Department of Musical Folklore at the Bulgarian Academy of Sciences was one of Bulgaria's most important folk music specialists. She had a broad vision and published the first Bulgarian collections of children's songs (*Du-li du-li, Gaida*, 1947) and was one of the first to take an interest in the Roma (Gypsy) musicians in town culture. As well as inspiring Bert she also introduced him to various influential people including Philip Koutev, conductor of the Ensemble for Folk Songs and Dances (now the Philip Koutev Ensemble) and Georgi Boyadjiev (head of the folk music section at Radio Sophia), useful contacts for future visits. Thanks to Katsarova's guidance and contacts Bert returned with recorded examples of some of Bulgaria's finest singers and musicians as well as performers who would become famous a couple of decades down the line. Some of these ended up in the BBC Sound Archives, some went into the

Alan Lomax collection and some appeared ten years later on the 1964 Topic album *Folk Music of Bulgaria.*

1954 ended with a Christmas present for Bert from Dr Jaap Kunst of the Royal Tropical Institute, Amsterdam – a copy of Kunst's *Cultural Relations Between the Balkans and Indonesia* inscribed 'For Mr A.L. Lloyd with kind regards from Jaap Kunst'. A bit of Christmas light reading.

TOPIC – A COTTAGE INDUSTRY

'A small company like Topic will be thanked by history for recording peoples' music straight when the big companies were mainly concerned with popping it up for quick cash.'

Pete Seeger

Through much of the 1960s and 1970s Topic and Leader records were recording the cream of the revival singers and the finest of the remaining traditional singers, Bill Leader was invariably the recording engineer and producer. Many of the most popular, or perhaps significant, folk albums were recorded on Leader's Revox tape machine in the bedroom of his Camden Town flat. The proceedings were often interrupted by the noise of low-flying aircraft or car horns and the screeching of brakes from nearby Camden Road, and the floor was frequently ankle deep in recording-tape as Leader wielded his editor's razor blade, cutting and splicing tracks together, and sometimes mislaying the odd verse on the floor.

At Easter 1955, after starting up a branch of the WMA in Bradford with Alex Eaton, a fellow communist and founder of Bradford's Topic Folk Club, one of the earliest folk clubs, Bill Leader had come down to London. As an enthusiastic record buff he found a job in the London offices of the WMA (at £10 a week), managing their Topic Record label which had just started to produce LPs. Topic, a WMA members' record club, advertised 'Gramophone records of historical and social interest'. Initially, this included a high proportion of Eastern European and British choral material.

Until 1956 Topic didn't have its own recording machine, and a lot of recordings were done in Ewan MacColl's home in East Croydon on a machine that MacColl had acquired from the BBC. Some songs, including some early Jack Elliott material, were recorded in Russell Quaye and Hylda Sims' bohemian studio flat in Pelham Street, South Kensington, from where they briefly ran the noisy Studio Skiffle Club, until they were thrown out by their landlord and moved the club to the Princess Louise pub.

Topic's first album (catalogue number TRL1) had consisted of dubs of MacColl and Isla Cameron taken from earlier 78s. TRL2 was a collection of Negro spirituals and folk songs by the communist Afro-American baritone Aubrey Pankey, a classical concert performer who also dabbled in folk material. He had left America after the Second World War as a protest against racism and died in his adopted home of East Berlin in 1971, after being knocked down by a car. TRL3 was *The Singing Sailor*, featuring Bert, MacColl and

Harry H. Corbett. These early albums were issued in pressings of ninety-nine to avoid tax, and were advertised in the WMA's monthly newsletter. According to Leader[17] there was no great rush from the membership to grab them. As most of the members were more into workers' choirs, as promoted by Alan Bush, they often bought the folk records for reasons of fraternal support rather than any particular love of the music.

Bill Leader's first solo engineering job was Bert's LP *English Drinking Songs* (1956). When Will Sahnow, General Secretary of the WMA, received the commission from the American folklorist Kenneth Goldstein to produce albums of British folk music for the American Riverside label, Topic thought it was time to get their own recorder. Through the WMA technical manager, electronic wizard and dedicated Wiccan Dick Sweatenham, who paid his bills with a 'proper job' at EMI, they secured a tape recorder built by Master Sound Systems. As Leader recalled in *The Living Tradition*: 'It was a monster, but all ours. Now we could go out and record. What we were recording was mainly people singing. It wasn't elaborate. With a decent mic in the right place in a decent sounding room, not too much traffic, you can walk away with something bearable.'[18]

What they 'walked away with' in those early days was Bert and MacColl's important eight-LP Riverside set of *The English and Scottish Popular Ballads* and their *Great British Ballads Not Included in the Child Collection*, which all came out at the end of 1956. Notwithstanding Goldstein's fanciful biographical notes, and the claims that Bert learnt several of the ballads at his mother's or his 'fisherman' father's knees, it was an impressive and far-sighted project, produced and edited by Goldstein to: 'Make available to scholars, lecturers and instructors in the fields of folklore, balladry and English literature, recordings of the great traditional ballads appropriate for use in classroom and lecture work.' In all, Bert and MacColl recorded a marathon eighty-two ballads, providing a representative cross-section of the 302 ballads in Francis James Child's 'great textual compilation' *The English and Scottish Popular Ballads,* an area of research to which MacColl would return ten years later with Peggy Seeger when they produced the Decca ten-LP series *The Long Harvest: Traditional Ballads in their English, Scots and American Variants.*

Although he was three years behind MacColl in commercial recording, Bert had recorded eight songs in July 1951 for the BBC Sound Archive – 'Polly Vaughan'/'Lord Bateman', 'The Grand Conversation on Napoleon'/'Christ Did Me Ransome'/'The Captain's Apprentice', 'The Bonny Boy' ('Trees Grow High')/'The Cruel Brothers (part 1)' and 'Royal Duke of Grantham'/ 'The Cruel Brothers (part 2)' – and he soon made up for lost time with commercial discs.

Alan Lomax used Bert's 'Polly Vaughan' on the English volume of *The Columbia World Library of Folk and Primitive Music* (1955). It is easy to hear how Douglas Kennedy and Vaughan Williams were impressed with Bert's singing back in 1951. There's a feel of Phil Tanner about it. It's nicely paced, pitched a bit high and lightly decorated with a vibrato. Lomax declared Gower resident Tanner '*England's* best traditional singer'. Despite his globetrotting, British geography obviously wasn't one of Lomax's strong points. Bert had obviously worked on his singing and he must have been one of the very few revival singers at that time to approximate a traditional style. It certainly sounds more authentic than the contrived, theatrical dialect singing of MacColl on the same Columbia album.

In 1953 Douglas Kennedy had arranged for Bert to record two 78rpm records for HMV with whom the EFDSS had a recording and distribution arrangement. Kennedy wrote asking Bert to record something a bit brighter than MacColl's earlier HMV recordings:

> We have an opportunity to do some folk song recordings for H.M.V. during the next two months of our 'quota'. I would like you to do a session and make four sides, but Miss Davis of the Education Department is afraid that all your songs will be dark and gloomy! The recordings that were made by Isla Cameron and Ewan MacColl come under that category in her opinion and she thinks we ought, for the sake of balancing the Catalogue, to have some cheerful songs.[19]

Bert's idea of 'cheerful' was 'The Shooting of His Dear'/'Lord Bateman' and 'Down in Yon Forest'/'The Bitter Withy' – manslaughter, imprisonment, a bleeding corpse and a triple drowning! Not exactly a laugh a minute. What Miss Davis thought is unrecorded. After the 1954 Topic 78 'Bold Jack Donahue'/'Banks of the Condamine' 1956 saw, apart from the titles mentioned earlier, *Australian Bush Songs* and *English Street Songs*. In 1957 the WMA General Secretary, Will Sahnow, died. His successor was Gerry Sharp, a communist accountant, who had been running the business side of Unity Theatre and had been involved with the National Union of Students.

For the first decade of its life, Topic Records, as a WMA members' discounted record club, mainly produced music from Unity Theatre productions and choral and orchestral settings of Russian and British left-wing works. It was financially one of the least successful parts of the WMA and in potential danger of being closed down. Sharp, with financial help from Alan Bush, decided to separate it from the WMA and make it a limited company. A careful accountant, Sharp obviously believed he could keep Topic afloat by producing folk music albums for the nascent folk revival outside of the WMA, even if he didn't expect to make any huge profits, which indeed proved to be the case. When the WMA and Topic separated, Topic was left with five-figure debts.

Sharp moved Topic from the WMA premises in Bishopsbridge Road to the basement of his house in Nassington Road, Hampstead. This was a house that he and his wife, Peggy, could afford, thanks to her family's financial backing. The fact that Peggy was working, and not short of money, meant that Sharp could work for Topic without having to earn a large salary. He was not a great lover of traditional music, even if, as Bill Leader commented, 'He didn't actually grind his teeth every time he heard it', but as a communist he believed in the idea of a people's music.

Bert had been an artistic advisor to Topic in the WMA days, and his position was consolidated under Sharp's regime when Bert was invited to join the board of directors as Artistic Advisor, along with Paul Carter, James Boswell (considered by many, to be one of the finest graphic artists of the twentieth century), Dick Sweatenham and Bill Leader. Bert and Carter had an input on repertoire (Carter eventually went off to produce albums for Collector), Boswell on design and graphics, Sweatenham and Leader on the technical side, and Sharp juggled the finances. Being an accountant with no knowledge of folk music, Sharp was dependent upon Bert's artistic advice and opinion. This continued until Sharp's death in 1972, when Tony Engle, who had been working for Topic for three years or so, took over the running of the company.[20]

Until then, any album project was invariably run past Bert for his approval. Sometimes the lines of communication were not as good as they might have been. Sharp was once offered an EP of Martin Carthy before Carthy was signed to Fontana for his first album (it sold out of the first pressing in three weeks). The tapes were sent to Bert for his opinion. Bert wrote back to Sharp saying that all the songs were in the same key. Sharp took this to be a rejection, and Topic missed out on the lucrative chance of being Carthy's record company from the very beginning.

Bert's artistic influence within the organisation slowly diminished when Engle took over and began to implement his own vision for the company and perhaps redressed the balance a bit for southern revival and traditional singers and music with albums such as *The Art of William Kimber*, *Boscastle Breakdown*, *Songs of the Open Road*, *When Sheep-shearing's Done*, *Sussex Harvest* and many more. Bert was still nominally an artistic consultant, and continued to write many of the Topic sleeve-notes. The last notes he wrote were for the 1982 album *Walter Pardon: A Country Life*, a favourite singer of Bert's. Rather uncharitably, Tony Russell, who supervised Topic's American old-time to western swing label String, said in an interview that when Bert left, Topic became 'a real record company'.

One of the most important Topic projects and according to Topic, one of their 'most satisfying achievements' was the marvellous ten-volume LP set *The Folk Songs of Britain*, issued in 1968–9. For a number of years only available on the American Caedmon label, this huge sampling of the cream of British traditional singers, taken from the field recordings of Lomax, Kennedy, Henderson and others, opened the ears of many people to the wide and rich variety of our traditional song, and brought such iconic performers as Harry Cox, the Coppers, Paddy Tunny, Jeannie Robertson, Johnny Doherty, Phil Tanner, Robert Cinnamond and dozens of others into living rooms throughout the country. The striking sleeve designs were by James Boswell, and Bert contributed some liner notes. This infuriated Alan Lomax and did nothing to cement their rocky friendship. According to journalist Ken Hunt, writing in *Rock 'n' Reel*:

Lomax snarled at me, 'They got Bert Lloyd to write the introduction for us for some unknown reason. I don't know why they made that happen. As if Peter Kennedy and I didn't know enough to write notes on our own stuff! It was an act of British myopia!' A mirthless laugh followed. 'Very typical, I think, of the worst side of the British. They don't like to be discovered.'[21]

Bert probably didn't lose much sleep over it. As we've seen he didn't hold Lomax in very high regard, unlike Lomax senior, John Lomax, whom Bert admired very much and whose early field recording he had avidly listened to in the late 1930s on Alistair Cooke's BBC series *I Hear America Singing*.

During his association with Topic Bert had a significant impact on the company's catalogue but he was never on a huge director's salary. He, like all the directors, was paid for each individual project he undertook, as Charlotte Lloyd explained to me: 'He was only paid a retainer for a year. He was normally paid by the job. This didn't really give him any security, either mental or financial as his Topic commitments frequently got in the way of his other work.' Bert's Topic projects included the Waterson's classic *Frost and Fire* album (1965); the influential LP of industrial songs *The Iron Muse* (1963), a bestseller for Topic which helped put them onto a sounder financial footing; *The Bird in the Bush* (1966), erotic songs, *Leviathan!* (1967), whaling songs and many more. It was also Bert who encouraged the studio and field recordings of traditional singers, and Leader's recording trips to Connemara and Donegal to record, amongst others, the piper Willie Clancy and singer Paddy Tunney. And, of course, Bert could push his own and MacColl's albums which came out thick and fast as the folk revival got under way and a reasonable market developed for folk music. The prime motivation for the number of records he recorded was probably to provide the folk revival with material and a guiding (controlling?) hand rather than self-aggrandisement, although, of course, he also needed to earn a living.

His Topic position offered him the opportunity to steer the revival in the direction of his vision. As Anne Briggs recalled: 'He became a mentor to emergent young singers, encouraging and suggesting material for them. He was very protective and wonderfully generous with the material he'd collected; he'd give me songs and say he could imagine me singing them.' Topic also provided him with the chance to establish a widely copied sleeve-note style – erudite but eminently readable, with each song set in a sociological, historical and musical context. Each note was a mini-musicological lesson. It's a style of presentation that doesn't appeal to everyone, but if you don't like it you don't have to read it. The songs will sound just as good, or bad, either way.

It didn't take long for the major record companies such as Decca, Fontana, HMV, Transatlantic and CBS to jump on board the folk-album train. So too did small independent labels such as Doug Dobell's 77 label and Collector. As the 1960s drew to a close, Bill Leader, who was doing a lot of recording work for Transatlantic and progressively less for Topic, eventually went off and started his own highly regarded Leader and Trailer folk labels from his Camden Town bedroom. Topic managed, however, despite the competition, to keep its head above water, and it acquired an enviable reputation for quality and musical integrity. In the 1950s and 1960s this didn't necessarily translate into a lot of money sloshing around in the Topic coffers. The recordings of traditional performers, for which Topic has always been justifiably lauded, were often subsidised by the good will and enthusiasm of a number of experts without whom Topic would have been unable to undertake such worthwhile projects as the series *Voice of the People*,[22] the most ambitious overview of British musical folklore to date.

THE ROAR OF THE GREASEPAINT

'War is like love, it always finds a way.'
    Bertolt Brecht, *Mother Courage*

The July 1955 Theatre Workshop production of Brecht's *Mother Courage* was booked in as part of the Devon Festival of the Arts at Barnstaple. It was produced by Oscar Lewenstein. During the Second World War, groups of German exiles in London had put on German language productions of Brecht's *The Threepenny Opera* and *Fear and Misery in the Third Reich*. Through his contact with these groups, Lewenstein went to see Brecht in Spring 1955 to discuss a Theatre Workshop production of *Mother Courage* with lyrics by A.L. Lloyd, as he told Howard Goorney in *The Theatre Workshop Story* : 'I went to Berlin, saw Brecht and said I thought Joan would make a perfect Mother Courage and that Theatre Workshop was a company that ought to have his sympathy. He was very cooperative, and said we could use any of the designs, music and so on and he'd send a young assistant called Karl Weber to assist in the production.' Brecht's permission for the production was contingent on Joan Littlewood playing the lead in this, the first professional performance of a Brecht play in Britain.

Unfortunately, a couple of months before the play was due to go on, Theatre Workshop went through one of its regular crises. Harry H. Corbett and George Cooper told Littlewood they were leaving the company to take up other acting offers that actually paid some money. The Arts Council withdrew its miniscule £100 safety net against financial loss on a production, and Martin's Bank froze their account. Littlewood was so busy trying to salvage the company that she had no time to rehearse the lead and gave it to one of her other actresses.[23] On hearing this, Brecht wrote to her threatening to pull the plugs on the production, whilst also taking the opportunity to give Joan a patronising slap across the wrist for her directing and for refusing to let Weber attend rehearsals:

Our production contract was contingent on your playing the part of Courage and I can't change that under any circumstances. I regret that the presence of my associate at rehearsals should annoy you. I respect individual working methods, but I don't believe you should reject technical advice in connection with the new-style plays. If art is to keep pace with the times, artists must take cognizance of new methods ... . Forgive this lecture, which seems to have been necessary in the interests of my play. It bores me no less than it does you.

One can only imagine where the volatile Littlewood would have liked to have told him to stick his play.

Little known and little understood in Britain in the early 1950s, Brecht's 'epic theatre' eschewed naturalistic characterisation, which he believed lulled audiences into a state of complacency and dulled their perceptions. His actors were trained to play both themselves and their character, visible simultaneously to the audience. In theory, this would force the audience into a realisation of theatrical artifice, shake them out of empathetic complacency and encourage critical analysis. The effects were enhanced by specific set and prop devices, such as banners announcing scenes and curtain stage dividers. It's these very specific production details that Brecht's 'associate' would have been looking for.

There was no way in the time remaining that Littlewood could have produced an accomplished performance in Brecht's epic style. This was made doubly difficult because the definitive interpretation of Courage had been originally developed by Brecht's wife Helen Weigel, and was the yardstick against which all subsequent interpretations were measured. Littlewood took over just twenty-four hours before the curtain went up. Kenneth Tynan in the Observer of 3 July 1955 crucified the performance. 'Littlewood plays it in a lifeless mumble, looking both over-parted and under rehearsed. The result is a production in which discourtesy borders on insult, as if Wagner was to be staged in a school gymnasium.'

Littlewood, commenting in her autobiography Joan's Book on the less than rave review, said: 'I might have got away with it but for that fucking hen! I had to pluck it in the first scene and it was stinking. The smell from its backside turned my stomach. Mother Courage had to stop herself from vomiting for well nigh half the play.'

A year later Brecht brought his own original 1949 Berliner Ensemble production of Mother Courage to London's Palace Theatre, where Weigel demonstrated why hers was the definitive portrayal of Courage. Despite a lacklustre production, it was Theatre Workshop's Mother Courage together with Sam Wanamaker's production of The Threepenny Opera at the Royal Court (February 1956), which featured Ewan MacColl as the street singer, and a Times Literary Supplement review of Brecht's published work (March 1956), that prepared the ground for the Berliner Ensemble's successful London visit in August 1956.

It's a shame that Bert's collaboration with Theatre Workshop was a less than glorious occasion because Joan Littlewood had been keen to work with him on a play as far back as 1945, when she'd tried to put on a production of his translation of Lorca's Blood Wedding. Unfortunately, Lorca's sister had given the English rights to the South African poet Roy Campbell. This was a double whammy for Bert, who felt that Campbell didn't even know the Spanish language (or at least not well enough to do a creditable job on Lorca). What was even worse, and Bert couldn't forgive, was that Campbell was an unrepentant supporter of Franco's fascist regime and had said of the Republicans: 'The sodomites are on your side. The cowards and the cranks.' A crumb of consolation for Bert was a postcard of 5 September from Berlin referring to Bert's BBC translation of the complete play: 'Mr Brecht found your translation [of *Mother Courage*] rather good.'[24]

Brecht had been hustling for work in England in the autumn/winter of 1934, staying off Grays Inn Road with his new musical collaborator, the German-Austrian communist composer Hanns Eisler (1898–1962). Although this was a mere hop, skip and a jump from the Fitzrovia pubs and cafés that Bert patronised at that time, no evidence has come to light that the two of them met: a potential meeting in July 1955 in East Berlin was cancelled.[25] It seems likely, however, that Brecht would have found his way to nearby Parton Street and the office of *Left Review*, which published an article by him the following year. During the visit, Brecht went to the Group Theatre's production of W.H. Auden's *The Dance of Death*, and Eisler made contact and organised some future musical projects with Alan Bush, with whom, of course, Bert would also work a few years later. In 1935 Eisler put on a demonstration with a number of working-class organisations at Morley College, Westminster Bridge Road, illustrating the various ways in which music could be used to further the class struggle.

Bert's next venture into the theatre was hardly more auspicious than his Theatre Workshop collaboration. On 30 September 1958, John Arden's play *Live Like Pigs* opened at the Royal Court, London. It was directed by George Devine and Anthony Page. The cast included Robert Shaw. Bert sang a linking Brechtian-style narration throughout. It's a work that examines the social conflict when the Sawneys, a group of non-Romany Travellers, are 're-settled' on a council estate next to the Jackson family. Bert's enthusiasm for the play, which he thought 'a good one', wasn't shared by a number of critics including, surprisingly, an advocate of challenging contemporary theatre, Richard Findlater, who commented coolly in *Encore* that the play allowed 'Mr. A.L. Lloyd to appear before the curtain every now and then hollering a few meaningful snatches of loaded balladry'.[26] The *Daily Mail* called it 'Savage, brutal and squalid … an insult to pigs'. Arden was assailed from all sides – the left accused him of attacking the welfare state, the right of offering a defence of immorality and anarchy. The prescient *Sunday Times* reviewer, however, sensed that '… the English Stage Company has discovered another new dramatist'. So it proved to be, even if Arden did eventually abandon England for Ireland and the cause of Irish nationalism.

Happier was Bert's relationship with his friend, the character actor, writer and director Bernard Miles (Baron Miles, 1907–91) and his Mermaid Theatre, situated on the Thames at Puddle Dock in the City. December 1959 saw the first production of the Mermaid's *Treasure Island* in which Miles played a critically acclaimed Long John Silver. Bert provided shanties, including additional verses for the best known of all pirate songs, 'Fifteen Men on a

Dead-man's Chest, Yo-ho-ho and a Bottle of Rum'. The production proved a great success and was regularly performed at the Mermaid over the next few years as well as touring Britain and Canada. During the course of the play, the pirates built the ship, the *Hispaniola*, in full view of the audience while singing sea shanties. The minimalist set was designed by the Irish stage-designer and director Sean Kenny (1932–73), the first resident art director at the Mermaid and famous in the 1960s for his innovative scaffolding stage designs. In 1960 the music publishers Keith Prowse produced the slim seventeen-page *Sea Shanties and Sea Songs* (The *Treasure Island* Song Book), adapted and arranged with new lyrics by A.L. Lloyd.

In 1964 Miles opened the Mermaid on several Sundays for a music and poetry revue called *The Buxom Muse*. Bert was booked to perform alongside, amongst others, actors Joss Ackland and Barrie Ingham, who were appearing at the time in the Mermaid's production of *The Bacchae of Euripides*. Bert sang five songs (including 'The Bonny Black Hare' 'The Husband With no Courage in Him' and 'The Farm Servant') between poetry and other readings. After the first two or three weeks Bert had to go abroad on a trip, and he rang up Martin Carthy and asked him if he'd deputise for him for the rest of the shows. This was the first time Carthy had worked for Bert although, of course, he had known him from around the London folk clubs, and had first heard of him in the 1950s through Joe Lloyd and his school skiffle group.

In the same year the communist theatre producer Oscar Lewenstein came back into Bert's life. He'd been a fan of Brecht's work long before the German playwright was well known to English-speaking audiences in Britain and, despite the lukewarm reception of his *Mother Courage* at Theatre Workshop in 1955, he decided in 1964 to put on Brecht's explicitly Marxist play *St Joan of the Stockyards* in London's West End in a translation by Charlotte and Bert (presumably the translation they had done for the BBC in 1960). Although he couldn't afford to regularly produce plays that failed to fill theatres, Lewenstein was successful enough to be able to take a risk occasionally to satisfy a personal whim and, despite being a committed communist, had access to the deep pockets of several well-heeled theatre 'angels'. Since his early days as general manager of the Royal Court Theatre (1952) and his founding, with George Devine and Ronald Duncan, of the English Stage Company (1956), he had been at the forefront of the new wave of British theatre writing, and was also committed to producing the best contemporary plays from abroad.

Lewenstein put together a formidable team for *St Joan* – Tony Richardson (one of the most successful young directors to come out of the Royal Court), designer Jocelyn Herbert (she had worked with John Arden, Arnold Wesker, Samuel Beckett and John Osborne), and a strong cast headed by Siobhan McKenna (replacing Vanessa Redgrave, who had to pull out), the American actor Lionel Stander (later famous as Max in the 1970s TV detective series *Hart to Hart*) and Rachel Kempson. The play opened on 11 June 1964.

It was an overtly left-wing production. Stander, dubbed by Columbia Pictures' Harry Cohn 'A Red son of a bitch', had been blacklisted in the United States after refusing to kowtow to the House of Un-American

Activities Committee (HUAC), when he was among the first group of actors investigated for supposed communist activities. In 1953 he made headlines with his declaration to the HUAC: 'I am not a dupe, or a dope, or a moe, or a schmoe ... I was absolutely conscious of what I was doing and I am not ashamed of anything I said in public or private.' It was a company in which Bert would have felt very much at home.

In his memoir *Kicking Against the Pricks* (1994) Lewenstein says: 'To have it [*St Joan*] played at the Queen's Theatre in the very heart of the West End was a joy I shall not forget ... all it lacked was a working-class audience to enjoy it.' Unfortunately, the London theatre critics savaged Richardson for his apparent lack of understanding of the text and for failing to realise that the Shakespearean blank verse passages were supposed to be a parody. It precipitated an anti-Brecht feeling amongst certain critics who claimed him to be a fraud and a fad. This 'let's get rid of Brecht' mood was only dissolved a year later when Brecht brought his acclaimed Berliner Ensemble to the National Theatre with his *Arturo Ui*.

In October of the following year Douglas Cleverdon directed a Commonwealth Festival concert of Australian songs and ballads at the Royal Court, in which he used Bert and Martin Carthy along with contemporary poets. The stage design by the celebrated Australian artist Arthur Boyd involved slides of Boyd's paintings projected onto a twelve-foot screen.

As part of the same festival Bert performed a programme of sea shanties, accompanied by Alf Edwards on concertina, entitled *The Seven Seas*. For this, in addition to Martin Carthy, Bert brought in Enoch Kent, Anne Briggs and Bob Davenport (one of Bert's favourite singers). Bert sang 'Do Me Ama', 'The Maid on the Shore' and 'The Rambling Sailor'. Carthy sang 'The Dockyard Gate', 'The Ship in Distress' and 'The Green Beds', Briggs did 'Lowlands of Holland' and 'Lowlands', Davenport belted out 'Little Sally Racket', 'Go to Sea Once More', 'Greenland Fishery', 'Lord Franklin' and 'Rounding the Horn', Kent sang 'Lovely on the Water' and 'Farewell Nancy' and they all joined in on 'Heave Away My Johnny', 'The Diamond' and 'Leave Her Johnny Leave Her'.[27] The concerts were resounding successes and made up for Bert's rather cool critical reception on the same stage seven years earlier in the Royal Court's *Live Like Pigs*.

14
The Folk Survival of the Fittest

> London is sharp as the edge of a knife,
> The city is filled with fraction and strife;
> There's none so sweet as the country life,
> All you that want me to go to London.
>
> Harry Cox

Beneath what might appear to some to have been the placid surface of the folk song pond there was, in the 1950s and 1960s, a feeding frenzy going on.

The larger, fiercer fish were gobbling up the small fry. The big fish all wanted control in order to promote their own ideological views. Although the folk revival was not directly run by the CPGB most people with a political agenda realised the power of song in shaping attitudes and opinion. The English Folk Dance and Song Society desperately tried to make up for its lost decades, in which song had been thought dead and largely ignored, now that the cadaver had miraculously resurrected and the Society found itself largely irrelevant to the folk club scene. According to Bert: 'The EFDSS was slow [to get involved in the folk club scene] because they were into dance, and they were very suspicious of the revival when it began because they thought it was too indiscriminate, that it didn't discriminate between traditional products and commercial products, and also because politically it seemed a dubious venture.' The larger record companies, which had been caught on the hop by the musical bushfire of skiffle, were determined not to miss out on 'folk', that conveniently adaptable word when applied to anyone with a guitar who might bring in crisp, or even tatty, pound notes.

The politicos smelt a change in the air and mistook it for revolution instead of incipient capitalism, creeping self-interest, and the approaching end of the working class as they knew it. Others settled for a comfortable life recording and performing easy-listening music on television and in the concert halls. For some peripatetic troubadours, the romance of the Guthrie and Kerouac hard-travelling life-style sustained them. Despite the fact that they were all involved in what they all called 'folk music', there was little if any cross-party discussion and understanding of each other's view point. As Karl Dallas admitted in *English Dance and Song* magazine (Summer 2001): 'We fought like Kilkenny cats.' Friendships and alliances were made and broken at the speed of Sean McGuire's playing of 'The Mason's Apron'. Fists were shaken, reputations were trashed. A sly anonymous column appeared in *Folk Music* magazine.[1]

Plotting went on at a rate unseen since the bad old days of Renaissance Florence. All that was missing was the poison. Some, like Jimmie Macgregor and Robin Hall, were relieved to get a regular BBC TV slot on the *Tonight* programme because, as Macgregor said, it lifted them out of 'the back-stabbing folk scene'. What they didn't realise was that they were simply exchanging the frying pan for the fire. The corridors of Broadcasting House were just as dangerous; character and reputation assassins lurked in many a production office doorway, and every employee was under constant surveillance.

In 1954 John Hasted opened the 44 Club in Gerard Street, and soon other London Youth Choir members such as Hylda Sims and Leon Rosselson were involved in new clubs. Sims and Russell Quaye, as we've seen, ran the Studio Skiffle Club from their studio home in Chelsea before moving on to the Princess Louise and finally the Skiffle Cellar. Rosselson, his sister Tina and some other singers ran the Southerners Club in Hampstead. Across town, at the Horseshoe in Tottenham Court Road, Ewan MacColl and Dominic Behan (a roistering apostate Catholic who joined the Communist Party, and exchanged one set of intellectual strictures for another) once came to blows on stage over Behan's remarks about MacColl's 'best friend', Alan Lomax. They were separated by their respective managers, Malcolm Nixon and Bruce Dunnet. As Bob Davenport half-jokingly observed: 'If the singing wasn't that good one evening you could rely on the fisticuffs.' Behan also had an ongoing dispute with the singer and author Patrick Galvin over Galvin's book *Irish Songs of Resistance*.

Mervyn Plunkett, a middle-class Scottish communist who had been one of MacColl's early folk associates (they had lived in the same house at one time), withdrew and in January 1959 set up with Reg Hall and Peter Grant the short-lived and radical (for the time) magazine *Ethnic*, from the pages of which they could snipe (justifiably) at the EFDSS and others whilst promoting their brand of ethnic anti-intellectualism. In his notes for Jeannie Robertson's Collector album *The Gallowa' Hills*, Hamish Henderson had said that Robertson's singing was 'as near as you can get to the high ballad style'. When reviewing the album for *Ethnic*, Plunkett poured cold water on Henderson's rhetoric by saying, 'I do not know what the High Ballad style might be'.

In their regular 'Things They Say' feature, the editors took delight in puncturing pomposity and slipping the knife between the ribs of what they saw as academic pontificating, as in these quotes from Bert and Cecil Sharp, culled from their writings:

The majority of our English folk-tunes, say two thirds, are in the MAJOR or IONIAN mode. The remaining third is fairly evenly divided between the MIXOLYDIAN, DORIAN and AEOLIAN modes, with, perhaps, a preponderance in favour of the MIXOLYDIAN. (Cecil Sharp, *English Folk Song*, London, 1907)

...to this very day the commonest modes of English songs are DORIAN, AEOLIAN and LYDIAN. (A.L. Lloyd, *Folk*, London, 1945)

So far as I am aware, no English collector has yet found a folk-tune in the LYDIAN mode. (Cecil Sharp, *English Folk Song*, London, 1907)

DORIAN, PHRYGIAN, LYDIAN, MIXOLYDIAN, AEOLIAN ... These are the commonest modes of English folk song. The LYDIAN is pretty rare. (A.L. Lloyd, *The Singing Englishman*, London, 1945)

The PHRYGIAN mode occurs but rarely in English folk song. I do not think that more than half-a-dozen English folk airs in that mode have been recorded. (Cecil Sharp, *English Folk Song*, London, 1907)

In the belief that songs should be learned 'directly from live sources' *Ethnic*'s general policy was not to print the tunes to songs, but they would send a tape to any prospective 'traditional singer'. Plunkett was as proscriptive and anally retentive as any other in the revival. He was described by Karl Dallas in *Sing* in 1961 as 'a pompous clown who has made ethnic music a byword for capricious argument and a stubborn march backwards into the past'. He once told singer Ed Pickford and Bob Davenport's step-sister, Mary Helton, to leave his house when Pickford turned up carrying a guitar.

Putting his boorishness and aggressive attitude aside, Plunkett did a lot of thinking about traditional musical culture and was capable of moments of real clarity and insight. Out of all the parties interested in traditional music (Plunkett, perhaps wisely, abstained from using the term 'folk music') only he and younger musicians such as Reg Hall and other fellow members of the Rakes, who shared his views, actually embedded themselves in rural music-making, as is common ethnomusicological practice. They believed the singers and musicians and style of performance to be as important as the songs and tunes, and that collectors had a responsibility towards both. As Plunkett pointed out: 'In the pages of the early *Folk Song Journal* one may search in vain for any sign of concern with those problems of style and performance or of social responsibility for the life of the tradition that seems so important to us [to some] today.'[2]

They adopted a holistic approach in which the songs represented only one aspect of the traditional cultural spectrum. In Sussex in the 1950s and 1960s they sang and played in the convivial surroundings of village pubs and private houses, and socialised with dozens of country performers such as Scan Tester, George Belton, George Spicer and George 'Pop' Maynard. They became, inasmuch as outsiders can ever become, part of the music-making community. Later, Hall became well known for his unique acceptance as a musician into such traditional groups as Bampton Morris, Padstow's May Day Blue 'Oss team and the postwar London Irish community that congregated and played in pubs such a Camden Town's Bedford Arms and The Favourite, Holloway Road.

Bert, Lomax, MacColl, the Kennedys, the EFDSS, Cecil Sharp and all the earlier folk song collectors (with perhaps the exception of Alfred Williams and Elisabeth Greenleaf, who saw her informants as 'singing people' not 'song repositories' to be rifled), were initially more interested in the texts and tuncs. At least in the early days, they tended to ignore the sociocultural aspects of the music in their rush to hoover up and publish the last of the autumn leaves from the folk song tree. Later, MacColl and Seeger did produce some wonderful studies of singers such as Sam Larner and the Stewarts of Blair, and Bert made films such as his Doc Watson documentary with Barrie Gavin, but always from the outside looking in. In fairness to Cecil Sharp, he did keep in touch with many of his informants and sent regular gifts of tobacco to his old singing men. He even bought Louie Hooper a concertina – now on display at Cecil Sharp House. And in North Carolina he once paid for clothes so that the thirteen-year-old daughter of one of his singers might attend a mission school.

Whereas Plunket and MacColl were frequently aggressive in defence of their attitude to the folk revival Bert, although he could occasionally be patronising, tended to be a bit more circumspect and was generally less confrontational (the stiletto rather than the bludgeon), but his remarks about various 'commercial folk singers' elicited a strong reaction from the belligerent Dominic Behan in the *Melody Maker* mailbag for 3 February 1968:

Apparently A.L. Lloyd looks with deep contempt upon the efforts of people like Dylan and Donovan and the 'droopy haired girls from American universities – Miss Baez, Miss Felix, Miss St. Marie, Miss Hester'.

That I may dislike or like whatever these people do does not alter the fact that they have been responsible for bringing more people to listen to good folk songs among the bad in two years than Mr Lloyd, Mr MacColl or Dominic Behan were able to do in ten. They have achieved far more of what we set out to do in a much shorter time than any of us could have possibly hoped.

Behan was right. All of the above, plus Lonnie Donegan, the Settlers, the Leesiders, the Spinners, Robin Hall and Jimmie Macgregor, and later the Yetties, and other 'commercial' performers introduced, or exposed, more people to folk music through radio, television and records than Bert and MacColl ever did.

Ten years after his *Melody Maker* letter, Behan was still having a go at Bert. In *Folk News* No. 17, 1978, he referred to the 1950s Ballads and Blues concerts at the Theatre Royal:

Ewan got a loan of the Theatre Royal, Stratford East, from Joan Littlewood, and proceeded to hold folk evenings there on each Sabbath.

He invited among others me and the McEwan brothers [Rory and Alex] and a chap from Botany Bay way called Bert Lloyd who had possibly the worst voice and the most inane repertoire that all but gave reassurance to the public that transportation had its good points too.

Even as late as 1988 when his novel *The Public World of Parable Jones* was published Behan couldn't resist attacking Bert (although Bert had been dead for six years) by referring to him in the book as 'the pusillanimous Bert Lloyd'. Stan Kelly believes it was 'Dom's revenge for Bert's scathing review of *Posterity be Damned* [Behan's 1959 play]', Bert's summary of which was 'Nothing to Declare'.

Behan, with 'the chap from Botany Bay', Peggy Seeger and MacColl, was a resident at the Singers' Club, but he fell out with MacColl when MacColl started to impose his artistic policy on the club:

Ewan [and Seeger] decided that men should be indigenous, and women would be likewise. In other words Irishmen would sing Irish songs, Welsh would sing chapel (and hunt in choral packs), the Scots would sing those dreadful border and Highland ballads and the Tasmanians would sing anything that wasn't nailed down.

As a writer I naturally could not agree with this nonsense and, having said so, decided to start a club of my own. Max Sylvester paid for my first artistes and Bruce Dunnet looked after the affairs of Folk Song Unlimited, and many's the good drink we had in the Cranbourne [Enterprise?] pub which was our venue.

Behan went off and sang along with Kelly, Hall and Isabel Sutherland at Folk Song Unlimited, which was started by Dunnet and Douglas Moncrief on a Wednesday at the Enterprise in Long Acre

This Singers' Club eventual 'policy' (it had been much more catholic in the beginning) of insisting that guests and floor-singers performed songs only from their own culture in their native tongue (a policy with which Bert concurred) created, or perhaps helped perpetuate, schisms in the folk ranks. It was later justified by MacColl and Seeger (and Martin Carthy) on the grounds that it made a lot of British singers investigate their own national repertoire.

MacColl and Seeger themselves adroitly side-stepped the strict letter of the law and continued to sing in various Scots, English and American accents, often accompanied by Seeger's American banjo and guitar. Bert later circumvented the guitar problem by using Alf Edwards on concertina; this was no more 'authentic' but might have seemed so. Under their rules, the fact that Afro-American singer Elizabeth Cotton worked for the Seeger family should have in no way validated white, upper-middle-class Peggy's singing of her songs. It was a case of do as we say and not as we do. Surprisingly, this was accepted unquestioningly by many gullible singers and club organisers.

There is little difference between MacColl's theatrical impressions of a range of accents and dialects and the efforts of certain other British singers to adopt some sort of American accent when singing American songs, many of which had their roots in Britain anyway. This vexed (for some) problem of accents continues nowadays on the Bluegrass and Old Time music scene. While it is virtually impossible to sound as authentic as a native speaker, authenticity can be achieved instrumentally – there are some amazingly talented Japanese bluegrass banjo pickers and British Old Timey frailers, as good as any American.

Behan was not the only one to fall out with MacColl over the Singers' Club. In the early summer of 1961, according to Eric Winter, MacColl, recently returned from a successful North American tour with Peggy Seeger, rang Winter, told him they were going to start up a new club and talked about their ideas. According to Winter he suggested: 'Why not call it the Singers' Club? Which is what it is'. They thought it a good name, so the Singers' Club it became. Karl Dallas, however, later credited Bruce Dunnet with naming the club.

Winter's offer to become involved was taken up and he became the first Singers' Club organiser, and printed the challenging club manifesto in the August issue of *Sing*. Point 5 of it declared: 'Finally, we need standards. Already the race for the quick pound note is on in the folk song world. "Quaint" songs, risqué songs, poor instrumentation and no-better-than-average-voices coupled with a lack of respect for the material: against these we will fight.' According to Dallas, who was apparently on the magazine's editorial committee, Winter, as editor, took a unilateral decision to align the magazine with the club.

The Singers' Club duly opened its doors on 25 June 1961, at the headquarters of the ACTT (Association of Cinematograph Television and Allied Technicians) at 2 Soho Square, where the old Ballads and Blues club had previously been held. At the end of the first evening MacColl wound up with: 'Well, that's all for tonight, kids. Come back next week to the only genuine folk club in Britain.' Winter thought this an extravagant claim, especially as it had been months since MacColl and Seeger had set foot in anyone else's club and didn't know what they were like. He felt that these grandiose claims could make them look stupid, but MacColl persisted, and in a matter of weeks Winter resigned from the club.

He immediately wrote a critical article on the way MacColl was running things, and in *Sing* (December 1961) he criticised MacColl's presumption in describing the Singers' Club in an advertisement as 'the only genuine folk club in London' when he rarely went to any other club, and at a time when a number of other clubs had worked with the Singers' to promote a Pete Seeger tour and Benefit Concert at the Royal Albert Hall: 'The arrogance that lies behind this has isolated MacColl from the mainstream of the clubs' life – especially in London ... . Moreover, it is difficult to see how one so cut off from the club scene can set himself up as a judge of the clubs.'

Bert took up the cudgels on MacColl's behalf and wrote a patronising letter to *Sing* in February 1962:

Some sharp little teeth were shown in SING Dec. 61 over the question: Isn't the Singers' Club too exclusive? The longest wind was spent in complaining that one of the Club's singers (E. MacColl) performs only at the Singers' Club and not at other clubs. Now SING is a small magazine, and its space (one would think) is too valuable for lengthy exercises in fan-mag-ish triviality. Surely it's the singer's own business where he performs and how frequently ... . Let the critics do even half as much for the revival as Mr MacColl, and the situation will be happier, and standards of performance and repertory will improve; likewise perhaps the standards of folk song journalism.

MacColl also wrote, refuting Winter's claims, denying having discussed things with him or ever saying the things he claimed. Winter, an honourable man, didn't believe journalists should 'get more than one bite of the cherry', and so chose not to defend his article. From then on MacColl never spoke to him: Winter ceased to exist, beyond a comment in an article in *Folk Music*, and didn't warrant a mention in MacColl's autobiography, *Journeyman*. Conversely, the next time Winter saw Bert, there was no mention of the article and letter. According to Winter, Bert was incapable of holding a grudge. This is backed up by Chris Roche, the shanty singer, who once recalled the time he asked Bert to sing at his London club. Bert agreed to go along on the condition that he was picked up and dropped back at Greenwich. The chauffeuring job fell to two young women from the club and afterwards they told Roche that during the two car journeys Bert kept up a running commentary on the folk scene, the singers and club organisers: 'He didn't have a bad word to say about anybody.'[3]

In 1967, when Bert's *Folk Song in England* came out, Winter was offered a free section of the book for reprinting in *Sing* magazine. He chose a few pages on 'How Folk Songs Get Around' (Winter's title, not Bert's). In the same issue he reviewed the book and took up three-quarters of the review strongly disagreeing with Bert's dismissal of Bob Dylan and similar singer-songwriters as 'cabaret-style products that have nothing to do with musical folklore ... the compositions of a Dylan or a Donovan [are not] folk songs by any workable definition'. Winter was relieved that Bert never mentioned the review to him. Perhaps, as Bert had five pages of free publicity in that issue of *Sing*, he thought the review (which, in fact, finished by saying: 'It is doubtful that any more important book on folk song will be published in your lifetime') was a fair exchange.

In 1966 Karl Dallas, in his 'Focus on Folk' column in *Melody Maker*, wrote:

One of the dreams of my life, seeing Ewan MacColl and Alex Campbell on the same bill together, may be achieved on Friday 27 May when the Singers' Club features them in a discussion on folk singing along with A.L. Lloyd and Bob Davenport. It's to be hoped there'll be a little less shadow boxing than the last time a discussion was featured in the days of the old London Folk Music Centre.

The discussion, or 'The Great Debate' as it is titled in the MacColl/Seeger archive, on the state of the folk revival and where it was going took place at the John Snow public house in Broadwick Street, Soho, another early venue of the Singers' Club. Bert kept away from the potential 'action' on stage (MacColl had been known to threaten to 'bottle' someone at a folk concert) by sitting amongst the audience, from where he made some perceptive contributions. Julie Felix, presumably selected as a prime example of the commercialisation of folk music, had been invited to attend but couldn't (or wisely chose not to) make it. MacColl, who chaired the debate, was deflated when a young woman in the audience told him he was out of order when he got up and started to present his case. She pointed out that, as the Chair, his role was merely to sum up the various points made by the panel.

Alex Campbell, one-time 'husband of convenience' to Peggy Seeger (to get her legally into the country), was the antithesis of MacColl, and represented the Glasgow cowboys, and Jack Elliott and Derroll Adams acolytes. He was once, perhaps generously, described by the singer Allan Taylor as: 'The most important and influential folksinger of the folk song revival in Europe. Admired, respected and loved by his fellow performers and his audiences. An outrageous, hard drinking, hard travelling, hard living man.'

He was from the entertainer end of the folk music spectrum, in MacColl's eyes the shallow end of the folk gene pool, and had a tendency to become maudlin when drunk. He broke down in tears at the meeting and begged forgiveness for his apostasy from the true path, as signposted by MacColl and Bert, and about which MacColl had written in Dallas's magazine *Folk Music* in November 1963:

> The folk song entertainer generally tries to achieve the same sort of audience relationship as the variety and cabaret artist. He tries to maintain an atmosphere of gaiety, he strives to be witty, casual, and, at the right moment, introduces a touch of soulful sadness … . By applying the performance techniques of the cabaret and variety stages, the singer of folk songs robs his material of much of its vitality, transforms and, more often than not, reduces its special characteristics. The entertainer is required to put *himself*, or herself, over to the audience; the traditional singer is concerned with putting *the songs* over.

The entertainer was lumped in with a whole gallery of other figures on whom MacColl, never one to sit on the fence, poured scorn: 'The winsome little cuddly things, the tit-hawkers, the krazy-kollege-kids, the fake hoboes who wear funny hats and cultivate inarticulateness … and all the rest of the riff-raff that swarm over the body of our folk music.'

Bob Davenport was dismayed at the Scotsman's collapse, having expected in Campbell an ally in the battle against the intellectual appropriation and, as Davenport believed, the misunderstanding of, or ignorance of, the true nature of traditional music, promulgated by MacColl and, perhaps, to a lesser extent by Bert. Davenport saw them as intellectual mediators and arbiters of the communist gospel. An inveterate iconoclast, he believed the music should speak for itself. It should be imbibed, if not with mothers' breast milk, at least in a relaxed, convivial setting, with no lecturing or pontificating to create an artificial barrier between performer and imbiber. Davenport, along with Reg Hall and the Rakes, followed his grandfather's advice on running a social event, and 'kept the kettle boiling' with songs and music. An evening at their Thursday club, the Fox at Islington, was a social event, not a Singers' Club classroom lecture. In 1965 it was described by Stephen Sedley as 'probably the best club in London'.

As we can see and hear from the early photos and recordings of the Eel's Foot sessions, where the MC knew everybody and where to place them, the 'them and us' (performer/audience) demarcation is an artificial concept that frequently didn't exist when these songs were performed in their natural habitat with shared accents, interests and vocabulary. The songs belonged as much to the group as to the individual singer, and all were potentially performers and receivers. Bert and MacColl well understood this, as MacColl said in the *Folk Music* article: 'The modern urban folksinger is rarely a member of the community in that sense. His audience is made up of strangers or of casual acquaintances about whom he knows little or nothing and whose experiences, accent and social outlook may be very different from his own.'

It was this central question of how to present folk song in this new, artificial situation that was at the root of much of the squabbling within the folk movement. The main difference between the Fox and the Singers' Club was that, at the Singers' Club, the general feeling was that the Tradition was moribund ('debris' as Bert described it) and needed reviving. At the Fox, where traditional singers, musicians and dancers such as Bampton Morris were regularly invited and encouraged to do whatever pleased them, with no rules or regulations on repertory or style, tradition was very much alive and was being encouraged to continue and thrive.

In a review of the Veteran CD *Good Order – Traditional Singing and Music from the Eel's Foot* Mike Yates pointed out the problems of presenting traditional songs in revival folk clubs: 'If there is a difference, then the difference comes from the loss of the sense of community, with all that entails. Songs removed from this context become just songs! This is why politicians can stand up in Parliament and mock revival singers. This is why the songs, and the singing, can be open to ridicule and misunderstanding.'

Bert and MacColl didn't always see eye to eye on the stage management of the folk revival. Bert didn't agree with MacColl's theatrical approach to the songs, and his use of Theatre Workshop techniques and ideas, such as adapting Stanislavski's theories on artistic preparation to the performance of traditional songs.

Louis Killen remembered Bert's reaction to a letter that he wrote to Bert shortly before his death:

> ... [R]esponding to my appreciation for all he'd given myself and others, he rejected the idea that he was in any way responsible for 'teaching' us to sing or 'interpret' the songs. 'That was Ewan's affair,' he said, but he went on to say, 'If I did anything to instil a bit more understanding and respect for the more serious parts of the repertoire, the idea would please me.'[3]

As MacColl says in his autobiography *Journeyman*:

> In 1964 an established Tyneside singer resident in London said, in the course of an interview, that Lloyd and MacColl should share the benefits of their enormous experience with all those newcomers on the scene who

were anxious to improve themselves. After reading the article I rang Bert and suggested that it might be a good idea to start a discussion group. He was distinctly cool and refused to be involved.

The idea eventually came to fruition as the Critics Group, which was perceived, perhaps incorrectly, by outsiders (including Bert) as an elitist group who thought they were in some way superior to the rest of the folk scene. The rather pretentious biographical notes for the CND Stage Club's Folk Song Prom in April 1963, where we read that the Haverim Trio are 'currently researching, under the guidance of Ewan MacColl and Peggy Seeger, into their local heritage', or that Sandra Kerr 'has started researching into London material and is studying under the direction of Ewan MacColl and Peggy Seeger', did little to dispel the impression.

MacColl and Seeger, in addition to Stanislavskian theories, introduced Nelson Illingworth's Theatre Workshop voice exercises, and according to MacColl: 'We invented exercises based on Laban's effort-scales and we had exercises for relaxation and to improve articulation and the sense of pitch. These formed the basis of our purely physical work.' To this group work was added detailed analysis and the deconstruction of texts and performances. The result succeeded, in the opinion of many people, in turning out MacColl and Seeger clones. This is a claim that is stoutly denied by ex-Critics Group member Jim Carroll:

> Whenever I hear someone say that the singers in the Critics Group sounded like MacColl I am tempted to ask 'Which particular MacColl?' More than any singer I have listened to, MacColl approached his songs as separate items, each one requiring individual treatment, using chest tones, nasal tones, soft, hard, edgy, light ... whichever he thought the song required. The efforts he used were heavy, light, soft, hard, fast, slow ... again, determined by the song.
>
> Nobody in the Group sounded remotely like MacColl, and if they did, they would have been told about it, by him and by the other members. The only singers I ever heard who remotely sang like MacColl were those who tried to.
>
> The aim of the group was to enable singers to sound like themselves; whether it worked or not depended on how much work you put in.[4]

EFDSS employee Tony Foxworthy begged to differ, as he indicated in his review of the Critics Group's 1967 album *A Merry Progress to London*: 'The only criticism I have to make is that the men sound just like Ewan MacColl and the girls like Peggy Seeger. But this is really to be expected seeing that Ewan MacColl and Peggy Seeger trained them.'

Despite all the bickering, infighting and jockeying for position, the folk community frequently put aside its differences as musicians teamed up to do 'good works', such as the concert in support of Pete Seeger's battle with the Un-American Activities Committee. They were socially committed, as befitted a movement that owed a lot of its early impetus to the Communist Party through its musical wing, the Workers' Music Association (WMA). Throughout the 1950s and 1960s musical support at demonstrations, marches (as Peggy Seeger said, 'We marched, and marched and marched') and fundraising concerts were a regular feature of the folk scene. The 1955 Royal Albert Hall concert, where the myopic Special Branch spies credited Bert with accompanying the WMA choir on the accordion, was a Silver Jubilee celebration and fund-raiser for the *Daily Worker*.

The CPGB kept a list of musicians (not just folk musicians) who could be called on for fundraising and public relations events, they also kept a list of supportive writers and lecturers. In April 1953 a copy of a letter containing details of artists who 'can be approached for concerts' was intercepted by Special Branch and copied before being delivered. It contained the codicil: 'Of course some will perform without their names being published.'[5] The Security Services also acquired the names of the members of the London Journalists Group of the Communist Party. On a revised list in April 1950 was Bert's fellow *Picture Post* writer Francis Klingender. Presumably Bert, who at that time was primarily a journalist, would also have been on this list. Klingender had been under observation from the 1930s when he had contributed with Bert to *5 On Revolutionary Art*.

Information was also passed on to Special Branch by shadowy figures who appeared in official reports as a 'reliable and well-placed source'. Who were these shameful informants who could sit and drink with Bert, MacColl, Seeger, Lomax, Hasted, Bush and the rest, perhaps play music with them, and then scurry home and write a detailed account of every remark made amongst 'friends' and pass it on to Special Branch, with no care for, or perhaps with delight in, the consequence of their actions?

The Party and its hierarchy was fully aware that it was under surveillance, but did the Party foot-soldiers and fellow-travellers – the writers, artists, journalists, broadcasters, musicians, union organisers, actors etc. – realise to what extent *they* were being spied on and reported upon? Whenever Bert left the country, which he did frequently, information on the trip was added to his file. In January 1954 the Security Services monitored Bert's trip to Czechoslovakia: 'The Following British subjects left London Airport. Albert Lancaster Lloyd, passport 17113023. A Journalist. Czech visa. David Caplan. Artist. Czech visa. James Henry Miller (Ewan MacColl). Dramatist, Czech visa.'

In 1953 David Attenborough, then a young television director, had an idea for a folk music series. He was familiar with John Lomax's collection of cowboy songs and Lomax's son Alan's celebrated biography of Jelly Roll Morton. Knowing that Alan Lomax (whom Attenborough described as a 'magnet for folk music') was in London and working on various folk music collecting projects and folk music programmes for the BBC, Attenborough had a chat with Lomax and put in a programme proposal for a TV series called *Song Hunter*. It was to be a studio-based production, recorded in the small BBC studios at Alexandra Palace. Lomax would present the programmes, talk about his song-collecting trips around the British Isles and bring some of his 'discoveries' into the studio to perform. Attenborough had to rely on Lomax's greater knowledge of folk singers and had a hard time controlling Lomax's extravagances.

At that time BBC TV, the poor brother of radio, was dependent for its funding on the radio coffers and was kept on a tight financial rein. Lomax, either not knowing this or not caring, would book guests such as an entire group of tweed workers from the Isle of Barra to come down and sing their waulking songs, (rhythmic leader/chorus songs performed by the group seated around a big table on which the women pushed and pummelled the wet tweed cloth). Their return air fares from the Hebrides, plus hospitality, used up practically all of Attenborough's budget for the whole series. The series of six programmes, which went out at eight o'clock in the evening, had a very small audience – television in the UK had not yet become the all-seeing eye in every sitting room in the land. As Attenborough said: 'It was not a popular programme by any means.'[6] Unfortunately, in those early days of television there were no facilities for electronic recording. The programmes went out live and were immediately lost forever.

The fact that well-known communists like Bert (whom Attenborough described as a political 'hot potato') and MacColl had been booked to sing on the series, allied to the fact that Lomax was under surveillance from MI5 for his communist sympathies, meant that the mandarins in Broadcasting House cast a jaundiced eye over the project, and MI5 took a special interest in the series and listed all the singers who appeared, which, as well as Bert and MacColl, included Michael Gorman, Margaret Barrie, Bob Roberts, Bob Copper and the girls from Barra. All were checked out for possible communist sympathies or signs of possible contamination from the prevailing left-wing, workers' song atmosphere of the programme. Attenborough, a sensible and unprejudiced man, thought it 'absurd that the BBC should worry about putting too many communists in the series'. His main worry was to curb Lomax's profligate spending.

It was also standard Special Branch procedure to intercept Party headquarters' telephone conversations and to make detailed reports of even the most innocuous of conversations, such as MacColl's December 1952 call to Sam Aaranovitch arranging to have tea![7] It was in this area of phone tapping and bugging that Bert's fellow Rambler, John Hasted, came in useful. Around 1950 he devised testing equipment for the Party's King Street telephones, and found that many of them appeared to be fixed, so that even when the receiver was put back on its cradle at the end of a call the line stayed open. This meant that everything said in the room could be heard in a government listening centre. Rather than let the security services know they'd been rumbled, the CP simply used other rooms for confidential conversations.

In July 1954 Bert performed in a fundraising Ballads and Blues concert for Theatre Workshop, held in the new Royal Festival Hall. The programme notes spelt out the connection between (British) ballads and (American) blues:

'The Blues aint notin' but a good man feelin' bad. The Blues aint notin' but a woman on a poor man's mind. The Blues aint notin' but the poor man's heart disease.' That is how a Blues singer defines the Blues. The same definition might be applied to Lancashire songs such as 'The Four Loom Weaver' and 'Van Dieman's Land'; to ballads like 'Lord Randall', 'The Rocks of Baun' and 'The Sheffield Apprentice'.

The notes also show how Bert and MacColl saw the current position of the folk revival. Their critical comments on the practices of earlier folklorists smack very much of the pot calling the kettle black; they were no less guilty of mediating the material to suit their own ends:

> The nineteenth century folklorists, industrious and well-meaning as they were, did much to foster the myth that folk music was too fragile for this brutal age and too coarse for polite society. It was considered expedient to forget the social origins of folk music. The 'folk' was a nebulous grouping of merry Arcadians, coy rustics prancing perpetually round village maypoles and flirting archly with each other. To have confused the 'folk' with that great army of rural cottagers driven into the Bastilles and factories by successive poor-law acts, with the half-starved Irish navvies building the first railroads, or with the evicted Highland crofters, would have been unthinkable.
>
> The creation of this mythical 'folk' made it necessary to carry out certain structural alterations on the folk music; anthologists and editors pruned it down to respectable proportions, skilled composers and musicians 'improved' the melodies by robbing them of their vitality, and concert singers showed the people how their music should be sung.
>
> What distinguishes the present folk-music renaissance from previous revivals is the fact that the people are demanding that their music be served up 'neat', and unadulterated, in the authentic traditional style.

Bert was no less romantic about his industrial workers than Cecil Sharp had been about his rural peasants. And his and MacColl's idea of 'authentic' generally meant whatever the pair of them thought and did. For instance, the sea shanties, which Bert and MacColl pioneered on the British folk scene (although, as we've seen, concert singers such as John Goss had been recording shanties since the late 1920s), and which the folk audiences assumed to be authoritative because of Bert's whaling trip (!) were, according to Britain's last genuine shantyman, and nautical authority, Stan Hugill, somewhat less so:

> All the weird shanties they put over are good, perhaps, depending which way you look at them. But for Bert they had to be modal, they had to be Myxolydian, they had to be Dorian. They never sang the songs the real sailors sang: 'The Rio Grand', 'Shenandoah', 'The Banks of the Sacramento'.
>
> > As I was walking down the strand,
> > Hoo dah, hoo dah.
> > I spied two bitches hand in hand.
> > Oh, hoo dah day.

Chorus:

Blow, boys, blow, for Californi-o.
There's plenty of grass to wipe your ass
On the banks of the Sacramento.

I chose the one with the curly locks;
Hoo dah, etc.
She's the bugger that gave me the pox.
Oh, etc.

Those were the songs the sailors sang but they never looked at them. Bert did 'Sally Brown' but not the normal version, not the way any sailor ever did it. He sang a Bahamian boatman's rowing song as a deepwater shanty, but it was never sung in deepwater. It was only collected once in the early '60s but Bert's version had extra verses that he must have written. 'Little Sally Racket' came from a collection of Jamaican folk songs and, again, was not the version sung by sailors.[8]

Real shanty singing was not always a very pleasant sound with its whoops and yelps. It was not meant to be 'listening music'. It was rough, often obscene, and solely designed to get a job done. Bert, MacColl and the young revivalists who copied them came to a compromise in their performance style as well as with their use of set lyrics, which would usually have been improvised at the moment of performance, as Jim Carroll commented: 'Shanties were work songs – the shanty men were aiming to get the work done not make pretty sounds. When MacColl, Lloyd et al introduced the shanties in the early days [of the folk revival] they attempted to strike a balance between the function of the songs and the aesthetics – personally I thought they did a good job of it – it's stayed with me for forty years.'[9]

In a 1965 *Sing* review of the Topic collection *Farewell Nancy* Eric Winter had this to say about Bert's sleeve notes on shanty singing: 'Lloyd doesn't pretend in the sleeve notes that the shanties are presented authentically. But they are sung with great vigour, a clear understanding of what the texts are about and an affection for the songs.' Carroll added: 'Lloyd once remarked about a group who were notorious for producing pretty and complex harmonies on shanties: "They sound very nice but they wouldn't get a rowing boat across a park lake."'[10] Perhaps Bert should have given them one of his Bahamian rowing songs. If you look through the track listings of Bert and Ewan's early shanty and sea-song records, it's remarkable how many became folk club standards. They provided the songs, the singing style, and the background information on virtually that whole genre of revival song.

Bert was, of course, well aware of how the shanties were originally sung but believed that different situations allow for different interpretations:

Fore-bitters usually had fixed texts telling a coherent story. Shanties often consisted of whatever words floated into the shantyman's mind in the course of the job; they were made of scraps and might be expanded or contracted, forty verses or four, according to the length of the task in hand. As for style, some singers sang with plenty of ornaments – 'hitches', the sailors called them – while others sang undecorated. Some sang with free, hardly measurable rhythm, others sang bang on the beat. There were no rules, except for the crowd on the choruses of the work-songs; they had to sing full, plain and regular, if they were to pull together. To the debated question whether seamen sang the shanty refrains in harmony the answer seems to be: some might but most didn't. But nowadays, when shanties are sung for fun and not in earnest, it's usual to brighten them with harmonies, and to sing them faster and jerkier than their true purpose demanded. Both shanties and fore-bitters are well-nigh indestructible; they can stand any treatment except the quaint and genteel.

And elsewhere he said: '... folklore forms don't depend on their original environment for their continued existence; sailing ships are gone but the sea shanty is still sung: the function is altered but the song remains. The stuff is trans-cultural.'

The 5 July Festival Hall concert was an eclectic affair, a microcosm of the folk scene as it was at that time before the big bang when all the disparate musical elements shot off on their individual trajectories. The show opened with Scottish country-dance music from the house 'folk' band, an odd assortment of jazz, folk and session men that bore little resemblance to any traditional 'folk' band.

It's worth recalling, though, what Bert once wrote in 'What's Traditional?' (*Folk Music*, November 1963): 'The Romanians [at a folklore conference] explained that their viewpoint was: Any instrument may be considered a folk instrument, depending on the way it's handled.' It's not the instruments that make a piece of music 'folk music', it's what you do with them and the context in which they are played. In the nineteenth century the melodeon and concertina must have been alien and exotic to folk musicians brought up on the fiddle, pipe and tabor. Although a popular folk instrument, the use of a cimbalom by Stravinsky in his 1918 jazz composition 'Ragtime for Eleven Soloists' didn't turn the work into folk music. So perhaps the line-up of Bruce Turner (alto sax and clarinet), jazz and session guitarists Fitzroy Coleman and Brian Daly; Scottish fiddler George Harvey Webb and ex-circus, variety and recording artist as well as English-concertina player Alf Edwards was a perfectly legitimate folk band.

It was Bert and MacColl's frequent use of the virtuosic and reliable Edwards in live performance and on many of their records over the years, and Edwards' teaching of the English concertina to Peggy Seeger – who subsequently ran workshops on the concertina as an accompanying instrument for folk song – that brought the English concertina to folk music prominence following its general decline in the inter-war years.

In his introduction to *The Penguin Book of English Folk Songs* Bert wrote:

The ideal way to sing an English folk song, of course, is unaccompanied. Our melodies were made to be sung that way, and much of their tonal beauty and delightful suppleness comes from the fact that they have been traditionally free from harmonic or rhythmic accompaniment. They are best suited to stand on their own, and we rather agree with the Dorset countryman who commented on a professional singer of folk songs: 'Of course, it's nice for him to have the piano when he's singing, but it does make it awkward for the listener'.

Bert, ever the pragmatist, realised that, following the burgeoning of instrumental accompaniment (mainly on the American guitar and banjo) of songs in the skiffle era, and the expectations of young pop-fed urban audiences for a fuller sound than the unadorned voice, he should invest in some sort of accompaniment. He eventually settled for Alf Edwards' English concertina, possibly for some of the reasons suggested by Stuart Eydmann:

In reluctantly accepting the instrumental accompaniment of folk song, Lloyd was obliged to sanction treatment which was appropriate in ideological as well as musical terms. In doing so he turned to the concertina. The instrument was small, unobtrusive and portable. It was versatile, with a potential for many accompaniment styles including melodic, chordal or drone playing. However, there were other considerations. The instrument already enjoyed endorsement by Sharp and Grainger, it was British (i.e. non-American) and, most importantly, it was an instrument born in and of the industrial revolution and came laden with working class associations.[11]

In the sleeve notes to the original Prestige International album *The Best of A.L. Lloyd* Bert had this to say about Alf Edwards:

I chose to be accompanied by Alf Edwards' fine concertina-playing not because the concertina is 'more traditional' than the fashionable guitar (strictly speaking in England no portable instrument is more traditional than any other as accompaniment to folk song) but because I think it suits my kind of songs better and interferes less with the rhythm; also I like working with Alf.

At the Royal Festival Hall, following Edwards and the folk band, Isla Cameron, who had joined MacColl in Theatre Workshop as a sixteen-year-old in 1940, stepped up to the microphone and sang a couple of traditional ballads. MacColl then gave one of his theatrical renderings of the 'Dowie Dens of Yarrow' before Bert sang 'The Seven Gypsies' and a Kentucky version of 'Little Musgrave'.

With the first batch of ballads out of the way it was time for the Ken Colyer Skiffle Group to kick in with some blues – 'Boll Weevil Blues' and the chain-gang song 'Take This Hammer'. Ken Colyer took his authentic New Orleans jazz and his bluesy skiffle as seriously as Bert and MacColl took traditional British music. He was labelled by some an obscurantist for his purist approach to traditional jazz but widely admired by others. In the early 1950s he had worked his passage across to Mobile, Alabama, and then, clutching his trumpet, jumped ship and headed for the flesh-pots and jazz-joints of New Orleans. Despite the colour bar, he'd hung out and drunk and illegally played with his black jazz heroes, including George Lewis. He was eventually arrested and thrown in prison on immigration charges. While in prison he smuggled a series of letters detailing his picaresque adventures back to his brother Bill (the manager of Collet's record store in London), who published them in *Melody Maker*.

By the time he arrived back in England, in March 1953, Colyer was a jazz hero and was invited to take over Chris Barber's band (which included Lonnie Donegan and Monty Sunshine) and to call it the Ken Colyer Jazzmen. Colyer was evicted from the band a year later over a series of personnel disagreements. He assembled a new jazz band/skiffle group just in time for the Festival Hall concert. The Skiffle Group line-up was Colyer (guitar), Alexis Korner (guitar/mandolin), Bill Colyer (washboard) and Micky Ashman (bass).

From 1949 when Colyer put together his first band, the Crane River Jazzmen, he had always incorporated some guitar-based blues and jug-band music into the act creating a band within the band. These were songs learnt from 78s of Leadbelly, Lonnie Johnson and Big Bill Broonzy. Originally they simply called this 'breakdown' music, but it was what, a few years down the line, would be called 'skiffle' (the term was adopted by Bill Colyer from the 1940s American group Dan Burley and his Skiffle Boys). They played it between sets to give the front line a rest and to introduce the audience to the roots of jazz. Three months after the Festival Hall concert Colyer opened a Monday night jazz club at the 51 Club, 11 Great Newport Street, just off the Charing Cross Road. It was known affectionately simply as Colyer's and became a beacon for hordes of sandaled, black-sweater'd trad-jazz fans up from the sticks who called each other 'Dad' and who hop-jived the night away to Colyer's uncompromising traditional jazz.

Meanwhile, back at the Royal Festival Hall, following a spiritual from the Colyer Jazz Band, Bert teamed up with the skiffle group and sang 'Ghost Soldier Blues':

> My Mama told me not to go and fight the war,
> But I did, I did, I did.
> Though war is full of heroism and inspiration,
> It's also full of tiredness and desperation.
> My Mama told me not to go and fight the war,
> But I did, I did, I did.

A song popular with American troops during the First World War and later parodied by Ewan MacColl and Peggy Seeger in their song 'Space Girl'.

The idea of jazz and folk as radical musical bedfellows came originally from America, where the two art forms were taken up by the Communist Party and the Congress of Industrial Organisations as useful 'adjuncts to political and trade union work', and therefore had both anti-racist and radical connotations for British leftish audiences. That evening Bert also sang 'The Commissions Report' (Trinidad Calypso), 'Pay Day at Coal Creek' (American mining song), 'Cosher Bailey's Engine' (Welsh railway song), a couple of shanties with MacColl, and 'St James Infirmary' with MacColl and the jazz band. His repertoire at that time was nothing if not eclectic, and reflected what he'd been singing for the previous two or three years with the Ramblers.

A 1950s movement with which the left, skiffle, folk song and traditional jazz became indissolubly linked was the Campaign for Nuclear Disarmament (CND). In February 1958, following Aneurin Bevan's 1957 rejection of unilateral nuclear disarmament, a group of scientists, churchmen, philosophers and general peace activists got together and established CND. At Easter 1958 (4–7 April) thousands of people braved the cold, wet, unseasonable weather to march in protest from London to the Atomic Weapons Research Establishment near Aldermaston in Berkshire in an attempt to persuade the British Government to renounce unconditionally the use and production of nuclear weapons. For the next five years, until 1963, the Aldermaston March was an important date on the music calendar. According to their daughter Caroline, both Bert and Charlotte trudged the weary miles through sleet and rain on that first march, as did Peggy Seeger (recently back in the country) and MacColl, singing and playing and handing out copies of MacColl's 'Song of Hiroshima' (English words by MacColl from an original song by Koti Kinoshita). This was sung on the march by Hasted's London Youth Choir, who also introduced the March anthem 'The H-Bomb's Thunder', which had been put together a week previously by John Brunner and the *Sing* editorial team.

Karl Dallas was also there, encouraging the musicians and leading some of the singing, and helping to elevate the spirits of the marchers, as the journalist Colin Irwin recounted: '... they soldiered on rallied by the sound of the jazz bands, the church choirs and skiffle groups scattered through the miles and, almost imperceptibly along the route, the tradition of song as a soundtrack to political protest, lifting spirits and symbolising unity, was firmly established.'[12] The foot-weary column of mainly middle-class protesters of all political persuasions, most respectably dressed in dresses, suits, collars and ties and overcoats (although there were also plenty of iconic 1950s duffle coats and rebelliously dressed ravers) were led into Hounslow on their first night on the road by Ken Colyer's Jazz Band blasting out 'When the Saints Go Marching In'. Mark Steinhardt makes a reference to Bert and CND in his biography of the singer Audrey Smith: 'At the 1962 Aldermaston March (the one she missed because of illness) A.L. Lloyd, Ewan MacColl and half the folk elite played.' Whether Bert marched, or simply sang in Trafalgar Square at the end of the march, Steinhardt doesn't say.

Of this time Hylda Sims wrote: 'The Left, thinly disguised as the Peace Movement, have been making an effort to get us to revive and sing our own songs, and many old and wonderful ballads are entering our repertoire, usually sung a cappella á la Ewan MacColl and Bert Lloyd, who are at the head of the thing, collecting and singing and publishing the old English and Scottish ballads and making new, political songs in the tradition.'[13]

In his book *Who Wrote the Ballads*, the Australian Marxist John Manifold saw the retention of traditional culture in Scotland, Ireland and, to a lesser extent, Northumbria as a means of preserving national and regional identity in the face of being 'overshadowed, threatened and frequently invaded by a richer and more populous neighbour'. He believed that the anti-Americanism of many in the peace movement had similar origins:

> The United States is playing the part towards Britain today [1960s] which England played towards Scotland [and Ireland] yesterday and the day before. American culture dominates and threatens; English people are aware and resentful of it. Even those who are resigned to U.S. military 'aid' deplore the stranglehold of U.S. commodity culture. The peace movement tends to fuse the struggle against juke-box culture with the struggle against American military and political domination.[14]

Manifold found it faintly ironic that 'the young folksingers who join the Aldermarston marchers should owe as much as they do to the style of the American folk song revival'. One of the side benefits of the CND marches for the denizens of Soho who busked or played banjos and guitars in coffee bars such as the Gs, Sam Widges, the Nucleus, the Farm and the Partisan, was the mountain of sleeping bags and other equipment that was lost en route and ended up in the crypt of St Martin's-in-the-Field. This was rifled through and 'claimed' by those who would be following Alex Campbell, Wizz Jones, Davey Graham, Colin Wilkie and others, hitching down to Newquay and St Ives, or across to Paris and then down the National 7 to the south of France once the weather warmed up. Most of these itinerant folk troubadours represented the strand of the folk revival that owed more to Kerouac, Henry Miller and Woody Guthrie than to Bert and McColl. Their Mecca was the Parisian Left Bank 'Bar Monaco' rather than Moscow.[15]

Another aspect of the CND movement and marches which is often overlooked, but which Karl Dallas pointed out, was the boost they gave to the formation of folk clubs around the country:

> People came for the Aldermarston marches from all over the country and returned to form folk clubs. The result was that the movement [folk revival] really began to move...and became uncontrollable....this was exactly the sort of spontaneous explosion that the mandarins of 16 King Street [CPGB Headquarters] had feared. The folk revival had found its own dynamic.[16]

Dallas's contention, contrary to the opinion of Dave Harker and others, is that the folk revival, despite the number of communists who initiated it, was never run from King Street: '... it [CND] played a more significant role than the Communist Party in spreading the good news of folk throughout the length and breadth of the land.'

Arnold Rattenbury was also emphatic that the common belief that all artistic and creative CP members were controlled and instructed by Moscow via King Street was a 'great libel'. Harry Pollitt may indeed have taken his handkerchief out every time Stalin sneezed, but many Party members, even Stalin supporters like Bert, Hutt and MacColl, apparently had a degree of independence even if, as Rattenbury suggests, they didn't always exercise it:

> Bert was looking at folklore because the Party wanted him to? People were not writing poems for the middle class because the Party didn't want them to? Bollocks! Lies! It's all lies! We all had an enormous amount of independence, with always the proviso that because we were members of the bloody thing we had our own sense of loyalty (and were doubtless far too gullible about the Soviet Union), Party members like Bert and myself created our own velvet manacles.[17]

The Party apparatchiks apparently knew little, and understood less, of what was happening on the street, and cast a jaundiced, suspicious eye on the evolving movement. As we've seen, there was little consensus among the leading communist folk revival lights. Had there been it might have become more effective politically. So, plenty of communists but, as Dallas said, frequently 'heterophony rather than harmony'. The CPGB did, however, have an influence on the wider labour movement, an influence out of proportion to its membership numbers. Between the wars many trade union officials and other potentially useful people were trained in the Lenin School in Moscow before returning to influence the working-class battle in their own countries.

Over the 1958 August Bank Holiday the newspapers reported 'ferocious riots' in the Notting Hill area of London. Despite the police protestations at the time that the riots were not racially motivated, confidential Metropolitan Police papers released in 2002 revealed that the riots were instigated by 300- or 400-strong gangs of armed 'Keep Britain White' youths who went 'nigger hunting' amongst the West Indian community. Following the riots, the jazz musicians Johnny Dankworth and Cleo Lane believed that by getting top people in the music world to give the lead, one could stop young people being racist. They started the Stars Campaign for Racial Equality, which was supported by many skiffle and folk musicians around London. The City Ramblers got involved and put on gigs in support of the scheme in their famous Greek Street club, The Cellar (they'd dropped 'skiffle' from the club name in May as skiffle started to wane). Bert, who regularly played with Trinidadian guitarist Fitzroy Coleman, was happy to add his voice to the campaign. His old singing partner, Jean Jenkins, wrote an article for the Winter 1958 issue of *Universities and Left Review* about the racial problems in Georgia, Mississippi and Arkansas.

In April 1963 Bruce Dunnet, the Scots communist agent, folk club promoter (he was running the Singers' Club in 1963), hustler and organiser of the 1962

CENTRE 42 Trades Festivals, put together and compered the second CND fundraising Folk Song Prom in the Empire Rooms, Tottenham Court Road. Along with Bert there appeared Leon Rosselson, Bob Davenport, Dominic Behan, Enoch Kent, Sandra Kerr, the Rakes, and a young Anne Briggs who had been 'discovered' when auditioned by Bruce Dunnet at the Nottingham CENTRE 42 Festival the previous year. She became a protégée of Bert and one of his favourite female singers, and he used her on *The Iron Muse* (1963) and *Bird in the Bush* (1966) and produced her 1971 eponymous Topic album before she perhaps sensibly escaped from the folk scene and withdrew to live a reclusive life in rural Scotland.

Arnold Wesker's CENTRE 42 was one of the most important arts movements of the 1960s and grew out of the 1960 TUC resolution to enquire into the state of the arts. The resolution was number 42 on the agenda and as CENTRE 42 artistic director Wesker recounts:

> In response to it [the resolution] a number of writers, theatre directors and others involved in the arts said to the Trade Union Movement if you are interested in the arts we will set up an arts organisation of which you can take advantage for your members. CENTRE 42 was born in 1961 with the aim of finding audiences for the arts, NOT an audience for popular art as was its frequently mistaken description.

CENTRE 42 produced arts festivals for trades councils around the country. The first one was put together for Wellingborough Trades Council at their invitation, following an article entitled 'A Cultural Revolution' which Wesker wrote for *Reynolds News*. The festivals included jazz, poetry, contemporary and classic plays, and folk music. For the Wellingborough folk concert, Bruce Dunnet assembled a decidedly northern-flavoured group of singers, including: Belle and Alex Stewart, Ray Fisher and Matt McGinn (Scotland), Francis MacPeake (Northern Ireland), Louis Killen, Bob Davenport and Colin Ross (Northumberland) and MacColl, Peggy Seeger, Alf Edwards and Bert. The festival was such a success that other trades councils took up the offer, and festivals were put on in Birmingham, Hayes and Southall, Leicester, Nottingham and Bristol. Folk photographer Brian Shuel (whose father-in-law was James Boswell, Bert's old friend from the AIA days) photographed the Wellingborough rehearsals and took one of the classic smiling-singing Bert shots, with a suited Edwards sitting stiffly in front of his music stand, looking as much bank manager as folk musician (see plate 33).

Dave Swarbrick, who played with Bert and Edwards on several of the CENTRE 42 gigs feels that Edwards doesn't get the credit he deserves:

> It's a shame that Alf's not remembered more, because he kicked off the whole concertina thing. To this day he's not been bettered he used to warm up with Paganinni caprices. I wouldn't even contemplate doing the first two bars of any of them. We did all kinds of gigs, mostly town halls, big ones

– Aberdeen, Edinburgh, London, Birmingham Town hall. It would be part of a package. Anything Bert did he'd have meself and Alf on. CENTRE 42 concerts, we did quite a lot of those. We didn't usually travel together we'd meet up at the gig. But dear old Alf never gets thought of at all.

Alf always had a rather strange attitude towards traditional music because he couldn't ever really figure out that it wasn't composed by one person. So any time I started to improvise Alf would nudge me and say, 'Play it as the composer wrote it'.[18]

Bert, Edwards and MacColl had been driven up to the Friday evening Wellingborough concert by Peggy Seeger. Following an after-concert party, Seeger offered Bob Davenport a lift back to London in their large Citroen. A short way down the motorway everyone jumped out of their skins when there was a loud bang as the bonnet flew open and hit the roof. Deprived of vision, Peggy calmly ducked her head and, peering through a small gap at the bottom of the windscreen, below the bonnet, she steered the car safely onto the hard shoulder. Bert and the others were suitably impressed with her calm handling of a situation that might have wiped out the architects of the folk revival at one fell swoop.[19]

Each of the week-long festivals began with a folk concert on the Friday night with much the same line-up each time, depending on who was free.

In 1957 a young American language student and folk musician named Ralph Rinzler came across to Europe to study for a graduate degree in French. At Swarthmore College, Pennsylvania he had been involved with organising folk music events, in the course of which he'd become friendly with the Seeger family – Pete, Mike and Peggy having played at the college. Through hanging out with Mike while he was interviewing and recording old-time musicians, and as a result of conversations with Mike's musicologist father Charles Seeger, Rinzler developed an interest in ethnomusicology. While in France he took a call from Peggy Seeger in London saying that she had to go abroad for a few months and asking if he could fill in for some of her recording commitments with Ewan MacColl and Bert Lloyd. He didn't need much persuading to put his studies on hold and get across to England, as he told folklorist Richard Gagne in an interview in 1993:

So I gave up graduate school for a while, and stayed in England, and lived primarily at Bert's house, and that was like going to college, Bert was extraordinarily erudite, in a very informal way. I just lived in his house for a year. Between Ewan and Bert's work, I had another vision of how people use folklore in creative ways. Bert had worked on whaling factories, he'd been an overlander and sheepherder in Australia. And he knew the tradition from the inside. And he used to write – I mean, here he is a Communist, in 1957, writing for BBC programmes for schools. And everyone knew he was a Communist. The idea of anyone (a Communist) in this country [America] writing for schools for the national network would be unheard of. He wrote these brilliant little things, full of humour and insight, about the different occupations, and then sang the songs.

During his year in London as Bert's house guest, Rinzler also worked with Ewan MacColl and Alan Lomax, to whom Seeger introduced him when she got back to England. Seeger was always grateful to Bert for taking her in and letting her stay as an unpaid guest at Croom's Hill when she'd first arrived in England in March 1956, following a phone call to her Copenhagen youth hostel from Alan Lomax who needed a banjo player for a project. Initially, she'd lived in unprepossessing cheap lodgings that Lomax had found for her. A short while later, MacColl took her across to Greenwich to meet Bert, who offered her one of the attic bedrooms. Although not necessarily 'chums' with Peggy's father, the celebrated Charles, Bert had met and chatted with him in July 1952 at the Fifth International Folk Music Council Conference held at Cecil Sharp House. Her half-brother, Pete Seeger, was one of Bert's heroes, so he was pleased to offer hospitality to one of the family.

Later, he was on the committee of the Friends of Pete Seeger support group set up in 1961 to raise money to help with Seeger's legal fees, after he'd been found guilty of Contempt of Congress. The Friends officially kicked off with a St Pancras Town Hall concert involving Bert, MacColl, Peggy Seeger, Behan, Bob Davenport, Louis Killen and the Bruce Turner Jump Band. For his 'spot' on the concert Davenport was told by MacColl, who was running the event, to go out in front of the curtains and do a couple of numbers to cover while the Bruce Turner Band cleared the stage. Davenport went out and sang 'Durham Gaol' and the McPeakes' 'Wild Mountain Thyme' which, much to MacColl's discomfort and Davenport's satisfaction, brought the house down. Davenport left the stage to cheers and screams for more, but MacColl hustled him off declaring that there was no time for any more! Later in the year Pete Seeger was brought over to play the Albert Hall.

Bert's offer of accommodation to Seeger's half-sister Peggy was a generous gesture that probably went down less well with Charlotte who, one suspects, was not enamoured with the idea of Bert spending time with the vivacious young banjo player. Charlotte rarely, if ever, went to gigs with Bert and, according to some of Bert's friends, didn't like him being away from home. She was also, surprisingly (considering her own and Bert's history), prudishly critical of Seeger's relationship with the older, married MacColl, to the point that when Seeger and MacColl had their first child, Bert phoned up and suggested that it might be best not to bring the baby over to show them. Charlotte, after her fenestration operation, found Seeger's fiddle practising hard on the ears, so much so that Seeger used to retreat next door to play. She eventually gave up playing it after finding it enough trouble to hump a guitar, banjo and concertina around the country to gigs, without the addition of a fragile fiddle.[20]

When she first came to the metropolis, Seeger ran a banjo class for the WMA. Two of her young students were Wizz Jones (who went on to become one of the most admired British blues guitarists) and Pete Stanley (who stuck to the banjo and has become a respected 'elder-statesman' and historian of the instrument). Both are still performing. Another member of her class, Barry Murphy, became a good friend of Rinzler when he took over running the classes, and he visited him several times at 16 Croom's Hill, where he recalled that Rinzler had the run of the house:

> Ralph was really liked by them [the Lloyds] you could tell, and he had free range of the place, like he'd always lived there. Because of this I could turn up anytime Ralph called, and I remember more than once on hot days getting out onto the roof from Ralph's bedroom, right up at the top of the house, onto a flat bit of leaded roof and sit and try to play along with him, and look out over Greenwich Park.[21]

While Rinzler and Murphy precariously serenaded Greenwich from the rooftop, Bert was usually working away at his desk by the first-floor window, on sleeve notes, radio scripts and articles. Charlotte often sat quietly in the same room, working on some stumpwork embroidery, which she used to research on regular trips to the Victoria and Albert Museum. When they came down from the roof for a cup of tea, or if Charlotte was out, they'd sit at the table in the stone-flagged basement kitchen, where they sometimes used to play and, if Bert joined them, listen to stories of his time fence-riding in Australia or amusing nautical anecdotes.

Years later, when he was a respected folklorist, a Fellow of the American Folklore Society and founder of the prestigious Smithsonian Folklife Festival, Rinzler credited Bert along with his other early mentors – Seeger, MacColl and Lomax – with having opened his eyes, ears, and mind, and shown him how to use folklore in creative ways: 'They were all very nurturing, and they all had a vision. Different visions, but you saw that if you had a vision of something and it wasn't going to happen other than your doing it, you just figured out how to do it.'

Over the three decades that the Lloyds lived at Croom's Hill hundreds of people beat a path to their large front door. It was a door that impressed Australian Mark Gregory when he first visited the house in 1969:

> When Maree and I arrived in London in October 1969, just a month or so before the birth of our daughter Morgan, I decided to ring Bert. I thought if I offered to lend him a book that he might not have seen, collector John Meredith's *Folk Songs of Australia and the Men and Women who Sang Them*, he might be interested. I was invited over to Greenwich – quite a journey from World's End [Chelsea] by bus, tube and train. I remember being amazed at the size of his front door ... and there he was, beaming, as he opened the door. He seemed to somehow glide on his feet like a dancer.[22]

The Gregorys became involved with the radical documentary group Cinema Action and other political activities, and Mark, who worked as a fitter and turner, did occasional casual handyman work for Bert and Charlotte: 'The great thing about our visits was the range of our conversations, art, music, theatre and politics, and the feeling that these were exchanges. We were certainly aware of how amazing Charlotte was too in these visits. She was gracefulness itself allied to strong opinion. And the calm atmosphere of the grand old house reflected that.'

15
The Radio Ballads

In January 1958 Peggy Seeger returned to Britain from her travels in Russia, China and Poland. She moved back into her old attic room at Croom's Hill, picked up her relationship with MacColl, and immediately started work arranging the music for the first Charles Parker, MacColl and Seeger Radio Ballad – *The Ballad of John Axon* – which was transmitted in July 1958. It was followed in November 1959 by *Song of the Road*. By the time it was transmitted, a pregnant Seeger had vacated the Lloyd's attic and fled the country, after being reported ('by another banjo player's wife!') to the Home Office for having overstayed her visa limit. She listened to the 'faint' broadcast of that first Radio Ballad from Paris. Seeger has resisted the temptation to name the banjo player in question but there weren't that many married banjo players around in 1958.[1]

John Axon was the English answer to all those American railroad disaster songs – Axon was our Casey Jones, or perhaps the Edgeley loco shed's equivalent of Steve Brady, the working-class hero of the *Wreck of the Old 97* who died in the wreck with his hand on the throttle, 'scalded to death by steam'. Driver Axon and his guard were both killed on 9 February 1957, when their freight train lost its steam-brakes and ploughed into the back of the 8.45 a.m. Rosely to Edgeley train.

Bert was booked to sing in the first four Radio Ballad programmes – *The Ballad of John Axon* (1958), *Song of a Road* (1959), *Singing the Fishing* (1960) and *The Big Hewer* (1961). As we've seen, Peggy Seeger was very happy to have Bert on board because, even if he might not have had a 'perfect tone', she felt the general effect of his performance 'gave the song a natural feel. In *John Axon* – just how a railwayman might sound.' Bert turned in a professional, 'authentic sounding' performance on 'Saturday Afternoon':

Come all you British loco men who travel the iron way,
There's a long week-end and money to spend, it's time to draw your pay.
You've done your eighty-hour fortnight and now it's time for play
So off with your dirty dungarees, your time is yours today.

We'll give her some rock and we'll beat the clock and send her on her way,
For every train is an express train upon a Saturday.

In *Singing the Fishing* Bert got to share with MacColl one of the best songs to come out of the Radio Ballad series – 'The Shoals of Herring', a song that both Bob Davenport and Nigel Denver went on to popularise in the folk clubs. MacColl based it on the memories and speech of herring fishermen like Sam

Larner from Winterton, Norfolk, and Ronnie Balls from Yarmouth; it took three days, sixty-two different versions of the tune, and five alternative texts before he was happy with it. The finished song has such an air of authenticity that many people assume it's a traditional song that MacColl got from Larner. In fact, Seeger said she overheard Bert telling someone as much during the recording of the programme. It's surely unlikely he'd have said that, unless at that time he mistakenly believed it.

Singing apart, the other advantage of using Bert for the technically complex, multi-layered and critically-timed productions, was that he was a radio professional, who could take, and act upon, direction, and could be relied on to always turn in a sound workmanlike performance. Mary Baker, a recording engineer and tape editor on the Radio Ballads, explained the pressure put on everyone by Parker's search for 'perfection': '... take after take after take, sometimes into the teens of them, as we had not at that time multi-track facilities. It was very trying for all concerned. Bert Lloyd was the absolute professional, subjecting himself to the disciplines, quiet, never ruffled and giving his best every time. It was a pleasure to have him there, alert, calm and dependable always.'

Seeger later recalled some of the problems encountered in *John Axon* when she was conducting the musicians, who had to be in time with the rhythm of a moving train but were unable to hear the train because the recording was only available in Seeger's headphones: '"When you've shovelled a million tons of coal" has to go hectically fast. On the other hand, the musicians found it hard to match the measured starting-off-uphill chug of "The Repair Was Done", but Bert Lloyd handles the song beautifully, a perfect parallel for the flat voice of fireman Scanlon.' She was equally impressed with his work on *Singing the Fishing*: 'He did wonders on *Singing the Fishing* – it was lovely what he did. He just slipped into the role and he took direction beautifully. Charles Parker was not easy to work with.'

Although Bert was a thorough professional it didn't stop him from indulging in the occasional bit of schoolboy fun, as Louis Killen recounted:

I got to know him quite well through the Radio Ballads. He was a very playful man. The first Radio Ballad I was in was *The Song of the Road*, which was recorded in London. Cyril Tawney [from Devon] and I were the two outsiders, everybody else were London based, and Bert started winding people up by pushing this whole thing that Alf Edwards was gay. And, of course Bert was a very touchy feely man, and people who didn't know his sense of humour were looking over their shoulders and wondering what was going on. He was always making fun, often of Ewan, not in a vicious way but in a jokey way; slicing the pretensions away.[2]

In his history of the Radio Ballads, *Set Into Song*, Peter Cox chronicled another example of Bert's quirky sense of humour. The Scottish singer Jimmie Macgregor had also been booked for *The Song of the Road*:

Bert Lloyd, lovely man. I was standing beside him when we sang a chorus about the rhythm of the big scrapers – it went 'Dig and Scrape and Load' – but I realised Bert was singing: 'Pig and Ape and Toad'. When we finished the thing, he shrugged and smiled. It really amused me – the idea of these two very eminent men scoring these boyish points off each other.[3]

It was Bert's sense of fun that Norma Waterson felt had usually been overlooked in interviews and articles: 'I've read lots of articles about him and so far there hasn't been one that said about his sense of humour. He had a great sense of humour. He was also a very loving man – a wonderful man.'[4]

When Peggy Seeger first came over to Britain she used to go around the clubs with Bert and MacColl and would occasionally accompany Bert's songs. However, this didn't last too long as Seeger felt that Charlotte wasn't over keen on her playing with Bert and generally 'palling around with him'. She also felt, probably correctly, that Charlotte didn't think much of MacColl. Seeger remembered how in those early days Bert and MacColl would joke around with each other:

They'd be sitting in the pub and Bert would say to Ewan: 'You what?' And Ewan would say: 'Yeah! Yeah! I know all that!' And they'd start arguing with each other at the tops of their voices. I didn't know this routine; I didn't know what was going on. The first time it happened Joe [Lloyd] was with us and he leant over to me and whispered: 'It's okay, just wait'. Then, just when it looked as if they were going to start a fight they'd both collapse in fits of laughter. They were good buddies. Bert had a good sense of humour – he was a funny guy, definitely.[5]

Seeger felt, on the other hand, that Charlotte had little sense of humour, as did Erica Bach, but as Seeger said: 'We often choose our opposites'.

Louis Killen's work on *Song of the Road* came about because Bob Davenport, who had been booked to do the programme, was taken ill. A frantic note was sent up to Killen in Newcastle:

I was working up in the Northeast and then Bob was ill and couldn't do it (although I didn't know this until later). I got a week's notice. I'd just got a job with British Rail, in the catering office up in Newcastle. At the end of three months I'd got my first free rail pass down to Doncaster, and I paid the rest of my way to London. I walked into the club on the Saturday night and Ewan said 'Ah, Louis, been looking all over the place for you. We'd like you to do this radio ballad with us'. I asked him when it started: 'Monday!' So I took immediate sick leave, did the programme with Bert, and Cyril Tawney and the rest of them, went back to Newcastle and got sacked. One of my many firings in the cause of folk music![6]

Both Davenport and Killen were much admired by Bert who used them over the years in numerous recorded and live projects. They both became very influential in the folk revival in different ways. Killen, whom Frankie Armstrong claims as one of her major influences (Bert being another), is a very skilful, thoughtful singer whose subtleties were, and are, much admired by other singers, especially on the ballads. MacColl held him in particularly high regard. Davenport is a bolder, louder singer. His more eclectic repertoire and down-to-earth attitude had been honed in the noisy, convivial atmosphere of working-men's clubs and Irish pubs. It was popularly rumoured on the folk scene that you could tell what key Davenport was singing in by the colour of his neck.

The Radio Ballads were an artistic and critical milestone in the use of newly written 'folk' song and recorded actuality on radio. The Director-General of the BBC, Hugh Carlton-Greene, thought *The Ballad of John Axon* 'the most originally conceived, the most brilliantly executed and the most moving radio programme I've ever heard'. High praise indeed. Similar acclamation came from most of the media critics.

While Parker was casting around for a follow-up to *John Axon*, one of his ideas had been a radio ballad on the whaling industry, which would have been right up Bert's street, but he settled instead on the more mundane building of the London–Yorkshire motorway – the M1.

Parker's plans for a ballad opera entitled *The White-Eye Whale*, written by Bert with a musical score by Matyas Seiber, was thrown into disarray when Seiber was killed in a motoring accident while on a lecture tour of South Africa in September 1960. Hungarian-born Seiber studied in Budapest under Kodaly, with whom he collected folk songs. He also knew and was influenced by Bartók, whom he championed and promoted in the West after fleeing the Nazis and settling in England in 1933. Like Bert, Seiber also had a gift for languages, so it's not surprising that with such a lot in common the two men became good friends, and worked together on several projects over the years. According to Seiber's daughter, Julia: 'They had a high regard for each other. I can remember several visits to Greenwich, and seeing Bert and Daddy working together – the Yugoslav and Hungarian folk songs in particular. I also remember them working in our garden at Caterham, on the lawn outside the music room.'[7]

In Bert's black foolscap notebook for 1961 he wrote the title: *The Silver Harpoon* – A Radio Opera. Text by A.L. Lloyd. Music by Edward Williams. In the same notebook is some of the script plus various whaling notes and his rewrite of the whaling song 'The Coast of Peru' beginning 'Come all you bold catchermen ...'. By February 1962, despite several discussions between Bert, Parker and composer Edward Williams, who had been brought on board following Seiber's death, no progress had been made on what Parker was still calling *The White-Eye Whale*. So, in a letter to the BBC Copyright Department (26 February) Parker decided to put the programme on ice, indefinitely.

A year later, in April 1963, Reggie Smith was attempting to persuade the BBC to produce the ballad opera now officially entitled *The Silver Harpoon*, written by Bert with music to be composed by Williams, who was very excited by the project but had not actually written anything. The BBC felt that, as well as being misogynistic, it was an inappropriate treatment of the subject for radio, and also that Williams, whose main work had been in film music, was not well-known enough as a composer. They turned it down.

Bert's descriptions of the flensing process, in which he described the whale as 'looking like an upturned frog' was deemed to be too redolent of schoolboy torture for Third Programme listeners. Williams said that Bert tried unsuccessfully to raise some funding to produce the opera and, disappointed, eventually gave up on it. Williams also tried to resurrect the project:

> Bert was always hoping we'd have got it off the ground. I had a copy of it, and tried to sell it to a radio producer down here [southwest of England] while Bert was still alive in the late '70s, but he turned it down because he said it was very sexist. I never got round to doing a score because I'm not very good at doing things before I'm paid. I need the guilt feeling from somebody having put down money![8]

And that was as far as the project got for some thirty years, until fiddler Dave Swarbrick got hold of a copy of the script, with a plan to compose a score for it and to record it:

> It's an astonishingly colourful vibrant work. Poetic. It's beautiful. Tony Engles wanted it for Topic. He was thrilled to bits with the idea and wanted to stage it for Topic's anniversary in 2009. Then he couldn't get any backing because it's un-PC. I'm quite happy about that because I think it should just be an album, and if anyone wants to stage it after that it's up to them. So long as I'm not involved.[9]

Bert's script might yet see the light of day.

Despite the publicity and acclaim the Radio Ballads received, all the essential elements – songs, music, recorded speech and sound effects – had been used before in programmes on which both Bert and MacColl had worked over the years for producers such as Bridson, Pudney, Cleverdon and the young and feisty Olive Shapley. Shapley, a communist, worked with Wilfred Pickles, MacColl and Joan Littlewood on BBC North Region programmes. She saw the potential advantages of the early outside broadcast recording vans, and developed, with the approval of the communist BBC North Region Programme Director Archie Harding, a style of actuality documentary programme in which she went out and interviewed real people, talking about their lives in their regional dialects. No mediation. No BBC actors reading from scripts and adopting working-class speech. Shapley produced groundbreaking 1930s programmes such as *Canal Journey*, for which she recorded men and women working on the Leeds–Liverpool canal. Other programmes included: *Night Journey* (the world of long-distance lorry drivers), *Homeless People* and *Miners' Wives*; keeping her linking commentary to a minimum, she let them tell their story in their own words. As the perceptive Georgina Boyes commented in *The Imagined Village:* '[The Radio Ballads] ... owed far more to pre-war North Region programmes than MacColl ever chose to acknowledge.'

Shapley's ground-breaking programmes, with some music and songs added, weren't a thousand miles away from Parker's 1950s idea for a vernacular ballad opera. This idea developed into something more exciting when he first got together with MacColl and they began listening to the rich, colourful language of the railwaymen (of which they recorded forty hours-worth). They decided to incorporate the language and images into the specially written songs which, inter-spliced with actuality and atmospheric music would carry the narrative along. Admittedly, not every railwayman, miner, taxi driver, fisherman or factory worker was an undiscovered Langland or Shakespeare, but there were many whose speech MacColl found to be: 'Full of the same kinds of symbols and verbal nuances which inform the ballads and folk songs of our tradition, and it was obvious we could not rewrite it without reducing it and falsifying it.'

So it was MacColl's, and later MacColl and Seeger's, job to convert some of this graphic language into script and song. Certain of the songs worked better than others and took on a life outside the programmes. Particularly popular were the songs written for *The Travelling People* which, as MacColl said in *Journeyman*, was a perfect radio ballad subject: 'Apart from any other considerations, the Travelling People are now among the chief carriers of the English and Scottish folk song traditions, a fact which made the choice of musical idiom a natural one. As custodians of many of the classic folk tales they number in their ranks storytellers of great skill. It was from these that the programme was to take its pace and overall style.' Two of the songs, 'Thirty-foot Trailer' and 'Freeborn Man', have been picked up by southern English Travellers and are occasionally heard at fairs or social evenings among the country and western favourites as nostalgic reminders of a vanished age.

The multi-layering of the spoken word, song, music, and sound effects was, in the surprisingly primitive 1950s BBC, a complex and expensive production job, permanently teetering on the edge of disaster. Parker would have understood Head of Music Robert Ponsonby's remark (recorded in Humphrey Carpenter's *The Envy of the World*) that 'working for the Corporation is like having sexual congress with an elephant – there's no pleasure involved, and no result of one's efforts for two years'.

Bert, who wasn't involved in the writing of the Radio Ballads, was ambivalent about the literary and poetic merit of the songs: 'I felt that with the radio ballads the melodies were often very superior to the words. Some smashing melodies but the words were often too directly factual. There wasn't enough lift to them.'

This was his opinion of most contemporary songwriting on the folk scene:

They're generally very humdrum in words but often rather good in melody. The words are often too literal ... never really take off. They're little bits of journalism rather than the sort of thing that shakes the heart. Frequently too full of message and the message is a directly expressed one which one automatically agrees with, and nod's one's head in agreement, but is not, perhaps, as deeply taken as many traditional songs and ballads can take one.

Bert acknowledged that it was frequently hard to pin down what it was about some songs that caught the imagination.

You have songs that have vitalised nations and it's bloody hard to see why! How does it happen that the 'Internationale' means so much to so many – dreadful set of words, trudgy melody, and yet, to many people, to Spanish workers, for instance, it's a clarion call?

I must confess I seldom encounter contemporary songs that really excite me. The connection to folklore is usually pretty remote. If they do remind you of folklore it's like meeting a relative of an old friend, but a pretty distant relative like as not.[10]

LIFE AFTER LOMAX

'Folk music is the vacant lot squeezed in between the fields of musicology and anthropology.'

Charles Seeger

From Bert's openly critical remarks about John and Alan Lomax and the issue of copyright in *Sing Out!* magazine, and his disdainful comment to Vic Gammon – 'Alan is a good journalist' – when asked for his opinion on Lomax's book *Folk Song Style and Culture*, one gets the impression that he was less enamoured of Alan Lomax than MacColl, Seeger and Shirley Collins – Lomax's lover for his last year in Britain.

For all the undoubted effort that Lomax had put into the second folk revival in his genuine desire to see Britain flower again as the singing 'Bonny Bunch of Roses', he had also commandeered a lot of radio and television airtime for his folk music programmes. Between 1951 and 1958 Lomax made over thirty radio and TV programmes and series for the BBC, which funded much of his European stay. As early as February 1951 he'd appeared in a two-part ballad series for G.D. Bridson (with whom he'd worked in New York on *The Martins and the Coys*), and on 13 February he started his own first series – three programmes entitled *Adventures in Folk Song*, looking at his work in the US for the Library of Congress. So, unlike the others, Bert's emotion was probably more relief than sorrow when Lomax finally left London in July 1958 and headed back to the States, having successfully avoided the worst of the 1950s McCarthyite witch hunts. Once he was out of the way, Bert could get on with establishing himself as Britain's leading folk music broadcaster.

On Christmas Day 1958 he presented his programme: *All Bells in Paradise: A Programme of English Traditional Carols*. It was produced by his old friend Douglas Cleverdon, who had been responsible for many of Bert's earlier classic music programmes such as *The Folk Music of Bulgaria* (January 1956), *The Folk Music of Rumania* (November 1956), *The Seeds of Love* (September

1957), and *The Origins of Polyphony* (February 1958). They'd first met during the Second World War in London where they had mutual friends in the BBC, the MOI, and the various arty pubs and drinking clubs of Soho and Fitzrovia. Cleverdon (1903–87) was the epitome of the Oxbridge-educated BBC features producer of the inter-war years. From 1922 to 1926 he read Greats at Oxford – Greek and Roman language, literature and philosophy, that wonderful cerebral combination which, in practical terms, prepared you for very little beyond teaching, lecturing, the Civil Service (the gentleman's club in which a Classical education was considered a good training for running the Empire), or a producer's job at the BBC. As the writer Peter Clayton said: 'Cleverdon and the original Third [BBC Third Programme] were naturals for each other. The Third, with its brave resolve to cater for intellectual minorities and to hell with the figures, was the perfect environment for Douglas Cleverdon with his concern only for quality.'[11]

As Cleverdon explained, a Classical discipline had helped him in his BBC researches because he had been trained to always go back to an original authority, to the source material. He was certainly no fool, yet like so many of the university-trained intellectuals that the autodidact Bert encountered during his life, he was, if not exactly in awe, certainly very impressed with Bert's seemingly all-encompassing knowledge and skills as a writer and broadcaster:

> Bert was absolutely reliable; he got things done on time, and knew so much. He was very easy to work with and never temperamental. Always very friendly to the people we met. Never patronising, very intelligent. Not an intellectual in the unpleasant sense. No side, always in accord due to background. He remained a devout communist, even after Hungary. He had a very steady faith in Communism. You just took it for granted that Bert was in the Party. He wasn't one of the great drunks, like some BBC employees, just a thoroughly nice chap.[12]

During his undergraduate years Cleverdon had circulated on the fringes of the Bloomsbury set and became a friend of the artist and art critic Roger Fry. Fry painted the sign for the specialist bookshop that Cleverdon opened in Bristol on leaving Oxford in 1926. He also became a publisher of special edition fine books. It was during the 1930s slump that he got involved with the BBC, doing some work for Western Region radio and in 1939 landing a junior producer's job on Children's Hour. He recorded Maude Karpeles' memories of Sharp's singers and, as we saw earlier, Louie Hooper, and the Marshfield Mummers. Following the bombing of his bookshop during the war he remained with the BBC Features Department for the next thirty years, initially under Bert's friend Jack Dillon. As well as many of Bert's major programmes Cleverdon was also responsible for many other important radio features.

His Albany Street home, near Broadcasting House, was a meeting place for other producers, writers and actors, popular as much for his wife Nest's cooking as for Cleverdon's conversation, as was noted in her obituary:

Nest cooked meals at all hours for them. Any day Richard Burton, Frank Duncan, Carleton Hobbs (a special favourite), Judi Dench or Derek Jacobi might be there trying out parts. Nest darned David Jones's vests, Flanders and Swann tried out new songs, David Gascoyne and Henry Reed agonized, John Betjeman and Stevie Smith sang *Hymns A & M*, with Nest (who knew all the words by heart) at the piano, and Dylan Thomas drank.[13]

And Bert enthused over his latest field trip to Romania or Albania, discussed proposals for drama documentaries and folk song series or planned concerts. For several years Cleverdon was also the Director of the Stratford-Upon-Avon Poetry Festival, and booked Bert to appear two or three times.

16

The Folk Revival

As far as folk music is concerned, nobody has the tablets from Mount Zion.

Eric Winter

A folk song in a book is like a photograph of a bird in flight.

Charles Seeger

The 'urban folk revival' ... was characterized by an eclectic, multigenre repertoire, reflecting a political stance of internationalism, to which English rural song contributed only one strand.

David Atkinson (*Journal of American Folklore* 114, 2001)

By the end of the 1950s, the seed-bed of the revival, Bert and the rest of the gang could look around with a certain degree of self-satisfaction. The infrastructure that Bert had felt was necessary for a national regeneration of people's music – clubs, concerts, festivals, records, radio and TV coverage – was in place. Although the effects of it varied in different parts of the British Isles (it was less in need of 'revival' in Scotland and Ireland), the folk movement that they'd envisaged and nurtured at the beginning of the decade was up and running – a musical juggernaut gathering momentum, which would ultimately prove to be beyond the powers of the English Folk Dance and Song Society and the left-wing song revivalists to control. It was running in two or three different lanes that, unlike the lines drawn to demonstrate perspective, would never end up meeting on some distant musical ecumenical horizon.

Bert, MacColl and Isla Cameron (who once modestly declared 'I hesitate to call myself the High Priestess of Folk'), three of the most influential performers on the London scene, which at that time was the epicentre of the folk revival, gradually dropped American material from their public performances, slowly bringing in more and more British songs and ballads. This, allied to their recordings, helped wean a growing number of young people off skiffle and American music into the embrace of British folk song.

We should perhaps remember that the traditional folk songs being pushed by Bert and others, wonderful though many of them were, did not represent the complete musical picture of popular traditional culture in Great Britain in the nineteenth and twentieth centuries. This was never Bert's, nor other people's, intention. Everyone seems to have been bent on reviving, rescuing and/or making museum pieces of very selective parts of our folk culture. The English revival, contrived, promoted and peopled by urban outsiders with romantic agendas, inexorably drifted further and further away from any roots it had, as Bert pointed out:

If an English person is interested and involved in musical folklore, it is invariably as a visitor to the tradition [or a part of the tradition], not as a resident within that tradition. His use of the traditional repertory [or part of the traditional repertory] is more and more audience-oriented, until, in modern terminology, folk music becomes yet another branch of popular commercially diffused music, in which the actual composition may be folkloric, but the treatment in performance may be that of modern popular professional style, e.g. electronic treatment of 'classic' folk ballads in the manner of the Fairport Convention or the late Steeleye Span.

The 'traditional repertory' that he was talking about was limited to songs and ballads prescribed by Sharp, Child and the rest, such as 'The Banks of the Sweet Primroses', 'Sovay, Sovay', 'Whaling in Greenland', 'The Gower Wassail', 'The Outlandish Knight', 'Barbara Allen' etc. It did not include the rest of the traditional singer's musical baggage of hymns, music-hall, pleasure garden, parlour, light operatic and national songs, although many so-called 'folk songs' had their origins in these genres. Universally popular songs, such as 'Knees Up Mother Brown', which were passed on orally as well as by record, print and the early radio, were of no interest.

Apart from his quibbles over the lack of interest amongst those he called the 'great collectors' with regard to industrial song and erotic song, and his natural antipathy towards the bourgeois middle-class song enthusiasts, Bert had no real disagreement with the selective and culturally atypical people's song and ballad canon dished up as the folk's music and printed in the *Journal* of the English Folk Dance and Song Society and elsewhere. Bert, like they, could tell a 'folk song' when he met one; it didn't have the 'soapy feel of the counterfeit coin'. What we now generally recognise as 'folk song' obviously existed but rarely in solitary splendour in an individual singer's or a community's repertory, a fact that was scarcely, if ever, commented on. Vic Gammon spelt this out:

> The only answer can be that he [Bert] so shared the Sharpian notion that folk song existed as a pure category that questions like this were ruled out of order. To Lloyd a folk song was something that had particular qualities, it could be distinguished by comparison with that which was not a folk song which did not have these qualities. He certainly held a notion of the deterioration of tradition, the urban songs of the 1820s and after being described as a 'miserable and undistinguished sort of thing' compared with what had been produced before.[1]

At times, it's difficult to know quite what Bert liked and disliked, and how he came to his decisions on what he considered 'folk song'. He could be contradictory and subject to blind spots, as, for example, his contention that it's what you do with an instrument that determines its folkloric quality rather than the instrument *per se*. However he could not see any merit in the recorder whatever it played, but was happy enough with Richard Thompson's electric guitar. International Brigaders in the Spanish Civil War had no such problems with the recorder; Bill Alexander remembered hearing their popular song 'Hold the Fort' sung to the 'unlikely accompaniment of recorder and spoons while marching to the cookhouse for meals'.

In his article 'The Tradition – What is it?' in the first Keele Folk Festival programme Bert admits:

> Being mostly transmitted orally, it doesn't circulate in set form but undergoes various transformations which are the sign of its 'folk' character. At the same time, hundreds of folk song texts in millions of copies have circulated in printed form (broadsides, etc.) among the bearers of the tradition so this oral business is but relative. Since it has generally been created independently of the world of bookish arts it presents, especially in its music, certain essential and definable differences from conventional 'author-made' compositions. Hmm. As usual with such ventures, this attempt at definition has more holes than a colander.

With so many holes in the 'authentic folk song' argument a lot of it comes down to the fact that for Bert, and others, folk song was what they chose it to be. As Vic Gammon points out, despite the contrary evidence of village bands, choirs, West Gallery church music and the several songs sent to her by Samuel Willett written out in parts (including a version of the 'Farmer's Boy' which he insisted 'people always sang in three parts'), collector Lucy Broadwood could ignore the harmonies when she published her folk songs and describe these same people as 'simple music lovers, unaccustomed to harmony, and therefore the more critically alive to the essentials of fine melody'.[2] A monodic image that Bert countered in his 1954 EFDSS *Journal* article on the Copper Family singing style. Although he does seem to suggest that solo unaccompanied singing is perhaps more authentic: 'Their repertoire is mainly made up of traditional pieces which have been current in their family for several generations. Individually, their manner of singing is the true folk singer's manner.'

Even though he didn't say so Bert, seemingly, didn't think much of some of the songs found in the Copper Family repertoire, even if they had 'been current in their family for several generations'. Partly, no doubt, because the idea of conservative, contented (servile?), rural agricultural workers didn't sit well with his vision of a déclassé peasantry in revolt against enclosures, unscrupulous employers and a privileged squirearchy, and partly because he considered a number of these songs (such as 'When Spring Comes On') to be more 'art' song than 'folk'. Referring to a version collected by the Hammond brothers and published in the 1968 *Folk Music Journal* he remarked in a rather contemptuous note: 'The text is characteristic enough of many idyllic pieces of educated amateur poetry that are not folkloric, though occasionally they are attached to good folk tunes. In this case, the text has no such benefit; the tune seems to me as artificial as the words.' In reply, Frank Purslow pointed out that 'The song *is* obviously a minor art production – but so are a large majority of what we call English "folk songs".' The fact that the song, and many like it, had been widely collected (Alfred Williams found many of the Coppers' songs in Wiltshire and Oxfordshire), and was obviously very popular with rural singers, including the Coppers, cut little ice with Bert, it didn't fit in with his idea of 'folkloric song'.

Tony Green, of Leeds University, agreed with Dave Harker that interest by Bert, the EFDSS and most other folk song luminaries, in the song-culture of 'real people in a real place at a particular time' was

> still conspicuously absent from our scholarship. It is still apparently possible to regard 'The Collier's Rant' as a more significant and 'genuine' example of working-class culture than 'Don't Go Down the Mine, Dad', despite the incontrovertible fact that ten miners sing the latter for every one that sings the former. Weight of numbers is not the only question, of course, but it is either stupid or dishonest to ignore it.[3]

Despite Bert's disregard for Neumann's *Rezeptionstheorie*, he was well aware (if not necessarily happy) that many fine, well known, 'folk songs' had actually undergone this descent through the social strata. Interestingly, though, rather than ending up as some form of inferior musical detritus, the 'folk songs' are invariably superior to the often verbose originals we find in early garlands, play texts and pleasure garden songsters. With the verbiage removed through oral transmission and popular print, the results are often smooth and polished. With so much textual and musical interaction across the whole strata of society over several hundred years, it's a brave man or woman, indeed, who can be dogmatic about what is and what isn't folk song.

During the 1950s much of the 'folk song' repertory was being accompanied in the clubs and coffee bars by guitar and banjo, following the lead of such role models as ex-army mule breaker Steve Benbow, some of whose most popular songs came from Bert. Benbow had accompanied Bert before he acquired Alf Edwards and Dave Swarbick (who one time played with the Ian Campbell Folk Group). Others taking the guitar and banjo route included Jimmie Macgregor, John Hasted, Peggy Seeger and Shirley Collins, and younger enthusiasts such as Martin Carthy who, after having spent months perfecting such iconic guitar pieces as Elizabeth Cotton's two-finger picked 'Freight Train' – and the somewhat less iconic 'Your Baby 'As Gorn Darn the Plughole' – underwent a conversion when in 1958 he heard the old Norfolk fisherman Sam Larner perform at the Ballads and Blues club.

Carthy would go on to become one of Bert's most successful and committed protégés as well as one of the most innovative guitarists performing traditional British material. It was to be a few years before such virtuoso players as Nic Jones, Martin Simpson, Chris Foster, Clive Woolf and Dick Gaughan caught up with Carthy and developed the now-widespread 'traditional' British guitar style (with its roots in American blues). Carthy was destined to spend countless hours on railway platforms around the country over the next fifty years; the corollary of his loyalty and commitment to the folk club scene. As Swarbrick recalled, many of the songs associated with the Swarbrick/Carthy duo came originally from Bert:

Bert was always egging you on to improvise. He'd say, 'This verse now, dear boy, I want you to play whatever you like'. And if you didn't go far enough out on a limb he'd do it again until you did. We used to practice, limited practice, usually in the studios pre-recording. Bert was very keen on me improvising on each verse. First words he ever spoke to me were, 'Try not to do that again.'

When he gave you a new song he'd always tell you a little story about it, where it came from, where he got it, not always, actually, but most of the time, and he'd tell you what time signature it was in. That wasn't important to me, what was important was the melody. I didn't care if it was 13/11 or 7/11 so long as I got the tune, and that pleased him. He was delighted with that attitude because he felt that that was the real way to play folk music. If you've got to start counting two threes and two and a one, or whatever, you're fucked aren't you? But Alf would play from the dots. But there wasn't anybody else and Alf had worked with Bert for a long time before I came on the scene.

But things like 'Sovay' I can't remember Alf playing or 'Byker Hill'. Bert was doing them before Martin and I did them, that's where they came from. I'm sure Martin heard Bert do them, but I'd been doing them with Bert long before I did them with Martin. 'Lovely Nancy', 'Trim-rigged Doxy', 'Byker Hill', 'Sovay', 'Reynardine' – there's a whole list. I did all those with Bert first, and many, many, more. Fifteen or so at least that Martin and I then did, or I took into Fairport [Convention].[4]

It's little known that both Bert and MacColl played guitar, but chose not to in public. Although he was happy to use accompanists, particularly in the early days, Bert was perfectly content to sing unaccompanied, and actually took a pride in being able to capture and hold an audience with just his voice and the power of the songs. John Brunner recalled seeing Bert win over a sceptical skiffle audience with his unaccompanied English songs in 1958 at a Nancy Whiskey club session at the Princess Louise pub:

Bert was brought forward and introduced. He looked thoughtful (in a certain way he had, which one might almost call mischievous, were he not so essentially dignified), and he addressed the audience. 'Well, everyone seems to have been singing American songs, so I'm going to sing some English songs, and they're going to be love songs'. The audience composed itself to listen. One could see an attitude which indicated they were prepared to look politely interested but reserved the right to feel bored. And Bert sang seven bawdy songs in a row. 'My Husband's got no Courage in Him' was the best, and the audience loved it.[5]

During the 1950s folk music moved out of the coffee bars and jazz cellars into an ever-expanding number of folk clubs. Pub landlords the length and breadth of Britain couldn't believe their luck – a new musical craze (as it was seen by many) which found thirsty musicians and audiences looking for places in which to indulge their craving for this alternative and, for then, somewhat subversive music. It was a marriage made in brewery heaven; pubs had cellars full of warm beer (things eventually improved on that front) and upstairs function rooms little used except for the occasional gathering round the watering hole by the Brethren of the Royal Antediluvian Order of Buffaloes (RAOB), and other such male groups. Folk clubs brought drinkers into the pubs, and the pubs provided smoky private rooms where consenting teens and adults could play and listen to folk music, safe from prying ears.

It's an interesting fact that the RAOB, founded in the 1820s by theatre staff, began life in the Harp Tavern, Great Russell Street, London, the same area in which the 1950s folk scene developed. The Order's song was the folk ballad 'Chase the Buffalo' which, according to Brother W.A.C. Hartmann, an Order historian, was hollered out at meetings right up to the beginning of the folk revival: 'The ballad was sung with a considerable amount of enthusiasm at R.A.O.B. lodge meetings as recently as the mid-1950s by many of our more long-serving members.' So the singing of folk songs, or at least one folk song, in rooms over pubs is not such a novelty as we might have thought. And in his book *A Social History of English Music* E.D. Makerness points out, if it needed pointing out, that prior to the opening of the music-halls in the mid-nineteenth century, concerts and popular sing-songs were held in pubs, and, of course, continued until driven out of the bar by the jukebox, fruit machines and changing tastes. It's paradoxical that often when one visits a folk club you walk through the bar, where many of the local 'folk' are drinking and socialising, and retreat upstairs away from the noise and life of the pub to sing to a group of cognoscenti the 'folk songs' that a few years earlier would have been sung in the bar by those very people downstairs.

Bert's 1950 decision to dedicate the rest of his life to the study, collection, performance and promotion of folk music, were aims not dissimilar to those of the English Folk Dance and Song Society, which declared its principal objectives as the preservation, promotion, and teaching of English folk dance and song, to make them known and to encourage the practice of them in their traditional forms. To be fair to the EFDSS, for all its air of Edwardian middle-class gentility and its hordes of jolly-hockey-stick-type spinster regional staff, volunteers and members, it was very active in the promotion of folk dance, though less so song except, sadly, in school. 'Dashing Away with the Smoothing Iron' and 'B.I.N.G.O' sung around the inevitable school piano did little to foster an enthusiasm for folk song among the young. It was Society Director Douglas Kennedy's worthy aim to 'take the living spark of tradition and fan it into flame'.

All over England, District Committees, regional representatives and enthusiastic dancers and singers ran festivals, concerts, dances and courses. In 1958 Society Districts put on over seventy courses and forty-three festivals in addition to events run at the London headquarters and regular dance meetings. So there was an already existing folk scene, a relic of Sharp's heyday, but it wasn't the sort of scene that Bert had in mind and was certainly not geared towards the working classes, as he pointed out in *Education* (May 1959), when he summed up the differences between the first and second folk revivals:

The revival that was produced and enriched by the work of the great collectors, Sharp, Hammond, Vaughan Williams and others, found its response chiefly among middle-class people. It led to folk song being taught in schools; but because folk song is taught in schools, that does not mean that folk traditions are continued. Youngsters leaving school found no use for folk song, had nothing to hook it on to.

Perhaps the trouble lay partly in the choice of song and the manner of teaching. Whatever the reason, folk song remained the preserve of a handful of devoted specialists and a circle of polite people ready to accept 'the trifles of the countryside' provided they were fitted with artistic accompaniment and sung in something approaching concert style.

He went on in his contrasting of the two revivals:

The present revival springs from different sources and affects rather different people. The newfound fans of British tradition, who have come to it of their own accord by way of jazz, American folk song and skiffle, are of all sorts. As a rule the song that catches their ear is not the song sung with the rather mask-like aloofness of the best country singers, and still less the song performed in the manner of the concert platform. They are attracted to listen to, and to perform, folk songs in an adapted style, a style containing many half-digested Americanisms, but a style they can somehow relate to their own needs and experiences.[6]

In 1953 two concerts at Cecil Sharp House had pointed up the differences between the old formal EFDSS, carefully planned, concert-platform presentation of folk music and a new iconoclastic, informal style, described admiringly by Douglas Kennedy as an evening of 'raw folk songs'. The former was a performance of *Music from the Countryside* by Society stalwarts Nan and Brian Fleming-Williams, Jean Forsyth and Pat Shuldham-Shaw. A typical Society audience was carried enthusiastically along. The other was an event announced simply as *An Evening of Folk Song*, during which Bert, MacColl, Seamus Ennis and the Kentucky singer Jean Ritchie sat around informally swapping songs, tunes and children's rhymes. As *English Dance and Song* (*ED&S*) *reported*: 'Here songs and even skipping rhymes were exchanged between singers who had learned to sing in the traditional manner. What programme there was had been sketched out over coffee beforehand and filled in as the singers' blood warmed. Nothing quite like it had been heard before at Cecil harp House.'

The August/September magazine printed a letter from an enthusiastic Society member lauding 'the informal ceilidh' which he said: 'Should have demonstrated to all those present the superiority of unaccompanied, unedited versions of folk songs over the edited accompanied versions which have been published or recorded.'

Following on, as it did, from the concert reports the implication was that the ceilidh presentation and style of singing was superior to the standard folk song recital. As the 'Folk Songs Raw and Civilised' article wasn't signed, it's impossible to know whether Kennedy, the Society's director, was rocking the boat or whether it was the *ED&S* editor, Sara Jackson. Either way, a wind of change blew through Cecil Sharp House that April evening. But it was to be a number of years before the EFDSS old guard, led by Maude Karpeles, who was intent on defending the status quo, and revival folkies found any common ground.

In October 1957 Douglas Kennedy and others, having realised that the Society had to buck up its ideas concerning song, put on the first English Folk Music Festival. In *ED&S* (January/February 1957) Kennedy explained that: 'The purpose of this Festival is to bring together some at least of the many singers and players who are eager to hear other styles and techniques and to share in the enjoyment of a simple yet subtle art.'

Unfortunately, instead of placing the Society at the centre of the song revival, it proved just how out of touch it was with traditional song and singers. Part of the festival was a singing competition in which elderly rural singers were stuck on stage in front of an unsympathetic adjudicating panel to battle for a place in the evening concert against a disparate mix of revival performers. Of the adjudicators only Peter Kennedy appears to have any idea of how to judge, if judge one must, traditional singers. Dr Sydney Northcote, Music Advisor for the Carnegie UK Trust, and ex-Guildhall lecturer, drew down the wrath of Eric Winter in a critical article in the December issue of *Sing*. 'It looked at one time', wrote Winter, 'as if Dr Northcote was going to rap on his glass as if to say he would take the other five or so verses as read.' And he was accused of saying various rude things 'to some of Britain's finest traditional singers, venerable old gentlemen who should have been treated with more respect'.

Later Fred (aka Karl) and Betty Dallas and Mervyn Plunkett queried the competence of the adjudicators to judge folk music, and declared the festival a fiasco, which had done the Society a great disservice. Another of the judges was Francis Collinson who had in fact collected songs from many rural singers in the southeast of England, including the Coppers, for the BBC's 1940s radio programme *Country Magazine*, so one would have expected him to be more sympathetic to the needs and singing style of the traditional contestants.

The Dallases also questioned the inclusion of non-traditional singers in the concert while 'many fine traditional singers who got nowhere in the competitions' were excluded – Scan Tester (solo instrument) and George Townshend (unaccompanied folk song) only received 'merits'. In its festival review, the *Daily Worker* felt it was too early to judge the folk song revival;

many of the singers were not yet in command of their instruments or their audiences.

Following the event, Reg Hall who, along with Mervyn Plunkett, had been involved in ferrying a group of traditional Sussex singers up to Cecil Sharp House for the day, wrote a critical letter to the Society in which he described the atmosphere in Cecil Sharp House as: 'A cross between a mortuary and an approved school [Hall, a probation officer, would know all about that]. Every attempt to liven up the proceedings was crushed ruthlessly.'

Bert, who sang on the evening concert, felt that the standard of the singing of traditional songs by the revivalist competitors generally left a lot to be desired. He criticised the tendency to imitate revival singers rather than traditional performers, and claimed to have heard 'a lady MacColl and a male Isla Cameron'. He concluded that if those revival singers who showed such 'skill and assiduity in impersonating' transferred 'half that doggedness towards creating a personal performance, we should all gain'. He added that on the debit side was 'the tendency of some adjudicators to judge folk singers' performances according to the standards of the concert platform ... when listening to folk song performers, genuine or revival, adjudicators have to be looking for a different set of artistic virtues from those immediately recognised by the singing teacher.'

On the other hand, Helen Kennedy, who was a very positive person and the director's wife, loyally declared that on the whole it had been 'a wonderful day and the evening concert [compered by Bob Copper] was grand'. And the Cornishman Charlie Bates, whose accordion-accompanied 'Padstow May Song' brought the house down, said it was just like being at home! So, a curate's egg, but deemed good enough in parts by the Society to justify further festivals.

After the third festival (October 1959) the Festival Organising Committee was dissolved due to (according to *Ethnic* magazine) the three-cornered fights between the neo-Victorians, the city-billies and the traditionalists. In their Autumn 1959 editorial the *Ethnic* editors, two of whom were on the committee, wrote: 'We believe that the publications of the details of this struggle would constitute a damning expose and indictment of the present policies of the EFDSS.' They pointed out that some people had 'irreverently' suggested that the festivals were really an opportunity for the concert-type singers to realise just how dreadful the country singers actually were!

The details of the 'struggle' weren't published, and eventually a new festival committee was set up which, at various times, included Bert, Avril Dankworth, Bob Rundle, Pat Shaw, Nan Fleming-Williams, Jean Forsyth, Sydney Carter and Eric Winter, and things gradually improved as the Society became more involved with the revival and more revival singers entered the portals of Cecil Sharp House and became involved in the Society. John Foreman 'The Broadside King' and authority on cockney song and folklore, and Redd Sullivan and Martin Winsor spring to mind for their popular Cecil Sharp House London events which helped to push the Society into the twentieth century.

Because of his early connections with folk music scholars in Eastern Europe where the changes in, and the creation of, musical folklore were widely scientifically studied (as well as being politically manipulated), Bert was interested in and supported innovation within the parameters of what he recognised as 'folk song' – as opposed to music 'with its face turned firmly towards Tin-Pan Alley', of which he had little interest. Less dogmatic than MacColl, he was never against change *per se*, as was shown later in their differing attitudes towards folk-rock. He acknowledged that change in folk music was inevitable and irrevocable, both within the folk revival and, more importantly, in the world at large: during the latter half of the twentieth century traditional musical cultures were changing at an unprecedented rate. Whether these changes were for the good or the bad depended on your perspective.

There is frequently a romantic streak in the outsider's view of tradition which abhors change; we want our traditional musicians to be fiddlers not saxophonists, untainted by the electronic age, and living in quaint thatched cottages with outside loos and damp bedrooms, and our customs, songs and rituals to have an ancestry lost in the mists of some earlier, pre-industrial, pre-nuclear Golden Age. Bert was certainly no less 'romantic' when it came to folk music but he understood that it is up to the traditional musicians and their communities to decide their own musical fate; what was appropriate for them in the context of changing social, economic and political conditions. In his 1959 editor's 'farewell' in *Recorded Folk Music* he regretted having to:

> … bow ourselves off the scene just now, at such a fascinating moment in the history of 'home-made' culture. There is a crisis in folk song, a crisis reaching to almost every corner of the world where traditional music is to be found alive. The animal is changing its shape; its behaviour is no longer easily predictable; the watching folklorist at least in our part of the world is filled with dubiety, perplexity, dismay. Even in regions where folk music seemed to have remained unchanged for centuries, suddenly innovation begins to have more prestige than tradition. The once 'classical' balladry of the Appalachians is transformed by hillbilly and rock. In the Balkans the great spring ritual dances become a stage-show rehearsed after factory hours and accompanied by a works band, including saxophones and all. The African cattle-herder adapts the guitar-breaks of Jimmy Rodgers to his native lyre, while his confrere on the Mongolian plains makes up space-travel songs whose melodies ring with the echoes of Soviet march-tunes. It's all very exciting for the folk, all very baffling for the scholars.

Since Bert wrote that, over fifty years ago, change has gone on apace, not least in British and Irish folk music. When we listen to Simon Care, Saul Rose, Andy Cutting, Tim Van Eyken and other contemporary melodeon players, what they are playing is often far removed from what was thought of as melodeon playing back in the 1950s when the role models were players such as George Tremain (North Skelton sword-dancers), Arthur Marshall (Loftus sword-dancers), Percy Brown (Norfolk step-dance musician) or Bob Cann playing tunes like the '7-Step Polka' on some early BBC recordings. Those old social musicians played stripped-down, functional dance music with less use of fancy chords and bass harmonies and quirky time patterns, their sole aim was to get people up and onto the dance floor. Sometimes, as in the case of Percy Brown, the 'wrong' bass buttons would be pumped, but it didn't matter, as long as the *rhythm* was right.

The repertoire, speed and general 'cleverness' of contemporary Irish fiddling is frequently a world away from the regional styles that were heard in the Camden Town pubs of the 1950s. It's now, as Bert said, more and more a music for listening to; geared to the concert hall and recording studio rather than the crossroads set-dance. Bob Davenport is less sanguine than Bert about these changes:

It's the social aspect that's important. Dance places, family places, drink and food places. Traditionally Saturday night is for a good time – it's not an education! From the beginning the way folk clubs developed had little relevance to working-class folk. The tunes were treated as art objects. When songs and tunes are divorced from their natural social setting and are introduced as 'such and such a version' they become art objects that take on art status and all that implies in terms of money value and exploitation.[7]

For Bert the decade that had started so precariously with his departure from the financial security of *Picture Post*, by dint of hard work had ended well. Two particularly important projects at that time were *The Penguin Book of English Folk Songs* (1959) and the dozen issues of Collet's *Recorded Folk Music* that he edited and wrote for between January 1958 and December 1959.

In 1956 Collet's had opened their jazz and folk shop at 70 New Oxford Street under the managership of Marjorie Clayton (folk) and Ray Smith (jazz). Humphrey Lyttelton, with Bert as one of the official guests, performed the opening. For the next seventeen or so years, especially during the 1960s and early 1970s reign of Gill Cook (ably assisted by Hans Fried), Collet's was as much a social centre and source for gossip as it was a provider of popular and arcane folk music – one of the original sources of what eventually became the now prolific world music scene. It was a folk Mecca for any singer living in or passing through London, including such internationally known singers as Pete Seeger, Dick Farina, Tom Paxton, Carolyn Hester and Paul Simon, although in those early days Simon was just an unknown young American singer doing the odd gig through the London City Agency for a few pounds a night.

Many of us impecunious British 1960s singers, who hung around the Soho coffee bars and clubs before sliding inexorably into turning 'professional', had Cook's generosity in buying second-hand albums to thank for a meal in the musicians' restaurant, The Star in Old Compton Street. A copy of Lomax's *Murderers' Home* sold back to Cook for a pound was good for a couple of spaghettis or that strange (now happily rare) dish, spam-fritters and chips. Collet's, as the Folk Shop was known on the folk scene (as if their other shops didn't exist), could become a veritable Tower of Babel on a busy day. When

Bert died, Cook bought up much of his large international record collection. On her death the remaining records passed to her (and Bert Jansch's) son Richard, and since *his* death they have been dispersed to the four corners of the music world.[8]

Eva Collet Reckitt, who inherited a large amount of money from her family (Reckitt & Colman's mustard), was, according to her MI5 report, known as the 'Milch cow' of the Communist Party for her generous contributions to Party funds. Through her connections with the CPGB and Moscow, her Collet's bookshops, along with the Party bookshop and distributor Central Books, had the sole rights on publications and records from behind the Iron Curtain. Records from all over the USSR (initially housed in Collet's Russian Shop) and nearly forty other national song traditions, including China, helped fill up the racks in the new folk shop. Added to these were speech records in various languages, recordings from the Bolshoi Theatre, classical Russian operas and the recorded works of Bertolt Brecht. As Thomas Russell, a one-time Folk Shop employee, recalled, Bert was 'enthusiastic about the opening of a shop specialising in folk music recordings', but was: '... critical of the meagre and often inaccurate information contained on the imported records or in the catalogues which went with them. At that time, the titles on most of the records were in the original languages, and the Cyrillic characters of the Russian language were an obstacle for record buyers.' As Russell went on to explain, this meant that folk enthusiasts had to take most of the recordings on trust. It was eventually decided that under Bert's editorship Collet's would publish a bi-monthly magazine that would provide 'a fuller and more accurate background to the whole field of folk music in general and to records imported by Collet's in particular'.

Recorded Folk Music – A Review of British and Foreign Folk Music was England's first (and last?) serious wide-ranging folk music magazine; serious in intent, catholic in taste, written by expert authorities and renowned musicians, and eschewing the cult of 'folk' personality. Bert commissioned ground-breaking articles by such authorities on British folk music, jazz and world musics as Peter Kennedy, Paul Oliver, Matyas Seiber, Alexis Korner, Eric Hobsbawm (a jazz enthusiast and jazz critic for the *New Statesman* as well as a historian), Zoltan Kodaly, Manuel Lazareno, David Rycroft (on the new South African township music that twenty-five years later would be the inspiration for Paul Simon's *Graceland*) and Deban Bhattacharya. However, the musicological core of the magazine was Bert's wide-ranging, highly readable bi-monthly articles with titles such as: 'So You Are Interested in Folk Music?', 'American Folk Song: The Present Situation', 'Rumanian Folk Music: In Reality and on Disc', 'Ethno-musicology and Edmundo Ross', 'Yugoslav Folk Music on Disc', 'The Street Singers of the French Revolution', 'How is Russian Folk Song Today?' and 'New Light on the Gypsy Musician'.

These articles, together with knowledgeable reviews of new records and overviews of the recorded music of various countries, made it essential reading for anyone with more than a passing interest in folk music. Unfortunately, it was, as with so much else in Bert's life, ahead of its time. The readership, if enthusiastic, was at that time relatively small, and at the end of the second year, before the folk and world music boom came along, Collet's decided to call it a day. In the December 1959 issue of *RFM* Bert said a rueful farewell:

This is the final issue of *Recorded Folk Music*. In these days, the life of a specialised journal is a hard battle, and perhaps we have been lucky to survive for two years. It would be pleasant to think that our appearance, short as it was, has been valuable, and that we leave our readers knowing more than they knew before about the complex and ill-understood matters of musical folklore. And now, readers, goodbye. I hope we meet again sometime, through the columns of some other, more successful, folk music review.

Success can be measured in myriad ways, and Bert's editorship of *Recorded Folk Music* was a journalistic and musicological success, it would have been icing on the cake had there been a large enough audience to support it. And, yes, anyone who read Bert's farewell message would almost certainly have met up with him again in countless magazines and journals over the following years, and would have been continually inspired and informed.

A longer-lived, seminal folk song publication was *The Penguin Book of English Folk Songs*, edited by Bert and Ralph Vaughan Williams. Bert first mooted the idea in October 1955 in a letter to Douglas Kennedy:

Dear Douglas, I would like to put an idea to you. There seems some demand, particularly from young people, for a handy pocket-sized selection of English folk songs, similar in format to the pocket edition of Burl Ives' songbook and other popular American compilations approximately of Penguin size. The demand seems to be for the kind of songs which match or surpass the good American songs in beauty and wit. The preference, in my experience, is for the songs to be printed as melody-lines only, with an indication of guitar chords.

Now, it occurs to me that in the volumes of the Society's Journal, there are a vast number of magnificent songs more or less hidden away from the general reader. Might it not be worth considering a popular selection of songs from the Journal, chosen with the preferences of today's young people in mind (I mean the Josh White and Burl Ives following, for instance).

If you think it's a good idea, I would be glad if you would put it before the Publications Committee for discussion. And if it is approved, I would be prepared for my name to be considered among the candidates for editorship, though I shan't be at all grieved if someone else does it.

Of course, the idea of compiling a songbook from versions at present only to be found in the *Journal* may have occurred to you all before. In which case my apologies.[9]

The idea was enthusiastically taken up by the Society and eventually resulted in the Penguin songbook, the Introduction to which begins: 'An old Suffolk labourer with a fine folk song repertory and a delicate, rather gnat-like voice, once remarked: "I used to be reckoned a good singer before these here *tunes* came in".'

This modest collection was arguably the best 3s 6d-worth of music to be published in 1959. Juliet Renny, a young freelance artist, designed its blue-striped iconic cover, with the broadside woodcut-style illustrations. It was, and remains to this day, a must-have book for performers of English traditional song, larger in ambition and quality than many collections twice its size, yet small enough to slip into a pocket or guitar-case. It was a pity that when the EFDSS republished the collection in 2003 under the title of *Classic English Folk Songs* they abandoned the original period cover design. However, the copyright on title and design remained with Penguin after the contents reverted back to the EFDSS. We should be grateful to the Socity for keeping this fine collection in print. It's a cornucopia of song, a seemingly inexhaustible source of material, as Martin Carthy found over the years: '[Bert's book] is probably the single most significant contribution made to the folk revival. It is in no way dated, and it continues to challenge the notion that folk music is easy; there are tunes in there that have taken me 25 years to come to terms with and material I once rejected as rubbish I am now singing.'

The songs were selected by Vaughan Williams and Bert from the two thousand or so musical items that had appeared in the *Journal of the Folk Song Society* and its continuation the *Journal of the English Folk Dance and Song Society* but which had not been published outside the covers of the journals. Restricted, as they were, to just seventy songs, they decided to leave out occupational and seasonal pieces in the hope that there might be a follow-up volume. We're still waiting for it. Vaughan Williams died in August 1958 just before the book went to press, leaving Bert to decide on the final presentation of the tunes, which he elected to transpose to finish on G or D to enable easier tune comparison, similar to continental practice.

The idea that the average folk fan or singer would bother, or be able, to make comparative analysis of melodies was perhaps crediting them with more dedication and musical skill than many possessed at that time. In 1974, when American folklorist Kenneth Goldstein conducted an informal survey amongst British revival singers, he found that less than 30 per cent could read music. The Lancashire singer Bernard Wrigley, whom Bert dubbed the 'Bolton Bullfrog,' recalled his own early attempts at music reading from *The Penguin Book of English Folk Songs*:

It was 1966 and Dave [Brooks] and I were about to leave school. Apart from being excited about that, we were to sing at the Liverpool Folk Festival in the Bluecoat Chambers. The event was not unlike a knockout competition, where performers sang in the afternoon and, if lucky, would be selected to perform in the evening concert, an event traditionally recorded by the EFDSS for release on an LP of the same name. As if that were not enough, one of the judges on the panel was A.L. Lloyd. He was revered from afar by us, since he had edited (along with Ralph Vaughan Williams) *The Penguin*

Book of English Folk Songs. This had been our bible for obtaining great songs. We liked to call it the *English Book of Penguin Folk Songs*, and it had been our key to unlocking the treasure trove of English folk music.

To our delight, Bert liked our performance of 'The Whale-catchers'. He asked us where we'd got that particular tune. We thought he was being silly, for it was obviously from the Penguin book. When we reminded him, he said 'No, that's a different tune'. It was then that we realised how poor we were at working out written music! At least he liked the variation.[10]

Bert would have appreciated that example of the 'folk process' as a demonstration of the protean nature of folk music.

Bert's daughter Caroline clearly remembers Vaughan Williams's visits to Greenwich whilst he and her father were working on the book: 'I have an image in my mind of Ralph Vaughan Williams and my dad in the sitting room of our house in Greenwich many years ago. Vaughan Williams is sitting very still by an open door leading out into the garden, and dad is busily moving around with a secret smile sorting papers into piles on a table. There is a quiet air of excitement.' Unfortunately, Ursula Vaughan Williams had nothing at all concerning the Penguin book amongst her husband's correspondence. We do know, however, from their joint introduction, that they were quite happy to use 'the editorial hand' where they felt it necessary in the interests of providing a coherent, singable text. However, the tunes, we are assured, are 'as the collector took them from the traditional singer'.

In the EFDSS reissue of the book the conscientious editor, the late Malcolm Douglas, went to inordinate lengths to establish just where the 'editorial hand' found the textual jigsaw pieces that were assembled to make the songs so singable. Douglas found that the degree of 'editing' was far greater in some cases than the reader would have supposed from Bert's and Vaughan Williams's introduction. Douglas's research is probably of more interest to the academic than the average singer, and in no way diminishes the quality of the songs. The Penguin collection seems to hold as much value for the latest generation of singers as it did for the earlier ones. It's a fitting, lasting, epitaph to all three editors.

It's regrettable that it was in the 1950s, as his folk music career was in the ascendant, that Bert's health went into decline. He was, however, determined not to let it dominate his life. Probably as a result of his more sedentary life style, as a frequently desk-bound journalist, Bert put on weight and in his mid-forties he was taken ill and it was discovered that he had had minor heart attacks a few years previously. He started to cut down on certain foods and decided that the walk up Croom's Hill to take Caroline to school in Blackheath would be an enjoyable way to get himself fitter. He was never 100 per cent fit for the rest of his life, although he refused to admit, or to accept, the fact.

Roy Harris received a typical chirpy response when he enquired after Bert's health following his 1969 treatment: 'When he went into hospital with irregular heartbeat problems I asked Charlotte how he was getting on. She replied that he was collecting songs from some ex-seafarers on the same ward! When he got out I rang him to ask how he was. He replied that his heart was now "As four-square as Bach". As for his health in general there was "Nothing wrong with me but antiquity".'[11]

Bert was in fact only sixty-one at the time – no great age at all – although he probably felt older. For all his light-hearted claims about his heart being 'as four-square as Bach' and 'antiquity' being his only problem, the heart condition of several years' standing inevitably led to other problems as Caroline recalled: 'Dad was very ill for a long time, and with heart conditions come a whole bunch of other problems – especially when the treatments available were far less sophisticated than they are now. He constantly astonished doctors with the strength of his will to live in the face of the gradual but general collapse of his body.'

He still had a number of unfulfilled ideas, ambitions and projects, and despite his increasing ill health worked away doggedly at them for the next thirteen years.

17
The Singing Sixties

The concept of folk song is a 'vaporous cloud of assertion and romanticism'.

David Harker

I do not know what English folk music is.

Peter Kennedy

By 1960, Bert, who had released around twenty-four albums both solo and with Ewan MacColl, was generally pleased with the revival and continued to be so until his death twenty years later. He was always encouraging and generous; he hated people sitting on material. He wanted songs to be out there in the clubs, on record, in people's ears and on their lips. This is why he abhorred seeing a potentially good song going to waste in a dilapidated condition trapped between the covers of a book, or hidden away from public sight in a collection of broadsides or manuscripts, awaiting the kiss of life, a resuscitation he was only too pleased to facilitate with a bit of judicious writing and, if necessary, the addition of a memorable, catchy, tune. 'It seems to me if a song's going to be nicer if you splice three or four variants of it together and make the story more or less complete, so much the better. It's better than having it hang around a ruin, a set of ruins. I don't feel in popular performance, the existing traditional model is sacrosanct.'[1]

He didn't let scholarly pedantry get in the way of a good song, as the playwright Willy Russell felt when he first saw Bert sing: 'When I first saw him singing in 1966 at (I think) the Keele Folk Festival I recognised that the knowledge and erudition he brought to the music would always be secondary to the joy of singing the stuff – something that's all too easily (and fatally) forgotten in so many areas of artistic endeavour.'[2]

For Bert, song was not merely a personal experience, but was also a philosophical and political statement, and he gave the matter a lot of thought. He came to the conclusion that a song had to, in some way, form people's opinion:

It might be very oblique. As for instance in a song such as 'Lovely Joan', in which a clever girl upends male superiority and succeeds in extricating herself with aplomb, or even triumph, from an awkward position:

> 'Oh place that ring into my hand,
> And I will neither stay nor stand,
> The ring would do more good for me
> Than twenty maidenheads,' said she.

But as he made for the pooks of hay,
She jumped on his horse and she rode away.
He called, he called, but t'was all in vain;
Young Joan she ne'er looked back again.

Or it may be a song that to some extent undermines the conventional mystification of Christianity or, not necessarily Christianity, of bourgeois illusion generally. Songs that tend towards a collective or communal feeling, away from an entirely personal navel-gazing one. Songs expressing an attitude either of social responsibility or of irony towards the more illusionistic kinds of institution that our masters try to fob us off with. I like to feel that my audience isn't quite the same after I've finished with them than when I began. It may sound a bit high-flown, but I like to feel it.[3]

Social responsibility, communality, individual worth, the exposure of cant and bourgeois hypocrisy and the celebration of ingenuity, these were some of the ideas that influenced Bert's choice of song as well as his political outlook on life. As the director Barrie Gavin said:

The Marxism wasn't a top dressing but a thread that ran through every aspect of his life. Some of his modesty stemmed from a genuine belief in the equality of everyone. I remember a review by Benny Green about one of our films, a nice review. Bert wrote a letter to the BBC saying how nice but that the film was a product of a joint effort between himself and the director. That was very characteristic of Bert. He had a genuine belief that everyone had something to offer.[4]

The complex worlds of communism, Stalinism, Marxism, Trotskyism, 1970s reformist Eurocommunism and all the other 'isms' are minefields in which political animals such as Dave Harker and Karl Dallas gambol with impunity, return unscathed, and write countless articles and books explaining the minutiae of the 'isms' and their relevance to folk music for the benefit of lesser mortals who just sing or enjoy listening. Surprisingly, both of the above mentioned folk music mavens, who normally have little in common, are in agreement about Bert's Marxism. Dallas finds himself in accord with Harker's statement: 'Lloyd's work is undoubtedly informed by many Marxist ideas, [but] it would be inaccurate to characterize his analyses as Marxist.'

Dallas is of the opinion that the architects of the second revival, including himself, didn't apply Marx's dialectical method properly 'to the problems and potential of the revival' and 'did not live up to the principles' they had set themselves. This would go along with Vic Gammon's critique of Bert's attempt to shoehorn a subjective middle class definition of folk music into a radical historic framework.

On the other hand, however, all of Bert's 1930s and 1940s friends and acquaintances, many of whom were very politically knowledgeable and considered themselves Marxists, thought of him as a Marxist and a Marxist interpreter of folk music, as did he and his family as well as later colleagues. Bert, like Marx, saw the 'fundamental conflict between workers and owners as the dialectical engine at the heart of history' and would have ticked all the boxes in the list of Marxist principles published in the Conference of Socialist Economists magazine *Capital and Class*:

1. An interest in the detail of the material conditions of people's lives and social relations among people.
2. A belief that people's consciousness of the conditions of their lives reflects these material conditions and relations, albeit a mediated one.
3. An understanding of class in terms of differing relations of production and as a particular position within such relations, class is never static.
4. An understanding of material conditions, technological change, and social relations as historically changeable and always changing.
5. A view of history according to which class struggle, the evolving conflict between classes with opposing interests, structures each historical period and drives historical change.
6. A sympathy and empathy for the working class or proletariat.
7. Finally, a belief that the ultimate interests of workers best match those of humanity in general.

Political beliefs that were more obviously conspicuous in his industrial song research and writing than his general English folk song work in which, as Gammon suggests, he attempted an aesthetic, artistic, emotional, radical, romantic, Marxist and historical juggling act.

By the mid-1960s the tentacles of the folk scene had spread to most parts of the British Isles. Many local village pubs had their folk club and in the cities clubs proliferated. In the February 1966 issue of *Folk Scene* magazine the editor, Dave Moran, printed Part One ('The Central Midlands') of a British Folk Club List in which were listed fifty-three clubs. In London, even with some fifty other clubs in competition, Les Cousins could successfully run for seven nights a week, plus two all-night sessions at the weekend, in the old Skiffle Cellar premises at 49 Greek Street. There were half-a-dozen specialist folk and jazz record stores – Collet's, Chris Wellard's (New Cross), Dobell's (75 Charing Cross Road), The Folk Shop (Cecil Sharp House), James Asman Ltd (off St Martin's lane), and Dobell's at 10 Rathbone Place (where Ron Gould, aka Red Nerk, was always 'happy to play you and even happier to sell you the latest folk records'). There were also several folk music artists/booking agencies.

It was a golden age for folk music in all its various forms. There was a loyal audience for the 'First Wave' of revival singers, such as Bert, MacColl and Seeger, Shirley Collins, Louis Killen, Bob Davenport and Cyril Tawney, and they were joined by the mid-to-late 1960s, by a 'Second Wave' of young professional singers performing English material in clubs and festivals all over Britain (Martin Carthy and Dave Swarbrick, Anne Briggs, Frankie Armstrong, the Watersons, the Young Tradition, Dave and Toni Arthur, etc.). There were also dozens of semi-pros and amateurs the length and breadth of the country who would turn professional as the club and festival scene continued to expand into the 1970s.

The majority of folk club audiences were eclectic in their tastes and were happy to listen to a broad spectrum of music, as long as it entertained. In any month a typical large folk club might book acts as varied as Bert, Alex Campbell, Julie Felix, Davey Graham, the Spinners and the Watersons. The top-selling folk artists for 1965 in Collet's, Wellard's and Dobell's were Bert Jansch, Alex Campbell, Tom Paxton, Bob Dylan, Joan Baez, Buffy Sainte Marie and Woody Guthrie. Only at the EFDSS Folk Shop were three of the top five albums traditional (the Coppers, Paddy Tunney and *Northumbrian Minstrelsy*), the other two being John Pierce's *Teach Yourself Folk Guitar* and Cyril Tawney's *Between Decks,* which included his haunting 'Sally Free and Easy', a song that Bob Dylan admired and occasionally sang.

Out of the various British (and American) folk music camps it was the 1960s singer-songwriters who had more of an impact on the popular music scene than the performers of traditional music. Their material became generally more personal and less universal, and the image of the singer-songwriter hunched over his guitar became just as much a satiric cliché on the folk scene and in the musical press as the 'finger-in-ear-traddie'; there was a certain amount of truth in both images.

Bert Jansch, Roy Harper, John Martyn, Al Stewart, Marc Brierley and Ralph McTell all gravitated to Soho, joining earlier Soho regulars such as Wizz Jones, Davey Graham and Alexis Korner. All of them at some point made their way to Greek Street and, guitars in hand, descended the steep staircase of Les Cousins, or more commonly simply 'the Cousins', which for a number of years was the hub of London's contemporary folk world, as earlier as 'the Cellar' it had been the hub of the skiffle scene. Bert on occasion popped in[5] – on his way to or from the BBC or a Topic board meeting – as did the then unknown Martyn Wyndham-Read, just back from seven years in Australia. The first night he turned up he sang 'The Old Keg of Rum' and stunned the audience with the power of his performance. A little later Australian singer Trevor Lucas, who eventually married Fairport's Sandy Denny, introduced Wyndham-Read to Bert at the Singers' Club. Bert was equally impressed with his singing and a month later Wyndham-Read received a phone call inviting him to sing on Bert's whaling album, *Leviathan!*.

All of the above-mentioned musicians were lumped under the one-size-fits-all folk umbrella, which just goes to show what a meaningless term it was by the 1960s. It meant so many different things to so many people as to be virtually worthless as a definition, covering everything from Bert's Romanian pear-leaf playing virtuosi to Led Zeppelin's Jimmy Page playing his acoustic concert-solo 'Black Mountain Side' (his take on the traditional Irish song 'Blackwater Side'). Page learnt it from Al Stewart via Bert Jansch and Anne Briggs, who taught it to Jansch, and ultimately from Bert, who had given the original Mary Doran Irish Traveller version to Briggs.

In October 1964 when Dave Moran and Stuart Wallace started up the magazine *Folk Scene*, Bert, Alex Campbell, Colin Wilkie and Shirley Hart, and the singing sailing-barge skipper Bob Roberts, wrote encouraging letters to Moran and Wallace who were intent on producing a publication with a more critical approach to folk music than many of the then current folk magazines, which they believed left a lot to be desired. Bert concurred:

> Devoted folk music magazines exist already, each with its shortcomings. They supply some information, often duplicated, and leave enormous gaps. I notice in Britain – and still more in America – that gossip about clubs and performers is plentiful but information about folk song is scanty. As if the singer, not the song, were more important. I feel the great need for a magazine devoted to repertory rather than to personalities. That means hard work of course, reading and research. But isn't it about time someone did a bit of that? Some club singers trot out song after song without any idea of the life of them – sometimes without any inkling of the real meaning of the piece. They never think to look in a library.
>
> There are perhaps too many publications to tell us about the clubs and singers and certainly too few to tell us about songs. Good luck to *Folk Scene*.

Bob Roberts's contribution was typically colourful: 'It will do a great service if it helps to stop money-worshipping young men from screaming into microphones like angry gorillas and reveals to them what the word 'song' really means.'

Bert did his bit by conscientiously passing on songs and background history to young singers, magazines (*Sing*, in particular, benefited from Bert's musical largesse), and in his album sleeve notes. Then around the mid-1960s as the number of folk club singers and audiences began to grow, Bert, the Workers' Music Association (WMA) and Party publishers Lawrence and Wishart saw the potential need and market for an updated and greatly expanded version of *The Singing Englishman*. Bert set to work. The necessary months of research and writing were funded by a joint subsistence grant from the WMA, the publisher and an unsolicited (by Bert) Arts Council grant. The 433-page *Folk Song in England*, was published in November 1967. Like *The Singing Englishman* it provided an overview (or, as Dave Harker saw it, 'a megalomaniac breadth') of English folk music from earliest times, but this time included erotic and, perhaps more importantly, his particular baby – industrial songs – alongside expanded sections on the more familiar early ballads, later lyrical country material, sea shanties etc. He was also at pains to acknowledge the influence of the broadside ballad on the folk song repertory, and that creative anonymity is not necessarily an essential hallmark of folk song. He gave examples of twentieth-century Eastern European and northern English 'folk songs' which, though the writers are known, nevertheless fulfil the rest of the International Folk Music Council's criteria (basically Cecil Sharp's Continuity, Variation and Selection) for folk song. He concluded that 'the famous anonymity of folk song is, in the main, an economic and social accident' and that if one day the author's name turned up for the 1830s Catnach broadside of 'The Dark Eyed Sailor' (from which all collected versions appear to derive) would it 'at that moment cease to be a folk song?'

Bert's view of history as the history of class struggle, and folk songs as lower-class songs which 'arise from the common experience of labouring people and express the identity of interest of those people, very often in opposition to the interests of the master' [very often?], was expanded from the earlier booklet, but, as Harker points out, was no more specific as to 'how (or even if) the common experience of an entire class is articulated through the songs he [Bert] cites'. However, this point and Bert's tendency to sometimes present unsubstantiated statements as categorical 'facts', were generally overlooked or not even noticed by the majority of readers.

If you tell the people what they want to hear, in a language that they can understand, you're on to a winner. Bert did just that with *Folk Song in England*. Fred McCormick had this to say online about the book: 'It conveys better than anything else I have ever read, the sheer richness and variety and artistic worth of folk song, and of the creative potential in ordinary people … so I would unhesitatingly put FSE down on anyone's reading list, with the proviso that it needs to be read carefully and sceptically. But what great work doesn't?'[6]

In the early days of the revival we wanted folk music to be a bit radical, a bit edgy, a bit rebellious. As in the song 'The Black Leg Miners' which Bert introduced to the folk revival:

> Join the union while you may
> Don't wait till your dying day
> For that may not be far away
> You dirty blackleg miner.

The Revival was a musical freemasonry to which the general public and the robber barons of the media industry weren't (initially) privy, with its own secrets, rituals, in-jokes and, depending on your folk regiment, uniform. It was also romantic, nostalgic, with deep taproots connecting some of us to earlier generations where we envisioned honest labouring folk earning their daily bread by the sweat of their brow, and at night in their cottages and pubs singing of brave deeds, romantic encounters and erotic dalliances.

Because Bert was there, yet again, at the right time, with a particular set of skills and had prepared the ground through countless earlier pronouncements and recordings, his *Folk Song in England* completely overshadowed every other general study of British folk music written in the twentieth century. Who, for instance, apart from dedicated folk song scholars and researchers has heard of, let alone read, poor old Frank Howes' worthy book *Folk Music of Britain and Beyond*, which came out a year after *Folk Song in England*. And despite Harker's critiques of Bert's theories in his book *Fakesong*, much of Harker's exposure has cut little ice with the folk scene:

Yet again, we are obliged to take his [Bert's] detailed attributions and unsupported generalizations on trust and to accept his right of veto. As with Child, we are told what is *not* 'folk song', not what *is*; and we are advised as to which cultural processes do *not* produce 'folk' materials, as opposed to those which *do*. In short, Lloyd swallows the IFMC's [International Folk Music Council] arbitrary concepts of 'tradition' whole, and, with some stretching upon the issue of broadsides. That of the essential orality of transmission, thereby collapsing what he knew of workers' culture and history back to the trammels of the Sharpian consensus.

Ignoring the ancient tradition of the sanctity of the messenger, Harker was widely savaged and designated the Devil's emissary on Earth for these sorts of comments. Karl Dallas, one of the earlier communists of the folk revival, and one of the folk scene's most prolific and, frequently, perceptive commentators, devotes a whole section of his website to trashing Harker's analysis of the folk revival and Bert's part in it.[7] Nonetheless, many of Harker's observations deserve to be aired and discussed. Everybody, it seems, has an opinion on Bert and the development of the Revival, and there seems to be little consensus on the matter.

In his university days, in the 1960s, Harker corresponded with Bert, seeking his advice on which areas of industrial folk music he should research. Bert, who after apologising for the delay in replying due to being hospitalised, pointed out that as far as industrial song was concerned the field was wide open; the surface had only been scratched (mainly by Bert with his mining songs). He helpfully suggested a variety of approaches including a serious study of the major broadside collections in an attempt to interpret the chronology, textual changes and geographical spread of songs. He also pointed out the importance of collecting not just songs, but stories, jokes, proverbs, and oral history concerning the various industries – the politics and craft skills of the workplace, and the investigation of industries other than mining, such as car manufacture, steel-making, textiles and so on.

So it was partly Bert's initial encouragement and inspiration that encouraged Harker to study folk and popular music, and ultimately to become one of Bert's most trenchant critics. But despite the criticisms of the likes of Harker, Georgina Boyes (in *The Imagined Village*) and Michael Brocken (in *The British Folk Revival 1944–2002*), many people still credit Bert with having written the most important book on English folk song to date.

Incidentally, Karl Dallas took Bert and MacColl to task on his website for failing to recognise the possible reason for the variation in the amount of musical folklore generated by different industries. As Dallas points out Bert and MacColl ascribed the differences to 'accident, or to the fact that no one can have looked hard enough in the industries seemingly deficient in folklore'. This led Dallas to describe the duo as quasi-Marxists, 'for Marx himself would never have missed the evidence before his eyes so unscientifically'. He continued:

What appears to me to distinguish those industries rich in folklore from those where it is rare or non-existent is the surviving collective nature of at least a part of the labour process, strongest in the mines even today, despite the National Coal Board's attempts to 'factoryise' them, surviving in cloth weaving for as long as the work retained vestiges of co-operative effort, and dying out as it became more and more fragmented with increasing mechanisation, never strong in railways where the hierarchical cleaner-fireman-driver structure tended to separate the men on the footplate from one another, but surviving in the quite different atmosphere of the engine sheds or off-duty in railway communities like Doncaster or Crewe.[8]

Be that as it may, for some the book took on the mantle of a Folk Bible (as had the original edition of *Come All Ye Bold Miners* in 1952), an oracular repository of universal truths and the fount of all folk knowledge. At least one folk club, Warrington, kept a copy on hand to settle any musical disputes that might arise among the residents or audience.

Despite the subsequent development of British folk song scholarship with the concomitant plethora of books, articles and essays, *Folk Song in England* has remained essential, if for some, contentious, reading for forty years. At the time of its appearance, there were very few people in Britain who knew as much about English folk song as Bert, and even less had his breadth of knowledge of international music. And today, with the academic tendency to specialise, many graduates from folk music and ethnomusicology programmes may be very knowledgeable in specific areas but most, one suspects, will lack his remarkable overview.

This was especially true in the 1960s with regard to Eastern European music; an area of expertise which enabled him to produce countless musical and theoretical examples and analogues to prove virtually any point he made. Examples that Vic Gammon admitted in 'A.L. Lloyd and History' (in Ian Russell, editor, *Singer, Song and Scholar*) left him with a feeling of 'great ignorance' when confronted with this material. Gammon, now one of our leading folk music scholars, was certainly not alone in not knowing much about Bert's Balkan sources, although he had a feeling that Bert 'used his Balkan evidence selectively'.

Despite Bert's opening sentence, which states that 'This is a book for beginners not specialists', most people, including Bert's more recent critics, agree that it is much more than that. The book received more favourable than critical reviews, although fellow *Folk Music Journal* board member Francis Collinson, while affirming that '[t]his is a book to be read for its wide knowledge and its industry of research, by everyone interested in English Folk Song, beginners or not', felt that 'it is also a book that will leave a bitter taste in the mouth by reason of its class prejudice'.[9]

The *Country Life* reviewer, however, enthusiastically declared that it was the book 'it seemed that no one was ever going to write'. The *New Statesman* thought it 'approaches folksong as living reality, as relevant to our present as to our past'. The *Musical Times* found it 'Very readable by reason of a racy vocabulary...breaks new ground...a rich book'. The *Times Educational Supplement* declared it to be 'scholarly, yet easy and absorbing to read'. Janos Marothy, of the Bartók Archive, Budapest, considered it to be: 'A marvellous book! A broad grasp united with captivating material and fascinating style; significant results obtained both by analysing the subject scientifically and appreciating it emotionally, and at the same time made accessible to the non-specialist reader.' Admittedly, few of the magazines had reviewers knowledgeable enough in this very specialised field (Marothy excepted), in which Bert reigned supreme, to give it a serious critique. That's not to say that what they wrote was necessarily wrong, but few could really get below the entertaining verbal window-dressing, and if you're not sure of your facts the easy thing is to fall back on platitudes.

But it was the first truly comprehensive book on the subject since Cecil Sharp had dipped his toe in the water and published the far less wide-ranging *English Folk-Song: Some Conclusions* some sixty years earlier. There had been a few other earlier titles such as Frank Kidson and Mary Neal's *English Folk Song and Dance* (1915) and Iolo Williams's *English Folk Song and Dance* (1935). (Williams was the father of the composer Edward Williams who later became a good friend of the Lloyds.) There were also a couple of English folk dance titles by Violet Alford and Douglas Kennedy, but none to match *Folk Song in England,* the range and variety of musicological references amused and impressed even Bert himself.

His daughter Caroline remembers well the process of compiling the book's index:

The indexing of *Folk Song in England* was a special occasion in the Lloyd household and took place at the kitchen table. As I remember it, Bert went through the proof copy calling out the references and we wrote them down on little cards with the page numbers. He was always passionate about the subject and was feeling euphoric that he had actually finished the hard, hard work of writing the book.

To my shame, I think I only helped a bit. For my liking (impatient and teenaged then) the business was constantly being interrupted by Bert turning pink and speechless with helpless giggles, or raising his impressive eyebrows in astonished surprise at the range of people, themes, and topics that cropped up.

'Well, what do you know?' he'd say, beaming with delight at meeting up with some reference again and then, of course, he'd have to tell us why he was so pleased. The joy in that index. The feast it hinted at for the text. It may have felt like a slow process at the time but it has lasted as a lovely memory.

Later I realised that my dad had only ever given me one piece of paternal advice. It was 'Use The Index'. It was fine advice.

The index included over 100 songs, ranging from songs of ceremony such as wassails, May-songs and wonderful-animals, with their roots in earlier more superstitious times, to contemporary industrial songs from the northern coal-fields. Although the bibliography includes most of the standard collections and writings on English folk music, over a third of Bert's notes refer to East European research and publications from the likes of Kodaly, Bartók, Marothy, Vargyas, Propp, Comisel and Brailoiu. American scholars, Wilgus, Charles Seeger, Bayard, Korson and Woodfill come in a poor third.

As well as being master of the little-known foreign reference, Bert was king of the metaphor and adjective: 'Generally speaking our folk song has not been much illuminated by learned comment. Some studious starlight falls on the carol, but most kinds of English traditional poetry and music remain in the darkness of a night pierced here and there by the hand-torch of the *Folk Song Journals*.'

For him, John Aubrey was 'curious', Miss Bell Robertson was 'redoubtable', the American folk song scholar Samuel P. Bayard was 'admirable', Ella Leather was 'diligent', Lucy Broadwood was 'indomitable', and the sixteenth-century author of *Anatomie of Abuses* was 'vinegary' Phillip Stubbs. All of which makes for a chatty, entertaining read, and, despite Collinson's claim, not one that I feel leaves a particularly bitter taste in the mouth. There are, admittedly, numerous references to 'capitalists' but that's what they were, so what else should he call them? And, surely, few can disagree that generally throughout history power has resided, and still resides, in the hands of a privileged few, and the 'peasants', 'proletariat', 'working-classes', 'workers' – or whatever you want to call them – have been subject to frequently draconian laws and exploitation in varying degrees by landowners, mine-owners, mill-owners, the Church, the army, the navy and others. As Bert points out, even the common sailors' hero, Horatio Nelson, as a young officer, did a stint as a hated and feared Press-Master.

The book brought together a lot of the things that Bert had been saying in folk magazines, album notes, lectures and interviews over the previous decade. Which, along with his claim for 'folk music' as being something recognisably different from other musics ('Not to knock one at the expense of the other, merely for convenience when studying folklore'), includes favourite items such as his investigations into the ancient and widespread lineage of the 'Lady Isabel and the Elf Knight' ('The Outlandish Knight'), in which he leans heavily on the researches of the Hungarian scholar Lajos Vargyas. This was the piece of musicological detective work that so impressed Mike Waterson at the first Keele Festival.

Bert's favourite carol with teeth, 'The Bitter Withy' appears again (he had been using it in articles and on record since the early *Picture Post* days), as does 'that most good-natured, mettlesome, and un-pacifistic of anti-militarist songs', 'Arthur McBride'. The song, detailing the trouncing of a recruiting sergeant by the eponymous McBride, was one of the earliest songs that Bert took into his repertoire (Hasted remembered him singing it with the Ramblers in 1950), and he was presumably that 'one' who 'recorded it for the BBC early in 1939', from 'a singer from Walberswick, Suffolk'. It appealed to

Bert because 'in temper and action it is something of a model for songs of disaffection and protest'.

Although his enthusiasm for his subject coupled with his political beliefs frequently caused him to jump in with both feet, he was, as Mike Waterson said, prepared to accept that in the light of further evidence his pronouncement on any given theme might ultimately prove to be 'bullshit'. This is confirmed by Gammon in 'A.L. Lloyd and History' where he prints a note sent by Bert to the *Folk Music Journal* in response to Gammon's critical essay on his writings on erotic song. Bert admits that 'over the years since *Folk Song in England* was published I have modified some of my views. Nowadays I would agree that as "spokesman" for the myth [of the uninhibited peasant] I wrote far too lyrically.'

Gammon speculates that had Bert lived another twenty years and possibly revised *Folk Song in England* he would in all probability 'have taken on board some of the subsequent criticism and discussion in the field'. Unfortunately it didn't happen, so it's up to the present day reader to approach it with an open and questioning mind in the knowledge of its subjectivity. It's a book that everyone should read who professes an interest in British traditional music. It is inspiring and thought-provoking and the ideal spring-board for further research.

There is no denying that the range of his learning, and the ease with which he could access it, was truly formidable. This, coupled with his colourful, easily assimilated writing style, explains the thrall in which he held much of the folk scene for so many years, and in which he continues to be a major controversial figure.

It wasn't just the British folk revival that pounced on *Folk Song in England* with the enthusiasm of Moses for the Ten Commandments. On the other side of the world, many in the Australian revival were just as keen to get their hands on an accessible history of English folk song, in the expectation that it might put their own musical efforts into some sort of context, as Mark Gregory recalled: 'In 1967 I airmailed Collet's in London from Melbourne with a cheque for Bert's *Folk Song in England*, the release of which I'd read about somewhere. That year I made liberal use of his chapter on Industrial Song that concluded his book when I organized a workshop at what is these days regarded as the first national folk festival in Australia – the 1967 festival in Melbourne.'

As Bert was writing *Folk Song in England*, Topic Records was going through an economic hard time. Their sales figures for 1965/6 of 23,590 albums fell to 16,761 in 1966/7 and hit a low of 14,461 in 1967/8. This fall in sales was due partly to increased competition, partly unsatisfactory service by wholesalers, but also because of the company's policy of issuing a greater proportion of albums of traditional performers. Just over a thousand albums a month sold across the whole Topic catalogue puts into perspective the extent of interest in traditional music at that time. A few bus-loads of purchasers a month out of a population of 55 million.

Although *Folk Song in England* would be considered Bert's magnum opus, and certainly his major piece of writing in the 1960s, it was by no means all he wrote in that decade. He wrote constantly for BBC Schools radio, averaging at least a programme a month from 1960 to 1968. Not, perhaps, a huge amount, but when added to his other radio work as writer, translator and performer, plus books, articles and editing, his work for Topic as director and recording artist, his theatre work, his collecting, lecturing and performing trips around the world, and his voluminous correspondence with friends, scholars and, more often than not, complete strangers, it's amazing just how he found the time to fit it all in. To his credit, he put as much care, research and information into his personal, non-paying, correspondence as he did into his professional work.

A case in point is a letter from Arnold Rattenbury in the summer of 1969, after having been out of touch for several years, asking for a piece of information on Methodist hymnology that he required for a project. Bert replied in August expressing delight at hearing from Rattenbury after so long, and apologising for the time he'd taken to reply. He explained he had been in hospital for over five weeks, and returned home to a mountain of paper that had accumulated on his desk. Then, after modestly declaring 'I can't tell you a great deal about Methodists as singing birds; it's rather out of my field', he launched into a two-thousand word essay on the history of Methodist hymn writers and performance. Not only was it meticulously researched, it was also a beautiful piece of writing that must have taken several hours to produce.[10]

An interesting project was his collaboration with his old AIA comrade Pearl Binder (latterly Lady Elwyn-Jones) on a children's book, *The Golden City*, published by Methuen in 1960. It's a *cante fable* of the adventures of a Victorian street urchin named Toby, his black West Indian friend Bingo, and Bingo's pet monkey Virginie and their dream of finding the Golden City. The story, written by Bert and brilliantly illustrated by Binder, is interlaced with traditional songs. London being a bustling Victorian port gave Bert the opportunity to slip in songs such as 'The Dark-Eyed Sailor', 'Whaling in Greenland' and the transportation ballad 'The Black Velvet Band' and several more. Binder's detailed colourful drawings are chock-full of historical detail of costume and social life in the streets, gin palaces, workhouses, parks, city streets and fairs of the Dickensian metropolis. The story finishes with Toby's realisation, like Dorothy's in *The Wizard of Oz*, that one's dream is often right under one's nose all the time. For Toby, London finally turned out to be the Golden City. Eric Winter thought it the best children's folk song book since Alan Lomax's *Harriet and her Harmonium* (with fourteen songs) which had been published in 1955, also illustrated by Pearl Binder.

Also in 1960, Keith Prowse published *Sea Shanties and Songs (The Treasure Island Song Book)* – Bert's songs for the Mermaid Theatre's production of *Treasure Island* – and Bert and Charlotte translated the German radio play *What Killed Goliath* by Josef Sryck. In 1965 the International Folk Music Council commissioned Bert and I.A. de R. Rivera to put together the collection of 150 songs and tunes *Folk Songs of the Americas*. During the 1960s Bert also took over editorship of the Royal Academy of Dancing's handbooks on Latin American dance, and wrote *Dances of Paraguay*. Two more of Bert's translations that we should mention here are Kurt Frieberger's *Simon Peter the Fisherman* (Heinemann, 1955) and Ion Creanga's *Recollections from Childhood*, published in 1956 by Lawrence and Wishart in their Library of Rumanian Literature Series.

During the 1960s and 1970s, Bert's name associated with a publication was guaranteed to endow it with an air of authority and gravitas. In 1962, although not always agreeing with Leslie Shepard's somewhat esoteric and spiritual view on ballad history and origins (in 1959 Shepard had spent a year in a temple on the banks of the Ganges studying religious philosophy and Indian music), he agreed to write the foreword for Shepard's *The Broadside Ballad: A Study of Origins and Meaning*.

From his *Picture Post* days, when he and Bert Hardy had tramped across Northumbria on a quest to find the source of the Tyne and interviewed the people they met en route, Bert had a particular interest in the folk culture of the northeast of England. Beside his researches into industrial song, he was fascinated by the Northumbrian pipes, which he successfully promoted through various Topic recordings. Whenever he was in the area he'd try and take a day or two out to research in the Black Gate Museum, the headquarters and library of the Society of Antiquaries of Newcastle upon Tyne. He was a friend of the Newcastle academic librarian and folk music scholar Frank Rutherford, and Rutherford's wife Vera:

> The first time he stayed with us was when we were living in Newcastle. It was in the cold dark of the year and he arrived at our house in the evening after a chilling day spent looking at North-East manuscripts in the Black Gate Museum, where their archives were in some disarray. When he arrived as well as being freezing cold he was ravenously hungry! He had a quiet, donnish, politely confident manner. He was not very tall, and thickset, going bald but with beetling eyebrows. His voice was light, and high for a man, but with an edge to it.[11]

When the indefatigable Kenneth Goldstein reprinted J. Collingwood Bruce and John Stokoe's important, if plagiarised (1882) *Northumbrian Minstrelsy: A Collection of the Ballads, Melodies, and Small-Pipe Tunes of Northumbria*, for Folklore Associates in 1965, Bert was at the top of the list of contributors to be invited to write the foreword. Later, in 1973, his interest in, and long-time promotion of, sea songs and shanties led John Foreman, the 'Broadsheet King', to ask him to write the introduction to his facsimile reprint of John Ashton's 1891 collection *Real Sailor Songs*.

The 1960s were Bert's Midas years, when everything he touched seems to have turned to gold. Many of his best remembered and most respected radio programmes were broadcast in the 1960s: *The Gypsy Minstrel* (1961); *Superman In Music* (1962); *Songs of the Durham Miners* (1963); *Bartók as Folklorist* (1964) two parts; *The Folk Music Virtuoso* (1966); *The Voice of the*

Gods (1967); *The Origins of Polyphony* (1968); and in 1974 the influential *The Savage in the Concert Hall*.

In 1963 he became involved in that strange BBC concept 'Radio-Vision', which, with its mix of radio, slides and pictures, one can't help thinking of as 'poor man's television', on a par with wind-up radios and similar alternative technologies useful in developing countries. Bert was the singer in the Radio-Vision schools programme *Courtship and Marriage in Painting* by Leo Aylen. In July 1965 he even did an item on *Woman's Hour*, 'Folk Music Festival at Keele University'.

In addition to the couple of dozen albums he'd recorded by 1960, between then and 1971 he recorded many more: *A Selection from the Penguin Book of English Folk Songs* (produced by Paul Carter for his Collector Records, 1960); *England and Her Folk Songs* (recorded April 1960, released November 1962); *Outback Ballads: Songs from the Australian Bush and Outback* (with Peggy Seeger, 1960); *All For Me Grog* (1961); *Gamblers and Sporting Blades* (with MacColl, 1962); *Whaler Out of New Bedford* (with MacColl and Seeger, 1962); *English and Scottish Folk Ballads* (with MacColl, 1964); *The Bird in the Bush: Traditional Erotic Songs* (with Frankie Armstrong and Anne Briggs, 1966); *First Person* (1966); *The Best of A.L. Lloyd* (1966); *Leviathan! Ballads and Songs of the Whaling Trade* (1967); *The Great Australian Legend* (1971). All these, plus re-issues in various combinations of his early sea songs and shanties with MacColl, provided the folk scene with a plethora of carefully selected, often 'improved' and arranged, ear-catching, toe-tapping and thought-provoking songs to see them through the 1960s.

THE TIMES THEY ARE A-CHANGING

'I believe the position of the traditionalist who would want to preserve strictly the forms and usages of nineteenth-century folk song and go no further is sheer antiquarianism and based on a misunderstanding of the dialectic and dynamics of tradition.'

Bert Lloyd

In his book *Worlds of Sound: The Story of Smithsonian Folkways*, Richard Carlin explains Moses Asch's (the founder of Folkways Records) attitude to the electrification of folk music:

By the mid-1960s [in the US], the folk revival was beginning to lose steam, being overwhelmed by rock'n'roll. Although it roiled the folk world at the time, Dylan's 'going electric' at the 1965 Newport Folk Festival was only one symbol of the changing world that would transform popular music styles. Like many of his generation, Asch did not understand electric folk-rock and felt that it was an attempt to court the popular audience, with all the evils associated with mass marketing and commoditization that folk music stood proudly against. This confusion of presentation with substance led many of the elders in the folk music movement to lose a vital connection with emerging performers.

Bert who, approaching sixty, could be classed as one of those 'elders' of the folk revival, was not of this opinion. Although he agreed with the 'evils' associated with mass marketing and commodification, he well understood the relationship between presentation and substance, as he pointed out as early as 1963 in his article 'What's Traditional?' in Karl Dallas's *Folk Music*:

> Can one use electric guitars to accompany folk song? Why not, provided that ways can be found of using the instrument in a manner that doesn't impoverish the material? (Mind you I'm not sure that such ways have been found yet).
>
> I was once present at a conference involving Rumanian and Bulgarian folklorists. The Bulgarians reproached the Rumanians for not doing enough to preserve the use of folk instruments in their villages. The Rumanians explained that their viewpoint was: Any instrument may be considered a folk instrument, depending on the way it's handled.
>
> They illustrated their point thus: In a group of West Rumanian villages fifty years ago, the dance music was provided by six-holed shepherd pipe. Gradually the peasants replaced this with the clarinet. Towards the end of the 1930s, the alto saxophone in turn replaced the clarinet. Now, in this region, brilliant hora-bands – mainly comprised of gypsies – provide saxophone music for the weekend collective folk dances. The melodies are ampler, the performances have more verve, but the character of the music, and its function, remains entirely folkloric. All that's missing is the element of handicraft charm that we Western city-folk often find more seductive than peasants do.[12]

Ten years later he reiterated this view in his article 'Folk-song Revivalists' in the *Observer Magazine*, of 23 October 1973: 'Whatever suits the times without impoverishing the song' has been the maxim, consciously or not, of folk singers ever since they began performing for others to listen to.' Bert was happy to take advantage of this opportunity for a double-page spread in a prestigious colour magazine to promote the folk revival.

Bert was very supportive of folk-rockers Fairport Convention, as Dave Swarbrick remembers, but of course it didn't hurt that the band's singer was Sandy Denny, of whom Bert was very fond, and whose singing he admired enormously. Caroline Clayton (Lloyd) said that after Joe's death the second most terrible for Bert was Sandy Denny's, also in 1978.

While he was relatively open-minded about traditional folk song accompaniment and instrumentation, and was perfectly happy to invent a new 'traditional' style by using Alf Edwards's English concertina and Swarbrick's idiosyncratic fiddling, Bert had little time for contemporary guitar-playing singer/songwriters – the 'Dylovans' of the commercial folk music world. He felt that Bob Dylan, Donovan, Tom Paxton, Paul Simon, Phil Ochs and

Jackson Frank, although labelled 'folk singers' (as was anyone with an acoustic guitar) by their record companies and the media, generally had little to do with musical folklore, as he explained to Michael Grosvenor Myer: 'I wouldn't quarrel with the word folk song that any non-folklorist chooses to apply, it's just that the donkey and the zebra are not quite the same animal, although the outlines might be similar.'[13]

He did, however, grow to become an admirer of Dylan. They first met on a freezing late-December evening in 1962 when Dylan dropped into the Singers' Club at the Pindar of Wakefield at King's Cross. The event was captured for posterity by the folk photographer Brian Shuel in a now famous black-and-white shot showing a young Dylan dressed in his trademark Huck Finn cap and sheepskin jacket, concentrating on his guitar playing. Sitting behind him is Bert, wearing an enigmatic smile, and MacColl who is either asleep or concentrating (see plate 31). Dylan sang two songs that evening. One was the grim 'Ballad of Hollis Brown' – a gothic tale of poverty, despair, murder and suicide, with its musical roots in the Appalachian murder ballad 'Pretty Polly'. The second song, to date, remains a mystery.

Dylan was in London for three weeks working for the TV director Philip Saville on the BBC film *Madhouse on Castle Street,* in which he played Lennie, a rebellious young guitar player. He stayed in the Cumberland Hotel, courtesy of the BBC, but hung out some of the time in Hampstead with Martin Carthy, who taught him 'Scarborough Fair' and 'Lord Franklin',[14] later reworked by Dylan as 'Girl From the North Country' and 'Bob Dylan's Dream'. Carthy trudged the wintry London streets as Dylan's guide to various folk venues including the King and Queen pub, Bungies Coffee House and the Troubadour, where Stephen Sedley remembers Dylan borrowing his guitar for a couple of songs. Three years later, Bert and Dylan both performed at the 1965 Newport Folk Festival, the occasion when Dylan split the folk world by going 'electric' and in so doing ushered in the electric folk age.

Bert was impressed with Dylan's grasp of politics. His daughter, Caroline, said she thought 'the scales fell away from his eyes' when he saw the apoplectic outcry at the Newport Sunday evening concert on 25 July 1965, by Alan Lomax, Pete Seeger and others as described by Robert Shelton in *No Direction Home: The Life and Music of Bob Dylan*:

> Backstage, there had been almost as much excitement as out front. At the first sound of the amplified instruments [Dylan's], Pete Seeger had turned a bright purple and began kicking his feet and flailing his arms ... he was furious with Dylan. Reportedly, one festival board member – probably Seeger – was so upset that he threatened to pull out the entire electrical wiring system. Cooler heads cautioned that plunging the audience into the dark might cause a real riot.

Earlier that day Dylan's agent, Albert Grossman, had come to blows with Lomax following his patronising introduction to the amplified Paul Butterfield Blues Band on the afternoon concert. Bert, whose own concert had been on the previous evening, was free to watch the Dylan performance. He sympathised with him after seeing his treatment by the 'old guard', and became enormously interested in Dylan's progress from then on.

MacColl, however, was quick to jump in and support his outraged 'best friend' Lomax, and made an embarrassing attack on Dylan in the pages of *Sing Out!* in September, 1965: 'Our traditional songs and ballads are the creations of extraordinarily talented artists working inside traditions formulated over time ... But what of Bobby Dylan? ... a youth of mediocre talent. Only a non-critical audience, nourished on the watery pap of pop music could have fallen for such tenth-rate drivel.'

In Karl Dallas's magazine *Folk Music*, MacColl, under the pseudonym Jack Speedwell, subjected Dylan to the smug and often cruel criticism that, from the safety of his anonymity, he dished out to members of the folk fraternity whom he held in contempt. MacColl, who on a bad day wrote such 'poetic' lines as: 'The rain was gently falling when they started down the line / And on the way to Buxton the sun began to shine' jeered that 'in Bobby [Dylan] we have a genius of the stature of McGonagall'. Dylan, obviously a more generous soul, always spoke well of MacColl.

A week before he witnessed Dylan turn the folk world on its head with his electric Newport set, Bert had been a guest workshop leader at the first Keele Folk Festival. Over the weekend of 16–18 July 1965, over 500 folk music enthusiasts turned up at the Keele University campus in Staffordshire for the festival. The need for an All-Britain Folk Festival had been suggested by the EFDSS National Folk Music Advisor, Peter Kennedy, in May 1964 at a folk club conference in London. This time they got it right. Rory McEwan chaired the Folk-Advisory Sub-Committee which organised this unique event, which was to become arguably the most prestigious English folk festival, bringing together the cream of surviving traditional performers and the best of the revivalists, plus workshops run by such folk luminaries as Ewan MacColl, Peggy Seeger, John Foreman, Peter Kennedy, Charles Parker, Johnny Handle, Colin Ross, Nan Fleming-Williams, Bill Clifton, Paul Oliver, Cyril Tawney, Eric Winter, Ian Campbell, John Pearce and, of course, Bert. Bert's ballad lecture at that first Keele Festival, which played to a full house was one of the highlights of the weekend and one that stayed in Mike Waterson's memory for the next forty years, as he recounted at the 2008 Bert centenary concert at Cecil Sharp House:

Bert was the man who knew everything that I wanted to know about folk music. I remember once I went to hear him give a two hour-long ballad lecture at Keele Folk Festival and I was awe-inspired by his description of the 'Outlandish Knight', he took it back and back until it ended up as two vases in the British Museum – a thousand-years old and I was gob-smacked. Afterwards I sat outside on the steps of the lecture hall and when he came down. I said, 'Bert, that was incredible.' He said, 'Michael, in the light of further evidence everything I've said today could be utter bullshit.

Eric Winter was also full of praise for Bert's contribution to the festival:

> Perhaps the one person who best represented a bridge between the traditional performers on the one hand and the revival singers and workshop leaders on the other was A.L. Lloyd who himself ran one of the best and certainly the best attended workshop at Keele. Bert's fascinating lecture/demonstration on ballads was learned, but in no way antiquarian.
>
> Bert sat at a table, smart in collar and tie and buttoned-up cardigan, fingers clasped, before a packed theatre of several hundred mainly young people, spellbound, at 10.00 am in the morning.[15]

Another of the workshops was Peggy Seeger's lecture on song accompaniment and how not to do it. She used the Irish tinker banjoist Maggie Barry as an example of how not to accompany songs. At the end of the lecture, Bert stood up and publicly remonstrated with Seeger about her comments on Barry's playing. He also publicly disputed a MacColl Keele lecture on traditional singing styles. One suspects that neither of these public challenges to Seeger and MacColl's authority would have further cemented the two men's earlier comradeship.

FRAIL BUT SO EXPRESSIVE

> 'A.L. Lloyd's strangely moving "unmusical" voice.'
> (Geoffrey Summerfield, University of York)

Even Bert's most avid supporters would admit he was not a great singer in the accepted sense of the word. In public Bert himself was rather disparaging about his own voice and claimed not to like it. This didn't, however, stop his regular rehearsals in front of the mirror, a fact that Charlotte teased him with one evening over dinner when he was telling me that he 'never practised' and that his singing style was 'artless'.

Throughout his life, colleagues and enemies remarked on his voice. Folk singer Audrey Smith, who ran the Nag's Head folk club in Battersea, remembered booking Bert around 1968: 'We brought him to the Nag's Head. I shall never forget him, a dumpy little figure on a chair in the middle of the stage, quietly and chillingly singing Tamlin. His singing was frail but so expressive and there was a delightful chuckle in his voice for comic songs. After the booking I drove him home to Greenwich and he never stopped talking and singing during the journey. Oh, he was a lovely man.'[16]

According to the journalist Ken Hunt, before one of Bert's stateside visits: 'Pete Seeger wrote approvingly of Bert's unaccompanied singing and earthiness, forewarning American listeners about what they might encounter.' Tom Paley, a founder member of the American Old Time string-band The New Lost City Ramblers and, for a short time, half of a duo with Woody Guthrie, recalled that he met Bert during this time and thought highly of him both as a singer and a folk music expert: 'I saw him several times at the Singers' Club after I moved over to London in 1965 and I was always impressed with his singing. He was a wonderful singer – not always perfectly on pitch, as I remember, but near enough not to destroy the song! I always thought he was one of the most interesting of the English revival singers.' When folk singer Martin Carthy, who had been a chorister at the Queen's Chapel of the Savoy, first heard Bert sing he thought it 'the weirdest thing I'd heard; it was very perplexing, but you heard the story. I've yet to hear one of Bert's songs that he handled badly.'[17]

For Louis Killen he was simply: 'The finest exponent of ballad singing I've ever heard. His telling of the stories was always fresh and full of invention, ornamentation and variation.'[18] In Peter Cox's history of the Radio Ballads, *Set Into Song*, Peggy Seeger said how she loved Bert's voice: 'Many people don't like Bert's singing because he floats, pitch wise, but I always loved his voice … He sang with a smile on his face, which gave it that sound.' And referring to his work on *John Axon*: 'Bert always smiled when he sang, with a perfect tone. If he wobbled a bit, it gave the song a natural feel: that's just how a railwayman might sound.' The BBC producer Madeau Stewart thought that: 'The most remarkable thing about Bert's broadcasting was that he had a most unsuitable voice. It was a head voice, rather high, and you'd think no this won't do at all, it's not going to carry the script, the words, the emphasis.'[19] But Douglas Cleverdon, who produced most of Bert's classic music programmes, felt that it was a 'highly individual voice' and that for radio it was better to have a recognisable sound.

The film director Barrie Gavin, after ten years of filmmaking with Bert, had this to say about his voice:

> There is a belief that there is a 'radio voice', and therefore something that's not a radio voice. But if someone speaks about their own thoughts, and imparts information with conviction it transcends the idea of good or bad. He had a light, skipping voice, but it was Bert. Sound recordists would sometimes say, 'Strange voice but, you're right, he's fascinating'.
> He had no inhibitions about his voice but he was a bashful performer; he didn't like to speak to camera, he would look away.[20]

The Australian folk collector John Meredith thought it 'gutless', and an unnamed person, quoted by Australian folk song researcher Brad Tate, thought it reminiscent of 'an old ram with its balls caught in a barbed wire fence'. But as Martin Carthy pointed out, 'you heard the story'. He drew audiences into the tales. This is a skill that many far better technical singers never achieve. James Cooke, in his book *Great Singers on the Art of Singing* claimed the same magic for certain vaudeville performers:

> Albert Chevalier, once heard, could never be forgotten. His pathetic lilt to *My Old Dutch* has made thousands weep. When he sings such a number he has a higher artistic control over his audience than many an elaborately trained singer trilling away at some very complicated aria. While Harry

Lauder had that appealing quality that simply commands an audience the moment he opens his mouth.

As Peggy Seeger said, Bert frequently 'smiled' as he sang. Sometimes it was a genuine smile of amusement, but often it was simply a facial expression divorced from humour and bonhomie, although most audiences didn't realise this. It was a conscious way of controlling his pitch and top notes through lifting the soft palate and creating more space. Smiling helps you stay on pitch: many classical sopranos control their high notes with a smile. Smiling also helps eliminate the microphone 'popping' on consonants such as B and P, and smiling, even humourless smiling, actually comes across on radio and record, as exemplified by the radio presenter Jim Lloyd, for many years the cosy voice of popular folk music on BBC Radio 2. He would switch on a 'smile' as soon as the green light came on in the studio, to give a friendly, if calculated, 'warmth' to his presentation.

Bert's smile could at times be a little disconcerting when it didn't reach his eyes, and some people got the feeling they were looking into a mask. When Mike Rosen interviewed Bert for *Isis* magazine in 1966, he commented on the smile in his article: 'Between phrases Lloyd would look up into the air; and his voice would wander off into high squeaky sounds that weren't quite words. And to underline something he'd turn his big mobile face at us with inexplicable big-eye smiles.'

Cecil Day Lewis, who was normally very easy to get on with, didn't find Bert terribly congenial, and he once remarked to his wife, Jill, that one of the things he found unsettling was 'the smile'. Jill, who spent more time with Bert, often sitting in his office listening to tapes of his latest travels, also commented on the smile: 'He was rather didactic. If you asked him something he'd give a little lecture. He had a funny, reedy, speaking voice, almost falsetto. He had a smile, or rather a trick of the lips, but not necessarily from the eyes. If you spoke he'd smile but it wasn't very warm.'[21]

As the folk revival progressed into its second decade, Bert and MacColl became less enamoured of each other's singing than would appear to have been the case in the early days, when they performed together in clubs and concerts and on the Riverside and Topic albums, and regularly used each other in radio programmes. This was partly because in the 1950s they had little choice. Singers with their radio experience and performance skills were as thin on the ground as London Symphony Orchestra melodeon players. In 1957, when Bert was looking for another male singer to perform in his radio programme of amatory folk songs, *The Seeds of Love*, he wrote in despair to the producer, Douglas Cleverdon, saying that as MacColl was away on holiday at the time of recording he didn't know who else to suggest, unless perhaps Bob Copper, whose quiet, thoughtful delivery might suit some of the love songs very well.

After the demise of the original Ramblers, Bert and MacColl did a lot of gigs together until Peggy Seeger arrived on the scene. Once MacColl had acquired an accomplished accompanist, with whom he was romantically attached, he had less need to work so closely with Bert, and they saw less of each other. According to Seeger, there was no actual 'falling out' between Bert and MacColl, as some people seem to think. She feels it was more of a drifting apart as their ideas and musical careers developed in different directions. However, she admits that MacColl was less than happy over Bert and Charlotte's attitude to his relationship with Seeger and the birth of their first child. Following the birth, Seeger never again visited Croom's Hill or saw Charlotte.[22]

When, after Bert's death in 1982, MacColl was approached for a contribution to the *Folk Music Journal* obituary, he simply said he couldn't help because he 'really knew nothing about him'![23] Although he was always very nice about Bert when he *did* mention him in interview or print, an attendee of some Critics Group meetings claims that MacColl spoke less well of Bert and his singing in private. This would neither have surprised or worried Bert, who had no great respect for the Critics Group, and MacColl's 'training methods':

> There are, of course, still plenty of people who despise any other music than fine art music, or pop music, or who feel that fine art music is bourgeois muck and so not for them, and that pop music is all a commercial con, and so not for them, and who look for the most rigid kind of traditional folk music to provide some kind of model for modern creations. Those people are few, but they exist and sometimes give themselves rather spiky titles like Critics Group, but those exclusive blokes are very few really.[24]

Most of the comments one hears or reads concerning Bert's singing, at least from British audiences and singers involved in the folk revival, are more concerned with the emotional effect he could have on an audience than on the nuts and bolts of his actual vocal style. Vic Gammon touched on it in his essay 'A.L. Lloyd and History', in *Singer, Song and Scholar*, in which he pointed out the Lloydian paradox of attempting a synthesis of radical history, as exemplified by J.L. and Barbara Hammond (*The Village Labourer 1760-1832*), A.L.Morton (*A People's History of England*) and, later, E.P. Thompson (*The Making of the English Working Class*), and Victorian and Edwardian middle-class folk song scholarship: '... the one concerned with an experiential account of the history of the lower classes, the other with an appropriation from lower class culture made to satisfy the romantic feelings of a middle class fraction around the turn of the [twentieth] century.'[25]

In attempting to bring these two disparate disciplines together, Bert evolved his theory of the two phases of folk song, an earlier style in which in general the melodies are 'more vigorous, squarer, franker in cast, their harmonic structure dominated by the common chord', and the later, early-eighteenth-century, post-enclosure period in which, according to Bert, the disenfranchised rural (folk singing) labouring class displayed their misfortune and distress by singing 'a looser, vaguer, less sure and confident style of melody'.

As Gammon and others have pointed out this theory doesn't square with the available evidence. We can't be certain from manuscript collections how songs sounded in performance in the eighteenth century and earlier, and Bert's picture of post-eighteenth-century folk singing is not borne out by the many twentieth-century sound recordings of rural singers whose styles are as varied as the number of singers. As Gammon says:

> Much of the repertory of traditional singers recorded in the last eighty years seems firmly set in Lloyd's earlier tradition, the singing is confident, the tunes are four-square and based upon the common chord and there seems little of hesitancy and vagueness … . I do not hear the qualities Lloyd writes of overmuch except in one place: the singing of A.L. Lloyd himself.

Graeme Smith commented in 'A.L. Lloyd and Australian Folk Revival Singing Style' that Bert's singing style: 'Is not a mimicked "traditional" style. It is distinctly individual and mannered. It incorporates techniques [use of melodic ornaments, subtle variation in vocal intimacy, the shape and placing of slides and vibratos etc.] used by English traditional singers, though in comparison to Lloyd, much more sparingly.' Smith continues:

> His melodic flexibility, his ornamentation, his profuse use of scoops and glides, all work to present his vocal melodies as repositories of little melodic secrets rather than as simple, clearly structured and commonplace. His persona is that of the introspective singer, and even when he moves from an intimate delivery into declamation, the emotional force always seems to be directed inwards.[26]

The Irish musician and storyteller Packie Byrne once said, 'the best storytellers were often introspective they would just sit there, still as a post, and draw you into the story' – a skill that Bert brought into his singing as much as his narration. He was a superb storyteller.

In mid- and later life he was a dumpy, avuncular little man with a rather high and, for some, unprepossessing voice. He was invariably clad conservatively in cardigan and collar and tie, more like the jovial Toby Jug of MacColl's affectionate description than a charismatic performer. Toby Jug or not, he could hold audiences spellbound with his carefully paced, brilliantly crafted tales and ballads.

As well as actual folk tales, such as the Australian cycle of Speewah tall tales, 'The Kush Maker', 'The Sleeve Job', and 'Hold On Hamilton' (which one suspects is Bert's Aussiefied remake of the Ozark cante-fable 'Fill, Bowl, Fill'), he had a fund of personal anecdotes about his experiences in Australia, on the *Southern Empress* and his later travels which he would use to introduce certain songs. Bert told Mark Gregory that during his time in Australia in the 1920s, stories were in 'much better condition than bush songs'.

> We used to tell tales to each other while we were mustering, or on similar jobs. Riding along rather slowly once the mob was together, moving from one paddock to another, or to the shearing shed or the railway yards. We

would often ride together instead of being spread out ... and we would spend hours in yarning, telling strings of anecdotes with sometimes quite complicated stories, lasting a quarter of an hour or more ... the kind of tales we used to swap were considerable almost epic.

What used to happen often was, because we were bored and most of us had little to read or to fill our minds with beyond talk, somebody would tell an anecdote, and that would stick in our heads, and perhaps three or four such anecdotes would begin to form a little cluster; and, lying in your bunk, you'd think it over and make an extended story with several narrative threads to it, just simply by putting anecdotes together and giving them an overall form. So that from, say, three two-minute stories, you'd make a ten or twelve-minute story simply by embedding them in a cocoon of nonsense, and you'd trot it out as an extended tale. That used to happen over and over again.

Bert didn't write down the bush tales but prided himself on his memory, which enabled him to re-create them whenever needed. As he said to Gregory:

I used to fancy myself as a re-creator of tales. An enormous lot of them have quite naturally dropped out of my head. But I still like to recall quite a number of the kind of tales that we used to tell. Those that I have in my head I have not as objects of received folklore, but as objects of reconstructed folklore. That is, I still tell many of them, but I don't tell them in the form I got them.

Which is how folktales should be told – with every telling a new creation.

Bert's re-worked narrative ballad 'Tamlin' (Child 39), which he first introduced to the folk revival in the late 1960s, is one of the finest of British ballads, and one whose magical (in both senses of the word) storyline never fails to delight audiences. The narrative is peppered with examples of ancient folkloric belief, superstition and symbolism, and the central tale of true love daringly overcoming all obstacles, including the power of the Queen of Faery, is an ageless universal theme, as relevant today as it was in 1549 when it was first mentioned in *The Complaynt of Scotland*.

The supernatural tale has inspired many paintings, poems and stories[27] and over the years numerous revival singers have put their spin on the ballad, with Bert's 'telling' of the story as the benchmark Ur-rendition. It's the song that, more than any other, people remember years later from Bert's performance repertoire. Many fellow singers remember first hearing Bert sing it and the significant effect it had, as Martyn Wyndham-Read recalls:

One of my most memorable experiences with Bert was a concert I did with him at the Vic Theatre, Stoke-on-Trent, and in a theatre which was designed in the round. This was crammed full with an audience of folk enthusiasts. I vividly remember, to this day, listening and watching Bert perform 'Tamlin'. Most people in the audience would have known this ballad word for word by then, but everyone was on the edge of their seats as the master ballad singer, Bert Lloyd, wove his magic. His performance was just gripping and memorable.

Martin Carthy:

I was with him [Bert] at the Singers' Club in 1968 when he sang 'Tamlin', it might have been the first time he sang it because the audience there hadn't heard it. Afterwards I went up to him and said, 'Bert, that was absolutely wonderful'. Before I'd got the sentence out he reached into his inside pocket and produced a set of the words and gave them to me. That's what he did. If you asked him about a song he'd just sung he always had several copies of the words that he'd hand to you and leave you to get on with it.

It's Carthy's contention (in Britta Sweers' *Electric Folk*) that Bert's introduction of 'Tamlin' onto the folk scene, and its subsequent recording by Fairport Convention, opened the floodgates for other ballads: '... had it not been for Bert. Nobody would have [recorded "Tamlin"], the song was considered too big. After that [Fairport's recording] you could sing a song of that length.' That might not actually be the case: Bert certainly introduced an original singable version of 'Tamlin' to the folk scene, but Bert, MacColl, several Scottish and Irish singers, and younger revival singers sang and/or recorded long ballads (including 'Tamlin') before Fairport's electric version. And, in fact, textually Fairport's version is not particularly long. When Dave Swarbrick joined Fairport he wanted to offer them some material for their planned English folk music inspired album and he asked the singer Marion Grey to put together a version for him from a ballad book she had lying around the house. This she did, and the result appeared soon after on Fairport's seminal British folk-rock album *Liege and Lief*.[28]

Although the acoustic guitar, especially in the hands of the likes of Carthy and later Nic Jones and Martin Simpson, was accepted by most sensible people on the traditional folk scene, the electric guitar was for some (as Bert witnessed at the Dylan Newport debacle) a step too far. With MacColl in the vanguard, some traditional music fans thought that Ballad Heaven would fall on their heads, to the cacophonous accompaniment of Fender Stratocasters and Gibson Les Pauls. They were wrong on various counts – the sky didn't fall, traditional music survived the 'electric shock', and folk-rock or electric-folk gave British folk music a rousing kick up the bottom and brought new audiences to the music. Many young people who subsequently went on to investigate and perform traditional music in an acoustic band, or unaccompanied setting, were first lured onto the folk music rocks in the 1970s by the brief siren song of Fairport Convention's Sandy Denny and, later, Steeleye Span's Maddy Prior.

Bert gave his blessing to Fairport when, after a car crash which killed their drummer Martin Lamble and Richard Thompson's girlfriend, Jeannie Franklyn, they transformed (under the influence of Sandy Denny, new band member Dave Swarbrick and the folk epiphany of bassist Ashley Hutchings) from being Britain's Jefferson Airplane to being trad-rockers. They took the folk scene by storm with *Liege and Lief*, with its multi-decibel, vari-rhythmed versions of traditional tunes and ballads such as 'Tamlin'.

In the notes to the 2002 reissue of *Liege and Lief*, Hutchings enthusiastically recalled the band's excitement and commitment when, having decided, after the accident, to change the direction of their music, to abandon their love affair with The Band, Joni Mitchell, Dylan and Americana, and to try and create a music as English as The Band's was American:

> [W]e made a uniformly conscious decision to tackle the business of playing old music on modern instruments but faced with the reality of making it work successfully how did we go about it? We set up our instruments in a circle in the largest living room downstairs [Record producer Joe Boyd had put them up in a large country house in Hampshire to work on the new repertoire] ... In this room came into being sounds, rhythms, patterns and magic that had never existed before.

Bert went along to the sell-out launch concert at the Royal Festival Hall in late 1969, and when Australians Mark and Maree Gregory beat a path to Bert's front door, he enthusiastically introduced them to Fairport's music. Mark didn't seem to notice Bert's somewhat back-handed compliment a while later when he remarked that Fairport's treatment of numbers such as 'Sir Patrick Spens' 'showed how tough these old ballads are'.

This is a good place to lay to rest the persistent myth that Bert was invited to join Fairport Convention. According to Swarbrick, there is no truth in the rumour, although he *was* invited to perform the cameo role of narrator on the band's 1971 concept album *Babbacombe Lee*, an offer he accepted and enjoyed doing.

With Swarbrick and Denny, his erstwhile accompanist and his favourite girl singer, in the band, it's no surprise that Bert lent a generally benign ear to their musical efforts. In a lecture as part of the Folk Music and Modern Sound conference at the University of Mississippi in 1980 he recalled that first concert:

> ...the first big 'all-electric, all-folk song' concert was presented in London in 1969 by the Fairport Convention Band, led by a gnomelike and somewhat gnomic fiddler, Dave Swarbrick, with a sweet, plump lady to whom I was devoted, Sandy Denny, as vocalist. Swarbrick said he was attracted to amplified music because he liked the sound, and because it offered great possibilities of exploring the dramatic content of the songs. With what success?[29]

He then played 'Reynardine' from *Liege and Lief*, which he obviously thought proved Swarbrick's point. This didn't mean, however, that he was 100 per cent convinced by folk-rock. It was 'interesting', and he was impressed by the atmospheric, powerful, soundscapes that the electric instruments (of

Swarbrick and Thompson in particular) were capable of creating around the songs, but he felt that they were 'often a little too heavy for what they had to say'. On the whole he felt the electrification of traditional music was 'an interesting enough exercise'. In an interview from the 1970s he explained what he saw as the advantages of 'e-e-e-e-lec-tricity', as Woody Guthrie called it:

> Folk Rock is an exploitation of the traditional repertory just as the treatments in the *Radio Ballads* were, and any sort of exploitation can bring down a good melody or it can enrich it. Certainly I don't feel any horror at the thought of electric treatment of folk music melodies. On the contrary, I find such treatments usually interesting, not always successful, goodness knows, but quite a lot that Fairport did in the past, Steeleye have been doing recently, that the Albion Band has produced, have seemed to me certainly not impoverishments of the material, and you know, properly handled, electronic sound can be enormously expressive. Musicians can envelop an audience of say 2000 or more in a web of sound, if properly handled, and can give them a very acute artistic experience, and this I've noticed working sometimes with the use of traditional music in quite interesting ways. For example in the old days when Sandy Denny was with Fairport they used to do a performance of 'Tamlin', and I didn't so much like the truncated text Sandy used, and I didn't so much like the rather off-centre melody which they fitted to the words; the story was told sketchily and then at the end the group would have an enormously long, purely instrumental coda, that would be an extension of the magical atmosphere of the ballad, but done in a way that really raised that atmosphere to a considerable pitch, a mixture of terror and triumph as the ballad itself has. It's a ballad full of anxieties that ends in triumph. Well handled electronic sounds can give the impression of elation, tragedy, in a way it takes enormous resources to achieve acoustically, and that kind of coda thing, applied to a folk music repertory can give that repertory a very heightened aspect. It's seldom done effectively because often the taste of pop music performers is not of the firmest and the musical ability is not always that great, although Fairport had competent musicians as do, on a slightly more modest scale Steeleye, but electronic treatment can cheapen a thing beyond recall but also has the possibility of raising it to an artistic pitch.[30]

Bert's lecture at Folk Music and Modern Sound is, in fact, one of his few disappointing pieces of work, and is ultimately little more than examples of folk-rock songs with a lightweight linking commentary. It would have made an easy-listening radio programme and doesn't really examine folk-rock – its origins and ramifications – in any depth. You can't help wondering if it warranted the 1980 flight to Oxford, Mississippi, to deliver. The printed essay, in *Folk Music and Modern Sound*, is the shortest piece in the collected lectures, at just over four pages, and lacks the gravitas of most of the American contributions. It reads like a piece of journalism, entertaining for what it is but not up to Bert's earlier standards when he was enjoying better health. This was as much enthusiasm and time as he was able to spend on the subject in the last couple of years of his life.

Bert's last recording project was an appearance on Norfolk singer Pete Bellamy's 1977 ballad opera, *The Transports*. *The Transports* came about by chance. In January 1975 while wandering around Norwich, Bellamy picked up a copy of the *Eastern Daily Press* in which he came across a short article by columnist Eric Fowler telling the story of Henry Cabell and his sweetheart, Susannah, who were transported to Australia in 1787 for burglary and for stealing a silver teaspoon. Theirs was the first wedding in Australia. The story caught Bellamy's imagination and he determined to write a cycle of songs for an album project telling their story.

He decided to get a group of his favourite singers to help out: Dolly Collins (musical arranger), Roddy Skeaping (musical director), Martin Carthy, Nic Jones, June Tabor, Swarbrick, Vic Legg, Cyril Tawney, Mike and Norma Waterson, Martin Winsor and Bert. Bert's character was that of Abe Carman, the burglar companion of Henry Cabell and his father. Nothing is known of Carman except that he was a robber, so as Bellamy said: 'I took some licence … I made him into a real rogue who gets the poor Cabells involved in his nefarious goings on. Having established that personality for Abe, Bert Lloyd was the obvious choice, so I wrote a tune which I felt would suit him.'

> My name it is Abe Carman
> My trade it is right charmin'
> For you know there is no harm in
> A little burglaree

And so it proved. It was, as Bellamy later said, 'an absolute natural for him'. The double album received enthusiastic reviews and was voted Folk Album of the Year.

Although happy to help out on the project, Bert, as a seasoned writer for radio and the theatre, had some reservations on the style and structure of the piece, as he explained to Bellamy on receipt of the script and tape of Carman's song:

> Dear Peter, Thank you for the script and cassette. Here's the script. I'd like to hang on to the cassette a little longer. The piece should make a nice enough little opus. The story is a bit short on action and relationships, considered as a scenario, and a bit short on lyricism, considered as a libretto. The latter comes, I suppose, from using broadside rather than 'classic ballad' models: it imposes a kind of journalistic narration, factual but what the Americans call low profiled; I like a bit of the sort of shock one gets from dream, such as the big ballads have here and there – a touch of madness perhaps, which gives a bite to the realism – but there …
>
> Anyway, let's hope the project not only gets off the ground but soars glorious.[31]

One wonders how Bellamy received Bert's negative reaction to his 'nice enough little opus'. Perhaps he was mollified by the general acclaim it engendered. In contrast to Bert, the journalist Karl Dallas has described it glowingly as: '... in every sense of the word a monumental work, and a great humanistic paean, from someone who always denied any didactic purpose in his work. Yet it would be impossible for even the aforesaid cloth-eared to experience the complete 75 minutes without being changed profoundly in their consciousness and mindset, which is surely the purpose of all great art.'

But, that was after Bellamy, an uncompromising advocate for traditional music, had committed suicide in September 1991, depressed and disheartened by the lack of interest in his idiosyncratic solo singing in Britain. After his death all those British folk club and festival organisers who hadn't filled his empty engagement diary with bookings came out of the woodwork, declaring his death 'a tragic loss to folk music.' They were right, but too late.

18
Teaching and Filmmaking

The first duty of the educator – like that of the journalist is to be understood, that simplicity, freshness and sympathy are the prime qualities needed, lack of which can be made up by no amount of intellectuality.

D.G. Bridson, 'Ariel and his Quality'

Bert dispensed information so simply without condescension. It was like a jolly lesson.

Madeau Stewart, BBC

A.L. Lloyd was a first-rate broadcaster – if a rather prolix lecturer.

Margaret Dean-Smith

Bert's two most satisfying areas of work came later in life, although, being luckier than some, he had already successfully fulfilled many earlier ambitions. The two areas were filmmaking and teaching, both of which gave him enormous satisfaction in the last decade of his life.

When he found out how much he enjoyed it, Bert often said that he wished he'd come to teaching earlier, but then he wouldn't have had the thirty-odd-years of musical experience to do the job so convincingly. It's an example of that arbitrary universal law that governs most of our lives – Sod's Law. The only consolation being that, unlike sex (where the more experienced and better you get at it the less able you are eventually to practice it), musical folklore studies have no such time limit apart from one's ultimate demise.

WHATEVER SUITS THE TIMES...

'Avant-garde music is a sort of research music. You're glad someone's done it but you don't necessarily want to listen to it!'

Brian Eno

From as early as his 1930s art criticism days, Bert had been interested in myth. He felt that one of the consequences of modern industrial society was the loss of myth as a spiritual and symbolic resource for artists and musicians. Some of these mythically disenfranchised creative souls, such as the modern Estonian composer Veljo Tormis, find inspiration in their traditional folk music; Tormis incorporates shamanic drumming and evokes ancient ritual in his compositions. The Finnish composer Pehr Henrik Nordgren turned to pagan folk poetry and old Ingrian rune melodies for his major work, *The Lights of Heaven*, and later to archaic laments and shepherd tunes for his fourth and fifth symphonies. Other modern composers looked further afield and resorted to more exotic non-European cultures for inspiration and sustenance.

In 1974 Bert gave a lecture at London University entitled 'The Savage in the Concert Hall' which looked at this cultural borrowing, one hesitates to say 'cross-fertilisation' because most of the positive traffic seems to be one way. While he was working on the lecture, he was interviewed by Michael Grosvenor-Myer for the magazine *Folk Review* in September 1974 and explained to him how: 'Several modern composers have gone for inspiration to primitive musics. Our civilisation is very short on mythological aids to support us in our troubles. Compare these two tapes: the first is ritual music from the mouth of the Orinoco, recorded by a French folklorist, the second is from a piece called *Leo,* from a suite by Roberto Gerhard, one of the most celebrated followers of Schoenberg.'

After listening to the two recordings and agreeing that they were remarkably similar, Grosvenor-Myer asked: 'But could it be a coincidence? Do you know for a fact that Gerhard had access to the Orinoco music?' 'Oh yes,' said Bert, 'I played it to him myself!' One wonders if Grosvenor-Myer felt that Bert had set him up for his own amusement?

Gerhard had been one of Arnold Schoenberg's star pupils in Berlin in the mid-1920s. Two more of Schoenberg's students with whom Bert became associated through the WMA, were Hanns Eisler and Matyas Scheiber. From around 1907 to 1923, when he introduced his *Method of Composing with Twelve Tones Which are Related Only with One Another,* Schoenberg was experimenting in composition without the framework of traditional keys or tonal centers. His first expressionist atonal piece, the *Second String quartet, Op. 10,* with soprano (1907), when listened to a hundred years on doesn't sound as avant-garde as it obviously did then. Perhaps our twenty-first-century ears are more used to dissonance. Gerhard went on to explore the world of electronic music, and it was through this that Bert and he met and became friends.

In his autobiography, *Prospero and Ariel,* D.G. Bridson wrote about his late-1950s BBC Radiophonic Workshop experiments with 'the avant-garde Spanish composer Roberto Gerhard in combining electronic music with spoken poetry'. The Radiophonic Workshop, which would achieve popular fame a few years down the line with Paddy Kingsland's soundtrack for *Doctor Who,* was originally set up in 1958 to provide innovative music and sounds to go with pioneering programming. It was run by Senior Studio Manager Desmond Briscoe and his assistant, Dick Mills. Until the early 1960s it was used mainly for radiophonic sound effects for experimental drama and 'radiophonic poems' as Bridson explained:

A radiophonic workshop had just been set up at Maida Vale, and this was doing interesting things for both radio and television. Many composers were now using electronic music experimentally, and both Roberto Gerhard and I were interested in the possibility of using it to reinforce the performance of poetry. We had done many programmes together, and Gerhard's interest in radio – apart from his brilliant originality as a composer – made him an ideal collaborator. Lorca's *Llanto por Ignacio Sanchez Mejias* quickly suggested itself as an ideal poem to set electronically.

The poem was recorded in Spanish and English with Stephen Murray reading Bert's translation, *Lament for the Death of a Bullfighter*, for which: 'Gerhard worked out a quite remarkable electronic background. As finally assembled in the Radiophonic Workshop, this gave almost a new dimension to the work, providing a commentary in pure sound as pictures might have provided a commentary in vision.'

Bridson regretted that Gerhard's: 'Immense creativity carried him on to so many purely orchestral works that he never had time to pursue the marriage of music and speech still further. In the sheer inventiveness of his treatment, he might have achieved the perfect consummation.'

The programme was broadcast on the Third Programme in May 1960: 'We present *Lament for the Death of a Bullfighter*, the poem by Federico Garcia Lorca. Translated into English by A.L. Lloyd. Set to electronic music by Roberto Gerhard, and read by Stephen Murray.' Gerhard introduced the programme:

I knew Lorca well in Spain, and I heard him on several occasions recite the lament. A poet with a good ear, and Lorca's was impeccable, can make entrancing word music of his own with no help from a composer. But, as I see it, the case is quite different when the poetry is set to electronic music. In such a setting the words become the main thread in a texture, which can be woven around them by other strands of sound. Let me tell you how I achieved such texture. First of all the whole piece was recorded on its own in English. This recording of the spoken poem I considered my even theme, as the main theme in the texture I was to weave with other strands of sounds. In other words I took over the whole internal economy of the poem.

Murray then read Bert's translation:

> At five in the afternoon.
> It was exactly five in the afternoon.
> A boy brought the white sheet
> At five in the afternoon.
> A frail of lime already prepared
> At five in the afternoon.
> The rest was death and death alone
> At five in the afternoon,
> etc.

This was followed by Lorca's friend the translator and writer R.M. Nadal reading the opening section in the original Spanish. The second half of the programme was Gerhard's electronic backing to Murray's reading of the poem. The contrast between the soft, pulsating sibilance of the Spanish with all Lorca's original rhymes, and the hard northern English consonants is very marked and make it a different poetic experience. One is internalised and one is externalised in a declamatory manner. One must agree with Pete Monro Jack who observed in the *New York Times* (3 September 1939) in his review of Stephen Spender and J.L. Gili's translations of Lorca's poems, that English is 'a dry and dull sound compared with the luscious Spanish'. Although here the 'dry and dull sound' was ameliorated somewhat by Gerhard's simple atmospheric electronic backing which helped Murray's spoken word transcend the visual straightjacket of punctuation, line, stanza and layout, and language. The programme finished to the electronic sound of wind through the olive trees:

> We shall wait long for the birth, if birth there is,
> Of an Andalusian so bright, so rich in adventure.
> I sing his elegance in words that moan
> And I remember a sad wind through the olive-trees.

IN THE LIGHT OF FURTHER RESEARCH...

When the AIA-affiliated Charlotte Street Centre opened in August 1943 to provide a contemporary gallery, and a social meeting-place for professional artists and those interested in the arts, Bert was one of the first members to be invited to lecture there. His subject was *Popular Songs of the 18th Century*. To provide some of the musical illustrations, Bert called in some old friends from the Unity Theatre, including Una Brandon-Jones.

Brandon-Jones, a leading light at Unity, was a feminist songwriter and actress who, in 1943, formed an all-female Unity revue troupe called The Amazons, in answer to actor Alfie Bass's complaint that there were too few women in the company. Brandon-Jones went on to appear in dozens of television films and series, and in 1987 had a part in Derek Jarman's cult film *Caravaggio*. In 1939/40 she had also recorded 'The Cutty Wren' (Topic) with the Topic Singers to a pipe and tabor accompaniment, as an 'English Medieval revolutionary song', four years before Bert made a similar claim in *The Singing Englishman*. Did she get it from Bert? Or the other way round?

Early in 1944 Bert returned to 84 Charlotte Street and delivered a lecture on the *Songs of the Yugoslav and Greek Partisans*, and in June 1948, as part of an AIA series of lectures, he gave another on *Industrial Folk Song*, illustrated by gramophone records, at the Lisle Street Gallery. It would be interesting to know what gramophone records Bert could have used to illustrate industrial song in 1948; presumably they were American. It was two years before Topic started recording MacColl's industrial songs such as 'The Four Loom Weaver'. Perhaps he sang some of the songs he'd researched and rewritten for Bridson's ballad opera *Johnny Miner* a year earlier?

In the 1950s, Mike Power, who became editor of *New Times*, was a Greenwich Young Communist League member along with Caroline Lloyd.

He remembers Bert going along to meetings and talking and playing his tapes for them, and in 1955 he ran classes in folk song at Hendon Technical College for the London County Council.

In the late 1950s, the Unity Theatre put on a series of illustrated talks under the heading of *Talking the Blues* – these were followed by a skiffle session. In December 1957 Bruce Turner discussed 'Improvisation' and in January 1958 Bert gave a talk on 'English Folk Song and Skiffle'. A couple of months later saw him in Cecil Sharp House giving a Library lecture on 'Jazz, Blues and Skiffle'.

Once the folk revival took off, Bert, as England's leading (and for a while) only serious left-wing folk song scholar, was in great demand at colleges and the folk festivals which mushroomed during the 1960s and 1970s. Of course, MacColl and Seeger also did an enormous amount of research and theorising, particularly amongst the British travelling community, but they never acquired the mantle of musical folklore scholarship to the same degree as Bert, certainly not internationally. Bert became an established workshop leader/lecturer at the Keele Festivals. Lively talks on favourite themes such as 'The Ballad', 'Industrial Song', 'Erotic Song', and 'Prehistoric Folk Song' were delivered to packed halls of enthusiastic young folk fans and revival performers keen to learn more about their new-found passion.

In 1962 he ran a weekend course at Barford with Tony Davis, Mick Groves and Alice Breenan from the Spinners folk group; morris dance and traditional music expert Dr Russell Wortley; and the wonderfully theatrical West Country dialect storyteller Ruth Tongue, who could give Bert a run for his money in being 'creative' with material and biography. 1966 saw him back at Cecil Sharp House for the October London Folk Music Festival where his subjects were 'Love Songs' and 'Occupational Songs'. In the evening he performed in a concert along with Martin Carthy and Dave Swarbrick, and the fine Scots ballad singer Isobel Sutherland. Four weeks later, he was up in Liverpool talking about song for the Liverpool Folk Meet festival of folklore, song and dance.

Between 1965 and 1968 he was a visiting lecturer at the University of Pennsylvania, where his old Riverside recording editor, Kenny Goldstein, ran the folklore department. And in 1967 at the invitation of Venetia Newall, the newly appointed Hon. Secretary of the Folklore Society, he gave a lecture for the Society. Newall has reason to remember his professionalism and good humour. The day of the lecture arrived and by six o'clock, the scheduled starting time, a large audience had assembled. At this point Newall realised that the person designated to provide a tape recorder for the occasion had forgotten it.

It was definitely one of the most awful moments of my life. But Bert was wonderful and kept the large audience happy for forty minutes(!) while two students searched and finally found a replacement machine in one of the departments of University College. I felt so awful and kept apologising to Bert, and he just couldn't have been nicer. 'That's all right, Venetia' he kept saying, 'Don't worry', and kept singing and chatting to the audience. The audience loved it. Most speakers, especially someone so well-known, would have turned pretty nasty, but not Bert. I have very warm and affectionate memories of him.[1]

In October 1967 he gave an illustrated talk at that year's annual EFDSS London Folk Music Festival on the history of folk instruments from their primitive origins. His recordings of Albanian shepherd-pipes and Chinese street music competed loudly with Nan Fleming-Williams's instrumental workshop which built in enthusiasm and volume as the afternoon wore on! During the 1970s he was booked by the British Council specialist tours department to go and wave the flag for Britain at Copenhagen University and tell the Danes about 'British Industrial Song', 'Epic Song' and 'Albanian Folk Music'. He also ran regular education lectures and courses at London University's Goldsmiths College, New Cross, which were generally fondly remembered by attendees.

Robert Carrington, a classical musician, teacher, and lecturer for the Workers' Education Authority (WEA) found Bert to be a fascinating speaker:

The talks/lectures were part of the evening classes organised by Goldsmiths College open to everyone. I attended them purely as an interested student. No essays or anything like that were required – no political agenda as I remember. ... I remember particularly his talks on Central European music. He played an amazing recording of music made on a fish scale. I knew who he was – radio broadcasts etc. – and already enjoyed and admired his work. I never heard him as a performer. People loved what he did – I never heard any criticism. It made a lifelong impression on me. For thirty-one years I was a teacher and folk was one of the things I included. I am a classical musician, but with many different musical interests. I didn't know at the time about his communist leanings – and it wouldn't have made any difference. I think most people felt honoured that we were his students. We were greatly informed and entertained. I thought he was wonderful. At present I work for the WEA, and many of my music courses for adults have a folk element in them, thanks to him.[2]

Dr Lionel Sawkins, a principal lecturer in music at the Roehampton Institute in London prior to retirement in 1985, was equally impressed:

I heard several of Lloyd's lectures at Goldsmiths between 1972 and 1975 and they were one of the highlights of the BMus course I was doing there He was infinitely more interesting and more erudite than most of the 'academic' lecturers – some of whom were appalling! We were a mature evening part-time group and admittedly rather critical.[3]

Bert's Goldsmiths lectures were so popular that Malcolm Barry of the Department of Adult Studies gave him *carte blanche* to lecture on what he liked, when he liked and however much he liked, within reason. However, not all classical music enthusiasts were as taken with Bert and traditional music as Carrington and Sawkins had been. In 1964 the WEA promoted a series of lectures on *The Folk Element in Music* at Manchester University which, according to a report:

> ... attracted not young folkies but mainly older people who attend any night classes as if they were some sort of religious observances. Although well illustrated from the lecturer's own record collection there was not much of a folk element. He responded by saying that the lectures were intended to be enjoyed by a large range of people and that traditional folk music tended to bore the classically minded majority. This he exemplified by playing A.L. Lloyd singing 'The Outlandish Knight' – the class was just not interested![4]

In May 1970, Discurio's Peter Mann organised an Australian lecture tour for Bert – three dates in Melbourne, three at Sydney University's Wallis Theatre, and one in Brisbane at the University of Queensland's St Lucia campus. The illustrated lectures covered 'Music of Spain', 'British Folk Music', 'Erotic Elements in English Folk song' and 'Folk Song in England'. The Sydney lectures were sponsored by the NSW Folk Federation and in their June newsletter they announced that they had:

> ...lost quite a large amount of money on Lloyd – but no regrets as the man presented us with knowledge in an interesting and entertaining manner, that only Lloyd could present ... it was money well spent. NSW people had many opportunities to meet Bert, and he proved most courteous and helpful to all. He was also made the first Honorary Member of the Federation and was presented with the newly designed and printed membership cards which he considered 'very attractive' with the NSW emblem on the front.

On the way back to the UK he stopped over for a week or so with Nigel and Joan Oram, friends of Ann and Edgar Waters, in Port Moresby, Papua New Guinea. Nigel Oram, an oral historian, and a British ex-colonial officer, was a lecturer at the University of Papua New Guinea. The Orams' daughter Jill and her husband, Jim Fingleton (who played in the folk band The Wild Colonial Boys), were staying with her parents during Bert's visit and have fond memories of the week spent in his company:

> Bert was an absolute delight. He fitted in easily with the Oram family, and he and Nigel had many conversations. Nigel played him tapes he had recorded of Papuan people singing long dirge-like ballads. He also listened to the Wild Colonial Boys LP record which had just come out, and was kind enough to say that I had 'an interesting singing style'. (I only sang one song on the record, 'The Flash Stockman', which was a blatant copy of Bert's own style, which goes to show how kind he was in complimenting me!) We had a large party at the Orams' and I was delighted to be able

to accompany Bert singing 'The Man from Kiandra' and other songs. He told stories and jokes, and we all went to the Port Moresby Races together.

While in Port Moresby Bert also met up with Ralph Bulmer the Professor of Anthropology at the University of Papua New Guinea, and he gave a couple of illustrated lectures, one on Australian music (a subject he'd avoided in Australia) and a general folk music one. With his 'bushy eyebrows and dumpy body' Bert reminded the Orams of a bird – a singing bird: 'His performance in concert was riveting. As soon as he broke into song, this marvellous sound filled the room. His animated delivery was unforgettable. He sang the songs illustrating his talk entirely unaccompanied, which only added to the uniqueness of the experience.'
By August 1970 he was back in Greenwich.

ROMANIAN GYPSY MUSIC

Earlier, in March 1962, the British Institute of Recorded Sound invited Bert to lecture on Balkan Gypsy music, especially that of the Romanian Gypsies. The lecture was published in *Recorded Sound*, the Institute journal in July 1965. The following year he was a guest speaker for the Royal Music Association on 'The Music of Rumanian Gypsies' (December, 1963), the text of which appeared in *Proceedings of the RMA 1963/64*. With regard to the RMA essay, Paul Nixon declared that: 'Bert's 1964 RMA piece on Romanian Gypsies merits belated correction. Persuasive in tone, deftly put together (as ever) and doubtless appealing to many who would never know the living realities, its suppressions are less than honourable. His empirical experience in E. Europe was extremely limited.'[5]

Nixon's point was, presumably, that Bert failed to mention the musical apartheid to which the Gypsy musicians were subject to under the communists. They were generally excluded, for instance, from the *Cintarea Romaniei* (Singing Romania), the lavish state traditional music shows created under Ceausescu to promote and glorify himself and state socialism. There was no place for dark-skinned Gypsies in the regime's promotion of an all-white Romanian nationalist folklore. The positive aspect of this was that the lack of interest in Gypsy music by the state meant that it fared better than other forms of musical folklore by being less subjected to 'arrangement' and what music journalist Garth Cartwright has called 'banalification'.

The recordings (or 'plunder' as musicologist Harold Dennis-Jones considered them) that Bert brought back from his numerous state-sponsored collecting trips provided him with exotic material for many radio lectures, as well as bringing in a small income from the sale of some of the material to the BBC Sound Archive and record projects such as the Topic albums *Folk Music of Bulgaria* and *Folk Music of Albania*. Some he used to interpret what he saw as a moribund English musical tradition:

Traditions that are in full flower can often throw light on traditions that are in a state of dilapidation. It happens often that things in their come-down state that appear mysterious become clarified in the light of what happens elsewhere in a flourishing form. We understand, for example, much more about the meaning of the Mummers' Play and the meaning of mumming through comparison with continental models than we would if we hadn't those continental models.[6]

Although continental and East European folklore traditions might indeed inform our researches into analogous British traditions, we should be careful in assuming like for like. One might argue that if, as Bert always avowed, musical folklore and customs are in a state of flux, reflecting economic and social changes, then attempting to compare like for like in societies as diverse economically, socially and historically as communist Albania and capitalist Britain might not be terribly helpful. We must also take into account the fact that the material Bert used as his folkloric yardstick was itself potentially contaminated by political interference. Even well-intentioned folklorists leave an indelible mark on the people or communities with whom they work. There is no contact without contamination.

Paul Nixon who, as a mature postgraduate student had attended Bert's Goldsmiths lectures, was made aware of the degree of state control and interference in folklore, and the high regard in which Bert was held by senior state folklorists, during the months he and his wife spent in Romania in the 1970s, researching in the Bucharest Folklore Institute:

Some staff behaved as if they had landed useful fish fed by their English godfather – he [Bert] had sent word on; 'a file' existed, institute Securitate officers revealed that everyone was under orders to contain our movements, monitor and document conversations, rule on what archive holdings could be talked about, etc. This was daily reality in high places, intimidating, un-conducive to open-minded exchange where we read fear in the faces of people with family responsibilities and much to lose if they appeared 'unreliable'. As with Bert, senior staff were dismissive of Western anthropology and sociology. It was suspect and unnecessary. They knew all there was to know and would instruct us.

Their statement of working methods asserted that THEY were the experts; peasants just performed without knowing what they were doing; 'experts' made sense of it and told the peasants what was good.[7]

The Nixons were apparently fed 'prize recordings in various genre' – copies of copies of copies – much of it material that they recognised from Bert's Goldsmiths lectures. Institute staff were affronted when asked for field documentation, notebooks, maps, and basic field data such as: 'Who had recorded what? When? In what circumstances? Who were the performers? How often did they do that sort of thing and for whom?' All of which fell on bemused and indignant ears. Why would they want such information? The music was lovely, the performers talented, the costumes colourful, the country beautiful and the political system sustained all this. What else was there to know? Word got back to Bert that his fellow countrymen were making waves and were being less than respectful to the system. Bert was furious, and in a telephone conversation accused Nixon of 'upsetting his good friends'.

Bert's generally uncritical use and promotion of Eastern European folk music and scholarship, and his lack of acknowledgement as to just how much it was mediated by the various regimes, also the extent to which their folklore researchers lived in fear of stepping out of line and appearing to be not sufficiently enthusiastic over such impositions as 'de-religionised ethnology and "Folk" praise for Comrade Stalin', has become more of a concern for academics in the years following Bert's death, especially in light of information made available since the break-up of the Soviet Union. As Nixon explained: 'Native specialists now distance themselves from coercive techniques, performance under orders such as they had to enforce. Authoritarian command-and-obedience structures have collapsed, and with them a great deal of the stuff that Bert passed off as living tradition. Many people are free to say that they can't stand folk music now.'

In his review of Frank Miller's *Folklore for Stalin: Russian Folklore and Pseudofolklore of the Stalin Era* (1991), John Cash of Indiana University had this to say of Socialist folklore:

> One of the tragic ironies of the intellectual history of Socialism is the way Stalinist regimes purported to create conditions for the natural growth of the arts – especially folk arts – unfettered by capitalist restrictions, while in fact subordinating all artistic activity to the service of the state. The resulting professional compromises in method, research, scholarship, and performance have left a climate of public and intellectual mistrust in central and Eastern Europe today.[8]

Despite critics such as Nixon, as with most areas of Bert's life, his academic admirers outweighed his detractors. He was as highly regarded for his knowledge of Eastern European music by many East European academics as he was amongst the British folk fraternity:

> I can hardly express how glad I was to receive your letter. I told my wife that I was more proud of your opinion than of any other kind of recognition including a Kossuth Prize [Hungary's highest cultural honour]. In fact, I often fear your judgement, because your knowledge of the facts is far greater than mine, and compared with it, I am afraid to fall into sterile speculation.[9]

This comes from the Marxist musical historian Janos Marothy who, before his death in 2001, was Professor of Aesthetics at the Budapest Institute for Art Theory and Media Studies, referring to complimentary comments Bert made concerning his 1974 book, *Music and the Bourgeois and Music and the Proletarian*. Marothy has been equally complimentary a few years earlier when *Folk Song in England* had been published, which he considered a 'marvellous book!'

A TUTOR IN ETHNOLOGY

With so few British academics possessed of Bert's impressive linguistic skills and overall view of folk music, for many years he went unchallenged and soon found himself invited into the world of academia and could rightfully claim on lecture material publicity to be 'tutor in Ethnology to the Music Department of London University'.

The worlds inhabited by most special interest groups tend to be a tad incestuous. Everybody knows everybody else. Like the literary and artistic left-wing mafia of the 1930s, to which Bert had belonged, musicologists and ethnomusicologists work together, read (and criticise) each others' papers, meet up at conferences and musicological jollies (wine tasting and boat trips up the Danube for Bert and the other delegates of the International Folk Music Council, IFMC), and Bert slipped easily into this arcane brotherhood.

In 1964 Thurston Dart, a musicologist, conductor and keyboard player, left his music professorship at Cambridge to take up the position of King Edward Professor of Music at King's College, London. While at King's, Dart started up a folk music and musical ethnography course. He died in 1971 and Bert was invited to take on some of his, mostly postgraduate, students. According to an off-the-cuff remark at the time by King's musicologist Professor Brian Trowell, Bert 'had been a known communist but he was too old to be dangerous anymore'. Is one ever too old to be dangerous?

It was a job that Bert loved. The students visited him at Croom's Hill for one-to-one tutorials, and he also lectured at Goldsmiths. He recalled that when the folk music course was started at King's: 'There was some trepidation among the faculty of the Music Department because none of them was a specialist in folk music or ethnomusicology, which is a hideous term, so it meant going outside for people to set papers and also to examine, also, of course to tutor.'[10]

After taking their BMus in fine art music, graduates could then take their MMus in musical folklore. Bert was very enthusiastic about the idea: 'At last there is a possibility of putting folk music studies onto a scientific basis instead of the thrashing about in the thickets that's been going on among amateurs, and also it means we may even see the beginning of the formation of a group of proper collectors and commentators on the material.'[11]

Two of Bert's MMus students who went on to make names for themselves in folk music and ethnomusicology are Dr Lucy Duran, Lecturer in African Music at London University's School of Oriental and African Studies, as well as being a regular presenter of Radio 3's world music programme *World Routes*, and the American musician and folk music scholar Jennifer Cutting.

Cutting, one of Bert's last students, was an ethnomusicology student, who, due to the lack of folk music specialists on the King's College teaching staff, was 'farmed out' for private tutorials with Bert. Every Wednesday she made her way by bus from her flat in Herne Hill, Dulwich, to Croom's Hill for a three-hour face-to-face tutorial. She was always let in by Charlotte and led upstairs to Bert's study where he sat waiting, surrounded by papers, books and tapes. Bert took his work for London University very seriously and didn't indulge in small talk, but was what Cutting described as 'every inch the professional lecturer'. If anything Cutting found him a bit 'stand-offish'. She felt that he was a little contemptuous of what she felt he saw as a rich, spoiled blonde with not a brain in her head.

Earning his grudging respect was a slow process. Her area of interest with Bert was the folk revival and in particular the electric folk bands. She saw the first crack in his reserve when she told him that she wanted to learn the melodeon as part of her course. He said it was a 'fine instrument' (despite having taken very little interest in it in the past). Cutting started taking lessons with Nigel Chippendale, and Bert, seeing her determination, warmed up and gave her a copy of Bob Cann's Topic album, *West Country Melodeon*. In a few days she had mastered Cann's 'Primrose Polka' and played it for Bert on her next visit, and she recalled, 'it was the first time he smiled'. Finally, realising how serious she was about the English revival and its repertory, Bert was very generous with his introductions to the likes of Martin Carthy and Fairport Convention. He was pleased that she was interested in the electric folk phenomenon.[12]

At the end of the course she brought in a year's worth of field tapes – Oyster Band, Steeleye Span, Home Service, Albion Band, Fairport Convention, etc. – and was given a good evaluation by Bert, although he did begin his report by saying that 'when she first arrived she was like an enthusiastic puppy'! Despite being somewhat peeved by the 'puppy' remark, Cutting says that she 'owes everything to him', and on returning to the States she dedicated her first folk-rock album *High Tea*, with her band the New St George, to Bert's memory, and included three tracks from *The Penguin Book of English Folk Songs*, a copy of which Bert had inscribed to her. As the sleeve notes to the album state, Cutting, 'after spending two years at the feet of English folk revival leader and mentor/guru/professor Bert Lloyd, moved to Washington DC, from London afire with desire to make creative British roots music on American shores'.

It's a pity that Bert didn't live long enough to hear the results of his work with Jennifer Cutting, because she went home and created an English-style folk-rock band as good as anything that came out of the English revival (and better than most). She is a fine musician (melodeon and keyboards) and arranger, and, during the New St George's existence, the leader of a group of truly talented innovative musicians. Bert would have enjoyed them.

The study of musical folklore was not picked up in England by the world of academe until comparatively recently, and then in relatively few universities – originally Leeds, Sheffield and London (Goldsmiths), and more recently Newcastle. Throughout his folk music writings Bert portrayed English folk song scholarship as a very amateurish affair ('thrashing about in the thickets'). Which, of course it was. In the United States and the USSR, it had long been a recognised academic discipline with an impressive publishing programme. Bert, unfairly, eschewed American folkloristics for Eastern European models. Here his linguistic skills enabled him to study the books, academic research papers and journal articles of musicologists such as Bartók, Kodaly (who, incidentally, once described Bert and MacColl as 'pop singers'), Katsorova, Tiberiu Alexandru and Brailoiu (and indeed translate them). Writings which most British folk singers, enthusiasts and researchers had no way of accessing. Vic Gammon said:

> We shouldn't forget that Bert wasn't a trained academic, he was a self-starter, he basically made it up as he went along. A guy sitting in a room in Greenwich pulled all this information together and attempted to make sense of it. His breadth of knowledge was unique in British folk music studies. Of course his work wasn't perfect, but it's pretty remarkable and represents folk music research at a certain time and place; things have changed a lot since his day, but he was there at the beginning, and contemporary folk music performance and scholarship would be less interesting, less penetrating without his groundwork, vision and incredible energy.[13]

If one passively and gratefully accepted Bert's beneficence and authority, which was generally the case owing to the fact that there was really no-one in any position to challenge his assertions, then Bert was invariably charming, helpful, and generous in the extreme with his time and information, as so many people testify.

Towards the end of his life, a number of people at the Open University tried to get Bert an Honorary MA. The award was agreed, and one morning the telephone rang at Croom's Hill and a young woman asked Bert for his measurements for his gown. After ascertaining the reason for the gown Bert went downstairs into the kitchen and told Charlotte that he'd been awarded an MA. She said, 'Why?' Bert's answer is unrecorded, but he would have undoubtedly taken it as a welcome confirmation and validation of his acceptance by the academic world. He received his Honorary Master of Arts on 13 May 1978.

A FILMING WE WILL GO...

Bert had been interested in working in television from the 1950s, when he first came back in out of the cold following his stint of being *persona non grata* at the BBC.

He had, apparently, written some music for a television play in 1957. In August that year he left London for the peace and quiet of Polgigga, a tiny remote hamlet a couple of miles east of Lands End, in west Cornwall, there to work on the music. He could hardly have found a more distant spot. Why Polgigga? The only connection between Bert and Polgigga seems to be that the Bloomsburyite Wyn Henderson had a cottage there from the 1930s. In 1931 Henderson ran the Hours Press from a Normandy farmhouse for Nancy

Cunard, and in 1938 she managed the newly opened Guggenheim Jeune Galley in London. For a short while she was Dylan Thomas's girlfriend and in April and May 1936 he stayed with her in the Polgigga cottage. (It was here the following year that Dylan brought his new paramour, Caitlin MacNamara, and, in true Dylan fashion, borrowed £3 from Henderson to buy a wedding licence for his marriage to Caitlin.)

Henderson and Bert obviously had several friends in common besides Dylan (she was very involved in the 1930s surrealist scene) and perhaps she still had the cottage twenty years later in the 1950s when Bert felt the need to 'retire' from Cobbett's 'Great Wen' for a couple of weeks' peace and quiet? It seems too much of a coincidence for there not to be a Henderson connection, even if, at the very least, it was Dylan waxing lyrical about the place one lunchtime over a pint in the Wheatsheaf.

Bert seems to have had little else, if anything, to do with television during the late 1950s and 1960s until at last, in 1969, at an age when most men are preparing to retire, Bert got the opportunity to make a sideways career move into television filmmaking. The opportunity came about through the good offices of his Greenwich neighbour Norman Swallow, the series editor for the BBC's flagship arts programme *Omnibus*. Swallow had joined the BBC after the Second World War. A Manchester Grammar School boy, he went up to Oxford and then into the army. While stationed in Palestine he picked up a copy of the *New Statesman* in the officers' mess and saw an advertisement for BBC staff. He immediately applied for a job and eventually arrived back in England within forty-eight hours of the interview deadline. He got the post and remained in broadcasting for the rest of his working life. He and his wife bought their £5,000 house on Croom's Hill in July 1959 and over the next twenty years they had the occasional meal with Bert and Charlotte, whom they considered friendly, charming and nice, but shy.[14]

TV film director Barrie Gavin, who had been making music programmes for BBC 2 since its inception in 1964, realised that he spent his entire working life in the concert hall and studio, directing chamber music and contemporary music documentaries and had never directed a programme on vernacular music. He decided that he wanted to make films from which he learnt something and, as he knew next to nothing about folk music, he determined to educate himself and the general public with a programme on British folk music 'as happening now. Not antique. The folk music of the cities and towns.' He spoke to Swallow about the idea and Swallow, who, Gavin said, 'had a facility for putting people together', suggested he got in touch with his neighbour Bert Lloyd, who was 'an expert on such things'.

Gavin travelled down to Greenwich for a preliminary chat with Bert: 'I outlined my idea for a film about the living music of our cities and industries. I was somewhat dashed by his [Bert's] response. "Well, that is a notion not without merit." Very quickly I was to learn that this was enthusiasm in the context of his rather quiet and mild personality.'[15]

He found Bert's knowledge impressive and invaluable, and he eventually left with contacts for several singers and local experts, including Harry Boardman and Bernard Wrigley in Lancashire, Pete and Pat Elliott in County Durham, Roy Palmer in the Midlands etc., and an agreement that Bert would be 'the writer and the musical guide on this journey through urban ethnography'.

Once the BBC had made official contact with the singers and arranged dates, Bert and Gavin set off on their first recording trip together. They left with no rigid plan in mind because Gavin believed that when making documentaries:

> As far as possible you should leave yourself open to whatever is going to happen in front of you. It was very much a collecting process of going to a place, usually a pub, where a number of musicians and singers would have gathered, and we'd say sing for us, do whatever you want to do. There was usually an audience, it was a social event. I didn't want it to be antiseptic and studio-bound. It was just like folk song collecting.

What this somewhat scattergun method of documentary filmmaking results in are some undoubted 'magical' serendipitous moments, as well as a lot more material than you can ever use.

Other BBC documentary makers, such as Philip Donellan, would disappear for weeks on end and arrive back with a room-full of rushes. Charles Parker was notorious within the BBC for recording hundreds of hours of speech and 'atmos' for an hour-long Radio Ballad. Despite the fact that in those halcyon BBC days, when money was plentiful, budgets frequently over-ran, and location lunch-breaks were lengthy, table-groaning affairs, and there seemed little danger of serious censure, Gavin was not as profligate as many of his colleagues. He generally managed his budget, stuck to his three or four weeks shooting time, and his film-stock allowance of forty or fifty ten-minute rolls, working at a ratio of about eight to one for a fifty-minute film.

It was Bert's dramatic and structural sense – from his radio work over many years, his journalistic training, and his musical knowledge – that Gavin found so useful when it came to selecting and assembling just fifty minutes of music, landscape and interviews into a seamless visual and auditory narrative, out of eight hours of film.

Once a rough cut of a film had been assembled from the many thousands of feet of film that they'd shot, Bert would go along and watch it and make some structural suggestions – cutting songs, putting songs over landscape etc. – and take note of what Gavin felt he still needed:

> He'd suggest taking this or that verse out here, and spreading it out, or condensing it, and we'd arrive at a fixed structure. Then he'd write the commentary. He was a marvellous writer. I'd say, 'Get me from Harris to Barra in thirty two seconds.' He'd say, 'Yes, all right.' And it would come out at exactly thirty-two seconds, and it would be alive and vivid. It would arrive in long-hand on broad paper. Spidery lines, elegant handwriting, and nine times out of ten it worked first time around – and then we'd record the commentary, the cement that held the whole thing together.

The eventual atmospheric, gritty, black and white 1970 film on industrial song and culture was titled *Rap Her to Bank,* taken from the northeast mining song of the same name. The phrase, which meant nothing to the Head of Arts Programming, referred to knocking (rapping) to tell the winder that miners wish to be drawn up to the top of the pit-shaft. A suggestion that it be changed to the more prosaic (and more understandable) *Music of the People* was resisted.

For many middle-class viewers, particularly in the south, the 'working-class culture' that was beamed into their sitting-rooms was shown not to be an oxymoron, but a living vibrant affair, a major component of which (as had also been shown in the Radio Ballads) was colourful, descriptive, regional speech – this was long before northern accents were commonplace on British national television and radio.

The first scene that Bert and Gavin filmed, that of the last of the Cradley Heath female chain-makers – a seventy-year-old woman sweating over her forge in a primitive workshop, half open to the elements, forging every chain-link by hand – was also a window onto the past. In fact, this programme has, like all the best documentaries, become a valuable historical document. The female, hand-forged, chain-making of the Black Country has long gone, as has the national coal industry, along with the jobs and communities of many of the working-class people filmed by Gavin in miners' social clubs singing about pit closures.

The two men became firm friends with a shared enthusiasm for traditional culture, and on Gavin's numerous visits to Greenwich throughout the 1970s Bert would invariably start their meetings off with 'I've got something upstairs that might just interest you'. Over the next ten years Bert and Gavin travelled together through the British Isles and the Appalachian mountains of North America, as well as exploring Hungary and Romania. Gavin found being with Bert a most illuminating musical education: 'Working with him and knowing him amplified your life. I feel very strongly and warmly about Bert, because my collaboration with him was different from any other I've ever had. It was something very particular, he was a very big figure in my life.'

According to Charlotte, Bert looked upon Gavin as a sort of surrogate son, thoughts that Bert himself would never have opened up enough to verbalise. Bert kept his life very compartmentalised, with few connecting doors, and in the light of information made available since his death, Gavin and others feel that they probably never really knew Bert at all, never really knew where he was coming from or where he was going, or what was going on behind his smiling public face.

After *Rap Her to Bank* there was a gap of a couple of years before Bert and Gavin got together again to produce *The Song of Maramures,* which was filmed up on Romania's northwest Russian border. It was an area in which Bartók had travelled some sixty years earlier collecting songs, and was renowned for its epic ballad singers and shepherds' music. Once again Bert's knowledge of the music, his political credentials and his contact list of friendly Romanian folklorists[16] proved invaluable for a stressful project, due partly to the problem of humping thirty cases of film equipment through rough country on unmade roads. This problem was exacerbated by the grumblings of an uncooperative BBC film crew, who would have felt that 'roughing it' meant having to go without a couple of bottles of wine with their lunch. The atmosphere wasn't helped when, before leaving London, the cameraman announced that he didn't like filming documentaries because he felt it compromised his art.

Sometimes the British film crews would be critical of the way of life in Romania or Hungary or wherever, and complain about the conditions they had to work under and the infuriating bureaucracy they encountered at every turn. Gavin recalled several discussions in hotels when the crew attacked Bert saying, 'You can't believe all of this, it's obviously no good. It doesn't work, it's inefficient.' Bert never lost his temper, nor was rattled by their criticisms, but answered them quietly and with certainty. There was a Marxist answer to everything that came up. Bert was always prepared to cut the Romanians a bit of slack, even when he drove forty-five miles over unmade roads to discover that the musician they had arranged to meet and film was away for a day or two. As there were no telephones in many villages, and frequently no electricity, it was usually impossible to confirm visits before setting off.

To get to Baia Mara in the northwest, where they intended filming, involved flying the length of the country from Bucharest up over the Carpathian Mountains. The cameraman warned the team that Romanian pilots, with a gun held to their heads, were forced to fly their planes in any weather,[17] despite the dangers. His attitude changed, however, when their plane was delayed due to bad weather and he eventually complained of the waiting. When they finally took off the flight turned out to be a stomach-churning, seriously bumpy ride, and when they stopped off in Cluj the ashen-faced cameraman and his assistant insisted on getting off and continuing the journey by train. Bert, Gavin, his wife and young son, and the rest of the crew continued by plane.

By the time they arrived at Baia Mara the clouds had blown away and the sun was out. They were met at the airport by a huge welcoming committee of party officials and local dignitaries who whisked them off for a tour of the region. It being a Sunday, everyone was out enjoying the sunshine; they saw dancers in the town square, singers, musicians and even a funeral procession with a coffin, and mourners carrying candles stuck into large round pieces of bread. Stage-managed? Unfortunately, the cameramen didn't arrive for eighteen hours, so Gavin was unable to film any of the colourful spectacles he'd witnessed.

According to Gavin one of the positive things about a dictatorship like Romania was that due to the huge emphasis on state control, the awareness of the value of their folk culture to the outside world, and their desire to know where everything and everybody was, they knew where most of the best folk musicians, dancers and singers could be found. Gavin would say he wanted to film a fiddler and they'd say: 'Oh yes, there's a great fiddler in such and such a village, he's on our register of folk musicians.'

The distinguished ethnographer, Tiberiu Alexandru, from the Bucharest folklore institute accompanied the BBC party. He was an old friend of Bert's and a few years later Bert revised the translation of his book *Rumanian Folk Music* (1980). A second minder was more of a Party official, in the obligatory B-film belted mackintosh, who spent much of his time trying to clear the dirtier people out of the shot. Eventually, Gavin and Bert cornered him and told him much to his horror that he was being very 'bourgeois' by trying to tidy everything up.

On their trips Bert demonstrated a certainty, a lack of political doubt, which Gavin believed most people would not be able to manage. He remained an unashamed advocate of Stalinism as Gavin saw on one of their filming trips in Budapest when Bert got up before a large gathering at a festival and 'sang for his supper' by glorifying the aims and successes of the Party and extolling the virtues of Albania:

> A lot of the young people we met in Budapest, which was a very lively, interesting place, full of lively, interesting people, all of them convinced socialists, were baffled and amused when they heard Bert extolling the virtues of Albania, for example, a country which they couldn't get into. It was as difficult for them as it would have been for an American, and they said to me, 'He's fascinating, but he's *so* old fashioned'.

The whole process of negotiating their way through both practical and beaurocratic minefields was very draining on Gavin, who was constantly forced to work round obstacles. In their first week in Romania they succeeded in recording just five hours of film.

One day in they went to film a group of women who worked in a collective factory making headscarves and ornamental shawls. They sang as they stitched and were duly filmed. Gavin then wanted to take an establishing shot of the outside of the grim looking factory. He'd just got the camera set up when the minder rushed over and told him he couldn't film the outside of the building because he hadn't acquired prior permission. Every shot had to be cleared by the authorities. Gavin had a brainwave, he turned to the cameraman and said, pointedly, 'Turn the camera OFF'. The cameraman, for once on the same wavelength said, 'Okay!' and switched the camera on. Gavin then pointed to the red running light and explained that a red light meant 'stop'. Gavin got his shot and the official was content.

Gavin and Bert acknowledged that some of what they filmed was set up for them and stage-managed by local House of Culture bosses, who, Paul Nixon claims, 'ordered favoured people to perform well drilled repertories under instruction', and that 'mock-weddings and tutored customs were enacted by industrial commuters dressed in best peasant attire'. And at least once a specialist was drafted in to rehearse the moves to ensure perfect film sequences. This is no doubt true and is not particularly surprising. It would however be inaccurate to assume that all music was successfully controlled and manipulated by the Party. Gavin explained:

There was a certain amount of stage-management but it was less a matter of the singers themselves but sometimes how they were presented. One time we were dragged off to a reproduction of a Romanian village and there was a woman who had a song but she wanted to do it to play-back. It didn't make it into the film. There was an occasional sense of people turning up to be filmed in their Sunday best, but that happens all over the place. It's what people do, they want to appear okay. It's not just an East European thing. But in the larger events the music itself was quite genuine and often very powerful. We were filming an old woman singing the *hora lunga*, this wonderfully elaborate style of singing, and she simply sat on a seat with her head shawl, she had just two teeth, one at the top and one at the bottom, I don't know whether or not she'd put on her best clothes, possibly she had. But the song was absolutely it, no question. Some of the Sunday dances we saw were certainly not put on for our benefit, they had them every Sunday.

An ex-Goldsmiths professor, Diane Waller, art psychotherapist and expert on Balkan textiles, who has worked and travelled extensively in Romania over many years, agreed that not all Romanian folk music was subject to State control. When she was at art school in Oxford she got in touch with Bert through a mutual friend for some advice about a proposed extended visit to Romania. Bert, as always, was very helpful with contacts and suggestions of places and things to see. Waller and a college friend subsequently hitch-hiked, apparently quite freely, all over Romania where they experienced great hospitality and found in the more remote parts of the country examples of impromptu rural music-making being performed below the state radar – local weddings and other family celebrations, weekend dances, and so on.

This was quite different from the large state-organised dance companies and choirs that she also saw, which, as Bert pointed out, were designed to promulgate a positive image of a colourful, virtuosic, socialist folk culture, and had little to do with genuine musical folklore. It's a moot point whether or not at least some of the material filmed by himself and Gavin fell into the same category.

The whole history of folk music under communism from the 1930s Russian appropriation and creation of folklore, which Laura Olson points out in *Soviet Approaches to Folk Music Performance*, was to 'be used widely for the promotion of a myth of a rural idyll; to ideologically re-educate the peasantry; and to boost patriotism', to the break-up of the Soviet Union fifty years later, is an area of research and publishing that has recently attracted a lot of interest in the United States, as well as in those former Iron Curtain countries where dissenting voices and opinions can at last be heard. I think Bert left the foundering ship just in time to prevent his last years being spent in a fighting withdrawal, justifying and defending political regimes and folklore practices that some might consider indefensible.

When Bert and Gavin set off for Romania to make the *Maramures* film, the BBC gave Bert a wad of money for foreign travel expenses, which he proceeded to spend freely. On their return the BBC Accounts Department asked him to give a detailed breakdown of his expenditure. He replied: 'Expenses £200 – all spent. A.L. Lloyd.' He absolutely refused to give an accounting as to where the money went. The next time they went abroad Gavin was made responsible for both their expenses. Bert found it very amusing to ask Gavin for his 'pocket money'. Gavin found it less funny because keeping tabs on Bert's spending meant extra work for him.

The BBC Accounts Department, however, has an elephantine memory and in May 1974 they wrote to Bert to point out that they were holding contracts for two programmes (*Nimmo in Australia* and *The Savage in the Concert Hall*) and after having consulted with their solicitor they were taking £126 out of his fee for the two programmes to cover the Romanian travel expenses still unaccounted for. All was not bad news, though, for what the BBC took away with one hand, the EFDSS replaced with the Society's Gold Badge for services to folk music.

Their third collaboration, which was filmed throughout 1972, was *The Passing of the Year*, an attempt to capture the seasonal ceremonies and rituals of the British folklore calendar, and to show that the British had as interesting and colourful a folk culture, if largely unrecognised, as anywhere else in the world. Again, Bert wrote and narrated the script and selected appropriate folk song recordings to ease the narrative along.

Although an atheist from his teenage years in Australia, Bert, nevertheless, had a deep interest in religious and pagan ritual, shamanism and folk magic, as evidenced by programmes such as *Voice of the Gods*, a study of the sacerdotal voice. In March 1979 he regretfully turned down an invitation from Dave Harker to attend a course on the occult and paranormal because it clashed with a week's course he was running for the Britten-Pears Music School in Aldburgh.

He was good friends with Topic's Dick Sweatenham, a practicing Wiccan whose coven practiced their magical rites in the small, ancient, timbered Witches' Cottage at Bricket Wood, Hertfordshire, the meeting place from 1946 of Gerald Gardner's first Gardnerian coven. Through Charlotte's first husband, William Ohly, Bert also got to know the British Museum ethnographer Cottie Burland, an authority and writer on Latin American pre-Hispanic cultures and author of *Echoes of Magic: A Study of Seasonal Festivals Through the Ages*. Bert was himself once described as 'a witch' by the bohemian, exotic Lady Gore Browne (Lorna Browne) who was apparently no admirer of Bert, but whether she meant literally a witchcraft practitioner or simply used the term as a derogatory epithet is unclear.

April 1976 saw Bert and Gavin, plus Bert's daughter Caroline, in Deep Gap in the northwest mountains of North Carolina, in the heart of the Southern Appalachians; a state in which Cecil Sharp had spent fourteen-and-a-half weeks between 1916 and 1918, and where he collected nearly 600 songs and tunes.

The focus of this *Omnibus* film, *Three Days With Doc*, was the fifty-three year-old blind guitarist, banjo-picker and singer Doc Watson, an icon, then as now, amongst folk music fans. The film opens with a long slow panning shot from left to right across the misty Blue Ridge Mountains, overlaid with an archetypal modal Old Time banjo and guitar instrumental. Then Bert announces 'Saturday, April 13, 1976, North Carolina' – and we're into the programme.

After a brief look at Doc performing to a noisy, cheering audience at a festival concert in the bustling town of Ashville, Bert and the rest of the crew headed off for the 100-mile drive to Deep Gap, a small rural community tucked into the folds of the mountains. Here Doc could retreat from the bustle of agents, record companies and radio stations that had become a way of life since his music, along with that of many other Old Time country musicians, took on a new lease of life in the 1950s when they were 'discovered' by the city-billys of the American folk revival. Young, often university educated, revival musicians, such as Tom Paley, Mike Seeger, John Cohen, Art Rosenbaum, Jack Elliott and Ralph Rinzler travelled down from New York into the southern mountains hunting for the Old Time musicians they'd unearthed on 78rpm records of the 1920s and 1930s.

The cabin-porch family gatherings and the Saturday night small-town dances were soon exchanged for university folk music clubs, concerts and festivals such as Newport and the Smithsonian Folk Life Festival, of which Bert's friend and ex-lodger Ralph Rinzler was one of the founders, and Artistic Director for many years. Interest and support, particularly from Rinzler, meant that Doc could give up picking his Les Paul electric guitar with the Jack Williams's country and western swing band, in which he played to support his wife Rosa Lee and their two children, and revert to his family's traditional repertoire of hymns, ballads and dance tunes, played on acoustic guitar and banjo. As he told Bert: 'When I went to the campuses and you could hear a pin drop, it was a little scary at first, but the most rewarding thing of my life was to do a song that I love dearly, that was dear to my heart, as they say, and find that people were sometimes in tears from the good old ballads and songs.'

A proud man, Doc was determined to pay his way in the world despite his disability. He declared he 'wouldn't have been worth the salt in his bread' if he couldn't have earned a living 'to put a few biscuits on the table and a couple of pairs of jeans for my little fellers as they were growing up'.

As Bert pointed out, 'in a [mountain] culture of hard scrabble and little gain' the family is the economic unit, and children can be economically profitable 'a problem therefore for a boy blind from babyhood'. Doc explained to Bert that it was a problem that both he and his father had to overcome. At fourteen, his father took him out to help him cut up some trees with a large cross-cut saw, and from then on Doc never looked back: 'That one thing, putting me to work, realising I was worth something, might have been the thing that gave me the nerve to tackle music as a profession and go and face the world.'

As a skilled interviewer, Bert always left plenty of space for people to talk and tell their story, and Doc was an ideal, eloquent, subject. Near the top of the film is a long sequence of Doc and Bert walking slowly towards the camera down a dusty country road. Bert dressed smartly in suit-jacket, dark trousers and, a surprisingly casual, white open-necked shirt, walks alongside Doc, hands thrust deep in his pockets, listening intently as Doc talks of his reasons for getting into music and his love of the songs and ballads he's been playing since his father made him his first banjo at the age of thirteen. The occasional sympathetic, quiet 'mmm' was all Doc needed to encourage him to tell his tale.

As well as being a virtuoso musician, he was steeped in his family's southern Appalachian mountain culture, and far from being a simple hillbilly, Doc was, and is, a cultivated performer and a thoughtful and articulate man. It's a thoughtful film which shows what an important part secular and religious music played in the lives of these independent, hardy mountain people who had emigrated from the British Isles in the eighteenth and nineteenth centuries in search of a better life, and who, when industry and urban ways finally got into the mountains, 'took most of the hard knocks of the American economy'.

It finishes with Doc's unaccompanied singing of a mournful Weslyan hymn before fading out on a final panning shot of the mountains.

> And am I born to die
> To lay this body down
> And must my trembling spirit fly
> Into a world unknown.

On a lighter note, during one of their conversations Bert somehow succeeded in falling off his seat and rolling off down the hill. This must have puzzled Doc, who could only imagine from the noise what was happening. Unfortunately it was a shot that never made it into the final cut.

On one of his visits to Croom's Hill, Gavin was introduced to recordings of Gaelic psalm singing and was hooked. The duo decided to explore Gaelic culture for their next project, and in 1978 were working on the Hebridean film *But Still We Sing*. Bert's suggested first port of call was the renowned Gaelic singer Flora MacNeil. Originally from the Isle of Barra, MacNeil moved to Edinburgh in 1948, where she was soon 'discovered' by Hamish Henderson who in 1951, with Alan Lomax, recorded her for the Scottish volume of the *Columbia World Library of Folk and Primitive Music*. She went on to spearhead the postwar revival of Gaelic song, and had traveled to Washington with Bert and the rest of the British contingent for the Smithsonian Bicentennial Festival.

On 18 October Bert and Gavin flew from Heathrow up to the Isle of Harris and checked into MacLeod's Hotel at Tarbert. They moved on to Stornaway and then the Isle of Barra, interviewing and recording in crofts and at ceilidhs along the way. They returned to London at the beginning of November with material for two films.

Following the news of Joe Lloyd's death Bert, who as we've seen had had heart problems for several years, suffered a heart attack before they made the Hebridean film, which then had to be delayed for a couple of months. From that point on, his health deteriorated quite rapidly. He had to be very careful not to overtax himself, and Gavin recalled how he paced himself beautifully. Their last couple of film trips reminded Gavin of Aesop's fable of the Tortoise and the Hare, particularly when they were making the Bartók film. While Gavin and the film crew were dashing about chasing their tails, Bert (who was also suffering from a touch of gout by this time), looking according to Gavin, 'like an English M'lord in his straw sun-hat, drifted serenely and happily through the six weeks filming, notebook in hand, never seeming to hurry but always getting to wherever he had to be, when he was needed'.

During conversations about his work with Bert, Gavin became conscious of just how little they had discussed families, wives and personal affairs over the dozen years of their close friendship and working partnership. Even when Joe died during the Hebridean programme Bert hardly mentioned it.

One of the few occasions that Bert did open up was when they were staying on the Isle of Barra and someone gave him an English translation of a collection of poems by the acclaimed Gaelic poet, Sorley MacLean. Bert came down to breakfast the next morning looking thoughtful, and he confided in Gavin that he'd been reading MacLean's Second World War poems, and that the short, bitter, 'Knightsbridge of Libya', which articulated many a soldier's fear of an unfaithful wife, had struck a chord with him, and brought back memories and emotions he thought long dead: 'Though I am to-day against the breast of battle, not here my burden and extremity; not Rommel's guns and tanks, but that my darling should be crooked and a liar.' Then, over the boiled eggs and toast, Bert told Gavin something of the almost Shakespearean web of love, intrigue, passion, betrayal and death that had enveloped Alan Hutt, Norma, Bert, William Ohly and Charlotte in the 1930s and 1940s.

Béla Bartók, as well as being Bert's favourite composer, was also a folk music inspiration and he gave several lectures on aspects of the Hungarian's work both on radio and live. In 1976 his illustrated lecture on Bartók's quartets and their provenance in his folk song collecting was enthusiastically received by the knowledgeable faculty and musicology students in the Harvard University music department in Cambridge, Massachusetts. Following what was apparently a scintillating and perceptive academic lecture, Bert put on his entertainer's hat and wowed the Harvard Folk Song Society with a dish of ballads, erotic songs and the inevitable tall tales and shaggy-dog stories.

Once, on his car radio, Gavin heard Bert giving a public lecture on Bartók, possibly Bert's lecture at Stoneyhurst College, Blackburn in September 1972, which was recorded and broadcast by the BBC. Gavin was captivated by the images that Bert conjured up and as soon as he got home he rang Bert up and said, 'That's a film!' And so it eventually proved.

In 1979 with the Bartók 1981 centenary looming, they set off for Hungary to follow Bartók's collecting trails. At the back of his mind, Gavin had the scene with which Bert had finished his radio lecture; a moving story of Bartók's discovery of a particularly wonderful lone female peasant singer in a remote valley. This was how Gavin intended to end his film. It would be a fitting epitaph.

During the filming, Bert and Gavin rented a flat from an eccentric landlady in Budapest because it was cheaper than a hotel. There they lived what Gavin described as a sort of Bertie Wooster and Jeeves set-up, with Bert an unlikely

Wooster and Gavin a willing Jeeves who would go down the hill to the shops and do the food shopping for the pair of them. The flat was in an idyllic setting up a hill above the city, surrounded by palms and cactuses. They would sit on the terrace in the morning sun enjoying Bert's favourite breakfast of soft-boiled eggs and peaches picked straight from the tree, while discussing the previous day's filming (of which Bert kept meticulous notes) and plan their next move.

They decided to call the film *The Miraculous Circumstance*, a term used by Bartók to describe the folk music riches he recorded in Eastern Europe. Produced for BBC Bristol and shown on BBC 2 as part of their 1981 Bartók centenary series, the film traced Bartók's folk music collecting trips and folk music's influence on his own compositions. Here Bert's encyclopedic knowledge of, and interest in, classical as well as folk music, came into its own. In *English Dance and Song* (Winter 2008) Gavin wrote: 'Bert's unrivalled knowledge of vernacular culture went along with a true understanding of the creative process. He could express how folk music and Bartók's own music exercised a subtle interplay, so that the greatest collector was also one of the founding fathers of twentieth century art music.'

While making the Bartók film, Gavin discovered that even Bert's impeccable political and musicological credentials in Eastern Europe were not necessarily an open sesame for every door. Czechoslovakia, where Bartók collected 4,500 Slovak folk song texts and many instrumental melodies, refused to allow Gavin's BBC team to enter the country. Gavin was furious at the ban and the general lack of cooperation from the Czech authorities. Bert, as to be expected, became an apologist for the Czech government. He pointed out that they'd had a lot of provocative visits from the BBC in the past, and that he felt that people should visit these countries with a little more understanding. This was of little consolation to Gavin who had to 'fudge' that part of the film.

On the last day of shooting the Bartók film Bert and the crew were in a village high up in the forested Padureni region of Transylvania. An isolated area with the villages strung out along the valleys, or the ridges in between, with few metalled roads. The filming had finished with a dance in the village square. To celebrate the successful conclusion of the work the village mayor laid on a delightful meal of cold meat and gherkins on a long table. A girl who had been in the film sang a beautiful song for their British guests. Bert returned the compliment with a song of his own. Gavin recalled: 'It completely stunned the table into silence. In his characteristic high, reedy, voice, he sang a song of such heart-breaking beauty that no-one ate, no-one touched their knives or forks till Bert had finished. It was very moving.'

Despite having to restrict their filming to Hungary and Romania, Gavin considered *The Miraculous Circumstance* to be their best effort. This opinion was obviously shared by the Judges of Ireland's Golden Harp Festival who awarded it First Prize. Gavin, who was in Galway for the Festival, rang Bert to tell him the good news, thinking that Bert would take it very casually but, in fact, to Gavin's surprise, Bert got extremely excited at the news.

Gavin and Bert always felt that they had been fighting a rearguard action with BBC television as far as folk music was concerned. According to

Gavin, 'No-one in the hierarchy of the BBC ever took folk music seriously. Executive producers would say patronisingly, 'Very nice! I think we should have something as exotic as this every once in a while.'

The major importance for the BBC, according to Gavin was Beethoven or Bach, whereas for Bert all music was of importance. 'He could be as knowledgeable about Beethoven, or Luigi Nono or Messiaen, as he could about folk music in Britain or the rest of the world.'

Bert was a good interviewer because he was genuinely interested in people, he really wanted to know about their lives and music; it was his natural empathy with ordinary people and his belief that everyone has something valuable to offer that had made him such a fine *Picture Post* journalist, and twenty years on, and in poor health, he hadn't lost that belief and curiosity in people and the passion to learn new things. By the time they returned to London from one of their filming trips, Bert would have his small notebooks filled with neatly written names and biographical details of the musicians they'd encountered, lyrics and tunes, and information on such things as the tunings of local instruments, historical, geographical and social comments and observations, information that proved invaluable weeks or months later when he came to write the scripts. Bert didn't take notes in shorthand but during his time as a journalist on *Picture Post* he developed a form of speed-writing, similar to today's abbreviated text-speak.

His meticulous attention to detail in some aspects of his life, such as these film notebooks, is strangely at odds with an earlier, sometimes, quite cavalier attitude to academic exactitude. He ruefully admitted this failing several times in correspondence. For the noted Bulgarian singer Dessislava Stefanova, however, his record notes were all she could have hoped for and were much appreciated, as she told the audience at Bert's centenary tribute concert at Cecil Sharp House in November 2008:

A.L. Lloyd had such good taste as I found when I first came to this country [to live] and a friend showed me his Bulgarian Topic record, that legendary record. When I looked at it, I saw the names of all the singers I had listened to and learned from, and I didn't know they had middle names! It showed me how much attention to detail A.L. Lloyd put into his work. All the little details were covered in those wonderful booklet notes inside the record sleeve.

Bert always protested to Gavin that he was not a good linguist. He could read and make sense of many more languages than he necessarily spoke proficiently. He was fluent in Spanish and German and, as Bert Hardy remembered from their wartime trips, he could speak Russian. He also picked up Norwegian during his six months as a whaler. How proficient he was in speaking some of the Eastern European languages is not clear, although Gavin remembers him speaking a certain amount of Hungarian. He didn't need to be fluent in all these east European languages because he always knew where to go to get stuff translated, and the various folklore institutes invariably supplied translators and guides, probably as much to keep an eye on the foreign visitors as to be helpful. Alun Hughes, a professional academic linguist, fluent in six or seven languages including Romanian doesn't remember Bert speaking Romanian:

> Lloyd's German and Spanish seemed to me to be very good indeed, on all levels. I knew that he had a reasonable working knowledge, for reading purposes, of several other languages, including Russian. I was never, however, too sure of the extent of his knowledge of Romanian. He certainly could read it, but never did I hear him actually speak Romanian. On his visits to Romania, the CSSR and elsewhere in Eastern Europe, he benefited greatly from official approval and help, with transport, interpretation and technical equipment.[18]

Barry Gavin was particularly impressed with Bert's 'marvellous Spanish'. While they were shooting the Bartók film, they took the opportunity in the evenings to start work on a programme about the Chilean communist poet and diplomat Pablo Neruda. Bert was less than impressed with the 'abominable translations' they had of Neruda's work, and in various hotel bedrooms over a few days Bert effectively retranslated most of the poems. He had long been an admirer of Neruda's work, and as early as July 1948 he had contributed an article and a translation of the poem 'Song for Bolivar' to *Our Time* – possibly the first British translation of Neruda's poetry.

Bert and Gavin made seven films over eleven years, but by 1981 it was evident to Gavin that Bert was a very sick man and that there'd be no more musical adventures. For Gavin the tragedy was that, had Bert lived, he could have made a lot more films, he had 'an immense storehouse of information to put across'. When Gavin went to visit Bert just before he died he said it was 'very painful'. Bert hadn't been out of the house for nearly a year. He had no physical energy left. He was very thin which accentuated his wild bushy eyebrows, and sitting in his room on a wooden chair he reminded Gavin of a figure from a Becket play. He knew what was happening to him and for a while it was difficult to talk as they both skirted round the central fact of Bert's imminent death.

19
Fare Thee Well

Can anything be sadder than work left unfinished? Yes, work never begun.

Christine Rossetti

The meaning of life is that it stops.

Franz Kafka

By the end of the 1970s Bert's body had finally betrayed him, and being too ill to undergo any sort of operation he survived the last couple of years through sheer determination, and the faint hope that some efficacious medical treatment might materialise. Caroline remembers the time as often being 'depressing, frightening and uncomfortable for him' despite his assertion that he was 'not so bad' when anyone enquired after his health.

Eventually, as he became less mobile, the man who as a teenager had roamed the seemingly limitless expanse of the Australian outback, and as a young man had sailed down to the southern ocean to hunt the whale, and who later travelled the world as a journalist and folklorist, was restricted to just three rooms at Croom's Hill, Greenwich. His bedroom, bathroom and office were all one level which, as Caroline said:

enabled him to 'scuttle'[Bert's description] from the bedroom to the workroom 'when the mists cleared' and get on with [translating] the Brailoiu. On more misty days he was still coming up with ideas for programmes that he wanted to make. And, at even mistier times, reflections on the ingenuity of man. A couple of days before he died he was contemplating the ingenuity of the invention of the teapot spout.

Caroline's husband, the actor Ted Clayton, took a job in London for the last couple of months of Bert's life in order to help Charlotte look after him. Three weeks before Bert died Charlotte rang up Barrie Gavin and said, 'Come and say hello to Bert'. Barrie knew she meant, 'Come and say goodbye to Bert'. So he went across to Greenwich and had dinner in Bert's room. Bert said: 'It's a bugger that I've got a head full of ideas but not the energy to write them down.' They discussed the idea of a machine that could extract all the unfulfilled thoughts and ideas and preserve them after death: Bert died three weeks later, on 29 September 1982. His death certificate stated 'Ethnomusicologist'. He left £70,500. His papers were, according to Caroline, 'in impeccable order'.

In the absence of such a machine, we'll have to make do with the thoughts and ideas that Bert *did* manage to put in print, in scripts and on film and record. His work in any one of these areas would be worthy of acclaim. The variety, erudition and skill that Bert displayed in all four of these areas was truly remarkable. Not everyone admired him, and not everyone agreed with all of his ideas and theories. Indeed, in the light of subsequent academic research, some of his early opinions on folk music need understandable revision. But his work over forty years was frequently groundbreaking and has been an inspiration to many, many people. In 1983 Louis Killen said in the American magazine *Come For To Sing*: 'His death has impoverished all of us, for there is no one to fill the place he has left behind.' Places do eventually get filled, but there's no doubt that the world would have been a poorer and different place without him.

He was a Marxist, he was his own man, and he believed in the working class. In private, Bert was ultimately critical of Stalin and his worst excesses. According to Ann Waters, who remained a good friend of Bert's after her split with Edgar and regularly visited the Lloyds on her trips to England, both she and Bert were unhappy with the CPGB (they were both Party members), but he saw the communist process as a much longer affair spanning decades, generations even, before coming to fruition, when the world would become a fairer place with enough of everything for everybody, and everybody being encouraged to fulfil their potential.

When asked by French radio interviewer Elise Pin how successful he felt the folk revival had been in terms of his own aims at the beginning, Bert said:

> It has been successful ... very successful really in restoring prestige to traditional music which had lost its prestige; to such an extent that even good traditional singers would seldom sing; would pack their songs away at the back of their memory because people simply did not want to hear it and because the general impression, even for the singers themselves sometimes, was that it was meaningless old stuff that had served its purpose. But that is no longer the case; the stuff has prestige now ... sometimes even an exaggerated prestige. That's the first thing. So the restoration of a certain amount of cultural validity to that kind of music has occurred. The other thing, the American invasion and swamping of our popular musics hasn't been halted; one didn't expect to halt it; one only expected to provide at best even a whisper of an alternative ... that whisper of alternative has occurred.
>
> Within the framework of the folk song clubs there is nowadays, I think, a bit more awareness of working-class problems, partly through the growing acquaintance with industrial songs, a bit more acquaintance with working-class problems among middle-class folk song audiences than was formerly the case. And also probably the organisation of folk song clubs has provided here and there a platform for directly political and agitational song – some of it made in the imitation of folk song, some of it not. But on the whole acceptable to folk song club audiences. By and large I think that even if the folk song revival fizzles out in a few years it will have served a very valuable purpose.[1]

If the true Socialist revolution dreamed of by those idealistic young men and women of the 1930s hasn't yet come about, it's our fault not theirs. We might yet live to regret that we settled for the spoils of a self-serving capitalism. A.L. Morton, Bert's early Marxist mentor, and a friend for more than fifty years, believed that: 'Bert's friends will always remember him as an outstanding Marxist humanist, abundant in ideas but always close to the earth, who loved and shared what he made the object of his study. An enemy of pretension and humbug and a delightful companion, whose wit was always employed not to wound but give pleasure and to provide more light.'

Bert's final piece of writing, was the posthumously published translation and editing of Constantin Brailoiu's *Problems of Ethnomusicology* (reissued by Cambridge University Press as a paperback in 2009), which, until the reissue, Caroline had: 'rather avoided reading, because he was so ill while he was working on it and it was hard to watch. It had sad memories for me.'

But Bert's 'End-Piece' to the book, a short commentary on, and translation of, Brailoiu's *Ale Mortului: Din Gorj* (Songs 'To the Dead' from Gorj, published in Bucharest, 1936), is superb, and as Caroline said:

I now realise that I was very wrong to wish that he would give in and sit back in peace – it must have been thrilling for him to work on this book and weigh the words in these translations. Pretty well to the last days of his life he remained fascinated by work and pleased when he could get on with it. To an outsider it looked as though he was driving himself too hard and would be far better off having a little lie down, but he managed to achieve work that is respectful and scholarly and in those last pieces he seems to me to look at death with his big heart open to both the finality of dying and the magnificent expression the people found to express the deep grief of those who are left. He had very nearly finished the translation when he died.

Although Bert, the atheist, eschewed the ritual of a traditional funeral for himself he appreciated the power and importance of such funeral rituals for those peasants of Gorj, in southern Romania, who sang their pagan liturgy to Brailoiu in the 1930s. Here is the 'Song of the Burial' the last of the 'Songs to the Dead'; a fitting coda to a remarkable life:

> Pray, O pray
> To the seven masons,
> Seven master masons,
> To build you a wall.
> Let them leave for you
> Seven little windows
> With seven lattices.
> Through one will come
> Soul-cakes and light;
> Through one will come
> A fresh-water spring

Recalling your father;
Through one will come
The smell of flowers,
Recalling your sisters;
Through one will come
Spikes of wheat
With all their grains;
Through one will come
Tendrils of vine
With all its fruit;
Through one will come
The rays of the sun
With all its warmth;
Through one will come
The wind with its freshness,
To refresh you
So you do not rot.

20
A Final Assemblage of Memories[1]

A.L. Lloyd is rumoured to be doing 'Blind Date'.

Folk Scene, October 1965

Many songs have beautiful tunes and words that make good sense; and some have their secrets beyond that. I like a song that treads softly but has claws.

Bert Lloyd

I said at the beginning of this book that it wasn't going to be a hagiography, but that doesn't mean that we can ignore all the good things Bert did throughout his life, and this is as good a time as any to mention a couple of things which show how much he valued friendship and was a man of his word. For me, generosity is one of the cardinal virtues and there are countless examples of Bert's generosity with information and musical material, but he was also generous with money (which he could often ill afford), as Bert Hardy pointed out in his autobiography: 'Bert Lloyd was one of the most brilliant men I have ever met ... He was a card carrying Communist, but for all the right reasons. He just didn't think that money should matter. He didn't keep account of anything borrowed or lent, and he was a kind and generous man.'

Bert's disdain for money dated from his early days in Australia and was influenced at least in part by his reading of Richard Jeffries' spiritual autobiography *The Story of My Heart* in which Jeffries dreamt of a Utopian society where work is kept to an absolute minimum, but being so well organised that everyone has sufficient for their needs, allowing them the time to develop their spiritual and artistic side. In the autumn of 1929 Bert wrote a letter to his aunts after just having read *The Story of My Heart*:

The fact is that working for a living bores me. I feel sure that I was intended by nature to be a member of the leisured classes – even if only the leisured class that sleeps under newspapers in parks – for I have an unlimited capacity for amusing myself, and very little appetite for anything else. 'But,' you'll say, 'why not work for a few years till you have enough money, and then pursue your interests.' To which I can only reply that the thought of trying to amass a reasonable sum appals me. I'm not *interested* in money. It is disgusting, fantastic, when one comes to realise how much of one's little life one fritters away in such trivialities as the necessity for working for a living when one might be doing so much more for oneself. When I realise what work can do for me, the ghastly brain-bound platitudes that issue from self-made and prosperous business men, I am yet more fully convinced of the absurdity of the whole business They are lunatics with an infinite capacity for the ruthless acquirement and storing up of metal counters or the paper equivalents thereof. A more futile occupation is hard to realise and in any rational community such maniacs would be locked up in asylums.

TOM HOPKINSON

Tom Hopkinson told me a story that is as amusing as it is important in showing Bert's integrity. It appears that in the 1930s Bert met a Tom Murphy (not J.T. Murphy, the founding member of the CPGB) who had known Lenin when Lenin lived in London in the early 1900s. They became friends and, as Murphy was broke, Bert wrote up his Lenin story and got it published in *Lilliput* (of which Hopkinson was editor) under Tom Murphy's name, so that he would be paid for the piece. Around 1943, the year Bert joined the MOI, Murphy died and in his will named Bert as his executor. As there were no possessions and no money to deal with, the only responsibility Bert had was to fulfil Murphy's last request for his body to be taken to Birmingham for cremation, and for Bert to play the communist anthem, the 'Internationale', as the coffin was consigned to the flames. Bert took his responsibilities very seriously, and succeeded in arranging a date for the cremation and to have the coffin put on a train at Euston. On the appointed day, they set off for Birmingham with Tom in the guard's van, and Bert, crammed in the corridor amongst hordes of soldiers in transit, clutching a wind-up gramophone and a 78rpm copy of the Topic recording of the 'Internationale', recorded a couple of years earlier by the Topic Singers.

Finally, after a fraught journey, Bert, Tom, the gramophone and the record arrived at the crematorium where everything was handed over to an attendant.

Things eventually got under way and it came time for the coffin to slowly disappear behind the curtain, on its way to the incinerator. The gramophone needle was carefully placed on the record and Tom Murphy's coffin slid from sight to the cheerful strains of: 'I'm the man, the very fat man / That waters the workers' beer!'

The attendant had put the record on upside down and got Unity Theatre's Paddy Ryan singing his composition, 'The Man Who Put the Water in the Workers' Beer'. But Bert had done his best, fulfilled his obligation, and Tom could have hoped for no more.

COLIN WILKIE

Sadly, the generous open-house policy, which the Lloyds seem to have run, can lay itself open to abuse (or in this case attempted abuse) as Colin Wilkie recounted:

One absolutely wonderful tale Bert told us was of a visiting American performer who went to the Lloyd's gaff in Greenwich. They were all sat chatting in the garden and having tea and cakes, when the visiting American performer arose and headed for the lavatory. He was gone a long time and Bert began to worry a bit, so he went into the house to see if all was well.

'As I passed my library,' he said, 'I saw the VAP taking books from the shelves and putting them into his guitar case.'

'What did you do?'

'Oh, I waited, and after he'd closed the case, and returned to the garden, I opened it and took all the books out and put them back in their places.'

'Didn't you say anything?'

Bert stroked his face, in that gentle, thoughtful, way he had, and said: 'No, but I often wonder what he thought when he got back to his hotel and found the guitar case was empty.'

WILLY RUSSELL

There have been attempts to document what I have done in the theatre and why I write in the style that I do, but it does not take into account the fact of years spent thrashing about in earnest debate the likes of which you can only ever know if you are part of one of those zealous revivalist movements like the folk song movement. I had the great good fortune during those years to come into contact with some of the best writers, some of the wisest people, like Bert Lloyd, probably the greatest of the folk artists, a folk song expert, a great man, who never functioned as an academic, and I met him because he came to sing at festivals. He was a massively self-educated man, extremely wise. I was sitting at dinner once with Michael Seagroatt. Now, Michael was a seventy-year-old authority on European films and Bert started talking about films and it was just fascinating to see the two of them together. Bert had the most fantastic spread of film experience. A lot of people in the folk song movement were in it purely because they couldn't function anywhere else. Now this wasn't true of Bert. He was a broadcaster, singer, collector, composer, he worked in films, he worked in the theatre and folk song was just one of his interests.

I'd hate to create the false impression that I was a close friend of Bert's or that I personally knew him that well. In total I probably met him no more than six or seven times at the most. Nevertheless, I've always felt that Bert was one of those crucial influences on me and my work. As well as being influenced by his ideas – and particularly his honouring and acknowledgement of the intrinsic quality and power in a language which was either routinely disregarded or lampooned – I had the great benefit of his genuine interest in me as a young writer. By the time I had my first TV play screened I'd largely lost touch with the folk scene but a couple of days after transmission I was delighted to receive a note of congratulation from Bert.

At the 2008 Bert Centenary Day at Cecil Sharp House, Audrey Winter, then in her eighties, came along and added to my pleasures of the day with a story of Bert's kindness to her nearly fifty years before.

AUDREY WINTER

When Eric and I lived in Cambridge back in the sixties Bert came up to sing at the St Lawrence Society [Cambridge University Folk Song Society]. Eric asked the organisers if he could stay with us. At that time I was some seven months pregnant with our son Simon, and although I wanted to hear Bert I couldn't face the idea of an evening in a smoky folk club. They all seemed to be smoky in those days.

Eric went to the club and by the time he and Bert got back I was tucked up in bed. They came in to see me in the bedroom and I sat up and chatted to them. I told Bert how sorry I was to have missed his gig and I asked him what he'd sung. He just sat on the chair by the side of the bed and sang his whole set again – a private performance – just for me. He sang for nearly two hours and introduced all the songs as if I'd been a proper audience. It was quite extraordinary. I've never forgotten the pleasure it gave me.

He was a man with a great sense of responsibility. I can't imagine him ever breaking a promise.

I can't remember anyone that Bert didn't get on with. He was a man with wonderfully catholic tastes.

Folk music journalist Colin Irwin, writing in *Folk Roots*, tells a similar story of Bert's kindness and his obvious delight in sharing his music. Irwin bumped into Bert at a Reading folk festival and said that he hoped that Bert would sing 'Tamlin' on stage later in the day: 'He did better than that – he took me to an oak tree in a quiet corner of the field and sang the whole thing there and then as if his life depended upon it. It remains one of the most gripping performances I've ever seen.'

Bert could be equally generous and encouraging to complete strangers, particularly young people setting out in life and looking for road signs and compass points to help them find and develop the potential that Bert believed everyone possessed. Kind and encouraging words can do wonders at critical stages in one's life and are rarely forgotten, as in the case of David Toop who, thirty years on from his first auditory contact with Bert, is an acclaimed ambient musician, music curator and author of *Ocean of Sound* (1995), which *Wire* magazine's Tony Herrington pronounced 'An extraordinary and revelatory book ... reads like an alternative history of 20th century music, tracking the passage of organised sound into strange and new environments of vapour and abstraction.'

DAVID TOOP

At the beginning of the 1970s I was immersed in a life-changing discovery of sound and music. Since I didn't have any money, a lot of what I learned came from the radio. Avidly listening to BBC Radio 3 I grew frustrated with their output and wrote to the corporation. To my surprise, I received a reply from Madeau Stewart, a producer of remarkable generosity and vision who let me loose in the BBC Sound Archive and commissioned three programmes. One of the few presenters I admired at that time was Bert Lloyd. His *Voice of the Gods* covered exactly that use of sound in ritual that so fascinated me, made me hunger to hear more of these uncanny instruments and eerie voices. Of course, what he had that I didn't was a wonderfully warm, engaging radio voice that drew you into his subject, no matter how arcane. I was very young and quite forward about approaching people who I thought might understand my odd position within avant-garde music, sound poetry and a very non-academic ethnomusicology. [In September 1973 Toop sent Bert a copy of a paper he had recently written entitled *Language and Paralanguage of The Sacred*] Bert was hugely supportive; never mind the fact that I was out on the margins and quite an unknown quantity.

Through working with Bob Cobbing I used to play at the Poetry Society in Earls Court, and heard Bert give a wonderful lecture in the bar there one evening. In mid-sentence he would stop speaking and sing the example of a song he had been discussing. It was a simple thing to do yet somehow shockingly intimate and affecting. Then in the early 1980s, not long before he died, I went to hear him talk about Albanian music. He didn't look in good health but the lecture was spellbinding, given an extra frisson by the two surly gentlemen sitting at the back in KGB-issue leather coats. Without an occasional supportive word from open-minded mavericks like Bert, Madeau Stewart, Laurence Picken and Jean Jenkins, I don't know if my confidence would have sustained me through some very trying times.

One of the last things that Bert wrote, a month before he died, was *Bouquet for the Watersons*, a eulogistic piece to be read at the Waterson's EFDSS Gold Badge Award ceremony. I'm sure he was delighted, in what he knew by then were the closing days of his life, to be 'praise singer' for his favourite folk group, and the group most closely identified with Bert during his heyday at Topic Records:

What a pleasure to be honouring the Watersons! They've been on the go for a good while now but nobody tires of them and nobody will. More than any other singers in the Folk Song Revival they have been a powerful influence, not only on account of their skill but because of the honesty, modesty and affectionate care they bring to the songs of their choice. Also they're prize examples when it comes to seeking and finding songs that are little known but capable of pulling down the stars.

NORMA WATERSON

So many things connect Bert to our career. Although we never called it a career, we called it an accident. When they made the film about the group called *Travelling for a Living* we called it *Grovelling for a Pittance*. I can't say how much of an influence he was on our lives. We met him after we'd started singing, we'd sung together when we were young, so it wasn't that he started us singing, but once we met him he became an enabler. We thank him for that. He took us to America in 1976, it was the celebration of the Bicentennial. We did all the bits we were supposed to do and one day he came along and said, 'Look, you've got to all be in your best bibs and tuckers tomorrow because you're meeting the Queen on the Mall.' There were quite a lot of us, there was Walter pardon, Flora McNeil, there were a whole lot of us from the British Isles. We said, 'Where are you going to be, Bert?' He said, 'Oh I won't be there.' I said, 'Why aren't you doing it?' 'Oh no, I've got to be somewhere else.'

We used to go down and visit Bert at Croom's Hill and have some tea or a meal with him and he'd keep us well entertained. We used to take our John with us [bass-singer cousin John Harrison]. Taking John was a dicey thing, you never knew what sort of a mood he was in. We were all sat down one time, talking discussing the subjects about which songs were written, and our John sat there with whatever it was he was eating with ketchup on. And he said, 'I'll bet there's never been a song written about ketchup.' And Bert said, 'Ah, wait a moment, I'll be back.' He came back with a book, opened it up, and there was a song about ketchup.

When we recorded *Frost and Fire* at Bill Leader's flat, Bert was there on some of the days, and so was Caroline and I remember jumping up and down on Bill Leader's bed with her. Bert gave us a whole host of songs. We've still got the folder. Every now and then when we all get together we open the folder and there's all these little things that Bert sent us – little bits of paper with songs and scraps of songs on them, and little postcards from outlandish places. He also had a great sense of humour, you were never in his company for long before you were laughing your head off.

MIKE WATERSON

Half way through working on the *Frost and Fire* album we went round to Bert's to see how we were progressing, because he'd inundated us with ceremonial songs. We all sat around and he said, 'What have you done with so and so?' We mentioned a particular song and he said, 'Well, sing it.' So we sang it and he said, 'Sing it again.' And he said, 'Sing it again.' And we sang it again and Norma said, 'What's wrong with it?' 'Nothing,' he said, 'Just personal indulgence.'

Another singer whose life was changed by Bert was Frankie Armstrong, she spoke warmly of his friendship and influence at the 2008 Memorial Concert.

FRANKIE ARMSTRONG

I think it was in 1964 that he brought out *Folk Music of Bulgaria* on Topic. And that was such an ear-opener to so many of us. I'd already started listening to the traditional singers of these islands, really seriously listening to vocal styles, largely helped and encouraged by Louis Killen. I'd already started experimenting with different vocal qualities, and when I heard these women from Bulgaria it made the hair on the back of my neck stand up. I had a miserable little bed-sitting room overlooking a railway line, and in there I used to try out all these vocal styles, and later when I was invited to the States to sing I met Ethel Raim, whose speciality was Eastern European, Balkan, particularly Bulgarian singing. I went to lots of her workshops and learnt all these wonderful songs. And that process of Bert opening my ears to the different vocal qualities around the world really changed my life. I became a lapsed social worker. About 1985 I gave up social work for singing.

LOUIS KILLEN

Bert wasn't dogmatic at all, he was very erudite and we all appreciated that. If we wanted information he'd supply it. He was very encouraging, he never laid down laws like you've got to sing like this. As he said in a letter to me just before he died, 'That was Ewan's job, what to sing, how to sing.'

He used to come up to Newcastle and do research on the manuscripts at the Black Gate Museum, especially the Bell manuscripts. One time I took him down to see the Elliotts at Birtley, I drove him down because he didn't drive, this would be around 1961 or 1962. During the drive we got onto something MacColl had said to me that was a little at odds with my experiences. 'Ah, yes,' said Bert, 'Ewan's got a romantic idea about the working class, it comes from all that bohemian agit-prop theatre.' It was then I realised that Bert was the stiletto man, distinct from MacColl who was a bludgeon man. It was an eye-opener to me because I hadn't realised there was any difference of opinion between them.

ROY HARRIS

The first time I met him to talk to was at one of the Keele Festivals. I had sung 'McCafferty' in a singaround and to my surprise Bert asked me about it afterwards, where did I learn it? From whom? And he was complimentary about my singing. He would have been very familiar with 'McCafferty' so for him to talk to me about it meant an awful lot to me. Thereafter we talked a lot, in person and by telephone, and I can tell you I've never talked to a more entertaining and stimulating, informative, witty and wise person. He was an exceptional man. I often phoned him with questions about songs. Occasionally I would get a letter from him with a song text and the note 'I think you could sing this'. He always used a sheet of notepaper turned sideways, writing lengthways in a spiky hand that wasn't too easy to read. I remember 'The Dockyard Gate' coming to me this way, also 'Bold Lovell', several shanties, and the bawdy gem 'Little Piece of Wang'.

One day in the 1970s the American singer Jerry Epstein was staying at our house. He asked me if I knew anything about a particular song. I couldn't help him but suggested I ring Bert for an answer. I rang, Bert replied in that familiar squeaky voice, and I handed the phone to Jerry to ask his question. Forty-five minutes later the call ended, and with a look of awe on his face Jerry described how Bert without moving away from the phone had given him chapter and verse on the song and half a dozen variants and analogues.

Bert once rang me to tell me he had just returned from a trip to Albania where he had been a guest at a government banquet. There, one of the bigwigs asked him a question that he (Bert) thought I was better qualified to answer. Just imagine my astonishment at this, and the delusions of grandeur that swept over me. 'I'll do my best Bert,' I said, mock modestly, 'what is it?' 'Oh,' says Bert 'He wanted to know if Trevor Francis is really worth one million pounds?' Trevor Francis had just been transferred from Birmingham to Nottingham Forest in the first £1million transaction in British football. Bert knew I had been a lifelong Forest supporter. The way he led me on was typical of Bert's witty approach to life.

He liked football. I once met him the day after a dull, defensive match had been shown on TV, I asked his opinion of the match. He rolled his eyes and said 'No Poetry'.

BERNARD WRIGLEY

After recording a second LP for Topic, *Rough and Wrigley*, with Bert again doing his superb sleeve notes, I did a songbook of my own writing, and asked Bert if he'd mind doing an introduction. What I got from him was a superbly crafted piece all about "schwankballads" and "Rabelaisian themes", in which he kindly described me as being the next torchbearer for these earthy songs and stories.

I recorded some contributions to Bert's shanties album in 1976, which involved visiting his house on Croom's Hill. It was fascinating to see his working environment, and I was pleased to be asked to contribute. Even though I'd gone to Transatlantic to do a couple of live albums I was still in love with sea songs. To this day I look on Bert's *Leviathan!* album from 1967 as one of the greatest folk albums ever recorded.

In 1980 Bert asked me if I'd like to do a concert with him at the Victoria Theatre in Stoke. A silly question! He dotted down some tunes on which he asked me to play accompaniment for him. So there we were, the two of us, doing a concert together. It was a momentous occasion for me, made more so by the fact that he died not long after, and I realized I'd played with him on one of his last concerts ever.

He was a unique, erudite, lovely man, and it's a great pleasure to have been associated with him.

Notes

Interviews, conversations and emails and correspondence are with the author unless otherwise stated.

INTRODUCTION

1. All comments and information from Bert Hardy throughout the book are taken from interviews at his Limpsfield farmhouse, 1983, unless otherwise stated.
2. 'Fallen Angel! The Political Cartoons of Jimmy Friell' by Peter Mellini, in *Cartoon History,* the Political Cartoon Society, www.political cartoon.co.uk.
3. All comments and information from Barrie Gavin are taken from interviews and telephone conversations.

CHAPTER 1

1. All quotes from Douglas Cleverdon are taken from interviews and correspondence, early 1980s.
2. Early family history comes from research into birth, death and marriage records, census returns, and Caroline Clayton.
3. All information on Ernest Lloyd's army life comes from First World War army records.
4. SS *Euripides* passenger records.
5. Information on 1920s migration is mainly from the Sydney Public Library, the 1925 edition of the *Australian Encyclopaedia* and G.A.W. Smith's *Once a Green Jackaroo.* Smith made the same trip as Bert in the mid-1920s.
6. *Stringybark and Greenhide*, Vol. 4 No. 3, 1983.
7. Email from Jim Fingleton, 2009.
8. Information by and about John Hasted comes from interviews with Hasted in 1992; his quirky biography *Alternative Memoirs* (1992); and snippets from his 'A Singer's Notebook' column in the early copies of *Sing* magazine.
9. Stephen Sedley interview and personal correspondence, 2008/9.
10. Vic Gammon 'A.L. Lloyd and History' in *Singer, Song and Scholar* (Sheffield Academic Press, 1986).
11. Mike Rosen, conversation, 2007. In an email of 2007, Rosen confirmed, 'I never saw the Oz diaries, nor spoke about them'.
12. 'A.L. Lloyd and his Place in Australian Folk Song' edited by Ron Edwards in the *Australian Folklore Society Journal*, No. 32, June 1996.
13. Kevin Bradley, email, 2008.
14. *Daily Worker* (1930–66) was founded in January 1930 as the organ of the Communist Party of Great Britain.

CHAPTER 2

1. Unless otherwise noted, Leslie Morton's memories of Bert and the 1930s used in this biography are taken from two interviews with Morton and his wife at their Suffolk home in the early 1980s.
2. Jenny Stein (née Hutt) interview in a London nursing home in February 2008.
3. *The Journal of Political Economy*, Vol. 42, No. 4. 1934.
4. Christina Foyle interviews, 1980s.

5. Ben Weinreb interviews, Hampstead, 1992.
6. All quotes by George and Doreen Rudé are from conversations at their house in Rye, 1980s.
7. David Gascoyne, *Collected Journals 1936–42* (a nightmare for research, as there are 402 pages and no index!).
8. Valuable information on the founding of the AIA is to be found in the personal memoirs of the participants in *AIA: The Story of the Artists International Association* (Museum of Modern Art, Oxford, 1983).
9. AIA Statement, *The Studio*. December 1934.
10. In the idiosyncratic *Eimi* (reprinted in 2007 after being out of print for fifty years). cummings famously described the Soviet Union as an 'uncircus of noncreatures'.
11. Ben Weinreb interview, 1992.
12. T.S. Eliot considered Barker (1913–91) 'a genius' and provided him with a modest income through Faber & Faber. Nowadays Barker is perhaps better known as the unnamed 'demon lover' of Elizabeth Smart's cult prose poem *By Grand Central Station I Sat Down and Wept*.
13. Reprinted by Faber & Faber in 2008.
14. BBC written archives.
15. Reprinted by Faber & Faber in 2008.
16. In 'Remembered: James Boswell' by James Friell, on Boswell's website, www.jboswell.info.
17. Gascoyne, *Collected Journals 1936–42*.
18. Sheila Legge remains a little-known, shadowy figure. Gascoyne recalled she was in her mid-twenties when she first wrote to him in 1935. Doreen Rudé told me that Legge ended up marrying a writer, and at thirty-eight died of pneumonia in a fishing village in Provence, where she was then living. John and Maisie Bignall, who were friends of Bert and Norma, the Rudés and Sheila Legge, and who ran a bookshop (Bignall for Books) in Parkway, Camden Town, in the 1930s, made a pilgrimage to Provence to lay flowers on Legge's grave.
19. *Left Review* was the organ of the British section of the Writers' International with the second largest circulation of any literary magazine in the UK. Its concern with reconciling aesthetics with left politics was serious, and during Rickword's editorship (II:4 to III:5) it published a considerable body of significant writing. Its final period, under Swingler's editorial control, was marked by greater control by the CP and a more political/doctrinaire tone (see www. Biblio.com).
20. Charles Montagu Slater was a writer and librettist for Benjamin Britten's opera *Peter Grimes*. He also worked with the legendary documentary maker John Grierson on films such as *Coal Face*. In 1937 he wrote the strike drama *Stay Down, Miner*.
21. Interview with Arnold Rattenbury at his home in Wales in the 1980s.

CHAPTER 3

1. Caroline Clayton correspondence.
2. Dr Alun Hughes of the Welsh Communist Party, interviewed in his home in Wales, 1980s.
3. John Lewis, *The Left Book Club*.
4. Alun Hughes interview, 2009.
5. Harold Dennis-Jones interview at his Tunbridge Wells flat in 1983, and subsequent correspondence when he went to do research in the Bucharest folklore archives.
6. Soon, according to a 2009 BBC radio programme, Churchill's government would be secretly paying Franco millions of pounds to stay out of the Second World War and remain neutral and leaving Britain access to the Mediterranean.

CHAPTER 4

1. Important sources for descriptions of the 1937/8 whaling season on the *Southern Empress* include a 1983 interview with ex-whaleman Bernard Campbell from Hull, who sailed on Bert's sister-ship; Bert's whaling diary; his sleeve notes for the Topic LP *Leviathan!*; and Alun Owen's *The Whalers of Anglesey*.

CHAPTER 5

1. 'The Donkey and the Zebra' *Folk Review,* September 1974. Michael Grosvenor Myer interview.
2. Information on Bert's BBC radio work came from, among other sources, the A.L. Lloyd Archive at Goldsmiths College, Caroline Clayton's collection of scripts, the BBC written archives, listening copies of programmes and interviews with BBC personnel, such as Charles Chilton, Madeau Stewart and Douglas Cleverdon, one of Bert's major producers.
3. Not strictly an invention, because in William Toone's 1834 *Glossary and Etymological Dictionary* we find: 'Hogsnorton a town in Oxfordshire properly spelt Hoch [Hook] Norton.' An early insult was, 'You were born at Hogs Norton, where pigs play on the organ.' Some early writers place the town/village in Leicestershire.
4. Incident related by Bert Hardy.
5. Olive Mary Shapley (1910–99) BBC pioneer in vox pop recording. She worked for BBC North Region in the 1930s under the left-wing radical Archie Harding with Joan Littlewood and Ewan MacColl. Perhaps an unacknowledged influence on MacColl's later *Radio Ballads?*
6. Laurence Gilliam, *Picture Post,* November 1940.
7. Ben Harker, *Class Act* p. 273.
8. Tom Hopkinson interview, 1983.
9. Cheesman 'Poetries On and Off the Air at the BBC World Service' *Diasporas, Migration and Identities*: www.open.ac.uk/socialsciences/diasporas/themes/poetries_on_and_off_air.htm.

CHAPTER 6

1. Jenny Stein (née Hutt) interview in a London nursing home in February 2008.
2. Eric Scott correspondence.
3. Harriette Flory, 'The Arcos Raid and the rupture of Anglo-Soviet relations', *Journal of Contemporary History 12* (1977) Also various ARCOS internet sites.
4. Jennings helped found Mass Observation and organise the 1936 Surrealist Exhibition.
5. Jill Balcon interview, 1992.
6. Erika Bach interview, Bristol, 1991.
7. Peter Cox, correspondence.

CHAPTER 7

1. Dan Davin, conversations, 1980s.
2. 'The Sign of the Cross', *Observer Magazine,* 30 October 1983.
3. Army records.
4. See Michael Anglo's *Service Newspapers of the Second World War.*

CHAPTER 8

1. See: Vladimir O. Pechatnov 'The Rise and Fall of Britansky Soyuznik: A Case study in Soviet Response to British Propaganda of the Mid-1940s', *The Historical Journal* 41, 1 (1998), Cambridge University Press.
2. Leslie Morton, conversation.
3. Tom Hopkinson, conversation.
4. Ibid.
5. Bert Hardy, 1983.

CHAPTER 9

1. Charlotte Lloyd conversation, 1982.
2. Jill Balcon interview.

3. Willy Russell interview, 2009.
4. Bert Hardy, 1983.
5. Tom Hopkinson interview.
6. Michael Rosen, conversation, 2008. Rosen is currently a regular BBC broadcaster.
7. Geoffrey Bridson, *Prospero and Ariel: The Rise and Fall of Radio, A personal Recollection*, Gollancz, 1971.
8. Arnold Rattenbury interview, 1980s.
9. According to Camilla Raab (who worked for the WMA at the time): interview, 1983.
10. Pat Shaw (1917–77): musician, folksong collector, composer and editor, with Emily Lyle and others, of the magnificent eight volume *Greig-Duncan Folk Song Collection*, Mercat Press, 1981–2002.
11. Norma Waterson, interview.
12. Vol. 1 No. 4 Jan/Feb 1955. For information, and confirmation, regarding Edgar Waters, and his time in London, I am indebted to Kevin Bradley of the National Library of Australia for letting me hear his in-depth biographical interviews with Waters for the Library. Other sources include correspondence between Edgar and Ann Waters and Dave Arthur, the A.L. Lloyd Archive at Goldsmiths College, London, and articles and letters by Waters in Australian folk magazines and journals, particularly the *Australian Folklore Society Journal* No. 32 June 1996, in which Waters answers what he called an 'outrageous and defamatory' article 'Laying Lloyd to Rest', by Jamie Carlin in the *Cornstalk Gazette*, March 1966.
13. NLA interview. For those who wish to follow the fascinating history of the song there is Ted Anthony's book *Chasing the Rising Sun: The Journey of an American Song* (Simon and Schuster, 2007).
14. NLA interview.
15. *Australian Folklore Society Journal* No. 32, 1996.
16. This was probably the one 'collected and edited' by John Manifold and published by Ron Edwards' Ram Skull Press between 1951–55 as part of the series of ballad broadsheets Entitled *Bandicoot Ballads*.
17. Letter from Waters to Bert, A.L. Lloyd Archive, Goldsmiths College.
18. Ibid.
19. *Old Bush Songs* (Angus and Robertson, 1957).
20. 'The Great Australian Folk Song That Wasn't' *Quadrant* vol. L111, No. 3, 2009.
21. Kevin Bradley interview with Waters for NLA.

CHAPTER 10

1. Timothy Neat, Hamish Henderson's biographer, correspondence.
2. In the 1956 album notes by Kenneth Goldstein for the Riverside series of Child Ballad recordings by Bert and MacColl, in which Bert is credited with learning songs from his East Anglian fisherman father!
3. *Recorded Folk Music*, Vol. 2, January/February 1959.
4. Information on the arcane workings of the EFDSS and the characters involved comes from personal knowledge and the back issues of *EFDSS News* and *English Dance and Song* magazine, which I edited for over twenty years.
5. For a while in the 1920s Amice Mary Calverley studied music under Ralph Vaughan Williams and was a noted English-born artist and inveterate adventurer and traveller who filmed peasant life in Egypt, the Balkans and on Crete. She eventually settled in Canada.
6. Paul Nixon, correspondence.
7. Mike Yates interview, 1983. Bert was still on the editorial board in 1971, when I was invited to join by the editor Dr Russell Wortley (1912–80; *Folk Music Journal* editor, 1965–71). When Bert and I left Cecil Sharp House to drive home to south London following our meetings, Bert invariably had a couple of Eastern European books under his arm for review, in languages incomprehensible to the rest of us.
8. A.L. Lloyd archive, Goldsmiths College.

9. Ibid.
10. Chris Roche interview, at his house in Croydon in 1980s.
11. Mudcat Café, www.mudcat.org. A.L. Lloyd: history and anecdotes thread.
12. Letter from Bert to Dave Harker.
13. Tom Hopkinson interview.
14. Those who want to participate in the Did He, Didn't He? Bert Lloyd Songwriting Detective Game could do worse than start by checking out the numerous Lloyd threads at www.mudcat.org. Despite the hope expressed a couple of times in the Bert threads that this biography will clear up once and for all which songs he did and didn't re-write, I'm afraid I've had neither the time nor space to go far down that line of investigation. Folk sleuths such as Brian Peters, Stephen Winick and the late Malcolm Douglas have been doing a good job of unravelling the provenance of many of Bert's songs.
15. Mike Parry, correspondence, 2008.
16. John Pilgrim, *Skiffle: The Roots of British Rock,* written for the 1998 Royal Albert Hall concert 'The Roots of British Rock'. Available at www.thecreativecartel.org/lonnigans.html.
17. Peggy Seeger, conversation.
18 Edward and Judy Williams interview, Bristol, 1993.
19. Pilgrim, *Skiffle.*

CHAPTER 11

1. 'Take It Easy, But Take It', *JAFL* [Journal of the American Folk-Lore Society], Vol. 83 No. 327, 1970.
2. Copy of proposal in A.L. Lloyd Archive, Goldsmiths College.
3. The main sources of information on the Ramblers are interviews with John Hasted, Jay Butler and Alun Hughes.
4. *Music in the World of Islam* three-CD series, Topic TSCD901–3.
5. *Bert: A Personal Memoir,* broadcast on Channel 4, 5 January 1986.
6. Leslie Shepard 'A.L. Lloyd: A Personal View', in *Singer, Song and Scholar* (Sheffield Academic Press, 1986), Shepard's account of meeting Bert, and the Coal Board song-collecting scheme that Shepard instigated.
7. MacColl talking in *Bert: A Personal Memoir.*
8. Transcription from recording of the lecture in the New South Wales Folk Federation Collection. Thanks to Mark Gregory and the Federation for the dubbed copies.
9. Bert in interview with French radio journalist Elise Pin, 1972.

CHAPTER 12

1. Copy of letter sent to me by Ken Bell.
2. Jean Ritchie interview.
3. Peggy Seeger, conversation.
4. Spencer Leigh's article *Hello Me Ol' Mateys* in which he examined the BBC Written Archives for an appraisal of the late 1950s teenagers music shows *Skiffle Session, Saturday Skiffle Club* and *Saturday Club* at: www.spencerleigh.demon.co.uk/Feature_Satclub.htm.

CHAPTER 13

1. Later, of course, in the late 1960s and early 70s, bands such as Crosby, Stills, Nash & Young gave voice to the fears and concerns of many young people in their songs dealing with anti-war politics and countercultural issues, such as 'Ohio', their 1970 song condemning the Kent State 'massacre' of students protesting against an escalation of the Vietnam war.
2. *Sing Out!*, February/March 1962. There's also a letter from Bert on p. 61 of the same issue on the lack of protest songs in Eastern Europe.

3. *Leadbelly and Ironhead* blog (15 November 2008), http://bartbull.blogspot. com/2008_11_01_archive.html.
4. Stephen Sedley interview and correspondence, 2008/9.
5. Ibid.
6. *Folk Song in England* (Lawrence & Wishart, 1967).
7. Ken Bell, correspondence.
8. Eric Winter interview.
9. Bert's obituary of Willie Clancy (1919–72) in *English Dance and Song*, Vol. XXXV No. 2, 1973.
10. Photocopy of article sent from Camilla Raab, 1980s. Also available at http://issuu.com/ leftspace/docs/ourhistorybulletin_6
11. Hylda Sims, singer and poet, and an early member of the choir, conversations.
12. Arnold Rattenbury interview.
13. Alun Hughes interview.
14. See Huxley's book *A Scientist Among the Soviets* (1932) for confirmation of his credulity as far as the Soviet Union was concerned.
15. Duncan Thompson, *Pessimism of the Intellect?: A History of New Left Review* (Merlin Press, 2007), and John Saville, *Memoirs from the Left* (Merlin Press, 2003).
16. Shirley Collins, conversations.
17. Bill Leader, conversations.
18. *The Living Tradition* (No. 68, May/June 2006).
19. A.L. Lloyd Archive, Goldsmiths College.
20. Sweatenham, Leader and Engle, conversations, and Topic material in the A.L. Lloyd Archive, Goldsmiths College.
21. *Rock 'n' Reel*, March/April 2008.
22. *Voice of the People*, 20 CD series (Topic TSCD651–670, 1998).
23. Joan Littlewood, *Joan's Book* (Methuen, 1994).
24. BBC written archives.
25. Ibid.
26. Charles Marowitz (ed.) *The 'Encore' Reader: A Chronicle of the New Drama* (Methuen, 1965).
27. Concert programme from Douglas Cleverdon.

CHAPTER 14

1. The column, written under the name of Speedwell, eventually turned out to have been written by Ewan MacColl.
2. Unpublished manuscript.
3. Louis Killen interview, 2008.
4. Mudcat Café, www.mudcat.org.
5. Special Branch documents released by The National Archives.
6. David Attenborough, conversation, 2009.
7. Special Branch files at The National Archives.
8. Stan Hugill interview.
9. Note on the Mudcat Café website, www.mudcat.org, 2008.
10. Ibid.
11. 'The Concertina as an Emblem of the Folk Music Revival in the British Isles', *British Journal of Ethnomusicology*, Vol. 4, 1995.
12. 'Power to the People', *Observer*, 10 August, 2008.
13. Hylda Sims, *On That Train and Gone: The Fifties, Skiffle and Stuff*, originally at www. hylda.co.uk/articles.html#anchortrain (link now defunct).
14. John S. Manifold, *Who Wrote the Ballads: Notes on Australian Folksong*, Australasian Book Society, Sydney, 1964.
15. Dave Arthur (ex-denizen) personal recollections.

16. www.karldallas.com/OldIndex07-03-19.html.
17. Arnold Rattenbury, 1993.
18. Talk with Dave Arthur at Bert's centenary celebration at Cecil Sharp House, November 2008.
19. Bob Davenport interview, 2008.
20. Peggy Seeger, conversation.
21. Barry Murphy, conversation.
22. Mark Gregory email.

CHAPTER 15

1. Peggy Seeger, conversation.
2. Louis Killen, converstation, Cecil Sharp House, 2008.
3. Peter Cox, conversation.
4. Norma Waterson, interview.
5. Peggy Seeger, conversation.
6. Louis Killen, conversation.
7. Julia Seiber, conversation.
8. Edward Williams interview.
9. Dave Swarbrick, conversation.
10. Barry Taylor interview, 1974.
11. *Sunday Telegraph*, 30 September 1990.
12. Douglas Cleverdon interview.
13. *Independent*, 5 January 2004.

CHAPTER 16

1. 'A.L. Lloyd and History', *Singer, Song and Scholar,* Sheffield Academic Press, 1986.
2. Vic Gammon, 'Folk Song Collecting in Sussex and Surrey, 1843–1914', *History Workshop,* Autumn 1980.
3. *English Dance and Song,* Summer, 1972, p. 73. A.E. Green, review of reprint of John Bell's *Rhymes of the Northern Bards,* Introduction by Dave Harker, Frank Graham, Newcastle upon Tyne.
4. Dave Arthur interview, 2008.
5. *Keynote* magazine, January 1959.
6. Thomas Hardy gave an interesting take on 'revivals' in *The Return of the Native*: 'A traditional pastime is to be distinguished from a mere revival in no more striking feature than this, that while in the revival all is excitement and fervour, the survival is carried on with a stolidity and absence of stir ... .'
7. Bob Davenport interview.
8. I now regret not having taken up Gill Cook's offer to go round to her flat and 'go through' Bert's collection, but at that time the possibility of a Bert biog was pretty remote and I was involved in other things.
9. A.L. Lloyd Archive, Goldsmiths College.
10. Bernard Wrigley, email, 2008.
11. Roy Harris, communication.

CHAPTER 17

1. Barry Taylor interview, 1974.
2. Willy Russell, correspondence, 2009.
3. Barry Taylor interview.
4. Barrie Gavin interview.

5. A couple of times during 1967, when my wife and I ran a Wednesday evening 'trad' night at the Cousins (the Young Tradition frequently hosted the Saturday all-nighters) for those who wanted a mid-week 'Cousins fix' but also a brief respite from DADGAD-tuned guitars.

6. Writing on the *Folk Song in England* thread on the Mudcat Café website, www.mudcat. org.

7. www.Karldallas.com/WorksInProgress/ (link currently defunct).

8. Ibid.

9. *Folk Music Journal*, 1968.

10. Arnold Rattenbury interview.

11. Vera Rutherford, correspondence.

12. *Folk Music*, Vol. 1 No. 1, November 1963.

13. Interview by Grosvenor Myer for *Folk Review,* September, 1974.

14. Martin Carthy, conversation. Carthy confirmed that, despite rumours to the contrary, Dylan did not stay with him.

15. *Keele Folk Festival 1965*, Sing Productions.

16. Audrey Smith, correspondence.

17. Martin Carthy, conversation.

18. Louis Killen, conversation.

19. Madeau Stewart interviewed on Barrie Gavin's Channel 4 TV film *Bert: A Personal Memoir* (1986).

20. Barrie Gavin, conversation.

21. Jill Balcon, interview.

22. Peggy Seeger, conversation, 2008.

23. *Folk Music Journal* obituary by Dave Arthur, 1982.

24. Taped interview with Bert sent to me in the 1980s. Source unknown.

25. Vic Gammon, 'A.L. Lloyd and History', *Singer, Song and Scholar*, Sheffield Academic Press, 1986, p. 160.

26. *Australian Folklore Society Journal*, December 1996.

27. In the 1960s, my ex-wife, Toni, and I were involved as 'magical advisors' to the film producer Stanley Mann when he decided to bring the story 'up to date' in the cinema (*Tam-lin*, 1970), directed by Roddy McDowell, and including songs from Pentangle.

28. When my then wife, Toni, and I heard Bert sing 'Tamlin' around 1968 it appealed to us, and this, along with a couple of traditionally collected versions sent to us by Hamish Henderson, inspired us to put our own version together, which we sang around the folk clubs, as well as to Swarbrick. As we were planning a 'magical' ballad album (*Hearken to the Witches' Rune*) we said we'd rather not have our version pre-empted by Fairport, hence Swarbrick making the approach to Marion Grey.

29. Later published as 'Electric Folk Music in Britain' in *Folk Music and Modern Sound*, University Press of Mississippi, 1982.

30. Barry Taylor interview, 1974.

31. A.L. Lloyd Archive, Goldsmiths College. See also www.thetransports.com.

CHAPTER 18

1. Venetia Newall, correspondence.

2. Robert Carrington, correspondence.

3. Dr Lionel Sawkins, correspondence.

4. 'The Folk Element in Music' *Ballads and Songs*, No. 3, 1965.

5. Dr Paul Nixon, correspondence.

6. Barry Taylor interview, 1974.

7. Dr Paul Nixon, correspondence.

8. *Folklore Forum*, 27:2, 1996.

9. A.L. Lloyd Archive, Goldsmiths College.

10. Barry Taylor interview, 1974.

11. Ibid.
12. Jennifer Cutting interview, 2009. Jennifer, who now performs and records with her current electric folk band OCEAN, is a Folklife Specialist at the American Folklife Center at the Library of Congress in Washington, DC.
13. Vic Gammon, conversation, 2009.
14. Norman Swallow interview, 1983.
15. All quotes by Barrie Gavin are from interviews, 1983–2009.
16. As early as 1952 Bert had toured Romania and visited the Bucharest folk music institute as part of a British-Rumanian Friendship Association delegation. And in 1959 he spent the whole summer travelling around the main 'Lautar' centres of south and central Romania interviewing and recording Gypsy musicians. A trip which resulted in the 1960 radio programme *The Gypsy Fiddler*.
17. Interestingly, following the 1989 Romanian Revolution, President Nicolae Ceausescu and his wife Elena attempted to flee from the scene of his crimes by commandeering a car. Elena, the Lady Macbeth of Romanian politics, held a gun to the driver's head during their escape attempt. When eventually caught they were both summarily executed.
18. Alun Hughes interview.

CHAPTER 19

1. Elise Pin interview, 1972.

CHAPTER 20

1. Unless otherwise stated, these memoirs were written for this biography.

Bibliography and Select Discography

BIBLIOGRAPHY

Here is a selection of the books, journals and websites that I found most useful during the writing of this biography. Not all of them are necessarily quoted from but all were read and informed my take on Bert's life. Also consulted were many hundreds of letters, personal and business, a gallimaufry of folk magazines from the early 1960s through to the 1980s, countless other websites, and most of Bert's written output from the 1930s to his death in 1982. Also my own memories and opinions of the folk scene from my misspent youth as a young skiffling teenager to my misspent mature years as performer and writer.

My interim bibliography of Bert's writing was published in the 1986 Sheffield Academic Press collection of essays *Singer, Song and Scholar*. Too large to include here, it can be read on my website at www.bertlloyd.org, as can a longer essay on Bert as a storyteller, which didn't get into the biography due to considerations of size.

Addison, Paul (1982) *The Road to 1945*, Quartet Books.
Aistrop, Jack and Reginald Moore (eds) (1945) *Bugle Blast: A Third Anthology From the Services*, George Allen and Unwin.
Alexander, Bill (n.d.) *George Orwell and Spain*, reprinted from *Inside the Myth* edited by Christopher Norris (Lawrence & Wishart, 1984).
Allen, Eleanor (1988) *Young in the Twenties*, A & C Black.
Allsop, Kenneth (1985) *The Angry Decade: The Cultural Revolt of the 1950s*, John Goodchild Publishers, Wendover.
Anderson, Hugh (1970) *The Story of Australian Folksong*, Oak Publications, New York.
Anglo, Michael (1977) *Service Newspapers of the Second World War*, Jupiter Books.
—— (1977) *Nostalgia: Spotlight on the Fifties*, Jupiter Books.
Armstrong, Frankie with Jenny Pearson (1992) *As Far as the Eye Can Sing: An Autobiography*, The Women's Press.
Armstrong, W.H. (ed.) (1930) *Song Book: Containing 25 Popular Songs of the late Thomas Armstrong*, Noel Wilson, Chester-le-Street.
Ashraf, Mary (1975) *Political Verse and Song from Britain and Ireland*, Lawrence & Wishart.
Ashton, John (with an introduction by A.L. Lloyd) (1973) *Real Sailor Songs*, The Broadsheet King (reprint of 1891 edition).
Atkinson, David (2001) 'The English Revival Canon: Child Ballads and the Invention of Tradition', *The Journal of American Folklore* Vol. 114, No. 453, 2001, University of Illinois Press on behalf of American Folklore Society.
Bakewell, Michael (1999) *Fitzrovia: London's Bohemia*, National Portrait Gallery Publications.
Bell, Quentin (1990) *Bloomsbury*, Weidenfeld & Nicolson.
Bird, Brian (1958) *Skiffle*, Robert Hale.
Blacking, John (1990) *A Common-sense View of all Music*, Cambridge University Press.
—— (1976) *How Musical is Man?*, Faber & Faber.
Bold, Alan (1970) *The Penguin Book of Socialist Verse*, Penguin Books.
Boldizsar, Ivan (ed.) (1981) *The New Hungarian Quarterly* (three articles on Bela Bartok's collecting, research and classification of folk song), Lapkiado Publishing House, Budapest.
Boyd, Joe (2006) *White Bicycles: Making Music in the 1960s*, Serpent's Tail.
Boyes, Georgina (1993) *The Imagined Village*, Manchester University Press.
—— (2004) 'The Singing Englishman: An Introduction and Commentary', *Musical Traditions* www.mustrad.org.uk.

Brailoiu, Constantin (ed. and trans. A.L. Lloyd) (1984) *Problems of Ethnomusicology*, Cambridge University Press.

Brand, Oscar (1967) *The Ballad Mongers: Rise of the Modern Folk Song*, Minerva Press.

Branson, Noreen and Margot Heinemann (1971) *Britain in the Nineteen Thirties*, Weidenfeld & Nicolson.

Bridson, D.G. (1971) *Prospero and Ariel: The Rise and Fall of Radio, A Personal Recollection*, Victor Gollancz.

Brill, Lesley (1997) *John Huston's Filmmaking*, Cambridge University Press.

British Broadcasting Corporation (1938) *BBC Handbook*, British Broadcasting Corporation.

Brocken, Mike, Alistair Banfield and Rod Stradling, 'The Complete Topic Records Discography', *Musical Traditions Internet Magazine*, www.mustrad.org.uk/discos/discog.htm.

—— (2003) *The British Folk Revival 1944–2002*, Ashgate Publishing, Aldershot.

Burland, C.A. (1972), *Echoes of Magic: A Study of Seasonal Festivals*, Peter Davies.

Burns, Emile (1935) *A Handbook of Marxism*, Victor Gollancz.

Bush, Alan (1980) *In my Eighth Decade and Other Essays*, Kahn and Averill.

Cable Street Group (1995) *The Battle of Cable Street 1936*, The Cable Street Group, London.

Cameron, James (1968) *Point of Departure: An Autobiography*, Arthur Barker.

Carey, John (1992) *The Intellectuals and the Masses: Pride and Prejudice Among the Literary Intelligentsia, 1880–1939*, Faber & Faber.

Carlin, Richard (2008) *Worlds of Sound: The Story of Smithsonian Folkways*, Smithsonian.

Carpenter, Humphrey (1996) *The Envy of the World: Fifty Years of the BBC Third Programme and Radio 3*, Phoenix Giant.

Carrington, R.C. (1971) *Two Schools: A History of St Olave's and St Saviour's Grammar School Foundation*, the Governers of the St Olave's and St Saviour's Grammar School Foundation.

Carthy, Martin (1987) *A Guitar in Folk Music*, New Punchbowl Music.

Chen, Jack (1944) *Soviet Art and Artists*, The Pilot Press.

Chipp, Herschel B. (1968) *Theories of Modern Art*, University of California Press.

Chisholm, Anne (1985) *Nancy Cunard*, Penguin Books.

Clarke, John, Chas Cricher and Richard Johnson (eds) (1979) *Working Class Culture*, Hutchinson University Library.

Colcord, Joanna C. (1964) *Songs of American Sailormen*, Oak Publications, New York.

Collins, Shirley (2004) *America Over the Water*, SAF Publishing.

Cleverdon, Douglas (Director of Poetry Productions) (1965) *Verse and Voice: A Festival of Commonwealth Poetry*, Poetry Book Society.

Communist Review (the Communist Party's monthly journal). Began May 1921, changed name to *The Communist* (1927), reverted to *Communist Review* (1929), ceased publication 1935.

Cooke, James (1996) *Great Singers on the Art of Singing*, Dover.

Cope, David (1999) *Central Books: A Brief History 1939–1999*, Central Books.

Cornforth, Maurice (ed.) (1978) *Rebels and their Causes: Essays in Honour of A.L. Morton* (contributors include Edgell Rickword, Eric Hobsbawm, Jack Lindsay, Christopher Hill and A.L. Lloyd), Lawrence & Wishart.

Coulton, Barbara (1980) *Louis MacNeice in the BBC*, Faber & Faber.

Cox, Peter (2008) *Set into Song*, Labatie Books (history of the Radio Ballads).

Craig, David (1973) *The Real Foundation: Literature and Social Change*, Chatto & Windus.

Creaton, Heather (1998) *Sources for the History of London 1939–45*, British Records Association.

Creighton, Helen (1932) *Songs and Ballads from Nova Scotia*, Toronto.

Croft, Andy (1990) *Red Letter Days: British Fiction in the 1930s*, Lawrence & Wishart.

Cummings, E.E. (1933, reprinted 2007) *Eimi: A Journey Through Soviet Russia*, Liveright Publishing Corporation, New York.

Cunningham, Valentine (1988) *British Writers of the Thirties*, Oxford University Press.

—— (ed.) (1986) *Spanish Front: Writers on the Civil War*, Oxford University Press.

Cutforth, Rene (1976) *Later than we Thought: A Portrait of the Thirties*, David and Charles.

David, Hugh (1989) *The Fitzrovians*, Sceptre.

Day Lewis, C (1960) *The Buried Day* (Autobiography), Chatto & Windus.

Ellis, Royston (1959) *Jiving to Gyp: A Sequence of Poems*, Scorpion Press.

English Dance and Song (1936–), magazine of the English Folk Dance and Song Society.

Ermarth, Michael (1991) *Kurt Wolff: A Portrait in Essays and Letters*, University of Chicago Press.

Eyerman, Ron and Andrew Jamison (1998) *Music and Social Movements*, Cambridge University Press.

Farson, Daniel (1974) *Out of Step*, Michael Joseph.

—— (1987) *Soho in the Fifties*, Michael Joseph.

Ferris, William and Mary L. Hart (1982) *Folk Music and Modern Sound*, University Press of Mississippi, Jackson.

Fitzgibbon, Constantine (1970) *The Blitz*, MacDonald.

Flanner, Janet (1975) (edited by Irving Drutman), *London Was Yesterday 1934–1939*, Viking Press, New York.

Folk Music Journal (1965–), English Folk Dance and Song Society.

Flory, Harriette (1977) 'The Arcos Raid and the Rupture of Anglo–Soviet Relations, 1927', *Journal of Contemporary History* Vol. 12, No. 4.

Foreman, John (1967) *The Folk Almanac 1967*, Broadsheet King.

—— (1968) *A Folk Almanac for 1968*, Broadsheet King.

Frame, Pete (2007) *The Restless Generation: How Rock Music Changed the Face of 1950s Britain*, Rogan House.

Gabriel (1941) *We're In The Army Now!*, Daily Worker Defence League.

Gammon, Vic (1980) 'Folk Song Collecting in Sussex and Surrey, 1843–1914' *History Workshop Journal*, Issue 10, Oxford University Press.

Garfield, Simon (2004) *Our Hidden Lives: The Everyday Diaries of a Forgotten Britain 1945–1948*, Ebury Press.

Gascoyne, David (1991) *Collected Journals 1936–42*, Skoob Books.

—— (1935) *A Short Survey of Surrealism*, Cobden-Sanderson.

Gibson, Ian (1983) *The Assassination of Federico Garcia Lorca*, Penguin Books.

Gili, J.L. (selected and translated) (1983) *Lorca Selected Poems*, Penguin Books.

Gilliam, Laurence (ed.) (1950) *B.B.C. Features*, Evans Brothers.

Goorney, Howard and Ewan MacColl (eds) (1986) *Agit-Prop to Theatre Workshop*, Manchester University Press.

—— (1981) *The Theatre Workshop Story*, Methuen.

Graves, Robert and Alan Hodge (eds) (1940) *The Long Weekend: A Social History of Great Britain 1918–1939*, Faber & Faber.

Greenleaf, Elizabeth B. and Grace Y. Mansfield (1933) *Songs of Newfoundland*, Harvard University Press, Cambridge, MA.

Gregory, E. David (1997) 'A.L. Lloyd and the English Folk Song Revival, 1934–44', *Canadian Journal for Traditional Music*.

—— (1999/2000) 'Starting Over: A.L. Lloyd and the Search for a New Folk Music, 1945–49', *Canadian Journal for Traditional Music* (1999/2000).

—— (2002) 'Lomax in London' *Folk Music Journal* Vol. 8 No. 2, English Folk Dance and Song Society.

Gregory, Mark (2009) *A.L. Lloyd interviewed, 1970*, Musical Traditions Internet Magazine www.mustrad.org.uk/articles/lloyd.htm.

Grierson, Philip (1943) *Books On Soviet Russia 1917–1942*, Methuen.

Hammond, J.L. and Barbara Hammond (1911) *The Village Labourer 1760–1832*, Longmans, Green and Co. (reprinted 1995 Alan Sutton, Stroud).

Hardy, Bert (1985) *My Life*, Gordon Fraser Gallery.

Harker, Ben (2007) *Class Act: The Cultural and Political Life of Ewan MacColl*, Pluto Press.

Harker, Dave (1980) *One for the Money: Politics and Popular Song*, Hutchinson.

—— (1985) *Fakesong*, Open University Press, Milton Keynes.

Harper, Colin (2006) *Dazzling Stranger: Bert Jansch and the British Folk and Blues Revival*, Bloomsbury.

Hasted, John (1992) *Alternative Memoirs*, Greengates Press, West Sussex.

Hawtree, Christopher (ed.) (1985) *Night and Day: July–Dec 1937*, Chatto & Windus.

Heinemann, Margot and Willie Thompson (eds) (1990) *History and the Imagination: Selected Writings of A.L. Morton*, Lawrence & Wishart.

Henderson, Hamish (1992) *Alias MacAlias* (Writings on Songs, Folk and Literature), Polygon, Edinburgh.

Heppenstall, Rayner (1960) *Four Absentees*, Barrie and Rockliff.

Hewison, Robert (1977) *Under Siege: Literary Life in London 1939–45*, Weidenfeld & Nicolson.

—— (1988) *In Anger: Culture in the Cold War 1945–60*, Methuen.

Hill, Douglas (1977) *Tribune 40: The First Forty Years of a Socialist Newspaper*, Quartet Books.

History Workshop: A Journal of Socialist Historians (1976–), Oxford Journals, Oxford University Press.

Hinkley, David (2002) 'Patronage or Pillage?' *New York Daily News*, 28 July 2002 (criticism of Lomax).

Hobsbawm, Eric (2002) *Interesting Times: A Twentieth Century Life,* Allen Lane.

—— (1997) *On History*, Weidenfeld & Nicolson.

Hoggart, Richard (1962) *The Uses of Literacy*, Pelican Books.

Hood, Grahame (2008) *Empty Pocket Blues: The Life and Music of Clive Palmer*, Helter Skelter Publishing.

Hopkinson, Tom (1982) *Of This Our Time*, Hutchinson.

—— (ed.) (1970) *Picture Post 1938–50*, Penguin Books.

—— (Introduction) (1975) *Bert Hardy: Photojournalist*, Gordon Fraser Gallery.

Howes, Frank (1969) *Folk Music of Britain – and Beyond*, Methuen.

Huberman, Leo (1937) *Man's Worldly Goods: The Story of the Wealth of Nations*, Victor Gollancz.

Hugill, Stan (1961) *Shanties from the Seven Seas*, Routledge & Kegan Paul.

—— (1969) *Shanties and Sailors' Songs*, Herbert Jenkins.

Hurren, Kenneth (1958) *Soho Annual 1958*, The Soho Association.

Huston, John (1980) *An Open Book*, Alfred A. Knopf, New York. Paperback reprint 1994, Da Capo Press, Cambridge, MA.

Hynes Samuel (1979) *The Auden Generation*, Faber & Faber.

Irwin, Colin (2001) *The Carthy Chronicles*, Free Reed Music.

Jacobs, Nicholas, and Prudence Ohlsen (eds) (1977) *Bertolt Brecht in Britain*, TQ Publications.

Jackson, Gordon, (1978) *The British Whaling Trade*, A & C Black.

Journal of the Folk-Song Society (1899–1931), English Folk Song Society.

*Journal of the English Folk Dance and Song Society (*1932–64), English Folk Dance and Song Society.

Journal of the International Folk Music Council (1948–), W. Heffer & Sons, Cambridge.

Johnson, Richard, Gregor McLennan, Bill Schwarz and David Sutton (eds) (1982) *Making Histories: Studies in History Writing and Politics*, University of Minnesota Press, Minneapolis.

Jose, Arthur Wilberforce and Herbert James Carter (eds) (1925) *The Illustrated Australian Encyclopaedia*, Angus & Robertson, Sydney.

Kee, Robert (ed.) (1989) *The Picture Post Album: A 50th Anniversary Collection*, Guild Publishing.

Kersh, Gerald (1938, reprinted 2007) *Night and the City*, London Books Classics.

Kettle, Arnold (1976) *Poetry and Politics*, The Open University.

King, James (1990) *The Last Modern: A Life of Henry Read*, Weidenfeld & Nicolson.

Klein, Joe (1981) *Woody Guthrie: A Life*, Faber & Faber.

Klingender, Francis D. (1972) *Art and the Industrial Revolution*, Paladin Books.

Laing, Dave, Karl Dallas, Robin Denselow and Robert Shelton (1975) *The Electric Muse*, Methuen.

Left Review (1934–38) (edited variously by Montagu Slater, Edgell Rickword, Randall Swingler, et al.), Organ of the British section of the Writers' International.

Leach, Robert and Roy Palmer (1978) *Folk Music in School* (includes 'The Meaning of Folk Music' by A.L. Lloyd), Cambridge University Press, Cambridge.

Lehmann, John (ed.) (1946) *Poems from New Writing 1936–1946*, John Lehmann.

—— (ed.) (1937) *New Writing 3*, Spring 1937, Lawrence & Wishart.

—— (ed.) (1952) *Pleasures of New Writing: An anthology*, John Lehmann.

—— (1955) *The Whispering Gallery: Autobiography, Vol. 1*, Longmans, Green and Co.

—— (1960) *I Am My Brother: Autobiography, Vol. 2*, Longmans, Green and Co.

—— (1966) *The Ample Proposition: Autobiography, Vol. 3*, Eyre and Spottiswoode.

Lewis, John (ed.) (1946–53) *Modern Quarterly* (contributors included: Bush, Bernal, Garman, Hill, Saville, Klingender, Dob, Lloyd, Hobsbawn) Lawrence & Wishart.

—— (1970) *The Left Book Club: An Historical Record*, Victor Gollancz.

Lewis, Peter (1978) *The 50s*, William Heinemann.

Lindsay, Jack (1982) *Life Rarely Tells: An Autobiography in Three Parts*, Penguin Books.

Ling, Jan (1997) *A History of European Folk Music*, University of Rochester Press, Rochester, NY.

Littlewood, Joan (1994) *Joan's Book*, Methuen.

Lloyd, A.L. (1935) (contributor with Henry Read, F.D. Klingender, Eric Gill and Alick West) *5 On Revolutionary Art*, Artists International Association and Martin Lawrence.

—— (1940) (trans.) (with Igor Vinogradoff) *Shadow of the Swastika*, John Lane/The Bodley Head.

—— (1940–50) *Picture Post*.

—— (1944) *The Singing Englishman*, Keynote Series Book 4.

—— (1945) (selected by) *Corn on the Cob: Popular and Traditional Poetry of the U.S.A*, Fore Publications.

—— (1952) (compiler) *Come all ye Bold Miners*, Lawrence & Wishart.

—— (1952) (contributor with Maurice and Kitty Cornforth, Jack and Ann Lindsay and others) *A Month in Rumania*, British-Rumanian Friendship Association.

—— (1958–9) (ed.) *Recorded Folk Music*, Collet's Holdings.

—— (1959) *The Penguin Book of English Folk Songs*, Penguin Books.

—— (1967) *Folk Song in England*, Lawrence & Wishart (reprinted 2008 by Faber & Faber).

—— (1978) (compiler) (revised and enlarged) *Come all Ye Bold Miners*, Lawrence & Wishart.

—— (2003) Vaughan Williams, R. and A.L. Lloyd (eds) (revised by Malcolm Douglas) *Classic English Folk Songs* (originally *The Penguin Book of English Folk Songs)*, English Folk Dance and Song Society.

Lomax, Alan (1968) *Folk Song Style and Culture*, American Association for the Advancement of Science, Washington, DC.

Longmate, Norman (1971) *How We Lived Then: A History of Everyday Life During the Second World War*, Hutchinson & Co.

Lorca, Federico Garcia (1937) *Lament for the Death of a Bullfighter and Other Poems* (in the original Spanish with English translation by A.L. Lloyd), William Heinemann.

—— (1961) *Three Tragedies: Blood Wedding, Yerma, The House of Bernada Alba*, Penguin Plays.

Lucas, John (1978) *The 1930s: A Challenge to Orthodoxy*, Harvester Press, Sussex.

Lyle, E.B. (ed.) (1976) *Ballad Studies*, D.S. Brewer and Rowman and Littlefield for the Folklore Society.

MacColl, Ewan (1954) *The Shuttle and Cage: Industrial Folk-Ballads*, Workers' Music Association.

—— (1990) *Journeyman: An Autobiography*, Sidgwick and Jackson.

Mackenzie, R.W. (1928) *Ballads and Sea Songs from Nova Scotia*, Harvard University Press, Cambridge, MA.

Mackinnon, Niall (1993) *The British Folk Scene*, Open University Press, Buckingham.

Maclaren-Ross, Julian (1984) *Memoirs of the Forties*, Penguin Books.

—— (1944) *The Stuff to Give the Troops*, Jonathan Cape.

Marowitz, Mark (1965) *The 'Encore' Reader: A Chronicle of the New Drama*, Methuen.

Marx Memorial Library and Workers School (1943) *Books Against Barbarism: What, How and Where to Read*, Lawrence & Wishart.

Matthew, Brian (1962) *Trad Mad*, World Distributors.

Maxwell, D.E.S. (1969) *Poets of the Thirties*, Routledge and Kegan Paul.

McKenry, Keith (2009) 'The Great Australian Folk Song that Wasn't', *Quadrant* Vol. L111 No. 3, 2009.

Mellins, Peter, 'Fallen Angel: The Political Cartoons of Jimmy Friell' in *Cartoon History* on the Political Cartoon Society website at www.politicalcartoons.co.uk.

Melly, George (1989) *Revolt into Style: The Pop Arts in the '50s and '60s*, Oxford University Press.

Minns, Raynes (1999) *Bombers and Mash: The Domestic Front 1939–45*, Virago Press.

Montagu, Ivor (1970) *The Youngest Son* (autobiography), Lawrence & Wishart.

Montgomery, John (1965) *The Fifties*, George Allen & Unwin.

Moore, Reginald (ed.) (1944) *Selected Writing*, Nicholson & Watson.

Morgan, Kevin (1989) *Against Fascism and War: Ruptures and Continuities in British Communist Politics 1935–41*, Manchester University Press.

—— (1993) *Harry Pollitt,* (Lives of the Left) Manchester University Press.

Morris, Lynda and Robert Radford (eds) (1983) *AIA: The Story of the Artists International Association 1933–1953*, Museum of Modern Art, Oxford.

Morton, A.L. (1938) *A People's History of England*, Victor Gollancz.

Muggeridge, Malcolm (1940, reprinted in paperback 1971) *The Thirties*, Fontana Books.

Munton, Alan (1989) *English Fiction of the Second World War*, Faber & Faber.

Neat, Timothy (2007) *Hamish Henderson: A Biography. Volume 1 – The Making of the Poet (1919–1953)*, Polygon, Edinburgh.

—— (2009) *Hamish Henderson: A Biography. Volume 2 – Poetry Becomes People (1954–2002)*, Polygon, Edinburgh.

Normand, Tom (1992) *Wyndham Lewis the Artist*, Cambridge University Press.

Olson, Laura (2006) *Soviet Approaches to Folk Music Performance*, NCEEER, Washington, DC.

Owen, Alun (1983) *The Whalers of Anglesey*, Gwynedd Archives Service.

Owen, Frank (1945) *The Royal Armoured Corps*, HMSO.

Palmer, Roy (ed.) (Facsimile reprint 1998) *A Book of British Ballads*, Llanerch Publishers, Felinfach.

Pechatnov, O. Vladimir (1998) 'The Rise and Fall of Britansky Soyuznik: A Case Study in Soviet Response to British Propaganda of the Mid-1940s', *The Historical Journal*, 41, 1 (1998), pp. 293–301, Cambridge University Press.

Pegg, Bob (1976) *Folk*, Wildwood House.

Peret, Benjamin (1936) *Remove Your Hat* (20 poems selected and translated by Humphrey Jennings and David Gascoyne), Roger Roughton Contemporary Poetry and Prose Editions.

Pickering, Michael, Emma Robertson and Marek Korczynski (2007) 'Rhythms of Labour: The British Work Song Revisited', *Folk Music Journal,* English Folk Song and Dance Society.

Pilgrim, John (1998) *Skiffle: The Roots of British Rock*, Square Peg Productions, available at www.thecreativecartel.org/lonnigans.html.

Platt, John (1985) *London's Rock Routes*, Fourth Estate.

Pollitt, Harry (1940) *Serving My Time*, Lawrence & Wishart.

Radford, Robert (1987) *Art for a Purpose: The Artists' International Association 1922–1953*, Winchester School of Art Press.

Rattenbury, (1981) *Dull Weather Dance: Poems*, Harry Chambers/Peterloo Poets.

Read, Herbert (1938) *Poetry and Anarchism*, Faber & Faber.

—— (1946) *Art and Society*, Faber & Faber.

Reed A.W. (1969) *Place-names of New South Wales*, A.H. & A.W. Reed, Sydney.

Reeves, James (ed.) (1958) *The Idiom of the People*, Heinemann.

—— (1960) (ed.) *The Everlasting Circle*, Heinemann.

Remy, Michel (1986) (introduction to exhibition catalogue) *British Surrealism Fifty Years On*, Mayor Gallery, London.

Rickword, Edgell/Writers Group of CPGB (1954) *Nothing is Lost: Ann Lindsay 1914–54*, Fore Publications (Ann Lindsay was active in the CP, Unity Theatre and a key figure in Fore Publications).

—— (1976) *Behind the Eyes* (Collected Poems and Translations), Carcanet New Press, Manchester.

Rollins, Hyder E. (1967) (reprint of original 1924 edition) (compiler) *An Analytical Index to the Ballad-Entries (1557–1709) in the Registers of the Company of Stationers of London*, Tradition Press, Hatboro, Pennsylvania.

Roughton, Roger (ed.) (1936) *Contemporary Poetry and Prose*, Roger Roughton.

Russell, Ian (ed.) (1986) *Singer, Song and Scholar*, Sheffield Academic Press.

—— and David Atkinson (2004) *Folk Song: Tradition, Revival and Re-creation*, The Elphinstone Institute, University of Aberdeen.

Saville, John and Joyce M. Bellamy (eds) (1976) 'Boswell, James Edward Buchanan (1906–71)', *Dictionary of Labour Biography* Vol. 3. No. 2.

Saville, John (2003) *Memoirs from the Left*, Merlin Press.

Seal, Graham (2006) 'A.L. Lloyd in Australia: Some Conclusions' *Folk Music Journal*, English Folk Dance and Song Society.

Seaman, L.C.B. (1970) *Life in Britain Between the Wars*, Batsford.

Sedley, Stephen (1967) *The Seeds of Love*, Essex Music.

Self, Geoffrey (1986) *The Music of E.J. Moeran*, Toccata Press.

Shapley, Olive (1988) *Broadcasting a Life: The Autobiography of Olive Shapley*, Scarlet Press.

Sheldon, Michael (1991) *Orwell*, William Heinemann.

Shelton, Robert (1986) *No Direction Home: The Life and Music of Bob Dylan*, William Morrow & Co.

Shepard, Leslie (Foreword by A.L. Lloyd) (1962) *The Broadside Ballad*, Herbert Jenkins.

Shields, Hugh (ed.) (1985) *Ballad Research*, Folk Music Society of Ireland, Dublin.

Sinclair, Andrew (1989) *War Like A Wasp: The Lost Decade of the Forties*, Hamish Hamilton.

Sked, Alan and Chris Cook (eds) (1979) *Post-War Britain: A Political History*, Pelican Books.

Skelton, Robin (1981) *Poetry of the Thirties*, Penguin Books.

Slobin, Mark (ed.) (1996) *Retuning Culture: Musical Changes in Central and Eastern Europe*, Duke University Press, North Carolina.

Socialist Platform (1992) *The Spanish Civil War: The View from the Left*, Revolutionary History Vol. 4, Nos 1/2. Socialist Platform.

Smith, G.A.W. (1975) *Once a Green Jackaroo*, Robert Hale.

Smith, Graeme (1996) 'A.L. Lloyd and Australian Folk Revival Singing Style', *Australian Folklore Society Journal*, No. 34, December 1996.

Spector, Jack (1997) *Surrealist Art and Writing 1919/39*, Cambridge University Press.

Spender, Stephen (1942) *Life and the Poet*, Searchlight Book 18, Secker and Warburg.

Stanford, Derek (1977) *Inside the Forties: Literary Memoirs 1937–1957*, Sidgwick and Jackson.

Stansky, Peter and William Abrahams (1966) *Journey to the Frontier: Julian Bell and John Cornford: Their Lives and the 1930s*, Constable.

Steinhardt, Mark (2000) *Audrey Smith: A Biography*, Stone Books.

Summers, Keith (late 1977/early 1978) *Sing, Say or Pay! A Survey of East Suffolk Country Music*, Traditional Music Nos 8 & 9.

Sweers, Britta (2005) *Electric Folk*, Oxford University Press, Oxford.

Symons, Julian (1960) *The Thirties: A Dream Revolved*, Faber & Faber.

Thompson, Duncan (2007) *Pessimism of the Intellect?: A History of New Left Review*, Merlin Press.

Thompson, E.P. (1991) *Customs in Common*, Merlin Press.

Thompson, John (1984) *Orwell's London*, Fourth Estate.

Thompson, Willie (1993) *The Good Old Cause: British Communism 1920–1991*, Pluto Press.

Thomson, George (1945) *Marxism and Poetry*, Lawrence & Wishart.

Tolley, A.T. (1975) *The Poetry of the Thirties*, St Martin's Press, New York.

Toop, David (1995) *Ocean of Sound*, Serpent's Tail.

Tremayne, Sydney D. (ed.) (1944) *Seven* (quarterly magazine of people's writing), Seven Magazine.

Unstead, R.J. (1974) *The Thirties*, MacDonald.

Upward, Edward (1969) *In the Thirties*, Penguin Books.

Vazquez, Adolfo Sanchez (1973) *Art and Society: Essays in Marxist Aesthetics*, Merlin Press.

Wannan, Bill (1964) *The Australian*, Angus and Robertson.

Warburg, Frederic (1973) *All Authors Are Equal*, Hutchinson.

Watson, Ian (1983) *Song and Democratic Culture in Britain*, Croom Helm.

Webb, Kaye (ed.) (1985) *Lilliput Goes to War*, Hutchinson.

West, Alick (1969) *One Man in his Time: An Autobiography* (of the communist, literary critic and activist), Allen and Unwin.

West, W.J. (1987) *Truth Betrayed* (radio propaganda in the Second World War), Duckworth.

Wheen, Francis (1990) *The Soul of Indiscretion: Tom Driberg*, Fourth Estate.
Whitehead, Kate (1989) *The Third Programme: A Literary History*, Clarendon Press, Oxford.
Wilgus, D.K. (1959) *Anglo-American Folksong Scholarship Since 1898*, Rutgers University Press, New Brunswick, NJ.
Willens, Doris (1988) *Lonesome Traveller: The Life of Lee Hays*, Norton, New York.
Willetts, Paul (2005) *Fear and Loathing in Fitzrovia* (biography of Julian MacLaren-Ross), Dewi Lewis Publishing, Stockport.
Williams, Alfred (1923) *Folk-Songs of the Upper Thames*, Duckworth.
Winick, Stephen D. (2004) *A.L. Lloyd and Reynardine: Authenticity and Authorship in the Afterlife of a British Broadside Ballad*, Folklore Vol. 115.
Wood, Neal (1959) *Communism and British Intellectuals*, Gollancz.
Wood, Pete (2008) *The Elliotts of Birtley*, David Herron Publishing, Todmorden.
Worsley, T.C. (1967) *Flannelled Fool*, Alan Ross.
Yass, Marion (1983) *This is Your War: Home Front Propaganda in the Second World War*, HMSO.
Zierke, Reinhard, *A.L. Lloyd Discography*, www.informatik.uni-hamburg.de/~zierke/lloyd/records/index.html.
—— *Index of A.L. Lloyd's Songs*, www.informatik.uni-hamburg.de/~zierke/lloyd/songs/index.html.

SELECT DISCOGRAPHY

Songs and 78s

'Polly Vaughan'/'Lord Bateman' (BBC Lib no. 16421, 1951).
'The Grand Conversation on Napoleon'/'Christ Did Me Ransome'/'The Captain's Apprentice' (BBC Lib no. 16420, 1951).
'The Bonny Boy' ('Trees Grow High')/'The Cruel Brothers (part 1)' (BBC Lib no 16418, 1951).
'Royal Duke of Grantham'/'The Cruel Brothers (part 2)' (BBC Lib no. 16419, 1951).
'Down in Yon Forest'/'The Bitter Withy' (HMV B 10594, 1953).
'Bold Jack Donahue'/'The Banks of the Condamine' (Topic TRC84, 1954).
'Polly Vaughan' on *The Columbia World Library of Folk and Primitive Music* (Columbia SL-206, 1955).

Albums and EPs

Australian Bush Songs (Riverside RLP 12-606, 1956).
The English and Scottish Popular Ballads (Riverside RLP 12-621/628).
English Drinking Songs (with Ewan MacColl, Riverside RLP 12-618, 1956).
English Street Songs (Riverside RLP 12-614, 1956).
Great British Ballads Not Included in the Child Collection (with Ewan MacColl, Riverside RLP 12-629, 1956).
The Singing Sailor (with Ewan MacColl, Topic TRL3, 1956).
The Banks of the Condamine and Other Bush Songs (Wattle C4, 1957).
The Blackball Line (with Ewan MacColl, Topic 8T8, 1957).
Convicts and Currency Lads (with Ewan MacColl, Wattle B2, 1957).
Singing Sailors (with Ewan MacColl, Wattle C5, 1957).
Shanties and Fo'c'sle Songs (with Ewan MacColl, Wattle C6, 1957).
Thar She Blows (with Ewan MacColl, Riverside RLP 12-635, 1957).
Across the Western Plains (Wattle D1, 1958).
Blow Boys Blow (with Ewan MacColl, Tradition TLP 1026, 1960).
Outback Ballads: Songs from the Australian Bush and Outback (with Peggy Seeger, Topic 12T51, 1960).
A Selection from the Penguin Book of English Folk Songs (produced by Paul Carter, Collector Records, JGB 5001, 1960).
All For Me Grog (Topic EP TOP66, 1961).

England and Her Folk songs (recorded April 1960, Collector EP JEB 8, 1962).

Gamblers and Sporting Blades (with Ewan MacColl, Topic EP TOP71, 1962).

A Sailors Garland (with Ewan MacColl, Prestige International INT 13043, 1962).

Whaler Out of New Bedford and Other Songs of the Whaling Era (with Ewan MacColl and Peggy Seeger, Folkways FS 3850, 1962).

The Iron Muse – A Panorama of Industrial Folk Music (Topic 12T86, 1963).

English and Scottish Folk Ballads (with Ewan MacColl, Topic 12T103, 1964).

First Person (Topic 12T118, 1966).

The Best of A.L. Lloyd (Prestige LP PL-13066 [USA], Transatlantic XTRA 5023 [UK], 1966).

The Bird in the Bush: Traditional Erotic Songs (with Frankie Armstrong and Anne Briggs, Topic LP 12T135, 1966).

Leviathan! Ballads and Songs of the Whaling Trade (Topic 12T174, 1967).

The Great Australian Legend (Topic 12TS203, 1971).

The Transports (by Pete Bellamy, Free Reed Records,1977; reissued by Topic, TSCD459, 1992). Bert's last recording project.

Good Order (Veteran VT140CD, 2002).

Index

Compiled by Sue Carlton